African States and Rulers

African States
and Rulers

*An Encyclopedia of Native,
Colonial and Independent States
and Rulers Past and Present*

by
John Stewart

McFarland & Company, Inc., Publishers
Jefferson, North Carolina, and London

British Library Cataloguing-in-Publication data available

Library of Congress Cataloguing-in-Publication Data

Stewart, John, 1952–
    African states and rulers : an encyclopedia of native, colonial and independent states and rulers past and present / by John Stewart.
      p.   cm.
    Bibliography: p. 303.
    Includes index.
    ISBN 0-89950-390-X (lib. bdg.; 50# acid-free natural paper) ∞
    1. Africa — History — Dictionaries. 2. Africa — Kings and rulers — Biography — Dictionaries. I. Title.
DT17.S74   1989
960′.03 — dc19
                         88-7945
                          CIP

Printed in the United States of America.

McFarland & Company, Inc., Publishers
  Box 611, Jefferson, North Carolina 28640

For Susan

Contents

vii

Contents viii

ix

Contents

Contents xviii

Preface

The history of Africa falls into three distinct phases — native, colonial and independent.

Until the European powers carved up the continent between them, Africans lived largely within natural tribal areas, and the degree of power of each tribe determined the boundaries of its country. The Europeans generally disregarded these "natural" frontiers, instead creating their own lines of demarcation where their conquests ended. Upon independence, these "artificial" countries were inherited, and that inheritance is a major cause of today's African problems.

It is the aim of this book to tell succinctly the political story of the Dark Continent, making it clear what happened in each country and when — changes of names, rulers, and so on. By Africa is meant herein not only the continental mass, but also the offshore islands which, geographically or politically, have an obvious African connection.

The standard entry gives the following information: official name of country (in **bold**); dates during which it went by that name (the Gregorian calendar is used); location; capital(s); other names by which that country might have gone during that time; a brief history of the country, including cross-references (in **bold**) to previous and later incarnations; and a list of rulers, with dates where known.

These complete entries will be found only under official names; common names are cross-referenced to official appellations. Thus the entry for the common name "Egypt" instructs the reader to "see these **names,**" offering a chronological (working backwards from the present) list of every official name that state has borne, with dates (e.g. "Arab Republic of Egypt, 1971– ; United Arab Republic, 1958–1971; Republic of Egypt, 1953–1958," etc.). Variant spellings are also cross-referenced, e.g. "**Tchad** *see* **Chad.**"

Many rulers' names, especially Arabic ones, are transliterated into Roman script. I have been uniform in my spellings of Muhammad (at the expense of Mahomet, Mohamed, etc.), and in most other cases have striven for uniformity. But where the most familiar form of a person's name would have to be changed for the sake of this uniformity, I have not done so.

As for the colonial rulers, I have given the names by which they were known, not necessarily their full names (which in the case of some Europeans, can be excessively long). Sometimes a ruler's name is unknown.

The index of 10,500 names at the back of the book will enable the reader to find any ruler's country quickly. Most variations of names are given and cross-referenced to the spelling given in this book.

Inevitably there will be omissions. Any book of this scope, size and type must have them. It is hoped that none will be thought glaring. Many dates are not complete; month and day were often unavailable. All colonial and independent polities and rulers are listed through Jan. 1, 1989, but as far as native (or pre-colonial) states go, a certain amount of selection was necessary.

By far the most valuable source for compiling this book was the writer's own notes taken in the 1970s and based on hundreds of direct African and European sources. Because the writer had no idea, a decade ago, that this research would ever turn up in published book form, the vast majority of these on-the-spot documents and oral sources are now unable to be credited accurately. However, much of this data has been corroborated by many of the books in the Bibliography. Errors, omissions, or opinions voiced in this book are the responsibility of the writer alone.

Aside from the authors listed in the Bibliography, I would like to thank the powers that made possible the many libraries I used over the years in Africa and Europe, and the African oral sources, too numerous to mention by name, who pointed me in the right directions—but especially my immortal friends Mufid Habib Basta and Ambassador Osman Mirza Ali Baig, wherever they are. I did a vast amount of research and double-checking in the downtown library of Winston-Salem, North Carolina, where I choose to live, and I thank the gracious staff there for their support—Bill Sugg, my good friend, you bring fun to a library. However, most of my research material was available at the astonishing library of Wake Forest University; enormous thanks to Ellen Knott and other members of her staff who did me favors which were probably little to them but big to me.

Inspirational help: Aside from my wife, all I needed were three people, and I got them—Mary Lyons Rearden, Dwight Shaw and Robbie Franklin, not to mention all my friends in Winston-Salem who felt frustrated because they couldn't help me out of the vise of time, but who in fact did help by their encouragement.

Every married male author acknowledges his wife. I always do. I met Susan in the Middle East one summer afternoon when I was 27. Some people have a turning point in their lives. That was mine. Without Susan I'd be living in a mud hut on the banks of the Blue Nile—if I were lucky. Thanks, Kid!

African States

1 **Abbasid Egypt [i]**. 9 Aug. 750–15 Sept. 868. *Location:* Egypt. *Capital:* al-Askar. *Other Names:* Egypt.

History: In Baghdad the Omayyad Caliphate (see **Omayyad Egypt**) gave way to the new dynasty of Abbasids. In 868 the Tulunids (see **Tulunid Egypt**) began a 37-year rule in Egypt which lasted until the Abbasids regained power there (see **Abbasid Egypt [ii]**).

Governors: 9 Aug. 750–2 Apr. 751 Salih ibn Ali; 2 Apr. 751–27 Oct. 753 Abu Awn; 27 Oct. 753–21 Feb. 755 Salih ibn Ali; 21 Feb. 755–26 Aug. 758 Abu Awn; 26 Aug. 758–28 Apr. 759 Musa ibn Ka'ab; 28 Apr. 759–18 Dec. 760 Muhammad ibn al-Ashath; 18 Dec. 760–14 Feb. 762 Humeyd ibn Kahtaba; 14 Feb. 762–30 Apr. 769 Yezid ibn Hatim; 30 Apr. 769–Feb. 772 Abdallah ibn Abderrahman; Feb. 772–18 Sept. 772 Muhammad ibn Abderrahman; 18 Sept. 772–14 Sept. 778 Musa ibn Olayy; 14 Sept. 778–18 March 779 Isa ibn Lukman; 18 March 779–1 June 779 Wadih; 1 June 779–Aug. 779 Mansur ibn Yezid; Aug. 779–15 Sept. 780 Abu Salih Yahya; 15 Sept. 780–6 Sept. 781 Salim ibn Sawada; 6 Sept. 781–1 July 784 Ibrahim ibn Salih; 1 July 784–10 July 785 Musa ibn Musab; 10 July 785–11 Aug. 785 As Ama ibn Amr; 11 Aug. 785–Apr. 786 al-Fadl ibn Salih; Apr. 786–15 Sept. 787 Ali ibn Suleiman; 15 Sept. 787–15 Feb. 789 Musa ibn Isa; 15 Feb. 789–28 Dec. 789 Maslama ibn Yahya; 28 Dec. 789–2 June 790 Muhammad ibn Zuheyr; 2 June 790–15 June 791 Dawud ibn Yezid; 15 June 791–June 792 Musa ibn Isa; June 792–1 Jan. 793 Ibrahim ibn Salih; 1 Jan. 793–12 Oct. 793 Abdallah ibn al-Mussayab; 12 Oct. 793–1 Nov. 794 Ishaq ibn Suleiman; 1 Nov. 794–9 Jan. 795 Harthama ibn Ayan; 9 Jan. 795–27 March 796 Abd al-Malik ibn Salih; 27 March 796–2 Nov. 796 Obeydallah ibn al-Mahdi; 2 Nov. 796–17 Aug. 797 Musa ibn Isa; 17 Aug. 797–2 Nov. 797 Obeydallah ibn al-Mahdi; 2 Nov. 797–4 Aug. 798 Ismail ibn Salih; 4 Aug. 798–10 Dec. 798 Ismail ibn Isa; 10 Dec. 798–21 June 803 al-Leyth ibn al-Fadl; 21 June 803–15 Sept. 805 Ahmad ibn Ismail; 15 Sept. 805–30 July 806 Obeydallah al-Abbasi; 30 July 806–24 Feb. 808 al-Hussein ibn Gemil; 24 Feb. 808– 25 Dec. 808 Malik ibn Delhem; 25 Dec. 808–11 July 810 al-Hassan ibn at-Takhtah; 11 July 810–25 March 811 Hatim ibn Harthama; 25 March 811–25 March 812 Gabir ibn al-Ashath; 25 March 812–13 Nov. 813 Abbad al-Balkhi; 13 Nov. 813–21 June 814 al-Muttalib; 21 June 814–4 Sept. 814 al-Abbas ibn Musa; 4 Sept. 814–3 Apr. 815 al-Muttalib; 3 Apr. 815–30 Sept. 816 as-Sari ibn al-Hakam; 30 Sept. 816–28 Feb. 817 Suleiman ibn Ghalib (pretender); 28 Feb. 817–10 Dec. 820 as-Sari ibn al-Hakam; 10 Dec. 820–7 Jan. 822 Muhammad ibn as-Sari; 7 Jan. 822–17 Apr. 826 Obeydallah ibn as-Sari; 17 Apr. 826–Dec. 828 Abdallah ibn Tahir; 21 Jan. 829–27 Jan. 829 Isa ibn Yezid; 27 Jan 829–28 Apr. 829 Omeyr ibn al-Wehid; June 829–830 Isa ibn Yezid; 830–28 Feb. 830 al-Motasim; 28 Feb. 830–18 Feb. 831 Abdaweyh ibn Gabela; 18 Feb. 831–832 Isa ibn Mansur; 832–March 832 al-Mamun (also Caliph); March 832–June 834 Nasr ibn Abdallah (or Keydar); June 834–9 Sept. 834 al-Muzaffar ibn Keydar; 9 Sept. 834–12 Feb. 839 Musa al-Hanafi; 12 Feb. 839–5 Feb. 841 Malik ibn Keydar; 5 Feb. 841–6 Oct. 843 Ali ibn Yahya; 6 Oct. 843–Dec. 847 Isa ibn Mansur; 15 Feb. 848–3 Apr. 849 Harthama ibn an-Nadr; 3 Apr. 849–3 May 849 Hatim ibn Harthama; 3 May 849–27 May 850 Ali ibn Yahya; 27 May 850–27 May 851 Ishaq ibn Yahya (or Khut); 27 May 851–24 Sept. 852 Abd al-Wahid ibn Yahya; 24 Sept. 852–22 Nov. 856 Anbasa ibn Ishaq; 22 Nov. 856–13 March 867 Yezid ibn Abdallah; 13 March 867–7 Apr. 868 Muzahim ibn Khakan; 7 Apr. 868–June 868 Ahmad ibn Muzahim; June 868–15 Sept. 868 Arguz Tarkhan.

2 Abbasid Egypt [ii]. 10 Jan. 905– 2 Sept. 935. *Location:* Egypt. *Capital:* al-Fustat. *Other Names:* Egypt.

History: In 905 the Abbasid general Muhammad ibn Suleiman re-conquered Egypt for his Caliph, from the Tulunid interlopers (see **Tulunid Egypt**). In 935 it was lost to the Ikhshids (see **Ikhshid Egypt**) who brought some control to the troubled land.

Military Commanders: 10 Jan. 905–Aug. 905 Muhammad ibn Suleiman.

Military Governors: Aug. 905–Aug. 905 Muhammad ibn Suleiman.

Governors: Aug. 905–Sept. 905 Isa; Sept 905–May 906 Muhammad al-Khalangi (usurper); May 906–9 May 910 Isa; 13 June 910–23 June 910 Abu'l Abbas; 23 June 910–27 Aug. 915 Tekin al-Khassa al-Gezeri; 27 Aug. 915–8 Aug. 919 Dhuka ar-Rumi; 8 Aug. 919–22 July 921 Tekin al-Khassa al-Gezeri; 22 July 921–25 July 921 Mahmun ibn Hamal; 25 July 921–14 Aug. 921 Tekin al-Khassa al-Gezeri; 14 Aug. 921–17 Aug. 923 Hilal ibn Bedr; 17 Aug. 923–12 Feb. 924 Ahmad ibn Keyghalagh; 12 Feb. 924–16 March 933 Tekin al-Khassa al-Gezeri; 16 March 933–30 Sept. 933 Muhammad ibn Tekin; 933–933 Muhammad ibn Tughh ("The Ikhshid") (did not take office); 30 Sept. 933–934 Ahmad ibn Keyghalagh; 934–2 Sept. 935 Muhammad ibn Tekin.

3 Abd-al-Wadid Kingdom. 1236–1550. *Location:* northern Algeria. *Capital:* Tlemcen (comes from "Tilmisan"—Moorish term for "springs"). *Other names:* Tlemcen, Zayyanid Kingdom, Tlemsen, Banu Zayyan Dynasty, Banu Abd-al-Wad.

History: Related to the Merinids (see **Merinid Kingdom**), the Banu Abd-al-Wad were loyal subjects of the **Almohad Empire** until, with the absolute decline of that empire the Abd-al-Wadid chieftain Abu Yahya Yaghmurasan ibn Zayyan, then Governor of the town of Tagrart, declared his independence and he united the towns of Tagrart and Agadir (the Algerian Agadir — not the Moroccan one) to form his capital of Tlemcen. Most of the time the kingdom was at war with the Merinids or the Hafsids (see **Hafsid Empire**), and several times, often for long stretches of time, the Abd-al-Wadids were forced out of their capital. The dynasty came to an end in 1550 and Tlemcen was captured by Algerian Turks in 1559.

Kings: 1236–March 1283 Abu Yahya Yaghmurasan ibn Zayyan; March 1283–6 June 1304 Abu Sa'id Uthman I; 6 June 1304–14 Apr. 1308 Abu Zayyar I Muhammad; 14 Apr. 1308–22 July 1318 Abu Hammu I Musa; 22 July 1318–May 1336 Abu Tashufin I Abdal Rahman; May 1336–1348 occupied by the Merinids; 1348–1352 Abu Sa'id Uthman II Abdal Rahman (joint); 1348–1352 Abu Thabit (joint); 1352–9 Feb. 1359 occupied by the Merinids; 9 Feb. 1359–20 May 1360 Abu Hammu II ibn Abi Yaqub; 20 May 1360–1360 Abu Zayyan Muhammad; 1360–1370 Abu Hammu II ibn Abi Yaqub; 1370–1372 Muhammad II; 1372–1383 Abu Hammu II ibn Abi Yaqub; 1383–1384 Muhammad II; 1384–1387 Abu Hammu II ibn Abi Yaqub; 1387–1387 Muhammad

II; 1387–1389 Abu Hammu II ibn Abi Yaqub; 1389–29 May 1393 Abu Tashufin II Abdal Rahman; 29 May 1393–8 July 1393 Abu Thabit II Yusuf; 8 July 1393–Nov. 1393 Abu Hajjaj Yusuf; Nov. 1393–1397 Abu Zayyan II Muhammad; 1397–1400 Abu Muhammad Abdallah I; 1400–1411 Abu Abdallah Muhammad I; 1411–1411 Abd al-Rahman ibn Musa; 1411–Nov. 1412 Abu Sa'id ibn Musa; Nov. 1412–May 1424 Abu Malik Abd al-Wahid; May 1424–1427 Abu Abdallah Muhammad II; 1427–1429 interregnum; 1429–1430 Abu Malik Abd al-Wahid; 1430–1430 Abu Abdallah Muhammad II; 1430–Jan. 1462 Abu al-Abbas Ahmad; Feb. 1462–1468 Abu Abdallah Muhammad III; 1468–1468 Abu Tashufin III; 1468–1504 Abu Abdallah Muhammad IV; 1504–1517 Abu Abdallah Muhammad V; 1517–1527 Abu Hammu III Musa; 1527–Jan. 1541 Abu Muhammad Abdallah II; Jan. 1541–7 March 1543 Abu Zayyan Ahmad; 7 March 1543–June 1543 Abu Abdallah Muhammad VI; June 1543–1550 Abu Zayyan Ahmad; 1550–1550 al-Hasan ibn Abdallah.

4 Abeokuta. ca. 1830–1893. *Location:* southwestern Nigeria. *Capital:* Abeokuta (name means "refuge among rocks"). *Other Names:* Egbaland.

History: founded about 1830 by Sodeke, a refugee from **Ibadan.** Many Yoruba people came to live here, mostly from a disintegrating **Oyo.** The Battle of Abeokuta in 1851 was the high point of a war with the **Dahomey Kingdom.** After the Yoruba Civil Wars (1877–93), the **Egba United Government** was formed.

Military Leaders: ca. 1830–1844 Sodeke. *Sabuas (Chiefs):* 1844–1854 Okukenu. *Alakes (Kings):* 1854–1861 Okukenu. *Regents:* 1861–1868 Shomoye. *Alakes (Kings):* 1869–1877 Ademola; 1877–1880 [unknown]; 1880–1881 Oyekon; 1881–(?) [unknown]; (?)–1920 Gbadebo; 1920–1962 Ladapo Ademola; 1962– Oyebadu Lipede.

5 Abomey Kingdom. ca. 1600–1730. *Location:* Benin Republic. *Capital:* Abomey.

History: about 1600 Do-Aklin left **Allada** when his father Madokun died. One of Do-Aklin's brothers stayed to rule Allada. These people, the Adja, who had migrated to Allada several years before (possibly as early as 1440), now intermarried in Abomey with the Gedevi tribe, who lived where Do-Aklin established his new kingdom. One of Do-Aklin's relatives founded the later **Porto-Novo Kingdom [i].** Thus the Fon ethnic group was formed. Agasu, the Leopard, was the mythical founder of the Abomey dynasty, but in reality it was Do-Aklin who founded the dynasty which was to last almost three hundred years. Wegbaja was the great king of this dynasty. Abomey captured Allada in 1724 and **Whydah Kingdom** in 1729, and in 1730 the name of the country changed to Dahomey (see **Dahomey Kingdom**).

Kings: ca. 1600–ca. 1625 Do-Aklin; ca. 1625–1645 Dakodonu; 1645–1645 Ganye Hesu; 1645–1685 Wegbaja; 1685–1708 Akaba (or Wibega) (joint). *Queens:* 1685–1708 Hangbe (joint). *Kings:* 1708–1730 Agaja (or Tossu).

6 Abuja. 1828–1902. *Location:* northern Nigeria-Niger border. *Capital:* Abuja.

History: In 1828 Abu Ja (Abu the Red) founded the independent Hausa emirate of Abuja. Prior to this, in 1804, the ruler of **Zaria,** Makau, was driven out of **Zaria** by the **Fulani Empire** and sought refuge at Zuba, his vassal state. Zuba now became his capital, from which he waged war against the Fulani. His brother Jatau (Abu Ja) founded the town and emirate of Abuja. The British occupied it in 1902 (see **Northern Nigeria Protectorate**).

Emirs: 1828–1851 Abu Ja (or Jatau); 1851–1877 Abu Kwaka; 1877–1902 Ibrahim Iyalai; 1902–1917 Muhamman Gani; 1917–1944 Musa Angulu; 1944– Suleimanu Barau.

Abyssinia see **Ethiopia**

7 Abyssinian Italian Protectorate. 2 May 1889–26 Oct. 1896. *Location:* Ethiopia. *Capital:* None.

History: In 1889 Italy declared a protectorate over the **Ethiopian Empire [ii],** just as their interpretation of the Treaty of Uccialli guided them to do. Gradually recognized by more and more countries, this protectorate was never recognized by Ethiopia. On Feb. 9, 1891 Menelik II denounced it, and on March 1, 1896 the Italians were soundly defeated at the Battle of Adowa. The "protectorate" was terminated a few months later by the Treaty of Addis Ababa.

Rulers: None', except the Ethiopians themselves (see **Ethiopian Empire [ii]**).

8 Adal [i]. ca. 900–1285. *Location:* the Zeila area of Somalia. *Capital:* Zeila. *Other names:* Adal.

History: A sultanate founded about 900, it was the center of Arab trade with the interior of what is today Somalia and Ethiopia. In 1285 it became part of **Zagwe Ethiopia.**

Rulers: unknown.

9 Adal [ii]. 1415–1526. *Location:* eastern Shoa, Ethiopia-Somalia borders. *Capital:* Harar (from ca. 1522). *Other names:* Adal.

History: In 1415 the old Sultanate of **Ifat** was conquered and made part of the **Ethiopian Empire [i].** About the same time the ruling Walashma dynasty of Ifat recreated in the same area the old kingdom of Adal (see **Adal [i]**) and ruled there until 1526, when it was conquered by the first Emir of **Harar.** Harar, the town, had in fact become the capital of the last sultan of Adal. Adal then became incorporated into the new Emirate of **Harar.**

Sultans: 1415–1422 Sabr ud-Din II; 1422–1425 al-Mansur II; 1425–1432 Jamal ud-Din II; 1432–1445 Badlai (or Shahah ud-Din); 1445–1471 Muhammad I; 1471–1472 Ibrahim I; 1472–1487 Shams ud-Din; 1487–1488 Ibrahim II; 1488–1518 Muhammad II; 1518–1519 Ali; 1519–1520 Fakhr ud-Din; 1520–1526 Abu Bakr.

10 Adamawa. 1806–Sept. 1901. *Location:* Cameroun/Nigeria border. *Capital:* Yola (from 1841); Jobolio (1839–41); Ribadu (1830–39); Gurin (1806–30). *Other names:* Fumbina, Fombina, Yola.

History: Founded and named by Adama, son of Ardo Hassana, a Fula noble, Adamawa was a Muslim emirate subject to the **Fulani Empire.** In 1901 it was partitioned between **Northern Nigeria Protectorate** and **Kamerun,** and became known as Yola Province. The name Adamawa was revived in 1926 in Adamawa Province.

Lamidos (Emirs): 1806–1848 Adama; 1848–1872 Hamman Lawal; 1872–1890 Saanda; 1890–1901 Zubeiru; 1901–1909 Bobbo Ahmadu; 1909–1910 Muhammadu Yerima Iya; 1910–23 Aug. 1924 Abba; 1924–1928 Muhammadu Bello (or Maigari); 1928–1946 Mustafa; 1946–June 1953 Ahmadu; June 1953–Aliyu Mustafa.

11 Adam Kok's Land. 1826–26 Dec. 1861. *Location:* southern Orange Free State. *Capital:* Philippolis (founded 1821 by Dr. John Philip, a missionary). *Other names:* Philippolis.

History: In 1820 Adam Kok II left **Griquatown** which he had ruled jointly with Barend Barends since 1813 and set up in **Campbell Lands.** From 1824–26 he lived as a rustler, and then he moved southeast to create a state around the town of Philippolis, thus creating the difference between the East and West Griquas (see **Waterboer's Land**). Kok died in 1835 and in 1838 his lands were defined by treaty. In 1861 Adam Kok III, after whom the state was actually named, sold the area to the **Orange Free State** and, with his people, trekked over the Drakensberg Mountains to form **Griqualand East.**

Kaptyns (Captains): 1826–12 Sept.

1835 Adam Kok II; 12 Sept. 1835–July 1837 Abraham Kok; July 1837–Sept. 1837 Barend Lucas (acting); Sept. 1837–26 Dec. 1861 Adam Kok III.

Adja-Tado see **Allada**

Adjatché, Adjatshé see **Porto-Novo Kingdom**

12 Adrar. ca. 1800–9 Jan. 1909. *Location:* Mauritania. *Capital:* Atar.
History: Around 1800 the dynasty of Ulad Yahya ibn Uthman began to rule in Adrar and lasted until the French proclaimed a protectorate, and brought the country into **Mauritania Civil Territory.**
Emirs: ca. 1800–(?) Uthman Ould Fadl Ould Sinan; (?)–(?) Sidi Ahmad; (?)–(?) Muhammad; (?)–1871 Ahmad II; 1871–1891 Sidi Ahmad III; 1891–ca. 1899 al-Mukhtar Ahmad; ca. 1899–1909 Sheikh Hassana; 1909–March 1932 Sidi Ahmad IV.

13 Afars and Issas Territory. 6 July 1967–27 June 1977. *Location:* as **Djibouti.** *Capital:* Djibouti. *Other names:* French Territory of the Afars and Issas, Térritoire Français des Afars et des Issas, Territory of the Afars and Issas.
History: The main inhabitants of the area are the Issas (Somalis) and the Afars (Danakils), both belonging to the Hamitic group. In 1967 **French Somaliland Overseas Territory** (as the country was then known) became the Territory of the Afars and Issas, once again by native vote (held as a referendum on March 19, 1967 and effective as from July 6, 1967). In 1977 the country became fully independent of France, as **Djibouti.**
High Commissioners: 6 July 1967–5 Feb. 1969 Louis Saget; 5 Feb. 1969–21 Aug. 1971 Dominique Ponchardier; 21 Aug. 1971–Dec. 1974 Georges Thiercy; Dec. 1974–9 Feb. 1976 Christian Dablanc; 9 Feb. 1976–27 June 1977 Camille d'Ornano. *Presidents of the Council of Government:* June 1974–May 1977 Ali Aref Bourhan. *Presidents:* 24 June 1977–27 June 1977 Hassan Gouled Aptidon. *Prime Ministers:* 6 July 1967–June 1974 Ali Aref Bourhan.

Africa Occidental Española see **Spanish West Africa**

14 Africa Nova. 46 B.C.–29 B.C. *Location:* **Numidia,** in Algeria. *Capital:* Cirta. *Other names:* New Africa.
History: In 46 B.C. Caesar conquered **Numidia** and formed out of it the Roman Province of Africa Nova. In 29 B.C. Augustus united it with **Africa Vetus** to form **Africa Roman Province [i].**
Praetors: 46 B.C.–44 B.C. Publius Sitius; 44 B.C.–ca. 29 B.C. Arabion.

15 Africa Proconsularis. 320–442. *Location:* Tunisia and Western Libya. *Capital:* Leptis Magna. *Other names:* Proconsular Africa.
History: In 320 **Tripolitania Roman Province** and **Byzacena Roman Province** became component parts of the greater colony of Africa Proconsularis, although the two parts remained autonomous colonies, except from 320 they reported to the Praetorian Prefect or the Consul of Africa Proconsularis. In 442 the whole Roman set-up in North Africa became part of **Vandal North Africa.**
Praetorian Prefects: 320–322 Menander; 322–333 [unknown]; 333–336 Lucius Aradius Valerius Proculus Felix; 336–337 Gregorius; 337–337 Nestorius Timonianus; 337–339 [unknown]; 339–340 Euagrius; 340–341 Antonius Marcellinus; 341–342 Aconius Catullinus; 342–344 [unknown]; 344–346 Placidus; 346–347 Vulcacius Rufinus; 347–349 Ulpius Limenius; 349–350 Hermogenes; 350–352 Anicetus; 352–353 Vulcacius Rufinus; 353–354 Flavius Philippus; 354–355 Maecilius Hilarianus; 355–355 Volusianus Lampadius; 355–356 Taurus; 356–356 Lollianus Mavortius; 356–361 Taurus. *Proconsuls:* 358–358 Sextus Petronius Probus. *Praetorian Prefects:*

362–365 Mamertinus; 365–367 Vulcacius Rufinus; 367–375 Sextus Petronius Probus. *Proconsuls:* 373–373 Quintus Aurelius Symmachus; 373–374 Constantius. *Praetorian Prefects:* 375–377 [unknown]; 377–378 Antonius. *Proconsuls:* 377–378 Nicomachus Flavianus. *Praetorian Prefects:* 378–382 Hesperius. *Proconsuls:* 378–380 Fallonius Probus Alypsius; 380–380 Alfenius Ceionius Camenius. *Praetorian Prefects:* 382–382 Severus; 382–382 Syagrius; 382–383 Hypatius; 383–384 Sextus Petronius Probus; 383–384 Atticus; 384–385 Praetextatus; 385–385 Neoterius. *Proconsuls:* 385–385 Pastorius. *Praetorian Prefects:* 385–386 Principius; 386–387 Eusignias; 387–388 Sextus Petronius Probus; 388–389 Trifolius; 390–390 Polemius. *Proconsuls:* 390–390 Pacatus Drepanius. *Praetorian Prefects:* 390–393 [unknown]; 393–394 Flavianus. *Proconsuls:* 393–394 Magnilius; 394–394 Macianus. *Praetorian Prefects:* 395–395 Dexter; 395–396 Eusebius; 396–396 Hilarius; 397–399 Mallius Theodorus; 399–400 Valerius Messala; 400–405 Rufius Synesius Hadrianus; 406–407 Longinianus; 407–408 Curtius; 408–409 Theodorus; 409–409 Caecillianus; 409–409 Liberius; 409–410 Lampadius; 410–410 Faustinus; 410–410 Macrobius; 410–412 Melitius; 412–413 Johannes; 413–414 Synesius Hadrianus; 414–415 Seleucus; 416–421 Junius Quartus Palladius; 422–422 Johannes; 422–423 Marinianus; 423–423 Venantius; 423–426 Proculus; 426–427 Bassus; 427–428 Portogenes; 428–429 Volusianus; 430–430 Theodosius; 430–431 Decius Acinancius Albinus; 431–432 Flavianus; 433–435 Petronius Maximus; 435–435 Flavius Bassus; 435–437 Petronius Maximus; 437–439 Flavius Bassus; 439–442 Petronius Maximus.

16 Africa Roman Province [i]. 29 B.C.–297 A.D. *Location:* Tunisia and western Libya. *Capital:* Colonia Julia Carthago (or Carthage). *Other names:* Africa.

History: In 29 B.C. the Emperor Augustus united **Africa Nova** and **Africa Vetus** to form Africa, a large Roman province. In 297 A.D. the Emperor Diocletian, in his reformation of the Empire, split that province into three: **Byzacena Roman Province, Tripolitania Roman Province,** and a smaller province in Northern Tunisia called **Africa Roman Province [ii].**

Praetors: 29 B.C.–12 A.D. [unknown]; 12 A.D.–15 Lucius Nonius Asprenas; 15–16 Lucius Aelius Lamia; 16–17 Aulus Vibius Habitus; 17–18 Marcus Furius Camillus; 18–21 Lucius Apronius; 21–23 Quintus Junius Blaesus; 23–24 Publius Cornelius Dolabella; 24–26 [unknown]; 26–29 Caius Vivius Marsus; 29–35 Marcus Junius Silanus; 35–36 Caius Rubellius Blandus; 36–37 Servius Cornelius Cethegus; 37–38 [unknown]; 38–39 Lucius Calpurnius Piso; 39–40 [unknown]; 40–41 Lucius Salvius Otho; 41–43 Quintus Marcius Barea Soranus; 43–44 [unknown]; 44–46 Servius Sulpicius Galba; 46–47 Marcus Servilius Nonianus; 47–51 [unknown]; 51–52 Lucius Tampius Flavianus; 52–53 Titus Statilius Taurus; 53–56 Marcus Pompeius Silvanus Staberius Flavinus; 56–57 Quintus Sulpicius Camerinus Peticus; 57–58 Cnaeus Hosidius Geta; 58–59 Quintus Curtius Rufus; 59–60 [unknown]; 60–61 Aulus Vitellius; 61–62 Lucius Vitellius; 62–63 Servius Cornelius Scipio Salvidienus Orfitus; 63–64 Titus Flavius Vespasianus; 64–68 [unknown]; 68– 68 Caius Vipstanus Apronianus; 68– 121 [unknown]; 121–121 Lucius Minicius Natalis; 121–139 [unknown]; 139– 140 Minicius; 140–141 Titus Prifernius Paetus Rosianus Geminus; 141–142 Sextus Julius Major; 142–143 Publius Tullius Varro; (?)–(?) Ennius Proculus; 153–ca. 154 Lucius Minicius Natalis Quadronius Verus; ca. 154–ca. 155 Marcellus; ca. 155–ca. 157 Severus; ca. 157–158 Lucius Hedius Rufus Lollianus Avitus; 158–160 Claudius Maximus; 160–161 Egrilius Plarianus; 161–162 Titus Prifernius Paetus Rosianus Geminus; 162–163 Quintus Voconius Saxa Fides; 163–164 Sextus Cocceius Severianus Honorinus; 164–164 Servius Cornelius Scipio Salvidienus Orfitus; 164–165 Marcus Antonius Zeno; 165–297 [unknown].

17 Africa Roman Province [ii]. 297–439. *Location:* northern Tunisia. *Capital:* Colonia Julia Carthago (Carthage). *Other names:* Africa.

History: Founded in 297 by the Emperor Diocletian from **Africa Roman Province [i]**, as were **Byzacena Roman Province** and **Tripolitania Roman Province**. In 439 the Roman Province of Africa went to the Vandals (see **Vandal North Africa**). This province, although it had the same name as its predecessor (**Africa Roman Province [i]**) was much smaller and confined to the north of what is today Tunisia. *Rulers:* 297–439 [unknown].

18 Africa Vetus. 146–B.C.–29 B.C. *Location:* Tunisia. *Capital:* Utica. *Other names:* Old Africa.

History: In 146 B.C. **Carthage** was wiped out by the Romans, who cursed the capital of Carthage and forbade human habitation there. They replaced the Carthage Empire with their own province of Africa Vetus and moved the capital to Utica. In 29 B.C. Augustus united Africa Vetus with **Africa Nova** to form **Africa Roman Province [i]**.

Only known Praetor: Publius Sextilius, ca. 88 B.C.

African Republic see **Dutch African Republic**

Afrique Équatoriale Française see **French Equatorial Africa**

Afrique Occidentale Française see **French West Africa**

19 Agaie. 1832–24 June 1898. *Location:* Niger State, northern Nigeria. *Capital:* Agaie. *Other names:* Agaie Emirate, Argeyes.

History: Originally there were the Mama. These people were superseded by the Dibo (or Zitako, or Ganagana). The loose group of peoples was taken over by the **Fulani Empire** in 1822, and in an enlarged form this area became an emirate in 1832. In 1898 it was taken over by the Royal Niger Company (see **Niger River Delta Protectorate**) and in 1900 came to form part of the **Northern Nigeria Protectorate**. In 1908 it became part of the newly-formed Niger Province of Nigeria.

Governors: 1822–1832 Mallam Baba. *Regents:* 1832–1848 Mallam Baba. *Emirs:* 1832–1857 Abdullahi; 1857–1877 Muhammadu (or Mamman Diko); 1877–1900 Nuhu; 1900–24 July 1919 Abubakar I; 19 Aug. 1919–1926 Abubakar II; 1926–Apr. 1935 Abdullahi; Apr. 1935–1953 Aliyu; Oct. 1953– Muhammadu Bello.

20 Agalega Islands. See these **names:**
Agalega Islands Dependency

21 Agalega Islands Dependency. *Location:* about 600 miles north of Mauritius, in the Indian Ocean. *Capital:* Sainte Rita (on South Island). *Other names:* The Agalegas.

History: Two islands, North and South, dependencies of **Mauritius**. Population: ca. 250.

Rulers: ruled from Mauritius.

22 Aghlabid Empire. 9 July 800–26 March 909. *Location:* Tunisia and eastern Algeria (i.e. Ifriqiyah). *Capital:* joint capitals of Tunis and al-Qayrawan. *Other names:* Ifriqiyah, Ifriqa, Ifrikiyah, Banu al-Aghlab Dynasty.

History: This was an orthodox Muslim Arab dynasty which controlled much of North Africa for a century, in 827 conquering Sicily and eventually taking a lot of Southern Italy before being subdued by the Fatimids (see **Fatimid Egypt** and **Fatimid Tunisia**).

Sultans: 9 July 800–5 July 812 Ibrahim ibn al-Aghlab; Oct 812–25 June 817 Abdallah I; 25 June 817–10 June 838 Ziyadat-Allah I; 10 June 838–18 Feb. 841 Abu-Iqal al-Aghlab; 18 Feb. 841–10 May 856 Muhammad I; 10 May 856–28 Dec. 863 Ahmad; 28 Dec. 863–23 Dec. 864 Ziyadat-Allah II; 23 Dec. 864–16 Feb. 875 Muhammad II; 16 Feb. 875–902 Ibrahim II; June 903–28 July 903 Abdallah II; 28 July 903–26 March 909 Ziyadat-Allah III.

23 Aghlabid Tripoli. 9 July 800–26 March 909. *Location:* Tripolitania, Libya. *Capital:* Tripoli. *Other names:* Tripoli (Aghlabid).

History: In 800 the **Aghlabid Empire** took Tripoli from the Arabs who had ruled the area in a loose confederation from the time of the end of the Vandal period in North Africa (see **Vandal North Africa**). In 909 the Aghlabids made way for the Fatimids (see **Fatimid North Africa** and **Fatimid Tripoli**).

Governors: There is only one recorded governor, Muhammad ibn Qurhub, ca. 869.

24 Aiyubid Empire. 10 Sept. 1171–2 May 1250. *Location:* as **Bahrite Mameluke Empire.** *Capital:* Damascus (in Syria); Cairo (capital of Egypt). *Other names:* Ayyubid Empire.

History: In 1171 Saladin founded the Aiyubid Empire, thus ending Fatimid rule in Egypt (see **Fatimid Egypt**). In 1250 the Sultan's bodyguards, the Bahrite Mamelukes, revolted, creating their own dynasty (see **Bahrite Mameluke Empire**).

Sultans: 10 Sept. 1171–4 March 1193 Saladin (or Yusuf ibn Aiyub); 4 March 1193–29 Nov. 1198 al-Aziz Uthman; 29 Nov. 1198–1200 Nasir ad-Din Muhammad; Feb. 1200–31 Aug. 1218 al-Adil Abu Bakr I (or Saphadin); 2 Sept. 1218–8 March 1238 Malik al-Kamil; 8 March 1238–31 May 1240 al-Adil Abu Bakr II; 1 June 1240–21 Nov. 1249 as-Salih Aiyub. *Queens-Regent:* 21 Nov. 1249–27 Feb. 1250 Sheger ad-Durr.

Sultans: 27 Feb. 1250–2 May 1250 Turanshah.

Ajashe see **Porto-Novo Kingdom**

Ajuda see **Whydah**

25 Akim. ca. 1500–1899. *Location:* Ghana. *Capital:* Nsauoen.

History: Founded about 1500, the kingdom of Akim lasted 400 years until it was taken into the **Gold Coast Northern Territories** by the British. Its first dynasty ended about 1733, its second about 1817, its third in 1866, and its fourth in 1912.

Kings: ca. 1500–ca. 1520 Kuntunkrunku; ca. 1520–ca. 1540 Apeanin Kwaframoa Woyiawonyi; ca. 1540–ca. 1560 Damram; ca. 1560–ca. 1580 Pobi Asomaning; ca. 1580–ca. 1600 Oduro; ca. 1600–ca. 1620 Boakye I; ca. 1620–ca. 1640 Boakye II; ca. 1640–ca. 1660 Agyekum Owari I; ca. 1660–ca. 1680 Boakye III; ca. 1680–ca. 1700 Agyekum Owari II; ca. 1700–ca. 1733 Agyekum Owari III; ca. 1733–ca. 1738 Ofori Panin; ca. 1738–1742 Bakwante; 1742–ca. 1744 Pobi; ca. 1744–ca. 1750 Owusu Akyem Ohenkoko (The "Red King"); ca. 1750–ca. 1760 Twum Ampoforo Okasu; ca. 1760–1770 Obirikorane; 1770–(?) Apraku; (?)–1811 Atta Wusu Yiakosan; 1811–ca. 1815 Kofi Asante Baninyiye; ca. 1815–1817 Twum. *Queens:* 1817–1851 Dokua. *Kings:* 1851–(?) [unknown]; (?)–(?) Atta Panyin; (?)–1866 Atta Biwom; 1866–1888 Amoaka Atta I; 1888–1911 Amoaka Atta II; 1911–1912 Amoaka Atta III; 1912–1943 Nana Ofori Atta I; 1943– Nana Ofori Atta II.

Aksum see **Axum**

26 Aku. ca. 1826–1880. *Location:* Sierra Leone. *Capital:* Aku.

History: Founded about 1826, Aku was brought into **Sierra Leone Territory [iii]** in 1880.

Kings: ca. 1826–1840 Thomas Will; 1840–5 Dec. 1867 John Macaulay (or

Atapa); 5 Dec. 1867–1880 Isaac Benjamin Pratt.

27 Akwamu. 1560–1730. *Location:* southern Ghana. *Capital:* Ayandawaase (from 1575); Aseremankese (1560–75).

History: In 1560 Otumfo Asare of **Twifo-Heman** founded Akwamu, one of the two famous Akan (or Bron) states (the other being **Ashanti**), making his capital at Aseremankese. Fifteen years later the capital was moved to Ayandawaase. In 1730 **Akim** conquered Akwamu.

Nanas (Kings): 1560–1575 Otumfo Asare; 1575–1585 Akotia; 1585–1600 Ansa Saseraku I; 1600–1621 Ansa Saseraku II; 1621–1638 Ansa Saseraku III; 1638–1660 Abuako Dako; 1660–1682 Afera Kuma; 1682–1689 Ansa Saseraku IV; 1689–1702 Manukure; 1702–1726 Akwano Panyini; 1726–1730 Dako Booman.

28 Alawid Morocco. 1659–4 Aug. 1907. *Location:* Morocco. *Capital:* mostly Rabat and Fez, but at times Meknes or Marrakesh; Tafilalt (1631–66). *Other names:* Morocco, Fez and Morocco, Empire of Morocco, Filali Morocco, Moroccan Empire.

History: The Alawis came from Arabia in the times of the **Merinid Empire** and based themselves in the oases of Tafilalt. By 1631 they had risen to enormous power in **Sa'did Morocco** and by 1659, and the end of the Sa'dids, the Alawis took over, Mulay Rashid being proclaimed sultan officially in 1666. The Alawis have ruled Morocco ever since, with a little help from the French (see **French-Occupied Morocco** and **French Morocco**), the Spanish (see **Spanish Captaincy-General of North Africa, Ceuta, Melilla, Ifni, Tangier** and **Spanish Morocco**), as well as from the Portuguese and the British at times.

Sheikhs: 1631–1635 Muhammad I ash-Sharif; 1635–3 Aug. 1664 Muhammad II; 3 Aug. 1664–1666 Mulay Rashid. *Sultans:* 1666–27 March 1672 Mulay Rashid; 27 March 1672–21 March 1727 Ismail as-Samin; 21 March 1727–Apr. 1728 Ahmad ad-Dhahabi; Apr. 1728–June 1728 Abd al-Malik; June 1728–5 March 1729 Ahmad ad-Dhahabi; 5 March 1729–29 Sept. 1734 Abd Allah; 29 Sept. 1734–12 May 1736 Ali al-Arag; 12 May 1736–1736 Abd Allah; 1736–1738 Muhammad III; 1738–1740 al-Mustadi ibn Ismail; 1740–1745 Abd Allah; 1745–1745 Zain ul-Abidin; 1745–1748 Abd Allah; 1748–1748 Muhammad III; 1748–1757 Abd Allah; 1757–11 Apr. 1790 Muhammad III; 11 Apr. 1790–15 Feb. 1792 Yazid; 15 Feb. 1792–1793 Hisham; 1793–19 Nov. 1822 Suleiman; 19 Nov. 1822–28 Aug. 1859 Abd ar-Rahman; 28 Aug. 1859–12 Sept. 1873 Muhammad IV; 25 Sept. 1873–7 June 1894 Hassan I; 7 June 1894–4 Aug. 1907 Abdul Azziz.

29 Aldabras. See these **names:** Aldabra Islands

30 Aldabra Islands. see below. *Location:* about 600 miles northeast of the Seychelles, in the Indian Ocean. *Capital:* none. *Other names:* The Aldabras.

History: Four uninhabited islands: South Island (the biggest), West Island, Polymnie and Middle Island. Part of the administration of the Seychelles until Nov. 8, 1965 when they became part of the British Indian Ocean Territory (a British colony). They were returned to the Seychelles on June 28, 1976.

Rulers: ruled direct from Victoria, Seychelles.

31 Alexandrian Egypt. 332 B.C.–13 June 323 B.C. *Location:* as **Egypt.** *Capital:* Alexandria. *Other names:* Egypt.

History: In 332 B.C. Alexander the Great conquered Egypt (see **Egypt Persian Province**), ruling through a governor, until his death in 323 B.C. He founded the town of Alexandria and his satrap, Ptolemy, founded the **Egyptian Satrapy** which followed Alexander's death.

Emperors: 332 B.C.–13 June 323 B.C. Alexander the Great. *Military Governors:* 332 B.C.–13 June 323 B.C. Kleomenes of Naucratis.

32 Algeria. See these **names:**
Algerian Democratic and Popular Republic (1962–)
Algeria (1962–1962)
Algerian Republic (Provisional Government) (1958–1962)
French Algeria (1881–1962)
French Algeria Military Province (1842–1881)
French Algerian Possessions (1839–1842)
French Possessions in North Africa (1830–1839)
Algiers Regency (1671–1830)
Algiers Pashalik [ii] (1525–1671)
Kabyle Algiers (1520–1525)
Algiers Pashalik [i] (1516–1520)
Constantine (1637–1837)
Mascara (1832–1847)
Oran (Turkish) [ii] (1792–1831)
Oran (Spanish) [ii] (1732–1792)
Oran (Turkish) [i] (1708–1732)
Oran (Spanish) [i] (1509–1708)
Abd-al-Wadid Kingdom (1236–1550)
Hammamid Kingdom (1014–1152)
Rustumid Emirate (776–911)
Mauretania Sitifensis (297–435)
Mauretania Caesariensis (42–ca. 395)
Mauretania (Roman) (33 B.C.–42 A.D.)
Mauretania [ii] (38 B.C.–33 B.C.)
Mauretania East (ca. 100 B.C.–38 B.C.)
Mauretania [i] ([?]–ca. 100 B.C.)
Numidia (201 B.C.–46 B.C.)
Africa Nova (46 B.C.–29 B.C.)

33 Algeria. 3 July 1962–25 Sept. 1962. *Location:* as **Algerian Democratic and Popular Republic.** *Capital:* Algiers.
History: In 1962 **French Algeria** gained its independence and later in 1962 it declared itself the **Algerian Democratic and Popular Republic.**
President of Provisional Executive Council: 3 July 1962–4 Aug. 1962 Abdur Rahman Farès. *Provisional Prime Ministers:* 5 July 1962–4 Aug. 1962 Yusuf Ben Khedda; 4 Aug. 1962–25 Sept. 1962 Ahmed Ben Bella.

34 Algerian Democratic and Popular Republic. 25 Sept. 1962– . *Location:* North Africa. *Capital:* Algiers (or al-Djazaiir) (founded by the Phoenicians and known throughout antiquity as Icosium, "al-Jaza'ir" means "the islands," which once existed in Algiers Bay). *Other names:* al-Jaza'ir, Algeria, The Democratic and Popular Republic of Algeria, Algérie.
History: In 1962 **French Algeria** came to an end, and the **Algerian Republic (Provisional Government),** waiting in exile in the wings, took over (see **Algeria**). Declared the Democratic and Popular Republic of Algeria on September 25.
Presidents: 20 Sept. 1963–19 June 1965 Ahmed Ben Bella; 19 June 1965–27 Dec. 1978 Houari Boumedienne; 27 Dec. 1978–9 Feb. 1979 Rabah Bitat (interim); 9 Feb. 1979– Chadli Bendjedid. *Prime Ministers:* 25 Sept. 1962–26 Sept. 1962 Ahmed Ben Bella (provisional); 26 Sept. 1962–20 Sept. 1963 Ahmed Ben Bella; 8 March 1979–22 Jan. 1984 Muhammad Abdelghani; 22 Jan. 1984–5 Nov. 1988 Abdelhamid Brahimi; 5 Nov. 1988– Kasdi Merbah. *Note:* in times of no Prime Minister, the President held that office.

35 Algerian Republic (Provisional Government). 18 Sept. 1958–3 July 1962. *Location:* Algeria, but the provisional government worked out of Tunis. *Capital:* Tunis, Tunisia (and previously Cairo, Egypt). *Other names:* Gouvernement Provisoire de la République Algérienne, GPRA.
History: In 1956 Ferhat Abbas went to Cairo to join the FLN (Front de Libération National) and in 1958 an Algerian Government in Exile was put together in Cairo, later moving to Tunis. In 1962 it came to power in Algeria at the end of **French Algeria**

and the beginning of **Algeria** and independence.

Presidents: 28 March 1962-3 July 1962 Abdur Rahman Farès. *Prime Ministers:* 18 Sept. 1958-22 Dec. 1959 Ferhat Abbas; 22 Dec. 1959-19 Jan. 1960 Krim Belkassim; 19 Jan. 1960-27 Aug. 1961 Ferhat Abbas; 27 Aug. 1961-3 July 1962 Yusuf Ben Khedda.

Algiers see **Algeria**

36 Algiers Pashalik [i]. 1516-1520. *Location:* Algiers and surrounding area. *Capital:* Algiers. *Other names:* Algiers Regency, Algiers.

History: In 1516 Aruj the Corsair conquered the Algiers area and in 1520 his brother Khair ad-Din (Barbarossa) lost it to the Kabyles (see **Kabyle Algiers**).

Pashas: 1516-Oct. 1518 Aruj; Oct. 1518-1520 Khair ad-Din (Barbarossa).

37 Algiers Pashalik [ii]. 1525-1671. *Location:* the Algiers coastline. *Capital:* Algiers. *Other names:* Algiers Regency, Algiers.

History: In 1525 Khair ad-Din reconquered Algiers from the Kabyles (see **Kabyle Algiers**). From then on Algiers and all the surrounding area were ruled by a "beylerbey" or bey of beys who delegated Algiers to a "khalifah" when he was out of the country. In 1587 the Beylerbeys were abolished. In 1671 the Turks took Algiers and it became **Algiers Regency**.

Beylerbeys in Residence: 1525-15 Oct. 1535 Khair ad-Din (Barbarossa) (Beylerbey until 1546). *Khalifahs (Governors):* 15 Oct. 1535-Dec. 1543 Hassan Agha; Dec. 1543-1544 Hajji Beshir Pasha; 1544-4 July 1546 Hassan Pasha. *Beylerbeys in Residence:* 4 July 1546-Sept. 1551 Hassan Pasha. *Khalifahs:* Sept. 1551-May 1552 Saffah. *Beylerbeys in Residence:* May 1552-1556 Salah Raïs. *Khalifahs:* 1556-June 1557 Hassan Corso. *Beylerbeys in Residence:* June 1557-June 1557 Tekelerli. *Khalifahs:* June 1557-1557 Yusuf;

1557-1557 Yahya. *Beylerbeys in Residence:* 1557-May 1561 Hassan Pasha. *Khalifahs:* June 1561-Sept. 1562 Hassan Agha; Sept. 1562-1562 Ahmad. *Beylerbeys in Residence:* 1562-1567 Hassan Pasha. *Khalifahs:* 1567-March 1568 Muhammad ibn Salah Raïs. *Beylerbeys in Residence:* March 1568-10 Oct. 1571 Eulj Ali (Beylerbey until 1577). *Khalifahs:* 10 Oct. 1571-1574 Arab Ahmad; 1574-May 1577 Ramdan. *Pashas:* May 1577-1580 Hassan Veneziano; 1580-1582 Ja'far; 1582-1588 Hassan Veneziano; 1588-1589 Deli Ahmad; 1589-1592 Hizr; 1592-1594 Hajji Shaban; 1594-1594 Mustafa; 1594-1596 Hizr; 1596-1598 Mustafa; 1598-1599 Hassan; 1599-1603 Suleiman; 1603-1605 Hizr; 1605-1607 Köse Mustafa; 1607-1610 Rizvan; 1610-1613 Köse Mustafa; 1613-1616 Sheikh Hussein; 1616-1616 Köse Mustafa; 1616-Jan. 1617 Suleiman Katanya; Jan. 1617-1619 Sheikh Hussein; 1619-1621 Sherif Koja; 1621-1621 Hizr; 1621-1622 Mustafa; 1622-1622 Khusrev; 1622-1623 vacant; 1623-1626 Murad; 1626-1627 vacant; 1627-1629 Hussein; 1629-1629 Yunus; 1629-1634 Hussein; 1634-1636 Yusuf; 1636-1638 Abu'l Hassan Ali; 1638- Aug. 1640 Sheikh Hussein; Aug. 1640-1642 Abu Jemal Yusuf; 1642-1645 Mehmed Brusali; 1645-1645 Ali Bijnin; 1645-1647 Mahmud Brusali; 1647-1650 Yusuf; 1650-1653 Mehmed; 1653-1655 Ahmad; 1655-1656 Ibrahim; 1656-1658 Ahmad; 1658-1659 Ibrahim; 1659-1671 Ismail. *Aghas (Military Commanders):* 1659-1660 Halil; 1660-1661 Ramadan; 1661-1665 Shaban; 1665-1671 Hajji Ali.

38 Algiers Regency. 1671-5 July 1830. *Location:* the Algerian coastline. *Capital:* Algiers.

History: In 1671 the Turks took Algiers and set it up as a regency of the Ottoman Empire. In 1830 the French took it (see **French Possessions in North Africa**).

Deys: 1671-Jan. 1682 Muhammad I; Jan. 1682-22 July 1683 Hasan I; 22 July

1683–1686 Husain I; 1686–Dec. 1688 Ibrahim; Dec. 1688–July 1695 Shaban; July 1695–Dec. 1698 Ahmad I; Dec. 1698–1699 Hasan II; 1699–Oct. 1705 Mustafa I; Oct. 1705–Apr. 1706 Husain II Khoja; Apr. 1706–March 1710 Muhammad II Bektash. *Pashas/Deys:* March 1710–17 June 1710 Ibrahim I; 17 June 1710–4 Apr. 1718 Ali I; 4 Apr. 1718–18 May 1724 Muhammad III; 18 May 1724–1731 Kurd Abdi; 1731–Nov. 1745 Ibrahim II; Nov. 1745–Feb. 1748 Kuchuk Ibrahim II; Feb. 1748–11 Dec. 1754 Muhammad IV. *Deys:* 11 Dec. 1754–Feb. 1766 Ali II; Feb. 1766–11 July 1791 Muhammad V; 11 July 1791–June 1798 Hasan III; June 1798–1 July 1805 Mustafa II; 1 July 1805–15 Nov. 1808 Ahmad II; 15 Nov. 1808–Feb. 1809 Ali III ar-Rasul; Feb. 1809–March 1815 Ali IV; March 1815–11 Apr. 1815 Muhammad VI; 11 Apr. 1815–2 May 1817 Umar; 2 May 1817–1 March 1818 Ali V Khoja; 1 March 1818–5 July 1830 Husain III.

39 Allada. ca. 1440–18 Nov. 1891. *Location:* Benin. *Capital:* Allada. *Other names:* Ardrah, Ardrah Empire, Empire of Ardrah, Adja-Tado, Ardra.

History: Founded about 1440, the country of Allada grew into a small empire, and about the year 1600 three brothers went different ways. Kopon stayed to rule Allada, Do-Aklin went north to found the **Abomey Kingdom,** while Te-Agdanlin founded the kingdom of Adjatché, or Porto-Novo as it became known (see **Porto-Novo Kingdom [i]**). Between 1724 and 1742 Allada was ruled by its sister state of Abomey, the great power in the area, and in 1891 the French placed a protectorate over Allada (see **Allada Protectorate**).

Kings: ca. 1440 Aholuho Adja; ca. 1445 De Nufion; ca. 1450 Djidomingba; ca. 1458–Dassu; ca. 1470 Dassa; ca. 1475 Adjakpa; ca. 1490 Yessu; ca. 1495 Azoton; ca. 1498 Yessu; ca. 1510 Akonde; ca. 1520 Amamu; ca. 1530 Agagnon; ca. 1540 Agbangba; ca. 1550 Hueze; ca. 1560 Agbande; ca. 1580 Kin-Ha; ca. 1585 Mindji; ca. 1587–ca. 1590 Akolu; ca. 1590–1610 Kopon (the first historic king); 1610–(?) Hunungungu; (?)–ca. 1660 Lamadje Pokonu; ca. 1660–(?) Tezifon; (?)–(?) gBagwe; (?)–March 1724 De Adjara; March 1724–1742 ruled direct from Abomey Kingdom; 1742–(?) Mijo; (?)–1845 [unknown]; 1845–(?) Deka; (?)–(?) Ganhwa; (?)–1879 Gangia Sindje; 1879–4 Feb. 1894 Gi-gla No-Don Gbé-non Mau; 4 Feb. 1894–ca. 1898 Gi-gla Gunhu-Hugnon; ca. 1898–15 Dec. 1923 Djihento.

40 Allada Protectorate. 18 Nov. 1891–22 June 1894. *Location:* Benin. *Capital:* Allada. *Other names:* Ardrah Protectorate.

History: In 1891 France declared a protectorate over **Allada,** and in 1894 it became part of **Dahomey Colony.**

Kings: 18 Nov. 1891–4 Feb. 1894 Gi-Gla No-Don Gbe-non Mau; 4 Feb. 1894–22 June 1894 Gi-Gla Gunhu-Hugnon.

41 Almohad Empire. 3 Apr. 1147–1268. *Location:* Algeria, Morocco and Tunisia. *Capital:* Marrakesh (from 1147); Tinmallal (1123–47). *Other names:* Muwahhid Dynasty.

History: The Almohads began in 1121, their first ruler, Muhammad ibn Tumart starting a long rebellion against the **Almoravid Empire.** Muhammad ruled his people from 1121–29, and was succeeded by Abd al-Mu'min (1129–63). In 1147 the Almohads finally took over the old Almoravid territory, and extended it greatly over the years. By 1152 they had taken what is today Algeria, and by 1155 what is today's Tunisia and the Tripolitania part of Libya. In 1268 they relinquished it in turn to the **Merinid Empire.**

Emirs: 1147–May 1163 Abd al-Mu'min; May 1163–29 June 1184 Yusuf I; 10 Aug. 1184–Dec. 1198 Yakub al-Mansur; Jan 1199–27 Dec. 1213 Muhammad an-Nasir; 28 Dec. 1213–6 Jan. 1224 Yusuf II al-Mustansir; 7 Jan.

1224–5 Sept. 1224 Abd al-Wahid al-Makhlu; 5 Sept. 1224–Oct. 1227 Abdallah al-Adil; Oct. 1227–1230 Yahya al-Mu'tasim (joint); Oct. 1227–1230 Idris al-Ma'mun (joint); 1230–16 Oct. 1232 Idris al-Ma'mun; 17 Oct. 1232–22 Dec. 1242 Abd al-Wahid II; 23 Dec. 1242–1248 Ali as-Sa'id; 1248–Oct. 1266 Umar al-Murtada; Oct. 1266–1268 Abu l'Ula al-Wathiq (or Abu Dabbus).

42 Almohad Tripoli. 22 Jan. 1160–ca. 1247. *Location:* Tripolitania, Libya. *Capital:* Tripoli. *Other names:* Tripoli (Almohad).

History: In 1160 **Norman Tripolitania** was taken by the **Almohad Empire,** and a governor installed. Rule vacillated for the next 80 or so years between the Almohads and the Aiyubids (see **Aiyubid Egypt**), but the governor of Tripoli remained, for the most part, an Almohad. In the 1220s the Hafsids rose to prominence and in 1236 proclaimed the **Hafsid Kingdom.** About 1247 they supplanted the Almohads in Tripoli (see **Hafsid Tripoli [i]**).

Zirid Governors for the Almohads: 1160–23 Aug. 1172 Sheikh Abu Yahya. *Aiyubid Governors:* 23 Aug. 1172–1190 Qaraqush. *Almohad Governors:* 1190–(?) [unknown]. *Aiyubid Governors:* (?)–1202 Qaraqush. *Almohad Governors:* 1202–1204 [unknown]; 1204–1207 Yahya al-Miruki; 1207–25 Feb. 1221 Abu Muhammad Abdul-Wahid; March 1221–June 1221 Abu Sa'id Abdarrahman; 1221–1221 Sayid Abu'l Ala Idris; 1221–1222 Ibrahim ibn Ismail Al-Hafs (acting); 1222–1223 Sayid Abu'l Ala Idris; 1223–1223 Abu Yahya Amran; 1224–1224 Abu Zaiyid; 1224–Aug. 1226 Abu Amran Musa; Aug. 1226–1228 [unknown]; 1228–1236 Yahya; 1236–ca. 1247 Abdarrahman Yaqub.

43 Almohad Tunis. July 1159–1236. *Location:* Tunisia. *Capital:* al-Mahdiya. *Other names:* Tunis.

History: In 1160 Tunis (see **Banu Khurasan Tunis**) fell under the **Almohad Empire** and became a province of that organization, ruled by an Almohad governor. In 1236 Tunis was declared independent as the **Hafsid Kingdom.**

Governors: July 1159–(?) Abu Ishak Ibrahim; (?)–1168 Abu Yahya al-Hassan; 1168–1195 [unknown]; 1195–1200 Abd al-Karim ar-Ragrag; 1200–May 1207 [unknown]; May 1207–Feb. 1221 Abu Muhammad Abd al-Wahid; Feb. 1221–May 1221 Abu Sa'id Abdarrahman; May 1221–Nov. 1221 Abu Ishak Ibrahim; Nov. 1221–1223 Saiyid Abu'l Ala Idris; 1223–Nov. 1226 Abu Sa'id Abdarrahman; Nov. 1226–June 1228 Abu Muhammad Abdallah Abu; June 1228–1236 Abu Zakariyya Yahya.

44 Almoravid Empire. 1031–3 Apr. 1147. *Location:* Morocco, western Algeria, southern Spain. *Capital:* Marrakesh (from 1086); Fez (1065–86); Ajmat (1031–65).

History: The al-Murabitun (Warrior Monks) or Almoravids were a grouping of Berber tribes of the Sanhajah clan of the Sahara. They ruled much of the Maghrib as successors to the old **Idrisid State,** and most of Spain. In 1147 they were succeeded in turn by the **Almohad Empire.**

Emirs: 1031–(?) Yahya ibn Ibrahim; (?)–1056 Yahya ibn Umar; 1056–1061 Abu Bakr ibn Umar; 1061–2 Sept. 1106 Yusuf ibn Tashufin; 3 Sept. 1106–1142 Ali ibn Yusuf; 1142–22 Feb. 1145 Tashufin ibn Ali; 22 Feb. 1145–1146 Ibrahim ibn Tashufin; 1146–3 Apr. 1147 Ishaq ibn Ali.

Aloa, Alodia, Alva see **Alwah**

45 Alwah. (?)–1504. *Location:* Sudan. *Capital:* Soba (or Subah). *Other names:* Alva, Alodia, Aloa.

History: One of the major kingdoms of the Nilotic Sudan in the Dark Ages, it became Christian in 580, and in 1504 gave way to the **Funj Sultanate.**

Rulers: [unknown].

Amasuta see **Basutoland Kingdom**

Amathembuland see **Tembuland**

46 Ambas Bay British Protectorate.
19 July 1884–28 March 1887. *Location:*
Ambas Bay, Cameroun. *Capital:* Victoria (founded in 1858 and named for
Queen Victoria). *Other names:* Victoria Colony.
History: In 1884 **Victoria Colony** was
re-named Ambas Bay, a protectorate
being placed over it because of the
heavy German involvement in the area
(see **German Crown Land of North
West Africa**). In 1887 it nonetheless
became part of the German lands.
Rulers: 19 July 1884–28 March 1887
[unknown].

Amboland see **Ovamboland**

Andries-Ohrigstad see **Ohrigstad**

47 Andruna. ca. 1550–1852. *Location:* Comoros. *Capital:* [unknown].
History: The first Comoran sultanate after **Mayotte** to become part of the
French **Mayotte Protectorate**. This
happened in 1852.
Sultans: ca. 1550–1835 [unknown];
1835–1852 Tsimiharo.

Anecho see **Little Popo**

Angaziya see **Gran Comoro**

48 Anglo-Egyptian Sudan. 19 Jan.
1899–22 Oct. 1952. *Location:* as **Sudan
Republic.** *Capital:* Khartoum. *Other
names:* Sudan, The Sudan, Anglo-Egyptian Condominium.
History: In 1899 **Sudan** became an
Anglo-Egyptian Condominium, occupied by the forces victorious over the
Mahdist State (i.e. the British and the
Egyptians). Technically ruled by Britain and Egypt, in fact Britain ruled
alone. In 1952 the Sudan won self-rule
(see **Sudan [Self-Rule]**).
Governors-General: 21 Jan. 1899–23
Dec. 1899 Lord Kitchener; 23 Dec.
1899–31 Dec. 1916 Sir Reginald Wingate; 1 Jan. 1917–20 Nov. 1924 Sir Lee
Stack; 21 Nov. 1924–5 Jan. 1925 Wasey
Sterry (acting); 5 Jan. 1925–17 July
1926 Sir Geoffrey Archer; 31 Oct. 1926–
10 Jan. 1934 Sir John Maffey; 10 Jan.
1934–19 Oct. 1940 Sir Stewart Symes; 19
Oct. 1940–19 Oct. 1940 Sir Bernard
Bourdillon (never took office); 19 Oct.
1940–8 Apr. 1947 Sir Hubert Huddleston; 8 Apr. 1947–22 Oct. 1952 Sir
Robert Howe.

49 Angola. See these **names:**
Angola People's Republic (1975–)
Angola Democratic People's Republic (1975–1976)
Angola Revolutionary Government
in Exile (1962–1975)
Angola Overseas Province (1951–1975)
Angola Colony (1914–1951)
Portuguese West Africa Colony
(1885–1914)
Portuguese West Africa (1589–1885)
Angola Donatária (1575–1589)
Dutch West Africa (1641–1648)
Ndongo (ca. 1358–ca. 1675)

50 Angola Colony. 15 Aug. 1914–11
June 1951. *Location:* as **Angola Overseas Province** (includes the exclave of
Cabinda). *Capital:* Nova Lisboa (Huambo) (from 1927); Luanda (until
1927). *Other names:* Angola, Portuguese West Africa.
History: In 1914 **Portuguese West
Africa Colony** became Angola. In 1951
Angola became an Overseas Province
of Portugal (see **Angola Overseas
Province**).
Governors-General: 15 Aug. 1914–
1915 José Norton de Matos; 1915–1916
António de Eça; 1916–1917 Pedro do
Amorim; 1917–1918 Jaime de Castro
Morais; 1918–1919 Filomeno Cabral;
1919–1920 Mimosa Guera (acting);
1920–1921 Vizconde de Pedralva. *Governors-General/High Commissioners:*
1921–1924 José Norton de Matos; 1924–
1924 João Soares; 1924–1925 Antero de
Carvalho; 1925–1926 Francisco
Chaves; 1926–1928 António Ferreira;
1928–1929 António Mora; 1929–1930

Filomeno Cabral; 1930–1931 José Sousa Faro; 1931–1934 Eduardo Viana; 1934–1935 Júlio Lencastre; 1935–1939 António Mateus; 1939–1941 Manuel Mano; 1941–1942 Abel Souto-Maior; 1942–1943 Álvaro Morna; 1943–1943 Manuel Figueira; 1943–1947 Vasco Alves; 1947–1947 Fernando Mena; 1947–11 June 1951 José Carvalho.

51 Angola Democratic People's Republic. 23 Nov. 1975–11 Feb. 1976. *Location:* as **Angola People's Republic.** *Capital:* Huambo (founded 1912, and from 1928–1975 called Nova Lisboa). *Other names:* Democratic People's Republic of Angola.

History: On November 11, 1975 **Angola Overseas Province** became independent as **Angola People's Republic,** with its capital in Luanda. Agostinho Neto, the leader of the Soviet-backed MPLA (Popular Movement for the Liberation of Angola) formed a government. But the other two freedom groups, UNITA (National Union for the Total Independence of Angola), led by Dr. Jonas Savimbi, and the FNLA (National Front for the Liberation of Angola), led by Holden Roberto (see also **Angola Revolutionary Government in Exile**), wanted to be in power too, and joined forces later in November to form their own joint government at Huambo. The Communist and Capitalist powers of the world lined up over this squabble. Cuban troops helped the MPLA win the war and take Huambo in February 1976. The Organization of African Unity recognized the MPLA as a member on February 11, and from this date the rival government was finished politically, although FNLA and UNITA continued guerrilla warfare until 1984 when the FNLA members surrendered. Only UNITA remains as a "problem."

Prime Minister (UNITA): 23 Nov. 1975–11 Feb. 1976 José Ndele. *Prime Minister (FNLA):* 23 Nov. 1975–11 Feb. 1976 Johnny Pinnock.

52 Angola Donatária. 1 Feb. 1575–1589. *Location:* Angola coast. *Capital:* São Paulo de Loanda. *Other names:* São Paulo de Loanda.

History: The Angolan coast was discovered by the Portuguese navigator Diogo Cam in 1482. Portuguese missionaries went out and then the army. In 1575 Paulo Dias de Novais was given a stretch of land as a donatária by the Portuguese government. This land lay south of the Congo Estuary. This was the germ of the later colony of **Portuguese West Africa,** which the area became after the death of de Novais in 1589.

Donatários: 1 Feb. 1575–1589 Paulo Dias de Novais.

53 Angola Overseas Province. 11 June 1951–11 Nov. 1975. *Location:* West Africa (includes the exclave of Cabinda). *Capital:* Nova Lisboa (founded 1912. Named Huambo from 1912–27 and from 1975 on). *Other names:* Angola, Portuguese West Africa.

History: In 1951 **Angola Colony** became an overseas province of Portugal. On January 31, 1975 a transitional government (i.e. a local autonomous government) was set up, but collapsed in July of that year. In November 1975 the country became totally independent as **Angola People's Republic.** (See also **Angola Revolutionary Government in Exile.**).

Governors-General/High Commissioners: 11 June 1951–1955 José Carvalho; 1955–1956 Manuel Gaivão (acting); 1956–15 Jan. 1960 Horácio Rebêlo; 15 Jan. 1960–23 June 1961 Álvaro Távares; 23 June 1961–26 Sept. 1962 Venâncio Deslandes; 26 Sept. 1962–27 Oct. 1966 Jaime Marquês; 27 Oct. 1966–Oct. 1972 Camilo de Miranda Rebocho Vaz; Oct. 1972–May 1974 Fernando Santos e Castro; May 1974–15 June 1974 Joaquim Pinheiro (acting); 15 June 1974–24 July 1974 Jaime Marquês; 24 July 1974–24 Jan. 1975 António Coutinho (acting); 24 Jan. 1975–

Aug. 1975 António Cardoso; Aug. 1975–Aug. 1975 Ernesto de Macedo (interim); Aug. 1975–11 Nov. 1975 Leonel Cardoso. *Presidents of Military Junta:* 24 July 1974–1974 António Coutinho. *Presidents of Provisional Government:* 1974–1974 António Coutinho. *Prime Ministers:* 31 Jan. 1975–July 1975 António Coutinho.

54 Angola People's Republic. 11 Nov. 1975– . *Location:* West Africa. *Capital:* Luanda (founded 1576, it became the capital in 1627. Formerly known as São Paolo de Loanda, it was named for the ancient chiefdom of Luanda). *Other names:* People's Republic of Angola, República Popular de Angola, Angola.

History: In 1975 **Angola Overseas Province** achieved its independence (see also **Angola Democratic People's Republic**), and this was the culmination of the work of the **Angola Revolutionary Government in Exile,** which had been set up since 1962, as well as of Agostinho Neto's MPLA (Popular Movement for the Liberation of Angola) and Jonas Savimbi's UNITA (National Union for the Total Independence of Angola). *Presidents:* 11 Nov. 1975–10 Sept. 1979 António Agostinho Neto; 21 Sept. 1979– José Eduardo dos Santos. *Prime Ministers:* 14 Nov. 1975–9 Dec. 1978 Lopo do Nascimento. *Note:* in times of no Prime Minister, the President held that office.

55 Angola Revolutionary Government in Exile. 5 Apr. 1962–11 Nov. 1975. *Location:* based out of **Zaire.** *Capital:* based at Kinshasa (Leopoldville) in **Zaire (Congo).** *Other names:* Governo Revolucionário de Angola no Exilio, GRAE.

History: In 1962 the FNLA (Frente Nacional de Libertaçao de Angola), the Revolutionary Front for the Liberation of Angola, set up a government in exile, based in Zaire. In 1963 it was recognized by its host country **Congo**

(Leopoldville) as well as by the Organization of African Unity, and in 1972 it was renamed The Supreme Council for the Liberation of Angola, under the auspices of the OAU. In 1975 Portugal granted complete independence to **Angola Overseas Province,** and it became **Angola People's Republic.**

Prime Ministers: 5 Apr. 1962–11 Nov. 1975 Holden Roberto.

56 Anjouan. ca. 1500–1866. *Location:* Comoros, in the Indian Ocean. *Capital:* Domoni (latterly); Mutsamudu (formerly). *Other names:* Ansuani, Nzwani, Anjouan Sultanate, Joanna (pirates' slang).

History: Founded about 1500, the Sultanate of Anjouan (the "Joanna" of the Red Sea Pirates) became part of the **Mayotte Protectorate** in 1866. *Sultans:* ca. 1500–ca. 1506 Muhammad I; ca. 1506–(?) Hassan; (?)–(?) Muhammad II; (?)–(?) Msindra. *Queens:* (?)–(?) Alimah I. *Regents:* ca. 1590–ca. 1605 Sayid Alawi. *Sultans:* ca. 1605–ca. 1610 Hussein. *Regents:* ca. 1610–ca. 1619 Sayid Idarus; ca. 1619–ca. 1632 Sayid Abu Bakr. *Queens:* ca. 1632–ca. 1676 Alimah II; ca. 1676–ca. 1711 Alimah III. *Sultans:* ca. 1711–1741 Sheikh Salim; 1741–1782 Sheikh Ahmad; 1782–1788 Abdallah I. *Queens:* 1788–1792 Halimah. *Sultans:* 1792–1796 Abdallah I; 1796–1816 Alawi; 1816–1832 Abdallah II; 1832–1833 Ali; 1833–1836 Abdallah II; 1836–1837 Alawi II; 1837–1852 Salim; 1852–Feb. 1891 Abdallah III; Feb. 1891–2 Apr. 1891 Salim II; 2 Apr. 1891–14 Apr. 1892 Sayid Umar; 14 Apr. 1892–25 July 1912 Sayid Muhammad.

Ankhole, Ankole see **Nkore**

57 Annobón (Portuguese). 7 Jan. 1494–1 March 1778. *Location:* Pagalu, Equatorial Guinea. *Capital:* San António (local headquarters), but administered from Santa Isabel on Fernando Po. *Other names:* Annobón.

History: In 1494 Annobón, until

then a Portuguese possession (see **Annobón [Portuguese Possession]**) became a colony of Portugal. In 1778 it went to Spain (see **Annobón [Spanish Possession]**).
Rulers: ruled direct from Fernando Po (Portuguese).

58 Annobón (Portuguese Possession). 1 Jan. 1474–7 Jan. 1494. *Location:* Pagalu, Equatorial Guinea. *Capital:* none.
History: Discovered in 1474, Annobón Island became a colony of Portugal in 1494 (see **Annobón [Portuguese]**).
Rulers: none.

59 Annobón (Spanish Possession). 1 March 1778–1926. *Location:* Pagalu, Equatorial Guinea. *Capital:* San António (local headquarters), but ruled from Santa Isabel on Fernando Po. *Other names:* Annobón.
History: In 1778 the Spanish took over Annobón (see **Annobón [Portuguese]**). In 1926 the island became part of **Spanish Guinea.**
Rulers: ruled direct from Fernando Po, except during the time of the British occupation of Fernando Po (see **Fernando Po [British]** from 1827–55).

Ansouani see **Anjouan**

Antemoro see **Madagascar Kingdom**

60 Anyidi Revolutionary Government. 15 July 1969–1970. *Location:* southern Sudan. *Capital:* none. *Other names:* ARG.
History: Founded in 1969 by Emidio Tafeng, an Anya Nya commander, as a partner to the **Nile Provisional Government** in the Southern Sudan, it was soon swallowed up by Joseph Lagu's Southern Sudan Liberation Front (SSLF) (see **Nile Provisional Government** and **Southern Sudan Provisional Government** for further details).
Presidents: 15 July 1969–1970 Emidio Tafeng Lodongi.

Aoukar see **Ghana Empire**

Arab Democratic Republic see **Saharan Arab Democratic Republic**

61 Arab Islamic Republic. 12 Jan. 1974–14 Jan. 1974. *Location:* **Tunisia Republic** and **Libyan Republic** joined. *Capital:* Tunis.
History: In 1974 President Bourguiba of **Tunisia Republic** and Colonel Qaddafi of the **Libyan Republic** signed the Djerba Declaration uniting the two countries as The Arab Islamic Republic. The closeness of the two countries may have warranted this move, but two days later Bourguiba reneged on the arrangement and the republic dissolved.
Presidents: 12 Jan. 1974–14 Jan. 1974 Habib Bourguiba. *Vice-Presidents:* 12 Jan. 1974–14 Jan. 1974 Muammar al-Qaddafi.

62 Arab North Africa [i]. 647–649. *Location:* North Africa (Libya, Tunisia, Algeria). *Capital:* al-Qayrawan. *Other names:* Ifriqa, Ifriqiyah.
History: In 647 the Arabs conquered **Byzantine North Africa [i].** In 649 the Byzantines re-conquered it (see **Byzantine North Africa [ii]**).
Governors: 647–649 Abdallah ibn Sa'd.

63 Arab North Africa [ii]. 667–697. *Location:* North Africa (Libya, Tunisia, Algeria). *Capital:* al-Qayrawan. *Other names:* Ifrika, Ifriqiyah.
History: In 667 the Arabs re-conquered **Byzantine North Africa [ii]**, but in 697 lost it again (see **Byzantine North Africa [iii]**).
Governors: 667–669 Mu'awaiyah; 669–675 Uqba; 675–682 Abul Muhagir Dinar; 682–683 Uqba; 683–686 during this time the area which is today Tunisia was in Berber hands; 686–689 Zuhayr; 689–689 Abdul Malik; 689–697 Hassan.

64 Arab Republic of Egypt. 2 Sept. 1971– . *Location:* northeast Africa.

Capital: Cairo (founded in 969 and named al-Qahir, meaning "the planet Mars," under whose sign the city was founded). *Other names:* Egyptian Arab Republic, Egypt.

History: In 1971 the **United Arab Republic** became The Arab Republic of Egypt. In 1979 Begin of Israel and Sadat of Egypt made peace after 31 years of enmity and war between the two countries, and Sinai was returned to Egypt.

Presidents: 2 Sept. 1971–6 Oct. 1981 Muhammad Anwar as-Sadat; 10 Oct. 1981–13 Oct. 1981 Sufi Abu Talib (acting); 13 Oct. 1981– Muhammad Hosni Mubarrak. *Prime Ministers:* 2 Sept. 1971–17 Jan. 1972 Mahmoud Fawzi; 17 Jan. 1972–27 March 1973 Aziz Sidqi; 25 Sept. 1974–13 Apr. 1975 Abdul Aziz Hegazy; 13 Apr. 1975–2 Oct. 1978 Mamdouh Salem; 2 Oct. 1978–12 May 1980 Mustafa Khalil; 7 Oct. 1981–13 Oct. 1981 Muhammad Hosni Mubarrak; 2 Jan. 1982–5 June 1984 Ahmad Fuad Mohieddin; 5 June 1984–17 July 1984 Kamal Hassan Ali (acting); 17 July 1984–4 Sept. 1985 Kamal Hassan Ali; 4 Sept. 1985–12 Nov. 1986 Ali Lutfi; 12 Nov. 1986– Atif Sidqi. *Note:* in times of no Prime Minister, the President held that office.

Ardra, Ardrah see **Allada**

Argeyes see **Agaie**

65 Argungu. 1827–1902. *Location:* as **Kebbi.** *Capital:* Argungu. *Other names:* Kebbi.

History: In 1827 the rebel Sarkin of **Kebbi,** Samaila, established his new emirate at Argungu, and the country that grew up here was also called Argungu. In 1831 the **Fulani Empire,** which had previously conquered **Kebbi,** conquered Argungu, and ruled until 1849, when the Kebbawa people kicked out the invader. In 1902 Argungu became part of **Northern Nigeria Protectorate** and in 1906 a considerable portion of it in the West was given to

French West Africa.

Emirs: 1827–1831 Samaila (or Karari). *Emirs in Exile:* 1831–1849 Yakubu Nabame. *Emirs:* 1849–1854 Yakubu Nabame; 1854–1859 Yusufu Mainassara; 1859–1860 Muhammadu Ba Are; 1860–1883 Abdullahi Toga; 1863–1915 Samaila II (or Sama); 1915–1920 Suleimana; 1920–1934 Muhammadu Sama; 1934–1942 Muhammadu Sani; 1942–1953 Samaila III; 1953–1959 Muhammadu Shefe; 1959– Muhammadu Mera.

Asante see **Ashanti**

66 Ascension. See these **names:** Ascension Dependency (1922–) Ascension (1815–1922)

67 Ascension. 6 Oct. 1815–1922. *Location:* as **Ascension Dependency.** *Capital:* administered from Jamestown, Saint Helena.

History: Discovered by the Portuguese navigator João da Nova Castela on Ascension Day 1501, it was uninhabited until 1815, when Napoleon arrived on Saint Helena. A few British troops were based here from that time. The island was administered from Saint Helena (see **Saint Helena British Crown Colony, Saint Helena [East India Company] [ii]** and **Saint Helena Colony**). In 1922 it became **Ascension Dependency.**

Rulers: ruled from Jamestown, Saint Helena.

68 Ascension Dependency. 1922– . *Location:* 700 miles northwest of Saint Helena. *Capital:* administered from Jamestown, Saint Helena.

History: Since 1922 (see **Ascension**), this island has been a dependency of **Saint Helena Colony.**

Rulers: ruled by the Governor of Saint Helena Colony, through an administrator on Ascension.

Aseb see **Assab**

69 Ashanti Colony. 26 Sept. 1901–6 March 1957. *Location:* mid-Ghana. *Capital:* Kumasi. *Other names:* Asiante, Ashantee, Sianti.

History: In 1901 **Ashanti Protectorate** was taken into **Gold Coast** as Ashanti Colony and administered separately, the administration reporting to Accra (cf **Gold Coast Northern Territories** and **Gold Coast Colony Region**). In 1957, at Ghana's independence (see **Ghana Dominion**), Ashanti Colony became defunct, and the Ashanti themselves became little more than a memory as far as the rest of the world went.

Residents: 26 Sept. 1901–1902 Donald Stewart. *Chief Commissioners:* 1902–1904 Sir Donald Stewart; 1904–1920 Francis Fuller; 1920–1923 Charles Harper; 1923–1931 John Maxwell; 1931–1933 Harry Newlands; 1933–1936 Francis Jackson; 1936–1941 Hubert Stevenson; 1941–1946 Edward Hawkesworth; 1946–1951 Charles Butler; 1951–1952 William Beaton. *Regional Officers:* 1952–1954 William Beaton; 1954–1955 Arthur Loveridge; 1955–6 March 1957 Arthur Russell. *Note:* for Ashanti kings before, during and after this period, see **Ashanti Empire.**

70 Ashanti Empire. ca. 1680–27 Aug. 1896. *Location:* central Ghana. *Capital:* Kumasi (from ca. 1695. Named for the "kum" tree); Asumenya Santemanso (until ca. 1695). *Other names:* Sianti, Ashantee, Asante, Asiante, Ashanti Kingdom.

History: Osei Tutu united the Twi-speaking people of the **Ashanti State** and founded the famous Ashanti Empire about 1680. In 1874 came the first Ashanti War with Britain, the second in 1900 (see **Ashanti Protectorate** and **Ashanti Colony**). In 1896 Britain placed a protectorate over Ashanti land (see **Ashanti Protectorate**). (See also **Denkyira, Ghana Dominion,** and the **Gold Coast** entries.)

Asantahenes (Kings): ca. 1680–Dec. 1712 Osei Tutu; 1712–1717 [unknown]; 1717–1720 vacant; 1720–May 1750 Osei Apoko Ware; May 1750–1764 Kwasi Obodun; 1764–1777 Osei Kojo (or Kwadwo); 1777–1801 Osei Kwame; 1801–1801 Opuku Fofie; 1801–21 Jan. 1824 Osei Bonsu (or Osei Tutu Quamina); 21 Jan. 1824–1838 Yau Akoto; 1838–1867 Kwaka Dua I; 1867–4 Feb. 1874 Karikari; 4 Feb. 1874–1883 Mansa Bonsu; 1883–1884 Civil War contenders; 1884–June 1884 Kwaka Dua II; June 1884–23 March 1888 vacant; 23 March 1888–17 Jan. 1896 Prempeh I (or Kwaka Dua III); 17 Jan. 1896–2 Jan. 1935 vacant; 2 Jan. 1935–June 1970 Prempeh II; 6 July 1970–   Opoku Ware II.

71 Ashanti Protectorate. 27 Aug. 1896–26 Sept. 1901. *Location:* as **Ashanti Colony.** *Capital:* Kumasi. *Other names:* Ashantee, Asanti, Sianti, Asiante.

History: In 1896 the **Ashanti Empire** came to an end, a British protectorate being placed over it. For some years there was alarming resistance to this move, but in 1901 the **Ashanti Colony** was created.

Residents: 27 Aug. 1896–1900 Donald Stewart; 1900–1901 Cecil Armitage (acting); 1901–26 Sept. 1901 Donald Stewart. *Note:* for list of Kings of Ashanti before, during and after this period, see **Ashanti Empire.**

72 Ashanti State. ca. 1570–ca. 1680. *Location:* middle Ghana. *Capital:* Asumenya Santemanso. *Other names:* Sianti, Ashantee, Asante, Asiante.

History: About 1570 Twum founded the Twi-speaking Akan state of Ashanti, a people bound loosely together until about 1680 when Osei Tutu founded the **Ashanti Empire.** His predecessor, Obiri, founded the capital at Kumasi.

Chiefs: ca. 1570–ca. 1590 Twum; ca. 1590–ca. 1600 Antwi; ca. 1600–ca. 1630 Kobia Amanfi; ca. 1630–ca. 1659 Oti Akenten; ca. 1659–ca. 1678 Obiri Yeboa; ca. 1678–ca. 1680 Osei Tutu.

Asiante see **Ashanti**

73 Assab. Dec. 1882–1 Jan. 1890.
Location: southern Eritrean coast.
Capital: Assab. *Other names:* Aseb,
Assab Protectorate.
History: In 1882 the Italians estab-
lished a protectorate over Assab. In
1885 they did the same to **Massawa,**
and in 1888 with the Danakil country.
They all combined in 1890 to form
Eritrea Colony.
Commandants: Dec. 1882–1885 Giu-
lio Pestalozza; 1885–1 Jan. 1890
[unknown].

Assinie see **Ivory Coast Protectorate**

Awfat see **Ifat**

Awlad Muhammad Dynasty see **Fezzan**

Awome see **New Calabar**

74 Axum. 250–ca. 950. *Location:*
Ethiopia-Sudan. *Capital:* Nazaret (now
Adama) (latterly); Azum (formerly).
Other names: Axume, Axumite Em-
pire, Axumite Kingdom.
History: Settled by the Habashi from
Abaseni in Arabia, Axum extended
over much of present-day Ethiopia and
Sudan. About 950 the dynasty was over-
thrown by Agau chief Judith. Axum
was abandoned. In 1150 the Zagwe
Dynasty re-established the kingdom at
Roha (see **Zagwe Kingdom**).
Kings: 250–ca. 300 Aphilas Bisi-
Dimele; ca. 300–325 unknown kings
reigned; 325–328 Ezana (or Aiezanes);
328–356 Ezana (or Aiezanes) (joint);
328–356 Shiazana (joint); 356–370 Ella
Abreha (joint); 356–370 Ella Asfeha
(joint); 356–370 Ella Shahel (joint);
370–374 Arfed; 374–379 Adhana; 379–
380 Rete'a; 380–381 Asfeh; 381–386
Asbeha; 386–401 Ameda; 401–401
Abreha; 401–402 Shahel; 402–404 Gobaz; 404–408 Suhal; 408–418 Abreha;
418–424 Adhana; 424–434 Yo'ab; 434–
436 Sahan; 436–446 Ameda; 446–448

Shahel; 448–451 Sabah; 451–466 Sa-
hem; 463–474 Gobaz (joint king for the
first 3 years); 474–475 Agabe (joint);
474–475 Lewi (joint); 475–486 Ella
Amida; 486–489 Jacob (joint); 486–489
David (joint); 489–504 Armah;
504–505 Zitana; 505–514 Jacob II;
514–542 Caleb (or El-Eshaba); 542–550
Beta Esrael; 550–564 Gabra Masqal;
564–578 Quastantinos; 578– 591 Wasan
Sagad; 591–601 Feresanay; 601–623
Adreaz; 623–633 Eklewudem; 633–648
Germa Safar; 648–656 Zergaz; 656–677
Mikael; 677–696 Baher Ikela; 696–720
Hezba Seyon; 720–725 Asagum;
725–741 Latem; 741–762 Tulatem;
762–775 Adegos; 775–775 Ayzur;
775–780 Dedem Almaz; 780–790 We-
demdem; 790–820 Demawedem; 820–
825 Rema Armah; 825–845 Degnajan;
845–846 Gedajan. *Queens:* 846–885
Judith. *Kings:* 885–905 Degnajan;
905–ca. 950 Del Nead.

Ayyubid see **Aiyubid**

Azania see **South Africa**

Babur see **Biu**

Bade see **Bedde**

75 Baguirmi. 1513–21 March 1899.
Location: the Baguirmi area of present-day **Chad Republic.** *Capital:* Cekna
(from 1902); Massenya (until 1902).
Other names: Bagirmi.
History: A Barma people situated
between **Bornu** and **Wadai,** they
formed a kingdom at their capital of
Massenya, in 1513. The history of
Baguirmi is one of wars with, and pay-
ing tribute to, its two large neighbors.
In 1892, the Sudanese adventurer Rabih invaded and destroyed Baguirmi,
and in 1897 the Sultan (or Mbang)
asked France for protection. In 1899 it
was taken into the French sphere of influence, in 1900 becoming part of **Chad
Military Territory and Protectorate.** In
1918 the Mbangs became chefs-de-
canton of the Massenya District of

Chad, the Sultanate being abolished in 1960, but re-instated in 1970.

Mbangs: 1513–1528 Birni Bessé; 1528–1540 Lubatko; 1540–1561 Malo; 1561–1602 Abdallah; 1602–1620 Omar; 1620–1631 Dalai; 1631–1661 Bourkomanda I; 1661–1670 Abderrahman Woli; 1670–1676 Dalo Birni; 1676–1704 Abdel Kadir Woli; 1704–1719 Bar; 1719–1734 Wanga; 1734–1739 Bourkomanda Tad Lélé; 1739–1749 Loel; 1749–1784 Muhammad al-Amin; 1784–1806 Abderrahman Guarang I; 1806–1806 Ngarba Bira; 1806–1846 Bourkomanda II; 1846–1858 Abd al-Kedir; 1858–1882 Abou Sekin Muhammad; 1882–1885 Bourkomanda III; 1885–1918 Abderrahman Guarang II; 1918–1935 Abd al-Kedir (or Manga); 1935–1960 Yusuf.

76 Bahr al-Ghazal Province. 29 Jan. 1869–30 Apr. 1884. *Location:* southern Sudan. *Capital:* Waw. *Other names:* Bahr el-Ghazal, Bahr al-Jazal.

History: In 1869 the Egyptians created Bahr al-Ghazal Province, part of **Egyptian Sudan.** In 1885 it fell to the **Mahdist State.**

Governors: 29 Jan. 1869–1872 Hajji Mehmed Nazir; 1872–March 1878 Zubeir Pasha; March 1878–June 1878 Idris Wad Daftar; June 1878–1879 Mehmed; 1879–Sept. 1880 Romolo Gessi Pasha; Sept. 1880–Dec. 1881 unknown acting governor; Dec. 1881–28 Apr. 1884 Frank Lupton; 28 Apr. 1884–30 Apr. 1884 Ali Musa Bey Sawqi.

77 Bahrite Mameluke Empire. 2 May 1250–26 Nov. 1382. *Location:* Egypt, Libya, the Levant and the Red Sea coasts. *Capital:* Cairo. *Other names:* Mameluke Empire, Bahri Sultanate of Egypt.

History: In 1250 Saladin's dynasty, the Aiyubids (see **Aiyubid Empire**) was overthrown by the Sultan's bodyguards, the Bahrite Mamelukes, and their leader became the new dynastic Sultan. In 1382 the Circassian Mamelukes took over (see **Circassian Mameluke Empire**).

Queens: 2 May 1250–31 July 1250 Sheger ed-Durr. *Sultans:* 31 July 1250–10 Apr. 1257 Aibak; 15 Apr. 1257–Nov. 1259 Noor-ed-Din; Nov. 1259–24 Oct. 1260 el-Mudhaffar Kutz; 24 Oct. 1260–1 July 1277 Beibars I; 3 July 1277–Aug. 1279 Said Barekh Khan; Aug. 1279–Nov. 1279 el-Adil Selamish; Nov. 1279–10 Nov. 1290 el-Mansaur Qalaun; 12 Nov. 1290–12 Dec. 1293 el-Ashraf Khalil; 14 Dec. 1293–Dec. 1294 Muhammad en-Nasir; Dec. 1294–7 Dec. 1296 el-Adil ed-Din Ketbugha; 7 Dec. 1296–16 Jan. 1299 el-Mansaur Lagin; 16 Jan. 1299–March 1309 Muhammad en-Nasir; Apr. 1309–5 March 1310 Beibars II; 5 March 1310–6 June 1341 Muhammad en-Nasir; 8 June 1341–1341 Abu-Bekr; 1341–1342 Ala ed-Din Kujuk; 1342–1343 Ahmad; 1343–1344 Ismail; 1344–1345 Shaabaan I; 1345–Dec. 1347 Haggee I; Dec. 1347–1351 Hassan; 1351–1354 Salih; 1354–1361 Hassan; 1361–1363 el-Mansaur ed-Din Muhammad; 1363–1368 Shaabaan II; 1368–1380 el-Mansaur Ala-ed-Din; 1380–26 Nov. 1382 es-Salih Haggee.

78 Bakgatlaland. ca. 1470–30 Sept. 1885. *Location:* Botswana. *Capital:* Mochudi. *Other names:* Bakgatla Kingdom.

History: The Bakgatla (Kgatla) formed one of the major divisions of what became **Bechuanaland Protectorate [i]** in 1885.

Kings: ca. 1470–(?) Malekeleke; (?)–(?) Masilo; ca. 1500–(?) Legabo; (?)–(?) Pogopi; (?)–(?) Botlolo; ca. 1600–(?) Mogala; (?)–(?) Matshego; (?)–(?) Kgafela; (?)–(?) Tebele; (?)–(?) Pheto I (Masellane); (?)–(?) Mare; ca. 1700–(?) Modimokwana; (?)–(?) Kgwefane; (?)–ca. 1780 Molefe; ca. 1780–ca. 1790 Makgotso; ca. 1790–ca. 1805 Pheto II; ca. 1805–ca. 1810 Senwelo; ca. 1810–ca. 1817 Letsebe; ca. 1817–ca. 1817 Senwelo; ca. 1817–ca. 1823 Motlotle; ca. 1823–ca. 1833 Molefi I; ca. 1833–ca. 1836 Kgotlamaswe; ca. 1836–ca. 1836 Molefi I; ca. 1836–ca. 1848 Pilane; ca.

1848-1874 Kgamanyane; 1874-1875 Bogatsu; 1875-1924 Lentswe. *Regents:* 1924-1929 Isang; 1929-1936 Kgosi Molefi II; 1936-1942 Mmusi; 1942-1945 Bakgatla; 1945- Molefi II.

Bakongo see **Kongo**

79 Bakwenaland. ca. 1570-30 Sept. 1885. *Location:* Botswana. *Capital:* Molepolole. *Other names:* Bakwena Kingdom, Land of the Crocodile People.

History: The Bakwena (or Kwena) were a major tribe of **Bechuanaland Protectorate [i],** or rather that protectorate which in 1885 took over all land of the tribes which make up present-day **Botswana.**

Kings: ca. 1570-(?) Masilo I; (?)-(?) Malope; ca. 1600-(?) Kwena; (?)-(?) Phokotsea; (?)-(?) Kgabo I; (?)-(?) Tebele; ca. 1700-(?) Kgabo II; (?)-(?) Masilo II; (?)-ca. 1770 Motsodhi; ca. 1770-ca. 1785 Motswasele I; ca. 1785-ca. 1795 Seitlhamo; ca. 1795-ca. 1803 Legwale; ca. 1803-ca. 1803 Malehe; ca. 1803-ca. 1807 Tshosa; ca. 1807-1821 Motswasele II; 1821-1829 Morvakgomo; 1829-1892 Setshele I; 1892-1911 Sebele I; 1911-1917 Setshele II; 1917-1931 Sebele II; 1931- Kgosi Kgari Setshele III.

80 Bamaleteland. ca. 1470-30 Sept. 1885. *Location:* Botswana. *Capital:* Gaberones (see also **Batlokwaland,** which shared the same capital). *Other names:* Bamalete Kingdom.

History: The Bamalete formed a country which, in 1885, became part of **Bechuanaland Protectorate [i].**

Kings: ca. 1470-(?) Badimo; (?)-(?) Phatle; (?)-(?) Malete; ca. 1500 Lesokwana; (?)-(?) Mokgware; (?)-(?) Digope; (?)-(?) Dira; (?)-(?) Mmusi; ca. 1600 Maphalaola; (?)-(?) Maoke; (?)-(?) Mongatane; (?)-(?) Maio; (?)-(?) Kgomo; ca. 1700 Mokgwa; (?)-(?) Marumo; (?)-ca. 1780 Poo I; ca. 1780- ca. 1805 Mokgojwa; ca. 1805-ca. 1820 Poo II; ca. 1820-1886 Mokgosi I;

1886-1896 Ikaneng; 1896-1906 Mokgosi II; 1906-1917 Bailutle; 1917-1937 Seboko; 1937-1945 Ketswerebothata; 1945- Mokgosi III.

81 Bamangwatoland. ca. 1610-30 Sept. 1885. *Location:* Botswana. *Capital:* Serowe. *Other names:* Bamangwato Kingdom.

History: The Bamangwato (or Ngwato) were the main tribe of what became **Bechuanaland Protectorate [i].**

Kings: ca. 1610-(?) Ngwato; (?)-(?) Molwa; (?)-(?) Tamasiga; (?)-(?) Seogola; (?)-(?) Madirana; ca. 1710 Kesitihoe; (?)-(?) Makgasama; (?)-ca. 1770 Molete; ca. 1770-ca. 1780 Mokgadi; ca. 1780-ca. 1795 Mathiba; ca. 1795-ca. 1817 Khama I; ca. 1817-ca. 1827 Kgari. *Regents:* ca. 1827-1833 Sedimo. *Kings:* 1833-1835 Khama II; 1835-1857 Sekgoma I; 1857-1858 Matsheng; 1858-1866 Sekgoma I; 1866-1872 Matsheng; 1872-1873 Khama III; 1873-1875 Sekgoma I; 1875-1923 Khama III; 1923-1925 Sekgoma II; 1925-1926 Gorewang; 1926-1956 Seretse Khama; 1956-5 May 1979 Rasebolai Kganane; 5 May 1979- Ian Seretse Khama.

Bambara Kingdoms see **Kaarta** and **Segu**

82 Bamoun Sultanate. 1394-14 July 1884. *Location:* around the Cameroun town of Foumban. *Capital:* Bamoun (or Mfom Ben, or Foumban). *Other names:* Bamum, Bamoum, Bamun.

History: Nehare, founder of the Bamoun dynasty, son of a Tikar chief, set out on a conquering expedition going south, and established himself in the Bamoun area, proclaiming himself King of the Pambans, and subjugating eighteen chiefs. Then he founded the town and sultanate of Bamoun. The kingdom was extended in the last half of the 18th century, and in 1884 the Sultan came under German domination in **German Crown Lands of North West Africa** (later known as **Kamerun**), although the Sultanate of Bamoun still exists.

Sultans: 1394–1418 Nehare Yen; 1418–1461 Ngoupou; 1461–1498 Monjou; 1498–1519 Mengap; 1519–1544 Ngouh I; 1544–1568 Fifen; 1568–1590 Ngouh II; 1590–1629 Ngapna; 1629–1672 Ngouloure; 1672–1757 Koutou; 1757–1814 Mbouombouo; 1814–1817 Gbetnkom; 1817–1818 Mbeikuo; 1818–1865 Ngouhouo; 1865–1865 Ngoungouré; 1865–1889 Nsangou; 1889–1931 Nyoja Ibrahim; 1931–1933 vacant; 1933– al-Hajj (or El Hadj) Saeidou Nyimoluh Nyoju.

83 Banana Island. ca. 1770–1820. *Location:* off the coast of Sierra Leone. *Capital:* Banana Island.
History: Four famous native kings ruled Banana Island until it was incorporated into **Sierra Leone Crown Colony** in 1820. The Caulkers then went on to rule **Bumpe.**
Kings: ca. 1770–1791 James Cleveland; 1791–1797 William; 1791–1810 Stephen Caulker; 1810–1820 Thomas Caulker.

84 Bangwaketseland. ca. 1650–30 Sept. 1885. *Location:* Botswana. *Capital:* Kanye. *Other names:* Bawanketseland, Bangwaketse Kingdom.
History: Founded about 1650, this was one of the major tribes (the Bangwaketse or Ngwaketse) of Bechuanaland, as it became in 1885 (see **Bechuanaland Protectorate [i]).**
Kings: ca. 1650 Ngwaketse; (?)–(?) Seepapitso; (?)–(?) Leema; (?)–(?) Khutwe; (?)–(?) Khutwane; (?)–ca. 1770 Makaba I; ca. 1770–ca. 1795 Mongala (or Molete); ca. 1795–1825 Makaba II. *Regents:* 1825–1843 Sebego (joint); 1825–1845 Segotshane (joint until 1843). *Kings:* 1845–July 1889 Gaseitswiwa; July 1889–1 July 1910 Bathoen; 1 July 1910–1916 Seepapitso II. *Regents:* 1916–1918 Kgosimotse; 1918–1919 Malope; 1919–1923 Tshosa; 1924–1925 Gagoangwe; 1925–1928

Ntebogang. *Kings:* 1928–1 July 1969 Kgosi Bathoen.

Banjol see **Bathurst Colony**

Banu al-Aghlab see **Aghlabid**

Banu al-Wadid see **Abd-al-Wadid**

Banu Hafs see **Hafsid**

Banu Hammad see **Hammamid**

85 Banu Khurasan Tunis. 1059–July 1159. *Location:* Tunisia. *Capital:* Tunis. *Other names:* Banu Hurasan Tunis, Tunis.
History: In 1059 the house of Khurasan began to rule Tunis as representatives of the **Zirid Kingdom,** which held sway over the area at that time. In 1159 with the collapse of the Zirids, Tunis fell to the Almohads (see **Almohad Tunisia** and **Almohad Empire**).
Sultans: 1059–1095 Sheikh Abu Muhammad ibn Khurasan; 1095–17 Nov. 1105 Sheikh Abu Muhammad Abdul Aziz; 17 Nov. 1105–8 March 1107 Abu Tahir Ismail; 8 March 1107–1128 Ahmad; 1128–(?) Abu'l Futuh Karama; (?)–(?) Muhammad; (?)–1149 Ma'add; 1149–1149 Abu Bakar; 1149–1158 Abdallah; 1158–July 1159 Ali.

Banu Rustum see **Rustumid**

Banu Wattas see **Wattasid**

Banu Zayyan see **Abd-al-Wadid**

86 Baol. ca. 1550–1877. *Location:* Senegal coast. *Capital:* Lambaye.
History: A satellite state of **Dyolof,** Baol was conquered by **Kayor** about 1550 and was a vassal state of Kayor until 1686. In 1877 the French took it as part of **Senegal Colony.**
Kings: ca. 1550–ca. 1560 Niokhor; ca. 1560–1593 Amari; 1593–(?) Mamalik Thioro; (?)–(?) Tié N'Della; (?)–(?) Tié Kura; (?)–(?) Mbissan Kura; (?)–ca. 1664 Tiande; ca. 1664–ca. 1690 M'Bar; ca. 1690–1693 Tié Yaasin

Demba; 1693–1697 Tié Tieumbeul; 1697–1719 Lat Sukaabe; 1719–1719 Mali Kumba Dyaring; 1719–1749 Ma-Kodu Kumba; 1749–ca. 1752 Mawa; ca. 1752–ca. 1758 M'Bissan N'Della; ca. 1758–1777 Ma-Kodu Kumba; 1777–1809 vacant; 1809–1815 Tié-Yaasin Dieng; 1815–1815 Tié-Kumba Faatim; 1815–ca. 1822 Amadi Dyor; ca. 1822–1832 Birayma Fatma; 1832–1832 Ma-Kodu Kodu Dyuf; 1832–1855 Isa Tein-Dyor; 1855–ca. 1857 Tié-Yaasin Ngone; ca. 1857–1859 Ma-Kodu Kodu Kumba; 1859–1862 Mali Kumba N'Gone; 1862–1890 Tié-Yaasin Gallo; 1890–3 July 1894 Tanor Gogne.

87 Barbary. A term used in the 18th and 19th centuries to denote the Maghrib. Term comes from Berber, original inhabitants of the area (Tripoli, Algiers, Tunis and Morocco).

Barca see **Cyrenaica**

Barnu see **Bornu**

88 Barolongland. ca. 1470–30 Sept. 1885. *Location:* Botswana. *Capital:* Lobatsi. *Other names:* Barolong Kingdom.
History: One of the oldest South African tribes, the Barolong (or Rolong) formed a major division of **Bechuanaland Protectorate [i]**, as the area became in 1885. In 1760, the Barolong had split into the Tshidi branch, staying in Bechuanaland, and the Seleka branch, going into South Africa proper.
Kings: ca. 1470–(?) Morolong; (?)–(?) Noto; ca. 1500 Morare; (?)–(?) Mabe; (?)–(?) Mabudi; (?)–(?) Maloto; ca. 1600 Mabeo; (?)–(?) Modiboya; (?)–(?) Tshesebe; (?)–(?) Setlhare; ca. 1700 Masepha; (?)–(?) Mokgopha; (?)–(?) Thibela; (?)–ca. 1760 Tau; ca. 1760–(?) Ratshidi (or Tsile); (?)–ca. 1805 Thutlwa; ca. 1805–(?) Leshomo; (?)–1849 Tawana; 1849–19 Oct. 1896 Montshiwa; 1896–1903 Besele; 1903–1911 Badirile; 1911–1915 Lekoko; 1915–1917 Joshua; 1917–1919 Bakolopang; 1919– Letla Moreng.

89 Barotseland. ca. 1550–11 June 1891. *Location:* Zambia (since 1969 the Western Province of Zambia; from 1964–69 the Barotse Province of Zambia). *Capital:* Lealui. *Other names:* Lozi Empire, Lotse Empire, Kololo-Rotse Empire (1838–64 only).
History: The Barotse (or Lozi, or Lotse) peoples were originally called the Aluyi. They founded the Lozi Empire around the middle of the 16th century. The nation was solidified around 1800 by Mulambwa. In 1838 they were conquered by the Kololo, a neighboring clan (the Lozi word "Aluyi" is translated into Kololo as "Barotse"), but in 1864 Prime Minister Njekwa threw the Kololo out. In the 1880s the Barotse gradually became subject to Britain, and in 1891 it became part of **Zambesia**. From that time it formed a large part of **Northern Rhodesia** (later **Zambia**). In the 1950s and 1960s the Barotse Native Government sought independent statehood, but this was rejected by Britain in 1961.
Litungas (Kings): ca. 1600 Mboo (or Mwana Silundu, or Muyunda); (?)–(?) Inyambo; (?)–(?) Yeta I; (?)–(?) Ngalama; (?)–(?) Yeta II; (?)–(?) Ngombala; (?)–(?) Yubya; (?)–(?) Mwanawina I (or Musanawina); (?)–1780 Mwananyanda (or Musananyanda); 1780–1830 Mulambwa; 1830–1838 Silumelume (joint); 1830–1838 Mubukwanu (joint) (also King of South Barotseland from ca. 1820–1830); 1838–1841 Mubukwanu; 1841–1860 Imasiku. *Regents:* 1860–1864 Sipopa (or Sepopa) (joint); 1860–1864 Njekwa (joint). *Litungas (Kings):* 1864–1876 Sipopa (or Sepopa); 1876–1878 Mwanawina II; 1878–1884 Lubosi (or Lewanika); 1884–1885 Tatila Akufuna (usurper); 1885–4 Feb. 1916 Lubosi (or Lewanika); 4 Feb. 1916–1945 Litia (or Yeta III); 1945–1948 Imwiko Lewanika; 1948–1968 Mwanawina III; 1968–1977 Godwin Mbikusita. *Kololo*

Rulers: 1838–1851 Sebitwane (King); 1851–1851 Mamosecane (Queen); 1851–1864 Sekeletu (King). *Prime Ministers:* 1864–1871 Njekwa; 1871–1878 [unknown]; 1878–1884 Silumbu; 1884–1885 Mataa; 1885–1898 Mwauluka; 1898–1919 [unknown]; 1919–(?) Mataa.

Barqah see **Cyrenaica**

Bashar see **Wase (Basharawa)**

Basotho-Qwaqwa see **Qwaqwa**

90 Bassa Cove. July 1835–1 Apr. 1839. *Location:* Liberia. *Capital:* Bassa Cove. *Other names:* Colony of Bassa Cove.
History: Sometime in July 1835 the Young Men's Colonization Society of Pennsylvania (Black Quakers) founded the Liberian settlement of Bassa Cove, on the ashes of **Port Cresson.** In 1837 it gained extra territory with the inclusion of **Edina,** and in 1839 the enlarged Bassa Cove Colony became part of the **Liberia Commonwealth.** In 1841 it changed its name to Buchanan.
Chief Magistrates: July 1835–Jan. 1836 Edward Hankinson; Jan. 1836–4 Aug. 1837 Thomas Buchanan; 4 Aug. 1837–June 1838 John Matthias; June 1838–1 Apr. 1839 Dr. Wesley Johnson.

Bastaards, Baster Gebiet see **Rehoboth**

91 Basutoland Crown Protectorate. 12 March 1868–11 Aug. 1871. *Location:* as **Lesotho.** *Capital:* Maseru (from March 11, 1869. Founded as the administrative capital by James Bowker); Thaba Bosiu (until 1869).
History: In 1868 the **Basutoland Protectorate** became a crown protectorate, i.e. a British agent was sent to advise the local king. In 1871 this state of affairs resulted in annexation of the country by the Cape (see **British Cape Colony**). (See **Basutoland Territory.**).
Kings: 12 March 1868–11 March 1870

Moshoeshoe I; 11 March 1870–11 Aug. 1871 Letsie I. *High Commissioner's Agents:* 14 March 1868–Apr. 1868 Walter Currie; Apr. 1868–11 March 1869 James Bowker (acting); 11 March 1869–May 1870 James Bowker; May 1870–Aug. 1871 William Surmon; Aug. 1871–11 Aug. 1871 Charles Griffith.

92 Basutoland High Commission Territory. 18 March 1884–1 Aug. 1964. *Location:* as **Lesotho.** *Capital:* Maseru. *Other names:* Basutoland.
History: In 1884 **Basutoland Territory** became a separate British area, one of the High Commission Territories (cf **Swaziland** and **Bechuanaland**). In 1964 it was granted self-rule (see **Basutoland [Self-Rule]**).
Kings: 18 March 1884–20 Nov. 1891 Letsie I; 20 Nov. 1891–19 Aug. 1905 Lerotholi; 19 Sept. 1905–28 Jan. 1913 Letsie II; 11 Apr. 1913–July 1939 Griffith; Aug. 1939–Dec. 1940 Seeiso. *Queens Regent:* Dec. 1940–12 March 1960 MaNtsebo. *Paramount Chiefs:* 12 March 1960–1 Aug. 1964 Moshoeshoe II. *Resident Commissioners:* 18 March 1884–18 Sept. 1894 Marshall Clarke (knighted 1886); 18 Sept. 1894–1895 Godfrey Lagden; 1895–1895 Herbert Sloley (acting); 1895–1901 Godfrey Lagden (knighted 1897); 1901–1913 Herbert Sloley (knighted 1911); 1913–1913 James MacGregor (acting); 1913–1915 Sir Herbert Sloley; 1915–1917 Robert Coryndon; 1917–Apr. 1926 Edward Garraway (knighted 1926); Apr. 1926–March 1935 John Sturrock (knighted 1934); March 1935–Aug. 1942 Edmund Richards (knighted 1941); Aug. 1942–Nov. 1946 Arden Clarke (from 1951 Sir Charles Arden-Clarke); Nov. 1946–24 Oct. 1951 Aubrey Forsyth-Thompson; 24 Oct. 1951–Sept. 1956 Edwin Arrowsmith; Sept. 1956–1961 Alan Chaplin; 1961–1 Aug. 1964 Alexander Giles. *Note:* see **Union of South Africa (Self-Rule)** for list of High Commissioners, who, after 1931 were no longer responsible for South Africa, only for the High Com-

ission Territories of Basutoland, Bechuanaland and Swaziland.

93 Basutoland Kingdom. 1822–13 Dec. 1843. *Location:* Southern Africa, in fact more or less as **Lesotho**. *Capital: Thaba Bosiu (from July 1824); Butha-Buthe (until July 1824). Other names:* Basutoland, Amasuta.
History: In 1822 Moshoeshoe I, leader of the Basotho, arrived in the area and built a kingdom. In 1843 it became **Basutoland Protectorate.**
Kings: 1822–13 Dec. 1843 Moshoshoe I.

94 Basutoland Protectorate. 13 Dec. 1843–12 March 1868. *Location:* as **Lesotho**. *Capital:* Thaba Bosiu (name means "The Hill of Night").
History: In 1843 Britain recognized the Kingdom of Basutoland (see **Basutoland**) and agreed to offer it protection. In 1868 it became **Basutoland Crown Protectorate.**
Kings: 13 Dec. 1843–12 March 1868 Moshoeshoe I.

95 Basutoland (Self-Rule). 1 Aug. 1964–4 Oct. 1966. *Location:* as **Lesotho**. *Capital:* Maseru (founded 1869). *Other names:* Basutoland.
History: In 1964 **Basutoland High Commission Territory** was granted self-rule, but it was still a British territory. In 1966 it gained complete independence, as **Lesotho.**
Kings: 1 Aug. 1964–4 Oct. 1966 Moshoeshoe II. *Prime Ministers:* 1 May 1965–5 July 1965 Chief Sekhonyana Maseribane; 5 July 1965–4 Oct. 1966 Chief Leabua Jonathan. *Resident-Commissioners:* 1 Aug. 1964–Apr. 1965 Alexander Giles (knighted 1965). *British Government Representatives:* Apr. 1965–4 Oct. 1966 Sir Alexander Giles. *High Commissioners for Basutoland, Bechuanaland and Swaziland:* 1 Aug. 1964–4 Oct. 1966 Sir Hugh Stephenson.

96 Basutoland Territory. 11 Aug.

1871–18 March 1884. *Location:* as **Lesotho**. *Capital:* Maseru.
History: In 1871 **Basutoland Crown Protectorate** was annexed to the Cape (see **British Cape Colony),** albeit as an autonomous territory. In 1884 it became **Basutoland High Commission Territory.**
Kings: 11 Aug. 1871–18 March 1884 Letsie I. *Governor's Agents:* 11 Aug. 1871–1877 Charles Griffith; 1877–9 Dec. 1877 Emile Rolland (acting); 9 Dec. 1877–1878 Charles Griffith; 1878–10 Oct. 1878 Emile Rolland (acting); 10 Oct. 1878–25 Aug. 1881 Charles Griffith; 25 Aug. 1881–16 March 1883 Joseph Orpen (acting); 17 March 1883–18 March 1884 Matthew Blyth (acting).

Batawana see **Batwanaland**

97 Bathurst Colony. 23 Aug. 1816–17 Oct. 1821. *Location:* as **Fort James.** *Capital:* Bathurst (founded 1816 and named for Henry Bathurst, British Colonial Secretary). *Other names:* Banjol, St. Mary.
History: In 1816 the British occupied Banjol and renamed the island Saint Mary. The town was called Bathurst. Power was in the hands of Captain Alexander Grant and the Royal African Corps, and the colony prospered. In 1821 all forts and settlements in West Africa were put under the rule of Sierra Leone (see **Gambia Territory [i]).**
Administrators: 23 Aug. 1816–17 Oct. 1821 Alexander Grant.

98 Bathurst Settlement and Dependencies in the Gambia. 12 Dec. 1829–11 Apr. 1843. *Location:* Banjul, Gambia, and parts of the interior. *Capital:* Bathurst.
History: In 1829 the first lieutenant-governor arrived in the Gambia (see **Gambia Territory [i]),** and the name of the area changed to Bathurst Settlement and Dependencies in the Gambia. In 1843 Gambia became a separate colony (see **Gambia Colony [i]).**
Lieutenant-Governors: 12 Dec.

1829–23 Feb. 1830 Lt.-Col. Alexander Findlay; 23 Feb. 1830–22 Sept. 1837 George Rendall; 22 Sept. 1837–Oct. 1838 Thomas Ingram (acting); Oct. 1838–May 1839 William Mackie; May 1839–Jan. 1840 Thomas Ingram (acting); Jan. 1840–Oct. 1841 Sir Henry Huntley; Oct. 1841–11 Apr. 1843 Thomas Ingram (acting).

Batlokoa Lands see **Sekonyela's Land**

99 Batlokwaland. ca. 1660–30 Sept. 1885. *Location:* Botswana. *Capital:* Gaberones (as also **Bamaleteland**). *Other names:* Batlokoaland, Batlokwa Kingdom.
History: Founded about 1660, the Batlokwa tribe formed one of the major divisions of what became **Bechuanaland Protectorate [i].**
Kings: ca. 1660 ca. 1680 Tshwaana; ca. 1680–ca. 1700 Mosime; ca. 1700–ca. 1730 Mothubane; ca. 1730–ca. 1750 Mokgwa; ca. 1750–ca. 1770 Taukobong; ca. 1770–ca. 1780 Makabe; ca. 1780–ca. 1815 Bogatswe; ca. 1815–ca. 1820 Kgosi; ca. 1820–1825 Leshage; 1825–1835 Bashe; 1835–1880 Matlapeng; 1880–1931 Gaborone I; 1931–1948 Matlala; 1948– Kgosi Gaborone II.

100 Batwanaland. ca. 1795–30 Sept. 1885. *Location:* Botswana. *Capital:* Maun. *Other names:* Batwana Kingdom, Batawana, Twanaland, Tawanaland.
History: One of the major divisions of Bechuanaland, which in 1885 became a British protectorate (see **Bechuanaland Protectorate [i]**).
Kings: ca. 1795–ca. 1820 Tawana; ca. 1820–ca. 1828 Moremi I; ca. 1828–ca. 1830 Sedumedi; ca. 1830–ca. 1840 Mogalakwe; ca. 1840–1874 Letsholathebe; 1875–1876 Meno; 1876–1876 Dithapo I; 1876–4 Nov. 1890 Moremi II; 1891–1891 Dithapo II; 1891–1906 Sekgoma; 1906–1906 Sekgathole; 1906–1933 Mathiba; 1933–1934 Monaamabura; 1934–1936 Dibolayang; 1936–

1937 Guetsalwe; 1937–1946 Moremi III. *Queens:* 1947– Dulano Seezo (or Elizabeth).

101 Bauchi Emirate. 1805–Feb. 1902. *Location:* northern Nigeria. *Capital:* Rauta (1877–1902); Bauchi (1809–77); Inkil (1805–09). *Other names:* Bautschi, Inkil (its name before 1809).
History: Uthman Dan Fodio, creator of the **Fulani Empire,** went on a jihad (holy war) from 1804–1809, conquering most of the kingdoms in Northern Nigeria and surrounding areas. Most of these kingdoms became emirates. Some emirates were created with no kingdom of that name preceding it. Such was Bauchi. Dan Fodio had 14 Masu-tuta (flag-bearers) who led his jihad. All were Fulani, except Yakubu, who was a Gerawa and a long-time disciple of Dan Fodio. In 1809 Yakubu founded the town of Bauchi. In 1902 Bauchi Emirate became part of **Northern Nigeria Protectorate,** as Bauchi Province.
Emirs: 1805–1843 Yakubu; 1843–1879 Ibrahim; 1879–1885 Usman; 1885–1902 Umaru; 1902–1903 Muhammadu; 1903–1908 Hassan; 1908–1941 Yakubu II; 1941–1954 Yakubu III; 1954– Adamu Jumba.

102 Baule. ca. 1710–ca. 1840. *Location:* Ivory Coast. *Capital:* Wareba.
History: The Baule people, an Ashanti-Bron tribe, came to their destination about the middle of the 18th century under the leadership of their queen, Awura Pokou. The kingdom disintegrated by 1840, and became part of the later **French Ivory Coast.**
Queens: ca. 1710–ca. 1750 Asae Pokou; ca. 1750–ca. 1760 Awura Danse Pokou; ca. 1760–ca. 1770 [unknown]. *Kings:* ca. 1770–ca. 1790 Akwa Bini; ca. 1790–ca. 1840 [unknown].

Baure see **Daura-Baure**

Bautschi see **Bauchi**

Bawanketseland see **Bangwaketseland**

103 Bechuanaland. 1 Aug. 1964–3 March 1965. *Location:* as **Botswana.** *Capital:* Mafeking (South Africa) (name means "among the stones").

History: In 1964 **Bechuanaland High Commission Territory** ceased to exist, as did all of the High Commission Territories in South Africa (cf **Swaziland** and **Basutoland**). In 1965 Bechuanaland gained self-government (see **Bechuanaland [Self-Rule]**).

Commissioners: 1 Aug. 1964–3 March 1965 Peter Fawcus. *Chief Native Administrators:* 1 Aug. 1964–3 March 1965 Rasebolai Khamane.

104 Bechuanaland High Commission Territory. 9 May 1891–1 Aug. 1964. *Location:* as **Botswana.** *Capital:* Mafeking (in South Africa).

History: In 1891 **Bechuanaland Protectorate [ii]** and **British Bechuanaland Crown Colony** were delimited and the protectorate (the northern part) became a High Commission Territory. On November 11, 1895 the southern part was annexed to the Cape. In 1964 the High Commission Territories (see also **Basutoland** and **Swaziland**) ceased to exist and the country became **Bechuanaland**.

Resident Commissioners: 9 May 1891–19 Nov. 1895 Sir Sidney Shippard; 19 Nov. 1895–21 Dec. 1897 Francis Newton; 21 Dec. 1897–Jan. 1901 Hamilton Goold-Adams; Jan. 1901–1906 Ralph Williams; 1906–1916 Francis Panzera; 1916–1917 Edward Garraway; 1917–1920 James MacGregor; 1920–1920 Jules Ellenberger (acting); 1920–1923 James MacGregor; 1923–1926 Jules Ellenberger; 1926–1926 Rowland Daniel (acting); 1926–1927 Jules Ellenberger; 1927–1930 Rowland Daniel; 1930–1937 Charles Rey (knighted 1932); 1937–1942 Arden Clarke (from 1951 Sir Charles Arden-Clarke); 1942–1946 Aubrey Forsyth-Thompson; 1946–1950 Anthony Sillery; 1950–1953 Edward

Beetham; 1953–1955 William Mackenzie; 1955–1959 Martin Wray; 1959–1 Aug. 1964 Peter Fawcus. *Chiefs of the Bamangwato:* 9 May 1891–2 Feb. 1923 Khama III; 2 Feb. 1923–1925 Sekgoma II; 1925–5 Feb. 1950 Seretse Khama. *Regents:* 1925–1952 Tshekedi Khama. *Chief Native Administrators:* 1952– Rasebolai Khamane. *Note:* see **Union of South Africa (Self-Rule)** for list of High Commissioners.

105 Bechuanaland Protectorate [i]. 23 March 1885–30 Sept. 1885. *Location:* same as modern day **Botswana,** plus the Bechuanaland part of north Cape Colony. *Capital:* None. *Other names:* Bechuanaland.

History: In 1885 the area generally known as Bechuanaland (i.e. the land of the Tswana peoples, or the Batswana) became a British protectorate. The kingdoms which comprised Bechuanaland were numerous, but the salient ones were **Batlokwaland, Batwanaland, Bakwenaland, Bangwaketseland, Bamangwatoland, Barolongland, Bakgatlaland** and **Bamaleteland.** Later in 1885 the protectorate was split up, the north becoming **Bechuanaland Protectorate [ii]** and the south **British Bechuanaland Crown Colony.**

Military Commanders: 23 March 1885–24 Sept. 1885 Sir Charles Warren; 24 Sept. 1885–30 Sept. 1885 Lt.-Col. Frederick Carrington.

106 Bechuanaland Protectorate [ii]. 30 Sept. 1885–9 May 1891. *Location:* as **Botswana.** *Capital:* Mafeking (in South Africa). *Other names:* North Bechuanaland.

History: In late 1885 the British took the area occupied by most of the Tswana tribes and known as **Bechuanaland Protectorate [i]** and divided it into the Bechuanaland Protectorate [ii] in the north and the **British Bechuanaland Crown Colony** in the south. The chief of the Bamangwato was overlord of all Bechuanaland. In 1891 the newer protectorate became **Bechuanaland High**

Commission Territory. *Chiefs of the Bamangwato:* 30 Sept. 1885–9 May 1891 Khama III. *British Administrator:* 30 Sept. 1885–9 May 1891 Sidney Shippard (knighted 1887).

Bechuanaland Republic see **United States of Stellaland**

107 Bechuanaland (Self-Rule). 3 March 1965–30 Sept. 1966. *Location:* as **Botswana.** *Capital:* Gaberones.

History: In 1965 **Bechuanaland [ii]** gained self-government. In 1966 it became fully independent as **Botswana.**

Commissioners: 3 March 1965–1965 Sir Peter Fawcus; 1965–30 Sept. 1966 Hugh Norman-Walker.

108 Bedde. 1825–1902. *Location:* northeastern Nigeria. *Capital:* Gorgoram. *Other names:* Bade (name comes from "Birnin-Bedr," their Arabian ancestral home).

History: The Bade tribe left **Kanem** and the Lake Chad area in the 13th century and kept on the move until they reached Dadigar. There they seem to have split up, one group staying at Dadigar and three others going elsewhere, one of them to Tagali. The Tagali group became dominant around 1475, and the later Royal Family (whose list of rulers appears below) left Dadigar in the 18th century and moved to Gazai, then united with their cousins at Tagali, then on to Gayin, Gidgid, Agama Kasha, Sagmaga, Satako, and finally to Gorgoram, which they built in 1825. Rabih (see **Rabih's Empire**) captured Gorgoram in 1893 and in 1902 it became Bedde Emirate of **Northern Nigeria Protectorate,** its capital later moving to Gashua.

Mais (Kings): (?)–(?) Dugum Bugia; (?)–(?) Dugum Akuya; ca. 1820–1842 Lawan Babuje; 1842–1893 Alhaji; 1893–1897 Duna; 1897–Apr. 1919 Saleh; Feb. 1920–1941 Sule; 1942–1945 Umara; 1945– Umar Suleiman.

109 Beledugu. ca. 1670–1870. *Location:* Mali. *Capital:* Nyoro (from 1846); Gemuo; Kodie; Sunsana (or Suntian) (1670–1709).

History: Founded about 1670, it became part of the **Tukolor Empire** in 1870.

Kings: ca. 1670–ca. 1690 Sunsa; ca. 1690–ca. 1690 Massa; ca. 1690–ca. 1700 Bemfa; ca. 1700–ca. 1709 Fulakoro; ca. 1709–1760 Sebe; 1760–1780 Denibabo; 1780–1788 Sirabo; 1788–1802 Dase; 1802–1812 Musa Kurabo; 1812–1815 Tegenkoro; 1815–1818 Sekuba; 1818–1835 Bodian Moriba; 1835–1844 Garan; 1844–1854 Kandia Mamadi; 1854–1870 Diringa Mori; 1870–1870 Bussei.

110 Belgian Congo. 15 Nov. 1908–30 June 1960. *Location:* as **Zaire.** *Capital:* Léopoldville (1923–60) (founded in 1881 by Henry M. Stanley and named for King Léopold of the Belgians); Boma (1908–23). *Other names:* Congo Belge.

History: In 1908 **Congo State (Belgian)** became the Belgian Congo. In 1960 it gained independence as **Congo (Léopoldville),** thus named to distinguish it from the other Congo across the Congo River (i.e. **Congo [Brazzaville]**). In 1933 Katanga had been brought into the Belgian Congo as its richest province.

Governors: 15 Nov. 1908–20 May 1912 Joseph Wahis; 20 May 1912–20 Aug. 1916 Félix Fuchs; 20 Aug. 1916–Jan. 1921 Joseph Henry; Jan. 1921–1923 Maurice Lippens; 1923–27 Dec. 1927 Joseph Rutten; 27 Dec. 1927–14 Sept. 1934 Auguste Tilkens; 14 Sept. 1934–31 Dec. 1946 Pierre Ryckmans; 1 Jan. 1947–Jan. 1951 Eugène Jungers; Jan. 1951–5 July 1958 Léon Pétillon; 5 July 1958–30 June 1960 Henri Cornelis. *Presidents:* 24 June 1960–30 June 1960 Joseph Kasavubu. *Prime Ministers-Designate:* 17 June 1960–19 June 1960 Joseph Kasavubu. *Prime Ministers:* 19 June 1960–21 June 1960 Joseph Kasavubu; 21 June 1960–30 June 1960 Patrice Lumumba.

111 Belgian Ruanda-Urundi. 21 May 1916–30 May 1919. *Location:* East Africa **(Rwanda** and **Burundi).** *Capital:* Boma **(Belgian Congo),** with local headquarters at Bujumbura. *Other names:* Ruanda-Urundi.

History: In 1916 the Belgian troops took German Ruanda-Urundi (part of **German East Africa [ii])** and administered it until 1919 when it was officially awarded to Belgium as **Ruanda-Urundi Territory.**

Governors: 21 May 1916–30 May 1919 Justin Malfeyt. *Kings of Ruanda:* 21 May 1916–30 May 1919 Yuhi IV Musinga. *Kings of Burundi:* 21 May 1916–30 May 1919 Mwambutsa II.

112 Benadir Coast Protectorate. 3 Aug. 1889–15 May 1893. *Location:* Somalia. *Capital:* Mogadishu.

History: Acquired by Italy in 1889, this stretch of the coast of what is today **Somalia Democratic Republic** was not administered until 1893, when the Filonardi Company took it over (see **Benadir Coast Protectorate [Filonardi Company]).**

Rulers: none.

113 Benadir Coast Protectorate (Filonardi Company). 15 May 1893–1896. *Location:* as **Italian Somaliland Colony.** *Capital:* Mogadiscio (Mogadishu). *Other names:* Italian Benadir.

History: In 1893 the **Benadir Coast Protectorate** became a company-run area, by the Filonardi Company. In 1896 it became **Benadir Coast Protectorate (Royal Commission).**

Governors: 15 May 1893–1896 Vincenzo Filonardi.

114 Benadir Coast Protectorate (Milanese Commercial Society). 25 May 1898–16 March 1905. *Location:* as **Italian Somaliland Colony.** *Capital:* Mogadiscio (Mogadishu). *Other names:* Benadir Coast Protectorate (Benadir Company).

History: In 1898 the **Benadir Coast Protectorate (Royal Commission)** was placed in the hands of the Milanese Commercial Society, also called the Benadir Company, founded by Antonio Cecchi (killed in 1896). In 1905 the country became an Italian colony (see **Italian Somaliland Colony).**

Governors: 25 May 1898–16 March 1905 Ernesto Dulio.

115 Benadir Coast Protectorate (Royal Commission). 1896–25 May 1898. *Location:* as **Italian Somaliland Colony.** *Capital:* Mogadiscio (Mogadishu). *Other names:* Benadir Coast.

History: Between the rule of the Filonardi Company (see **Benadir Coast Protectorate [Filonardi Company])** and the Milanese Commercial Society (see **Benadir Coast Protectorate [Milanese Commercial Society]),** the Italian Government administered what was later named **Italian Somaliland.**

Royal Commissioners: 1896–1897 Vincenzo Filonardi; 1897–1897 Ernesto Dulio; 1897–25 May 1898 Giorgio Sorrentino.

116 Benin [Dahomey]. See these names:

Benin Republic (1975–)

Dahomey Republic (1960–1975)

Dahomey Autonomous Republic (1958–1960)

Dahomey Overseas Territory (1946–1958)

Dahomey Colony and Dependencies (1911–1946)

Dahomey Colony (1894–1911)

Porto-Novo Colony (1893–1894)

Porto-Novo Protectorate [ii] (1882–1893)

Cotonou (1868–1894)

Whydah French Protectorate (1891–1894)

Allada Protectorate (1891–1894)

Dahomey Portuguese Protectorate (1885–1887)

Porto-Novo Protectorate [i] (1863–1865)

Allada (ca. 1440–1891)

Porto-Novo Kingdom [ii] (1865–1882)

Porto-Novo Kingdom [i] (1688–1863)
Dahomey Kingdom (1730–1894)
Abomey Kingdom (ca. 1600–1730)
Whydah Kingdom (ca. 1580–1891

117 Benin. 1170–18 Feb. 1897. *Location:* southern Nigeria. *Capital:* Usama (or Benin City).

History: In 1897 the British pronounced a protectorate over the ancient and venerable chiefdom of Benin, as well as allied city states along the Nigerian coastline, thus bringing them into the **Niger Coast Protectorate.**

Obas (Chiefs): 1170–1200 Oranmiyan; 1200–1220 Eweka I; 1220–1231 Uwakhuahen; 1231–1255 Ehenmihen; 1255–1280 Ewedo; 1280–1295 Oguola; 1295–1299 Edoni; 1299–1334 Udagbedo; 1334–1370 Ohen; 1370–1390 Egbeka; 1390–1410 Orobiru; 1410–1440 Uwaifiokun; 1440–1473 Ewuare; 1473–1477 Ezoti; 1477–1481 Olua; 1481–1504 Ozolua; 1504–1550 Esigie; 1550–1578 Orhogbua; 1578–1608 Ehengbuda; 1608–1640 Ohuan (or Odogbo); 1640–1661 Ahenzae; 1661–1669 Akenzae; 1669–1675 Akengboi; 1675–1684 Ahenkpaye; 1684–1689 Akenbedo; 1689–1700 Oreoghene; 1700–1712 Ewuakpe; 1712–1713 Ozuere; 1713–1735 Akenzua I; 1735–1750 Eresonyen; 1750–1804 Akengbuda; 1804–1816 Obanosa; 1816–1817 Ogbebo; 1817–1848 Osemwede; 1848–1888 Adolo; 1888–1897 Ovonramven; 1897–1914 unrecognized; 1914–5 Apr. 1933 Egbeka II; 5 Apr. 1933– Akenzua II.

118 Benin Republic. 4 Dec. 1975– . *Location:* northwest Africa. *Capital:* Porto-Novo (Portuguese name for "new port"). *Other names:* République Populaire du Bénin, People's Republic of Benin, Benin.

History: In 1975 **Dahomey Republic** changed its name to Benin (named for the Bight of Benin).

Presidents: 1 Dec. 1975– Mathieu Kerekou (after Sept. 29, 1980 re-named Ahmed Kerekou).

119 Berber Tunisia. 26 March 909–6 Jan. 910. *Location:* Tunisia. *Capital:* Tunis. *Other names:* Tunis.

History: Between the **Aghlabid Empire** and the installation of **Fatimid North Africa** rulers in 910, about 10 months elapsed during which Tunis was ruled by the Berbers.

Kings: 26 March 909–6 Jan. 910 Abu Abdallah as-Si'i al-Muhtasab.

Betsimisaraka see **Madagascar Kingdom**

120 Biafra. 30 May 1967–15 Jan. 1970. *Location:* eastern Nigeria. *Capital:* Enugu (from May–Oct. 1967) (Enugu was founded in 1917. "Enu ugwu" means "at the top of the hill"). *Other names:* The Republic of Biafra (named for the Bight of Biafra).

History: After unsuccessful talks with other regions of **Nigeria Federal Republic,** the Ibo-populated eastern region of Nigeria broke away after demanding that the power of the country's central government be diminished. Military Governor Ojukwu led the secession in May and in July war began with Nigeria. By Oct. Enugu had been taken by Nigeria and by late 1968 Biafra (which in 1967 had unilaterally declared a republic) had been reduced to one-tenth its original size and did not have a real capital city. Most of its towns had been taken and its people bombed and starved into submission. In 1970 it rejoined Nigeria and occupies what are now the four states of Cross River, Anambra, Imo, and Rivers.

Presidents: 30 May 1967–8 Jan. 1970 Odumegwu Ojukwu; 8 Jan. 1970–15 Jan. 1970 Phillip Effiong (acting).

121 Bight of Benin. 1 Feb. 1852–6 Aug. 1861. *Location:* around Lagos, Nigeria. *Capital:* Lagos.

History: In 1852 another British sphere of influence came into being— The Bight of Benin (cf **The Bight of Biafra**) with headquarters at Lagos. In 1861 the Kingdom of Lagos (see **Lagos**

Kingdom) came to an end, and **Lagos** came into being, with the Lagos administration (and a year later that of **Lagos Settlement**) ruling over the Bight of Benin interests. In 1867 **The Bight of Biafra** assumed responsibility for the Bight of Benin and the two became the **Bights of Biafra and Benin.**
Consuls: May 1852–1853 Louis Fraser; 1853–Apr. 1859 Benjamin Campbell; Apr. 1859–1860 George Brand; 1860–Jan. 1861 Henry Hand; Jan. 1861–May 1861 Henry Foote; May 1861–6 Aug. 1861 William McCoskry (acting).

122 Bight of Biafra. 30 June 1849–1867. *Location:* eastern Nigeria coast. *Capital:* Fernando Po; Bonny (local headquarters).
History: In 1849 a British consul was appointed to safeguard British interests in the area. He was also the governor of **Fernando Po (British).** In 1867 it took in the **Bight of Benin** (see also **Lagos** and **Lagos Settlement**) and the two combined to form the British sphere of influence called **The Bights of Biafra and Benin.**
Consuls: 30 June 1849–10 June 1854 John Beecroft; 10 June 1854–1855 James Lynslager (acting); 1855–1861 Thomas Hutchinson; 1861–Dec. 1864 Richard Francis Burton; Dec. 1864–1867 Charles Livingstone.

123 Bights of Biafra and Benin. 1867–5 June 1885. *Location:* southern Nigeria, i.e. as the **Oil Rivers Protectorate.** *Capital:* Fernando Po; Bonny (local headquarters).
History: In 1867 the **Bight of Biafra** took in the area around Lagos (but not including Lagos the city) named the Bight of Benin (see also the entry **Bight of Benin**), and it was renamed the Bights of Biafra and Benin. It was a sphere of British influence only, and in 1884 the British started to declare protectorates over the local kingdoms (see **Oil Rivers Protectorate** for details). In 1885 they declared a British protec-

torate over the whole coast (see **Oil Rivers Protectorate**), including **Lagos Settlement.**
Consuls: 1867–1873 Charles Livingstone; 1873–1878 George Hartley; 1878–13 Sept. 1879 David Hopkins; 13 Sept. 1879–5 June 1885 Edward Hyde Hewett.

124 Biram. ca. 1100–1805. *Location:* northern Nigeria-Niger border. *Capital:* Biram.
History: Founded by Garin Gabas as an early native state of the Hausa persuasion, it had a long and mostly unrecorded history until taken over by the **Fulani Empire** in 1805, as part of **Hadeija Emirate.**
Kings: ca. 1100 Biram; (?)–(?) Bomi; (?)–(?) Tumku; (?)–(?) Maji; (?)–(?) Kurada; (?)–(?) Yarima; ca. 1210 Kumari; (?)–(?) Dankwafan; (?)–(?) Jatau; (?)–(?) Amale; (?)–(?) Mamadu; ca. 1300 Dango; (?)–(?) Yahaya; (?)–(?) Dan Asan; (?)–(?) Abore; (?)–(?) Sakaina; (?)–(?) Musa I; ca. 1405 Kujera; (?)–(?) Adam; (?)–(?) Ali; (?)–(?) Tagwai; (?)–(?) Jimami; ca. 1500 Barikurgu; (?)– (?) Gamajiya da Yau; (?)–(?) Bako; (?)– (?) Burwai; (?)–(?) Gwarma; (?)–(?) Buri; ca. 1600 Usuman; (?)–(?) Gadbo; (?)–(?) Abdu; (?)–(?) Tukur; (?)–(?) Buba; ca. 1700 Kankarau; (?)–(?) Asawa; (?)–(?) Muhamman Bako; (?)–(?) Kawu; (?)–(?) Barwa; (?)–1805 al-Hajj Abu Bakar; 1805–1805 Musa II.

125 Bissau [i]. 1687–1707. *Location:* as **Bissau [ii].** *Capital:* Bissau.
History: In 1687 the second settlement in what is today **Guinea-Bissau** was founded—Bissau (see also **Cacheu**). In 1707 it was terminated as an administration.
Rulers: 1687–1696 no fixed rule; 1696–1699 José da Camara (Capitão-Mor); 1699–1707 Rodrigo da Fonseca (Capitão-Mor). *Note:* The Capitão-Mor was a Captain-Major, ruler of a Portuguese captaincy.

126 Bissau [ii]. 1753–1879. *Location:* southern **Guinea-Bissau.** *Capital:* Bissau.

History: In 1687 **Bissau [i]** was established, but it was five years before an administration was begun. From 1707 until 1753 the Captaincy of Bissau was non-existent, but it was revived in 1753 as Bissau [ii]. By the early 1800s Bissau was more important than the first settlement of **Cacheu,** and in 1879 Bissau, the Cacheu area and all the other Portuguese settlements in what is now **Guinea-Bissau** became **Portuguese Guinea.**

Capitães-Mores: 1753–(?) Nicolau Pino de Araújo; ca. 1757–1759 Manuel Pires; 1759–(?) Duarte Róis; ca. 1763–(?) Filipe de Souto-Maior; 1770–ca. 1775 Sebastião da Cunha Souto-Maior; ca. 1775–ca. 1777 [unknown]; ca. 1777–(?) Inácio Baião; 1793–ca. 1796 José António Pinto; ca. 1796–1799 [unknown]; 1799–(?) João de Neves Leão; 1803–(?) António Faria; 1805–1811 Manuel de Gouveia; 1811–(?) António Figueiredo; ca. 1820–ca. 1821 João Semedo; ca. 1821–1822 [unknown]; 1822–(?) Joaquim de Matos; (?)–1825 Domingos de Abreu Picaluga; 1825–1827 Joaquim de Matos; 1827–(?) Francisco Muacho; ca. 1829–1830 Caetano Nozolini; 1830–(?) Joaquim de Matos; (?)–1834 Caetano Nozolini; 1834–(?) Joaquim de Matos; 1836–1836 José Vieira; 1836–1839 Honório Barreto; 1839–1840 José Barbosa; 1840–1841 Honório Barreto; 1841–1842 José Machado; 1842–1842 António Santos; 1842–1843 António Torres; 1843–1844 José Coelho; 1844–1845 Alois Dziezaski; 1845–1847 Joaquim Alpoim; 1847–1848 Carlos de Sousa; 1848–1850 Caetano Nozolini; 1850–1851 [unknown]; ca. 1851–(?) Alois Dziezaski; 1852–1852 Libánio dos Santos; 1852–1853 José da Ávila; 1853–1854 José da Silva; 1854–1854 Pedro Ferreira; 1854–1855 [unknown]; 1855–1858 Honório Barreto; 1858–1858 António de Albuquerque Cota Falcão; 1858–1859 Honório Barreto; 1859–1860 [unknown];

1860–1862 António Zagalo; 1862–1863 [unknown]; 1863–(?) Joaquim Marquês; 1867–1868 Bernardo Moreira; 1868–1869 Manuel Meira; 1869–1871 Álvaro Caldeira; 1871–1871 José do Crato; 1871–(?) Joaquim Marquês; ca. 1877–1879 António Vieira. *Note:* Capitães-Mores is the plural of Capitão-Mor (Captain-Major).

127 Biu. ca. 1535–27 Dec. 1899. *Location:* northeastern Nigeria. *Capital:* Biu (from 1878, and permanent from 1904); Kogu (ca. 1763–1878); Limbur (until ca. 1763). *Other names:* Babur.

History: Founded by **Bornu** emigrees, it resisted the **Fulani Empire** and was taken into the brand new **Northern Nigeria Protectorate** in 1899 (effective from January 1, 1900). In 1920 the area was created an emirate.

Mais (Kings): ca. 1535–1580 Yamtara-Wala; 1580–(?) Mari Vira Hyel; (?)–(?) Dira Wala; (?)–(?) Yamta Amba; (?)–ca. 1670 Yamta Kupaya Wadi; ca. 1670–(?) Mari Watila Tampta; (?)–(?) Yamta ra Bangye; (?)–(?) Mari Luku; (?)–(?) Jakwa Birtitik; (?)–(?) Thlama Bahara; (?)–(?) Tayar Warinki; (?)–ca. 1740 Dakwai; ca. 1740–ca. 1750 Mari Kopchi (or Kwabchi); ca. 1750–ca. 1760 Di Forma; ca. 1760–ca. 1770 Garga Moda; ca. 1770–ca. 1780 Dawi Moda; ca. 1780–ca. 1783 Di Biya; ca. 1783–1783 Di Rawa; 1783–1793 Garga Kopchi (or Kwabchi); 1793–1838 Mari Watirwa; 1838–1873 Ari Paskur; 1873–1891 Mari Biya; 1891–1908 Garga Kwomting; 1908–1935 Ari I (or Dogo); 1935–1951 Ari II (or Gurgur); 1951–1959 Muhammad Aliyu (or Maidalla Madu); 1959– Maidalla Mustafa Aliyu.

Boina see **Madagascar Kingdom**

128 Bonaparte. 1801–8 July 1810. *Location:* as **Réunion,** in the Indian Ocean. *Capital:* Saint Denis. *Other names:* Île Bonaparte.

History: In 1801 **Réunion** was renamed yet again, this time in honor of Napoleon Bonaparte. In 1810 it was taken by the British and renamed Bourbon (see **Bourbon [British]**).

Governors: 1801–1803 Philippe Jacob de Cordemoy; 1803–1806 François Magallon de Lamorlière; 1806–1809 Nicolas de Regnac des Brulys; 1809–8 July 1810 Jean Brunteau de Sainte-Suzanne.

129 Bonny. ca. 1450–5 June 1885. *Location:* on the Nigerian coast. *Capital:* Bonny. *Other names:* Grand Bonny, Ibani, Ubani, Okoloba.

History: Originally a chiefdom, it became a kingdom dealing in slaves. In the 1830s, with the abolition of the slave market, Bonny became a leading trader in palm oil, and hence was one of the Oil River States (cf **Brass**). In 1885 it became part of the **Oil Rivers Protectorate.**

Chiefs: ca. 1450–(?) Alagbariye; (?)–(?) Okapara Ndole; (?)–(?) Opu Amakubu; (?)–(?) Okpara Asimini. *Kings:* (?)–(?) Asimini; (?)–(?) Edimini; (?)–(?) Kamba; (?)–(?) Kamalu; (?)–(?) Dappa; (?)–(?) Amakiri; (?)–(?) Appinya (or Apia); ca. 1705 Warri. *Joint-Kings:* (?)–(?) Awusa (or King Holiday); (?)–(?) Egbani (or Igbani); (?)–(?) Bupuor; (?)–(?) Ipuor. *Kings:* ca. 1750–1792 Perekule (or Captain Pepple); 1792–1792 Fubra (or Agbaa). *Joint-Kings:* 1792–(?) Fubra II; 1792–1829 Opobo. *Kings:* 1829–1830 Bereibibo. *Regents:* 1830–1835 Madu. *Kings:* 1835–23 Jan. 1853 Dappa (or William, or Bill Pepple); 23 Jan. 1853–13 Aug. 1855 Agba Fubra (or Dappo). *Regents:* 13 Aug. 1855–1861 ruled by a series of regents. *Kings:* 1861–1863 Dappa (or William, or Bill Pepple); 1863–1865 Jaja (or George); 1885–25 Aug. 1891 Oko Jumbo.

130 Bono. ca. 1420–1723. *Location:* Ghana (Takyiman State). *Capital:* Bono-Mansu.

History: An Akan state of Ghana, formed about 1420 by the Fante tribe

from the Sudan, it was a great gold mining and distributing center. Bono was finally subjugated by the **Ashanti Empire** in 1723.

Nanas (Kings): ca. 1420–ca. 1430 Asaman. *Regents:* ca. 1430–ca. 1440 Ameyaw Kese. *Nanas (Kings):* ca. 1440–ca. 1450 Akumfi I; ca. 1450–ca. 1480 Obunumankona; ca. 1480–ca. 1500 Takyi Akwamo; ca. 1500–ca. 1520 Gyako I; ca. 1520–ca. 1550 Dwambera Kwame; ca. 1550–ca. 1560 Afena Yaw; ca. 1560–1577 Berempon Katakyira; 1577–1591 Yebowa Ananta; 1591–1600 Ati Kwame; 1600–1615 Ameyaw Kurompe; 1615–1621 Afena Diamono; 1621–1631 Owusu Aduam; 1631–1641 Akumfi II; 1641–1646 Kofi; 1646–1651 Owusu Akyempo; 1651–1666 Gyamfi; 1666–1674 Boakyi; 1674–1694 Kyereme; 1694–1723 Ameyaw Kwaakye.

131 Bophuthatswana. 6 Dec. 1977– . *Location:* South Africa. *Capital:* Mmabatho. *Other names:* Bophuthatswana Republic, Republic of Bophuthatswana, Repaboliki ya Bophuthatswana.

History: On June 1, 1972 Bophuthatswana became self-governing, with Lucas Mangope as Chief Minister. In 1977 this homeland, or Bantustan (of the Tswana tribe), became independent from **South Africa,** as six scattered enclaves throughout the Transvaal and Orange Free State Provinces. It was the second Bantustan to gain independence, and like the others (see **Transkei, Venda, Ciskei**), it is recognized by only **South Africa** and each other.

Presidents: 6 Dec. 1977– Lucas Mangope.

132 Bornu Empire [i]. ca. 1400– March 1808. *Location:* as **Kanem-Bornu.** *Capital:* Birni Ngazargamu (founded 1475); Yamia (or Muniyo) (until 1475). *Other names:* Bornu, Kanem-Bornu, Bornu Empire, Regnum Organa.

History: Around 1400 the Empire of

Kanem-Bornu became simply the Bornu Empire, because emphasis of power shifted from Kanem to Bornu. In the early 1500s Kanem was re-conquered from the Bulala (see **Kanem State** for details) and the land of Aïr was also taken. The latter half of the 17th century saw the beginning of the collapse of the empire, with Tuaregs invading, as well as famine, and by 1700 it was in a state of decadence. After the Fulani invasions of the early 19th century (see **Fulani Empire**), Bornu became split into several emirates, but by 1824 the Fulani had been expelled and the Bornu Empire was re-activated (see **Bornu Empire [ii]**).

Mais (Kings): 1400–1432 Biri III; 1432–1433 Uthman III Kaliwama; 1433–1435 Dunama III; 1435–1442 Abdullah III Dakumuni; 1442–1450 Ibrahim II; 1450–1451 Kadai; 1451–1455 Ahmad Dunama IV; 1455–1456 Muhammad II; 1456–1456 Amr; 1456–1456 Muhammad III; 1456–1461 Ghaji; 1461–1466 Uthman IV; 1466–1467 Umar II; 1467–1472 Muhammad IV; 1472–1504 Ali Ghajideni; 1504–1526 Idris Katarkamabi; 1526–1545 Muhammad V Aminami; 1545–1546 Ali II Zainami; 1546–1563 Dunama V Ngumaramma; 1563–1570 Dala (or Abdallah); 1570–1580 Aissa Kili; 1580–1603 Idris Alooma (or Alawma); 1603–1617 Muhammad Bukalmarami; 1617–1625 Ibrahim III; 1625–1645 Umar III; 1645–1685 Ali III; 1685–1704 Idris IV; 1704–1723 Dunama VI; 1723–1737 Hamdan; 1737–1752 Muhammad VII Erghamma; 1752–1755 Dunama VII Ghana; 1755–1793 Ali IV ibn Haj Hamdun; 1793–March 1808 Ahmad ibn Ali. *Note:* for rulers between 1808 and 1824 see **Bornu Empire [ii]**.

133 Bornu Empire [ii]. 1824–1902. *Location:* as **Bornu Empire [i]**. *Capital:* Yerwa (from 1907); Kukawa (1814–1907); Ngazargamu (until 1814). *Other names:* Bornu, Kanem-Bornu, Bornou Empire, Bornu Empire.

History: In 1824 the inhabitants of Bornu kicked the Fulani invaders out of their country (see **Bornu Empire [i]**) and re-established their empire, the state regaining strength. In 1846 the Sefawa dynasty of Mais (Kings) ended and a series of Shehus (Sheikhs) ruled until 1893, when the empire ended, being conquered by Rabih (see **Rabih's Empire**). In 1898 it became part of the French and British spheres of influence, and in 1902 part of it went into the **Northern Nigeria Protectorate**; another part had gone (in 1900) to **Chad Military Territory and Protectorate**. In 1907 the capital moved to Yerwa (erroneously known as Maiduguri).

Mais (or Sultans, or Kings): 1808–1810 Dunama Lafiami; 1810–1814 Muhammad VIII; 1814–1817 Dunama Lafiami; 1817–1846 Ibrahim; 1846–1846 Ali Delatumi. *Protectors of Bornu:* 1817–1824 al-Kanemi; 1824–1846 Umar. *Shehus (or Sheikhs):* 1846–1853 Umar; 1853–1854 Abdarrahman; 1854–1881 Umar; 1881–1884 Bukar Kura; 1884–1885 Ibrahim; 1885–1893 Hashim; 1893–1893 Kiyari Muhammad al-Amin. *Conqueror and ruler:* 1893–22 Apr. 1900 Rabih Zubeir. *Ruler:* 22 Apr. 1900–23 Aug. 1901 Fadl-Allah (son of Rabih). *Shehus (or Sheikhs):* 1902–Feb. 1922 Bukar Garbai; 1922–1937 Umar Sanda Kura; 1937–1969 Umar Sanda Kiyarimi; 1969– Umar Baba Ya Mairami.

134 Bornu State. ca. 850–ca. 1260. *Location:* northeast Nigeria, west of Lake Chad. *Capital:* unknown. *Other names:* Bornu, Bornou, Barnu.

History: One of several small states founded on the dissolution of the old **Zaghawa Kingdom** (see also **Kanem State**) around 850, this one by the Sao peoples. On the southwest of Lake Chad, it lived in the shadow of its neighbor, Kanem State across the water until about 1200 when the Kanuri from Kanem began expanding into Bornu, taking it over totally about 1260. It then became part of the growing **Kanem-Bornu.**

Rulers: unknown.

Borozwi see **Rozwi**

135 Botswana. See these **names:**
Botswana (1966–)
Bechuanaland (Self-Rule) (1965–1966)
Bechuanaland (1964–1965)
Bechuanaland High Commission Territory (1891–1964)
Bechuanaland Protectorate [ii] (1885–1891)
British Bechuanaland Crown Colony (1885–1895)
Bechuanaland Protectorate [i] (1885–1885)
Batlokwaland (ca. 1660–1885)
Batwanaland (ca. 1795–1885)
Bakwenaland (ca. 1570–1885)
Bangwaketseland (ca. 1650–1885)
Bamangwatoland (ca. 1610–1885)
Barolongland (ca. 1470–1885)
Bakgatlaland (ca. 1470–1885)
Bamaleteland (ca. 1470–1885)

136 Botswana. 30 Sept. 1966– .
Location: Southern Africa. *Capital:*
Gaborone (formerly Gaberones)
(founded about 1892 and named for
Chief Gaberone Matlapin). *Other
names:* The Republic of Botswana,
Botswana Republic.
History: **Bechuanaland (Self-Rule)**
became independent in 1966 as The
Republic of Botswana, still remaining
within the British Commonwealth.
Presidents: 30 Sept. 1966–13 July
1980 Sir Seretse Khama; 13 July 1980–18
July 1980 Quett Masire (acting); 18 July
1980– Quett Masire.

137 Bou Regreg. 1627–1641. *Loca-
tion:* Salé-Rabat, Morocco. *Capital:*
Salé. *Other names:* Bu Regreg, Bu
Ragrag, Bou Ragrag, Republic of Bou
Regreg, Morisco Republic, Salé-Rabat.
History: In 1608 expatriate Moriscos
(Spanish Muslims) were kicked out of
Spain, settled in Rabat in Morocco,
and strongly fortified it. More Mor-
iscos settled across the Bou Regreg
River in Salé. Thus two cities were set
up by these Hornacheros (Moriscos

from Hornacho in Spain) – Sla al-
Qadim (Old Salé) and Sla al-Jadid
(New Salé, or Rabat). From this base
the Hornachero pirates, especially the
dreaded Sallee Rovers (the most notorious of all the Barbary Pirates) raided
shipping in the Atlantic with the protection of the Moroccan sultan (see
Sa'did Morocco). The two cities combined to form the pirate republic of
Bou Regreg. Incorporated into **Sa'did
Morocco** in 1641, the pirates continued
to raid unimpeded from Rabat-Salé until the 1750s.
Presidents: 1627–1641 Abu Abdallah
Muhammad ibn Ahmad az-Ziyani.
Governors of Rabat: 1629–1630 Muhammad ibn Abdel Kadir; 1630–1637
Ahmad ibn Ali; 1637–1641 Abdallah
ibn Ali al-Kasri.

138 Bourbon [i]. 1649–1764. *Location:* as **Réunion,** in the Indian Ocean.
Capital: Saint Denis (ca. 1736–1764);
Saint Paul (1649–ca. 1736). *Other
names:* Île de Bourbon.
History: The Portuguese had had a
claim on what they called **Santa Apollonia,** and in 1649 the French officially
took it over (they had taken it in 1642 –
see **Santa Apollonia [French]**), the first
colonists coming in 1662 from France.
In the early 1730s refugee Madagascar
pirates (French) arrived from the big
island and from 1674–1764 Bourbon
was ruled by the Compagnie des Indes
Orientales. In the latter year it became
a Crown Colony (see **Bourbon Colony**).
Commandants: 1649–1665 no central
administration; 1665–1671 Étienne Reg-
nault; 1671–1674 Jacques de Lahure;
1674–1678 Henri Esse d'Orgeret; 1678–
1680 Germain de Fleuricourt; 1680–
1686 Bernardin de Quimper; 1686–1689
Jean-Baptiste Drouillard; 1689–1690
Henri Habet de Vauboulon; 1690–1696
Michel Firélin; 1696–1698 Joseph Bas-
tide; 1698–1701 Jacques de la Cour de la
Saulais; 1701–1709 Jean-Baptiste de
Villers; 1709–1710 Francois Desbordes
de Charanville; 1710–1715 Pierre Parat

de Chaillenest; 1715–1718 Henri Justamont; 1718–1723 Joseph Beauvollier de Courchant; 1723–1725 Antoine Boucher-Desforges; 1725–1727 Hélie Dioré; 1727–1735 Pierre-Benoît Dumas; 1735–1739 Alfred Lémery-Dupont; 1739–1744 Pierre d'Héguerty; 1744–1745 Didier de Saint-Martin; 1745–1745 Jean-Baptiste Azéma; 1745–1746 Gaspard de Ballade; 1746–1748 Didier de Saint-Martin; 1748–1749 Gaspard de Ballade. *Governors:* 1749–1753 Jean-Baptiste Bouvet de Lozier; 1753–1756 Joseph Brénier; 1756–1763 Jean-Baptiste Bouvet de Lozier. *Commandants:* 1763–1764 François Bertin d'Avesnes.

139 Bourbon [ii]. Apr. 1815–1848. *Location:* as **Réunion,** in the Indian Ocean. *Capital:* Saint Denis.
History: In 1815 Bourbon, for five years a British possession (see **Bourbon [British]**) became a French colony again. In 1848 it changed its name again, to **Réunion Colony.**
Governors: Apr. 1815–1817 Athanase Bouvet de Lozier; 1817–1818 Hilaire Lafitte de Courteil; 1818–1821 Pierre-Bernard de Milius; 1821–1826 Louis Desaulses de Freycinet; 1826–1830 Achille de Penfentenio de Cheffontaines; 1830–1832 Étienne Mengin Duval d'Ailly; 1832–1838 Jacques Cuvillier; 1838–1841 Adm. Louis de Hell; 1841–1846 Charles Bazoche; 1846–1848 Joseph Graëb.

140 Bourbon (British). 8 July 1810–Apr. 1815. *Location:* as **Réunion,** in the Indian Ocean. *Capital:* Saint Denis. *Other names:* Bourbon.
History: In 1810 the British captured **Bonaparte** in the Indian Ocean, and renamed the island Bourbon. In 1815 it was handed back to France (see **Bourbon [ii]**).
Governors: 8 July 1810–1811 Robert Farquhar; 1811–1811 Henry Warde; 1811–Apr. 1815 Henry Keating.

141 Bourbon Colony. 1764–1793. *Location:* as **Réunion,** in the Indian Ocean. *Capital:* Saint Denis. *Other names:* Île de Bourbon.
History: In 1764, **Bourbon [i],** until then governed by the French East India Company (La Compagnie des Indes Orientales), became a colony of the French Crown. In 1793 its name was changed to **Réunion,** a not unexpected dropping of the Bourbon image, given events in the mother country at the time.
Commandants: 1764–1767 François Bertin d'Avesnes; 1767–1767 Martin-Adrien Bellier. *Governors:* 1767–1773 Guillaume de Bellecombe; 1773–1776 Jean Steinauer; 1776–1779 François de Souillac; 1779–1781 Joseph Murinay de Saint-Maurice; 1781–1785 André Chalvet de Souville; 1785–1787 Hélie Dioré; 1787–1790 David Charpentier de Cossigny; 1790–1792 Dominique de Chermont; 1792–1793 Jean-Baptiste Vigoureux du Plessis.

Boussouma see **Mossi States**

142 Brakna. ca. 1650–18 Oct. 1904. *Location:* Mauritania. *Capital:* Shamama (from 1780).
History: Around 1650 the dynasty of Ulad Nurmash began ruling in Brakna, and by 1780 the dynasty of Ulad Abd-Allah (or Ulad Saiyyid) had taken over. In 1904 the French took it over as part of **Mauritania Civil Territory.**
Emirs: ca. 1650–(?) Nurmash; (?)–1728 Muhammad al-Hiba; 1728–1762 Ahmad al-Hiba; 1762–1780 Ali; 1780–1780 Ahmayada; 1780–1800 Muhammad; 1800–1817 Sidi Ali I; Jan. 1818–1841 Ahmaddu I; 1841–1842 Moukhtar Sidi; 1842–1851 Muhammad ar-Rajal; 1851–Dec. 1858 Muhammad Sidi; Dec. 1858–1893 Sidi Ali II; 1893–Dec. 1903 Ahmaddu II; Dec. 1903–18 Oct. 1904 Sidi Muhammad. *Rebel Leaders:* Dec. 1903–28 Oct. 1910 Sheikh Mahl Aynin; 28 Oct. 1910–6 May 1912 Hamid al-Hiba. *Sultans:* 6 May 1912–1919 Hamid al-Hiba; 1919–1919 Talib Hiyar; 1919–7 Apr. 1934 Maribbi Rabbu.

143 Brandenburger Gold Coast Set-

lements. May 1682–1701. *Location:* Gold Coast. *Capital:* Gross-Friedrichsburg (founded 1683). *Other names:* Gross-Friedrichsburg, Hollandia.

History: In 1682 the Brandenburg Electorate (later Prussia) founded settlements along the coast of what is today **Ghana Republic.** In 1701, when Brandenburg became the nucleus of the Kingdom of Prussia, they became the **Prussian Gold Coast Settlements.** Fort Dorothea (Accada) was their secondary fort.

Governors: May 1682–1683 Phillip Bloncq; 1683–1684 Nathaniel Dillinger; 1684–1686 Karl Von Schnitter; 1686–1691 Johann Niemann; 1691–1693 Johann Tenhoof; 1693–1695 Jakob Tenhoof; 1695–1697 Gijsbrecht Van Hoogveldt; 1697–1699 Jan Van Laar; 1699–1701 Jan de Visser.

144 Brass. ca. 1450–5 June 1885. *Location:* right on the Delta of the Niger River, **Nigeria.** *Capital:* Brasstown (named for the "Barasin," which means "let go," it was also called Brass, and formerly Nembe). *Other names:* Nembe, Nimby, Itebu, Debe.

History: The origins of the Nembe area are obscure, but it is likely that people from **Benin** came to the Delta under the leadership of Kala-Ekule. One of the early amanyanabos (or kings) was called Nembe, and from him came the name of the country. Like **Bonny,** Brass became a major slave-dealing, then palm-oil dealing, city-state, and in 1885 became part of the **Oil Rivers Protectorate.**

Note on the capital: The original capital of Nembe was Nembe, about 35 miles inland. Until the end of the 19th century this was called Brass by the white men. Then, due to expediency, the capital (of trade, at least) was shifted to the mouth of the Brass River, to Tuwon (or Twon), which was erroneously called Town by the white men. Hence Brass Town (or Brasstown).

Amanyanabos (Kings): ca. 1450–ca.

1500 Ekule; (?)–(?) Ogbodo; (?)–(?) Nembe; (?)–(?) Owagi; (?)–(?) Ogio; (?)–(?) Peresuo; (?)–(?) Obia; ca. 1700 Basuo; (?)–(?) Mingi (or Mingi I); ca. 1780 Ikata (or Mingi II); (?)– 1800 Gboro (or Mingi III); 1800–1830 Kulo (or King Forday, or Mingi IV); 1830–1846 Amain (or King Boy, or Mingi V); 1846–1863 Kien (or Mingi VI); 1863–1879 Ockiya VII (or Mingi VII); 1879–1889 interregnum; 1889–1898 Koko (or Mingi VIII); 1898–1926 ruled directly by the British; 1926–1936 Anthony Ockiya (or Mingi IX); 1936– Allagoa (or Mingi X).

145 British Bechuanaland Crown Colony. 30 Sept. 1885–16 Nov. 1895. *Location:* in the north of **British Cape Colony,** i.e. the southern part of **Bechuanaland Protectorate [i].** *Capital:* Vrijburg (Vryburg). *Other names:* British Bechuanaland.

History: In 1885 **Bechuanaland Protectorate [i]** was split into two. The northern section became **Bechuanaland Protectorate [ii],** which in 1891 became the germ of modern day **Botswana,** and the south became a Crown Colony and included the **United States of Stellaland.** In 1895 this southern part became part of **British Cape Colony (Self-Rule).**

Military Commander: 30 Sept. 1885–23 Oct. 1885 Lt.-Col. Frederick Carrington. *Administrator:* 23 Oct. 1885–16 Nov. 1895 Sidney Shippard.

146 British Cameroons Territory. 4 March 1916–22 July 1920. *Location:* western Cameroun–eastern Nigeria. *Capital:* Lagos, Nigeria; Buea (local headquarters). *Other names:* British Cameroons, Western Cameroons.

History: In 1916 **Cameroun French-British Condominium** came to an end and the British and the French created their own territories out of the conquered German colony (see **Kamerun**). The French got four-fifths of the whole country—(see **French Cameroun Territory**) and the British got the rest, the small western portion bordering **Nigeria Colony and Protectorate.** The British section was administered from Lagos, being attached to the Eastern Provinces of Nigeria, and divided into three districts. In 1920 it became **Cameroons British Mandate.**

Rulers: ruled from Lagos, Nigeria (see **Nigeria Colony and Protectorate**).

147 British Cape Colony. 13 Aug. 1814–1 Dec. 1872. *Location:* the southern province of **South Africa,** since 1910 called The Cape of Good Hope Province. *Capital:* Cape Town (founded April 6, 1652 as De Kaapsche Vlek (The Cape Hamlet), by Jan Van Riebeeck. *Other names:* Cape Colony, Cape of Good Hope Colony.

History: In 1814 **British-Occupied Cape Colony [ii]** became legally British. It was a reluctant acquisition, done so as the only means of preventing other powers from blocking Britain's trade to the East Indies. It was in the 19th century that Cape Colony did most of its expansion. In 1872 it achieved self-government (see **British Cape Colony [Self-Rule]**).

Governors: 13 Aug. 1814–12 Jan. 1820 Lord Charles Somerset; 13 Jan. 1820–30 Nov. 1821 Sir Rufane Donkin (acting); 30 Nov. 1821–5 March 1826 Lord Charles Somerset; 5 March 1826–9 Sept. 1828 Richard Bourke (acting); 9 Sept. 1828–10 Aug. 1833 Sir Lowry Cole; 10 Aug. 1833–16 Jan. 1834 Thomas Wade (acting); 16 Jan. 1834–20 Jan. 1835 Sir Benjamin D'Urban; 20 Jan. 1835–30 Dec. 1835 John Bell (acting); 30 Dec. 1835–22 Jan. 1838 Sir Benjamin D'Urban; 22 Jan. 1838–18 March 1844 Sir George Napier; 18 March 1844–10 Oct. 1846 Sir Peregrine Maitland. *High Commissioners/Governors:* 10 Oct. 1846–27 Jan. 1847 Sir Peregrine Maitland; 27 Jan. 1847–1 Dec. 1847 Sir Henry Pottinger; 1 Dec. 1847–31 March 1852 Sir Harry Smith; 31 March 1852–26 May 1854 Sir George Cathcart; 26 May 1854–5 Dec. 1854 Charles Darling (acting); 5 Dec. 1854–20 Aug. 1859 Sir George Grey; 20 Aug. 1859–4 July 1860 Robert Wynyard (acting); 4 July 1860–15 Aug. 1861 Sir George Grey; 15 Aug. 1861–15 Jan. 1862 Robert Wynyard (acting); 15 Jan. 1862–20 May 1870 Sir Philip Wodehouse; 20 May 1870–31 Dec. 1870 Charles Hay (acting); 31 Dec. 1870–1 Dec. 1872 Sir Henry Barkly. *Prime Ministers:* 29 Nov. 1872–1 Dec. 1872 Sir John Molteno.

148 British Cape Colony (Self-Rule). 1 Dec. 1872–30 May 1910. *Location:* as Cape of Good Hope Province, **South Africa.** *Capital:* Cape Town. *Other names:* Cape Colony, Cape of Good Hope.

History: In 1872 **British Cape Colony** achieved self-rule and a prime minister was elected. In 1910 it became one of the four colonies to make up the **Union of South Africa.**

High Commissioners/Governors: 1 Dec. 1872–31 March 1877 Sir Henry Barkly; 31 March 1877–15 Sept. 1880 Sir Bartle Frere; 15 Sept. 1880–27 Sept. 1880 Henry Clifford (Officer Administering); 27 Sept. 1880–22 Jan. 1881 Sir George Strahan (Officer Administering); 22 Jan. 1881–30 Apr. 1881 Sir Hercules Robinson; 30 Apr. 1881–Aug. 1881 Sir Leicester Smythe (Officer Administering); Aug. 1881–25 Apr. 1883 Sir Hercules Robinson; 25 Apr. 1883–26 March 1884 Sir Leicester Smythe (Officer Administering); 26 March 1884–7 Apr. 1886 Sir Hercules Robinson; 7 Apr. 1886–7 July 1886 Sir Henry Torrens (Officer Administering); 7 July 1886–1 May 1889 Sir Hercules Robinson; 1 May 1889–13 Dec. 1889 Henry Smyth (Officer Administering); 13 Dec. 1889–14 Jan. 1891 Sir Harry Loch; 14 Jan. 1891–1 Dec. 1892 Sir William Cameron (Officer Administering); 1 Dec. 1892–May 1894 Sir Harry Loch; May 1894–July 1894 Sir William Cameron (Officer Administering); July 1894–30 May 1895 Sir Harry Loch; 30 May 1895–21 Apr. 1897 Sir Hercules Robinson (created Baron Rosmead in

1896); 21 Apr. 1897–5 May 1897 Sir William Goodenough (Officer Administering); 5 May 1897–2 Nov. 1898 Sir Alfred Milner; 2 Nov. 1898–14 Feb. 1899 Sir William Butler (Officer Administering); 14 Feb. 1899–6 March 1901 Sir Alfred Milner. *High Commissioners:* 6 March 1901–1 Apr. 1905 Sir Alfred Milner (created Baron Milner in 1901 and Viscount Milner 1902); 2 Apr. 1905–17 June 1909 2nd Earl of Selborne; 17 June 1909–21 Sept. 1909 Sir Walter Hely-Hutchinson (acting); 21 Sept. 1909–30 May 1910 Sir Henry Scobell (acting). *Governors:* 6 March 1901–30 May 1910 Sir Walter Hely-Hutchinson. *Prime Ministers:* 1 Dec. 1872–5 Feb. 1878 Sir John Molteno; 6 Feb. 1878–8 May 1881 Gordon Sprigg; 9 May 1881–12 May 1884 Sir Thomas Scanlen; 13 May 1884–24 Nov. 1886 Sir Thomas Upington; 25 Nov. 1886–16 July 1890 Sir Gordon Sprigg; 17 July 1890–12 Jan. 1896 Cecil Rhodes; 13 Jan. 1896–13 Oct. 1898 Sir Gordon Sprigg; 14 Oct. 1898–17 June 1900 William Schreiner; 18 June 1900–21 Feb. 1904 Sir Gordon Sprigg; 22 Feb. 1904–2 Feb. 1908 Sir Starr Jameson (formerly Dr. Leander Starr Jameson); 3 Feb. 1908–30 May 1910 John Merriman.

149 British Central Africa Protectorate. 22 Feb. 1893–6 July 1907. *Location:* as **Malawi Republic.** *Capital:* Zomba. *Other names:* Nyasaland, British Central Africa.

History: In 1893 **Nyasaland** changed names to the Protectorate of British Central Africa. In 1907 it reverted to Nyasaland (see **Nyasaland Protectorate**).

Commissioners/Consuls-General: 22 Feb. 1893–1894 Harry Johnston; 1894–1894 John S. Brabant (acting); 1894–1894 Alfred Sharpe (acting); 1894–16 Apr. 1896 Harry Johnston (knighted 1896); 16 Apr. 1896–14 July 1897 Alfred Sharpe (acting); 14 July 1897–1903 Alfred Sharpe; 1903–1903 Francis Pearce (acting); 1903–31 March 1907 Sir Alfred Sharpe; 1 Apr. 1907–6

July 1907 Francis Pearce (acting).

150 British Cyrenaica. 21 Dec. 1942–21 Nov. 1949. *Location:* eastern Libya. *Capital:* Benghazi (from 1943); al-Marj (Barce) (1942–43). *Other names:* Cyrenaica, Barca, Barqah.

History: Cirenaica, the eastern area of Libya, was the first major section of the **Libya Italian Colony** to be taken by the Allies in World War II. In 1943 the Tripolitania area and the Fezzan area were captured and the Italians changed sides. The French and British split up the former Italian colony among themselves as **British Cyrenaica, British Tripolitania** and **French Fezzan.** On June 1, 1949 the Emir, Idris, proclaimed the independence of Cyrenaica, calling it the Kingdom of Libya. The British didn't quite agree, but did give autonomy to the area in preparation for the real independence which was to come for all of Libya in 1951. (See **Cyrenaica [Autonomous]**).

British Military Administrators: 21 Dec. 1942–10 March 1943 Duncan Cumming. *Chief Administrators:* 10 March 1943–30 Oct. 1945 Duncan Cumming; 30 Oct. 1945–1946 Peter Acland; 1946–1948 James Haugh; 1948–17 Sept. 1949 Eric Vully de Candole. *Residents:* 17 Sept. 1949–21 Nov. 1949 Eric Vully de Candole. *Emirs:* 21 Dec. 1942–21 Nov. 1949 Idris al-Mahdi as-Sanusi. *Prime Ministers-Designate:* 5 July 1949–7 Nov. 1949 Fathi al-Kikhya (never took office). *Prime Ministers:* 9 Nov. 1949–21 Nov. 1949 Umar Mansur al-Kikhya.

151 British East Africa Colony. 3 Sept. 1888–1 July 1895. *Location:* as **British East Africa Protectorate.** *Capital:* Mombasa. *Other names:* East Africa Colony.

History: In the late 1880s the scramble for East Africa between Germany and Britain resulted in the Imperial British East Africa Company taking what is now **Kenya** as a means of access to **Uganda.** The Uganda venture ruined the company and in 1895 the British Government took over the colony as the **British East Africa Protectorate**. *Commissioners:* 3 Sept. 1888–May 1890 George Mackenzie; May 1890–Feb. 1891 Sir Francis de Winton; Feb. 1891–1891 George Mackenzie; 1891–1892 Ernest Berkeley; 1892–Jan. 1895 John Pigott. *Consuls-General in Zanzibar:* Jan. 1895–1 July 1895 Arthur Hardinge.

152 British East Africa Protectorate. 1 July 1895–23 July 1920. *Location:* as **Kenya Republic**, but with the addition of the Zanzibar coast. *Capital:* Nairobi (1905–20); Mombasa (1895–1905) (founded by Arabs in the 11th century and most likely named for Mombasa in Oman). *Other names:* East Africa Protectorate.

History: In 1895 the **British East Africa Colony**, ruled by the Imperial British East Africa Company, became a crown protectorate of Britain. The Consul-General in **Zanzibar Protectorate** was also commissioner of the new protectorate of British East Africa from 1895–1904. In 1920 it became **Kenya Colony and Protectorate**.

Commissioners: 1 July 1895–Oct. 1900 Arthur Hardinge (knighted 1897); Dec. 1900–20 June 1904 Sir Charles Eliot; 20 June 1904–12 Dec. 1905 Sir Donald Stewart; 12 Dec. 1905–31 Dec. 1905 James Sadler. *Governors:* 31 Dec. 1905–16 Sept. 1909 James Sadler (knighted 1907); 16 Sept. 1909–July 1912 Sir Percy Girouard; July 1912–3 Oct. 1912 Charles Bowring (acting); 3 Oct. 1912–22 July 1919 Henry Belfield (knighted 1914); 22 July 1919–23 July 1920 Sir Edward Northey.

153 British Eritrea. 5 May 1941–11 Sept. 1952. *Location:* the northern Ethiopian coastline. *Capital:* Asmara. *Other names:* Eritrea.

History: In 1941 British troops occupied **Eritrea Province** and it became British. In 1952 it became **Eritrea Autonomous State**.

Chief Administrators: 5 May 1941–4 May 1942 William Platt; 4 May 1942–9 Sept. 1944 Stephen Longrigg; 9 Sept. 1944–14 Aug. 1945 C.D. McCarthy; 14 Aug. 1945–1 Nov. 1946 John Benoy; 1 Nov. 1946–19 Feb. 1951 Francis Drew; 19 Feb. 1951–11 Sept. 1952 Duncan Cumming. *U.N. Commissioners:* 19 Feb. 1951–11 Sept. 1952 Edoardo Matienzo.

154 British Gold Coast (Committee of Merchants). 25 June 1828–1843. *Location:* as **English Gold Coast Settlements**. *Capital:* Cape Coast Castle. *Other names:* British Gold Coast Territory (Committee of Merchants).

History: In 1828 a committee of merchants took over the reins of government when the British Crown relinquished control temporarily from 1828–43. (See **British Gold Coast Crown Colony** for what the area became after 1843; see **Gold Coast Territory [i]** for what the area was prior to 1828.) Throughout this fifteen year period, though, it still remained part of the **West African Territories**.

Governors: 25 June 1828–19 Feb. 1830 John Jackson (acting); 19 Feb. 1830–26 June 1836 George Maclean; 26 June 1836–15 Aug. 1838 William Topp (acting); 15 Aug. 1838–1843 George Maclean.

155 British Gold Coast (Company of Merchants). 23 June 1751–7 May 1821. *Location:* as **English Gold Coast Settlements**. *Capital:* Cape Coast Castle.

History: In 1751 the Company of Merchants Trading to Africa became the controlling power on the British Gold Coast, a stronger government thus being formed over the previous **British Gold Coast Settlements**. In 1821 it became a Crown Colony (see **Gold Coast [British]**).

Governors: 23 June 1751–23 Jan. 1756 Thomas Melvill; 23 Jan. 1756–17 Feb. 1756 William Tymewell; 17 Feb. 1756–15 Oct. 1757 Charles Bell (acting);

15 Oct. 1757–10 May 1761 Nassau Senior (acting); 10 May 1761–15 Aug. 1763 Charles Bell; 15 Aug. 1763–1 March 1766 William Mutter; 1 March 1766–11 Aug. 1766 John Hippisley; 11 Aug. 1766–21 Apr. 1769 Gilbert Petrie; 21 Apr. 1769–11 Aug. 1770 John Grossle; 11 Aug. 1770–20 Jan. 1777 David Mill; 20 Jan. 1777–25 March 1780 Richard Miles; 25 March 1780–20 May 1781 John Roberts; 20 May 1781–29 Apr. 1782 John Weuves (acting); 29 Apr. 1782–29 Jan. 1784 Richard Miles; 29 Jan. 1784–24 Jan. 1787 James Mourgan; 24 Jan. 1787–27 Apr. 1787 Thomas Price; 27 Apr. 1787–20 June 1789 Thomas Norris; 20 June 1789–15 Nov. 1791 William Fielde; 15 Nov. 1791–31 March 1792 John Gordon; 31 March 1792–16 Dec. 1798 Archibald Dalzel; 16 Dec. 1798–4 Jan. 1799 Jacob Mould; 4 Jan. 1799–28 Apr. 1800 John Gordon; 28 Apr. 1800–30 Sept. 1802 Archibald Dalzel; 30 Sept. 1802–8 Feb. 1805 Jacob Mould; 8 Feb. 1805–4 Dec. 1807 George Torrane; 4 Dec. 1807–21 Apr. 1816 Edward White; 21 Apr. 1816–19 Jan. 1817 Joseph Dawson; 19 Jan. 1817–7 May 1821 John Hope Smith.

156 British Gold Coast Crown Colony. 1843–13 Jan. 1850. *Location:* southern Ghana. *Capital:* Cape Coast Castle. *Other names:* Gold Coast, British Gold Coast, Gold Coast-Sierra Leone Colony.

History: In 1843 the British Crown resumed control of its Gold Coast territories (for fifteen years they had been in the hands of a committee of merchants—see **British Gold Coast [Committee of Merchants])** and linked them with Sierra Leone. In 1850 the area became the **Gold Coast Colony.**

Governors: 1843–8 March 1845 Worsley Hill; 8 March 1845–15 Apr. 1846 James Lilley (acting); 15 Apr. 1846–31 Jan. 1849 William Winniett; 31 Jan. 1849–13 Jan. 1850 James Fitzpatrick (acting).

157 British Gold Coast Settlements (Royal African Company). 1 May 1707–23 June 1751. *Location:* as **English Gold Coast Settlements.** *Capital:* Cape Coast Castle. *Other names:* British Gold Coast (Royal African Company).

History: In 1707 the Union of England and Scotland took place, and the **English Gold Coast Settlements (Royal African Company)** became British instead of English with the automatic name-change back home. It was still run by the Royal African Company in the same way. In 1751 the Company of Merchants took over control of the British Gold Coast Settlements from the dying Royal African Company (see **British Gold Coast [Company of Merchants]),** thus forming a more central and stable government.

Governors: there is only one known governor: 1 May 1707–1708 Sir Thomas Dalby.

158 British Kaffraria Colony. 17 Dec. 1847–7 March 1860. *Location:* as **Queen Adelaide Land.** *Capital:* King William's Town (rebuilt by Sir Harry Smith in 1847). *Other names:* British Kaffraria.

History: In 1847 Sir Harry Smith annexed **Queen Adelaide Land** as a separate British colony called British Kaffraria. In 1860 its dependency on the Cape was removed and it became **British Kaffraria Crown Colony.**

Chief Commissioners: 23 Dec. 1847–Oct. 1852 George Mackinnon; Oct. 1852–7 March 1860 John Maclean.

159 British Kaffraria Crown Colony. 7 March 1860–17 Apr. 1866. *Location:* as **British Kaffraria Colony.** *Capital:* King William's Town (permanently established in 1847 and named for King William IV of Great Britain). *Other names:* British Kaffraria.

History: In 1860 **British Kaffraria Colony** became a separate colony, and in 1866 it merged into the Cape (see

British Cape Colony), becoming the two districts of King William's Town and East London. Later on, this region became the **Ciskei.**
Lieutenant-Governors: 7 March 1860-24 Dec. 1864 John Maclean. *Governor's Deputies:* 24 Dec. 1864-17 Apr. 1866 Robert Graham.

160 British-Occupied Cape Colony [i]. 16 Sept. 1795-20 Feb. 1803. *Location:* as **British Cape Colony,** minus territory acquired later. *Capital:* Cape Town. *Other names:* Cape Colony, Cape of Good Hope.
History: In 1795, the British, by the Capitulation of Rustenburg, seized the Cape from the Dutch East India Company, and at the end of their war, Britain handed it to the Dutch government. For history of the area before 1795, see **Cape of Good Hope Colony.** For history after 1803, see **Dutch Cape Colony.**
Military Commanders: 16 Sept. 1795-15 Nov. 1795 Admiral Sir George Elphinstone; 16 Sept. 1795-15 Nov. 1795 General Alured Clark; 16 Sept. 1795-15 Nov. 1795 General James Craig. *Commandants:* 15 Nov. 1795-5 May 1797 James Craig (knighted 1797). *Governors:* 5 May 1797-20 Nov. 1798 George, Earl MacCartney; 21 Nov. 1798-9 Dec. 1799 Francis Dundas (acting); 10 Dec. 1799-20 Apr. 1801 Sir George Yonge; 20 Apr. 1801-20 Feb. 1803 Lord Glenbervie (did not leave Britain); 20 Apr. 1820-20 Feb. 1803 Francis Dundas (acting).

161 British-Occupied Cape Colony [ii]. 10 Jan. 1806-13 Aug. 1814. *Location:* as **British Cape Colony,** minus territory acquired later. *Capital:* Cape Town. *Other names:* Cape Colony, Cape of Good Hope.
History: In 1806 Britain, at the Capitulation of Papendorp, took **Dutch Cape Colony.** In 1814 it became legally British (see **British Cape Colony**).
Governors: 10 Jan. 1806-17 Jan. 1807 David Baird (acting); 17 Jan. 1807-

May 1807 Henry Grey (acting); 22 May 1807-4 July 1811 Alexander, Earl of Caledon; 4 July 1811-5 Sept. 1811 Henry Grey (acting); 6 Sept. 1811-18 Oct. 1813 Sir Francis Cradock; 18 Oct. 1813-7 Jan. 1814 Robert Meade (acting); 7 Jan. 1814-6 Apr. 1814 Sir Francis Cradock; 6 Apr. 1814-13 Aug. 1814 Lord Charles Somerset.

162 British-Occupied Egypt. 15 Sept. 1882-18 Dec. 1914. *Location:* as **Egypt.** *Capital:* Cairo. *Other names:* Egypt.
History: In 1882 the British occupied **Ottoman Egypt [ii],** because of Turkey's problems with the country. The country was, in theory, an Ottoman state until 1914, when the **Egyptian Protectorate** came into being. The Khedive of Egypt was the nominal ruler throughout the occupation.
Khedives: 15 Sept. 1882-7 Jan. 1892 Tewfiq; 7 Jan. 1892-18 Dec. 1914 Abbas II Hilmi. *Agents/Consuls-General:* 15 Sept. 1882-11 Sept. 1883 Sir Edwin Malet; 15 Sept. 1883-1891 Sir Evelyn Baring; 1891-1892 Arthur Hardinge (acting); 1892-24 Apr. 1907 Sir Evelyn Baring (created Baron Cromer in 1892, Viscount Cromer in 1899 and Earl Cromer in 1901); 7 May 1907-12 July 1911 Sir Eldon Gorst; 16 July 1911-18 Dec. 1914 Lord Kitchener. *Prime Ministers:* 15 Sept. 1882-8 Dec. 1882 Riaz Pasha; 8 Dec. 1882-30 Oct. 1883 Nubar Pasha; 30 Oct. 1883-7 Jan. 1884 Sherif Pasha; 7 Jan. 1884-8 June 1888 Nubar Pasha; 8 June 1888-12 May 1891 Riaz Pasha; 13 May 1891-15 Jan. 1893 Mustafa Fehmy Pasha; 18 Jan. 1893-16 Apr. 1894 Riaz Pasha; 16 Apr. 1894-11 Nov. 1895 Nubar Pasha; 12 Nov. 1895-12 Nov. 1908 Mustafa Fehmy Pasha; 12 Nov. 1908-20 Feb. 1910 Butros Ghali; 22 Feb. 1910-3 Apr. 1914 Muhammad Said Bey; 5 Apr. 1914-18 Dec. 1914 Hussein Rushdi Pasha.

163 British-Occupied German East Africa. 9 Oct. 1916-10 Jan. 1920. *Location:* **German East Africa Protectorate**

[ii], minus **Ruanda-Urundi.** *Capital:* Dar es-Salaam.

History: In 1916 Britain occupied **German East Africa Protectorate [ii],** or rather what became (in 1920) the Tanganyika part of it. **Ruanda-Urundi** went to the Belgian occupying forces. In 1920 Tanganyika was born (see **Tanganyika Mandate).** *Administrators:* 9 Oct. 1916–10 Jan. 1920 Horace Byatt (knighted 1919).

164 British-Occupied Mauritius. 3 Oct. 1810–30 May 1814. *Location:* as **Mauritius.** *Capital:* Port Louis. *Other names:* Mauritius, Île de France.

History: In 1810 the British occupied **Île de France Colony** during the Napoleonic Wars. In 1814 it was ceded to Britain and re-named **Mauritius Colony.** *Governors:* 3 Oct. 1810–1811 Sir Robert Farquhar; 1811–1811 Henry Warde (acting); 1811–30 May 1814 Sir Robert Farquhar.

165 British Occupied Séchelles. 1794–1810. *Location:* as **Seychelles Republic.** *Capital:* Mahé.

History: In 1794 the British captured **Séchelles French Colony,** but the French commandant and administration remained until 1810 when it became **Seychelles Colony.** *Commandants:* 1794–1810 Jean-Baptiste Quéau de Quincy.

166 British Pondoland. 25 Sept. 1894–30 May 1910. *Location:* as **Pondoland.** *Capital:* none. *Other names:* Pondoland (British).

History: In 1894 **Pondoland East** and **Pondoland West** were annexed to **British Cape Colony (Self-Rule),** and governed from there. The area was called British Pondoland until 1910 when the **Union of South Africa** came into existence, and then it simply disappeared into history. *Rulers:* 25 Sept. 1894–30 May 1910 direct Cape rule.

167 British Somaliland. 1884–20

July 1887. *Location:* northeast Africa. *Capital:* Berbera.

History: In 1884 Britain established possession of **Egyptian Somaliland** after the Egyptians left the area. In 1887 a protectorate was declared (see **British Somaliland Protectorate).** *Residents/Political Agents:* 1884–20 July 1887 Frederick Hunter.

168 British Somaliland Protectorate. 20 July 1887–26 June 1960. *Location:* as **British Somaliland.** *Capital:* Hargeysa (from 1941); Berbera (until 1941. Founded about 300 B.C. by Ptolemy Philadelphus, the name means "Land of the Barbarians"). *Other names:* British Somaliland, Somali Protectorate.

History: In 1887 **British Somaliland** became a protectorate. In 1960 it became independent as **Somalia State.** In between those dates certain British protectorates merged into British Somaliland Protectorate, i.e. Mussa Island in 1888, Bab Island the same year, and Aubad Island, also in 1888. British Somaliland was occupied briefly by the Italians from 1940–41.

Residents/Political Agents: 20 July 1887–1888 Frederick Hunter; 1888–1893 Edward Stace; 1893–1896 Charles Sealy; 1896–1897 William Ferris; 1897–1898 James Sadler. *Consuls-General:* 1898–1901 James Sadler; 1901–1903 Eric Swayne; 1903–1904 Harry Cordeaux (acting); 1904–1905 Eric Swayne. *Administrators:* 1905–1907 Harry Cordeaux; 1907–1907 Sir William Manning (acting); 1907–Jan. 1910 Harry Cordeaux; Jan. 1910–Jan. 1910 Horace Byatt (acting); Jan. 1910–July 1911 Sir William Manning; July 1911–1912 Horace Byatt; 1912–1913 Geoffrey Archer (acting); 1913–May 1914 Horace Byatt. *Commissioners:* May 1914–Oct. 1919 Geoffrey Archer. *Governors:* Oct. 1919–1920 Geoffrey Archer (knighted 1920); 1920–1921 Arthur Lawrance (acting); 1921–17 Aug. 1922 Sir Geoffrey Archer; 17 Aug. 1922–1925 Gerald Summers (knighted 1925); 26 Jan.

1926-18 June 1932 Harold Kittermaster (knighted 1928). *Commissioners:* 18 June 1932-1935 Arthur Lawrance (knighted 1934). *Governors:* 1935-2 March 1939 Sir Arthur Lawrance; 2 March 1939-18 Aug. 1940 Vincent Glenday; 18 Aug. 1940-29 March 1941 Italian occupation. *Military Governors:* 29 March 1941-3 March 1943 Arthur Chater; 3 March 1943-1948 Gerald Fisher. *Governors:* 1948-1954 Gerald Reece (knighted 1950); 1954-1959 Theodore Pike (knighted 1956); 1959-26 June 1960 Sir Douglas Hall. *Prime Ministers:* 19 May 1956-26 June 1960 Abdullah Issa.

169 British Tangier. 29 Jan. 1662-6 Feb. 1684. *Location:* northern Morocco. *Capital:* Tangier. *Other names:* Tangier.
History: In 1662 when Charles II married Catherine of Braganza, Tangier came with her. From 1471 Tangier had been Portuguese (see **Portuguese Tangier**). A long siege by the Sultan of Morocco caused the British to abandon the town and fortress in 1684, and it became part of **Alawid Morocco**.
Governors: 29 Jan. 1662-1663 Earl of Peterborough; 1663-3 May 1664 Earl of Teviot; 3 May 1664-1664 Sir Tobias Bridges (acting); 1664-Apr. 1665 John Fitzgerald; Apr. 1665-1666 Baron Belasyse; 1666-1669 Sir Henry Norwood; 1669-1670 Earl of Middleton; 1670-1672 Sir Hugh Cholmondeley (acting); 1672-1674 Earl of Middleton; 1674-1675 Budgett Meakin (acting); 1675-1680 Earl of Inchiquin; 1680-1681 Sir Edward Sackville; 1681-1683 Sir Piercy Kirke; 1683-6 Feb. 1684 Baron Dartmouth.

170 British Togoland. 27 Dec. 1916-30 Sept. 1920. *Location:* Ghana. *Capital:* Ho. *Other names:* West Togo.
History: In 1916 the **Togoland French-British Condominium** came to an end, and Togo was divided into West (British) and East (French). In 1920 France and Britain both received League of Nations mandates for their areas (see **Togoland French Mandate** and **Togoland British Mandate**).
Rulers: 27 Dec. 1916-30 Sept. 1920 ruled direct from Gold Coast.

171 British Tripolitania. 15 Dec. 1942-24 Dec. 1951. *Location:* northwestern Libya. *Capital:* Tripoli. *Other names:* Tripolitania.
History: In 1942-43 the British captured **Libya Italian Colony** and created a tri-partite state, composed of British Tripolitania, **French Fezzan** and **British Cyrenaica**. In 1951 these areas joined as Libya gained its independence (see **Libyan Kingdom**).
Deputy Chief Civil Affairs Officers: 15 Dec. 1942-23 Jan. 1943 Maurice Lush; 23 Jan. 1943-1944 Travers Blackley. *Chief Administrators:* 1944-Apr. 1949 Travers Blackley. *Residents:* Apr. 1949-24 Dec. 1951 Travers Blackley.

172 British West Africa. See these names:
West Africa Settlements (1874-1888)
West African Settlements (1866-1874)
West African Territories (1821-1850)

173 British Zululand. 21 June 1887-1 Dec. 1897. *Location:* Zululand, northern Natal, South Africa. *Capital:* Eshowe. *Other names:* Zululand British Protectorate.
History: In 1887 **Zululand Province** became British Zululand, under British law. In 1897 it was annexed to the Cape (see **British Cape Colony [Self-Rule]**).
Paramount Chiefs: 21 June 1887-1 Dec. 1897 Dinuzulu. *Resident-Commissioners:* 21 June 1887-1893 Sir Melmoth Osborn; 1893-1 Dec. 1897 Marshall Clarke.

Bu Regreg see **Bou Regreg**

174 Buganda. 1395-26 Dec. 1890. *Location:* Uganda. *Capital:* Nabulagala (1882-90); Lubaga (1880-82); Kikandwa (1879-80); Lubaga (1875-

79); Kabodha (1872–75); Nabulagala (1870–72); Nnakawa (1865–70); Bbanda (1862–65); Nakatema (1860–62); Nabulagala (1856–60); Mulago (1850–56); Mengo (until 1850). *Other names:* Uganda Kingdom.

History: For centuries Buganda was a native kingdom dominated by **Bunyoro**. In the 16th and 17th centuries it gradually broke free, but by 1890 had been taken over by Britain. In that year it became part of **Uganda,** although the kings of Buganda continued to have influence on local chiefs and in the administration of the colony, until the monarchy was abolished in 1967.

Kabakas (Kings): 1395–1408 Kintu; 1408–1420 Cwa I Nabaka; 1420–1447 Kimera; 1447–1474 Tembo; 1474–1501 Kiggala; 1501–1528 Kiyimbo; 1528–1555 Kayima; 1555–1582 Nakibinge; 1582–1609 Mulundo (joint); 1582–1609 Jemba (joint); 1582–1609 Suna I (joint); 1609–1636 Sekamanya (joint); 1609–1636 Kimbugwe (joint); 1636–1663 Katerrega; 1663–1690 Juuko (joint); 1663–1690 Mutebi (joint); 1663–1690 Kayemba (joint); 1690–1717 Tebandeke (joint); 1690–1717 Ndawula (joint); 1717–1744 Kagulu (joint); 1717–1744 Mawanda (joint); 1717–1744 Kikulwe (joint); 1744–1771 Kagulu (joint); 1744–1771 Namagula (joint); 1744–1771 Kyabaggu (joint); 1771–1798 Junju (joint); 1771–1798 Semakookiru (joint); 1798–1825 Kamanya; 1825–1852 Suna II; 1852–10 Oct. 1884 Mutesa I Walugembe Mukaobya; 10 Oct. 1884–1888 Danieri Mwanga; 1888–Oct. 1888 Mutebi II Kiwena; Oct. 1888–Oct. 1889 Kalema; Oct. 1889–July 1897 Danieri Mwanga; July 1897–Nov. 1897 no king ruled; Nov. 1897–20 Nov. 1939 Daudi Cwa II; 20 Nov. 1939–30 Nov. 1953 Mutesa II; 30 Nov. 1953–17 Oct. 1955 tribe unrecognized; 17 Oct. 1955–8 Sept. 1967 Mutesa II.

175 Bumpe. 1820–1888. *Location:* Sierra Leone. *Capital:* Bumpe.

History: The Caulkers had ruled **Banana Island,** until it fell under British rule in **Sierra Leone Crown Colony.** They moved to Bumpe, which they ruled till 1888, when it became part of **Sierra Leone Territory [iii].**

Kings: 1820–1832 Thomas Caulker; 1832–1842 Charles Caulker; 1842–1857 Canreba; 1857–1864 Thomas Theophilus Caulker; 1864–1888 Richard Canreba Caulker; 1888–1895 vacant; 1895–1898 Richard Canreba Caulker; 1898–1901 vacant; 1901–(?) James Canreba Caulker.

176 Bunyoro. ca. 1400–30 July 1896. *Location:* Uganda. *Capital:* Mparo. *Other names:* Unyoro Kingdom.

History: Founded by northern invaders the kingdom became pre-eminent in the area. Finally, by the 18th century, it lost sway to **Buganda.** In 1896 it became absorbed into **Uganda Protectorate,** by having "protection" thrust upon it by the British. The monarchy was abolished in 1967 (cf. **Buganda**).

Omukamas (Kings): ca. 1400 Isingoma Mpuga Rukidi; (?)–(?) Ochaki Rwangira; (?)–(?) Oyo Nyimba; (?)–(?) Winyi I Rubembeka; (?)–(?) Olimi I Kalimbi; (?)–(?) Nyabongo I Rulemu; ca. 1550 Winyi II Rubangiramasega; fl. 1582 Olimi II Ruhundwangeye; (?)–(?) Nyarwa Omuzarra Kyaro; (?)–(?) Cwa I Mali Rumoma Mahanga. **Queens:** (?)–(?) Mashamba. *Omukamas (Kings):* (?)–(?) Kyebambe I Omuzikiya; (?)–(?) Winyi III Ruguruka; ca. 1710 Nyaika (joint); ca. 1710 Kyebambe II Bikaju (joint); (?)–1731 Olimi III Isansa; 1731–1782 Duhaga I Cwa Mujwiga; 1782–1786 Olimi IV Kasoma; 1786–1835 Kyebambe III Nyamutukura; 1835–1848 Nyabongo II Mugenyi; 1848–1852 Olimi V Rwakabale; 1852–1869 Kyebambe IV (or Kamurasi); 1869–1870 Kabigumere; 1870–1898 Cwa II Kabarega; 1898–1902 Kitahimbwa Karukare; 1902–1924 Duhaga II Bisereko; 1924–8 Sept. 1967 Winyi IV Gafabusa.

177 Burkina Faso. See these **names:**

Burkina Faso (1984–   )
Upper Volta Republic (1960–1984)
Upper Volta Autonomous Republic (1958–1960)
Upper Volta Overseas Territory (1947–1958)
Upper Ivory Coast (1938–1947)
Upper Volta Colony (1919–1933)
Upper Volta Protectorate (1895–1919)
Gurma (1204–1895)
Gwiriko (1714–1890)
Kenedugu (ca. 1650–1898)
Wagadugu (ca. 1495–1896)
Yatenga (1540–1895)
Mossi States—explanation and referral entry

178 Burkina Faso. 4 Aug. 1984–   .
Location: northwest Africa. *Capital:* Ouagadougou (founded about 1050). *Other names:* Burkina, Burkina Faso Republic, Republic of Burkina Faso.
History: In 1984 **Upper Volta Republic** became Burkina Faso (the name means "country of honest men") and in 1986 Sankara declared it a Jamhariyya (Republic).
Heads of State: 4 Aug. 1984–15 Oct. 1987 Thomas Sankara; 15 Oct. 1987– Blaise Compaore.

179 Burundi. ca. 1675–6 Apr. 1903.
Location: Burundi Republic. *Capital:* Usumbura (what is today Bujumbura).
History: About 1675 the Tuti king Ntare I built a kingdom in what is now **Burundi Republic,** and in his reign conquered the areas of Nkoma, Bututsi, Kilimiro, and Buyenzi. Conquest and internecine struggles marked the history of Burundi until in 1903 it became part of the **German East Africa Protectorate [i],** although the Germans never really ruled the area (cf **Ruanda**). After World War I its fate was inexorably bound up with that of **Ruanda** (see **Ruanda-Urundi**).
Mwamis (Kings): ca. 1675–ca. 1705 Ntare I Rushatse; ca. 1705–ca. 1725 Mwezi I; ca. 1725–ca. 1760 Ntare II Kivimira; ca. 1760–ca. 1768 Mwezi II;

ca. 1768–ca. 1795 Mwambutsa I; ca. 1795–1810 Mutaga I Seenyamwiiza; 1810–1852 Ntaare II Rugaamba; 1852–21 Aug. 1908 Mwezi II Kisabo; 21 Aug. 1908–10 Nov. 1915 Mutaga II; 16 Dec. 1915–8 July 1966 Mwambutsa II; 8 July 1966–28 Nov. 1966 Ntare III Ndiziye.

180 Burundi Autonomous Kingdom. 29 Sept. 1961–1 July 1962. *Location:* as **Burundi Republic.** *Capital:* Bujumbura. *Other names:* Burundi, Urundi, Autonomous Kingdom of Burundi.
History: In 1961 Urundi (then one-half of the **Ruanda-Urundi Trust Territory**—the other half being Ruanda) was given limited self-rule as Burundi, being ruled by the Tutsi minority who had, as in Ruanda, ruled nominally throughout foreign occupation. In 1962, on the breaking up of the Trust Territory, **Burundi Kingdom** came into being, as the state gained full independence from Belgium.
Kings: 29 Sept. 1961–1 July 1962 Mwambutsa II. *Prime Ministers:* 29 Sept. 1961–13 Oct. 1961 Prince Louis Rwagasore; 20 Oct. 1961–1 July 1962 Chief André Muhirwa. *Governors of Ruanda-Urundi:* 29 Sept. 1961–1 July 1962 Jean-Paul Harroy.

181 Burundi Kingdom. 1 July 1962–28 Nov. 1966. *Location:* east central Africa. *Capital:* Bujumbura. *Other names:* Kingdom of Burundi, Burundi.
History: In 1962 when **Ruanda-Urundi Trust Territory** was broken up, two separate independent states emerged—**Rwanda Republic** and the Kingdom of Burundi. Each had evolved from an autonomous state within the trust territory (see **Rwanda Autonomous Republic** and **Burundi Autonomous Kingdom**). In 1966 Burundi became a republic (see **Burundi Republic**) and the monarchy was abolished.
Mwamis (Kings): 1 July 1962–6 July 1966 Mwambutsa II; 8 July 1966–28 Nov. 1966 Ntare III (or Charles Ndizeye). *Prime Ministers:* 1 July 1962–10

June 1963 Chief André Muhirwa; 17 June 1963-1 Apr. 1964 Pierre Ngendamdumwe; 1 Apr. 1964-7 Jan. 1965 Albin Nyamoya; 7 Jan. 1965-15 Jan. 1965 Pierre Ngendamdumwe; 15 Jan. 1965-25 Jan. 1965 Pie Masumbuko (acting); 25 Jan. 1965-30 Sept. 1965 Joseph Bamina; 1 Oct. 1965-9 July 1966 Léopold Biha; 13 July 1966-28 Nov. 1966 Michel Micombero.

182 Burundi Republic. 28 Nov. 1966– . *Location:* as **Burundi Kingdom.** *Capital:* Bujumbura. *Other names:* Republic of Burundi, Burundi, République du Burundi.

History: In 1966 **Burundi Kingdom** became a republic and the monarchy was abolished.

Presidents: 28 Nov. 1966-1 Nov. 1976 Michel Micombero; 9 Nov. 1976– Jan. 1980 Jean-Baptiste Bagaza (Head of the Supreme Council of the Revolution); Jan. 1980-3 Sept. 1987 Jean-Baptiste Bagaza; 3 Sept. 1987-9 Sept. 1987 Maj. Pierre Buyoya (Leader of the Military Committee for National Salvation). 9 Sept. 1987– Pierre Buyoya. *Prime Ministers:* 14 July 1972-6 June 1973 Albin Nyamoya; 13 Nov. 1976– Jan. 1980 Édouard Nzambimana. *Note:* In times of no Prime Minister, the President held that office.

183 Byzacena Roman Province. 297-442. *Location:* southern Tunisia. *Capital:* Hadrumatum. *Other names:* Byzacium.

History: In 297 Diocletian reformed the Roman Empire, and out of **Africa Roman Province [i]** cut three new provinces: **Africa Roman Province [ii], Tripolitania Roman Province** and Byzacena. From about 395 Byzacena came under the Prefecture of Italy (Subdivision: Diocese of Africa), and in 442 it went to the Vandals (see **Vandal North Africa**).

Rulers: 297-442 [unknown].

184 Byzantine Egypt [i]. 395-616. *Location:* Egypt. *Capital:* Alexandria. *Other names:* Egypt.

History: In 395 control of Egypt passed from Rome (see **Egyptian Diocese of Rome**) to Constantinople, and the Byzantines ruled it until 616 when the Persians temporarily took it for 12 years (see **Persian Egypt**).

Prefects: 395-5 Feb. 396 Charmosynus; 5 Feb. 396-30 March 396 Gennadius (or Torquatus); 30 March 396-17 June 397 Remigius; 17 June 397-(?) Archelaus; (?)-(?) [unknown]; 403-404 Pentadius; 404-(?) Euthalius; (?)-(?) [unknown]; 415-(?) Orestes; 422-(?) Callistus; 435-(?) Cleopater; 442-(?) Charmosinus; 451-(?) Theodorus; 453-(?) Florus; 468-(?) Alexander; (?)-(?) [unknown]; 476-477 Boethus; 477-478 Anthemius; 478-479 Theoctistus; 479-(?) Theognostus; 482-482 Apollonius; 482-(?) Pergamius; 485-(?) Eutrechius; 487-487 Theodorus; 487-(?) Arsenius; 501-(?) Eustathius; ca. 510-(?) Theodosius; 520-(?) Licinius; 527-(?) Hephaestus; 535-(?) Dioscorus; 537-(?) Rhodon. *Duci:* 539-542 Petrus Marcellinus Felix Liberius; 542-(?) Ioannes Laxarion; ca. 560-(?) Favorinus; 566-(?) Iustinus; 582-(?) Ioannes; ca. 585-(?) Paulus; ca. 588-(?) Ioannes; ca. 592-(?) Constantinus; ca. 595-(?) Menas; 600-603 Petrus (or Iustinus); ca. 606-(?) Ioannes; 614-(?) Niketas. *Note:* Duci is the plural of Dux (Duke).

185 Byzantine Egypt [ii]. 628-17 Sept. 642. *Location:* Egypt. *Capital:* Alexandria. *Other names:* Egypt.

History: In 628 Egypt was won by Heraclius I, Emperor of Rome, from the Persians (see **Persian Egypt**), who had held the country for the previous twelve years. But the Muslims were on the scene now and were irresistible. In 639 they marched into Egypt and took town after town until, in 642, the Byzantines left (see **Egypt [Arab]**).

Military Prefects: 628-629 [unknown]; 629-641 Anastasius; 641-17 Sept. 642 Theodorus.

186 Byzantine North Africa [i]. Apr. 534-647. *Location:* North Africa

(Libya, Tunisia and Algeria). *Capital:* Carthage.

History: In 534 the Byzantines expelled the Vandals (see **Vandal North Africa**) from Africa, and set up a province under Constantinople. In 647 the Arabs invaded and captured it (see **Arab North Africa [i]**).

Prefects: Apr. 534–May 534 Archelaus. *Military Commanders:* May 534–Sept. 534 Belisarius; Sept. 534–535 Salomon. *Prefects:* 535–Dec. 536 Salomon; Dec. 536–Dec. 536 Symmachus. *Military Commanders:* Dec. 536–539 Germanus. *Prefects:* 539–543 Salomon; 544–Dec. 545 Areobindus; Dec. 545–May 546 Athanasius. *Military Commanders:* May 546–546 Artabanus; 546–Sept. 552 Johannes Troglita. *Prefects:* Sept. 552–555 Paulus; 555–Oct. 558 Boethius; Oct. 558–Dec. 562 Johannes Troglita. *Military Commanders:* Dec. 562–June 563 Johannes Rogathinos. *Prefects:* June 563–563 Areobindus. *Military Commanders:* 563–565 Marcianus. *Prefects:* 565–565 Thomas; 565–569 Lucius Mappius. *Military Commanders:* 569–May 570 Theodorus; May 570–571 Theoctistus; 571–574 Amabilis; 574–578 [unknown]; *Prefects:* 578–578 Thomas. *Military Commanders:* 578–578 Gennadius; 578–Aug. 582 Vitalius. *Prefects:* Aug. 582–590 Theodorus; 590–July 591 Johannes; July 591–594 Gennadius. *Exarchs:* 594–Oct. 598 Pantaleon; Oct. 598–July 600 Gennadius. *Prefects:* July 600–602 Innocentius. *Exarchs:* 602–611 Heraclius; 611–614 [unknown]; 614–617 Caesarius; 617–619 [unknown]; 619–June 627 Nicetas. *Prefects:* June 627–633 Gregorius. *Exarchs:* 633–641 Petrus. *Prefects:* 641–July 645 Gregorius. *Exarchs:* July 645–647 Gregorius.

187 Byzantine North Africa [ii]. 649–667. *Location:* North Africa (Libya, Tunisia, Algeria). *Capital:* Carthage.

History: In 649 the Byzantines conquered **Arab North Africa [i]** and in 667 lost it again (see **Arab North Africa [ii]**).

Rulers: [unknown].

188 Byzantine North Africa [iii]. 697–703. *Location:* North Africa (Libya, Tunisia, Algeria). *Capital:* Carthage.

History: In 697 the Byzantines reconquered North Africa from the Arabs (see **Arab North Africa [ii]**). In 703 they lost it for the last time (see **Omayyad North Africa**).

Governors: 697–703 Johannes.

Cabo Verde see **Cape Verde**

189 Cacheu. 1614–1852. *Location:* north Guinea-Bissau. *Capital:* Cacheu.

History: Nuno Tristão, the Portuguese discoverer, was probably the first to visit the area which is today **Guinea-Bissau** — in 1446. In the 1500s it was settled from **Cape Verde Islands**. In 1614 an administration was begun, subject to the Cape Verde government. In 1687 **Bissau [i]** was founded to the south, but by 1850 Cacheu had lost its importance as a captaincy. In 1879 the area, along with **Bissau [ii]** and others along the coast, merged into **Portuguese Guinea**.

Capitães-Mores: 1614–(?) João de Sousa; ca. 1615–ca. 1616 Baltasar de Castelo Branco; ca. 1616–ca. 1622 [unknown]; ca. 1622–(?) Francisco de Távora; 1625–(?) Francisco Sodré Pereira; (?)–1634 Francisco Nunes de Andrade; 1634–1634 Domingos Reimão; 1634–(?) Paulo da Silva; (?)–(?) Manuel da Silva Botelho; (?)–1641 Luis de Magalhães; 1641–1644 [unknown]; 1644–1649 Gonçalo de Gamboa Ayala; 1649–1650 Gaspar Vogado; 1650–1654 João Fidalgo; 1654–1655 [unknown]; 1655–(?) Francisco da Cunha; 1658–1662 Manuel Contrim; 1662–1664 António Ornelas; 1664–(?) João Moutinho; (?)–(?) Manuel de Almeida; (?)–(?) Ambrósio Gomes; ca. 1674–(?) Sebastião da Rosa; 1676–1682 António

Bezerra; 1682–1685 Gaspar Pacheco; 1685–1686 João de Oliveira; 1686–1687 [unknown]; 1687–1688 António Bezerra; 1688–1689 Rodrigo da Fonseca; 1689–1690 José da Camara; 1690–1691 Domingos de Carvalho; 1691–1707 Santos Castanho; 1707–(?) Paulo de Abreu e Lima; 1715–1718 António Bezerra, Jr.; 1718–(?) Inácio Ferreira; ca. 1721–(?) António Bezerra, Jr.; ca. 1723–(?) Pedro de Barros; 1726–(?) Manuel Lobo; ca. 1729–1731 João Perestrelo; 1731–(?) António Bezerra, Jr.; 1733–ca. 1734 João de Carvalho; ca. 1734–ca. 1737 [unknown]; ca. 1737–(?) Damião de Bastos; ca. 1741–(?) Nicolau Pino de Araújo; 1748–1751 João de Távora; 1751–ca. 1755 Francisco Souto-Maior; ca. 1755–ca. 1765 [unknown]; ca. 1765–1770 Sebastião Souto-Maior; 1770–1775 [unknown]; 1775–(?) António Vaz de Araújo; (?)–1785 António de Meneses; 1785–1786 João Barreto; 1786–(?) Luis de Araújo e Silva; 1798–(?) Lopo Henriques; 1800–(?) Manuel de Gouveia; ca. 1802–1803 José Torvão; 1803–(?) João Pinto; 1811–1814 Joaquim de Figueiredo e Góis; 1814–1815 [unknown]; 1815–(?) João Goodolfim; (?)–1819 João de Meneses Drumont; 1819–1820 [unknown]; ca. 1820–1821 José Correia de Barros; 1821–(?) João de Araújo Gomes; 1823–ca. 1825 João Goodolfim; 1825–1826 [unknown]; ca. 1826–(?) António Santos; ca. 1835–(?) José Ferreira; 1838–(?) Delfim dos Santos; 1842–1844 António Chaves; 1844–1846 José do Crato; 1846–1847 Honório Barreto; 1847–ca. 1849 José do Crato; ca. 1849–1852 [unknown]; 1852–1852 Honório Barreto. *Note:* Capitães-Mores is the plural of Capitão-Mor (Captain-Major).

Calabar, Calbaria see **New Calabar**

190 Cameroons British Mandate. 22 July 1920–13 Dec. 1946. *Location:* western Cameroun–eastern Nigeria. *Capital:* Lagos (Nigeria); Buea (local headquarters). *Other names:* British Cameroons.

History: On June 28, 1919, at the Treaty of Versailles, France and Britain were each granted League of Nations mandates of their territories in the Cameroons (effective from July 22, 1920) (see also **French Cameroun Mandate**). For the name of the area prior to this see **British Cameroons Territory.** In 1946 it became a U.N. Trust Territory (see **Cameroons British Trust Territory**).

Rulers: ruled from Lagos, Nigeria (see **Nigeria Colony and Protectorate**).

191 Cameroons British Trust Territory. 13 Dec. 1946–1 Oct. 1954. *Location:* western Cameroun–eastern Nigeria. *Capital:* Lagos (Nigeria); Buea (local headquarters). *Other names:* British Cameroons.

History: In 1946 **Cameroons British Mandate** became a United Nations Trust Territory. In 1954 British Cameroons became one of the autonomous regions of **Nigeria Federation,** being divided into Northern Cameroon and Southern Cameroon.

Rulers: ruled from Lagos, Nigeria (see **Nigeria Colony and Protectorate**).

192 Cameroun. See these names:
Cameroun Republic [ii] (1984–   )
Cameroun United Republic (1972–1984)
Cameroun Federal Republic (1961–1972)
Cameroun Republic [i] (1960–1961)
Cameroun Autonomous Republic (1959–1960)
Cameroun French Trust Territory (1946–1959)
Cameroun Autonomous French Mandate (1921–1946)
Cameroun French Mandate (1920–1921)
French Cameroun Territory (1916–1920)
Cameroons British Trust Territory (1946–1954)
Cameroons British Mandate (1920–1946)
British Cameroons Territory (1916–

1920)

Cameroun French-British Condominium (1914–1916)

Kamerun (1900–1916)

German Crown Land of North West Africa (1884–1900)

Ambas Bay British Protectorate (1884–1887)

Victoria Colony (1858–1884)

Adamawa (1806–1901)

Bamoun Sultanate (1394–1884)

Kom (ca. 1720–1884)

Mandara (ca. 1500–1902)

193 Cameroun Autonomous French Mandate. 23 March 1921–13 Dec. 1946. *Location:* as **Cameroun Republic [i].** *Capital:* Douala (1940–46), Yaoundé (1922–40), Douala (1921–1922). *Other names:* East Cameroon.

History: In 1921 **Cameroun French Mandate** was given autonomy and in 1946 it was made into a United Nations Trusteeship (see **Cameroun French Trust Territory**).

Commissioners: 23 March 1921–24 April 1921 Auguste Bonnecarrère (acting); 24 Apr. 1921–March 1923 Jules Carde; March 1923–29 Apr. 1923 Albéric Fournier (acting); 29 Apr. 1923–27 Dec. 1924 Théodore Marchand; 27 Dec. 1924–11 May 1925 Ernest Bleu (acting); 11 May 1925–2 March 1926 Théodore Marchand; 2 March 1926–31 Oct. 1926 Ernest Bleu (acting); 31 Oct. 1926–26 Apr. 1929 Théodore Marchand; 26 Apr. 1929–26 Oct. 1929 Ernest Bleu (acting); 26 Oct. 1929–19 June 1931 Théodore Marchand; 19 June 1931–6 Feb. 1932 Ernest Bleu (acting); 6 Feb. 1932–31 Aug. 1932 Théodore Marchand; 31 Aug. 1932–7 July 1934 Auguste Bonnecarrère; 7 July 1934–1936 Jules Repiquet; 1936–Jan. 1937 Gaston Guibet (acting); Jan. 1937–7 Oct. 1937 Pierre-François Boissons; 7 Oct. 1937–9 March 1938 Pierre Aubert (acting); 9 March 1938–16 Nov. 1938 Pierre-François Boissons; 16 Nov. 1938–29 Aug. 1940 Richard Brunot. *Governors:* 29 Aug. 1940–12 Nov. 1940 Philippe Leclerc de Hauteclocque; 12 Nov. 1940–20 July 1943 Pierre Cournarie; 20 July 1943–15 Nov. 1944 Hubert Carras; 15 Nov. 1944–16 Jan. 1946 Henri Nicolas; 16 Jan. 1946–16 March 1946 Alexis Leger (acting). *High Commissioner:* 16 March 1946–13 Dec. 1946 Robert Delavignette.

194 Cameroun Autonomous Republic. 1 Jan. 1959–1 Jan. 1960. *Location:* as **Cameroun Republic.** *Capital:* Yaoundé. *Other names:* Cameroun, East Cameroun, Autonomous Republic of Cameroun.

History: In 1959 the **Cameroun French Trust Territory** became an autonomous republic within the French Community. In 1960 it became fully independent as **Cameroun Republic [i].**

High Commissioners: 1 Jan. 1959–1 Jan. 1960 Xavier Torré. *Prime Ministers:* 1 Jan. 1959–1 Jan. 1960 Ahmadou Ahidjo.

195 Cameroun Federal Republic. 1 Oct. 1961–2 June 1972. *Location:* as **Cameroun United Republic.** *Capital:* Yaoundé.

History: In 1961 **Cameroun Republic [i]** became a federal republic with the merger of **Cameroun Republic [i]** and the Southern Cameroons of Nigeria, the latter having voted to join the **Cameroun Republic [i].** This created a federal government which consisted of two parts, East and West Cameroun—the East being French-speaking and the West being English-speaking. The President was to be French- and the Vice-President to be English-speaking. In 1972 Cameroun became a unitary state (see **Cameroun United Republic**).

Presidents: 1 Oct. 1961–2 June 1972 Ahmadou Ahidjo. *Prime Ministers of East Cameroun:* 1 Oct. 1961–June 1965 Charles Assalé; June 1965–20 Nov. 1965 Vincent de Paul Ahanda; 20 Nov. 1965–2 June 1972 Simon Tchoungi. *Prime Ministers of West Cameroun:* 1 Oct. 1961–11 Jan. 1968 John Foncha; 11 Jan. 1968–2 June 1972 Solomon Tandeng.

196 Cameroun French-British Condominium. 26 Sept. 1914–4 March 1916. *Location:* as **French Cameroun Territory** and **British Cameroons Territory.** *Capital:* Douala. *Other names:* Cameroun.

History: In 1914 the British and French captured much of **Kamerun** from the Germans and set up a military joint condominium. In 1916 the Germans finally and formally surrendered, and in March 1916 **French Cameroun Territory** and **British Cameroons Territory** came into being as two separate countries.

Military Commanders: 26 Sept. 1914–7 Apr. 1915 Joseph Aymerich. *Administrators:* 7 Apr. 1915–4 March 1916 Joseph Aymerich.

197 Cameroun French Mandate. 22 July 1920–23 March 1921. *Location:* Cameroun. *Capital:* Douala. *Other names:* East Cameroons, French Cameroons, Cameroun Français, French Cameroun League of Nations Mandate.

History: In 1920 the League of Nations made **French Cameroun Territory** a mandate. In 1921 this mandate was given autonomy (see **Cameroun Autonomous French Mandate**).

Governors: 22 July 1920–Oct. 1920 Jules Carde; Oct. 1920–23 March 1921 Auguste Bonnecarrère (acting).

198 Cameroun French Trust Territory. 13 Dec. 1946–1 Jan. 1959. *Location:* Cameroun. *Capital:* Yaoundé. *Other names:* Cameroun, French Cameroun, French Cameroun United Nations Trust Territory, East Cameroons, French Cameroun United Nations Trusteeship.

History: In 1946 France accepted a trust territory for Cameroun (until then it had been **Cameroun Autonomous French Mandate**). In 1959 it became **Cameroun Autonomous Republic.**

High Commissioners: 13 Dec. 1946–25 March 1947 Robert Delavignette; 25 March 1947–Apr. 1947 Robert Casimir (acting); Apr. 1947–7 July 1949 René Hoffherr; 7 July 1949–10 Jan. 1950 Robert Casimir (acting); 10 Jan. 1950–2 Dec. 1954 Jean-Louis Soucadaux; 2 Dec. 1954–17 Apr. 1956 Roland Pré; 17 Apr. 1956–29 Jan. 1958 Pierre Messmer; 29 Jan. 1958–19 Feb. 1958 Jean Paul Ramadier; 19 Feb. 1958–1 Jan. 1959 Xavier Torré. *Prime Ministers:* 15 May 1957–18 Feb. 1958 Andre Maria Mbida; 18 Feb. 1958–1 Jan. 1959 Ahmadou Ahidjo.

199 Cameroun Republic [i]. 1 Jan. 1960–1 Oct. 1961. *Location:* as **Cameroun Republic [ii]**, excluding Southern Cameroons Province of Nigeria. *Capital:* Yaoundé. *Other names:* Republic of Cameroun, Cameroun.

History: In 1960 **Cameroun Autonomous Republic** became independent as The Republic of Cameroun. In 1961 the autonomous Nigerian province of Southern Cameroons elected to go into the Republic of Cameroun instead of staying with **Nigeria.** This formed the **Cameroun Federal Republic.**

Presidents: 5 May 1960–1 Oct. 1961 Ahmadou Ahidjo. *Prime Ministers:* 1 Jan. 1960–5 May 1960 Ahmadou Ahidjo; 14 May 1960–1 Oct. 1961 Charles Assalé. *Note:* in times of no Prime Minister, the President held that office.

200 Cameroun Republic [ii]. 21 Jan. 1984– . *Location:* as **Cameroun United Republic.** *Capital:* Yaoundé (founded 1888). *Other names:* Cameroun, République du Cameroun.

History: In 1984 President Paul Biya discarded the old term **Cameroun United Republic** and the country became just Cameroun Republic again. The name "Cameroun" comes from "Rio de Cameroẽs"—"River of Prawns," the name given by the early Portuguese to the Wouri River Estuary.

Presidents: 21 Jan. 1984– Paul Biya.

201 Cameroun United Republic. 2 June 1972–21 Jan. 1984. *Location:* northwest Africa. *Capital:* Yaoundé. *Other names:* République du Cameroun, Republic of Cameroun, United Republic of Cameroun, Cameroun United State, United State of Cameroun.
History: In 1972 **Cameroun Federal Republic** became a unitary state. In 1984 it returned to the name Cameroun Republic (see **Cameroun Republic [ii]**).
Presidents: 2 June 1972–6 Nov. 1982 Ahmadou Ahidjo; 6 Nov. 1982–21 Jan. 1984 Paul Biya. *Prime Ministers:* 30 June 1975–6 Nov. 1982 Paul Biya; 6 Nov. 1982–22 Aug. 1983 Bello Bouba Maigari; 22 Aug. 1983–21 Jan. 1984 Luc Ayang.

202 Campbell Lands. 1813–May 1824. *Location:* Orange Free State, **South Africa.** *Capital:* Campbell.
History: In 1813 the Rev. John Campbell established a Griqua state with its capital at Campbell. From the London Missionary Society, Campbell gave the Griquas their name (they were a mixture of races), and the area was loosely ruled until 1819 when Adam Kok II left **Griquatown** and established his rule in Campbell. In 1824 Cornelis Kok II, Adam's younger brother, succeeded to the captaincy and the area became known as **Cornelis Kok's Land** (see also **Adam Kok's Land**).
Residents: 1813–1819 John Campbell. *Captains:* 1819–May 1824 Adam Kok II.

203 The Canary Islands. See these names:
Canary Islands (Self-Rule) (1983–)
Las Palmas de Gran Canaria Province (1927–1983)
Santa Cruz de Tenerife Province (1927–1983)
Canary Islands Protectorate (1912–1927)
Canary Islands Province (1821–1912)
Gran Canaria Territory [iii] (1625–1821)

Tenerife Territory [ii] (1625–1821)
Canary Islands Captaincy-General [ii] (1625–1821)
Gran Canaria [ii] (1595–1625)
Tenerife [ii] (1595–1625)
Gran Canaria Territory [i] (1589–1595)
Tenerife Territory [i] (1589–1595)
Canary Islands Captaincy-General [i] (1589–1595)
Gran Canaria [i] (1480–1589)
Tenerife [i] (1495–1589)
Canary Islands Kingdom (1405–1480)
Fortunate Islands ([?]–1405)

204 Canary Islands Captaincy-General [i]. 1589–1595. *Location:* as **Canary Islands.** *Capital:* Las Palmas. *Other names:* The Canaries, The Canary Islands, Islas Canárias.
History: In 1589 a Captain-General was appointed over the Canaries as a group (see also entries **Gran Canária** and **Tenerife**). The Captaincy-General lasted six years and then each of the individual islands, which until 1589 had been running themselves, resumed their authority (again, see individual entries for islands). In 1625, however, the Captaincy-General was reinstituted (see **Canary Islands Captaincy-General [ii]**).
Captains-General: 1589–1591 Marques de Bedmar; 1591–1595 [unknown]. *Note:* although they do not have individual entries in this book, the islands of Lanzarote, Gomera, La Palma, Hierro and Fuerteventura shared a parallel fate to the larger, more important **Gran Canária** and **Tenerife.**

205 Canary Islands Captaincy-General [ii]. 1625–1821. *Location:* as **Canary Islands Captaincy-General [i].** *Capital:* Las Palmas. *Other names:* Islas Canárias, Canary Islands, The Canaries.
History: In 1625 the Captaincy-General was reinstituted (see **Canary Islands Captaincy-General [i]** for fur-

ther details) over the Canaries. In 1821 the Canaries became a metropolitan province of Spain (see **Canary Islands Province**).

Captains-General: 1625–1626 Francisco de Andía Irarrazábal y Zárate; 1626–1629 [unknown]; 1629–1634 Juan de Rivera y Zambrana; 1634–1638 Iñigo de Brizuela y Urbina; 1638–1644 Luís de Córdoba y Arce; 1644–1650 Pedro de Guzmán; 1650–1659 Alfonso Dávila y Guzmán; 1659–1661 Sebastián de Corcuera y Gaviría; 1661–1665 Jerónimo de Quiñones; 1665–1666 Juan de Toledo; 1666–1671 Conde de Puertollano; 1671–1676 Juan Mogrobejo; 1676–1677 [unknown]; 1677–1681 Jerónimo de Velasco; 1681–1685 Conde de Guaro; 1685–1689 Francisco Barahona; 1689–1697 Marqués de Fuensagrada; 1697–1701 Conde del Palmar; 1701–1705 Miguel de Otazo; 1705–1709 Agustín Laurenzana; 1709–1713 Francisco Medina y Salazar; 1713–1718 Ventura de Landaeta y Horna; 1718–1719 José de Chaves y Osorio; 1719–1722 Juan de Mur Aguirre y Argaiz; 1722–1723 [unknown]; 1723–1735 Marqués de Valhermoso; 1735–1741 Francisco Emparan; 1741–1744 Andrés Pignately; 1744–1745 José de Lima; 1745–1746 Luís Salazar; 1746–1747 [unknown]; 1747–1764 Juan de Urbina; 1764–1764 Pedro Moreno y Perez de Oteyro; 1764–1768 Domingo Gómez; 1768–1775 Miguel de Heredia; 1775–1779 Marqués de los Tabalosos; 1779–1784 Marqués de la Cañada Ibáñez; 1784–1789 Marqués de Branciforte; 1789–1791 José de Avellaneda; 1791–1799 Antonio de Otero y Santallana; 1799–1803 José de Perlasca; 1803–1809 Marqués de Casa Cagigal; 1809–1810 Carlos Luján; 1810–1810 Duque del Parque; 1810–1811 Ramon Carvajal; 1811–1820 Pedro de la Buría; 1820–1821 [unknown].

206 Canary Islands Kingdom. 15 Dec. 1405–6 March 1480. *Location:* The Canary Islands. *Capital:* Acatife.

History: In 1404 and 1405 Juan de Bethencourt set about conquering the Fortunate Islands, as the Canaries were then called, and established a regal dynasty there on the orders of Henry III of Castile. In 1480 Gran Canária, the only island of the Canary Group really civilized by that year, became a Spanish colony (see **Gran Canária [i]**).

Kings: 15 Dec. 1405–1418 Maciot de Bethencourt; 1418–(?) Enrique de Guzman; (?)–(?) Guillen Peraza I; (?)–1444 Guillen Peraza II; 1444–1476 Diego de Herrera; 1476–6 March 1480 [unknown].

207 Canary Islands Protectorate. 1912–1927. *Location:* Canary Islands. *Capital:* Las Palmas.

History: Named "Canary" because of the large amount of big dogs on the islands in the ancient days (Latin: canis = dog). In 1912 **Canary Islands Province** became a protectorate of Spain, and in 1927 the islands were split up into two separate provinces — **Santa Cruz de Tenerife Province** and **Las Palmas de Gran Canária Province**.

Rulers: [unknown].

208 Canary Islands Province. 1821–1912. *Location:* Canary Islands. *Capital:* Las Palmas.

History: In 1821 the **Canary Islands Captaincy-General [ii]** came to an end, to be replaced by the Spanish Province of the Canary Islands, In 1912 it became **Canary Islands Protectorate**.

Rulers: [unknown].

209 Canary Islands (Self-Rule). 8 May 1983– . *Location:* 7 main islands and 6 islets off the coast of Morocco. The islands are Gran Canária, Tenerife, Lanzarote, Hierro, Fuerteventura, La Palma, and Gomera. Three of the islets are inhabited — Alegranza, Graciosa and Lobos. *Capital:* Las Palmas (founded 1478 and named for the palms in the area). *Other names:* Islas Canárias.

History: In 1983 the Canary Islands, a fundamental part of Spain, became autonomous. Until then the archipelago had been composed of two Spanish provinces, **Las Palmas de Gran Canária Province** and **Santa Cruz de Tenerife Province.** *Presidents of the Government:* 8 May 1983– Jerónimo Saavedra. *Presidents of the Parliament:* 8 May 1983– Pedro Guerra Cabrera.

Canem see **Kanem**

Cape Colony see main **South Africa** heading

210 Cape Mesurado Colony. 15 Dec. 1821–15 Aug. 1824. *Location:* around Monrovia, Liberia. *Capital:* Thompson Town. *Other names:* Christopolis (named by Jehudi Ashmun).
History: Named by Portuguese explorer Pedro de Sintra as Cape Montserado, this area of the Grain Coast was bought from the Dei chieftains in 1821 by Eli Ayres of the American Colonization Society, as the site of the first Liberian colony ("liber" meaning "free," and named by Robert Goodloe Harper, the same person who named Monrovia, and in turn who had a town—Harper—named for him). The American Colonization Society (ACS) was formed by a few white North American philanthropists and clergymen on January 1, 1817 with the plan to send a few blacks to Africa to found a state, to convert the continent to Christianity, to begin the expansion of American trade, and to rid the USA of the free negroes—or rather "those considered undesirables." Among the early settlers were Lott Carey (arrived 1821) and representatives of U.S. firms. An unpopular, hard-won country, 19,000 blacks were settled here from the U.S. between 1822 and 1867. Malaria and African hostiles killed many, and their motto was (and still is) "The Love of Liberty Brought Us Here." In 1824 the Colony expanded and became **Liberia Colony.**
Colonial Agents: 15 Dec. 1821–25 Apr. 1822 Dr. Eli Ayres; 25 Apr.

1822–4 June 1822 Frederick James (acting); 4 June 1822–8 Aug. 1822 Elijah Johnson (acting); 8 Aug. 1822–2 Apr. 1823 Jehudi Ashmun (acting); 2 Apr. 1823–14 Aug. 1823 Elijah Johnson (acting); 14 Aug. 1823–15 Aug. 1824 Jehudi Ashmun (acting).

211 Cape of Good Hope Colony. 6 Apr. 1652–16 Sept. 1795. *Location:* as **British Cape Colony,** minus territory acquired later. *Capital:* Cape Town (known simply as Kaapstad by about 1690, it was known as Cape Town by the British from 1773). *Other names:* Table Bay, Hottentot Hollandia.
History: Between 1487, when the Portuguese explorer Diaz discovered the Cabo da Boa Esperança (Cape of Good Hope) and 1652, there were several landings made by Europeans in the area. A few settlements were considered, but nothing came of them, until the Dutch East India Company decided to set up a colony at Cape Town to serve as a refreshment station en route to the East Indies. Gradually the Cape Colony area widened, taking in the local Bantu chiefdoms. The original inhabitants of the Cape were the San, or Bushmen, pushed out by the Khoikhoi, or Hottentots. It was these Hottentots whom the Dutch encountered when they landed in 1652. The Dutch East India Company ruled until the British seized the Cape in 1795 (see **British-Occupied Cape Colony [i]**).
Commanders: 7 Apr. 1652–6 May 1662 Jan Van Riebeeck; 6 May 1662–27 Sept. 1666 Zacharias Wagenaar; 27 Sept. 1666–18 June 1668 Cornelis Van Quaelbergen; 18 June 1668–25 March 1670 Jacob Borghorst; 25 March 1670–30 Nov. 1671 Pieter Hackius; 30 Nov. 1671–25 March 1672 Coenrad Van Breitenbach (Leader of the Council of Policy); 25 March 1672–2 Oct. 1672 Albert Van Breughel (acting); 2 Oct. 1672–14 March 1676 Isbrand Goske; 14 March 1676–29 June 1678 Johann Bax; 29 June 1678–12 Oct. 1679 Hendrik Crudop (acting); 12 Oct. 1679–1 June

1691 Symon Van Der Stel. *Governors:* 1 June 1691–11 Feb. 1699 Symon Van Der Stel; 11 Feb. 1699–3 June 1707 Willem Van Der Stel; 3 June 1707–1 Feb. 1708 Johan D'Ableing (acting); 1 Feb. 1708–27 Dec. 1711 Louis Van Assenburgh; 27 Dec. 1711–28 March 1714 Willem Helot (acting); 28 March 1714–8 Sept. 1724 Pasques de Chavonnes; 8 Sept. 1724–25 Feb. 1727 Jan de la Fontaine (acting); 25 Feb. 1727–23 Apr. 1729 Pieter Noodt; 23 Apr. 1729–8 March 1730 Jan de la Fontaine (acting); 8 March 1730–31 Aug. 1737 Jan de la Fontaine; 31 Aug. 1737–19 Sept. 1737 Adriaan Van Kervel; 20 Sept. 1737–14 Apr. 1739 Daniel Van Den Henghel (acting); 14 Apr. 1739–27 Feb. 1751 Hendrik Swellengrebel; 27 Feb. 1751–11 Aug. 1771 Ryk Tulbagh; 12 Aug. 1771–18 May 1774 Joachim Van Plettenberg (acting); 4 Sept. 1772–23 Jan. 1773 Pietre Van Oudtshoorn (died on voyage out); 18 May 1774–14 Feb. 1785 Joachim Van Plettenberg; 14 Feb. 1785–24 June 1791 Cornelis Van De Graaff; 24 June 1791–3 July 1792 Johan Rhenius (acting). *Commissioners-General:* 3 July 1792–2 Sept. 1793 Sebastian Nederburgh; 3 July 1792–2 Sept. 1793 Simon Frijkenius; 2 Sept. 1793–16 Sept. 1795 Abraham Sluysken.

212 Cape Verde. See these **names:**
Cape Verde Republic (1975–   )
Cape Verde Autonomous Republic (1974–1975)
Cape Verde Overseas Province (1951–1974)
Cape Verde Colony (1587–1951)
Ribeira Grande (1495–1587)
Cape Verde Islands (1462–1495)

213 Cape Verde Autonomous Republic. 19 Dec. 1974–5 July 1975. *Location:* as **Cape Verde Republic.** *Capital:* Praia. *Other names:* Cape Verde, Autonomous Republic of Cape Verde, Cabo Verde.
History: In 1974 the Portuguese government signed an agreement with the African Party for the Independence of Guinea-Bissau and The Cape Verde Islands, and the islands became an autonomous republic, effective December 31, 1974. In 1975 independence finally came, as **Cape Verde Republic.**
High Commissioners: 19 Dec. 1974–31 Dec. 1974 Antonio dos Santos; 31 Dec. 1974–5 July 1975 Almeida D'Eça. *Ruling Council:* 30 Dec. 1974–5 July 1975 Carlos Reis; 30 Dec. 1974–5 July 1975 Amaro da Luz; 30 Dec. 1974–5 July 1975 Manuel Faustino.

214 Cape Verde Colony. 1587–11 June 1951. *Location:* as **Cape Verde Republic.** *Capital:* Villa de Praia (from 1769); Cidade de Ribeira Grande (until 1769).
History: In 1587 Portugal was ruled by Spain. Madrid wished to centralize the different Cape Verde governments, or donatárias, and bring them under one governor. Hence the important captaincy-general of **Ribeira Grande** and the other islands of São Antão, São Vicente, São Tiago, São Nicolau, Maio, Bõa Vista, Sal, Fogo and Brava (all grouped together as **Cape Verde Dominion**) all became component parts of the new colony. In 1951 Cape Verde became an overseas province of Portugal (see **Cape Verde Overseas Province**).
Governors: 1587–1591 Duarte da Gama; 1591–1595 Brás de Melo; 1595–1596 Amador Raposo; 1596–1603 Francisco da Gama; 1603–1606 Fernão de Brito; 1606–1611 Francisco da Silva; 1611–1614 Francisco de Sequeira; 1614–1618 Nicolau de Castilho; 1618–1622 Francisco de Moura; 1622–1622 Francisco Rolim; 1622–1624 Manuel de Guerra (acting); 1624–1628 Francisco da Cunha; 1628– 1632 João Corte-Real; 1632–1636 Cristóvão de Cabral; 1636–1639 Jorge de Castilho; 1639–1640 Jerónimo de Cavalcanti e Albuquerque; 1640–1645 João da Cunha; 1645–1646 Lourenço Garro; 1646–1648 Jorge de Araújo; 1648–1648 Roque de Barros do Rego; 1648–1650 Council of Government; 1650–1650

Gonçalo de Gamboa Ayala; 1650–1651 Pedro Cardoso; 1651–1653 Jorge Castelo Branco; 1653–1658 Pedro Barreto; 1658–1663 Francisco de Figueroa; 1663–1667 Antonio Galvão; 1667–1671 Manuel da Costa Pessôa; 1671–1676 Manuel de Melo; 1676–1676 João Pássaro; 1676–1678 Council of Government; 1678–1683 Manuel da Costa Pessôa; 1683–1687 Inácio Barbosa; 1687–1688 Veríssimo da Costa; 1688–1690 Vitoriano da Costa; 1690–1691 Diogo Esquivel; 1691–1692 Council of Government; 1692–1696 Manuel da Camara; 1696–1696 António Mena; 1696–1698 Council of Government; 1698–1702 António Salgado; 1702–1707 Gonçalo de Lemos Mascarenhas; 1707–1711 Rodrigo da Fonseca; 1711–1715 José da Camara; 1715–1716 Council of Government; 1716–1720 Serafim de Sá; 1720–1725 António Vieira; 1725–1726 Council of Government; 1726–1728 Francisco de Nóbrega Vasconcelos; 1728–1733 Francisco Grans; 1733–1737 Bento Coelho; 1737–1738 José Barbosa; 1738–1741 ruled by a Chamber Senate; 1741–1752 João de Santa Maria; 1752–1752 António de Faria; 1752–1757 Luis António da Cunha d'Eça; 1757–1761 Manuel de Sousa e Meneses; 1761–1761 Marcelino de Ávila; 1761–1764 António Bezerra; 1764–1766 Bartolomeu de Sousa Tigre; 1766–1767 João Henriques; 1767–1768 Council of Government; 1768–1777 Joaquim Lobo; 1777– 1781 António de Sousa e Meneses; 1781–1782 Duarte de Almeida; 1782– 1783 Francisco de São Simão (acting); 1783–1785 Council of Government; 1785–1790 António de Faria e Maia; 1790–1795 Francisco Carneiro; 1795–1796 José d'Eça; 1796–1802 Marcelino Bastos; 1802–1803 Council of Government; 1803–1818 António de Lencastre; 1818–1822 António Pussich; 1822–1826 João da Mata Chapuzet; 1826–1830 Caetano de Vasconcelos; 1830–1831 Duarte Macedo; 1831–1833 José de Lencastre; 1833–1835 Manuel Martins; 1835–1836 Joaquim Marinho; 1836–1837 Domingos Arouca; 1837–1839 Joaquim Marinho; 1839–1842 João de Melo; 1842–1845 Francisco Paula; 1845–1847 José de Noronha; 1847–1848 Council of Government; 1848–1851 João de Melo; 1851–1854 Fortunato Barreiros; 1854–1858 António Arrobas; 1858–1860 Sebastião Meneses; 1860–1861 Januário de Almeida; 1861–1864 Carlos Franco; 1864–1869 José de Carvalho e Meneses; 1869–1876 Caetano de Almeida e Albuquerque; 1876–1878 Lopes de Macedo; 1878–1879 Vasco de Carvalho e Meneses; 1879–1881 António de Sampaio; 1881–1886 João de Vasconcelos; 1886–1889 João de Lacerda; 1889–1890 Augusto de Carvalho; 1890–1893 José de Melo; 1893–1894 Fernando de Magalhães e Meneses; 1894–1898 Alexandre Serpa Pinto; 1898–1900 João de Lacerda; 1900–1902 Arnaldo de Rebelo; 1902–1903 Francisco de Paula Cid; 1903–1904 António de Freitas; 1904–1907 Amáncio Cabral; 1907–1909 Bernardo de Mecedo; 1909–1910 Martinho Montenegro; 1910–1911 António Ortigão; 1911–1911 Artur de Campos; 1911–1915 Joaquim Biker; 1915–1918 Abel da Costa; 1918–1919 Teófilo Duarte; 1919–1921 Manuel da Maia Magalhães; 1921–1922 Filipe de Carvalho; 1922–1924 Council of Government; 1924–1926 Julio de Abreu; 1926–1927 João de Almeida; 1927–1931 António Guedes Vaz; 1931–1941 Amadeu de Figueiredo; 1941–1943 José Martins; 1943–1949 João de Figueiredo; 1949–11 June 1951 Carlos Roçadas.

215 Cape Verde Islands. 1462–1495. *Location:* about 365 miles off the coast of northwest Africa. *Capital:* none. *Other names:* Arquipélago de Cabo Verde.

History: The Portuguese have the first substantial claim to discovery of the islands, in 1460. The island of São Tiago was settled in 1462, and the town of Ribeira Grande (the oldest European town in the tropics) was built on Santo Antão soon after. In 1495 the islands became the Portuguese colony

of **Ribeira Grande.**
Rulers: unknown, if any.

216 Cape Verde Overseas Province.
11 June 1951–19 Dec. 1974. *Location:* as
Cape Verde Republic. *Capital:* Villa de
Praia.
History: **Cape Verde Colony** became
a Portuguese overseas territory in 1951,
and in 1974, self-governing (see **Cape
Verde Autonomous Republic**).
Governors: 11 June 1951–1953 Carlos
Roçadas; 1953–1957 Manuel Amaral;
1957–1958 António Correia (acting);
1958–1963 Silvinio Marques; 1963–Dec.
1970 Leão Monteiro; Jan. 1971–19 Dec.
1974 António dos Santos.

217 Cape Verde Republic. 5 July
1975– . *Location:* off the coast of
Senegal. *Capital:* Praia. *Other names:*
The Republic of Cape Verde, Repub-
lica de Cabo Verde.
History: In 1975 **Cape Verde Autonomous Republic,** a Portuguese territory, gained its independence, and
allied itself politically to **Guinea-Bissau.**
Presidents: 8 July 1975– Aristides
Pereira. *Prime Ministers:* 15 July
1975– Pedro Pires.

218 Carthage. ca. 550 B.C.–146 B.C.
Location: Tunisia. *Capital:* Carthage
(the name means "new town." Today it
is a suburb of Tunis). *Other names:*
Carthago, Karchedon, Kart-Hadasht.
History: Carthage was traditionally
founded by Phoenicians in 814 B.C.
(legend says by Dido, the Tyrian princess). The inhabitants were called Poeni
by the Romans. The state of Carthage
(not the city) dates from about 550 B.C.
The city and state fell in 146 B.C., to the
Romans, who created **Africa Vetus** out
of it.
Sufets (Judges): ca. 500 B.C. Mago;
ca. 400 B.C. Himilco; ca. 240 B.C.
Hamilcar; ca. 235 B.C. Hanno; ca. 220
B.C. Hasdrubal; ca. 210 B.C. Mago II;
ca. 196 B.C. Hannibal; ca. 149 B.C.
Hasdrubal II.

Cayor see **Kayor**

Cazembe see **Kazembe**

219 Central African Empire. 4 Dec.
1976–21 Sept. 1979. *Location:* as **Central African Republic.** *Capital:* Bangui.
Other names: Empire Centrafricaine.
History: In 1976 Jean-Bedel Bokassa, Marshal of the **Central African
Republic [i],** proclaimed his country an
empire, and he himself was crowned a
year later. In 1979 he was deposed in a
bloodless coup and the name of the
country reverted to the **Central African
Republic [ii].**
Emperors: 4 Dec. 1976–21 Sept. 1979
Bokassa I. *Prime Ministers:* 8 Dec.
1976–14 July 1978 Ange Patassé; 14 July
1978–21 Sept. 1979 Henri Maidou.

Central African Federation see **Federation of Rhodesia and Nyasaland**

220 Central African Republic. See
these **names:**
Central African Republic [ii]
(1979–)
Central African Empire (1976–1979)
Central African Republic [i] (1960–
1976)
Central African Republic (Auton-
omous) (1958–1960)
Ubangi-Shari Overseas Territory [ii]
(1946–1958)
Ubangi-Shari Overseas Territory [i]
(1937–1946)
Ubangi-Shari Region (1934–1937)
Ubangi-Shari Colony [ii] (1916–1934)
Ubangi-Shari Territory (1906–1916)
Ubangi-Shari Colony [i] (1894–1906)
Ubangi-Bomu Territory (1893–1894)

221 Central African Republic [i]. 13
Aug. 1960–4 Dec. 1976. *Location:*
north central Africa. *Capital:* Bangui.
Other names: République Centrafricaine, C.A.R.
History: In 1960 the **Central African
Republic (Autonomous)** became independent. A coup at the end of 1965
removed the ineffectual Dacko and
replaced him with the insane tyrant
Bokassa, who in 1976 made himself
emperor and changed the name of the

country to **Central African Empire.**
Presidents: 13 Aug. 1960–17 Nov.
1960 David Dacko (interim President);
17 Nov. 1960–31 Dec. 1965 David
Dacko; 1 Jan. 1966–22 Feb. 1972 Jean-
Bedel Bokassa; 22 Feb. 1972–7 Apr.
1976 Jean-Bedel Bokassa (President for
Life); 7 Apr. 1976–5 Sept. 1976 Jean-
Bedel Bokassa (Marshal of the Repub-
lic). *Prime Ministers:* 2 Jan. 1975–7
Apr. 1976 Elizabeth Domitienne; 5
Sept. 1976–4 Dec. 1976 Ange Patassé.
Note: In times of no Prime Minister,
the President filled that office.

222 Central African Republic [ii]. 21
Sept. 1979–   . *Location:* north central
Africa. *Capital:* Bangui (named for the
Ubangi [Oubangui] River), on which it
lies. *Other names:* République Cen-
trafricaine, C.A.R.
History: In 1979 the **Central African
Empire** became a republic again, after
the excesses of Bokassa's regime.
Presidents: 21 Sept. 1979–1 Sept. 1981
David Dacko; 1 Sept. 1981–21 Sept.
1985 André Kolingba (Chairman of the
Committee of National Recovery); 21
Sept. 1985– André Kolingba. *Prime
Ministers:* 26 Sept. 1979–22 Aug. 1980
Bernard Ayandho; 12 Nov. 1980–4
Apr. 1981 Jean-Pierre Lebouder; 4
Apr. 1981–1 Sept. 1981 Simon Bozanga.
Note: In times of no Prime Minister,
the President filled that office.

**223 Central African Republic
(Autonomous).** 1 Dec. 1958–13 Aug.
1960. *Location:* as **Central African
Republic.** *Capital:* Bangui. *Other
names:* Central African Republic,
République Centrafricaine, C.A.R.,
Ubangi-Shari, Oubangui-Chari.
History: In 1958 **Ubangi-Shari Overseas Territory [ii]** became an autonomous republic within the French Community. In 1960 it achieved full independence as the **Central African Republic [i].**
High Commissioners: 1 Dec. 1958–13
Aug. 1960 Paul Bordier. *Prime Ministers:* 8 Dec. 1958–29 March 1959 Bar-

thélémy Boganda; 30 March 1959–5
May 1959 Abel Goumba (acting); 5
May 1959–13 Aug. 1960 David Dacko.

224 Ceuta Comandáncia. 27 Nov.
1912–7 Apr. 1956. *Location:* northern
Morocco. *Capital:* Ceuta. *Other
names:* Ceuta.
History: In 1912 **Ceuta District** became a comandáncia of **Spanish
Morocco,** and in 1918 it and **Melilla
Comandáncia** enlarged slightly as the
third comandáncia, Larache, became
extinct. In 1956 Ceuta became a presidio (or plaza), a part of Metropolitan
Spain. The Mayor of Ceuta represents
the exclave in the Spanish cortes.
Rulers: ruled by the Governor-General of Spanish Morocco through a
commander in Ceuta.

225 Ceuta District. 1847–27 Nov.
1912. *Location:* Ceuta. *Capital:* Ceuta.
Other names: Ceuta.
History: In 1847, on the establish-
ment of the **Spanish Captaincy-Gen-
eral of North Africa, Ceuta (Spanish)**
became a district of the Captaincy-
General. In 1912, with the establish-
ment of **Spanish Morocco,** it became
Ceuta Comandáncia (cf **Melilla**).
Governors: see Captains-General of
**Spanish Captaincy-General of North
Africa.**

226 Ceuta (Portuguese). 1415–1640.
Location: Ceuta, Morocco. *Capital:*
Ceuta. *Other names:* Ceuta.
History: In 1415 Portugal captured
Ceuta from the Merinids (see **Merinid
Kingdom**). This was Europe's first
modern colony. From 1580 to 1640,
although Spain ruled Portugal, Por-
tugal maintained her overseas posses-
sions. In 1640, Ceuta went to Spain (see
Ceuta [Spanish]).
Captains-General: 1415–1430 Pedro,
Conde de Viana; 1430–1434 Duarte,
Conde de Viana; 1434–1437 Pedro,
Conde de Viana; 1437–1438 Duarte,
Conde de Viana; 1438–1445 Fernão,
Conde de Vila Real; 1445–1447 An-

tónio Pacheco; 1447–1450 Duque de Bragança; 1450–1460 Conde de Odemira; 1460–1461 [unknown]; 1461–1464 Pedro, Conde de Vila Real; 1464–1479 João Rodrigues de Vasconcelos Ribeiro; 1479–1481 Rui Mendes de Vasconcelos Ribeiro; 1481–1487 João de Noronha; 1487–1491 Conde de Linhares; 1491–1509 Fernão, Conde de Alcoutim; 1509–1512 Pedro Alardo; 1512–1517 Pedro, Conde de Alcoutim; 1517–1518 [unknown]; 1518–1519 Conde de Portalegre; 1519–1521 Gomes da Silva de Vasconcelos; 1521–1522 [unknown]; 1522–1524 João de Noronha; 1524–1525 Pedro, Conde de Alcoutim; 1525–1529 Gomes da Silva de Vasconcelos; 1529–1539 Nunho de Noronha; 1539–1540 [unknown]; 1540–1549 Affonso de Noronha; 1549–1549 Antão de Noronha; 1549–1550 Martim da Silva; 1550–1553 Pedro de Meneses; 1553–1553 Pedro da Cunha; 1553–1553 João Rodrigues Pereira; 1553–1555 Martim da Silva; 1555–1557 Jorge Vieira; 1557–1562 Fernão de Meneses; 1562–1563 Conde de Vila Real; 1563–1564 Fernão de Meneses; 1564–1565 Pedro da Cunha; 1565–1566 [unknown]; 1566–1567 Francisco Pereira; 1567–1574 Duque de Vila Real; 1574–1577 Diogo Lopes de França; 1577–1578 Duque de Vila Real; 1578–1580 Dionísio Pereira; 1580–1586 Jorge Pessanha; 1586–1591 Gil da Costa; 1591–1592 Francisco de Andrade; 1592–1594 Duque de Caminha; 1594–1597 Mendo de Ledesma; 1597–1601 Duque de Caminha; 1601–1602 [unknown]; 1602–1605 Affonso de Noronha; 1605–1616 Duque de Caminha; 1616–1622 Conde de Vila Real; 1622–1623 [unknown]; 1623–1623 Duque de Caminha; 1623–1624 António Albuquerque; 1624–1625 Conde da Tôrre; 1625–1625 Gonçalo Alcoforado; 1625–1626 Duque de Caminha; 1626–1627 [unknown]; 1627–1627 Dinís de Mascarenhas de Lencastre; 1627–1634 Jorge de Mendonça Pessanha; 1634–1636 Brás Teles de Meneses; 1636–1637 [unknown]; 1637–1637 Fernão Teles de Meneses; 1637–1641 Fran-cisco de Almeida.

227 Ceuta (Spanish). 1640–1847. *Location:* Ceuta, Morocco. *Capital:* Ceuta. *Other names:* Ceuta.

History: In 1640 **Ceuta (Portuguese)** became Ceuta (Spanish). In 1847, with the establishment of the **Spanish Captaincy-General of North Africa**, Ceuta, like **Melilla (Spanish)** became a district of that body (see **Ceuta District**).

Governors: 1640–1641 no appointed rule; 1641–1644 Marqués de Miranda de Auta; 1644–1645 [unknown]; 1645–1646 Marqués de Malagón; 1646–1653 Marqués de Torcifal; 1653–1661 Marqués de Tenorio; 1661–1662 [unknown]; 1662–1665 Marqués de Castelo Mendo; 1665–1672 Marqués de Sentar; 1672–1677 Conde de Torres Vedras; 1677–1677 Antonio Chacón y Ponce de León; 1677–1678 Diego de Portugal; 1678–1679 Antonio Chacón y Ponce de León; 1679–1681 Conde de Puñonrostro; 1681–1689 Francisco de Velasco y Tovar; 1689–1692 Francisco Varona; 1692–1695 Marqués de Valparaíso; 1695–1698 Marqués de Valdecañas; 1698–1702 Marqués de Villadarias; 1702–1704 Marqués de Gironella; 1704–1705 [unknown]; 1705–1709 Juan de Araña; 1709–1715 Gonzalo Chacón y Arellano Sandoval y Rojas; 1715–1719 Francisco Fernández y Rivadeo; 1719–1719 Francisco Pérez Mancheño; 1719–1720 Príncipe de Campo Flórido; 1720–1720 Juan de Araña; 1720–1725 Francisco Fernández y Rivadeo; 1725–1731 Comte de Charny; 1731–1738 Marqués de Santa Cruz de Marcenado; 1738–1739 Antonio Manso Maldonaldo; 1739–1745 Marqués de Campofuerte; 1745–1745 Juan Antonio Tineo y Fuertes; 1745–1746 Juan de Palafox y Centurión; 1746–1751 José Horcasitas y Oleaga; 1751–1751 Marqués de la Matilla; 1751–1755 Marqués de Croix; 1755–1760 Miguel Carreño; 1760–1763 Marqués de Warmarch; 1763–1776 Diego Osorio; 1776–1783 Marqués de Casa Tremañes; 1783–1784 Domingo de Salcedo; 1784–1791 Miguel Porcel y

Manrique de Araña Menchaca y Zaldívar; 1791–1792 José de Sotomayor; 1792–1794 José de Urrutia y las Casas; 1794–1795 Conde de Santa Clara; 1795–1795 Diego de la Peña; 1795–1798 José Vassallo; 1798–1801 José Bautisto de Castro; 1801–1805 Antonio Terrero; 1805–1807 Francisco de Horta; 1807–1808 Ramón de Carvajal; 1808–1809 Carlos Luján; 1809–1810 Carlos Gand; 1810–1813 José María Alós; 1813–1813 José María Lastres; 1813–1813 Pedro Grimarest; 1813–1814 Fernando Gómez de Buitrón; 1814–1815 Pedro Grimarest; 1815–1816 Luis Antonio Flores; 1816–1818 Juan de Pontons y Mujica; 1818–1820 José de Miranda; 1820–1820 Vincente Rorique; 1820–1822 Fernando Gómez de Buitrón; 1822–1823 Álvaro Chacón; 1823–1823 Manuel Fernández; 1823–1823 Antonio Quiroga; 1823–1824 Juan María Muñoz; 1824–1826 José de Miranda; 1826–1826 Joaquín Bureau; 1826–1826 Julio O'Neill; 1826–1830 Juan María Muñoz; 1830–1833 Carlos Ullmann; 1833–1835 Mateo Ramírez; 1835–1835 Carlos Espinosa; 1835–1836 Joaquín Gómez Ansa; 1836–1837 Francisco Sanjuanena; 1837–1837 Bernardo Tacón; 1837–1844 José María Rodríguez Vera; 1844–1847 Antonio Ordóñez.

228 Chad. See these **names:**
Chad Republic (1960–   )
Chad Autonomous Republic (1958–1960)
Chad Overseas Territory [ii] (1946–1958)
Chad Overseas Territory [i] (1937–1946)
Chad Region (1934–1937)
Chad Colony (1920–1934)
Chad (1916–1920)
Chad Territory (1906–1916)
Chad Protectorate (1902–1906)
Chad Military Territory and Protectorate (1900–1902)
Baguirmi (1513–1899)
Bornu Empire [ii] (1824–1902)
Bornu Empire [i] (ca. 1400–1808)

Kanem-Bornu (ca. 1256–ca. 1400)
Kanem (784–ca. 1260)
Wadai (ca. 1500–1909)
Zaghawa Kingdom ([?]–ca. 1350)

229 Chad. 12 Apr. 1916–17 March 1920. *Location:* southern Chad, i.e. the southern portion of what is today Chad. *Capital:* Fort Lamy. *Other names:* Tchad.
History: In 1916, with the break-up of the **Ubangi-Shari-Chad Colony, Chad Territory** became simply **Chad** while waiting to be granted colonial status of its own, which it achieved in 1920 (see **Chad Colony**). In that interim it was ruled by administrators who in turn were subject to Bangui (see **Ubangi-Shari Colony [ii]**).
Military Commandants: 12 Apr. 1916–1918 Clément Martelly; 1918–17 March 1920 Albert Du Carré.

230 Chad Autonomous Republic. 28 Nov. 1958–11 Aug. 1960. *Location:* as **Chad Republic.** *Capital:* Fort Lamy (founded in 1900 and named for Major Lamy of the French Army, who was killed nearby). *Other names:* Autonomous Republic of Chad, République du Tchad, Chad Republic, Republic of Chad, Chad, Tchad.
History: In 1958 **Chad Overseas Territory [ii]** became self-governing within the French Community. In 1960 full independence came (see **Chad Republic**).
Presidents of Government Council: 28 Nov. 1958–16 Dec. 1958 Daniel Doustin. *High Commissioners:* 16 Dec. 1958–11 Feb. 1959 Daniel Doustin; 11 Feb. 1959–12 March 1959 M. Sahoulba (acting); 12 March 1959–23 March 1959 Ahmand Koulamallah. *Prime Ministers:* 24 March 1959–11 Aug. 1960 François Tombalbaye.

231 Chad Colony. 17 March 1920–30 June 1934. *Location:* Chad. *Capital:* Fort Lamy. *Other names:* Tchad.
History: In 1920 **Chad** became a colony. On February 18, 1930 Tibesti became part of Chad, and the rough outlines of present-day **Chad Republic**

were born. In 1934 Chad became a region of **French Equatorial Africa Colony,** and became known as **Chad Region.**
Military Commanders: 17 March 1920–10 Aug. 1920 Albert Du Carré.
Lieutenant-Governors: 10 Aug. 1920–30 Jan. 1923 Fernand Lavit; 30 Jan. 1923–1925 Dieudonné Reste; 1925–9 Apr. 1925 Antoine Touzet; 9 Apr. 1925–25 Jan. 1926 Dieudonné Reste; 25 Jan. 1926–13 Jan. 1928 Jules de Coppet (acting); 13 Jan. 1928–21 Apr. 1929 Adolphe Deitte; 21 Apr. 1929–22 Nov. 1929 Émile Buhot-Launay; 22 Nov. 1929–14 May 1932 Jules de Coppet; 14 May 1932–26 Jan. 1933 Georges Prouteaux (acting); 26 Jan. 1933–30 June 1934 Richard Brunot.

232 Chad Military Territory and Protectorate. 5 Sept. 1900–5 July 1902. *Location:* as **Chad Protectorate.** *Capital:* Fort Lamy (founded Apr. 13, 1900). *Other names:* Tchad.
History: In 1900 the area of Chad was formed into an administration. On September 5, 1900 Borku was declared French; this formed the nucleus of what became Chad. In 1902 it became **Chad Protectorate.** (See also **Baguirmi** and **Bornu Empire [ii]).**
Military Commandants: 5 Sept. 1900–1901 Georges Destenave; 1901–5 July 1902 Col. Julien.

233 Chad Overseas Territory [i]. 31 Dec. 1937–13 Oct. 1946. *Location:* as **Chad Republic.** *Capital:* Fort Lamy. *Other names:* Chad, Tchad.
History: In 1937 **Chad Region** became an overseas territory of France, but still answerable to the Governor-General of the **French Equatorial Africa Colony.** In 1946 Chad became an overseas territory of the Fourth Republic in France (see **Chad Overseas Territory [ii]).**
Chefs du Territoire: 31 Dec. 1937–28 March 1938 Max De Masson de Saint Félix; 28 March 1938–19 Nov. 1938 Émile Buhot-Launay (acting); 19 Nov.

1938–14 Dec. 1938 Félix Éboué; 14 Dec. 1938–1939 Charles Dagain (acting); 1939–12 Nov. 1940 Félix Éboué; 12 Nov. 1940–30 July 1941 Pierre Lapie; 30 July 1941–5 Nov. 1943 André Latrille; 5 Nov. 1943–10 Aug. 1945 Jacques Rogué; 10 Aug. 1945–13 Oct. 1946 Léon Auguste Éven (acting).

234 Chad Overseas Territory [ii]. 13 Oct. 1946–28 Nov. 1958. *Location:* Chad. *Capital:* Fort Lamy. *Other names:* Tchad, Chad.
History: In 1946 **Chad Overseas Territory [i],** then part of **French Equatorial Africa Colony,** became an overseas territory of the Fourth Republic of France. It maintained its status within the AEF Colony, however, until 1958, when it became an autonomous republic within the French Community (see **Chad Autonomous Republic).**
Governors: 13 Oct. 1946–24 Nov. 1948 Jacques Rogué; 24 Nov. 1948–1949 Paul de Layec; 1949–1950 Henri de Mauduit; 1950–27 Jan. 1951 M. Casamata (acting); 27 Jan. 1951–29 Oct. 1951 Charles Hanin (acting); 29 Oct. 1951–3 Nov. 1956 Ignace Colombani; 3 Nov. 1956–28 Nov. 1958 Jean Troadec.
Presidents of Govt. Council: 13 May 1957–28 Nov. 1958 Daniel Doustin.

235 Chad Protectorate. 5 July 1902–11 Feb. 1906. *Location:* southern Chad (today's Chad, that is). *Capital:* Fort Lamy. *Other names:* Tchad.
History: In 1902 **Chad Military Territory and Protectorate** became the French Protectorate of Chad. In 1906 it became **Chad Territory,** part of **Ubangi-Shari-Chad Colony.**
Military Commandants: 5 July 1902–1904 Étienne Largeau; 1904–11 Feb. 1906 Henri Gouraud.

236 Chad Region. 30 June 1934–31 Dec. 1937. *Location:* as **Chad Republic.** *Capital:* Fort Lamy. *Other names:* Region of Chad, Région du Tchad, Tchad, Chad.
History: In 1934 **Chad Colony** came to an end, and it became a region of

French Equatorial Africa Colony. In 1937 it became an overseas territory, but still part of AEF Colony (see **Chad Overseas Territory [i]**).
Governors-Delegate: 30 June 1934–17 Aug. 1934 Richard Brunot; 17 Aug. 1934–21 May 1935 Adolphe Deitte; 21 May 1935–30 May 1935 Richard Brunot; 30 May 1935–23 Oct. 1936 Pierre Bonnefont (acting); 23 Oct. 1936–24 Oct. 1936 Émile Buhot-Launay (acting); 24 Oct. 1936–31 Dec. 1937 Max de Masson de Saint-Félix.

237 Chad Republic. 11 Aug. 1960– .
Location: central north Africa. *Capital:* N'Djamena (until Sept. 6, 1973 called Fort Lamy). *Other names:* Chad, Tchad, République du Tchad, Republic of Chad.
History: In 1960 **Chad Autonomous Republic** became independent. The French continued to administer B.E.T. (Borkou-Ennedi-Tibesti) in the north until January 23, 1965 when they pulled out and the prefecture was incorporated into the Republic of Chad.
Heads of State: 12 Aug. 1960–23 Apr. 1962 François Tombalbaye (or Ngarta Tombalbaye). *Presidents:* 23 Apr. 1962–13 Apr. 1975 François Tombalbaye (or Ngarta Tombalbaye); 13 Apr. 1975–15 Apr. 1975 General Odingar (acting); 15 Apr. 1975–23 March 1979 Félix Malloum (President of the Supreme Military Council); 23 March 1979–29 Apr. 1979 Goukouni Oueddi (Chairman of Provisional Government); 29 Apr. 1979–22 Aug. 1979 Lol Muhammad Shawa (Chairman of Provisional Government); 22 Aug. 1979–7 June 1982 Goukouni Oueddi (President of Provisional State Council); 7 June 1982–19 June 1982 Hissen Habré (Leader of Revolutionary Council). *Heads of State:* 19 June 1982–21 Oct. 1982 Hissen Habré. *Presidents:* 21 Oct. 1982– Hissen Habré. *Prime Ministers:* 11 Aug. 1960–12 Aug. 1960 François Tombalbaye (or Ngarta Tombalbaye); 29 Aug. 1978–23 March 1979 Hissen Habré; 19 May 1982–7 June 1982

Djidingar Done Ngardoum (acting). *Note:* in times of no Prime Minister, the President or Head of State held that office.

238 Chad Territory. 11 Feb. 1906–12 Apr. 1916. *Location:* the southern portion of present-day **Chad Republic.** *Capital:* Fort Lamy. *Other names:* Chad.
History: In 1906 **Chad Protectorate** became a territory within **Ubangi-Shari-Chad Colony.** It was administered by military commandants responsible to Bangui (the capital of the greater colony) (for more details see **Ubangi-Shari-Chad Colony**). On June 3, 1909 **Wadai** came into the Chad fold, and in 1916, on the breakup of the Ubangi-Shari-Chad Colony, the Territory of Chad became simply **Chad,** while waiting for colonial status.
Military Commandants: 11 Feb. 1906–1908 Étienne Largeau; 1908–1909 Constant Millot; 1909–9 Nov. 1910 Alexandre Moll; 9 Nov. 1910–1911 Joseph Maillard; 1911–1912 Étienne Largeau; 1912–1912 James-Édouard Hirtzman; 1912–1913 Gabriel Briand; 1913–1915 Étienne Largeau; 1915–12 Apr. 1916 Gabriel Briand.

Changamire see **Rozwi**

Christopolis see **Cape Mesurado Colony**

239 Circassian Mameluke Empire. 26 Nov. 1382–22 Jan. 1517. *Location:* as **Bahrite Mameluke Empire.** *Capital:* Cairo. *Other names:* Mameluke Empire, Egypt.
History: In 1382 the Circassian Mamelukes founded a new dynasty in the old **Bahrite Mameluke Empire,** and in later years this new empire fell more and more under the power of the emirs until in 1517 it was conquered by Turkey (see **Ottoman Egypt [i]**).
Sultans: 26 Nov. 1382–1 June 1389 Barquq; 1 June 1389–1 Feb. 1390 es-Salih Haggee (temporary Bahrite reign); 1 Feb. 1390–20 June 1399

Barquq; 20 June 1399–20 Sept. 1405
Faraq; 20 Sept. 1405–20 Nov. 1405 Ab-
dul Aziz; 20 Nov. 1405–28 May 1412
Faraq; 28 May 1412–6 Nov. 1412 al-Adil
al-Musta'in; 6 Nov. 1412–13 Jan. 1421
Sheikh al-Mu'aiyad; 13 Jan. 1421–29
Aug. 1421 al-Muzaffar Ahmad; 29 Aug.
1421–30 Nov. 1421 ed-Dehir Tatar; 30
Nov. 1421–1 Apr. 1422 es-Salih Muhammad; 1 Apr. 1422–7 June 1438 el-
Ashraf Barsabey; 7 June 1438–9 Sept.
1438 el-Aziz Yusuf; 9 Sept. 1438–1 Feb.
1453 Abu Sa'id Jaqmaq; 1 Feb. 1453–19
March 1453 Abu s-Sadat Othman; 19
March 1453–26 Feb. 1461 Eynal; 26
Feb. 1461–28 June 1461 Ahmad; 28
June 1461–9 Oct. 1467 Khoshkhakham;
9 Oct. 1467–3 Dec. 1467 Bilbay; 3 Dec.
1467–31 Jan. 1468 Temerbeg; 31 Jan.
1468–7 Aug. 1496 Qait Bey; 7 Aug.
1496–31 Oct. 1498 Muhammad; 21 Nov.
1498–28 June 1500 Khansoo; 30 June
1500–25 Jan. 1501 Janbalat; 27 Jan.
1501–20 Apr. 1501 Tooman Bey 1; 22
Apr. 1501–15 Oct. 1516 el-Ghuri; 17
Oct. 1516–22 Jan. 1517 Tooman Bey I.

240 Cirenaica Colony. 17 May 1919–
24 Jan. 1929. *Location:* eastern Libya.
Capital: Benghazi. *Other names:* Cyrenaica Colony, Barqah, Barca.
History: In 1919 the Italians made
their **Cirenaica Protectorate** into a colony. In 1929 they reunited it and
Tripolitania Colony into one possession, **Libya.**
Governors: 17 May 1919–5 Aug. 1919
Vincenzo Garioni; 5 Aug. 1919–23
Nov. 1921 Nobile Giacomo de Martino;
23 Nov. 1921–1 Oct. 1922 Luigi Pintor;
1 Oct. 1922–1 Dec. 1922 Eduardo Bac-
cari; 1 Dec. 1922–7 Jan. 1923 Oreste de
Gasperi; 7 Jan. 1923–24 May 1924 Luigi
Bongiovanni; 24 May 1924–22 Nov.
1926 Ernesto Mombelli; 2 Dec. 1926–18
Dec. 1928 Attilio Teruzzi; 21 Jan.
1929–24 Jan. 1929 Domenico Siciliani.

241 Cirenaica Protectorate. 15 Oct.
1912–17 May 1919. *Location:* eastern
Libya. *Capital:* Benghazi. *Other
names:* Cyrenaica Protectorate ("Cire-

naica" is the Italian spelling).
History: By 1912 the Italians had
conquered the three areas of Libya.
Tripoli Ottoman Province was the first
to go, in 1911, followed by **Fezzan
Pashalik,** and **Cyrenaica Ottoman
Province,** both in 1912. The Italians re-
divided the country into two protector-
ates – Cirenaica and Tripolitania (see
Tripolitania Protectorate). In 1919
both of these became colonies (see
Cirenaica Colony and **Tripolitania
Colony**).
Governors: 15 Oct. 1912–Oct. 1913
Ottavio Briccolo; Oct. 1913–5 Aug.
1918 Giovan-Battista Ameglio; 5 Aug.
1918–17 May 1919 Vincenzo Garioni.

242 Ciskei. 4 Dec. 1981– . *Loca-
tion:* eastern Cape Province, **South
Africa.** *Capital:* Bisho. *Other names:*
Republic of Ciskei, Iriphabliki Yecis-
kei.
History: On August 1, 1972 the Bantustan (or native homeland) of Ciskei
won self-government, with J.T.
Mabandla as Chief Minister. On May
21, 1973 Mabandla was succeeded by
Lennox Sebe, who has continued to
rule ever since. On September 1, 1976
J.J. Engelbrecht was appointed
Commissioner-General from South
Africa, and in 1981 the country (a
homeland of the Xhosa peoples)
became the fourth Bantustan to
achieve independence, and the first to
opt for independence using the referendum system. Like **Transkei, Bophuthatswana** and **Venda** it is not recognized internationally.
Presidents: 4 Dec. 1981– Lennox
Sebe. *Note:* Sebe is also Prime Minister.

243 Communist Ethiopia. 10 Sept.
1984–10 Sept. 1987. *Location:* northeastern Africa. *Capital:* Addis Ababa
(the name means "new flower," and was
founded in 1887, and named by the
Empress Taitu, wife of Menelik II).
Other names: Ethiopia (the ancient
name for "blacks").
History: In 1984 Ethiopia, until then

a socialist state (see **Ethiopian Military State**) became officially a Communist country when it established the Workers' Party of Ethiopia as the only legal political party. Its problems are vast and seemingly unsolvable: famine, poverty, illiteracy and the threat from **Somalia Democratic Republic** and Eritrea (see **Eritrean Autonomous State**). In 1987, the government handed over power to the people (see **Ethiopia People's Democratic Republic**).

Secretaries-General: 10 Sept. 1984–10 Sept. 1987 Mangistu Haile Mariam.

244 Comoros. See these **names:**
Comoros Republic (1975–)
Mayotte Department (1976–)
Comoros Autonomous State (1961–1975)
Comoros Overseas Territory (1946–1961)
Comoros Dependent Colony (1914–1946)
Comoros Dependent Territory (1908–1914)
Comoros Protectorate (1887–1908)
Mayotte Protectorate (1841–1887)
Mayotte (ca. 1515–1841)
Anjouan (ca. 1500–1866)
Mohéli ([?]–1886)
Gran Comoro (ca. 1515–1893)
Andruna (ca. 1550–1852)

245 Comoros Autonomous State. 22 Dec. 1961–6 July 1975. *Location:* the Comoros Islands, plus Mayotte. *Capital:* Moroni (from 1962); Dzaoudzi (1961–62).

History: In 1961 **Comoros Overseas Territory** became an autonomous state. In 1968 it won the right to form parties and hold elections, and in 1975 it gained independence from France as the **Comoros Republic.**

Administrators-Superior: 22 Dec. 1961–27 Feb. 1962 Louis Saget. *High Commissioners:* 27 Feb. 1962–22 May 1962 Louis Saget; 22 May 1962–15 Feb. 1963 Yves de Daruvar; 15 Feb. 1963–26 July 1966 Henri Bernard; 26 July 1966–1969 Antoine Columbani; 1969–6

July 1975 Jacques Mouradian. *Prime Ministers:* 22 Dec. 1961–16 March 1970 Sa'id Muhammad Sheikh; 16 March 1970–16 July 1972 Sa'id Ibrahim ibn Ali; 16 July 1972–Oct. 1972 Sa'id Muhammad Gafar al-Angadi; 26 Dec. 1972–6 July 1975 Ahmad Abdallah.

246 Comoros Dependent Colony. 23 Feb. 1914–13 Oct. 1946. *Location:* as **Comoros Dependent Territory.** *Capital:* Dzaoudzi (local headquarters); Tananarive (Madagascar). *Other names:* Province de Mayotte et Dependences, Mayotte Dependent Colony.

History: In 1914 **Comoros Dependent Territory** was annexed to Madagascar and became its province. In 1946 it became an overseas territory of the Fourth Republic of France (see **Comoros Overseas Territory**).

Rulers: see **Madagascar Colony** and **Madagascar British Military Territory** for the rulers of the Comoros during this period.

247 Comoros Dependent Territory. 9 Apr. 1908–23 Feb. 1914. *Location:* as **Comoros Republic,** but with the island of Mayotte included too. *Capital:* Dzaoudzi.

History: In 1908 the **Comoros Protectorate** became a dependent territory (dependent on Madagascar). In 1914 it became **Comoros Dependent Colony** (still dependent on Madagascar).

Administrators: 9 Apr. 1908–8 Sept. 1908 Fernand Foureau; 8 Sept. 1908–1 May 1911 Charles Vergnes. *Governors:* 1 May 1911–28 Sept. 1911 Frédéric Estèbe; 28 Sept. 1911–21 Feb. 1913 Gabriel Garnier-Mouton; 21 Feb. 1913–23 Feb. 1914 Honoré Catron.

248 Comoros Overseas Territory. 13 Oct. 1946–22 Dec. 1961. *Location:* as **Comoros Dependent Territory.** *Capital:* Dzaoudzi.

History: In 1946 **Comoros Dependent Colony** became an overseas territory of France, once again an autonomous unit. In 1958 it voted to remain part of France, and in 1961 it became

Comoros Autonomous State.
Administrators-Superior: 13 Oct.
1946–31 Dec. 1948 Eugène Alaniou; 31
Dec. 1948–Dec. 1950 Roger Remy (acting); Dec. 1950–21 Apr. 1956 Pierre
Coudert; 21 Apr. 1956–11 Feb. 1958
Georges Arnaud (acting); 11 Feb. 1958–
30 June 1959 Georges Arnaud; 30 June
1959–14 Dec. 1960 Gabriel Savignac
(acting); 14 Dec. 1960–22 Dec. 1961
Louis Saget.

249 Comoros Protectorate. 5 Sept.
1887–9 Apr. 1908. *Location:* The Comoros Islands (the name comes from the
Arabic "kamar" meaning "moon").
Capital: Dzaoudzi.
History: In 1887 **Mayotte Protectorate** became the French Protectorate
of the Comoros. In 1893 **Moroni** became part of it also, and so all the in-
gredients were now in the Comoros
cake. In 1908 the islands became a dependent territory of Madagascar (see
Comoros Dependent Territory).
Administrators: 5 Sept. 1887–4 May
1888 Paul Celeron de Blainville; 4 May
1888–1893 Clovis Papinaud; 1893–30
March 1896 Étienne Lacascade; 30
March 1896–5 Aug. 1897 Gentien Pere-
ton; 5 Aug. 1897–7 March 1899 Louis
Micon; 7 March 1899–18 Sept. 1900
Clovis Papinaud. *Governors:* 18 Sept.
1900–15 Oct. 1902 Pierre Pascal; 15 Oct.
1902–28 Feb. 1905 Albert Martineau;
28 Feb. 1905–3 March 1906 Jean Joliet;
3 March 1906–9 Apr. 1908 Fernand
Foureau.

250 Comoros Republic. 6 July
1975– . *Location:* three principal
islands are Grande Comore (Ngazidja),
Anjouan (Ndzouani) and Mohéli
(Moili). **Mayotte Department,** although
a main constituent part of the geo-
graphic Comoros Islands, and politically part of the Comoros for 6 months
(1975–76), is now an overseas department of France, and treated separately
in this work. *Capital:* Moroni (on the
island of Ngazidja). *Other names:* Republic of the Comoros, République des

Comores, Les Comores, The Comoros, Comoro Archipelago, Federal
Islamic Republic of The Comoros.
History: In 1975 **Comoros Autonomous State** became independent as a
republic, having declared a UDI (Unilateral Declaration of Independence) to
that effect. In 1976 Mayotte (the fourth
island) voted to remain a territorial collectivity of France (see **Mayotte Department**). In 1983 France assumed sole
responsibility for the defense of the
Comoros.
Presidents: 7 July 1975–3 Aug. 1975
Ahmad Abdallah; 3 Aug. 1975–5 Aug.
1975 Ali Soilih (Provisional Head of
State); 5 Aug. 1975–3 Jan. 1976 Prince
Sa'id Muhammad Jaffar (President of
National Executive Council); 3 Jan.
1976–13 May 1978 Ali Soilih; 13 May
1978–21 May 1978 Sa'id Attourmani; 21
May 1978–3 Oct. 1978 Ahmad Abdallah (co-president); 21 May 1978–3
Oct. 1978 Muhammad Ahmad (co-
president); 22 Oct. 1978– Ahmad Ab-
dallah. *Prime Ministers:* 6 Jan. 1976–22
Dec. 1978 Abdullahi Muhammad; 22
Dec. 1978–25 Jan. 1982 Salim Ben Ali;
8 Feb. 1982–31 Dec. 1984 Ali Mroudjae.
Note: in times of no Prime Minister,
the President held that office.

251 Congo. See these **names:**
Congo People's Republic (1970–)
Congo (Brazzaville) (1960–1970)
Congo Autonomous Republic (1958–
1960)
Moyen-Congo Overseas Territory
[ii] (1946–1958)
Moyen-Congo Overseas Territory [i]
(1937–1946)
Moyen-Congo Region (1934–1937)
Moyen-Congo Colony [ii] (1903–
1934)
Moyen-Congo District (1902–1903)
Moyen-Congo Territory (1888–1902)
Moyen-Congo Colony [i] (1886–
1888)
Moyen-Congo (1886–1886)
Moyen-Congo Protectorate (1883–
1886)
Portuguese Congo (1884–1884)

Congo see also **Congo** and main **Zaire** heading

252 Congo Autonomous Republic. 28 Nov. 1958–15 Aug. 1960. *Location:* as **Congo People's Republic.** *Capital:* Brazzaville. *Other names:* Autonomous Republic of the Congo, République du Congo.
History: In 1958 **Moyen-Congo Overseas Territory [ii]** became a self-governing republic within the French Community. In 1960 it became fully independent as **Congo (Brazzaville).**
High Commissioners: 28 Nov. 1958–7 Jan. 1959 Charles Dériaud (acting); 7 Jan. 1959–15 Aug. 1960 Gui-Noël Georgy. *Prime Ministers:* 28 Nov. 1958–8 Dec. 1958 Jacques Opangoult; 8 Dec. 1958–15 Aug. 1960 Fulbert Youlou.

253 Congo (Brazzaville). 15 Aug. 1960–1 Jan. 1970. *Location:* as **Congo People's Republic.** *Capital:* Brazzaville. *Other names:* Congo Republic, République du Congo, Republic of the Congo.
History: In 1960 **Congo Autonomous Republic** became independent of France. For the first decade it was most popularly known as Congo (Brazzaville) in order to distinguish it from its neighbor across the Congo River, **Congo (Leopoldville),** or as that state later became, **Congo (Kinshasa).** In 1970 it became **Congo People's Republic.**
Presidents: 15 Aug. 1960–15 Aug. 1963 Fulbert Youlou; 16 Aug. 1963–19 Dec. 1963 Alphonse Massemba-Débat (acting); 19 Dec. 1963–2 Aug. 1968 Alphonse Massemba-Débat; 2 Aug. 1968–4 Aug. 1968 Marien Ngouabi (Head of National Revolutionary Council); 4 Aug. 1968–4 Sept. 1968 Alphonse Massemba-Débat; 4 Sept. 1968–1 Jan. 1969 Alfred Raoul; 1 Jan. 1969–1 Jan. 1970 Marien Ngouabi. *Prime Ministers:* 24 Dec. 1963–15 Apr. 1966 Pascal Lissouba; 6 May 1966–12 Jan. 1968 Ambroise Noumazalay. *Note:*

In times of no Prime Minister, the President held that office.

254 Congo Democratic Republic. 1 Aug. 1964–1 July 1965. *Location:* as **Zaire.** *Capital:* Léopoldville (founded 1881 by Henry M. Stanley, the explorer and agent for King Léopold of the Belgians, for whom Stanley named the town). *Other names:* Democratic Republic of the Congo, Congo (Léopoldville).
History: In 1964 **Congo (Léopoldville)** changed its name to the Democratic Republic of the Congo. Congo (Léopoldville) had had many names, and this change added more fuel to the fire of confusion between this state and **Congo (Brazzaville).** In 1965, on the renaming of Léopoldville, the country became known as **Congo (Kinshasa).**
Presidents: 1 Aug. 1964–1 July 1965 Joseph Kasavubu. *Prime Ministers:* 1 Aug. 1964–1 July 1965 Moise Tshombe.

255 Congo Free State. 1 July 1885–18 Oct. 1908. *Location:* Zaire. *Capital:* Boma (from 1886). *Other names:* État Indépendant du Congo, Congo State, Kongo Free State, Independent State of the Congo.
History: On Feb. 5, 1885 (effective from July 1) the **International Association of the Congo** became Congo Free State. In 1908 the Belgian government took it over, as **Congo State (Belgian).**
Kings: 1 July 1885–18 Oct. 1908 King Léopold of the Belgians. *Administrators-General:* 1 July 1885–26 March 1887 Francis de Winton. *Governors-General:* 26 March 1887–1 March 1888 Camille Janssen; 1 March 1888–1889 Hermann Ledeganck (acting); 1889–17 Apr. 1891 Camille Janssen. *Governors:* 17 Apr. 1891–8 May 1891 Henri-Ernest Gondry; 8 May 1891–26 Aug. 1892 Camille-Aimé Coquilhat; 26 Aug. 1892–4 Sept. 1896 Joseph Wahis; 4 Sept. 1896–21 Dec. 1900 Francis Dhanis; 21 Dec. 1900–Dec. 1900 Col. Bartels (acting); Dec. 1900–18 Oct. 1908 Joseph Wahis.

256 Congo (Kinshasa). 1 July 1965–21 Oct. 1971. *Location:* as **Zaire.** *Capital:* Kinshasa (until 1 July 1965 it was called Léopoldville). *Other names:* Congolese Republic, République Congolaise, Independent Congo Republic, Republic of the Congo.

History: In 1965 **Congo Democratic Republic** changed its name to Congo (Kinshasa), but the confusion remained with the name of the country across the River Congo, i.e. **Congo (Brazzaville).** This confusion was cleared up in 1971 when Congo (Kinshasa) changed its name again, this time to **Zaire.**

Presidents: 1 July 1965–25 Nov. 1965 Joseph Kasavubu; 25 Nov. 1965–1 Dec. 1965 Joseph Desiré Mobutu (Provisional President); 1 Dec. 1965–21 Oct. 1971 Joseph Desiré Mobutu. *Prime Ministers:* 1 July 1965–13 Oct. 1965 Moise Tshombe; 13 Oct. 1965–25 Nov. 1965 Léonard Mulamba. *Note:* in times of no Prime Minister, the President held that office.

257 Congo (Léopoldville). 30 June 1960–1 Aug. 1964. *Location:* as **Zaire.** *Capital:* Léopoldville. *Other names:* Independent Congo Republic. Democratic Republic of the Congo.

History: In 1960 the **Belgian Congo** became independent as Congo (Léopoldville). These early years of the new state were indescribably troublous and complex (see also **South Kasai Republic, Katanga Republic** and **Stanleyville Republic**). In 1964 it changed its name to **Congo Democratic Republic.**

Presidents: 30 June 1960–1 Aug. 1964 Joseph Kasavubu. *Prime Ministers:* 30 June 1960–5 Sept. 1960 Patrice Lumumba; 5 Sept. 1960–9 Feb. 1961 Joseph Ileo (PM elect); 9 Feb. 1961–1 Aug. 1961 Joseph Ileo; 1 Aug. 1961–10 July 1964 Cyrille Adoulla; 10 July 1964–1 Aug. 1964 Moise Tshombe. *Military Commanders:* 14 Sept. 1960–9 Feb. 1961 Joseph Desiré Mobutu. *Chairmen of High Commission:* 20 Sept. 1960–9 Feb. 1961 Justin Bomboko.

258 Congo People's Republic. 1 Jan. 1970– . *Location:* west central Africa. *Capital:* Brazzaville (founded 1883 and named for the French explorer and administrator Pierre Savorgnan de Brazza. Built on the site of Nntamo). *Other names:* Congo, République Populaire du Congo, People's Republic of the Congo.

History: In 1970 **Congo (Brazzaville)** changed its name to the People's Republic of the Congo. The country is named for the Congo River, which in turn was named for the **Kongo** Kingdom.

Presidents: 1 Jan. 1970–5 Jan. 1970 Marien Ngouabi; 5 Jan. 1970–25 Aug. 1973 Marien Ngouabi (President of State Council); 25 Aug. 1973–18 March 1977 Marien Ngouabi; 18 March 1977–5 Feb. 1979 Joachim Yhombi-Opango (Chairman of Military Committee); 8 Feb. 1979–31 March 1979 Denis Sassou-Nguesso (interim President); 31 March 1979– Denis Sassou-Nguesso. *Prime Ministers:* 25 Aug. 1973–11 Dec. 1975 Henri Lopes; 13 Dec. 1975–7 Aug. 1984 Louis Sylvain Ngoma (or Goba); 11 Aug. 1984– Ange-Édouard Poungui. *Note:* in times of no Prime Minister, the President held that office.

259 Congo State (Belgian). 18 Oct. 1908–15 Nov. 1908. *Location:* as **Zaire.** *Capital:* Boma.

History: In 1908 Léopold's excesses in the **Congo Free State** caused the Belgian government to take over what was Léopold's private concern. This happened on Aug. 20, 1908 and was confirmed by an act of the Belgian parliament on October 18, 1908. For a month it was known as the Congo State (Belgian), then it became the **Belgian Congo.**

Governors: 18 Oct. 1908–15 Nov. 1908 Joseph Wahis.

Congolese People's Republic see **Stanleyville People's Republic**

260 Constantine. 1637–1837. *Location:* northern Algeria. *Capital:* Qusantina (or Constantine). *Other names:* Qusantina.

History: In 1637 Qusantina (Constantine) was created a separate Beylik by the Turks, and subject to the Beylerbey of Algiers. In 1837 it became part of the **French Possessions in North Africa.**

Beys: 1637–(?) Ferhad Bey; (?)–(?) [unknown]; ca. 1700–1713 Ali Kojja Bey; 1713–1736 Kalyan Hassan; 1736–1754 Hassan; 1754–1756 vacant; 1756–1771 Ahmad al-Kollo; 1771–1792 Salah; 1792–1826 during this period a total of 17 Beys ruled, including Mustafa Inglis; 1826–1830 [unknown]; 1830–1837 Ahmad.

261 Cornelis Kok's Land. May 1824–1857. *Location:* Orange Free State. *Capital:* Campbell. *Other names:* Campbell Lands.

History: In 1824 Cornelis Kok succeeded to the captaincy of **Campbell Lands** and from that time the land became known as Cornelis Kok's Land. During his lifetime his boundaries were re-structured by all of the neighboring white powers and sometime in 1857 Kok and his lands passed into oblivion, becoming part of the **Orange Free State.**

Captains: May 1824–1857 Cornelis Kok II.

Côte d'Ivoire see **Ivory Coast**

262 Cotonou. 19 May 1868–22 June 1894. *Location:* Kotonou, Benin. *Capital:* Cotonou. *Other names:* Kotonu, Cotonou Territory.

History: In 1868 the French established a protectorate over the coastal kingdom of Kotonu. An administration does not seem to have been set up until 1878, in the form of a French consul. In 1883 the power at Cotonou became vested in the Resident of **Porto-Novo Protectorate [ii].** In 1894 it became part of **Dahomey Colony.**

Consuls: 1878–1881 Albert Ardin d'Elteil; 1881–1883 Victor Bareste; 1883–22 June 1893 ruled by Porto-Novo Protectorate [ii]; 22 June 1893–22 June 1894 ruled by Porto-Novo Colony.

Crocodile People see **Bakwenaland**

Cush see **Kush**

Cyrenaica see also **Cirenaica**

263 Cyrenaica (Autonomous). 21 Nov. 1949–24 Dec. 1951. *Location:* as **British Cyrenaica.** *Capital:* Benghazi. *Other names:* Cyrenaica, Barca, Barqah.

History: In 1949 **British Cyrenaica** was granted autonomy. In 1951 it, **French Fezzan** and **British Tripolitania** merged to form the **Libyan Kingdom.**

Residents: 21 Nov. 1949–24 Dec. 1951 Eric Vully de Candole. *Emirs:* 21 Nov. 1949–24 Dec. 1951 Idris al-Mahdi as-Sanusi. *Prime Ministers:* 21 Nov. 1949–18 March 1950 Umar Mansur al-Kikhya; 18 March 1950–24 Dec. 1951 Muhammad as-Saqizli. *United Nations High Commissioners:* 17 March 1950–24 Dec. 1951 Adrian Pelt.

Cyrene see **Pentapolis**

Dagbon see **Dagomba**

264 Dagomba. ca. 1440–1896. *Location:* mid-Ghana. *Capital:* Yendi. *Other names:* Dagbon.

History: Legend has it that the Dagomba Kingdom was founded in the 14th century, but around 1440 seems more correct. About 1680 Dagomba was subjugated by the **Ashanti Empire** and remained so until 1874 when the Ashanti were defeated by the British. In 1896 it continued to hitch its wagon to the British star by becoming part of **Ashanti Protectorate.**

Kings: ca. 1440 Nyagse; ca. 1475 Zulande; ca. 1500 Nagalogu; ca. 1520 Datorli; ca. 1525 Buruguyomda; ca.

1530 Zoligu; ca. 1560 Zonman; ca. 1600 Ninmitoni; ca. 1630 Dimani; ca. 1640 Yanzo; ca. 1645 Darizegu; ca. 1660 Luro; ca. 1680 Tutugri; ca. 1690 Zagale; ca. 1695 Zokuli; ca. 1700 Gungobili; ca. 1710 Zangina; ca. 1720 Andani Sigili; ca. 1730 Ziblim Bunbiogo; ca. 1745 Gariba; ca. 1760 Ziblim Na Saa; ca. 1780 Ziblim Bandamda; ca. 1785 Andani I; ca. 1815 Mahama I; ca. 1820 Ziblim Kulunku; ca. 1830 Sumani Zoli; ca. 1845 Yakubu I; ca. 1863 Abdullai I; ca. 1882–1899 Andani II; 1899–1900 Darimani; 1900–1920 al-Hassan; 1920–1938 Abdullai II; 1938–1948 Mahama II; 1948–1953 Mahama III; 1953–1968 Abdullai III; 1968–1969 Andani III; 1969–1974 Muhammad Abdullai IV; 1974– Yakubu II.

265 Dahomey Autonomous Republic. 4 Dec. 1958–1 Aug. 1960. *Location:* as **Benin Republic.** *Capital:* Cotonou. *Other names:* Autonomous Republic of Dahomey, Dahomey.

History: In 1958 **Dahomey Overseas Territory** became self-ruling within the French Community. In 1960 it gained independence as **Dahomey Republic.**

High Commissioners: 4 Dec. 1958–1 Aug. 1960 René Tirant. *Prime Ministers:* 4 Dec. 1958–22 May 1959 Sourou Apithy; 22 May 1959–1 Aug. 1960 Hubert Maga.

266 Dahomey Colony. 22 June 1894–24 June 1911. *Location:* the coastline of **Benin Republic.** *Capital:* Cotonou. *Other names:* Dahomey.

History: In 1894 **Porto-Novo Colony,** already French, became the capital territory of the southern part of what is today **Benin Republic.** This was effected because in 1894 the French conquered **Dahomey Kingdom** in the interior and took the name Dahomey for their colony, which included Porto-Novo. In 1900 the Kingdom of Dahomey was abolished and the area annexed to the French Government. In 1911, after the subduing of lands further north, the country became known as **Dahomey Colony and Dependencies.**

Lieutenant-Governors: 22 June 1894–3 July 1899 Victor Ballot; 3 July 1899–8 Oct. 1899 Jean-Baptiste Fonssagrives (acting); 8 Oct. 1899–26 Nov. 1900 Pierre Pascal (acting); 26 Nov. 1900–30 June 1902 Victor Liotard; 30 June 1902–Oct. 1902 Charles Marchal (acting); Oct. 1902–1 Sept. 1903 Victor Liotard; 1 Sept. 1903–15 Jan. 1904 Eugène Décazes (acting); 15 Jan. 1904–28 June 1904 Jean Penel (acting); 28 June 1904–5 May 1906 Victor Liotard; 5 May 1906–9 June 1906 Joseph Lhuerre (acting); 9 June 1906–16 July 1906 Charles Marchal (acting); 16 July 1906–8 March 1908 Charles Marchal; 8 March 1908–22 Sept. 1908 Antoine Gaudart (acting); 22 Sept. 1908–9 Oct. 1908 Charles Brunet (acting); 9 Oct. 1908–25 Apr. 1909 Jean Peuvergne; 25 Apr. 1909–29 June 1909 Henri Malan; 29 June 1909–10 Feb. 1910 Raphaël Antonetti (acting); 10 Feb. 1910–6 March 1911 Henri Malan; 6 March 1911–24 June 1911 Raphaël Antonetti.

267 Dahomey Colony and Dependencies. 24 June 1911–13 Oct. 1946. *Location:* as **Benin Republic.** *Capital:* Cotonou. *Other names:* Dahomey.

History: In 1911 **Dahomey Colony** was added to by its hinterland, which became its dependencies. In 1946 the whole region became an overseas territory of the Fourth Republic of France (see **Dahomey Overseas Territory**).

Lieutenant-Governors: 24 Jan. 1911–9 May 1912 Émile Merwart; 9 May 1912–11 July 1912 Charles Noufflard (acting); 11 July 1912–7 Apr. 1917 Charles Noufflard; 7 Apr. 1917–July 1919 Gaston Fourn (acting); July 1919–1 May 1921 Gaston Fourn; 1 May 1921–28 Feb. 1922 Pierre Chapon (acting); 28 Feb. 1922–1 Apr. 1924 Gaston Fourn; 1 Apr. 1924–26 Nov. 1924 Alphonse Choteau (acting); 26 Nov. 1924–29 Aug. 1928 Gaston Fourn; 29 Aug. 1928–4 April. 1929 Lucien Geay (acting); 4 Apr. 1929–8 Feb. 1931 Dieudonné Reste; 8 Feb. 1931–7 Jan. 1932 Théophile Tellier; 7 Jan. 1932–2 Aug. 1932 Louis Blacher; 2 Aug. 1932–22 July 1933 Louis Aujas (acting); 22 July 1933–24 Aug. 1934 Jules de Coppet; 24 Aug. 1934–15 Feb. 1935 Jean de Santi (acting); 15 Feb. 1935–22 Sept. 1935 Maurice Bourgine; 22 Sept. 1935–1936 Jean de Santi (acting); 1936–12 Jan. 1937 Maurice Bourgine; 12 Jan. 1937–7 Aug. 1937 Henri Martinet (acting); 7 Aug. 1937–7 Apr. 1938 Ernest Gayon (acting); 7 Apr. 1938–1 June 1938 Henri Martinet (acting). *Governors:* 1 June 1938–27 Aug. 1940 Armand Annet; 27 Aug. 1940–18 Sept. 1940 Pierre Saliceti (acting); 18 Sept. 1940–26 Aug. 1943 Léon Truitard; 26 Aug. 1943–21 May 1946 Charles Assier de Pompignan; 21 May 1946–13 Oct. 1946 Robert Legendre (acting).

268 Dahomey Kingdom. 1730–22 June 1894. *Location:* **Benin Republic.** *Capital:* Allada. *Other names:* Dahomey, Kingdom of Dahomey.

History: In 1730 **Abomey Kingdom** became Dahomey after acquiring much land by conquest. On December 3, 1891 the French established a military protectorate over the country, and in 1894, when the French colony of Dahomey came into being officially (see **Dahomey Colony**), so the kingdom came to a close, although kings continued to rule nominally for a while.

Kings: 1730–Apr. 1732 Aguja (or Tossu); Apr. 1732–17 May 1774 Tegbesu (or Avissu); 17 May 1774–1789 Kpengla (or Gnansunu); 17 Apr. 1790–1797 Agonglo (or Sindozan). *Regents:* 1797–1804 Adanzan. *Kings:* 1804–1818 Adanzan; 1818–1858 Gezo (or Gangkpe); 1858–29 Dec. 1889 Gelele (or Glele); 30 Dec. 1889–15 Jan. 1894 Gbehanzin; 15 Jan. 1894–1898 Agbo Agoli.

269 Dahomey Overseas Territory. 13 Oct. 1946–4 Dec. 1958. *Location:* as

Benin Republic. *Capital:* Cotonou. *Other names:* Dahomey.

History: In 1946 **Dahomey Colony and Dependencies** became an overseas territory of the Fourth Republic of France. In 1958 it became self-governing within the French Community (see **Dahomey Autonomous Republic**).

Governors: 13 Oct. 1946–14 Jan. 1948 Robert Legendre (acting); 14 Jan. 1948–13 Jan. 1949 Jean-Georges Chambon; 13 Jan. 1949–19 Sept. 1949 Jacques-Alphonse Boissier; 19 Sept. 1949–Nov. 1951 Claude Valluy (acting); Nov. 1951–21 June 1955 Charles Bonfils; 21 June 1955–21 March 1958 Casimir Biros; 21 March 1958–15 July 1958 Bernard Hepp (acting); 15 July 1958–4 Dec. 1958 René Tirant (acting).

270 Dahomey Portuguese Protectorate. 5 Aug. 1885–22 Dec. 1887. *Location:* Benin. *Capital:* none. *Other names:* Portuguese Dahomey.

History: The Portuguese "claimed" a protectorate over the Dahomey coastline, but in reality their only possession in the area was the old fort at Whydah. By 1887 they had relinquished all claims to France (see **Porto-Novo Protectorate [ii]**).

Rulers: 5 Aug. 1885–22 Dec. 1887 none.

271 Dahomey Republic. 1 Aug. 1960–4 Dec. 1975. *Location:* as **Benin Republic.** *Capital:* Cotonou. *Other names:* Dahomey, Republic of Dahomey, République du Dahomey (named for the Dahomey Kingdom ["Dan-Homey"—"on the stomach of Dan"]).

History: In 1960 **Dahomey Autonomous Republic** became fully independent. On November 30, 1975 (effective from Dec. 4), it changed its name to **Benin Republic.**

Heads of State: 1 Aug. 1960–11 Dec. 1960 Hubert Maga. *Presidents:* 11 Dec. 1960–28 Oct. 1963 Hubert Maga; 28 Oct. 1963–19 Jan. 1964 Christophe

Soglou (interim Pres.); 19 Jan. 1964–27 Nov. 1965 Sourou Apithy; 27 Nov. 1965–29 Nov. 1965 Justin Ahomadegbé; 29 Nov. 1965–22 Dec. 1965 Tairou Congacou; 22 Dec. 1965–17 Dec. 1967 Christophe Soglou; 17 Dec. 1967–22 Dec. 1967 Revolutionary Mil. Committee in power; 22 Dec. 1967–1 Aug. 1968 Alphonse Alley; 1 Aug. 1968–10 Dec. 1969 Emil Zinsou; 10 Dec. 1969–7 May 1970 Maurice Kouandété (Pres. of Committee); 7 May 1970–7 May 1972 Hubert Maga; 7 May 1972–26 Oct. 1972 Justin Ahomadegbé; 27 Oct. 1972–4 Dec. 1975 Mathieu Kerekou. *Prime Ministers:* 19 Jan. 1964–27 Nov. 1965 Justin Ahomadegbé; 22 Dec. 1967–1 Aug. 1968 Maurice Kouandété. *Note:* in times of no Prime Minister, the President held that office.

272 Damagaram. 1731–30 July 1899. *Location:* the Zinder area of southern Niger. *Capital:* Zinder (1822–99); Kianza (1802–22); Gueza (1731–1802). *Other names:* Zinder (from 1822).
History: Founded in 1731 as a vassal state of the **Bornu Empire [ii],** Damagaram became independent about 1800 and in 1899 was taken by the French as part of **French West Africa,** becoming in 1900 the base for **Zinder Autonomous Military Territory.**
Kings: 1731–1746 Mallam ibn Maina Kadey; 1746–1757 Babami; 1757–1775 Tanimun; 1775–1782 Assafa; 1782–1787 Abaza; 1787–1790 Mallam Babu Saba; 1790–1799 Dauda; 1799–1812 Ahmadu I; 1812–1822 Suleiman I; 1822–1841 Ibrahim I; 1841–1843 Tanimun II; 1843–1850 Ibrahim I; 1850–1851 Muhammad Kace; 1851–1884 Tanimun II; 1884–1884 Ibrahim II; 1884–1893 Suleiman II; 1893–30 July 1899 Ahmadu II; 30 July 1899–1906 Ahmadu III; 1906–1922 Bellama; 27 Feb. 1923–1950 Barma Mustafa; 1950– Umaru Sanda.

273 Danish Gold Coast Settlements. 1658–30 March 1850. *Location:* the eastern coast of Ghana. *Capital:* Fort Christiansborg (from 1685); Fort Frederiksberg (1658–1685). *Other names:* Danish Guinea.
History: In 1653 the Danes arrived on the Gold Coast to compete in trade with the other powers (cf. **English, Portuguese,** and **Dutch Gold Coast Settlements).** In 1658 they captured Fort Frederiksborg, the old Swedish capital (see **Swedish Gold Coast Settlements),** expelling the remaining Swedes from the Gold Coast. Until 1750 the Danish forts were run by the West India and Guinea Company, but after that year the Danish Crown managed affairs in the colony. In 1850 the forts and ports of Christiansborg (later the nucleus of Accra), Keta, Kongosteen, Fort Fredensborg and Fort Augustenborg were sold to the British, who incorporated them into the **Gold Coast Colony.** That year the Danes left the Gold Coast.
Opperhoveds (Chief Heads): 1658–16 Apr. 1659 Samuel Smidt; 16 Apr. 1659–Oct. 1659 no Danish rule; Oct. 1659–6 June 1662 Jost Cramer; 6 June 1662–10 Sept. 1664 Henning Albrecht (acting); 10 Sept. 1664–1669 Henning Albrecht; 1669–1674 Bartolomaus von Gronestein; 1674–1680 Conrad Crul (acting); 1680–1680 Peter With (acting); 1680–2 Feb. 1681 Peter Valck (acting); 2 Feb. 1681–1 July 1681 Magnus Prang; 1 July 1681–11 July 1684 [unknown]; 11 July 1684–1687 Hans Lykke; 1687–5 Jan. 1691 Nikolaj Fensman; 5 Jan. 1691–1692 Jørgen Meyer; 1692–1694 Harding Petersen; 1694–6 Dec. 1696 Thomas Jacobsen; 6 Dec. 1696–23 Dec. 1698 Erik Lygaard (acting); 23 Dec. 1698–31 Aug. 1703 Johan Trawne; 11 Sept. 1703–23 Apr. 1704 Hartvig Meyer. *Vice-Opperhoveds:* 23 Apr. 1704–5 May 1705 Peter Sverdrup; 5 May 1705–25 May 1705 Peter Petersen. *Opperhoveds:* 25 May 1705–17 Aug. 1711 Erik Lygaard; 17 Aug. 1711–26 Nov. 1717 Bfantz Boye; 26 Nov. 1717–6 Aug. 1720 Knud Röst; 6 Aug. 1720–24 Jan. 1722 Peter Østrup; 25 Jan. 1722–22 Jan. 1723 David Hernn; 22 Jan. 1723–30 Oct. 1723 Niels Østrup;

7 Nov. 1723–27 Apr. 1724 Christian Syndermann; 27 Apr. 1724–1 March 1727 Hendrik von Suhm; 4 March 1727–18 Sept. 1727 Fred Pahl; 18 Sept. 1727–24 Dec. 1728 Andreas Willennsen; 24 Dec. 1728–12 Aug. 1735 Anders Waerøe; 12 Aug. 1735–14 June 1736 Severin Schilderup; 14 June 1736–20 June 1740 Enewold Borris; 20 June 1740–26 May 1743 Peter Jørgensen; 26 May 1743–3 Feb. 1744 Christian Dorph; 3 Feb. 1744–11 March 1745 Jørgen Billsen; 11 March 1745–23 March 1745 Thomas Brock; 23 March 1745–23 April 1745 Johan Wilder; 23 Apr. 1745–21 June 1746 August Hackenborg; 21 June 1746–6 March 1751 Joost Platfusz; 6 March 1751–8 March 1751 Magnus Lützow; 8 March 1751–21 July 1752 Magnus Hacksen (acting); 21 July 1752–11 March 1757 Carl Engmann; 11 March 1757–14 Feb. 1762 Christian Jessen; 14 Feb. 1762–20 Oct. 1766 Carl Resch. *Govs. of Guinea:* 20 Oct. 1766–11 Jan. 1768 Christian Tychsen; 11 Jan. 1768–2 July 1769 Frantz Kyhberg (acting); 2 July 1769–11 June 1770 Gerhard Wrisberg; 11 June 1770–13 June 1770 Joachim Otto (acting); 13 June 1770–15 June 1772 Johan Frohlich (acting); 15 June 1772–24 June 1777 Niels Aarestrup (acting); 24 June 1777–2 Dec. 1780 Conrad von Hemsen; 2 Dec. 1780–21 Apr. 1788 Jens Kiøge (acting); 21 Apr. 1788–23 Oct. 1789 Johan Kipnasse (acting); 23 Oct. 1789–July 1792 Andreas Biørn; July 1792–25 Jan. 1793 Andreas Hammer (acting); 25 Jan. 1793–30 June 1793 Andreas Hammer; 30 June 1793–3 Aug. 1793 Bendt Olrich; 3 Aug. 1793–17 Aug. 1795 Frantz von Hager (acting); Oct. 1795–31 Dec. 1799 Johan Wrisberg; 31 Dec. 1799–3 Oct. 1802 Johan Ahnholm (acting); 3 Oct. 1802–15 Apr. 1807 Johan Wrisberg; 15 Apr. 1807–1 March 1817 Christian Schiønning (acting); 3 March 1817–5 Oct. 1817 Johan Richter; 5 Oct. 1817–6 May 1819 Jens Reiersen (acting); 6 May 1819–25 Nov. 1819 Philip Wrisberg (never took office); 6 May 1819–1 Jan. 1821 Christian Svanek-

jaer (acting); 1 Jan. 1821–5 Sept. 1821 Peter Steffens; 5 Sept. 1821–23 Dec. 1823 Matthias Thønning (acting); 23 Dec. 1823–7 May 1825 Johan von Richelieu; 7 May 1825–30 Sept. 1827 Niels Brøch (acting); 30 Sept. 1827–1 Aug. 1828 Jens Flindt; 1 Aug. 1828–20 Jan. 1831 Heinrich Lind (acting); 29 Jan. 1831–21 Oct. 1831 Ludwig von Hein; 21 Oct. 1831–4 Dec. 1831 Helmut von Ahrenstorff; 4 Dec. 1831–1 March 1833 Niels Brøch; 1 March 1833–21 July 1833 Heinrich Lind; 21 July 1834–26 Dec. 1834 Edvard von Gandil (acting); 26 Dec. 1834–19 Aug. 1837 Frederik Mørch (acting); 19 Aug. 1837–18 March 1839 Frederik Mørch; 19 March 1839–18 Aug. 1839 Hans Giede (acting); 18 Aug. 1839–24 May 1842 Lucas Dall (acting); 24 May 1842–26 Aug. 1842 Bernhardt Wilkens (acting); 26 Aug. 1842–15 March 1844 Edvard Carstensen (acting); 15 March 1844–5 July 1844 Edvard Ericksen (acting); 5 July 1844–9 Oct. 1844 Georg Lutterodt (acting); 9 Oct. 1844–10 Apr. 1847 Edvard Carstensen (created July 30, 1844); 10 Apr. 1847–20 Feb. 1850 Rasmus Schmidt (acting); 20 Feb. 1850–30 March 1850 Edvard Carstensen. *Nominal Govs.:* Apr. 1850–17 Aug. 1850 Edvard Carstensen.

274 Daniski. 1447–1806. *Location:* northern Nigeria. *Capital:* Daniski Hill.

History: The Bolewa people came from the Lake Chad area to northern Nigeria in 1447 and settled in the Daniski Hills, establishing their capital at Daniski Hill, and displacing the Ngamo tribe. In 1806 their sarki (king) founded **Fika** and left Daniski.

Sarkis: 1447–1454 Idriso; 1454–1463 Atman. *Mois (Kings):* 1463–1471 Moi Albo; 1471–1488 Mele Manso; 1488–1498 Anbanga; 1498–1554 Bunowo; 1554–1596 Barma dan Moi Bunowo; 1596–1611 Gandowo; 1611–1621 Langawa Daka; 1621–1639 Halbo; 1639–1674 Mama Kayi; 1674–1684 Bawa Kayi; 1684–1709 Mele Fusan; 1709–1710 Buraima Wamu; 1710–1721 Mama

Mulu; 1721–1728 Adam Bakam; 1728–1745 Mama Korya; 1745–1749 Mama Gimsi; 1749–1752 Sule Ladi; 1752–1770 Aji Daka; 1770–1787 Langawa; 1787–1796 Usman Gana; 1796–1804 Mammadi Gizze; 1804–1805 Mele Filata; 1805–1806 Moi Buraima.

275 Darfur Province. 24 Oct. 1874–Dec. 1883. *Location:* eastern Sudan. *Capital:* al-Fasher. *Other names:* Dar Fur, Darfur.
History: In 1874 **Darfur Sultanate** was conquered by the Egyptians and it became a province of **Egyptian Sudan.** In 1883 it was overrun by the **Mahdist State,** of which it became a fundamental part. In 1899 it was re-established (see **Darfur Sultanate [ii]).**
Governors: 24 Oct. 1874–1881 Hassan Bey Hilmi; 1881–Dec. 1883 Rudolf Karl Slatin.

276 Darfur Sultanate [i]. 1603–24 Oct. 1874. *Location:* eastern Sudan. *Capital:* al-Fasher (this was the first permanent capital, established as such about 1790). *Other names:* Darfur, Dar Fur, Fur.
History: In 1603 the Keira Dynasty was founded in Darfur, thus beginning the recorded history of that state. After about 1670 the Sultans established their "fasher" at a different place, until about 1790 when it was fixed at al-Fasher (meaning "the capital"). In 1874 it was taken by Egypt, and became the **Darfur Province** of **Egyptian Sudan.**
Sultans: 1603–1637 Suleiman Solong; 1637–1682 Musa ibn Suleiman; 1682–1722 Ahmad Bakr ibn Musa; 1722–1732 Muhammad I Dawra; 1732–1739 Umar Lele; 1739–1756 Abu'l Qasim; 1756–1787 Muhammad II Tairab; 1787–1801 Abdarrahman ar-Rashid; 1801–1839 Muhammad III al-Fadhl; 1839–1873 Muhammad IV Hussain; 1873–24 Oct. 1874 Ibrahim.

277 Darfur Sultanate [ii]. 21 March 1899–6 Nov. 1916. *Location:* eastern Sudan. *Capital:* al-Fasher. *Other*

names: Darfur, Darfur Province.
History: In 1899 the old Darfur Sultanate (see **Darfur Sultanate [i])** was re-established on the fall of the **Mahdist State** in the Sudan. It had been out of existence as a sultanate for 25 years, during which time it had been **Darfur Province** of the **Egyptian Sudan** (from 1874–1883), and then part of the **Mahdist State** (from 1884–1898). In 1915 the Sultan revolted against Anglo-Egyptian rule in the Sudan (see **Anglo-Egyptian Sudan**) and was killed in 1916, and Darfur became a province of the **Anglo-Egyptian Sudan.**
Sultans: 21 March 1899–6 Nov. 1916 Ali Dinar ibn Zakariyya.

278 Daura-Baure. ca. 1825–1903. *Location:* 36 miles southeast of **Daura Emirate.** *Capital:* Baure. *Other names:* Baure.
History: In 1805, when the **Daura Kingdom** was superseded by the **Daura Emirate,** two sets of Hausa nobles left Daura to form continuing, but separate, lines of the Royal House (see **Daura-Zango** for details). The Baure group, under Danshuhunni, resided at Dan Mairam until the king was killed, and his son Tsofo went to found the town of Baure, around which revolved the kingdom of Daura-Baure, as a rival to **Daura-Zango.** In 1903 it went to **Zinder Autonomous Military Territory.**
Sarkins: ca. 1825–(?) Tsofo; (?)–(?) Habu; (?)–(?) Jibo; (?)–(?) Zakari; (?)–(?) Abdu; (?)–1903 Hallaru.

279 Daura Emirate. 1805–1903. *Location:* northern Nigeria-Niger border. *Capital:* Daura. *Other names:* Daura, Daura Fulani.
History: In 1805 **Daura Kingdom** was taken over by the **Fulani Empire** and made an emirate. The ruling Hausa fled to other parts and about 1825 set up two individual, rival, Hausa kingdoms (see **Daura-Baure** and **Daura-Zango**). In 1903 Daura was divided by the French and the British, and a reformed

emirate was formed in **Northern Nigeria Protectorate.**

Emirs: 1805–(?) Mallam Ishaku; (?)–(?) Yusufu; (?)–(?) Muhamman; (?)–(?) Zubeiru; (?)–(?) Bello; (?)–(?) Altine; (?)–(?) Maigardo; (?)–(?) Sogiji; (?)–1906 Murnai.

280 Daura Kingdom. ca. 700–1805. *Location:* Niger-Nigeria border. *Capital:* Daura (this was the latter capital. Name means "blacksmith" in ancient Tuareg); Tsofon Birni (this was the original capital).

History: The senior of all the **Hausa States,** it was taken over in about 1000 by Kazuru. He arrived in the area and married the 17th Queen of Daura. In 1805 the Fulani took it over as an emirate (see **Daura Emirate**) (see also **Daura-Zango** and **Daura-Baure**).

Magajiyas (Queens): ca. 700 Kufuru (or Kofano); (?)–(?) Gino (or Gufano); (?)–(?) Yakumo (or Yakwano); (?)–(?) Yakunya (or Yakaniya); (?)–(?) Walzamu (or Waizam); (?)–(?) Yanbamu; (?)–(?) Gizirgizit (or Gadar Gadar); (?)–(?) Innagari (or Anagiri); (?)–(?) Daura; (?)–(?) Gamata; (?)–(?) Shata; (?)–(?) Batatume; (?)–(?) Sandamata; (?)–(?) Jamata; (?)–(?) Hamata; (?)–(?) Zama; (?)–(?) Shawata. *Sarkins (Kings):* ca. 1000–ca. 1030 Abayajidda (or Kazuru); ca. 1030–ca. 1070 Bawo; ca. 1070–ca. 1100 Gazaura; (?)–(?) Gakuna; (?)–(?) Jaaku; (?)–(?) Jaketake; (?)–(?) Yakama; ca. 1200 Jaka; (?)–(?) Ada Hamta; (?)–(?) Ada Jabu; (?)–(?) Dagamu; (?)–(?) Ada Yaki; (?)–(?) Hamdogu; (?)–(?) Yabau; ca. 1300 Naji; (?)–(?) Gani; (?)–(?) Wake; (?)–(?) Kamutu; (?)–(?) Rigo; (?)–(?) Gaga; (?)–(?) Jabu; ca. 1400 Zamnau; (?)–(?) Shashimi; (?)–(?) Ada Inda; (?)–(?) Doguma; (?)–(?) Ada Gamu; ca. 1500 Ada Sunguma; (?)–(?) Shafau; (?)–(?) Ada Sabau; (?)–(?) Ada Doki; (?)–(?) Nagama; (?)–(?) Ada Kube; (?)–(?) Hamama; ca. 1600 Dagajirau; (?)–(?) Kamu; (?)–(?) Ada Guguwa; (?)–(?) Hamida; (?)–(?) Abdu Kawo; (?)–(?) Nagama; (?)–(?) Hanatari; ca. 1700 Rifau; (?)–(?) Hazo; (?)–(?) Dango; (?)–(?) Bawan Allah; (?)–(?) Kalifah; (?)–(?) Tsofo; (?)–(?) Jiro; (?)–1805 Gwari Abdu.

281 Daura-Zango. ca. 1825–1903. *Location:* 12 miles east of **Daura Emirate.** *Capital:* Zango. *Other names:* Zango.

History: In 1805 when the Fulani emir Mallam Ishaku conquered **Daura Kingdom** and set up his emirate there (see **Daura Emirate**), the old king, Gwari Abdu, escaped and went to Kwargdom, Tsirkau, Murya and finally to Nguru. Then he stayed at Murya again. He waged war on the Fulani but was unable to re-capture Daura. He died about 1809 and his brother Lukudi became de jure Sarkin Daura of the Habe Dynasty. He forced the Fulani out of the Zango area and about 1825 set up a rival kingdom in Zango. There was another splinter group based at Baure (see **Daura-Baure**) which was also Hausa (as opposed to Fulani) and of the same Habe line. Zango spent most of its time as a vassal state of **Damagaram** (which had its capital at Zinder), as did Baure. It wasn't until 1903 when the British and the French carved up the area that Zango became truly free of Damagaram. Damagaram became part of **Zinder Autonomous Military Territory,** as did **Daura-Baure** and part of Daura-Zango, while the other part of Zango (the ruling section) and **Daura Emirate** went into **Northern Nigeria Protectorate.** In 1904 the old dynasty was restored at Daura.

Sarkins Daura: ca. 1825–1828 Lukudi; 1828–1843 Nuhu; 1843–1856 Muhamman Sha; 1856–1862 Haruna; 1862–1868 Dan Aro; 1868–1888 Tafida; 1888–1890 Suleimanu; 1890–1895 Yusufu; 1895–1904 Tafida; 1904–1911 Mallam Musa; 1911–1912 interregnum; 1912–1963 Abdurrahman; 1963– al-Hajj Muhammadu Bashar.

Debe see **Brass**

282 Denkyira. 1550–1701. *Location:* Ghana-Ivory Coast. *Capital:* Abankeseso. *Other names:* Denkyera.

History: In 1550 the Denkyira people founded their community, the state of Denkyira itself being formed in 1620. In 1701 the **Ashanti Empire** conquered it.

Chiefs: 1550–1560 Ayekeraa; 1560–1570 Yao Awirri; 1570–1590 Anim Kokobo Boadee; 1590–1601 Ahaha; 1601–1609 Ahihi; 1609–1649 Werempe Ampem (or Mumuromfi); 1649–1671 Boadu Akafo Berempon (or Adafo Biaka); 1671–1690 Boa Amponsem (or Boa Siante); 1690–1710 Ntim Gyakari.

Diallon see **Futa Jallon**

283 Diego Ruy's Island. 1507–1638. *Location:* as Rodrigues, in the Indian Ocean. *Capital:* none.

History: Discovered as an uninhabited island by the Portuguese in 1501, it was colonized by the French in 1638 (see **Rodrigues Colony**).

Rulers: none.

284 Diego Suarez Colony. 1886–6 Aug. 1896. *Location:* northern Madagascar. *Capital:* Diego Suarez.

History: In 1886 the local king ceded Diego Suarez to France as a colony in the far north of Madagascar. In 1896 it became part of **Madagascar Colony**, as Diego Suarez District.

Commandants: 1886–1887 Henri Caillet; 1887–6 Aug. 1896 Ernst-Emmanuel Froger.

Diggers' Republic see **Klipdrift Republic**

285 Diva Morgabin. 1502–9 Feb. 1513. *Location:* Reunion. *Capital:* none.

History: Discovered by the Portuguese in 1502 and named Diva Morgabin. In 1513 it was re-named **Santa Apollonia.**

Rulers: none.

Djallon see **Futa Jallon**

286 Djibouti. See these **names:**
Djibouti (1977–)
Afars and Issas Territory (1967–1977)
French Somaliland Overseas Territory (1958–1967)
French Somaliland (1896–1958)
Obock Colony (1884–1896)
French Coast of the Somalis (1862–1884)

287 Djibouti. 27 June 1977– . *Location:* northeast Africa, at the southern entrance to the Red Sea. *Capital:* Djibouti (built around 1880). *Other names:* République du Djibouti, Jamhariyya Djibouti, Republic of Djibouti, Jibuti, Djibuti, Djibouti Republic.

History: In 1977 the Territory of the Afars and Issas (see **Afars and Issas Territory**) became independent from France as Djibouti. Both Ethiopia and Somalia have laid claims to it.

Presidents: 27 June 1977– Hassan Gouled Aptidon. *Prime Ministers:* 12 July 1977–17 Dec. 1977 Ahmed Dini; 5 Feb. 1978–21 Sept. 1978 Abdallah Kamil; 30 Sept. 1978– Barket Gourad Hamadou. *Note:* in times of no Prime Minister, the President held that office.

Djolof see **Dyolof**

288 Doma. 1232–1901. *Location:* northern Nigeria. *Capital:* Doma. *Other names:* Gara.

History: In 1232 the kingdom of Doma was founded by Andoma. In 1901 it was taken by the British, as part of **Northern Nigeria Protectorate.**

Kings: 1232 Andoma; (?)–(?) Aseil; (?)–(?) Akau; ca. 1300 Akwei; (?)–(?) Adago; (?)–(?) Oka; ca. 1390 Okabu; (?)–(?) Okaku; ca. 1480 Aboshe; ca. 1500 Oga I; (?)–(?) Atta I; (?)–(?) Anao; ca. 1600 Akwe I; (?)–(?) Aboshi; (?)–(?) Adra; ca. 1700 Asabo; (?)–(?) Anawo; ca. 1800 Oga II; (?)–(?) Ogu;

(?)-(?) Atta II; (?)-ca. 1855 Ari; ca. 1855 Akwe II; (?)-(?) Amaku; (?)-(?) Atta III; (?)-(?) Ausu; (?)-(?) Agabi; (?)-(?) Agulu; (?)-1901 Agabo; 1901-1930 Atta IV.

Dongo see **Ndongo**

289 Dongola. ca. 675-1323. *Location:* Sudan. *Capital:* Dunqulah. *Other names:* Dunqulah.

History: About 675 **Mukurra** and the land of the Nobatae (see **Nubia**) united to form the kingdom of Dongola. It was a Christian state until 1323, when it became Muslim under the Mamelukes of Egypt (see **Bahrite Mameluke Empire**).

Kings: ca. 675-ca. 710 Merkurios; ca. 710-ca. 722 [unknown]; ca. 722-ca. 738 Kyriakos; ca. 738-ca. 744 Zacharias I; ca. 744-ca. 768 Simon; ca. 768-ca. 780 Markos; ca. 780-ca. 790 Abraham; ca. 790-ca. 810 Michael; ca. 810-ca. 822 Joannes; ca. 822-ca. 831 Zacharias III; ca. 831-ca. 831 Qanun (pretender); ca. 831-ca. 854 Zacharias III; ca. 854-ca. 860 Ali Baba; ca. 860-ca. 870 Israel; ca. 870-892 Georgios I; 892-ca. 912 Asabysos; ca. 912-ca. 943 Istabanos; ca. 943-ca. 958 Kubri ibn Surun; ca. 958-ca. 969 Zacharias IV; ca. 969-ca. 980 Georgios II; ca. 980-ca. 999 Simeon; ca. 999-ca. 1030 Rafael; ca. 1030-ca. 1080 Georgios III; ca. 1080-ca. 1089 Salomo; ca. 1089-ca. 1130 Basileios; ca. 1130-ca. 1158 Georgios IV; ca. 1158-ca. 1174 Moise; ca. 1174-ca. 1210 Aiyubid occupation; ca. 1210-ca. 1268 Yahya; ca. 1268-ca. 1274 David; ca. 1274-Apr. 1276 David II; Apr. 1276-ca. 1277 Shekanda; ca. 1277-1279 Mashqadat; 1279-1286 Barah; 1286-1293 Shamamun; 1293-1304 Mameluke occupation; 1304-1305 Amai; 1305-1312 Kudanbes; 1312-1323 Mameluke occupation.

Dunqulah see **Dongola**

290 Dutch African Republic. 17 Jan. 1852-16 Dec. 1856. *Location:* as **Potchefstroom.** *Capital:* Potchefstroom (for details on name see **Potchefstroom**). *Other names:* African Republic, South African Republic.

History: Formerly the Republic of Potchefstroom (see **Potchefstroom**) it became in 1856 the **South African Republic [i],** and its independence was recognized. The town of Pretoria was founded in 1855 (see **Transvaal [Self-Rule]** for details).

Commandants-General: 17 Jan. 1852-23 July 1853 Andries Pretorius; 23 July 1853-16 Dec. 1856 Marthinus Pretorius.

291 Dutch Cape Colony. 21 Feb. 1803-10 Jan. 1806. *Location:* as **British Cape Colony,** minus territory acquired later. *Capital:* Cape Town. *Other names:* Cape Colony, Cape of Good Hope.

History: In 1803, under the terms of the Treaty of Amiens at the end of the war between Holland and Britain, the Dutch (Batavian) Government took over control of the Cape, thus bringing to an end **British-Occupied Cape Colony [i].** In 1806 Britain took the Cape for the last time (see **British-Occupied Cape Colony [ii]**).

Commissioners-General: 21 Feb. 1803-25 Sept. 1804 Jacob de Mist. *Governors:* 1 March 1803-10 Jan. 1806 Jan Janssens.

292 Dutch Gold Coast Settlements. 1598-21 Feb. 1871. *Location:* Ghana coast. *Capital:* Elmina (from 1637); Moree (1598-1637).

History: In 1598 the Dutch arrived at the Gold Coast. In 1637 they captured the Portuguese fort of Elmina, and in 1642 they expelled the Portuguese entirely from the Gold Coast (see **Portuguese Gold Coast Settlements**). In the 1860s they began selling their posts to the British while it was **Gold Coast Territory,** and by 1871 had moved out of the Gold Coast. Their major posts were Elmina, Axim, Kormantin, Accra and Takoradi.

Directors-General: 1598–1624 unknown rulers; 1624–1 Oct. 1638 Adriaan Jacobs; 1 Oct. 1638–18 July 1639 Nikolaas Van Ypren; 18 July 1639–6 Jan. 1641 Arend Montfort; 6 Jan. 1641–18 Dec. 1645 Jacob Ruyghaver; 18 Dec. 1645–9 Apr. 1650 Jacob Van Der Well; 9 Apr. 1650–11 June 1650 Hendrik Doedens. *Governors:* 11 June 1650–15 March 1651 Arent Cocq. *Directors-General:* 15 March 1651–24 Jan. 1656 Jacob Ruyghaver; 24 Jan. 1656–27 Apr. 1659 Jean Valkenburg; 27 Apr. 1659–7 Apr. 1662 Jasper Van Houssen; 7 Apr. 1662–23 Dec. 1662 Dirk Wilré; 23 Dec. 1662–2 June 1667 Jean Valkenburg. *Governors:* 2 June 1667–12 Dec. 1668 Huybert Van Ongerdonk. *Directors-General:* 12 Dec. 1668–12 June 1675 Dirk Wilré; 12 June 1675–13 Sept. 1676 Johan Root; 13 Sept. 1676–26 March 1680 Abraham Meermans; 26 March 1680–1 Aug. 1683 Daniel Verhoutert; 1 Aug. 1683–15 July 1685 Thomas Ernsthuis; 15 July 1685–29 Jan. 1690 Nikolaas Sweerts; 29 Jan. 1690–25 March 1694 Joel Smits; 25 March 1694–9 June 1696 Jan Staphorst; 9 June 1696–2 June 1702 Jan Van Sevenhuysen; 2 June 1702–5 Nov. 1705 Willem de la Palma; 5 Nov. 1705–10 Oct. 1708 Pieter Nuyts. *Governors:* 10 Oct. 1708–14 Aug. 1709 Henrikus Van Wiessel. *Directors-General:* 14 Aug. 1709–16 Apr. 1711 Adriaan Schoonheidt; 16 Apr. 1711–11 June 1716 Hieronimus Haring; 11 June 1716–9 Apr. 1718 Abraham Robberts; 9 Apr. 1718–14 Oct. 1722 Willem Bullier; 14 Oct. 1722–28 May 1723 Abraham Houtman. *Governors:* 28 May 1723–14 Dec. 1723 Mattheus de Kraane. *Directors-General:* 14 Dec. 1723–11 March 1727 Pieter Valkenier; 11 March 1727–6 March 1730 Robert Norri; 6 March 1730–13 March 1734 Jan Pranger; 13 March 1734–21 Feb. 1736 Antonius Van Overbeek; 21 Feb. 1736–15 Oct. 1736 [unknown]; 15 Oct. 1736–16 March 1740 Francis de Bordes. *Governors:* 17 March 1740–7

March 1741 Francis Barbrius. *Directors-General:* 8 March 1741–11 Apr. 1747 Baron Jacob de Petersen; 11 Apr. 1747–14 July 1754 Jan Van Voorst; 14 July 1754–24 Oct. 1755 Nikolaas Van Der Nood de Gieterre. *Governors:* 25 Oct. 1755–16 Jan. 1758 Roelof Ulsen. *Directors-General:* 16 Jan. 1758–12 March 1759 Lambert Van Tets; 13 March 1759–2 March 1760 Jan Huydecooper; 2 March 1760–10 July 1763 David Erasmi. *Governors:* 11 July 1763–31 Aug. 1764 Hendrik Walmbeek. *Directors-General:* 31 Aug. 1764–11 Sept. 1764 [unknown]; 11 Sept. 1764–8 June 1767 Jan Huydecooper. *Governors-General:* 8 June 1767–10 June 1769 Jan Huydecooper. *Directors-General:* 10 June 1769–11 Apr. 1780 Pieter Woortman; 11 Apr. 1780–10 May 1780 [unknown]. *Governors:* 10 May 1780–30 Dec. 1780 Jacobus Van Der Puye. *Directors-General:* 30 Dec. 1780–12 March 1784 Pieter Volkmar. *Governors-General:* 15 March 1784–14 Feb. 1785 Servaas Gallé. *Directors-General:* 14 Feb. 1785–26 May 1786 Adolph Thierens. *Governors-General:* 2 June 1786–24 Aug. 1787 Servaas Gallé. *Presidents:* 8 Sept. 1787–19 March 1790 Lieven Van Burgen Van Der Grijp. *Directors-General:* 19 March 1790–23 March 1794 Jacobus de Veer; 23 March 1794–26 May 1794 [unknown]. *Presidents:* 26 May 1794–10 Jan. 1795 Lieven Van Burgen Van Der Grijp. *Governors:* 10 Jan. 1795–3 June 1796 Otto Duim. *Directors-General:* 3 June 1796–10 Aug. 1796 [unknown]; 10 Aug. 1796–1 May 1798 Gerhardus Van Hamel. *Governors-General:* 8 May 1798–28 Apr. 1804 Cornelis Bartels. *Presidents:* 29 Apr. 1804–15 June 1805 Izaak de Roever. *Governors-General:* 16 June 1805–21 July 1807 Pieter Linthorst. *Presidents:* 22 July 1807–11 Aug. 1808 Johannes Hoogenboom. *Directors-General:* 12 Aug. 1808–23 Feb. 1810 Jan Koning. *Commandants-General:* 23 Feb. 1810–1 March 1816 Abraham de Veer. *Governors-General:* 1 March 1816–22 Apr. 1818 Herman Daendels.

Presidents: 22 Apr. 1818–10 Jan. 1820 Frantz Christian Oldenborg. *Commanders/Presidents:* 10 Jan. 1820–27 July 1821 Johannes Oosthout. *Commanders:* 27 July 1821–11 Jan. 1823 Frederick Last (acting); 11 Jan. 1823–6 May 1823 Librecht Timmink (acting); 6 May 1823–14 May 1824 Willem Poolman; 14 May 1824–25 Dec. 1824 Hendrik Mouwe (acting); 25 Dec. 1824–2 Jan. 1825 Johan Pagenstecher (acting); 2 Jan. 1825–12 Nov. 1826 Frederick Last (acting); 12 Nov. 1826–4 Oct. 1828 Jacobus Van Der Breggen Paauw (acting); 4 Oct. 1828–17 Apr. 1833 Frederick Last; 17 Apr. 1833–17 May 1833 Jan Cremer (acting); 17 May 1833–2 Feb. 1834 Eduard Van Ingen (acting); 2 Feb. 1834–16 March 1834 Marthinus Swarte (acting); 16 March 1834–2 Dec. 1836 Christiaan Lans; 2 Dec. 1836–28 Oct. 1837 Hendrikus Tonneboeijer (acting); 29 Oct. 1837–5 Aug. 1838 Anthony Van Der Eb (acting). *Governors:* 5 Aug. 1838–7 March 1840 Hendrik Bosch; 7 March 1840–1846 Anthony Van Der Eb; 1846– 1847 W.G.F. Derx; 1847–1852 Anthony Van Der Eb; 1852–1856 Hero Schomerus; 1856–1856 P.J. Runckel; 1856–1857 W.G.F. Derx; 1857–1857 Jules Van Der Bossche; 1857–1862 Cornelis Nagtglas; 1862–1865 Col. Henry Elias; 1865–1866 A. Magnin; 1866–1867 Willem Van Idzinga; 1867–1869 Col. Georg Boers; 1869–1871 Cornelis Nagtglas; 1871–1871 Jan Hugenholz; 1871–21 Feb. 1871 Jan Fergusson (acting).

293 Dutch Mauritius [i]. 1598–31 July 1638. *Location:* as **Mauritius.** *Capital:* none. *Other names:* Mauritius.

History: Mauritius was discovered in 1507 by the Portuguese and named **Ilha do Cerne.** In 1598 the Dutch took possession and re-named it Mauritius, after Maurits von Nassau, Stadholder of Holland. It remained uninhabited (except by dodoes) until 1638, when it became a Dutch colony (see **Dutch Mauritius Colony [i]**).

Rulers: none.

294 Dutch Mauritius [ii]. 1658–1664. *Location:* as **Mauritius.** *Capital:* none. *Other names:* Mauritius.

History: In 1658 the Dutch abandoned Mauritius (see **Dutch Mauritius Colony [i]** in favor of the **Cape of Good Hope Colony,** which served as a way-station en route to the East. In 1664 it was partially re-settled (see **Dutch Mauritius Colony [ii]**).

Rulers: none.

295 Dutch Mauritius Colony [i]. 31 July 1638–1658. *Location:* as **Mauritius.** *Capital:* no central capital. *Other names:* Mauritius.

History: In 1638 the Dutch occupied Mauritius, which had been their property since 1598 (see **Dutch Mauritius [i]**). In 1658 they abandoned it (see **Dutch Mauritius [ii]**).

Commanders: 31 July 1638–1639 Cornelis Goyer; 1639–1645 Adriaan Van Der Stel; 1645–1648 Jacob Van Der Meerschen; 1648–1653 Reinier Por; 1653–1654 Jost Van Der Woutbeek (joint); 1653–1654 Maximilian de Jongh (joint); 1654–1656 Maximilian de Jongh; 1656–1658 Abraham Evertszoon.

296 Dutch Mauritius Colony [ii]. 1664–1710. *Location:* as **Mauritius.** *Capital:* no central capital. *Other names:* Mauritius.

History: In 1664 the Dutch partially resettled the island they had abandoned six years before as useless. In 1710 they finally got out, leaving it vacant until the French claimed it in 1715 (see **French Mauritius**).

Commanders: 1664–1664 Jacobus Nieuwland; 1664–1665 [unknown]; 1665–1667 Georg Wreede; 1667–1668 Jan Van Laar; 1668–1669 Dirk Smient; 1669–1672 Georg Wreede; 1672–1673 Pieter Col; 1673–1677 Hubert Hugo; 1677–1692 Isaäc Lamotius; 1692–1703 Roelof Dieodati; 1703–1710 Abraham Van de Velde.

297 Dutch West Africa. 1641–1648.

Location: the coastal areas of Angola. *Capital:* Luanda. *Other names:* Luanda.

History: In 1641 the Dutch, in their war against the Portuguese, captured the coastal areas of **Portuguese West Africa,** including Benguela and the capital Luanda. In 1648 the Portuguese, who had been pushed into the interior, recovered their possessions.

Directors: 1641–1642 Pieter Moorthamer; 1642–1648 Cornelis Ouman.

298 Dyolof. ca. 1350–July 1889. *Location:* Senegal. *Capital:* Linger (or Linguère). *Other names:* Djolof, Ouolof, Wolof Empire.

History: Founded about 1350, Dyolof lasted 500 years before becoming part of **Senegal Colony** in 1889.

Burbas (Kings): ca. 1350–ca. 1370 N'Dyadya N'Dyaye; ca. 1370–ca. 1390 Sare N'Dyaye; ca. 1390–ca. 1420 N'Diklam Sare; ca. 1420–ca. 1440 Tyukuli N'Diklan; ca. 1440–ca. 1450 Leeyti Tyukuli; ca. 1450–ca. 1465 N'Dyelen Mbey Leeyti; ca. 1465–ca. 1481 Birayma N'Dyeme Eter; ca. 1481–ca. 1488 Tase Daagulen; ca. 1488–ca. 1492 Birayma Kuran Kan; ca. 1492–ca. 1527 Bukaar Biye-Sungule; ca. 1527–ca. 1543 Birayma Dyeme-Kumba; ca. 1543–ca. 1549 Leele Fuli Fak; ca. 1549–ca. 1566 al-Buri Penda; ca. 1566–ca. 1597 Lat-Samba; ca. 1597–ca. 1605 Gireun Buri Dyelen; ca. 1605–ca. 1649 Birayma Penda; ca. 1649–ca. 1670 Birayma Mba; ca. 1670–ca. 1711 Bakar Penda; ca. 1711–ca. 1721 Bakan-Tam Gan; ca. 1721–ca. 1740 al-Buri Dyakher; ca. 1740–ca. 1748 Birayamb; ca. 1748–ca. 1750 Birawa Keme; ca. 1750–ca. 1755 Lat-Kodu; ca. 1755–ca. 1763 Bakaa-Tam Buri-Nyabu; ca. 1763–ca. 1800 Mba Kompaas; ca. 1800–ca. 1818 Mba Buri-Nyabu; ca. 1818–ca. 1838 Birayamb Kumba-Gey; ca. 1838–1845 al-Buri Tam; 1845–1847 Baka Kodu; 1847–1849 Birayamb Aram; 1849–1849 Birayma-Penda; 1849–1849 Mbanyi Paate; 1849–1849 Lat-Koddu; 1849–1850 interregnum; 1850–1855 Birayamb Ma-Dyigen; 1855–1856 al-Buri Peya Birayma; 1856–1858 Bakan-Tam Yaago; 1858–1863 Taanor; 1863–1871 Bakan-Tam Khaari; 1871–1875 Amadou Seeku; 1875–May 1890 Ali Buri N'Dyaye; 3 June 1890–3 Nov. 1895 Samba; 3 Nov. 1895–1900 Buuna.

East Africa see **British-, German-,** and **Portuguese East Africa**

East Mauretania see **Mauretania East**

299 East Nupe. 1796–1805. *Location:* northern Nigeria. *Capital:* Gbara. *Other names:* Nupe East.

History: In 1796 **Nupe Kingdom [i]** temporarily split into two, **East Nupe** and **West Nupe,** due to civil war between the two inheriting brothers. East Nupe retained the capital of Gbara, while West Nupe was founded with its capital at Raba (see **West Nupe** for further details). In 1805 the two rival states were reunited as **Nupe Kingdom [ii].**

Sarkins Gbara: 1796–1805 Jimada. *Note:* Sarkins Gbara is the plural of Sarkin Gbara (king at Gbara).

East Pondoland see **Pondoland East**

Eastern Cape Province see **Queen Adelaide Land**

Eastern Nigeria see **Nigeria Eastern Region**

300 Edina. 1832–1837. *Location:* on the opposite bank of the St. John's River from **Bassa Cove,** Liberia. *Capital:* Edina. *Other names:* Edina Colony.

History: In 1832 Edina was formed as a colony, or settlement, by the New York and Pennsylvania Colonization Societies. In 1837 it became part of **Bassa Cove.**

Rulers: unknown.

301 Egba United Government. 1893–
16 Sept. 1914. *Location:* southwestern
Nigeria. *Capital:* Abeokuta. *Other
names:* Egba Kingdom, Egbaland.

History: In 1893 the King of **Abeokuta** signed an agreement with the British Government which recognized the
independence of the Egba United Government. In 1914 it became part of
Nigeria Colony and Protectorate.
Alakes (Kings): 1893–(?) [unknown];
(?)–16 Sept. 1914 Gbadebo.

Egwanga see **Opobo**

302 Egypt. See these **names:**
Arab Republic of Egypt (1971–   )
United Arab Republic (1958–1971)
Republic of Egypt (1953–1958)
Egyptian Kingdom (1922–1953)
Egyptian Protectorate (1914–1922)
British-Occupied Egypt (1882–1914)
Ottoman Egypt [ii] (1801–1882)
French Egypt (1798–1801)
Ottoman Egypt [i] (1517–1798)
Circassian Mameluke Empire (1382–
1517)
Bahrite Mameluke Empire (1250–
1382)
Aiyubid Empire (1171–1250)
Fatimid Egypt (969–1171)
Ikhshid Egypt (935–969)
Abbasid Egypt [ii] (905–935)
Tulunid Egypt (868–905)
Abbasid Egypt [i] (750–868)
Omayyad Egypt (658–750)
Egypt (Arab) (642–658)
Byzantine Egypt [ii] (628–642)
Persian Egypt (616–628)
Byzantine Egypt [i] (395–616)
Egyptian Diocese of Rome (330–395)
Roman Egypt (30 B.C.–330 A.D.)
Egypt of the Ptolemies (305 B.C.–30
B.C.)
Egyptian Satrapy (323 B.C.–305
B.C.)
Alexandrian Egypt (332 B.C.–323
B.C.)
Egypt (Persian Province) (335 B.C.–
332 B.C.)
Egypt of Khababasha (338 B.C.–335
B.C.)

Egypt   (Ancient) — Dynasties   1
through 31 have separate entries covering the period ca. 3100 B.C.–338 B.C.
Upper Egypt ([?]–ca. 3100 B.C.)
Lower Egypt ([?]–ca. 3100 B.C.)

303 Egypt, 1st Dynasty. ca. 3100
B.C.–ca. 2890 B.C. *Location:* as **Arab
Republic of Egypt,** with noted differ-
ences. [For the remainder of the An-
cient **Egypt** listings, this heading,
"Location," will be omitted]. *Capital*
possibly Memphis (formerly called
"White Wall"); possibly Thinis (or
Ijene). *Other names:* for the **Egypt**
listings of Ancient times, this heading,
"Other names," will be omitted.

History: About 3100 B.C. Menes is
believed to have united **Lower Egypt**
and **Upper Egypt.** The dates, of course,
are very uncertain and highly speculative as far as accuracy is concerned, but
must have been in the general area of
time proposed. Menes's identity, and
even his existence, is doubted in many
areas of research, but someone united
the two kingdoms, and almost over-
night Egypt became a country of great
sophistication during the First Dynasty. About 2890 B.C. came **Egypt,
2nd Dynasty.**

Kings: ca. 3100 B.C. Menes (or
Narmer, or Min, or Meni); (?)–(?) Aha;
(?)–(?) Djer; (?)–(?) Djet; (?)–(?) Den;
(?)–(?) Anedjib; (?)–(?) Semerkhet;
(?)–ca. 2890 B.C. Qa'a.

Note: The Egyptians called their
country "Keme" or "Kmt" ("the black
land") because of the black alluvial soil
on the banks of the Nile. Egypt is from
the Greek "Aigiptos."

304 Egypt, 2nd Dynasty. ca. 2890
B.C.–ca. 2686 B.C. *Capital:* as **Egypt,
1st Dynasty.**

History: Successor to **Egypt, 1st
Dynasty.** The reasons for a change of
dynasty are not clear. Possibly a south-
north struggle, which led to a re-
unification under the first king of the
2nd Dynasty. By 2686 B.C. the dynasty
had come to an end, and the Old

Kingdom had begun (see **Egypt, 3rd Dynasty**).

Kings: ca. 2890 B.C.–(?) Hetepsekhemwy; (?)–(?) Re'neb; (?)–(?) Ninetjer; (?)–(?) Weneg; (?)–(?) Sened; (?)–(?) Peribsen; (?)–(?) Khasekhem; (?)–ca. 2686 B.C. Khasekhemwy (maybe the above).

305 Egypt, 3rd Dynasty. ca. 2686 B.C.–ca. 2613 B.C. *Capital:* Memphis (without doubt).

History: Successor to **Egypt, 2nd Dynasty,** this was the first dynasty of the so-called Old Kingdom. During the life of the dynasty Djoser built the Step Pyramid at Saqqarah, the first monument of any great size to be built completely of stone (Imhotep was the architect). Other pyramids were built during this dynasty. It was Djoser who fixed Egypt's southern boundary at the First Cataract. Succeeded by **Egypt, 4th Dynasty.**

Kings: ca. 2686 B.C.–ca. 2680 B.C. Sanakht; ca. 2680 B.C.–ca. 2661 B.C. Djoser (or Zoser); ca. 2661 B.C.–(?) Sekhemkhet; (?)–(?) Kha'ba; (?)–ca. 2613 B.C. Huni.

306 Egypt, 4th Dynasty. ca. 2613 B.C.–ca. 2496 B.C. *Capital:* Memphis.

History: Successor to **Egypt, 3rd Dynasty,** this was the great dynasty, the Golden Age of Pyramid building at Giza (pyramids proper as opposed to step pyramids), the dynasty which included Snefru and Khufu among its kings, expansion of territory, strong centralized government, peace and prosperity, innovation and huge technological advance. Succeeded by **Egypt, 5th Dynasty.**

Kings: ca. 2613 B.C.–ca. 2589 B.C. Snefru (or Snofru); ca. 2589 B.C.–ca. 2558 B.C. Khufu (or Cheops); ca. 2558 B.C.–ca. 2549 B.C. Ra'djedef; ca. 2549 B.C.–ca. 2530 B.C. Khafre (or Chephren); ca. 2530 B.C.–ca. 2512 B.C. Menkaure (or Mycerinus); ca. 2512 B.C.–ca. 2496 B.C. Shepsekaf.

307 Egypt, 5th Dynasty. ca. 2496 B.C.–ca. 2345 B.C. *Capital:* Memphis.

History: Successor to **Egypt, 4th Dynasty.** This was the dynasty which emphasized the cult of Ra (or Re) the Sun-God, at Heliopolis, and which built its tombs south of Giza, at Abu-Sir. Succeeded by **Egypt, 6th Dynasty.**

Kings: ca. 2496 B.C.–(?) Userkaf; (?)–(?) Sahure; (?)–(?) Neferirkare; (?)–(?) Shepseskare; (?)–(?) Neferefre; (?)–(?) Niuserre; (?)–(?) Menkauhor; (?)–(?) Djedkare Izezi; (?)–ca. 2345 B.C. Unas (or Unis).

308 Egypt, 6th Dynasty. ca. 2345 B.C.–ca. 2181 B.C. *Capital:* Memphis.

History: The government was decentralized in this dynasty, the successor to **Egypt, 5th Dynasty.** This led to provincial governorates, responsible to the king. The nomarchs (rulers of these governorates or nomes) gradually assumed more and more power. Trade with **Nubia** to the south was stepped up, and the nomarch of Elephantine (the southern boundary of Egypt at that time) was made governor of all Upper Egypt. Succeeded by **Egypt, 7th Dynasty.**

Kings: ca. 2345 B.C.–ca. 2340 B.C. Teti; ca. 2340 B.C.–ca. 2335 B.C. Userkare; ca. 2335 B.C.–ca. 2286 B.C. Pepi I Meryre; ca. 2286 B.C.–ca. 2281 B.C. Antyemsaf I Merenre; ca. 2281 B.C.–ca. 2187 B.C. Pepi II Neferkare; ca. 2187 B.C.–ca. 2184 B.C. Antyemsaf II Merenre; ca. 2184 B.C.–ca. 2182 B.C. Netjerykare; ca. 2182 B.C.–ca. 2181 B.C. Menkare. *Note:* Pepi II is said to have reigned 94 years.

309 Egypt, 7th Dynasty. ca. 2181 B.C.–ca. 2174 B.C. *Capital:* Memphis (?).

History: Successor to **Egypt, 6th Dynasty,** it is not known how long this dynasty lasted, or indeed, what the dynasty was. With the breakdown of centralized government in Egypt during the 6th Dynasty, and the establishment of powerful nomarchs throughout

Upper and Lower Egypt (especially the former), it seems likely that the 7th Dynasty was a line of kings or princes of Memphis, who survived only short terms at the helm of a nominal government. The country was in much confusion, and all direction was gone. The 7th Dynasty may have been succeeded by the 8th (see **Egypt, 8th Dynasty**).
Kings: unknown.

310 Egypt, 8th Dynasty. ca. 2174 B.C.–ca. 2160 B.C. *Capital:* Memphis (?).
History: Nothing much more is known about this dynasty than about its possible predecessor, **Egypt, 7th Dynasty.** They were probably based out of Memphis, and controlled a certain amount of Upper and Lower Egypt, but really Egypt was in the hands of the nomarchs. Succeeded by **Egypt, 9th Dynasty.**
Kings: unknown.

311 Egypt, 9th Dynasty. ca. 2160 B.C.–ca. 2130 B.C. *Capital:* Neni-Nesu (Greek – Heracleopolis).
History: This dynasty, the successor to **Egypt, 8th Dynasty** is an unclear one in history, but begins with Akhtoy, nomarch of Heracleopolis in Upper Egypt, who, about 2160 B.C. declared himself King of Egypt, and began to weld the neighboring nomes together. He took most of Egypt, but his successors did not have the same energy, and twilight falls over the rest of the dynasty, which marked the beginning of what is called The First Intermediate Period. It was followed by **Egypt, 10th Dynasty.**
Kings: ca. 2160 B.C.–(?) Akhtoy (or Achthoes); (?)–ca. 2130 B.C. unknown names of indeterminate number of kings.

312 Egypt, 10th Dynasty. ca. 2130 B.C.–ca. 2040 B.C. *Capital:* Neni-Nesu (Greek – Heracleopolis).
History: An extension of **Egypt, 9th Dynasty**, the 10th Dynasty created a

certain stability in the country, but failed to reunite Egypt as one nation. The rise of Thebes in the south happened during this dynasty, when Mentuhotep I became not only the founder of the 11th Dynasty, but ruler of Upper Egypt (see **Egypt, 11th Dynasty**).
Kings: indeterminate number of unknown names until
(?)–(?) Merikare
who was followed by one other king before the next dynasty took over.

313 Egypt, 11th Dynasty. ca. 2040 B.C.–ca. 1991 B.C. *Capital:* Nowe (or Nuwe) (Greek – Thebes).
History: About 2040 B.C. the rulers of Southern (or Upper) Egypt, who were based at Thebes, conquered the Delta, and re-unified the country (see **Egypt, 10th Dynasty**) under Mentuhotep II. His dynasty had been founded in the Nome of Thebes about 2133 B.C. 2040 B.C. also marks the beginning of what is called The Middle Kingdom. Succeeded by **Egypt, 12th Dynasty.**
Kings: ca. 2040 B.C.–ca. 2009 B.C. Mentuhotep II Nebhepetre; ca. 2009 B.C.–ca. 1997 B.C. Mentuhotep III Sankhkare; ca. 1997 B.C.–ca. 1991 B.C. Mentuhotep IV Nebtowere.
Note: The Theban Dynasty which ruled in Upper Egypt from about 2133 B.C. until the re-unification of Egypt in about 2040 B.C. was as follows:
Kings of Upper Egypt: ca. 2133 B.C.–ca. 2117 B.C. Mentuhotep I; ca. 2133 B.C.–ca. 2117 B.C. Sehertowy Intef; ca. 2117 B.C.–ca. 2068 B.C. Intef II; ca. 2068 B.C.–ca. 2060 B.C. Intef III; ca. 2060 B.C.–ca. 2040 B.C. Mentuhotep II Nebhepetre.

314 Egypt, 12th Dynasty. ca. 1991 B.C.–ca. 1786 B.C. *Capital:* Itj-Towy (it is near al-Fayyum, and is now called al-Lisht).
History: About 1991 B.C. the vizier of Egypt, Amenemhet, who was also Governor of Upper Egypt, seized the throne and established his own dy-

nasty, a great dynasty and moved his family to Itj-Towy. It was during this dynasty that contact with Asia and the Aegean flourished in a big way for the first time. At home the nomes were abolished, and the country split into three regions, all responsible to the vizier. During this dynasty the southern boundary reached the 2nd Cataract. The arts flourished as never before and peace and prosperity reigned. The cult of Osiris reached its peak. This dynasty succeeded **Egypt, 11th Dynasty** and in turn was succeeded by **Egypt, 13th Dynasty,** and its end marked the beginning of the Second Intermediate Period of Egyptian history.

Kings: ca. 1991 B.C.–ca. 1962 B.C. Amenemhet I Shetepibre; ca. 1972 B.C.–ca. 1928 B.C. Sesostris (or Senwosre) I Kheperkare; ca. 1929 B.C.–ca. 1895 B.C. Amenemhet II Nubkaure; ca. 1897 B.C.–ca. 1878 B.C. Sesostris (or Senwosre) II Khakheperre; ca. 1878 B.C.–ca. 1842 B.C. Sesostris (or Senwosre) III Khakaure; ca. 1842 B.C.–ca. 1798 B.C. Amenemhet III Nemare; ca. 1798 B.C.–ca. 1789 B.C. Amenemhet IV Makherure. *Queens:* ca. 1789 B.C.–ca. 1786 B.C. Sebekhnofru Sebbekhare.

315 Egypt, 13th Dynasty. ca. 1786 B.C.–ca. 1674 B.C. *Capital:* as **Egypt, 12th Dynasty.**

History: Successor to **Egypt, 12th Dynasty,** the 13th Dynasty controlled Egypt much as before, for about a hundred years, but gradually central control was lost. The 14th Dynasty (see **Egypt, 14th Dynasty**) co-existed with it for its entire duration, but the main threat was from Asiatics encouraged in the last dynasty. Grouped around the eastern Delta region, the Hyksos took over Egypt around 1674 B.C. (see **Egypt, 15th Dynasty**).

Kings: ca. 1786 B.C.–(?) Sebekhotep I; (?)–(?) Amenemhet V Sekhemkare; (?)–(?) Amenemhet VI Sehetepibre; (?)–(?) Sankhibre; (?)–(?) Hetepibre; (?)–(?) Sebekhotep II; (?)–(?) Rense-

neb; (?)–(?) Awibre Hor; (?)–(?) Sedjefakare; (?)–(?) Khutowere; (?)–(?) Sesostris (or Senwosre) IV Seneferibre; (?)–(?) Userkare Khendjer; (?)–(?) Semenkhkare; (?)–(?) Sebekemsaf I Sekhemre Wadjkhau; (?)–(?) Sebekhotep III Sekhemre Sewadjtowy; (?)–(?) Ncferholep I Khasekhemre; (?)–(?) Sebekhotep V Khaankre; (?)–(?) Neferhotep II Mersekhemre; (?)–(?) Sebekhotep VI Khahotepre; (?)–(?) Neferhotep III Sekhemre Sankhtowy; (?)–(?) Wahibre Iayeb; (?)–(?) Merneferre Iy; (?)–(?) Merhetepre Ini; (?)–ca. 1674 B.C. Djedneferre Dudimose.

316 Egypt, 14th Dynasty. ca. 1786 B.C.–ca. 1602 B.C. *Capital:* Xois (in the western Delta).

History: According to tradition a dynasty existed, based in the western Delta area, around the town of Xois. It lasted 184 years and had 76 kings. As it corresponded with a viable 13th Dynasty (see **Egypt, 13th Dynasty**) it can only have been of local importance, if it existed at all. It would have continued into the period of the 'Great Hyksos' (see **Egypt, 15th Dynasty**).

Rulers: unknown.

317 Egypt, 15th Dynasty. ca. 1674 B.C.–ca. 1567 B.C. *Capital:* Avaris.

History: About 1720 B.C. the Asiatics living in the eastern Delta area occupied the town of Avaris and formed the Seth Cult. As central administration during the last part of the 13th Dynasty (see **Egypt, 13th Dynasty**) weakened, so the power of the Asiatics grew. About 1674 B.C. Memphis was taken by them, and the Dynasty of the 'Great Hyksos' (as opposed to the 'Minor Hyksos'—see **Egypt, 16th Dynasty**) began. The name 'Hyksos' was given to these Asiatic rulers many centuries later, and means 'Shepherd Kings,' the name coming probably from the Egyptian 'heqa-khase' or 'ruler of a foreign principality.' They introduced the horse and chariot into

Egypt, and were Semitic peoples. It is doubtful whether they ruled all of Egypt—probably only Lower Egypt. About 1567 B.C. the dynasty crumbled when the (17th Dynasty) rulers of Upper Egypt, at Thebes, gradually extended control northward, and in 1552 B.C. formed the 18th Dynasty, and unified the country. (See **Egypt, 14th Dynasty; Egypt, 16th Dynasty; Egypt 17th Dynasty; Egypt, 18th Dynasty**).

Kings: ca. 1674 B.C.-(?) Mayebre Sheshi (or Salitis); (?)-(?) Meruserre Yakhuber; (?)-(?) Sewesewenre Khayan; (?)-(?) Auserre Apopi I; (?)-(?) Ahenenre Apopi II; (?)-ca. 1567 B.C. Asehere Khamudy.

318 Egypt, 16th Dynasty. ca. 1674 B.C.-ca. 1567 B.C. *Capital:* somewhere in the eastern Delta.

History: Contemporaneous with the 15th Dynasty (see **Egypt, 15th Dynasty**) there existed a second line of Hyksos rulers, called the 'Minor Hyksos,' to distinguish them from the 'Great Hyksos' of the 15th Dynasty. Not much is known of this dynasty, and by 1567 B.C. the Hyksos sway in both dynasties was finished, and the 18th Dynasty (see **Egypt, 18th Dynasty**) was ruling from Thebes.

Rulers: unknown.

319 Egypt, 17th Dynasty. ca. 1650 B.C.-ca. 1567 B.C. *Capital:* as **Egypt, 12th Dynasty.**

History: Probably descended from the 13th Dynasty rulers (see **Egypt, 13th Dynasty**), this dynasty ruled Southern, or Upper, Egypt from about 1650 B.C., as rivals (or colleagues) of the Hyksos kings further north (see **Egypt, 15th Dynasty**). By 1567 B.C. they had taken all of Egypt and united it, expelling the Hyksos after a war (see **Egypt, 18th Dynasty**).

Kings of Upper Egypt: ca. 1650 B.C. Sekhemre Wahkha Rahotep; (?)-(?) Sekhemre Wepmae Intef; (?)-(?) Sekhemre Herhimae Intef; (?)-(?) Sekhemre Shedtowe Sebekemsaf; (?)-(?)

Sekhemre Smentowe Djehuty; (?)-(?) Sankhenre Mentuhotep; (?)-(?) Swadjenre Nebirierau; (?)-(?) Neferkare Nebirierau; (?)-(?) Semenmedjatre; (?)-(?) Seuserenre; (?)-(?) Sekhemre Shedwast; (?)-(?) Nubkheperre Intef; (?)-(?) Senakhtenre; (?)-(?) Sekenenre Tao I; (?)-(?) Sekenenre Tao II; (?)-ca. 1570 B.C. Wadjkheperre Kamose; ca. 1570 B.C.-ca. 1567 B.C. Ahmose Nebpehtire.

320 Egypt, 18th Dynasty. ca. 1567 B.C.-ca. 1320 B.C. *Capital:* Thebes (ca. 1359 onward); Tell el-Amarna (or Akhenaton) (ca. 1374 B.C.-ca. 1359 B.C.); Memphis (ca. 1465 B.C.-ca. 1374 B.C.); Thebes (until ca. 1465 B.C.).

History: This was a direct continuation of **Egypt, 12th Dynasty,** but with the major difference being that Ahmose, the first ruler, unified Egypt again, after mopping up the Hyksos, whom his brother had routed around 1570 B.C. (see **Egypt, 15th Dynasty** and **Egypt, 17th Dynasty**), and thus beginning the period of Egyptian history known as the New Kingdom, with its capital at Thebes. This was the dynasty with the famous Pharaohs ("per'o" in Ancient Egyptian) or Kings—Thutmose III, the Amenhoteps (including Akhenaton) and best remembered of all, Tutankhamen. Wars increased territory (most of the Levant and Middle East) and revenue, and the pyramids gave way to rock-cut tombs as burial places for the kings. The southern boundary of the kingdom extended to the 4th Cataract during this dynasty. It was succeeded by **Egypt, 19th Dynasty.**

Kings: ca. 1567 B.C.-ca. 1546 B.C. Ahmose Nebpehtire; ca. 1546 B.C.-ca. 1526 B.C. Amenhotep I Djeserkare; ca. 1526 B.C.-ca. 1512 B.C. Thutmose I Akheperkare; ca. 1512 B.C.-ca. 1504 B.C. Thutmose II Akheperenre; ca. 1504 B.C.-ca. 1450 B.C. Thutmose III Mankheperre (he didn't become effective until ca. 1482 B.C.). *Queen Regent:* ca. 1504 B.C.-ca. 1482 B.C. Hatshepsut Makare (from ca. 1502 B.C.-ca.

1482 B.C. she ruled as effective king [sic]). *Kings:* ca. 1452 B.C.–ca. 1425 B.C. Amenhotep II Akheprure (joint until ca. 1450 B.C.); ca. 1425 B.C.–ca. 1417 B.C. Thutmose IV Menkheprure; ca. 1417 B.C.–ca. 1379 B.C. Amenhotep III Nebmare; ca. 1379–ca. 1374 B.C. Amenhotep IV Neferkheprure Waenre; ca. 1374 B.C.–ca. 1362 B.C. Akhenaton (formerly Amenhotep IV); ca. 1364 B.C.–ca. 1361 B.C. Smenkhare Ankheprure (joint until ca. 1362 B.C.); ca. 1361 B.C.–ca. 1359 B.C. Tutankhaton; ca. 1359 B.C.–ca. 1352 B.C. Tutankhamen Nebkheprure (formerly Tutankhaton); ca. 1352 B.C.–ca. 1348 B.C. Ay Kheperkheprure Itnute; ca. 1348 B.C.–ca. 1320 B.C. Horemheb Djeserkheprure.

321 Egypt, 19th Dynasty. ca. 1320 B.C.–ca. 1200 B.C. *Capital:* Pi-Ramesse (from ca. 1280 B.C.); Thebes (until ca. 1280 B.C.).

History: When Horemheb, the last of the 18th Dynasty Pharaohs (see **Egypt, 18th Dynasty**) died without male issue, he nominated his vizier (or wazir) Rameses to follow him on the throne. Wars with the Libyans and Hittites featured early in the dynasty. This was the time of the Biblical "Exodus," the relevant pharaoh probably being Merneptah. At the end of the dynasty myriad internal factions caused havoc and it was resolved by the 20th Dynasty (see **Egypt, 20th Dynasty**).

Pharaohs (Kings): ca. 1320 B.C.–ca. 1318 B.C. Rameses I Menpehtire; ca. 1318 B.C.–ca. 1304 B.C. Seti Menmare Merneptah; ca. 1304 B.C.–ca. 1237 B.C. Rameses II the Great Usermare Miamun; ca. 1237 B.C.–ca. 1223 B.C. Merneptah Binere Meryamun Hotphimae; ca. 1223 B.C.–ca. 1217 B.C. Amenmesse Menmire; ca. 1217 B.C.–ca. 1210 B.C. Seti II Usikheperure Merneptah; ca. 1210 B.C.–ca. 1203 B.C. Siptah Akhenre Merneptah. *King/Queen:* ca. 1203 B.C.–ca. 1200 B.C. Tausert (or Tewosre) Sitre Meryamun. *Note:* Tausert's gender is open to ques-

tion. Was she a queen who later revealed herself to be a king, was she both, or was she the widow of Siptah who ruled after he died? This last is the generally held theory.

322 Egypt, 20th Dynasty. ca. 1200 B.C.–ca. 1085 B.C. *Capital:* Pi-Ramesse.

History: Senakht, the founder of the dynasty, restored order after the havoc created at the end of **Egypt, 19th Dynasty**. His son, Rameses III, was the last great Pharaoh, and spent much of his reign repelling invasions. The rest of the dynasty saw the diminishing of the empire, and the rise of the highpriests in Egypt. On the death of Rameses XI, the Governor of Tanis, Smendes, became king (or Pharaoh), thus founding the 21st Dynasty (see **Egypt, 21st Dynasty**).

Pharaohs: ca. 1200 B.C.–ca. 1198 B.C. Senakht Userkhaure; ca. 1198 B.C.–ca. 1166 B.C. Rameses III Usermare Meryamun; ca. 1166 B.C.–ca. 1160 B.C. Rameses IV Hekamare Setpenamun; ca. 1160 B.C.–ca. 1156 B.C. Rameses V Usermare Sekhepereure; ca. 1156 B.C.–ca. 1148 B.C. Rameses VI Nebmare Meryamun; ca. 1148 B.C.–ca. 1145 B.C. Rameses VII Usermare Meryamun; ca. 1145 B.C.–ca. 1140 B.C. Rameses VIII Usermare Akhenamun; ca. 1140 B.C.–ca. 1121 B.C. Rameses IX Neferkare Setpenre; ca. 1121 B.C.–ca. 1113 B.C. Rameses X Khepermare Setpenre; ca. 1113 B.C.–ca. 1085 B.C. Rameses XI Menmare Setneptah.

323 Egypt, 21st Dynasty. ca. 1085 B.C.–945 B.C. *Capital:* Tanis.

History: During this dynasty, the successor to **Egypt, 20th Dynasty**, Egypt lost control of Nubia and its Asiatic empire. Pharaoh Siamon married his daughter to King Solomon of Israel. At Thebes a hereditary dynasty of highpriests developed late in the 20th Dynasty, and are often referred to as Dynasty 20 b. In 945 B.C. came the 22nd Dynasty (see **Egypt, 22nd Dynasty**).

Pharaohs: ca. 1085 B.C.–ca. 1059 B.C. Nesbanebded (or Smendes) Hedjkeperre; ca. 1059 B.C.–ca. 1054 B.C. Amenemnisu Hekawise Neferkare; ca. 1054 B.C.–ca. 1001 B.C. Psusennes I (or Psibkhaemne) Akheperre; ca. 1001 B.C.–ca. 983 B.C. Amenemope Usermare; ca. 983 B.C.–ca. 960 B.C. Siamon Nutekheperre; ca. 960 B.C.–945 B.C. Psusennes II (or Psibkhaemne) Titkheprure. *High Priests:* ca. 1094 B.C.–ca. 1087 B.C. Herihor; ca. 1087 B.C.–ca. 1074 B.C. Piankh; ca. 1074 B.C.–ca. 1050 B.C. Pinudjem I; ca. 1050 B.C.–(?) Menkheperre; (?)–(?) Nesbanebded; (?)–945 B.C. Pinudjem II.

324 Egypt, 22nd Dynasty. 945 B.C.–ca. 715 B.C. *Capital:* Bubastis.

History: In 945 B.C. Sheshonk, the leader of the Meshwesh Libyan captive race in Egypt took the throne and established the 22nd Dynasty, successor to **Egypt, 21st Dynasty.** He politically intermarried his people with the high-priest families of Thebes, thus trying to cement the whole kingdom. About 931 B.C. Sheshonk sacked Jerusalem. About 817 B.C. a rival dynasty sprang up in Thebes (see **Egypt, 23rd Dynasty**). About 715 B.C. both these dynasties, the 22nd and the 23rd, came to an end with the conquering of all Egypt by the 25th Dynasty (see **Egypt, 25th Dynasty**).

Kings: 945 B.C.–ca. 924 B.C. Sheshonk I Hedjkheperre (or Shishak); ca. 924 B.C.–ca. 890 B.C. Osorkhon I Sekhemkheperre; ca. 890 B.C.–ca. 889 B.C. Sheshonk II Hekenkheperre; ca. 889 B.C.–ca. 874 B.C. Takelot I Usermare; ca. 874 B.C.–ca. 850 B.C. Osorkhon II Usermare; ca. 850 B.C.–ca. 825 B.C. Takelot II Hedjkheperre; ca. 825 B.C.–ca. 773 B.C. Sheshonk III Usermare; ca. 773 B.C.–ca. 767 B.C. Pimay Usermare (or Pami); ca. 767 B.C.–ca. 730 B.C. Sheshonk V Akheperre; ca. 730 B.C.–ca. 715 B.C. Osorkhon IV Akheperre. *Note:* for Sheshonk IV see Egypt, 23rd Dynasty.

325 Egypt, 23rd Dynasty. ca. 817 B.C.–ca. 715 B.C. *Capital:* Thebes.

History: About 817 B.C. a 23rd, Theban, Dynasty arose in competition with the "official" dynasty of Egypt (see **Egypt, 22nd Dynasty**) at Tanis. About 730 B.C. the 24th Dynasty (see **Egypt, 24th Dynasty**) sprang up in the western Delta and tried to conquer Egypt. The Kushites (see **Kush** and **Egypt, 25th Dynasty**), founders of the 25th Dynasty in Egypt, countered from the south and defeated this rebel dynasty, and after another fifteen years of trouble from the 24th Dynasty, the 25th Dynasty took over Egypt (about 715 B.C.).

Kings: ca. 817 B.C.–ca. 793 B.C. Redebast Usermare (joint after ca. 804 B.C.); ca. 804 B.C.–ca. 783 B.C. Iuput I (joint until ca. 793 B.C.); ca. 783 B.C.–ca. 777 B.C. Sheshonk IV; ca. 777 B.C.–ca. 749 B.C. Osorkhon III (joint after 754 B.C.); ca. 754 B.C.–ca. 734 B.C. Takelot III (joint until ca. 749 B.C.); ca. 734 B.C.–ca. 731 B.C. Rudamen; ca. 731 B.C.–ca. 720 B.C. Iuput II; ca. 720 B.C.–ca. 715 B.C. Sheshonk VI.

326 Egypt, 24th Dynasty. ca. 730 B.C.–ca. 715 B.C. *Capital:* Sais.

History: About 730 B.C. the Libyan nobleman Tefnakhte tried to conquer Egypt from his base at Sais in the western Delta. He captured Memphis and proceeded south, to the annoyance of the Kushites (in modern day Sudan). Piy (or Piankhi), the Kushite King (see **Kush**) took Thebes in 730 and beat the northerners, retiring back to Kush. Tefnakhte then rebelled again and in 720 his son succeeded to the dynastic throne. This king was burned alive by Shabaka, the founder of the 25th Dynasty (see **Egypt, 25th Dynasty**). (See **Egypt, 23rd Dynasty** for information on Egypt just prior to 730 B.C.)

Kings: ca. 730 B.C.–ca. 720 B.C. Tefnakhte Shepsesre; ca. 720 B.C.–ca. 715 B.C. Bekenrinef (or Bocchoris) Wahkare.

327 Egypt, 25th Dynasty. ca. 715 B.C.–656 B.C. *Capital:* Thebes.

History: About 715 B.C. **Egypt, 24th Dynasty** and **Egypt, 23rd Dynasty** gave way to the 25th Dynasty—the Ethiopian Dynasty founded back in the early 8th Century (see **Kush**). King Shabaka of Kush (or Napata) became King of all Egypt about 715 B.C. Wars with Assyria were the main problem during this dynasty. About 656 B.C. the Assyrians finally kicked the Ethiopians out and returned to Assyria. Psamtik I of the Delta formed **Egypt, 26th Dynasty.**

Kings: ca. 715 B.C.–ca. 702 B.C. Shabaka; ca. 702 BC.–690 B.C. Shebitku; 690 B.C.–664 B.C. Taharqa; 664 B.C.–656 B.C. Tanuatamon.

328 Egypt, 26th Dynasty. 656 B.C.– 525 B.C. *Capital:* Sais.

History: In 656 B.C. Psamtik I, son of Necho (who had founded the dynasty around 668 B.C.) took all of Egypt (see **Egypt, 25th Dynasty**). There was a great Greek immigration during this period, as well as trading. In 525 B.C. the Persian Cambyses invaded and took Egypt (see **Egypt, 27th Dynasty**).

Kings: 664 B.C.–610 B.C. Psamtik I Wahibre; 610 B.C.–595 B.C. Necho II Wehembre; 595 B.C.–589 B.C. Psamtik II Neferibre; 589 B.C.–570 B.C. Apries (or Hophra, or Haaibre) Wahibre; 570 B.C.–526 B.C. Ahmose Khnemibre; 526 B.C.–525 B.C. Psamtik III Ankhkaenre.

329 Egypt, 27th Dynasty. 525 B.C.– 404 B.C. *Capital:* Memphis.

History: In 525 B.C. Cambyses conquered Egypt (see **Egypt, 26th Dynasty**) and it became a Persian province. Together with the Libyan oases and Cyrenaica, it formed the 6th Persian Satrapy. Until 486 B.C. the Persians governed it well, and with great tolerance, but that year Xerxes put down a rebellion in the Delta and from then on treated Egypt as a conquered province in fact as well as on papyrus. Xerxes was the first major Achaemenid ruler of Persia who never visited Egypt and he was assassinated in 465 B.C. This sparked off an Athenian-backed revolt in the Delta led by the Libyan Inaros, who, after 11 years of warfare was caught and crucified. Around 450 B.C. Herodotus made a celebrated trip to Egypt. In 404 B.C. came the 28th Dynasty (see **Egypt, 28th Dynasty**).

Emperors of Persia: 525 B.C.–1 July 522 B.C. Cambyses (or Kambujiyah II); 1 July 522 B.C.–522 B.C. Smerdis (or Bardiya-Gaumata); 522 B.C.–Nov. 486 B.C. Darius the Great (or Darayavahush I); Nov. 486 B.C.–Dec. 465 B.C. Xerxes I (or Khshayarsha I); Dec. 465 B.C.–424 B.C. Artaxerxes I (or Artakhshassa I); 424 B.C.–423 B.C. Xerxes II (or Khshayarsha II); 423 B.C.–July 423 B.C. Sogdianos; July 423 B.C.–March 404 B.C. Darius II (or Darayavahush II); March 404 B.C.–404 B.C. Artaxerxes II (or Artakhshassa II). *Governors:* 1 July 522 B.C.–517 B.C. Aryandes; 517 B.C.–485 B.C. Pherendates I; 485 B.C.–484 B.C. [unknown]; 484 B.C.–460 B.C. Achaimenes; 460 B.C.–404 B.C. [unknown].

330 Egypt, 28th Dynasty. 404 B.C.– 399 B.C. *Capital:* Sais.

History: In 404 B.C., with the Persians occupied elsewhere other than **Egypt, 27th Dynasty,** Amyrtaeus, a Libyan nobleman, revolted in the Delta after the death of Darius II in Persia. Amyrtaeus's rule was recognized all over Egypt. The dynasty was short-lived, and supplanted by **Egypt, 29th Dynasty.**

Kings: 404 B.C.–399 B.C. Amyrtaeus (or Amonirdisu).

331 Egypt, 29th Dynasty. 399 B.C.– 380 B.C. *Capital:* Mendes.

History: In 399 B.C. **Egypt, 28th Dynasty** came to an end, and a new one appeared out of the eastern Delta city of Mendes. This dynasty (under

Achoris) forged close political and military links with Greece in order to repel the Persians. In 380 B.C. came **Egypt, 30th Dynasty.**

Kings: 399 B.C.-393 B.C. Nefaurud (or Nepherites I); 393 B.C.-393 B.C. Setneptah Usire Pshenmut; 393 B.C.-380 B.C. Achoris (or Hakor) Khnemmaere; 380 B.C.-380 B.C. Nefaurud (or Nepherites II).

332 Egypt, 30th Dynasty. 380 B.C.-343 B.C. *Capital:* Sebennytus.

History: In 380 B.C. **Egypt, 29th Dynasty** came to an end when General Nectanebo usurped the throne and established his own dynasty. Much building took place during the dynasty, as well as three Persian invasions — the third, in 343 B.C. succeeding, Nectarebe the King fleeing to Nubia. Then came **Egypt, 31st Dynasty.**

Kings: 380 B.C.-362 B.C. Nectanebo (or Nekhtnebef Kheperkhare); 362 B.C.-360 B.C. Setpenanhur Irmaenre Djeho (or Takhos); 360 B.C.-343 B.C. Nectarebe (or Nekhtharehbe Snedjembre).

333 Egypt, 31st Dynasty. 343 B.C.-338 B.C. *Capital:* Sebennytus.

History: In 343 B.C. the Persians retook Egypt (see **Egypt, 30th Dynasty**), and the new 31st Dynasty was to last a mere five years before a Nubian prince named Khababasha gained control of Egypt for three years (see **Egypt of Khababasha**).

Persian Emperors: 343 B.C.-Sept. 338 B.C. Artaxerxes III (or Artakhshassa III); Sept. 338 B.C.-338 B.C. Arsha. *Governors:* 343 B.C.-338 B.C. Pherendates II.

334 Egypt (Arab). 17 Sept. 642-July 658. *Location:* Egypt. *Capital:* al-Fustat. *Other names:* Egypt.

History: In 639 the Arabs began an assault on **Byzantine Egypt [ii]**, and under Amr ibn al-As had conquered it by 642, and the Byzantines had gone. In 645 the Byzantines attempted to recapture Alexandria (their former Egyptian capital), but were quickly put down by the Arabs. The Muslims changed little of Byzantine provincial rule. They moved the capital to al-Fustat. In 658 the first of the Omayyad governors assumed office (see **Omayyad Egypt**).

Governors: 17 Sept. 642-644 Amr ibn al-As (or al-Asi); 644-654 Abdallah ibn Sa'd; 654-655 Keys ibn Sa'd; 655-656 Abdallah ibn Sa'd; 656-July 658 Muhammad ibn Abu Bakr.

335 Egypt of Khababasha. 338 B.C.-335 B.C. *Location:* as Egypt. *Capital:* Memphis. *Other names:* Hababasha's Egypt, Khababasha's Egypt.

History: In 338 B.C., after the death of Artaxerxes III, Emperor of Persia, **Egypt, 31st Dynasty** fell to a Nubian prince named Khababasha. By 335 B.C., however, Persia had regained control (see **Egypt [Persian Province]**).

Kings: 338 B.C.-335 B.C. Khababasha.

336 Egypt of the Ptolemies. 7 Nov. 305 B.C.-12 Aug. 30 B.C. *Location:* as Egypt. *Capital:* Alexandria. *Other names:* Egypt, Lagid Egypt, Ptolemaic Egypt, Egypt of the Lagids (Lagus was father of Ptolemy I).

History: In 305 B.C. Ptolemy I, the Alexandrine satrap of Egypt (see **Egyptian Satrapy**), became king and began the Ptolemaic dynasty, which was to rule Egypt until 30 B.C., when it became a Roman province (see **Roman Egypt**).

Kings: 7 Nov. 305 B.C.-ca. Jan. 282 B.C. Ptolemy I Soter I (called Soter only after 304 B.C.). *Queens:* 290 B.C.-ca. Jan. 282 B.C. Berenice I. *Kings:* 26 June 285 B.C.-24 Oct. 247 B.C. Ptolemy II Philadelphus. *Queens:* ca. 277 B.C.-July 270 B.C. Arsinoe II. *Kings:* 24 Oct. 247 B.C.-18 Oct. 221 B.C. Ptolemy III Euergetes I. *Queens:* 245 B.C.-18 Oct. 221 B.C. Berenice II. *Kings:* 18 Oct. 221 B.C.-28 Nov. 205

B.C. Ptolemy IV Philopator. *Queens:* 217 B.C.-204 B.C. Arsinoe III. *Kings:* 28 Nov. 205 B.C.-ca. May 180 B.C. Ptolemy V Epiphanes. *Queens:* ca. Feb. 193 B.C.-176 B.C. Cleopatra I. *Kings:* ca. May 180 B.C.-Oct. 164 B.C. Ptolemy VI Philometor. *Queens:* 173 B.C.-Oct. 164 B.C. Cleopatra II. *Kings:* 170 B.C.-163 B.C. Ptolemy VIII Euergetes (or Physcon); 163 B.C.-ca. July 145 B.C. Ptolemy VI Philometor. *Queens:* 163 B.C.-115 B.C. Cleopatra II (from 136 B.C.-28 June 116 B.C. as Rival Queen, and from 28 June 116 B.C.-115 B.C. as Queen Regent). *Kings:* 147 B.C.-Aug. 145 B.C. Ptolemy VII Neos Philopator; Aug. 145 B.C.-28 June 116 B.C. Ptolemy VIII Euergetes II (or Physcon). *Queens:* ca. 136 B.C.-28 June 116 B.C. Cleopatra III. *Kings:* 28 June 116 B.C.-Oct. 110 B.C. Ptolemy IX Soter II (or Lathyrus). *Queens:* 28 June 116 B.C.-115 B.C. Cleopatra IV; 115 B.C.-Oct. 110 B.C. Cleopatra V Selene; 115 B.C.-101 B.C. Cleopatra III (Queen Regent). *Kings:* Oct. 110 B.C.-ca. Feb. 109 B.C. Ptolemy X Alexander I; ca. Feb. 109 B.C.-March 107 B.C. Ptolemy IX Soter II (or Lathyrus). *Queens:* ca. Feb. 109 B.C.-March 107 B.C. Cleopatra V Selene. *Kings:* March 107 B.C.-88 B.C. Ptolemy X Alexander I. *Queens:* 101 B.C.-80 B.C. Berenice III. *Kings:* 88 B.C.-80 B.C. Ptolemy IX Soter II (or Lathyrus); 80 B.C.-80 B.C. Ptolemy XI Alexander II; 80 B.C.-58 B.C. Ptolemy XII Auletes. *Queens:* 80 B.C.-58 B.C. Cleopatra VI Tryphaeana; 58 B.C.-55 B.C. Berenice IV. *Kings:* 55 B.C.-51 B.C. Ptolemy XII Auletes; 52 B.C.-47 B.C. Ptolemy XIII Theos Philopator. *Queens:* 52 B.C.-12 Aug. 30 B.C. Cleopatra VII. *Kings:* 47 B.C.-July 44 B.C. Ptolemy XIV Theos Philapator II; July 44 B.C.-12 Aug. 30 B.C. Ptolemy XV Caesar (or Caesarion).

Note: the following Queens were at some stage sole rulers of Egypt: Berenice III (in 80 B.C., in between ruling with Ptolemy IX and Ptolemy XI), Cleopatra VI (in 58 B.C., after she had ruled with Ptolemy XII), Berenice IV (she did not reign with a king). *Note:* joint rule was the order of the day in Ptolemaic Egypt. Sons would begin to share the throne of the father in the latter's lifetime, wives would rule jointly with husbands (usually brothers in this incestuous society), and mothers would co-reign with their sons and daughters (in law?) as dowagers.

Note: the notable Prime Minister during the period was Sosibius, who really was the power behind the throne from October 18, 221 B.C. until 202 B.C. *Note:* THE Cleopatra was Cleopatra VII.

337 Egypt (Persian Province). 335 B.C.-332 B.C. *Location:* as Egypt. *Capital:* Sebennytus. *Other names:* Egypt, 31st Dynasty (Continuation).

History: In 335 B.C. **Egypt of Khababasha** was conquered by the Persians again. In 332 B.C. Alexander the Great walked in without a battle (see **Alexandrian Egypt**).

Persian Emperors: 335 B.C.-332 B.C. Darius III (or Darayavahush III). *Governors:* 335 B.C.-333 B.C. Sabakes; 333 B.C.-332 B.C. Mazakes.

338 Egyptian Diocese of Rome. 330-395. *Location:* Egypt. *Capital:* Alexandria. *Other names:* Egypt.

History: In 330 Constantine reorganized his Empire into Christian dioceses. Egypt was one of these (for Egypt before 330 A.D. see **Roman Egypt**). In 395 control passed from Rome to Byzantium (see **Byzantine Egypt [i]**).

Prefects: 330-28 March 338 Sabinianus; 28 March 338-26 Feb. 354 Flavius Antonius Theodorus; 26 Feb. 354-ca. 357 Longinianus; ca. 357-2 July 357 Parnasius; 2 July 357-360 Pomponius Metrodorus; 360-2 Dec. 362 Artemius; 2 Dec. 362-ca. 367 Ecdicius; ca. 367-370 Tatianus; 370-ca. 372 Publius; ca. 372-374 Tatianus; 374-375 Aelius Palladius; 375-377

Tatianus; 377–17 March 380 Hadrianus; 17 March 380–380 Julianus;
380–381 Paulinus; 381–14 May 382 Bas-
sianus; 14 May 382–8 May 383 Palladius; 8 May 383–384 Hypatius; 384–
18 Dec. 384 Antoninus; 18 Dec. 384–25
July 385 Florentius; 25 July 385–17
Feb. 386 Paulinus; 17 Feb. 386–30 Apr.
388 Florentius; 30 Apr. 388–18 Feb.
390 Erythrius; 18 Feb. 390–16 June 391
Alexander; 16 June 391–5 March 392
Evagrius; 5 March 392–9 Apr. 392
Potamius; 9 Apr. 392–22 June 392
Hypatius; 22 June 392–Aug. 392 Potamius; Aug. 392–392 Claudius Septimus Eutropius; 392–395 Potamius.

339 Egyptian Kingdom. 28 Feb.
1922–18 June 1953. *Location:* northeast
Africa. *Capital:* Cairo. *Other names:*
The Kingdom of Egypt, Egypt.

History: In 1922 the **Egyptian Protectorate** became a kingdom, the Sultan becoming King soon after. A
British High Commissioner remained
until 1936. On July 23, 1952 the Army
seized power, and Cols. Naguib and
Nasser assumed control (Sadat also
took part in the coup). In 1953 a
republic was declared (see **Republic of
Egypt**).

Sultans: 28 Feb. 1922–15 Mar. 1922
Fuad I. *Kings:* 15 Mar. 1922–28 Apr.
1936 Fuad I; 28 Apr. 1936–22 July 1952
Farouk; 26 July 1952–18 June 1953
Fuad II. *High Commissioners:* 28 Feb.
1922–26 Feb. 1925 Lord Allenby; 21
Oct. 1925–8 Aug. 1929 Sir George
Lloyd; 8 Aug. 1929–16 Dec. 1933 Sir
Percy Loraine; 8 Jan. 1934–1936 Sir
Miles Wedderburn Lampson. *Prime
Ministers:* 28 Feb. 1922–1 Mar. 1922
Adli Yegen Pasha; 1 Mar. 1922–30
Nov. 1922 Abdul Khalik Pasha Sarwat;
30 Nov. 1922–5 Feb. 1923 Tewfik
Pasha; 15 Mar. 1923–17 Jan. 1924 Yehia
Ibrahim Pasha; 28 Jan. 1924–24 Nov.
1924 Sa'd Zaghlul Pasha; 25 Nov.
1924–6 June 1926 Ahmad Pasha Ziwar;
6 June 1926–18 Apr. 1927 Adli Yegen
Pasha; 18 Apr. 1927–16 Mar. 1928 Ab-
dul Khalik Pasha Sarwat; 16 Mar.

1928–25 June 1928 Nahhas Pasha; 25
June 1928–2 Oct. 1929 Muhammad
Mahmud Pasha; 2 Oct. 1929–30 Dec.
1929 Adli Yegen Pasha; 31 Dec. 1929–21
June 1930 Nahhas Pasha; 21 June
1930–21 Mar. 1933 Ismail Sidqi Pasha;
24 Mar. 1933–6 Nov. 1934 Yehia Ibrahim Pasha; 15 Nov. 1934–22 Jan. 1936
Muhammad Tewfik Nessim; 30 Jan.
1936–10 May 1936 Ali Maher Pasha; 10
May 1936–30 Dec. 1937 Nahhas Pasha;
30 Dec. 1937–18 Aug. 1939 Muhammad
Mahmud Pasha; 18 Aug. 1939–22 June
1940 Ali Maher Pasha; 28 June 1940–14
Nov. 1940 Hassan Sabry; 14 Nov. 1940–
8 Feb. 1942 Hussein Sirry Pasha; 8 Feb.
1942–8 Oct. 1944 Nahhas Pasha; 9 Oct.
1944–24 Feb. 1945 Ahmad Pasha; 24
Feb. 1945–8 Feb. 1946 Nokrashy Pasha;
8 Feb. 1946–8 Dec. 1946 Ismail Sidqi
Pasha; 9 Dec. 1946–28 Dec. 1948
Nokrashy Pasha; 28 Dec. 1948–26 July
1949 Abdul Hidi Pasha; 26 July
1949–12 Jan. 1950 Hussein Sirry Pasha;
12 Jan. 1950– 27 Jan. 1952 Nahhas
Pasha; 27 Jan. 1952–1 Mar. 1952 Ali
Maher Pasha; 1 Mar. 1952–29 June
1952 Naguib al-Hilaili Pasha; 2 July
1952–20 July 1952 Hussein Sirry Pasha;
24 July 1952–7 Sept. 1952 Ali Maher
Pasha; 7 Sept. 1952–18 June 1953
Muhammad Naguib.

340 Egyptian Protectorate. 18 Dec.
1914–28 Feb. 1922. *Location:* as **Arab
Republic of Egypt**. *Capital:* Cairo.
Other names: British Protectorate of
Egypt, Protectorate of Egypt, Egypt.

History: In 1914 Britain declared a
protectorate over **British-Occupied
Egypt**. A High Commissioner ruled,
with a British-placed Sultan in nominal
office. In 1922 the **Egyptian Kingdom**
(and independence) came into being.

High Commissioners: 18 Dec. 1914–9
Jan. 1915 Sir Milne Chatham (acting);
9 Jan. 1915–1 Jan. 1917 Sir Arthur Mac-
Mahon; 1 Jan. 1917–17 Oct. 1919 Sir
Reginald Wingate; 17 Oct. 1919–28
Feb. 1922 Lord Allenby. *Khedives:* 18
Dec. 1914–19 Dec. 1914 Abbas II Hilmi.
Sultans: 19 Dec. 1914–9 Oct. 1917 Hus-

sein Khamil; 9 Oct. 1917–28 Feb. 1922 Fuad (or Ahmad Fuad I). *Prime Ministers:* 18 Dec. 1914–21 Apr. 1919 Hussein Rushdi Pasha; 21 Apr. 1919–28 Nov. 1919 Muhammad Said Pasha; 28 Nov. 1919–19 May 1920 Yusef Wahba Pasha; 19 May 1920–15 March 1921 Tewfik Nessim Pasha; 15 March 1921–28 Feb. 1922 Adli Yegen Pasha.

341 Egyptian Satrapy. 13 June 323 B.C.–7 Nov. 305 B.C. *Location:* as **Arab Republic of Egypt.** *Capital:* Alexandria. *Other names:* Egypt.
History: In 323 B.C., on Alexander the Great's death (see **Alexandrian Egypt**), Ptolemy, his satrap, ruled as such until 305 B.C., when he became king, and the era of **Egypt of the Ptolemies** began.
Satraps: 13 June 323 B.C.–7 Nov. 305 B.C. Ptolemy (later, from 304 B.C., called Ptolemy Soter).

342 Egyptian Somaliland. 7 Sept. 1877–1884. *Location:* as **British Somaliland.** *Capital:* Berbera. *Other names:* Somaliland (Egyptian).
History: Taken by the Egyptians as a step in their conquest of Africa (an ambition that wasn't as limited as near as the East African Lakes, as they claimed). Internal and domestic problems placed a strain on the new empire, however, and in 1884 the Egyptians were forced to pull out of Somaliland in order to concentrate on the Mahdi (see **Mahdist State**). At that point the British moved into the area (see **British Somaliland**).
Governors: 7 Sept. 1877–1878 Rauf Pasha; 1878–1884 [unknown].

343 Egyptian Sudan. 12 June 1821–6 Jan. 1884. *Location:* most of present-day **Sudan Republic.** *Capital:* Khartoum. *Other names:* Sudan.
History: In 1818 the Turkish-Egyptian army conquered the Red Sea coast of what is now the Sudan, including the strategic port of Suakin. **Massawa,** in **Eritrea,** was also included in the new territory of conquest the same year. **Nubia** was conquered from 1820–22, and the **Funj Sultanate** and **Kordofan** in 1821 and 1822 respectively. Khartoum was founded in 1823, and in 1871 **Equatoria** was included within the country, **Darfur** joining in 1874. Harrar also became an Egyptian province in 1874, later becoming **British Somaliland.** In 1881 the **Mahdist State** began to develop and by 1884 had taken over all of the former Egyptian Sudan, although the Egyptian Sudan did not officially come to an end until Gordon's death at Khartoum in 1885.
12 June 1821–1825 no fixed rule. *Governors-General:* 1825–1826 Uthman Bey; 1826–March 1826 Mahhu Bey; March 1826–June 1838 Khurshid Pasha; June 1838–6 Oct. 1843 Ahmad Pasha abu Wadan; 6 Oct. 1843–1844 [unknown]. *Military Commanders:* 1844–1845 Ahmad Pasha al-Manikli. *Governors-General:* 1845–1846 [unknown]; 1846–1849 Khalid Pasha; 1849–1850 [unknown]; 1850–Jan. 1851 Abd al-Latif Pasha; Jan. 1851–May 1852 Rustum Pasha; May 1852–1853 Ismail Pasha Abu Jabal; 1853–1854 Salim Pasha; July 1854–Nov. 1854 Ali Pasha Sirri; Nov. 1854–1855 [unknown]; 1855–1857 Ali Pasha Jarkis; 1857–1859 Arakil Bey al-Armani (acting). *Governors:* 1859–1861 Hasan Bey Salamah; 1861–1862 Muhammad Bey Rasileh; 1862–1865 Musa Pasha Hamdi; 1865–Nov. 1865 Omar Bey Fahri (acting). *Governors-General:* Nov. 1865–1866 Ja'far Pasha Sadiq; 1866–5 Feb. 1871 Ja'far Pasha Mazhar; 5 Feb. 1871–Oct. 1872 Mumtaz Pasha; Oct. 1872–1872 Edhem Pasha (acting). *Governors:* 1872–May 1877 Ismail Pasha; May 1877–Dec. 1879 Gordon Pasha (or Charles Gordon); Dec. 1879–Feb. 1882 Ra'uf Pasha; Feb. 1882–May 1882 Geigler Pasha (acting); May 1882–March 1883 Abd al-Qadir Pasha Hilmi; March 1883–5 Nov. 1883 Ala ad-Din Pasha Siddiq; 5 Nov. 1883–18 Feb. 1884 [unknown]; 18 Feb. 1884–26 Jan. 1885 Gordon Pasha (or Charles Gordon).

344   Egyptian Tripoli. 1412–1482. *Location:* Tripolitania, Libya. *Capital:* Tripoli. *Other names:* Tripoli (Mameluke), Tripoli (Egyptian).

History: In 1412 the **Circassian Mameluke Empire** took over Tripoli from the Hafsids (see **Hafsid Tripoli [ii]**). In 1482 they lost it to the Hafsids again (see **Hafsid Tripoli [iii]**).

Governors: 1412–1421 Barsabay; 1421–ca. 1480 [unknown]; ca. 1480–1482 Sheikh Abd as-Salaam al-Asman.

Ekwanga see **Opobo**

345 English Gold Coast Settlements. 1621–1632. *Location:* along the Ghana coast. *Capital:* Kormantin.

History: The British started arriving along the Gold Coast in 1618, and an administration of company factors was inaugurated in 1621. In 1632 the Company of Merchants (see **English Gold Coast Settlements [Company of Merchants Trading to Guinea]**) established a centralized government.

Governors: 1621–1623 Sir William St. John; 1623–1632 [unknown].

346 English Gold Coast Settlements (Company of London Merchants). 1651–1658. *Location:* along the Ghana coast. *Capital:* Kormantin.

History: In 1651 the **English Gold Coast Settlements (Company of Merchants Trading to Guinea)** became a territory of the London Company of Merchants. In turn they lost it, in 1658 (see **English Gold Coast Settlements [East India Company]**).

Rulers: unknown.

347 English Gold Coast Settlements (Company of Merchants Trading to Guinea). 1632–1651. *Location:* along the Ghana coast. *Capital:* Kormantin.

History: In 1632 the **English Gold Coast Settlements** were taken over by the Company of Merchants Trading to Guinea. They lost the area in 1651 (see **English Gold Coast Settlements [Company of London Merchants]**).

Rulers: unknown.

348 English Gold Coast Settlements (East India Company). 1658–10 Jan. 1662. *Location:* along the Ghana coast. *Capital:* Kormantin.

History: In 1658 the **English Gold Coast Settlements (Company of London Merchants)** became an East India Company territory. In 1662 they lost it in turn (see **English Gold Coast Settlements [Royal Adventurers]**).

Only known Governor: 1660 Governor Greenhill.

349 English Gold Coast Settlements (Royal Adventurers). 10 Jan. 1662–27 Sept. 1672. *Location:* along the Ghana coast. *Capital:* Cape Coast Castle (1664–72); Kormantin (1662–64).

History: In 1662 the Company of Royal Adventurers took over administration of the English Gold Coast from the East India Company (see **English Gold Coast Settlements [East India Company]**). In 1672 they lost control to the Royal African Company (see **English Gold Coast Settlements [Royal African Company]**).

Rulers: none known.

350 English Gold Coast Settlements (Royal African Company). 27 Sept. 1672–1 May 1707. *Location:* along the coast of present-day **Ghana Republic.** *Capital:* Cape Coast Castle.

History: In 1672 the Royal African Company took control of the English-speaking forts and settlements along the Guinea Coast of West Africa (today's Ghana) from the Royal Adventurers (see **English Gold Coast Settlements [Royal Adventurers]**), a company formed by Charles II. In 1707, by force of the English-Scottish Union, the name changed from English to British (see **British Gold Coast Settlements [Royal African Company]**).

Only known Governors: 1685 Henry Nurse; 1691 John Bloome; 1697–1701 Governor Baggs; 1701–1 May 1707 Sir Thomas Dalby.

351 Equatoria Province. 26 May 1871–1889. *Location:* southern Sudan. *Capital:* Gondokoro.

History: In 1871 Equatoria was made a province of the **Egyptian Sudan.** In 1889 it fell to the **Mahdist State.**

Governors: 26 May 1871–1873 Samuel Baker Pasha; 1873–1874 Mehmed Reuf Pasha; 1874–1876 Charles Gordon Pasha; 1876–1877 Henry Prout Bey; 1877–Aug. 1877 Alexander Mason Bey; Aug. 1877–1878 Ibrahim Pasha Fawzi; 1878–1889 Mehmed Emin Pasha.

352 Equatorial Guinea. See these names:
Equatorial Guinea (1968–   )
Equatorial Guinea (Self-Rule) (1963–1968)
Spanish Guinea Overseas Province (1959–1963)
Spanish Territories of the Gulf of Guinea (1938–1959)
Spanish Guinea (1926–1938)
Fernando Po (Spanish) [ii] (1855–1926)
Fernando Po (British) (1827–1855)
Fernando Po (Spanish) [i] (1778–1827)
Fernando Po (Portuguese) (1494–1778)
Annobón (Spanish Possession) (1778–1926)
Annobón (Portuguese) (1494–1778)
Annobón (Portuguese Possession) (1474–1494)
Formosa (1472–1494)
Rio Muni Colony (1900–1926)
Rio Muni Protectorate (1885–1900)

353 Equatorial Guinea. 12 Oct. 1968–   . *Location:* west central African coast. *Capital:* Malabo (formerly Santa Isabel). *Other names:* Republic of Equatorial Guinea.

History: A republic, the only independent Spanish-speaking state in Africa. **Equatorial Guinea (Self-Rule)** won independence in 1968. It consists of the mainland province of Rio Muni, the island province of Macías Nguema Biogo (previously called Fernando Po),

Annobón Island (since 1973 called Pagalu) off the coast of Gabon and the islands of Corisco and the Elobeys off the coast of Rio Muni.

Presidents: 12 Oct. 1968–14 July 1972 Francisco Macías Nguema Biyogo Negue Ndong; 14 July 1972–3 Aug. 1979 Francisco Macías Nguema Biyogo Negue Ndong (President for Life); 3 Aug. 1979–10 Oct. 1979 Teodoro Obiang Nguema Mbasogo (interim); 10 Oct. 1979–   Teodoro Obiang Nguema Mbasogo. *Prime Ministers:* 15 Aug. 1982–   Cristino Seriche Bioko. *Note:* in times of no Prime Minister, the President held that office. *Note:* On Sept. 26, 1975 Macías dropped the 'Francisco' part of his name, and in 1976 he changed 'Macías' to 'Macie.'

354 Equatorial Guinea (Self-Rule). 15 Dec. 1963–12 Oct. 1968. *Location:* as **Equatorial Guinea.** *Capital:* Santa Isabel (Malabo). *Other names:* Equatorial Guinea, Spanish Guinea.

History: In 1963 **Spanish Guinea Overseas Province** changed its name to Equatorial Guinea and gained partial self-rule. In 1964 Fernando Po was given autonomy status, and in 1968 the whole country became the Republic of **Equatorial Guinea.**

High Commissioners: 15 Dec. 1963–1964 Francisco Rodriguez; 1964–1966 Pedro Alcubierre; 1966–12 Oct. 1968 Victor Díaz del Rio. *Presidents of the Government Council:* 15 Dec. 1963–12 Oct. 1968 Bonifacio Ondo Edu.

355 Eritrea Colony. 1 Jan. 1890–9 May 1936. *Location:* as Eritrea, Ethiopia. *Capital:* Asmara (1935–36); Massawa (1890–1936). *Other names:* Eritrea (named by the Italians for the 'Mare Erythraeum'—the Red Sea of the Romans).

History: In 1890 the Colony of Eritrea was born, created by the Italians upon an extension of prior protectorates in the area, such as **Assab** and **Massawa.** In 1936 Eritrea became a province of **Italian East Africa.** (See also **Eritrea Province.**)

Commandants: 1 Jan. 1890–30 June 1890 Baldassare Orero; 30 June 1890–28 Feb. 1892 Giacomo Gandolfi; 28 Feb. 1892–22 Feb. 1896 Oreste Baratieri; 22 Feb. 1896–16 Dec. 1897 Antonio Baldissera. *Governors:* 16 Dec. 1897–25 March 1907 Ferdinando Martini; 25 March 1907–17 Aug. 1915 Giuseppe Salvago-Raggi; 17 Aug. 1915–16 Sept. 1916 Giovanni Cerrina-Ferroni (acting); 16 Sept. 1916–20 July 1919 Nobile Giacomo di Martino; 20 July 1919–20 Nov. 1920 Camillo de Camillis; 20 Nov. 1920–14 Apr. 1921 Ludovico Pollera; 14 Apr. 1921–1 June 1923 Giovanni Cerrina-Ferroni; 1 June 1923–1 June 1928 Jacopo Gasparini; 1 June 1928–16 July 1930 Corrado Zoli; 16 July 1930–15 Jan. 1935 Riccardo Astuto; 15 Jan. 1935–18 Jan. 1935 Ottone Gabelli (acting). *High Commissioners:* 18 Jan. 1935–27 Nov. 1935 Emilio De Bono; 28 Nov. 1935–9 May 1936 Pietro Badoglio.

356 Eritrea Province. 9 May 1936–5 May 1941. *Location:* Eritrea, Ethiopia. *Capital:* Asmara. *Other names:* Eritrea.

History: In 1936, on the establishment of **Italian East Africa, Eritrea Colony** became a province of that Empire. In 1941, after Britain re-captured the Italian East Africa possessions, Eritrea became **British Eritrea.**

High Commissioners: 9 May 1936–31 May 1936 Pietro Badoglio (also Viceroy of Ethiopia); 31 May 1936–June 1936 Alfredo Guzzoni; June 1936–9 Apr. 1937 Emilio De Bono; 9 Apr. 1937–15 Dec. 1937 Vincenzo de Feo; 15 Dec. 1937–2 June 1940 Giuseppe Daodice; 2 June 1940–5 May 1941 Luigi Frusci.

357 Eritrean Autonomous State. 15 Sept. 1952–14 Nov. 1962. *Location:* as Eritrea Province of Ethiopia. *Capital:* Asmara. *Other names:* Eritrea.

History: In 1952 **British Eritrea** became an autonomous state, independent except that it was ruled by Ethiopia, the two areas being called an Ethiopian-Eritrean Federation. In 1962 the province became the 14th Province of the **Ethiopian Empire [iii].** That year the ELF (Eritrean Liberation Front) was formed, as was the EPLF (Eritrean People's Liberation Front) later on. These groups at one time had captured most of Eritrea and set up a rudimentary government. In 1978, however, the Ethiopian army crushed (but did not kill) the rebels, who returned to guerrilla warfare. On Sept. 18, 1987, the new Ethiopian government (see **Ethiopia People's Democratic Republic**) granted autonomy to Eritrea.

Governors: 11 Sept. 1952–Aug. 1955 Ato Tedla Bairu; Aug. 1955–Dec. 1959 Betwoded Asfaha Wolde Mikael; Dec. 1959–1964 Abiye Abebe; 1964–Dec. 1970 Ras Asrata-Medhin Kassa; Dec. 1970–Aug. 1974 Debebe Haile Maryan; Aug. 1974–19 Feb. 1975 Immanuel Amde Michael; 19 Feb. 1975– General Getachew Nadu.

358 Ethiopia. See these **names:**
Ethiopia People's Democratic Republic (1987–   )
  Communist Ethiopia (1984–1987)
  Ethiopian Military State (1974–1984)
  Ethiopian Empire [iii] (1941–1974)
  Italian East Africa (1936–1941)
  Ethiopian Empire [ii] (1855–1936)
  Gonder Ethiopia (1632–1855)
  Ethiopian Empire [i] (1270–1632)
  Zagwe Ethiopia (1117–1268)
  Abyssinian Italian Protectorate (1889–1896)
  Assab (1882–1890)
  Massawa Protectorate (1885–1890)
  Eritrean Autonomous State (1952–1962)
  British Eritrea (1941–1952)
  Eritrea Province (1936–1941)
  Eritrea Colony (1890–1936)
  Shoa [ii] (1886–1889)
  Shoa [i] (ca. 1470–1856)
  Gojjam (ca. 1620–1855)

Harar (1526–1887)
Ifat (1285–1415)
Axum (250–ca. 950)

Ethiopia see also **Kush**

358a Ethiopia People's Democratic Republic. 10 Sept. 1987– . *Location:* as **Communist Ethiopia.** *Capital:* Addis Ababa. *Other names:* People's Democratic Republic of Ethiopia.
History: In 1987 Ethiopia ceased to be Communist (see **Communist Ethiopia**). Mariam was elected president by the people. On Sept. 18, "autonomous" status was granted to five regions: Eritrea, Tigrai, Assab, Dire Dawa, and Ogaden.
Presidents: 10 Sept. 1987– Mengistu Haile Mariam. *Prime Ministers:* 10 Sept. 1987– Fikre Selassie Wogderess.

359 Ethiopian Empire [i]. 1270–14 June 1632. *Location:* Ethiopia. *Capital:* Danqaz (the latter capital); Tegulat (the first capital). *Other names:* Abyssinia, Ethiopia.
History: In 1270 **Zagwe Ethiopia** came to an end, to be replaced by the Amhara, legitimate heirs of the old Axumite Kingdom (see **Axum**). They moved the capital to Tegulat in **Shoa**. In 1632, this dynasty came to an end, to be replaced with **Gonder Ethiopia.**
Emperors: 1270–1285 Yekuno Amlak (or Tasfa Iyasus); 1285–1294 Salomon I (or Yagbe'a Seyon); 1294– 1295 Bahr Asqad (or Senfa Ar'ed); 1295–1296 Hezba Asqad; 1296–1297 Kedma Asqad; 1297–1298 Djin; 1298– 1299 Saba Asqad; 1299–1314 Wedem Ar'ed; 1314–1344 Amda Seyon (or Gabra Maskal); 1344–1372 Newaya Krestos (or Safya Ar'ed); 1372–1382 Newaya Maryam; 1382–1411 Dawit I (or David I); 1411–1414 Tewodoros I (or Theodore I); 1414–Sept. 1429 Yeshaq I (or Isaac I); Sept. 1429–March 1430 Endreyas; March 1430–June 1433 Takla Maryam (or Hezba Nan); June 1433– Nov. 1433 Sarwe Iyasus (or Mehreka Nan); Nov. 1433–June 1434 Amda Iyasus; June

1434–6 Sept. 1468 Zara Yaqob (or Constantine I); 6 Sept. 1468– 19 Nov. 1478 Ba'eda Maryam I; 19 Nov. 1478–May 1494 Eskender; May 1494– Dec. 1494 Amda Seyon II; Dec. 1494–31 July 1508 Na'od (or Anbasa Bazar); 22 Aug. 1508–2 Sept. 1540 Lebna Dengel Dawit II (or David II); 13 Sept. 1540–23 March 1559 Galawdewos (or Claudius); 3 April 1559–23 Jan. 1563 Admas Sagad (or Minas); 31 Jan. 1563–2 Aug. 1597 Sarsa Dengel (or Malak Sagad); 2 Aug. 1597–1603 Yaqob I; Sept. 1603–24 Oct. 1604 Za Dengel (or Asnaf Sagad); 24 Oct. 1604–10 March 1607 Yaqob I; 10 March 1607–14 June 1632 Susneyos (or Seltan Sagad).

360 Ethiopian Empire [ii]. 11 Feb. 1855–9 May 1936. *Location:* as **Ethiopian Empire [iii].** *Capital:* Addis Ababa (1889–1936); Entoto (1880–1889); Magdala (1855–1880). *Other names:* Abyssinian Empire.
History: In 1855 Emperor Theodore II brought **Gojjam** and **Tigre** together and in 1856 brought in **Shoa [i].** He died in 1868; **Harrar** became part of the Empire in 1887, and **Shoa [ii]** in 1889. The beginning of Menelik II's reign marked the start of the modern era (within the modern Empire), and in 1936 the Italians invaded (see **Italian East Africa**). (See also **Abyssinian Italian Protectorate.**).
Emperors: 11 Feb. 1855–10 Apr. 1868 Lij Kasa (Tewodoros II) (Theodore II); 14 Apr. 1868–12 Jan. 1872 Takla Giyorgis II; 12 Jan. 1872–10 March 1889 Yohannes IV (John IV); 12 March 1889–3 Nov. 1889 Disputed succession; 3 Nov. 1889–15 May 1911 Sahle Mariam (Menelik II); 15 May 1911–27 Sept. 1916 Lij Iyasu; 30 Sept. 1916–2 Apr. 1930 Zauditu (Empress); 30 Sept. 1916–2 Nov. 1930 Ras Dejazmatch Tafari (Haile Selassie); 2 Nov. 1930–9 March 1936 Haile Selassie.

361 Ethiopian Empire [iii]. 5 May 1941–12 Sept. 1974. *Location:* as **Ethiopian Military State.** *Capital:* Addis

Ababa. *Other names:* Abyssinia, Ethiopia.

History: In 1941 Emperor Haile Selassie returned with British assistance (Orde Wingate) to his country, which since 1936 had formed the bulk of **Italian East Africa**. In 1962 Eritrea (see **Eritrea Autonomous State**) became part of Ethiopia. In 1974 Selassie, 'The Lion of Judah,' was deposed by a revolutionary council and the **Ethiopian Military State** came into being.

Emperors: 5 May 1941–12 Sept. 1974 Haile Selassie. *Governors-General:* 5 May 1941–19 May 1941 Duke of Aosta (acting); 19 May 1941–6 July 1941 Pietro Gazzera (acting); 6 July 1941–22 Nov. 1941 Guglielmo Nasi (acting). *Prime Ministers:* 5 May 1941–3 Apr. 1958 Makonnen Endalkatchon; 3 Apr. 1958–Dec. 1960 Abede Aragai; 17 Apr. 1961–28 Feb. 1974 Tshafe Tezaz Aklilu Habte-Wold; 28 Feb. 1974–22 July 1974 Makonnen Endalkatchon; 22 July 1974–12 Sept. 1974 Mikael Imru.

362 Ethiopian Military State. 12 Sept. 1974–10 Sept. 1984. *Location:* as **Ethiopian Empire**. *Capital:* Addis Ababa. *Other names:* Socialist Ethiopia, Ethiopia.

History: In 1974 Haile Selassie was deposed and a 120-member military government, The Dergue, was formed. Ethiopia (previously the **Ethiopian Empire [iii]**) has had a revolutionary character since then. The monarchy was abolished in March 1975, and in 1984 the country became **Communist Ethiopia.**

Kings (nominal): 12 Sept. 1974–21 March 1975 Asfa Wossen. *Chiefs of State:* 12 Sept. 1974–28 Nov. 1974 Aman Andom (Head of Provisional Military Government); 28 Nov. 1974–3 Feb. 1977 Teferi Benti (acting); 11 Feb. 1977–10 Sept. 1984 Mengistu Haile Mariam (Chairman of Military Council).

Fada N'Gourma see **Gurma**

363 Fatimid Egypt. 5 Aug. 969–10

Sept. 1171. *Location:* Egypt. *Capital:* Cairo (named al-Mansuriyah from 969–74). *Other names:* Egypt.

History: In 969 the Fatimid general Gohar conquered **Ikhshid Egypt** and made Cairo his new capital. The Fatimid Empire had been founded in 909 (see **Fatimid North Africa**), and named for Fatima, the daughter of the Prophet. Ruled by caliphs from Tunisia, the empire spread over North Africa and Arabia. In 1073 Badr, Commander of the Armies, seized power. These Commanders (also viziers [or wazirs]) actually ruled, and in 1171 Saladin (Salah ad-Din), the Vizier, brought an end to the Fatimid Empire (see **Aiyubid Empire**).

Military Administrators: 5 Aug. 969–June 973 Gohar. *Caliphs:* June 973–10 Dec. 975 al-Mu'izz; 10 Dec. 975–14 Oct. 996 al-Aziz; 14 Oct. 996–13 Feb. 1021 al-Hakim; 13 Feb. 1021–13 June 1036 az-Zahir; 13 June 1036–29 Dec. 1094 al-Mustansir; 31 Dec. 1094–8 Dec. 1101 al-Musta'li; 8 Dec. 1101–17 Oct. 1130 al-Amir; 1131–Oct. 1149 al-Hafiz; Oct. 1149–16 Apr. 1154 az-Zafir; 16 Apr. 1154–23 July 1160 al-Fa'iz; 23 July 1160–10 Sept. 1171 al-Adid. *Maliks (or Viziers, or Military Commanders):* June 973–23 Feb. 991 ibn Kallis; June 1050–March 1058 al-Yazuri; 27 Jan. 1074–Apr. 1094 Badr al-Jamali; Apr. 1094–Dec. 1121 al-Afdal Shahanshah; Dec. 1121–4 Oct. 1125 ibn al-Batai'hi (al-Mamun); 21 Sept. 1130–8 Dec. 1131 Abu Ali; 8 Dec. 1131–Aug. 1132 Yanis; 29 March 1134–15 Feb. 1137 Bahram; 15 Feb. 1137–14 June 1139 Rudwan; 14 June 1139–1143 [unknown]; 1143–ca. 1152 Salih ibn Ruzzik; ca. 1152–Apr. 1153 ibn as-Salar; Apr. 1153–1154 Abbas; 1154–1161 Salih ibn Ruzzik; 1161–1163 al-Adil Ruzzik; 1163–30 Aug. 1163 Shawar; 31 Aug. 1163–May 1164 Dirgham; May 1164–18 Jan. 1169 Shawar; 18 Jan. 1169–23 March 1169 Shirkuh; 23 March 1169–10 Sept. 1171 Saladin (or Salah ad-Din).

364 Fatimid North Africa. 6 Jan.

910–973. *Location:* Tunisia-eastern Algeria. *Capital:* al-Mahdiya (from 921) (established as a town in 912).

History: In 909 the first Fatimid Caliph, Mahdi Ubaydallah, conquered al-Qayrawan, the major **Aghlabid Empire** capital, and set up his first headquarters on the coast at al-Mahdiya. This was the first phase of the Fatimid Empire, the second being from 973 when al-Muizz transferred his capital to Cairo (see **Fatimid Egypt**). In 973 the Zirids took power in the part of North Africa previously under Fatimid control, although the Zirids remained vassals of the Fatimids until 1045.

Caliphs: 6 Jan. 910–4 March 934 al-Mahdi Ubaydallah; 4 March 934–18 May 946 al-Qa'im; 18 May 946–18 March 953 al-Mansur; Apr. 953–973 al-Mu'izz.

365 Fatimid Tripoli. 26 March 909–977. *Location:* Tripolitania, Libya. *Capital:* Tripoli. *Other names:* Tripoli (Fatimid).

History: In 909 the Fatimids (see **Fatimid North Africa** and **Fatimid Egypt**) took Tripoli from the Aghlabids (see **Aghlabid Empire** and **Aghlabid Tripoli**). In 977 they lost it to the Zirids (see **Zirid Tripoli** and **Zirid Kingdom**).

Only known governor: ca. 973 Abdallah ibn Yahluf.

Fazzan see **Fezzan**

366 Federation of Rhodesia and Nyasaland. 23 Oct. 1953–31 Dec. 1963. *Location:* present-day Malawi, Zimbabwe and Zambia. *Capital:* Salisbury, Southern Rhodesia. *Other names:* Central African Federation.

History: A British-controlled federation of three states — **Nyasaland Protectorate** (and in the final part of 1963 **Nyasaland [Self-Rule]**), **Northern Rhodesia Protectorate** and **Southern Rhodesia Colony.** Differences between the three caused the breakup of the federation.

Governors-General: 23 Oct. 1953–24 Jan. 1957 Lord Llewellin; 24 Jan. 1957–31 Dec. 1963 Earl of Dalhousie. *Prime Ministers:* 18 Dec. 1953–31 Oct. 1956 Sir Godfrey Huggins (created 1st Viscount Malvern in 1955); 1 Nov. 1956–31 Dec. 1963 Sir Roy Welensky. *Deputy Prime Ministers:* 18 Dec. 1953–31 Oct. 1956 Sir Roy Welensky.

367 Fernando Po (British). 1827–1855. *Location:* as **Fernando Po (Spanish) [i].** *Capital:* Santa Isabel.

History: In 1827 part of Fernando Po (see **Fernando Po [Spanish] [i]**) was settled by the British on a lease arrangement with Madrid. The Spanish and British had considered the island unfit for colonization but it was still used as a British naval base and as a consulate for the **Bight of Biafra** until 1855, when the Spaniards decided to try colonization again. The British consulate remained until 1885. (See **Fernando Po [Spanish] [ii]**).

Governors: 1827–1829 William Owens; 1829–1830 Edward Nicolls; 1830–1832 John Beecroft (acting); 1832–1833 Edward Nicolls; 1833–10 June 1854 John Beecroft; 10 June 1854–1855 James Lynslager.

368 Fernando Po (Portuguese). 7 June 1494–1 March 1778. *Location:* in the Bight of Biafra, about 60 miles south of Nigeria. *Capital:* Santa Isabel. *Other names:* Fernando Poo.

History: In 1494 **Formosa** became Fernando Po (or Fernando Poo, in Portuguese), a possession of Portugal. In 1778 it went to Spain (see **Fernando Po [Spanish] [i]**).

Rulers: unknown.

369 Fernando Po (Spanish) [i]. 1 March 1778–1827. *Location:* in the Bight of Biafra, about 60 miles south of Nigeria. *Capital:* Santa Isabel.

History: In 1778 the Spanish took Fernando Po from the Portuguese (see **Fernando Po [Portuguese]**). In 1781 they left the area, considering it un-

99		*Fezzan Pashalik*

suitable. Still a Spanish property in 1827, it was leased in that year (or rather part of it was) by the British (see **Fernando Po [British]**).
Rulers: 1 March 1778–1781 [unknown]; 1781–1827 none.

370 Fernando Po (Spanish) [ii].
1855–1926. *Location:* Macías Nguema Biyogo, Equatorial Guinea. *Capital:* Santa Isabel. *Other names:* Puerto de Isabel.
History: In 1855 **Fernando Po (British)** reverted to Spain (see also **Fernando Po [Spanish] [i]**). Adventurers went in to pacify the Rio Muni section on the mainland of Africa, and in 1885 a protectorate was placed over this new land (see **Rio Muni Protectorate**). In 1900 Rio Muni became **Rio Muni Colony,** and in 1926 **Rio Muni Colony, Annobón (Spanish Possession)** and Fernando Po were joined together to form **Spanish Guinea.**
Governors: 1855–1858 Domingo Mustrich; 1858–1858 Carlos Chacón y Michelena; 1858–1862 José de la Gándara y Navarro; 1862–1865 Pantaleón Ayllón; 1865–1868 José Barrera; 1868–1869 Joaquin Gallardo; 1869–1869 António Maymó; 1869–1870 Zoilo Acaña; 1870–1871 [unknown]; 1871–1871 Frederico Anrich; 1871–1872 [unknown]; 1872–1874 Ignacio Tudela; 1874–1875 [unknown]; 1875–1877 Diego Chamorro; 1877–1879 Alejandro Salgado; 1879–1880 Enrique Santaló; 1880–1883 José de Oca; 1883–1885 António Cano; 1885–1887 José de Oca; 1887–1888 Luís Navarro; 1888–1889 Antonio Guerra; 1889–1890 José de Ibarra; 1890–1890 José Barreda; 1890–1892 José de Barrasa; 1892–1892 Antonio Martínez; 1892–1893 Eulógio Merchán; 1893–1895 José de la Puente Basseve; 1895–1897 Adolfo de España y Gómez de Humarán; 1897–1898 Manuel Rico; 1898–1900 José Vera; 1900–1901 Francisco Dueñas; 1901–1905 José de la Ibarra; 1905–1906 José de la Serna; 1906–1906 Diego Saavedra y Magdalena; 1906–1907 Angel Barrera y Luyando;

1907–1908 Luis Ramos Izquierdo; 1908–1909 José Anchorena; 1909–1910 [unknown]; 1910–1924 Angel Barrera y Luyando; 1924–1926 Carlos Tovar de Revilla.

Fez and Morocco see **Alawid Morocco**

371 Fezzan. ca. 1566–1842. *Location:* southwest Libya. *Capital:* Murzuq. *Other names:* Awlad Muhammad Dynasty, Fazzan Kingdom.
History: About 1566 al-Mustansir ibn Muhammad set up a local rule in the Fezzan. In 1842 the Osmanli Turks conquered it and it became **Fezzan Pashalik.** During its lifetime the kingdom was constantly invaded by Tripoli.
Sultans: ca. 1566–1580 al-Mustansir ibn Muhammad; 1580–1599 an-Nasir; 1599–1612 al-Mansur. *Tripolitanian Governors:* 1612–1614 [unknown]. *Sultans:* 1614–1623 Tahir I. *Tripolitanian Governors:* 1623–1626 [unknown]. *Sultans:* 1626–1658 Muhammad I; 1658–1682 Jehim; 1682–1682 Nagib; 1682–1689 Muhammad II Nasir. *Tripolitanian Governors:* 1689–1689 Muhammad al-Mukni. *Sultans:* 1689–1689 Temmam; 1689–1690 Muhammad III. *Tripolitanian Governors:* 1690–1690 Ali al-Mukni. *Sultans:* 1690–1718 Muhammad II Nasir; 1718–1767 Ahmad I; 1767–1775 Tahir II; 1775–1789 Ahmad II; 1789–1804 Muhammad IV al-Hakim; 1804–1804 Muhammad V al-Mustansir; 1804–1805 Yusuf al-Mukni. *Ottoman Governors:* 1805–1831 [unknown]. *Sultans:* 1831–1842 Abdul-Jalil.

372 Fezzan Pashalik. 1842–15 Oct. 1912. *Location:* southern Libya. *Capital:* Murzuq. *Other names:* Fazzan.
History: In 1842 the Fezzan, a disputed area between Turks and local sects, became a Sanjak, or province (or Pashalik) of the Ottoman Empire. In 1912 the Italians captured and dismembered it.
Pashas: 1842–1846 Bekir; 1846–1855 Hassan al-Balazi; 1855–1859 [unknown]; 1859–1865 Halim; 1865–

1865 Hamid Bey (acting); 1865–1870 Halim; 1870–(?) [unknown]; (?)– ca. 1882 Mustafa Faik; (?)–(?) [unknown]; (?)–(?) [unknown]; ca. 1900– ca. 1906 Mahmud Bey; ca. 1906–1909 Samih Bey. *Sanusi Governors:* 1909–15 Oct. 1912 Sayid Muhammad al-Abid.

373 Fika. 1806–27 Dec. 1899. *Location:* Bornu Province, northeastern Nigeria. *Capital:* Fika (built around 1805 and called Lafiya Moi until about 1807).

History: Founded as an emirate in 1806 by King Buraima of the Bolewa tribe who had moved his kingdom from **Daniski.** It was never taken by the **Fulani Empire** or by the Sudanese adventurer Rabih (see **Rabih's Empire**) in the 1890s. In 1899 it became part of the soon-to-be-announced **Northern Nigeria Protectorate** and in 1924 the capital of the emirate was moved to Potiskum. Fika is known for its dates (the fruit).

Emirs: 1806–1822 Buraima; 1822–1844 Adam; 1844–1857 Disa Siri; 1857–1867 Mammadi Gaganga; 1867–1871 Ismaila; 1871–1882 Mammadi Buye; 1882–1882 Aji; 1882–1885 Mama (or Muhammad); 1885–1902 Sule (or Suleiman); 1902–1922 Disa (or Idrissa); 1922– Muhammadu ibn Idrissa.

Filali Morocco see **Alawid Morocco**

Filane Empire see **Fulani Empire**

374 Fingoland. 1835–1875. *Location:* Transkei. *Capital:* Nqamakwe.

History: In 1875 the Fingos (or Mfengu), who had been refugees displaced as a result of the Mfecane (or Zulu movements of the 1820s), were incorporated into the Cape (see **British Cape Colony [Self-Rule]**). They had first been granted lands for fighting on the British side during the Xhosa War of 1835, and over the years, and through successive Xhosa Wars, they increased their land at the expense of the Xhosa (see **Kaffraria Proper**).

Rulers: [unknown].

Fombina see **Adamawa**

375 Formosa. 1472–7 June 1494. *Location:* Fernando Po (Macías Nguema Biyogo), **Equatorial Guinea.** *Capital:* none.

History: The island was discovered by Fernão do Pó, a Portuguese navigator, and was named Formosa ("beautiful"). The original inhabitants were the Bubi. In 1494 it was renamed Fernando Poo (see **Fernando Po [Portuguese]**).

Rulers: none.

376 Fort-Dauphin Colony. 24 Sept. 1642–27 Aug. 1674. *Location:* southeastern Madagascar. *Capital:* Fort-Dauphin. *Other names:* Fort Dauphin, Fort-Dauphin.

History: In 1642 the French founded Fort-Dauphin as an East India trading base, but it was never used for this purpose. From 1667–1671 it was the headquarters of the Compagnie des Indes Orientales, but was abandoned in 1674 (see also the **Madagascar** headings).

Governors: 24 Sept. 1642–4 Dec. 1648 Jacques Pronis; 4 Dec. 1648–12 Feb. 1655 Étienne de Flacourt; 12 Feb. 1655–23 May 1655 Jacques Pronis (acting); 23 May 1655–1655 Jean des Perriers; 1655–1656 Martin Gueston (acting); 1656–29 May 1657 Luc de Champmargou (acting); 29 May 1657– 9 May 1661 Pierre de Rivau; 9 May 1661–8 July 1665 Luc de Champmargou; 8 July 1665–14 Dec. 1665 Pierre de Beausse; 14 Dec. 1665–Sept. 1666 Gilles Montauban; Sept. 1666–10 March 1667 Luc de Champmargou (acting); 10 March 1667–4 Dec. 1670 Marquis de Montdevergue; 4 Dec. 1670–26 June 1671 Jacob Blanquet de la Haye; 26 June 1671–6 Dec. 1672 Luc de Champmargou; 6 Dec. 1672–27 Aug. 1674 Jean de la Bretesche.

Fort James see **James Fort**

Fort Victoria see **Port Natal [iii]**

377 Fortunate Islands. (?)–15 Dec. 1405. *Location:* Canary Islands. *Capital:* [unknown]. *Other names:* Canary Islands.
History: The Guanches and the Canários were the local people of the Canary Islands (or Fortunate Islands as they were then known by the European world) before being exterminated by the Spanish from the time of their conquest of the islands in 1405 (see **Canary Islands Kingdom**).
Rulers: ca. 1400–(?) Guarafia (in Lanzarote); ca. 1350–(?) Gumidafe (in Gran Canária); ca. 1402–(?) Artemi (in Gran Canária).

Fourth Shore see **Libya**

Fouta Jalon see **Futa Jallon**

Fouta Toro see **Futa Toro**

378 Free Province of New Holland in South East Africa. 2 Dec. 1836–20 Oct. 1838. *Location:* Natal (i.e. as **Natalia**). *Capital:* no central administrative area. *Other names:* De Vrije Provincie van Nieuwe Holland in Zuid Oost Afrika.
History: Boer emigrants from Cape Colony (see **British Cape Colony**) under Gerrit Maritz, Jacobus Uys, Hendrik Potgieter and Piet Retief founded this polity in 1836. In 1838 it became **Natalia**.
Commandants-General: 2 Dec. 1836–6 June 1837 Gerrit Maritz. *Governors/Commandants-General:* 6 June 1837–6 Feb. 1838 Piet Retief; 6 Feb. 1838–23 Sept. 1838 Gerrit Maritz; 23 Sept. 1838–20 Oct. 1838 Andries Pretorius.

379 Freedom Province. 14 May 1787–Dec. 1789. *Location:* the coast of Sierra Leone. *Capital:* Granville Town. *Other names:* Sierra Leone.
History: In 1787 freed slaves from America settled this area, sponsored by Granville Sharp. In 1789 Granville Town was burned to the ground by King Jimmy, a local Temne chief. In 1791 the colony was restored, as **Sierra Leone.**
Administrators: 14 May 1787–Sept. 1787 Capt. B. Thompson. *Governors:* 1788–(?) John Taylor.

Freetown see **Sierra Leone**

380 French Algeria. 26 Aug. 1881–3 July 1962. *Location:* north Africa, between Morocco and Tunisia. *Capital:* Algiers. *Other names:* Algeria.
History: In 1881 **French Algeria Military Province** assumed a civil government, and the three northern départements of Algiers, Oran and Constantine were made integral parts of France. This situation ended on Dec. 31, 1896, and military rule returned. In the early 20th century France conquered most of the desert regions and brought the limits of Algeria close to those of today (see **Algerian Popular and Democratic Republic**).
Governors-General: 26 Aug. 1881–26 Nov. 1881 Albert Grévy (acting); 26 Nov. 1881–18 Apr. 1891 Louis Tirman; 18 Apr. 1891–28 Sept. 1897 Jules Cambon; 28 Sept. 1897–1 Oct. 1897 Auguste Loze (declined appointment); 1 Oct. 1897–26 July 1898 Louis Lépine; 26 July 1898–3 Oct. 1900 Édouard Julien-Laferrière; 3 Oct. 1900–18 June 1901 Celestin Jonnart (acting); 18 June 1901–11 Apr. 1903 Paul Revoil; 11 Apr. 1903–5 May 1903 Maurice Varnier (acting); 5 May 1903–22 May 1911 Celestin Jonnart (acting); 22 May 1911–29 Jan. 1918 Charles Lutaud; 29 Jan. 1918–29 Aug. 1919 Celestin Jonnart (acting); 29 Aug. 1919–28 July 1921 Jean-Baptiste Abel; 28 July 1921–17 Apr. 1925 Théodore Steeg; 17 Apr. 1925–12 May 1925 Henri Dubief; 12 May 1925–20 Nov. 1927 Maurice Viollette; 20 Nov. 1927–3 Oct. 1930 Pierre Bordes; 3 Oct. 1930–21 Sept. 1935 Jules Carde; 21 Sept. 1935–19 July 1940 Georges Le Beau; 19 July

1940–16 July 1941 Jean Abrial; 16 July 1941–20 Sept. 1941 Maxime Weygand (acting); 20 Sept. 1941–20 Jan. 1943 Yves Chatel; 20 Jan. 1943–3 June 1943 Marcel Peyrouton; 3 June 1943–8 Sept. 1944 Georges Catroux; 8 Sept. 1944–11 Feb. 1948 Yves Chataigneau; 11 Feb. 1948–9 March 1951 Marcel Naegelen; 11 Apr. 1951–26 Jan. 1955 Roger Léonard; 26 Jan. 1955–30 Jan. 1956 Jacques Soustelle; 30 Jan. 1956–6 Feb. 1956 Georges Catroux. *Residents-General:* 10 Feb. 1956–15 May 1958 Robert La Coste; 15 May 1958–28 May 1958 André Mutter. *Delegates-General:* 16 June 1958–19 Dec. 1958 Raoul Salan; 19 Dec. 1958–24 Nov. 1960 Paul Delouvrier; 24 Nov. 1960–19 March 1962 Jean Morin; 19 March 1962–3 July 1962 Christian Fouchet. *Presidents of the Provisional Executive Council:* 28 March 1962–3 July 1962 Abdur Rahman Farès.

381 French Algeria Military Province. Feb. 1842–26 Aug. 1881. *Location:* Algeria, but without the desert regions. *Capital:* Algiers.

History: In 1842 the **French Algerian Possessions** took on the name French Algeria Military Province. In 1881 it became a Civil Province, as **French Algeria.**

Governors-General: Feb. 1842–1 Sept. 1845 Thomas de la Piconnerie (from 1844 the Duc d'Isly); 1 Sept. 1845–6 July 1847 Christophe de Lamoricière (acting); 6 July 1847–27 Sept. 1847 Marie-Alphonse Bedeau (acting); 27 Sept. 1847–24 Feb. 1848 Duc d'Aumale; 24 Feb. 1848–29 Apr. 1848 Eugène Cavaignac; 29 Apr. 1848–9 Sept. 1848 Nicolas Changarnier; 9 Sept. 1848–22 Oct. 1850 Baron Charon; 22 Oct. 1850–10 May 1851 Comte d'Hautpoul; 10 May 1851–11 Dec. 1851 Aimable Pelissier; 11 Dec. 1851–31 Aug. 1858 Comte Randon. *Ministers for Algeria and the Colonies:* 24 June 1858–24 March 1859 Prince Napoléon Bonaparte; 24 March 1859–24 Nov. 1860 Comte de Chasseloup-Laubat; 24 Nov. 1860–22 May 1864 Aimable Pelis-

sier (from 1856 the Duc de Malakoff). *Governors-General:* 22 May 1864–1 Sept. 1864 Édouard de Martimprey; 1 Sept. 1864–27 July 1870 Duc de Magenta; 27 July 1870–23 Oct. 1870 Baron Durieu (acting); 23 Oct. 1870–16 Nov. 1870 Jean Walsin-Esterhazy (acting); 24 Oct. 1870–16 Nov. 1870 Henri Didier (did not take office); 16 Nov. 1870–8 Feb. 1871 Charles du Bouzet (acting); 8 Feb. 1871–29 March 1871 Alexis Lambert (acting); 29 March 1871–10 June 1873 Comte de Gueydon; 10 June 1873–15 March 1879 Antoine Chanzy; 15 March 1873–26 Aug. 1881 Albert Grévy (acting). *Note:* du Bouzet (1870–71) and Lambert (1871–71) were also Prefects of Oran.

382 French Algerian Possessions. 1839–Feb. 1842. *Location:* as **French Algeria Military Province.** *Capital:* Algiers.

History: Algeria as a name was first used in 1839. Until then the area had been called the **French Possessions in North Africa.** In 1842 it became a military province of France (see **French Algeria Military Province**).

Governors-General of the French Possessions in North Africa: 1839–Dec. 1840 Comte Valée; 22 Feb. 1841–Feb. 1842 Thomas de la Piconnerie.

383 French Cameroun Territory. 4 March 1916–22 July 1920. *Location:* Cameroun. *Capital:* Douala. *Other names:* Cameroun.

History: In 1916 the **Cameroun French-British Condominium** came to an end. The country was divided up between France and Britain, each getting a territory (see also **British Cameroons Territory**). In 1920 these territories were recreated as mandates by the League of Nations (see **Cameroun French Mandate** and **Cameroons British Mandate**).

Governors: 4 March 1916–8 Oct. 1916 Joseph Aymerich; 8 Oct. 1916–6 March 1919 Lucien Fourneau; 6 March 1919–22 July 1920 Jules Carde.

384 French Coast of the Somalis. 11 March 1862–24 June 1884. *Location:* the coast of Djibouti. *Capital:* Obock. *Other names:* Côte Française des Somalis, Obock Protectorate.
History: In the 1830s and 1840s the French explored this area of the Red Sea, signing treaties with the local Afar and Issas leaders in 1859. In 1862 they bought the seaport of Obock. In 1884 a commandant was appointed at Obock and the place was finally occupied by the French, when it was renamed **Obock Colony.** The name "French Coast of the Somalis" lingered on in France until 1967.
Rulers: none.

385 French Congo. 30 Apr. 1891–15 Jan. 1910. *Location:* as **French Equatorial Africa Colony.** *Capital:* Brazzaville. *Other names:* Congo Français et Dependances.
History: In 1891 **French Equatorial African Protectorate** became the French Congo. In 1910 it changed its name again, to **French Equatorial Africa.**
Commissioners-General: 30 Apr. 1891–28 Sept. 1897 Pierre Savorgnan de Brazza; 28 Sept. 1897–2 Dec. 1898 Henri de la Mothe; 2 Dec. 1898–Apr. 1899 Martial Merlin (acting); Apr. 1899–28 Apr. 1900 Henri de la Mothe; 28 Apr. 1900–Dec. 1900 Jean-Baptiste Lemaire (acting); Dec. 1900–2 March 1903 Louis Grodet; 2 March 1903–Oct. 1903 Émile Gentil (acting); Oct. 1903–21 Jan. 1904 Louis Grodet; 21 Jan. 1904–28 June 1908 Émile Gentil. *Governors-General:* 28 June 1908–24 Sept. 1909 Martial Merlin; 24 Sept. 1909–15 Jan. 1910 Charles Rognon (acting).

French Congo see also **Moyen-Congo**

386 French-Controlled Madagascar. 17 Dec. 1885–5 Aug. 1890. *Location:* Madagascar. *Capital:* Tananarive.
History: In 1885 the French gained such a hold over the island that it controlled its affairs as a prelude to establishing a protectorate (see **Madagascar Protectorate**) in 1890.
Queens: 17 Dec. 1885–5 Aug. 1890 Ranavalona III. *Residents-General:* 28 Apr. 1886–March 1888 Charles Le Myre de Villiers; March 1888–12 Dec. 1889 Arthur Larrouy; 12 Dec. 1889–5 Aug. 1890 Maurice Bompard.

387 French Egypt. 25 July 1798–27 June 1801. *Location:* northern Egypt. *Capital:* Cairo. *Other names:* Napoleonic Egypt.
History: In 1798 Napoleon conquered most of northern Egypt from the Ottomans (see **Ottoman Egypt [i]**). The following year he left General Kléber in charge, and in 1801 the French were defeated by the British and the Turks at Alexandria; Cairo was surrendered in June and in September the Napoleonic troops left Alexandria and Egypt became Turkish again (see **Ottoman Egypt [ii]**).
Military Commanders: 25 July 1798–22 Aug. 1799 Napoléon Bonaparte; 22 Aug. 1799–14 June 1800 Jean-Baptiste Kléber; 14 June 1800–27 June 1801 Jacques de Menou.

388 French Equatorial Africa. See these **names:**
French Equatorial Africa Colony (1934–1958)
French Equatorial Africa (1910–1934)
French Congo (1891–1910)
French Equatorial African Protectorate (1886–1891)
Ubangi-Shari-Chad Colony (1906–1916)
Lower Congo-Gabon Colony (1902–1903)
Ivory Coast-Gabon (1860–1883)
Moyen-Congo-Gabon (1888–1902)

389 French Equatorial Africa. 15 Jan. 1910–30 June 1934. *Location:* as **French Equatorial Africa Colony.** *Capital:* Brazzaville. *Other names:* French Equatorial Africa Federation, A.E.F., Afrique Équatoriale Française.

History: In 1910 **French Congo** became the A.E.F. (these French initials indicate the actual French name for this federation). In 1934 it became a colony (see **French Equatorial Africa Colony**). *Governors-General:* 15 Jan. 1910–3 May 1910 Charles Rognon (acting); 3 May 1910–18 July 1910 Adolphe Cureau (acting); 18 July 1910–17 Nov. 1910 Martial Merlin; 17 Nov. 1910–7 March 1911 Charles Rognon (acting); 7 March 1911–16 May 1911 Charles Vergnes (acting); 16 May 1911–1912 Martial Merlin; 1912–23 March 1913 Charles Vergnes (acting); 23 March 1913–17 Nov. 1913 Georges Poulet (acting); 17 Nov. 1913–14 Sept. 1914 Frédéric Estèbe (acting); 14 Sept. 1914–15 May 1917 Martial Merlin; 15 May 1917–17 June 1919 Gabriel Angoulvant; 17 June 1919–July 1919 Frédéric Estèbe (acting); July 1919–16 May 1920 Gabriel Angoulvant; 16 May 1920–5 Sept. 1920 Maurice Lapalud (acting); 5 Sept. 1920–9 Oct. 1921 Jean Augagneur; 9 Oct. 1921–19 July 1922 Matteo Alfassa (acting); 19 July 1922–21 Aug. 1923 Jean Augagneur; 21 Aug. 1923–8 July 1924 Robert de Guise (acting); 8 July 1924–16 Oct. 1924 Matteo Alfassa (acting); 16 Oct. 1924–15 May 1925 Raphaël Antonetti; 15 May 1925–14 Dec. 1925 Matteo Alfassa (acting); 14 Dec. 1925–15 Nov. 1929 Raphaël Antonetti; 15 Nov. 1929–30 Aug. 1930 Matteo Alfassa (acting); 30 Aug. 1930–9 Apr. 1931 Raphaël Antonetti; 9 Apr. 1931–5 Nov. 1931 Matteo Alfassa (acting); 5 Nov. 1931–4 Dec. 1932 Raphaël Antonetti; 4 Dec. 1932–11 Dec. 1933 Matteo Alfassa (acting); 11 Dec. 1933–30 June 1934 Raphaël Antonetti.

390 French Equatorial Africa Colony. 30 June 1934–28 Nov. 1958. *Location:* Chad, Central African Republic, Gabon and Congo (Brazzaville). *Capital:* Brazzaville. *Other names:* A.E.F., Afrique Équatoriale Française, French Equatorial Africa.
History: In 1934 **French Equatorial Africa** became a giant colony, with four component parts – **Chad Colony, Moyen-Congo Colony [ii], Gabon Colony [iii]** and **Ubangi-Shari Colony [ii]** – all becoming régions of the new colony (see each of these four names, but with "région" substituted for "colony"). In 1937 each of these régions became overseas territories of France, and in 1946 overseas territories of the Fourth Republic. But, as far as life in the tropics went, these four component parts remained the same and for the life of the A.E.F. Colony (1934–1958) they stayed as territorial parts, regardless of the precise and correct terminology applied to each by Paris. In 1958 the A.E.F. broke up, and autonomy was granted to all four components (see **Chad Autonomous Republic, Autonomous Central African Republic, Gabon Autonomous Republic** and **Congo Autonomous Republic**).
Governors-General: 30 June 1934–14 Oct. 1934 Raphaël Antonetti; 14 Oct. 1934–20 March 1935 Georges Renard; 20 March 1935–5 Apr. 1936 Marcel Marchessou (acting); 5 Apr. 1936–25 Nov. 1938 Dieudonné Reste; 25 Nov. 1938–9 Feb. 1939 Léon Solomiac (acting); 9 Feb. 1939–21 Apr. 1939 Dieudonné Reste; 21 Apr. 1939–3 Sept. 1939 Léon Solomiac (acting); 3 Sept. 1939–17 July 1940 Pierre Boissons; 17 July 1940–28 Aug. 1940 Louis Husson; 28 Aug. 1940–11 Aug. 1941 René de Larminat; 11 Aug. 1941–15 Feb. 1944 Félix Éboué; 15 Feb. 1944–2 Oct. 1944 Charles Bayardelle (acting); 2 Oct. 1944–8 March 1945 Charles Bayardelle; 8 March 1945–June 1945 Henri Sautot (acting); June 1945–3 Aug. 1946 Charles Bayardelle; 3 Aug. 1946–5 June 1947 Jean-Louis Soucadaux (acting); 5 June 1947–Aug. 1947 Laurent Péchoux (acting); Aug. 1947–17 Sept. 1947 Charles Luizet; 17 Sept. 1947–15 Nov. 1947 Jean-Louis Soucadaux (acting); 15 Nov. 1947–26 March 1948 Jean-Louis Soucadaux; 26 March 1948–21 Sept. 1951 Bernard Cornut-Gentille; 21 Sept. 1951–20 Jan. 1958 Paul Chauvet. *High Commissioners:* 20 Jan. 1958–15

July 1958 Pierre Messmer; 15 July 1958–28 Nov. 1958 Yvon Bourges.

391 French Equatorial African Protectorate. 27 Apr. 1886–30 Apr. 1891. *Location:* coastal areas of what was later **French Congo.** *Capital:* Brazzaville. *Other names:* Protectorat de l'Afrique Équatoriale Française.
History: In 1886 an administration was placed over all French possessions in the west central African country. In 1891 it was renamed **French Congo.**
Commissioners-General: 27 Apr. 1886–30 Apr. 1891 Pierre Savorgnan de Brazza.

392 French Fezzan. 29 Jan. 1943–24 Dec. 1951. *Location:* south Libya. *Capital:* Sabha. *Other names:* Fezzan, Fazzan.
History: In 1943 **Libya Italian Colony** came to an end (see **British Tripolitania** for further details). The Allied Forces of France and Britain split it up between them. The southern division went to France as French Fezzan. In 1951 it, **British Tripolitania** and **Cyrenaica (Autonomous)** merged to form the **Libyan Kingdom.**
Rulers: 29 Jan. 1943–1945 no fixed central administration; 1945–12 Feb. 1950 Ahmad Saif al-Nasir (Administrator); 1947–1950 Maurice Sarazac (Military Governor); 1950–24 Dec. 1951 Maurice Sarazac (Resident); 12 Feb. 1950–24 Dec. 1951 Ahmad Saif al-Nasir (Chief of Fezzan).

393 French Gambia. 11 Feb. 1779–3 Sept. 1783. *Location:* the Gambia River. *Capital:* Saint Louis.
History: In 1778 the French captured their former possessions in Senegal (see **Senegambia Colony**), and in 1779 took the British settlements on the Gambia River, thus effectively ending Senegambia Colony. From 1779 to 1783 (the Treaty of Paris—1783) Gambia was in French hands. In 1783 these settlements were returned to Britain, although not re-occupied until 1816 (see **Bathurst**

Colony).
Rulers: 11 Feb. 1779–3 Sept. 1783 Direct rule from Saint Louis, Senegal.

French Gold Coast see **Petit Dieppe, French Ivory Coast [i]** and **Ivory Coast Protectorate**

394 French Guinea Colony. 10 March 1893–13 Oct. 1946. *Location:* as **Guinea Republic.** *Capital:* Conakry. *Other names:* French Guinea, Guinée.
History: In 1893 the **Rivières du Sud Colony** became French Guinea. In 1946 it became an overseas territory of France (see **French Guinea Overseas Territory**).
Lieutenant-Governors: 10 March 1893–June 1893 Paul Cousturier (acting); June 1893–23 Apr. 1895 Noël Ballay; 23 Apr. 1895–28 May 1896 Paul Cousturier (acting); 28 May 1896–21 June 1898 Noël Ballay; 21 June 1898–12 Apr. 1900 Paul Cousturier (acting); 12 Apr. 1900–2 Nov. 1900 Noël Ballay; 2 Nov. 1900–28 Sept. 1904 Paul Cousturier; 28 Sept. 1904–15 Oct. 1904 Antoine Frezouls (acting); 15 Oct. 1904–27 Feb. 1906 Antoine Frezouls; 27 Feb. 1906–16 May 1907 Jules Richard (acting); 16 May 1907–25 July 1907 Joost van Vollenhouven (acting); 25 July 1907–18 Feb. 1908 Georges Poulet (acting); 18 Feb. 1908–24 Sept. 1909 Victor Liotard; 24 Sept. 1909–Jan. 1910 Georges Veillat (acting); Jan. 1910–4 July 1910 Victor Liotard; 4 July 1910–Nov. 1910 Georges Poulet (acting); Nov. 1910–9 May 1912 Camille Guy; 9 May 1912–7 March 1913 Jean-Louis Poiret (acting); 7 March 1913–6 March 1914 Jean Peuvergne; 6 March 1914–13 June 1914 Jean-Louis Poiret (acting); 13 June 1914–23 Oct. 1915 Jean Peuvergne; 23 Oct. 1915–12 Oct. 1916 Jean-Louis Poiret (acting); 12 Oct. 1916–9 Apr. 1919 Jean-Louis Poiret; 9 Apr. 1919–20 Jan. 1920 Fernand Lavit (acting); 20 Jan. 1920–15 Feb. 1922 Jean-Louis Poiret; 15 Feb. 1922–13 Nov. 1922 Jules Vidal (acting); 13 Nov. 1922–26 March 1925 Jean-Louis Poiret; 26

March 1925–Dec. 1925 Robert Simon (acting); Dec. 1925–7 Apr. 1927 Jean-Louis Poiret; 7 Apr. 1927–13 Apr. 1928 Antoine Paladi (acting); 13 Apr. 1928–21 Oct. 1928 Jean-Claude Tissier (acting); 21 Oct. 1928–21 July 1929 Jean-Louis Poiret; 21 July 1929–28 Feb. 1931 Louis Antonin (acting); 28 Feb. 1931–1 Jan. 1932 Robert de Guise; 1 Jan. 1932–13 June 1933 Joseph Vadier; 13 June 1933–6 Dec. 1933 Antoine Paladi (acting); 6 Dec. 1933–8 July 1935 Joseph Vadier; 8 July 1935–24 Nov. 1935 Louis-Placide Blacher (acting); 24 Nov. 1935–7 March 1936 Joseph Vadier. *Governors:* 7 March 1936–21 Nov. 1936 Louis-Placide Blacher (acting); 21 Nov. 1936–4 Sept. 1937 Louis-Placide Blacher; 4 Sept. 1937–26 Jan. 1938 Pierre Tap (acting); 26 Jan. 1938–10 June 1939 Louis-Placide Blacher; 10 June 1939–1 Oct. 1939 Félix Martiné (acting); 1 Oct. 1939–12 Feb. 1940 Louis-Placide Blacher; 12 Feb. 1940–Aug. 1942 Félix Giacobbi; Aug. 1942–25 March 1944 Horace Crocicchia; 25 March 1944–30 Apr. 1946 Jacques-Georges Fourneau (acting); 30 Apr. 1946–13 Oct. 1946 Éduard Terrac.

395 French Guinea Overseas Territory. 13 Oct. 1946–2 Oct. 1958. *Location:* as **Guinea Republic.** *Capital:* Conakry. *Other names:* French Guinea.

History: In 1946, with the establishment of the Fourth Republic in France, **French Guinea Colony** became an overseas territory. In 1958 it was the only state in **French West Africa** which elected not to go through the autonomous republic stage, and became independent as **Guinea Republic.**

Governors: 13 Oct. 1946–Jan. 1948 Éduard Terrac (acting); Jan. 1948–9 Feb. 1951 Roland Pré; 9 Feb. 1951–Apr. 1953 Paul Sirieix; Apr. 1953–23 June 1955 Jean-Paul Parisot; 23 June 1955–3 June 1956 Charles-Henri Bonfils; 3 June 1956–29 Jan. 1958 Jean-Paul Ramadier; 29 Jan. 1958–2 Oct. 1958 Jean Mauberna.

396 French Ivory Coast [i]. 1843–4 Aug. 1860. *Location:* along the coast of what is today the Ivory Coast. *Capital:* Grand Bassam. *Other names:* Ivory Coast, Grand Bassam, French Gold Coast Establishments.

History: In 1843 protectorates of a sort were established by the French at Grand Bassam and Assinie, and posts were set up. A little later, at Gabon, a similar thing happened (see **Gabon Settlements**). In 1860 the Ivory Coast became a territory (see **Ivory Coast Territory**) within the greater colony of **Ivory Coast-Gabon.**

Commandants: 1843–1843 Charles de Kerhallet; 1843–1844 Thomas Besson; 1844–1845 Joseph Pellegrin; 1845–1847 M. Conjard; 1847–1848 Adolphe Pigeon; 1848–1850 Jean-Jules Boulay; 1851–1853 Charles Martin des Pallières; 1853–1854 François Chirat; 1854–1855 Pierre Mailhetard; 1856–1856 Noël Bruyas; 1857–1857 Charles Brossard de Corbigny; 1858–1859 Pierre Mailhetard; 1859–4 Aug. 1860 [unknown].

397 French Ivory Coast [ii]. 16 Dec. 1883–10 Jan. 1889. *Location:* the coastline of the Ivory Coast. *Capital:* Grand Bassam. *Other names:* Ivory Coast, Côte d'Ivoire.

History: In 1883 **Ivory Coast-Gabon** came to an end, and each of the territories (see **Gabon Territory [i]** and **Ivory Coast Territory [Verdier & Co.]**) went their separate ways. French Ivory Coast, in 1889, became the **Ivory Coast Protectorate.**

Residents: 16 Dec. 1883–1886 Arthur Verdier; 1886–10 Jan. 1889 Marcel Treich-Laplène.

398 French Mauritius. 1715–1722. *Location:* as **Mauritius.** *Capital:* none. *Other names:* Mauritius, Île Maurice.

History: In 1715 the French East India Company claimed the island which five years before the Dutch had abandoned as useless (see **Dutch Mauritius Colony [ii]**). In 1722 the French began to populate it (see **Île de France**).

Governors: 1715–1718 none; 1718–1722 Joseph de Courchant.

399 French Morocco. 30 March 1912–2 March 1956. *Location:* Morocco, excluding Tangier and the northern, i.e. Spanish Morocco sector. *Capital:* Rabat. *Other names:* Maroc Français, French Protectorate of Morocco.

History: In 1912 the French, influential in the area since 1905, finally declared a protectorate over **French-Occupied Morocco,** i.e. most of the country, Spain taking the northern segment of the Rif (see **Spanish Morocco).** As early as July 20, 1901 Morocco had granted France control of the Frontier Police, so the move was inevitable. In 1956 both protectorates came to an end and Morocco became independent (see **Morocco [Independent Sultanate]).**

Residents-General: 24 May 1912–13 Dec. 1916 Hubert Lyautey; 13 Dec. 1916–7 Apr. 1917 Henri Gouraud (acting); 7 Apr. 1917–24 Sept. 1925 Hubert Lyautey; 4 Oct. 1925–1 Jan. 1929 Théodore Steeg; 1 Jan. 1929–July 1933 Lucien Saint; Aug. 1933–22 March 1936 Henri Ponsot; 22 March 1936–17 Sept. 1936 Marcel Peyrouton; 17 Sept. 1936–14 Nov. 1942 Augustin Noguès; 5 June 1943–3 March 1946 Gabriel Puaux; 3 March 1946–14 May 1947 Eirik Labonne; 14 May 1947–28 Aug. 1951 Alphonse Juin; 28 Aug. 1951–20 May 1954 Augustin Guillaume; 20 May 1954–20 June 1955 François La Coste; 20 June 1955–29 Aug. 1955 Gilbert Grandval; 29 Aug. 1955–9 Nov. 1955 Comte Boyer de la Tour du Moulin; 9 Nov. 1955–2 March 1956 André Dubois. *Sultans:* 30 March 1912–11 Aug. 1912 Abdul-Hafiz; 11 Aug. 1912–17 Nov. 1927 Yusuf; 17 Nov. 1927–14 Aug. 1953 Muhammad V; 14 Aug. 1953–16 Aug. 1953 Muhammad VI; 16 Aug. 1953–21 Aug. 1953 vacant; 21 Aug. 1953–30 Oct. 1955 Muhammad VI; 1 Nov. 1955–2 March 1956 Muhammad V. *Prime Ministers:* 7 Dec. 1955–2 March 1956 M'barek ben Mustafa el-Bakai.

400 French-Occupied Morocco. 4 Aug. 1907–30 March 1912. *Location:* as **Kingdom of Morocco.** *Capital:* Rabat. *Other names:* Morocco.

History: France's involvement with Morocco dates back to 1830 when France seized Algiers (see **French Possessions in North Africa)** and increased from then on. The rebel Abdelkader (see **Mascara)** caused a strain on this relationship in the 1830s and 1840s and France took portions of Morocco and added them to Algeria (see **French Algeria Military Province).** Basically France wanted to control North Africa, and by 1904 Morocco had become a French sphere of influence, although Moroccan independence was affirmed by all the world powers (see **Alawid Morocco** for information about the country prior to 1907). Also in 1904 France occupied the Figuig area south of Oujda, and in 1907 Oujda itself was occupied. A war between the two countries began, and Casablanca and Rabat were occupied by the French. The Sultan was deposed by his successor in late 1907. By 1911 Fez and Meknes were also occupied, and as it looked as if the French would take the whole country, Spain stepped in and seized the Rif (see **Spanish Morocco),** while the rest of the country became French (see **French Morocco).**

Sultans: 4 Aug. 1907–4 Jan. 1908 Abdul Azziz; 4 Jan. 1908–30 March 1912 Abdul-Hafiz.

401 French Possessions in North Africa. 5 July 1830–1839. *Location:* as **French Algerian Possessions.** *Capital:* Algiers.

History: The name Algeria was not used until 1839 (see **French Algerian Possessions)** to denote the French possessions taken in 1830 from the dey of Algiers (see **Algiers Regency).** Algiers was taken on July 5, 1830, Oran in 1831, Bone in 1832, and Constantine in 1837. (See **Constantine.)** With the exception of Constantine all of these major towns and the areas around them had been ruled by Turkey since 1518. (See also **Oran [Spanish]**).

Military Commanders: 5 July 1830–12 Aug. 1830 Comte Bourmont; 12 Aug. 1830–21 Feb. 1831 Comte Clausel; 21 Feb. 1831–6 Dec. 1831 Baron Berthezène; 6 Dec. 1831–29 Apr. 1833 Duc de Rovigo; 29 Apr. 1833–27 July 1834 Théophile Viorol (acting). *Governors-General of the French Possessions in North Africa:* 27 July 1834–8 July 1835 Comte D'Erlon; 8 July 1835–12 Feb. 1837 Comte Clausel; 12 Feb. 1837–12 Oct. 1837 Comte de Danrémont; 11 Nov. 1837–1839 Comte Valée.

402 French Somaliland. 1896–1958. *Location:* **Djibouti.** *Capital:* Djibouti. *Other names:* French Somaliland Protectorate, Côte Française des Somalis.

History: In 1896 **Obock Colony** became French Somaliland Protectorate. The interior was developed in the 1920s and 1930s. During part of World War II the British occupied it, but the French administration continued. Internal autonomy was granted in 1956, and in 1958 it became **French Somaliland Overseas Territory.**

Governors: 1896–7 March 1899 Léonce Lagarde; 7 March 1899–23 March 1899 Louis Mizon (acting); 28 March 1899–13 Apr. 1900 Alfred Martineau; 13 Apr. 1900–6 Dec. 1900 Gabriel Angoulvant (acting); 6 Dec. 1900–7 Sept. 1901 Adrien Bonhoure; 7 Sept. 1901–June 1902 Louis Ormières (acting); June 1902–23 May 1903 Adrien Bonhoure; 23 May 1903–Dec. 1903 Albert Dubarry (acting); Dec. 1903–2 Apr. 1904 Adrien Bonhoure; 2 Apr. 1904–5 Aug. 1904 Albert Dubarry (acting); 5 Aug. 1904–9 Sept. 1905 Pierre Pascal; 9 Sept. 1905–13 Oct. 1905 Raphaël Antonetti (acting); 13 Oct. 1905–19 May 1906 Louis Ormières (acting); 19 May 1906–19 June 1906 M. Patte (acting); 19 June 1906–July 1908 Pierre Pascal; July 1908–5 Jan. 1909 Jean-Baptiste Castaing (acting); 5 Jan.

1909–June 1911 Pierre Pascal; June 1911–Dec. 1911 Jean-Baptiste Castaing (acting); Dec. 1911–1915 Pierre Pascal; 1915–1916 Paul Simoni; 1916–1918 Victor Fillon; 1918–1924 Jules Lauret; 1924–1932 Pierre Chapon-Baissac; 1932–7 May 1934 Louis Blacher; 7 May 1934–18 July 1935 Jules de Coppet; 18 July 1935–20 Dec. 1935 Achille Silvestre; 20 Dec. 1935–1 May 1937 Armand Annet; 1 May 1937–27 Apr. 1938 François Pierre-Alype (acting); 27 Apr. 1938–2 May 1939 Hubert Deschamps (acting); 2 May 1939–1940 Hubert Deschamps; 1940–7 Aug. 1940 Gaëtan Germain; 7 Aug. 1940–4 Dec. 1942 Pierre Nouailhetas; 4 Dec. 1942–30 Dec. 1942 Christian Dupont; 30 Dec. 1942–22 June 1943 Charles Bayardelle; 22 June 1943–7 Jan. 1944 Michel Saller (acting); 7 Jan. 1944–1 May 1944 Michel Saller; 1 May 1944–14 May 1945 Jean Chalvet; 14 May 1945–Dec. 1945 Jean Beyriès (acting); Dec. 1945–30 Apr. 1946 Jean Chalvet; 30 Apr. 1946–1 March 1950 Paul Siriex; 1 March 1950–6 Apr. 1954 Numa Sadoul; 6 Apr. 1954–13 Aug. 1954 Roland Pré; 13 Aug. 1954–7 Aug. 1957 Jean Petitbon; 7 Aug. 1957–1958 Maurice Meker.

403 French Somaliland Overseas Territory. 1958–6 July 1967. *Location:* as **Djibouti.** *Capital:* Djibouti. *Other names:* French Somaliland.

History: In 1958 **French Somaliland** became an overseas territory of France by the choice of the native people (the Afars and Europeans said "yes"; the Issas said "no"). In 1967 it was renamed the Territory of the Afars and Issas (see **Afars and Issas Territory**).

Governors: 1958–16 Nov. 1962 Jacques Compain; 16 Nov. 1962–15 Sept. 1966 René Tirant; 15 Sept. 1966–6 July 1967 Louis Saget.

404 French Sudan. 4 Dec. 1920–13 Oct. 1946. *Location:* as **Mali Republic.** *Capital:* Bamako. *Other names:* Soudain Français.

History: In 1920 **Upper Senegal and**

Niger Colony became French Sudan. In 1946 it became an overseas territory of the French Fourth Republic (see **French Sudan Overseas Territory**).

Lieutenant-Governors: 4 Dec. 1920–Jan. 1921 Théodore Maillet (acting); Jan. 1921–21 Aug. 1921 Marcel Olivier; 21 Aug. 1921–26 Feb. 1924 Jean Terasson de Fougères (acting); 26 Feb. 1924–23 Apr. 1924 Jean Terasson de Fougères; 23 Apr. 1924–6 May 1924 Jean Joseph Carreau (acting); 6 May 1924–Feb. 1925 Albéric Fournier (acting); Feb. 1925–30 Apr. 1926 Jean Terasson de Fougères; 30 Apr. 1926–Nov. 1926 Gabriel Descemet (acting); Nov. 1926–2 Apr. 1928 Jean Terasson de Fougères; 2 Apr. 1928–28 Jan. 1929 Gabriel Descemet (acting); 28 Jan. 1929–31 Dec. 1930 Jean Terasson de Fougères; 31 Dec. 1930–4 Apr. 1931 Joseph Court (acting); 4 Apr. 1931–11 June 1931 Gabriel Descemet (acting); 11 June 1931–31 March 1933 Louis Fousset; 31 March 1933–22 May 1933 René Desjardins (acting); 22 May 1933–30 Nov. 1933 Léon Solomiac (acting); 30 Nov. 1933–19 Feb. 1935 Louis Fousset; 19 Feb. 1935–22 Nov. 1935 Félix Éboué (acting); 22 Nov. 1935–9 Nov. 1936 Matthieu Alfasa; 9 Nov. 1936–4 Dec. 1936 Ferdinand Rougier (acting); 4 Dec. 1936–1937 Ferdinand Rougier. *Governors:* 1937–28 March 1938 Ferdinand Rougier; 28 March 1938–15 Nov. 1940 Jean Desanti (acting); 15 Nov. 1940–17 Apr. 1942 Jean Rapenne (acting); 17 Apr. 1942–29 Dec. 1942 Auguste Calvel (acting); 29 Dec. 1942–15 May 1946 Auguste Calvel; 15 May 1946–13 Oct. 1946 Edmond Louveau.

405 French Sudan Civil Territory. 21 Nov. 1893–16 June 1895. *Location:* as **Mali Republic.** *Capital:* Kayès. *Other names:* French Sudan. *History:* In 1893 **French Sudan Military Territory** became a civil territory; in 1895, **French Sudan Colony.** *Lieutenant-Governors:* 21 Nov. 1893–Dec. 1893 François Bonnier (act-ing); Dec. 1893–16 June 1895 Louis Grodet.

406 French Sudan Colony. 16 June 1895–17 Oct. 1899. *Location:* Mali. *Capital:* Kayès. *Other names:* French Sudan. *History:* In 1895 **French Sudan Civil Territory** became a colony. In 1899 it became subject to Senegal (see **Senegal Colony**) and became **Upper Senegal and Niger Territory.** *Lieutenant-Governors:* 16 June 1895–12 July 1895 Louis Grodet; 12 July 1895–1898 Louis de Trentinian; 1898–1899 René Audéoud (acting); 1899–17 Oct. 1899 Louis de Trentinian.

407 French Sudan Military Territory. 27 Aug. 1892–21 Nov. 1893. *Location:* as **Mali Republic.** *Capital:* Kayès. *Other names:* French Sudan. *History:* In 1892 **French Sudan Territory** became a military territory. In 1893 it became **French Sudan Civil Territory.** *Lieutenant-Governors:* 27 Aug. 1892–Sept. 1892 Pierre Humbert (act-ing); 3 Oct. 1892–2 Aug. 1893 Louis Archinard; 2 Aug. 1893–21 Nov. 1893 François Bonnier (acting).

408 French Sudan Overseas Territory. 13 Oct. 1946–24 Nov. 1958. *Location:* as **Mali Republic.** *Capital:* Bamako. *Other names:* French Sudan. *History:* In 1946 **French Sudan** became an overseas territory. In 1958 it gained autonomy within the French Community (see **Sudanese Republic [Autonomous]**). *Governors:* 13 Oct. 1946–25 Feb. 1949 Edmond Louveau; 25 Feb. 1949–3 Feb. 1950 Lucien Geay (acting); 3 Feb. 1950–Apr. 1952 Edmond Louveau; Apr. 1952–10 July 1952 Victor Bailly; 10 July 1952–23 Feb. 1953 Salvador Jean Etcheber; 23 Feb. 1953–2 Dec. 1953 Albert Mouragues; 2 Dec. 1953–10 Feb. 1954 Lucien Geay (acting); 10 Feb. 1954–3 Nov. 1956 Lucien Geay. *High Commissioners:* 3 Nov. 1956–24 Nov. 1958 Henri Gipoulon. *Prime Ministers:*

Apr. 1957–24 Nov. 1958 Jean-Marie Koné.

409 French Sudan Territory. 18 Aug. 1890–27 Aug. 1892. *Location:* as **Mali Republic.** *Capital:* Kayès. *Other names:* French Sudan.
History: In 1890 **Upper Senegal Protectorate** became French Sudan, a territory of the French nation. In 1892 it became **French Sudan Military Territory.**
Commandants-Superior: 18 Aug. 1890–9 Oct. 1891 Louis Archinard; 9 Oct. 1891–27 Aug. 1892 Pierre Humbert.

French Territory of the Afars and Issas see **Afars and Issas Territory**

410 French Togoland. 27 Dec. 1916–30 Sept. 1920. *Location:* as **Togo.** *Capital:* Lomé.
History: In 1916 the **Togoland French-British Condominium** came to an end, each country getting a share of the conquered German territory (see **Togoland Colony**); viz. French Togoland and **British Togoland.** In 1920 each of these areas was made into a League of Nations mandate (see **Togoland French Mandate** and **Togoland British Mandate**).
Governors: 27 Dec. 1916–27 Apr. 1917 Gaston Fourn; 27 Apr. 1917–25 Jan. 1920 Alfred-Louis Woelfel; 25 Jan. 1920–30 Sept. 1920 Numa Sasias (acting).

411 French West Africa. See these names:
Senegambia (1982–   )
French West Africa (1895–1959)

412 French West Africa. 16 June 1895–6 Apr. 1959. *Location:* North West Africa—comprising Guinea, Mali, Ivory Coast, Senegal, Benin, Mauritania, Niger, Burkina Faso (or rather, the names by which those countries went between 1895 and 1958).

Capital: Dakar (from 1904); Gorée (1902–04); Saint Louis (1895–1902); *Other names:* A.O.F., Afrique Occidentale Française.
History: In 1895 the Federation of French West Africa was born, taking in **French Guinea, French Sudan Civil Territory, Ivory Coast Colony** and **Senegal Colony.** In 1899 **Dahomey Colony** joined, in 1919 **Upper Volta Colony** joined, in 1921 **Mauritania Colony** joined, and in 1922 **Niger Colony** joined. The A.O.F. became defunct in 1958.
Governors-General: 16 June 1895–28 Sept. 1895 Jean-Baptiste Chaudié (acting); 28 Sept. 1895–1 Nov. 1900 Jean-Baptiste Chaudié; 1 Nov. 1900–26 Jan. 1902 Noël Ballay; 26 June 1902–15 March 1902 Pierre Capest (acting); 15 March 1902–15 Dec. 1907 Ernest Roume; 15 Dec. 1907–9 March 1908 Martial Merlin (acting); 9 March 1908–14 Apr. 1915 Amédée Merlaud-Ponty; 14 Apr. 1915–3 June 1917 Joseph Clozel; 3 June 1917–22 Jan. 1918 Joost van Vollenhouven; 22 Jan. 1918–28 Feb. 1919 Gabriel Angoulvant; 28 Feb. 1919–16 Sept. 1919 Charles Brunet (acting); 19 Sept. 1919–27 May 1922 Martial Merlin; 27 May 1922–1 Dec. 1922 Marcel Olivier (acting); 1 Dec. 1922–18 March 1923 Martial Merlin; 18 March 1923–15 Oct. 1930 Jules Carde; 15 Oct. 1930–27 Sept. 1936 Jules Brévié; 27 Sept. 1936–14 July 1938 Jules de Coppet; 14 July 1938–28 Oct. 1938 Léon Geismar (acting); 28 Oct. 1938–18 Apr. 1939 Pierre Boissons; 18 Apr. 1939–25 June 1940 Léon Cayla. *High Commissioners:* 25 June 1940–1 July 1943 Pierre Boissons; 1 July 1943–May 1946 Pierre Cournarie; May 1946–27 Jan. 1948 René Barthes; 27 Jan. 1948–24 May 1951 Paul Béchard; 24 May 1951–21 Sept. 1952 Paul Chauvet (acting); 21 Sept. 1952–5 July 1956 Bernard Cornut-Gentille; 5 July 1956–July 1958 Gaston Cusin. *High Commissioners-General:* July 1958–21 Jan. 1959 Pierre Messmer; 21 Jan. 1959–6 Apr. 1959 no administrative rule.

413 Fulani Empire. 21 Feb. 1804–15 March 1903. *Location:* northern Nigeria, southern Niger and parts of Cameroun. *Capital:* Sokoto and Gwandu (from 1809); Sifawa (1807–1809); Gando (July 1805–1807); Sabon Gari (March 1805–July 1805). *Other names:* Sokoto Caliphate, Filane Empire.

History: Sokoto as a town had existed since 1200, within the old state of **Gobir,** and in 1809 Uthman Dan Fodio, the Muslim conqueror, established it as one of his capitals. These Fulani invaders, between 1804–1812, conquered the states of **Katsina, Kano, Zaria, Daura, Gombe, Misau, Kazaure, Katagum, Bauchi, Adamawa, Ilorin** and **Nupe,** a Caliphate being established over all these emirates. (See **Bauchi Emirate** for a different perspective on the Fulani Empire.) Dan Fodio's son Bello was the first Sultan, and in 1903 the Fulani Empire (or Sokoto Caliphate) became part of **Northern Nigeria Protectorate** (or rather, most of it did. Some of it went to **Zinder Autonomous Military Territory** and **Kamerun**).

Military Commanders: 21 Feb. 1804–21 Apr. 1817 Uthman (or Usman) Dan Fodio. *Sultans:* 21 Apr. 1817–1837 Muhammad Bello; 1837–1842 Abubakr Atiku I; 1842–1859 Aliyu; 1859–1866 Ahmada Atiku; 1866–1867 Aliyu Karami; 1867–1873 Ahmadu Rufai; 1873–1877 Abubakr Atiku II; 1877–1881 Mu'azu; 1881–March 1891 Umaru; March 1891–1902 Abdarrahman; 1902–1903 Atahiru Ahmadu (or Muhammad Atahiru I); 1903–1915 Muhammad Atahiru II; 1915–1924 Muhammad Maiturare; 1924–1931 Muhammad Tambari; 1931–1938 Hassan Shahu; 1938–Sidiq Abubakr.

Fumbina see **Adamawa**

Funchal see also **Madeira**

414 Funchal Donatária. 1418–1580. *Location:* Madeira Island, Madeira. *Capital:* Funchal (founded 1421 by João Gonçalves Zarco).

History: see **Porto Santo Donatária** for details of early history. In 1580 it became part of **Madeira Colony.**

Rulers: unknown.

415 Funj Sultanate. 1504–12 June 1821. *Location:* central Sudan. *Capital:* Sennar (from 1515). *Other names:* Sennar, Senaar, Fung Kingdom, Sennaar.

History: In 1504 Amara Dunkas founded the sultanate around Sennar. A peak in power was reached in the late 17th century, then it declined until 1762, when the Hamaj clan began ruling through puppet sultans. The Turkish-Egyptian Army conquered the area in 1821 and it became incorporated, along with **Nubia** and **Kordofan,** into the newly formed state of Sudan (see **Egyptian Sudan**).

Sultans: 1504–1534 Amara Dunkas; 1534–1551 Nayil ibn Amara; 1551–1558 Abd al-Kadir I; 1558–1569 Amara II Abu Sakaykin; 1569–1586 Dakin al-Adil; 1586–1587 Dawra ibn Dakin; 1587–1591 Tabl; 1591–1592 interregnum; 1592–1604 Unsa I; 1604–1606 Abd al-Kadir II; Nov. 1606–1611 Adlan I; 1611–1617 Badi I Sid al-Qum; 1617–1645 Rubat I; 1645–28 Dec. 1680 Badi II Abu Daqan; 28 Dec. 1680–6 June 1692 Unsa II; 6 June 1692–13 Apr. 1716 Badi III al-Ahmar; 13 Apr. 1716–8 June 1720 Unsa III; 8 June 1720–8 July 1724 Nul; 8 July 1724–25 March 1762 Badi IV Abu Shulukh; 25 March 1762–1769 Nasir ibn Badi; 1769–1776 Ismail ibn Badi; 1776–1789 Adlan II; 1789–1789 Tabl II; 1789–1790 Badi V; 1790–1790 Hassab Rabbihi; 1790–1791 Nawwar; 1791–1796 Badi VI; 1796–1803 Ranfi; 1803–12 June 1821 Badi VI.

Fur see **Darfur**

416 Futa Jallon. ca. 1700–14 July 1881. *Location:* Guinea. *Capital:* Timbo. *Other names:* Diallon, Djallon, Futa, Futa Jalon, Fouta Jalon, Futa Dyallo.

History: Formed around 1700 the kingdom of Futa Jallon, composed of Diallon peoples, was the major political unit of what became **Rivières du Sud Territory,** into which it merged in 1881.
Emirs: ca. 1700–1715 Muhammad Saidi; 1715–1720 Musa Ba Kikala; 1720–1720 Sambigu; 1720–1720 Nuhu Ba Kikala; 1720–1727 Malik Si; 1727–1776 Ibrahim Musa; 1776–1791 Ibrahima Sori I; 1791–1796 Sa'adu; 1796–1797 Ali Bilma; 1797–1799 Salihu; 1799–1799 Abdullahi Ba Demba; 1799–1810 Abdelkader; 1810–1814 Abdullahi Ba Demba; 1814–1822 Abdelkader; 1822–1822 Bu Bakar; 1822–1822 Yahya; 1822–1823 Ahmadu; 1823–1839 Bu Bakar; 1839–1840 Yahya; 1840–1843 Umaru Sori; 1843–1845 Bakari; 1845–1848 Ibrahima Sori II; 1848–1850 Umaru Sori; 1850–1852 Ibrahima Sori II; 1852–1854 Umaru Sori; 1854–1856 Ibrahima Sori II; 1856–1858 Umaru Sori; 1858–1860 Ibrahima Sori II; 1860–1862 Umaru Sori; 1862–1864 Ibrahima Sori II; 1864–1866 Umaru Sori; 1866–1868 Ibrahima Sori II; 1868–1870 Umaru Sori; 1870–1871 Ibrahima Sori II; 1871–1872 Umaru Sori; 1872–1873 Ibrahima Sori III; 1873–1875 Ahmadu Dara Alfaya; 1875–1877 Umaru Ba Demba; 1877–1879 Ahmadu Dara Alfaya; 1879–1881 Ibrahima Sori III; 1881–1883 Ahmadu Dara Alfaya; 1883–1885 Ibrahima Sori III; 1885–1887 Ahmadu Dara Alfaya; 1888–1890 Ibrahima Sori III; 1890–1892 Bu Bakar III; 1892–June 1894 Ahmadu Dara Alfaya; June 1894–Jan. 1896 Bu Bakar III; Jan. 1896–Feb. 1896 Modi Abdulaye; Feb. 1896–18 Nov. 1896 Bu Bakar III; 18 Nov. 1896–1 Dec. 1896 Umaru Ba Demba; 1 Dec. 1896–30 Oct. 1897 Alfa Ibrahima Sori; 26 Nov. 1897–1906 Baba Alimu; 1906–1912 Bu Bakar IV.

417 Futa Toro. 1513–24 Oct. 1877. *Location:* northern Senegal. *Capital:* Podor. *Other names:* Fouta Toro.

History: Founded by the Dia Ogo Dynasty about 850, then ruled by various peoples until 1513 when the Denyanke Dynasty came into being. In 1877 it became part of **Senegal Colony.**
Kings: 1513–1535 Dengella Koli I; 1535–1538 Dengella Koli II; 1538–ca. 1765 15 kings unknown by name today; ca. 1765–1776 Sule-Budu; 1776–1804 Abdelkedir; 1804–ca. 1859 [unknown]; ca. 1859–ca. 1868 Mustafa; ca. 1868–1875 Ahmadu Sego; 1875–Feb. 1891 Abdul Bu Bakar.

418 Gabon. See these **names:**
Gabon Republic (1960–   )
Gabon Autonomous Republic (1958–1960)
Gabon Overseas Territory [ii] (1946–1958)
Gabon Overseas Territory [i] (1937–1946)
Gabon Region (1934–1937)
Gabon Colony [iii] (1903–1934)
Gabon Territory [iv] (1902–1903)
Gabon Territory [iii] (1888–1902)
Gabon Colony [ii] (1886–1888)
Gabon Territory [ii] (1886–1886)
Gabon Colony [i] (1883–1886)
Gabon Territory [i] (1860–1883)
Gabon Settlements (1843–1860)
Gulf of Guinea Settlements (1839–1843)

419 Gabon Autonomous Republic. 28 Nov. 1958–17 Aug. 1960. *Location:* as **Gabon Republic.** *Capital:* Libreville. *Other names:* Autonomous Republic of Gabon.
History: In 1958 **Gabon Overseas Territory** became an autonomous republic on the way to independence, which was achieved in 1960 as **Gabon Republic.**
High Commissioners: 28 Nov. 1958–July 1959 Louis Sanmarco; July 1959–17 Aug. 1960 Jean Risterucci. *Chief Ministers:* 28 Nov. 1958–27 Feb. 1959 Léon M'Ba. *Prime Ministers:* 27 Feb. 1959–17 Aug. 1960 Léon M'Ba.

420 Gabon Colony [i]. 16 Dec. 1883–27 April 1886. *Location:*

Gabon. *Capital:* Libreville. *Other names:* Gabon and Gulf of Guinea Settlements.

History: In 1883 **Gabon Territory [i]** devolved from its connection with Ivory Coast (see **Ivory Coast-Gabon**), and became a separate colony. In 1886 it became a territory again (see **Gabon Territory [ii]**).

Commandants-Particulier: 16 Dec. 1883–1885 Jean Cornut-Gentille; 1885–27 Apr. 1886 Georges Pradier.

421 Gabon Colony [ii]. 29 June 1886–11 Dec. 1888. *Location:* as **Gabon Republic**. *Capital:* Libreville. *Other names:* Gabon.

History: In June 1886 **Gabon Territory [ii]** became an autonomous colony ruled by a lieutenant-governor. In 1888 it reverted to territorial status (see **Gabon Territory [iii]**) as part of **Moyen-Congo-Gabon**.

Lieutenant-Governors: 29 June 1886–27 Aug. 1887 Noël Ballay; 27 Aug. 1887–25 Dec. 1887 Capt. Gourgas (acting); 25 Dec. 1887–11 Dec. 1888 Noël Ballay.

422 Gabon Colony [iii]. 29 Dec. 1903–30 June 1934. *Location:* as **Gabon Republic**. *Capital:* Libreville. *Other names:* Gabun, Gaboon.

History: In 1903 **Gabon Territory**, part of **Lower Congo-Gabon** became a separate colony again. In 1934 it became part of **French Equatorial Africa Colony**, as **Gabon Region**.

Lieutenant-Governors: 29 Dec. 1903–21 Jan. 1904 Direct rule from Saint Louis, Senegal Colony (and after 1904 Senegal Colony and Protectorate); 21 Jan. 1904–19 Apr. 1905 Louis Ormières; 19 Apr. 1905–5 Aug. 1905 Paul Cousturier (acting); 5 Aug. 1905–27 Apr. 1906 Alfred Fourneau; 27 Apr. 1906–23 Apr. 1907 Charles Noufflard (acting); 23 Apr. 1907–26 Apr. 1907 Alfred Martineau; 26 Apr. 1907–Dec. 1908 Édouard Telle (acting); 20 Jan. 1909–10 Feb. 1909 Frédéric Weber (acting); 10 Feb. 1909–9 Nov. 1909 Charles Rognon (acting); 9 Nov. 1909–June 1911 Léon Richaud (acting); June 1911–21 Feb. 1912 Georges Poulet; 21 Feb. 1912–18 Apr. 1914 Paul Adam (acting); 18 Apr. 1914–1 June 1917 Casimir Guyon; 1 June 1917–12 June 1918 Georges Thomann (acting); 12 June 1918–30 June 1919 Maurice Lapalud; 30 June 1919–13 Apr. 1920 Jean Marchand (acting); 13 Apr. 1920–12 March 1921 Jean Marchand; 12 March 1921–Aug. 1921 Georges Thomann (acting); Aug. 1921–29 May 1922 Jean Marchand; 29 May 1922–15 June 1923 Edmond Cadier (acting); 15 June 1923–29 July 1924 Louis Cercus (acting); 29 July 1924–26 Sept. 1926 Joseph Bernard; 26 Sept. 1926–Aug. 1927 Adolphe Deitte (acting); Aug. 1927–13 Apr. 1928 Joseph Bernard; 13 Apr. 1928–Sept. 1929 Adolphe Deitte (acting); Sept. 1929–19 June 1931 Joseph Bernard; 19 June 1931–Sept. 1931 Louis Vingarassamy (acting); Sept. 1931–30 June 1934 Louis Bonvin.

423 Gabon Overseas Territory [i]. 31 Dec. 1937–13 Oct. 1946. *Location:* as **Gabon Republic**. *Capital:* Libreville. *Other names:* Gabon Region, Gabun, Gaboon.

History: In 1937 **Gabon Region** became an overseas territory of France, still part of the **French Equatorial Africa Colony**. In 1946 it became part of the Fourth Republic of France (see **Gabon Overseas Territory [ii]**).

Delegate-Governors: 31 Dec. 1937–29 Aug. 1938 Georges Parisot; 29 Aug. 1938–2 Nov. 1939 Georges Masson (acting); 2 Nov. 1939–14 Nov. 1940 Georges Masson; 14 Nov. 1940–26 March 1941 Lt.-Col. Parent (acting). *Governors:* 26 March 1941–30 May 1942 Victor Valentin-Smith; 30 May 1942–26 Aug. 1943 Charles Assier de Pompignan; 26 Aug. 1943–5 Nov. 1943 Paul Vuillaume; 5 Nov. 1943–Dec. 1943 André Servel (acting); Dec. 1943–19 Nov. 1944 Paul Vuillaume; 19 Nov. 1944–28 March 1946 Numa-François Sadoul; 28 March 1946–13 Oct. 1946 Roland Pré.

424 Gabon Overseas Territory [ii].
13 Oct. 1946–28 Nov. 1958. *Location:*
as **Gabon Republic.** *Capital:* Libreville. *Other names:* Gabun, Gaboon,
Térritoire du Gabon.

History: In 1946 **Gabon Overseas Territory [i]** became an overseas territory of the French Fourth Republic,
part of the **French Equatorial Africa Colony.** In 1958 it became **Gabon Autonomous Republic.**
Governors: 13 Oct. 1946–31 Dec.
1947 Roland Pré; 31 Dec. 1947–6 Apr.
1949 Numa-François Sadoul; 6 Apr.
1949–19 Oct. 1951 Pierre Pelieu; 19 Oct.
1951–25 Apr. 1952 Charles Hanin (acting); 25 Apr. 1952–29 Jan. 1958 Yves
Digo; 29 Jan. 1958–28 Nov. 1958 Louis
Sanmarco.

425 Gabon Region. 30 June 1934–31
Dec. 1937. *Location:* as **Gabon Republic.** *Capital:* Libreville. *Other names:*
Région du Gabon, Gabun, Gaboon.

History: In 1934 **Gabon Colony [iii]**
became a region of the **French Equatorial Africa Colony.** In 1937 it became
an overseas territory of France (see
Gabon Overseas Territory [i]).
Lieutenant-Governors: 30 June
1934–26 Sept. 1934 Louis Bonvin.
Superior-Administrators: 26 Sept.
1934–1935 Louis Bonvin; 1935–24 Oct.
1936 Charles Assier de Pompignan
(acting). *Delegate-Governors:* 24 Oct.
1936–11 Sept. 1937 Louis Bonvin; 11
Sept. 1937–31 Dec. 1947 Georges Parisot.

426 Gabon Republic. 17 Aug.
1960– . *Location:* west central Africa,
on the Atlantic coast.

Capital: Libreville (founded in 1847
for freed slaves — the name means "free
town"). *Other names:* Gabonese Republic, Republic of Gabon, République Gabonaise.

History: In 1960 **Gabon Autonomous Republic** became independent
from France as the Republic of Gabon.
The name comes from "gabão," Portuguese for "hooded cloak," which the

Gabon Estuary looked like to the early
explorers.

Presidents: 17 Aug. 1960–17 Feb.
1964 Léon Mba; 17 Feb. 1964–19 Feb.
1964 Jean Hilaire Aubame (Usurper
Head of State with title Provisional
Prime Minister); 20 Feb. 1964–27 Nov.
1967 Léon Mba; 28 Nov. 1967– Omar
Bongo (until 1973 known as Albert-Bernard Bongo). *Prime Ministers:* 16
Apr. 1975– Leon Mébiame. *Note:* in
times of no Prime Minister, the President held that office.

427 Gabon Settlements. 11 June
1843–4 Aug. 1860. *Location:* the coast
of what is today **Gabon Republic.**
Capital: Libreville (1849–60); Fort
d'Aumale (1843–49). *Other names:*
Gabon Protectorate.

History: In 1843 the French founded
Fort d'Aumale as a naval post on the
Gabon coast, and a commandant-particulier was installed to rule over the
territories acquired along the coast (see
Gulf of Guinea Settlements). On
March 28, 1844 the chiefdom of Glass
became French; on November 4, 1846
the area of George's Creek became part
of the settlements, as did the Como and
Remboue Rivers region (formerly part
of the Séké and Bakélé chiefdoms) on
Dec. 2, 1846; on February 14, 1848 the
Mondah became French (also formerly
Séké), and in August 1849 Libreville
was founded. Cape Esterias fell to the
French on September 18, 1852, and in
1860 the whole country became **Gabon Territory [i]**.

Commandants-Particulier: 11 June
1843–1844 Antoine Devoisins; 1844–
1844 Joseph-Marie Millet; 1844–1846
André Brisset; 1846–1847 Jean Carrilès; 1847–1847 André Brisset; 1847–25
March 1848 Victor-Joseph Roger; 25
March 1848–3 Aug. 1848 Alphonse
Sordeaux; 3 Aug. 1848–Dec. 1848
Eugène Desperles; Dec. 1848–10 Aug.
1849 Étienne Deschanel; 10 Aug. 1849–
15 Dec. 1850 Jean Martin; 15 Dec.
1850–1853 Alexis Vignon; 1853–1857
Théophile Guillet; 1857–1859 Alexis

Vignon; 1859–4 Aug. 1860 Pierre Mailhetard.

428 Gabon Territory [i]. 4 Aug. 1860–16 Dec. 1883. *Location:* Gabon. *Capital:* Libreville.
History: In 1860 **Gabon Settlements** became a territory of **Ivory Coast-Gabon.** On Jan. 18, 1868 Nkomiland became a French protectorate within Gabon Territory, and on August 6, 1873 Mandji did likewise. Cape Lopez also became part of this French territory during this period, and in 1883 the whole country became **Gabon Colony [i].**
Commandants-Particulier: 4 Aug. 1860–1861 César Pradier; 1861–1863 Paul Bruë; 1863–1866 Charles Baur; 1866–1867 Joseph Brunet-Millet; 1867–1868 Laurent Aube; 1868–1869 Frédéric Bourgarel; 1869–1871 Hippolyte Bourgoin; 1871–1873 Gustave Garraud; 1873–1875 Charles Panon de Hazier; 1875–1876 Félix Clément; 1876–1878 Jules Boitard; 1878–1879 Paul Caudière; 1879–1880 Augustin Dumont; 1880–1882 Jules Hanet-Cléry; 1882–16 Dec. 1883 Émile Masson.

429 Gabon Territory [ii]. 27 Apr. 1886–29 June 1886. *Location:* Gabon. *Capital:* Libreville. *Other names:* Gabon.
History: In April 1886 **Gabon Colony [i]** came under the direct rule of the **French Equatorial African Protectorate** as the Territory of Gabon. Two months later it became a separate colony (see **Gabon Colony [ii]**).
Governors: 27 Apr. 1886–29 June 1886 Pierre Savorgnan de Brazza.

430 Gabon Territory [iii]. 11 Dec. 1888–5 July 1902. *Location:* Gabon. *Capital:* Libreville. *Other names:* Gabon.
History: In 1888 **Gabon Colony [ii]** became a territory again, as part of **Moyen-Congo-Gabon.** In 1902, still maintaining its territorial status (see **Gabon Territory [iv]**) it became part of **Lower Congo-Gabon.**
Lieutenant-Governors: 11 Dec. 1888–12 March 1889 Noël Ballay; 12 March 1889–1 June 1894 Fortuné de Chavannes; 1 June 1894–1 May 1899 Albert Dolisie; 1 May 1899–5 July 1902 Émile Gentil.

431 Gabon Territory [iv]. 5 July 1902–29 Dec. 1903. *Location:* Gabon. *Capital:* Brazzaville (Congo) with Libreville as the local headquarters. *Other names:* Gabon.
History: In 1902 **Moyen-Congo-Gabon** became **Lower Congo-Gabon** and thus **Gabon Territory [iii]** became **Gabon Territory [iv].** In 1903 it became **Gabon Colony [iii].**
Rulers: 5 July 1902–29 Dec. 1903 Ruled direct from Brazzaville (**French Congo**). *Note:* Naturally, the country was called Gabon throughout its history. The nomenclatures used here are for convenience when trying to work out the epochal marks in the colony's history.

432 Galekaland. 1750–19 May 1835. *Location:* Kaffraria, South Africa. *Capital:* Kentani. *Other names:* Gcalekaland, Galakaland.
History: Gcaleka, after whom Galekaland was named, was left in control of his (the northern) branch of the Xhosa when his father Phalo emigrated to the south with his other son Rarabe (see **Queen Adelaide Land** for rulers of the Rarabe branch of the Xhosa) in 1750. (See also **Kaffraria Proper** for rulers of the Xhosa prior to 1750.) Galekaland began, effectively, at this time. From 1835–1886 it was known as **Kreli's Country,** and in 1886 it was annexed to the Cape (see **British Cape Colony [Self-Rule]**).
Chiefs: 1750–1792 Gcaleka; 1792–1804 Khawuta. *Regents:* 1804–1820 Nqoko. *Chiefs:* 1820–12 May 1835 Hintsa; 12 May 1835–19 May 1835 interregnum; 19 May 1835–Feb. 1893 Kreli (or Sarili) (see **Kreli's Country**); Feb. 1893–1902 Sigcawu; 1902–1921 Gwebin-

kumbi. *Regents:* 1921–1923 Daliza; 1923–1933 Ngangomhlaba; 1933–Zwelidumile

433 The Gambia. See these **names:**
The Gambia Republic (1970–   )
Gambia (1965–1970)
Gambia (Self-Rule) (1963–1965)
Gambia Colony and Protectorate (1894–1963)
Gambia Colony [ii] (1888–1894)
Gambia Territory [iii] (1874–1888)
Gambia Territory [ii] (1866–1874)
Gambia Colony [i] (1843–1866)
Bathurst Settlement and Dependencies in The Gambia (1829–1843)
Gambia Territory [i] (1821–1829)
Bathurst Colony (1816–1821)
French Gambia (1779–1783)
James Fort (Company of Merchants) (1750–1765)
James Fort (Royal African Company [ii] (1699–1750)
James Fort (French) (1695–1699)
James Fort (Royal African Company) [i] (1684–1695)
James Fort (Gambia Adventurers) (1668–1684)
James Fort (Royal Adventurers) (1661–1668)
Gambia (Dutch Possession) (1659–1661)
Gambia (Courlander Settlements) (1651–1659)

434 Gambia. 18 Feb. 1965–24 Apr. 1970. *Location:* Gambia. *Capital:* Bathurst.
History: In 1965 Gambia became independent within the British Commonwealth (see **Gambia [Self-Rule]**). In 1970 it was proclaimed a republic (see **The Gambia Republic**).
Governors-General: 18 Feb. 1965–9 Feb. 1966 Sir John Paul; 9 Feb. 1966–24 Apr. 1970 Sir Farimang Singhateh. *Prime Ministers:* 18 Feb. 1965–24 Apr. 1970 Dawda Jawara (knighted 1966).

435 Gambia Colony [i]. 11 Apr. 1843–19 Feb. 1866. *Location:* Gambia.

Capital: Bathurst. *Other names:* Gambia.
History: In 1843 **Bathurst Settlement and Dependencies in The Gambia** became a colony. In 1866 it became part of **West African Settlements,** as **Gambia Territory [ii].**
Governors: 11 Apr. 1843–Oct. 1843 Capt. Henry Seagram; Oct. 1843–1844 Edmund Norcott; 1844–1847 Commander Charles Fitzgerald; 1847–1852 Sir Richard Macdonnell; 1852–1852 Arthur Kennedy (never arrived); 1852–Sept. 1859 Col. Luke O'Connor; Sept. 1859–19 Feb. 1866 Col. George D'Arcy.

436 Gambia Colony [ii]. 28 Nov. 1888–1894. *Location:* the coastal and riverine sections of present-day **Gambia Republic.** *Capital:* Bathurst. *Other names:* Gambia.
History: In 1888 **Gambia Territory [iii]** became an independent colony again with the demise of the **West Africa Settlements.** In 1894, with the addition of the hinterland, it became **Gambia Colony and Protectorate.**
Administrators: 28 Nov. 1888–1891 Gilbert Carter (knighted 1890); 1891–1894 Robert Llewellyn.

437 Gambia Colony and Protectorate. 1894–3 Oct. 1963. *Location:* Gambia. *Capital:* Bathurst. *Other names:* Gambia.
History: In 1894 the hinterland of Gambia was opened up as a protectorate, and added to **Gambia Colony [ii].** In 1963 the modern country of Gambia gained self-rule (see **Gambia [Self-Rule]**).
Administrators: 1894–1900 Robert Llewellyn (knighted 1898); 1900–11 Jan. 1901 Sir George Denton. *Governors:* 11 Jan. 1901–21 Dec. 1911 Sir George Denton; 21 Dec. 1911–11 Apr. 1914 Sir Henry Galway (until 1911 known as Gallwey); 11 Apr. 1914–1918 Edward Cameron (knighted 1916); 1918–1919 Herbert Henniker (acting); 1919–1920 Sir Edward Cameron; 1920–3 Jan. 1921 Herbert Henniker (acting); 3 Jan. 1921–

10 March 1927 Cecil Armitage (knighted 1926); 10 March 1927–29 Nov. 1928 Sir John Middleton; 29 Nov. 1928–11 Sept. 1930 Sir Edward Denham; 11 Sept. 1930–12 Apr. 1934 Richmond Palmer (knighted 1933); 12 Apr. 1934–22 Oct. 1936 Arthur Richards (knighted 1935); 22 Oct. 1936–23 March 1942 Sir Thomas Southorn; 23 March 1942–29 March 1947 Hilary Blood (knighted 1944); 29 March 1947–1 Dec. 1949 Andrew Wright (knighted 1948); 1 Dec. 1949–19 June 1958 Percy Wyn-Harris (knighted 1952); 19 June 1958–29 March 1962 Sir Edward Windley; 29 March 1962–3 Oct. 1963 Sir John Paul. *Chief Ministers:* March 1961–May 1962 Pierre N'Jie. *Prime Ministers:* May 1962–3 Oct. 1963 Dawda Jawara.

438 Gambia (Courlander Settlements). 1651–1659. *Location:* St. Andrew's Island & the island of St. Mary, Gambia. *Capital:* St. Andrew's Island. *Other names:* Courlander Gambia Settlements, Kurlander Gambia Settlements, Gambia.

History: In 1651 James, Duke of Courland (a small Baltic state) saw in the Gambia a chance to improve the fortunes of his own country. His agents bought St. Andrew's Island from the King of Barra, and Banjol (the island of St. Mary) from the King of Kombo (Kombo and Barra were two local chiefdoms). They were the first to build a fort in the area (on St. Andrew's Island). Due to war at home the colonists were stranded and the Dutch West India Company took the colony over (see **Gambia [Dutch Possession]**).

Commandants: 1651–1654 Heinrich Fock; 1654–1659 Otto Stiel.

439 Gambia (Dutch Possession). 1659–19 March 1661. *Location:* as **Gambia (Courlander Settlements).** *Capital:* St. Andrew's Island. *Other names:* Dutch Gambia, Gambia.

History: In 1659 the Dutch West India Company made an arrangement with the Duke of Courland's agent in Holland whereby the company would take over the doomed Courlander settlement in the Gambia River (see **Gambia [Courlander Settlements]**). The Courlander commandant was expelled, and the colony was without any form of government until he was allowed to return in 1660. In 1661 the English took St. Andrew's Island, re-naming it James Island, or **James Fort.**

Commandants: 1659–June 1660 no fixed rule; June 1660–19 March 1661 Otto Stiel.

440 The Gambia Republic. 24 Apr. 1970– . *Location:* North West Africa, within Senegal. *Capital:* Banjul (named Bathurst until 1973, the original name of the island was Banjol Island). *Other names:* The Gambia, Republic of The Gambia.

History: In 1970 **Gambia** became The Gambia, a republic. (See also **Senegambia.**).

Presidents: 24 Apr. 1970– Sir Dawda Jawara.

441 Gambia (Self-Rule). 3 Oct. 1963–18 Feb. 1965. *Location:* Gambia. *Capital:* Bathurst. *Other names:* Gambia.

History: In 1963 **Gambia Colony and Protectorate** was granted self-rule. In 1965 it became an independent state within the British Commonwealth (see **Gambia**).

Governors: 3 Oct. 1963–18 Feb. 1965 Sir John Paul. *Prime Ministers:* 3 Oct. 1963–18 Feb. 1965 Dawda Jawara.

442 Gambia Territory [i]. 17 Oct. 1821–12 Dec. 1829. *Location:* Gambia. *Capital:* Bathurst.

History: In 1821 **Bathurst Colony** became, with all forts and settlements in West Africa under British control, subject to the rule of Sierra Leone (see **West African Territories**). In 1829, still thus administered, it changed its name to **Bathurst Settlement and Dependencies in The Gambia.**

Administrators: 17 Oct. 1821–1 Aug. 1826 Alexander Grant; 1 Aug. 1826–12 Dec. 1829 Lt.-Col. Alexander Findlay.

443 Gambia Territory [ii]. 19 Feb. 1866–17 Dec. 1874. *Location:* Gambia. *Capital:* Bathurst. *Other names:* Gambia.

History: In 1866 the **West African Settlements** were instituted, taking in **Gambia Colony,** which became a territory. In 1874, with the secession of **Gold Coast Territory [ii]** and **Lagos Territory [i]** from the W.A.S., the **West African Settlements** became the **West Africa Settlements,** with Gambia still a territory (see **Gambia Territory [iii]**).

Administrators: 19 Feb. 1866–1869 Admiral Charles Patey. *Officers Administering:* 1869–1871 Alexander Bravo. *Administrators:* 1871–1873 Thomas Callaghan; 1873–17 Dec. 1874 Sir Cornelius Kortright.

444 Gambia Territory [iii]. 17 Dec. 1874–28 Nov. 1888. *Location:* as **Gambia Territory [ii].** *Capital:* Bathurst. *Other names:* Gambia.

History: In 1874 **Gambia Territory [ii],** then under the **West African Settlements,** became Gambia Territory [iii], now under the reduced **West Africa Settlements.** In 1888 the area became **Gambia Colony [ii].**

Administrators: 17 Dec. 1874–1875 Sir Cornelius Kortright; 1875–1877 Dr. Samuel Rowe; 1877–1884 Dr. Valesius Gouldsbury; 1884–1886 Alfred Moloney; 1886–1886 James Hay; 1886–1888 Gilbert Carter (acting); 1888–28 Nov. 1888 Gilbert Carter.

Gando, Gandu see **Gwandu**

445 Gazaland. 1824–28 Dec. 1895. *Location:* southern Mozambique-Zimbabwe border. *Capital:* Xai Xai (or Chai Chai). *Other names:* Gaza, Gaza State, Shangana, Vatua, Landeen, Gaza Empire.

History: The Gaza Empire (named after a Bantu chief) was built in the early 1820s by Nguni leader Soshangane. In 1895 the Portuguese conquered it as part of **Mozambique Colony.**

Kings: 1824–11 Oct. 1858 Soshangane (or Manikusa); 11 Oct. 1858–1862 Mawewe; 1862–Aug. 1884 Mzila; Aug. 1884–28 Dec. 1895 Gungunyane.

446 Gazankulu. 1 Feb. 1973– . *Location:* northern Transvaal-Venda border, South Africa. *Capital:* Giyani. *Other names:* GazaNkulu National State.

History: GazaNkulu is the Bantustan (National homeland) for the Shangaan (or Thonga) peoples. In 1973 it achieved a status of self-government, but still part of **South Africa.**

Chief Ministers: 1 Feb. 1973– Prof. Hudson Ntsanwisi.

Gcalekaland see **Galekaland**

447 German Crown Land of North West Africa. 12 July 1884–1 Jan. 1900. *Location:* as **Cameroun Republic,** with some boundary differences. *Capital:* Buea. *Other names:* Crown Land of North-West Africa.

History: In 1884 the German flag was hoisted in what is now Cameroun. Various protectorates (e.g. Ambas Bay — July 19, 1884) followed until the German lands covered a vast area. On January 1, 1900 the name of the country changed to that of **Kamerun.**

Reichskommissars: 12 July 1884–19 July 1884 Gustav Nachtigal; 19 July 1884–1 Apr. 1885 Max Buchner (acting); 1 Apr. 1885–3 July 1885 Eduard von Knorr (acting). *Governors:* 3 July 1885–13 May 1887 Julius von Soden; 13 May 1887–4 Oct. 1887 Jesko von Puttkamer (acting); 4 Oct. 1887–17 Jan. 1888 Eugen von Zimmerer; 17 Jan. 1888–26 Dec. 1889 Julius von Soden; 26 Dec. 1889–17 Apr. 1890 Eugen von Zimmerer (acting); 17 Apr. 1890–3 Aug. 1890 Markus Graf Pfeil; 3 Aug. 1890–14 Aug. 1890 Herr Kurz (acting); 14 Aug. 1890–2 Dec. 1890 Jesko von

Puttkamer (acting); 2 Dec. 1890–7 Aug. 1891 Herr Leist (acting); 7 Aug. 1891–5 Jan. 1892 Bruno von Schuckmann (acting); 5 Jan. 1892–27 June 1893 Eugen von Zimmerer (acting); 27 June 1893–24 Feb. 1894 Herr Leist (acting); 24 Feb. 1894–31 Dec. 1894 Eugen von Zimmerer (acting); 1 Jan. 1895–27 March 1895 Jesko von Puttkamer (acting); 28 March 1895–4 May 1895 Herr von Lücke (acting); 5 May 1895–26 Oct. 1895 Jesko von Puttkamer (acting); 27 Oct. 1895–Sept. 1896 Theodor Seitz (acting); Sept. 1896–15 Aug. 1897 Jesko von Puttkamer (acting); 15 Aug. 1897–10 Sept. 1897 Theodor Seitz (acting); 11 Sept. 1897–12 Jan. 1898 Jesko von Puttkamer (acting); 12 Jan. 1898–13 Oct. 1898 Theodor Seitz (acting); 14 Oct. 1898–1 Jan. 1900 Jesko von Puttkamer (acting).

448 German East Africa Protectorate [i]. 27 May 1885–1 Jan. 1891. *Location:* as **German East Africa Protectorate [ii]**, but minus Ruanda-Urundi. *Capital:* Bagamoyo.

History: In 1885 Karl Peters, a German adventurer in East Africa, made several treaties with the local rulers (e.g. **Karagwe**), and wound up with a large stretch of land ruled over by his company, the German East African Company. The beginning of the Protectorate of Witu would seem to mark the inception of what can be called German East Africa, and other protectorate treaties followed in short order (e.g. Usagora—Aug. 14, 1885). Incidentally the British proclaimed a protectorate of their own over Witu on June 18, 1890. By 1890 the company was in trouble, and the German government established its own rule from October 28, 1890 (effective from January 1, 1891) (see **German East Africa Protectorate [ii]**).

Administrators: 27 May 1885–28 Apr. 1888 Karl Peters. *Reichskommissars:* 28 Apr. 1888–1 Jan. 1891 Maj. Herrmann von Wissmann.

449 German East Africa Protectorate [ii]. 1 Jan. 1891–14 Nov. 1918. *Location:* Tanganyika plus Ruanda-Urundi (Urundi from 1895, Ruanda from 1899). *Capital:* Dar es-Salaam (founded in 1862 by the Sultan of Zanzibar on the site of the village of Mzizima). *Other names:* German East Africa.

History: In 1891 the German East African Company (see **German East Africa Protectorate [i]**) lost control of the area to the German government. In World War I the British and Belgians occupied the area, dividing it up between them (see **Ruanda-Urundi; British-Occupied German East Africa; Tanganyika Mandate**). The Germans put up resistance right until November 14, 1918. By that time the war was over.

Military Commanders: 1 Jan. 1891–21 Feb. 1891 Maj. Herrmann von Wissmann. *Governors:* 21 Feb. 1891–1891 Julius von Soden; 1891–1891 Capt. Ruediger (acting); 1891–15 Sept. 1893 Julius von Soden; 15 Sept. 1893–1 May 1895 Friedrich von Schele; 1 May 1895–3 Dec. 1896 Herrmann von Wissmann; 3 Dec. 1896–12 Feb. 1901 Eduard von Liebert; 12 Feb. 1901–22 Apr. 1906 Graf Adolf von Götzen; 22 Apr. 1906–July 1912 Baron Albrecht von Rechenburg; July 1912–14 Nov. 1918 Heinrich Schnee.

450 German South-West Africa Colony. 14 Sept. 1892–15 July 1915. *Location:* as **Namibia**. *Capital:* Windhoek.

History: In 1892 **German South-West Africa Protectorate** became a colony. Effective control of the Hottentots and Hereros was not complete until 1906. In 1915 the Germans lost the country to South African troops, and it became **South-West Africa Protectorate.**

Landeshauptmänner: 14 Sept. 1892–15 March 1895 Kurt von François; 15 March 1895–1899 Theodor Leutwein. *Governors:* 1899–19 Aug. 1905 Theodor Leutwein; Nov. 1905–26 Aug.

1907 Friedrich von Lindequist; 26 Aug. 1907–20 June 1910 Bruno von Schuckmann; 17 Nov. 1910–15 July 1915 Theodor Seitz. *Military Commanders:* June 1904–19 Nov. 1905 Lothar von Trotha; 19 Nov. 1905–1906 Col. Dame; 1906–26 Aug. 1907 Col. Berthold von Deimling.

451 German South-West Africa Protectorate [i]. 24 Apr. 1884–1889. *Location:* as **Namibia.** *Capital:* Otjimbigwe.

History: Germany's first colonial move, this area was subdued in the early 1880s, the first settlements being made on April 24, 1883. The town of Lüderitz was taken in the same year, and the rest of the country in 1884. Prior to 1884 the area was split into three basic regions: **Ovamboland** in the north, **Damaraland** in the center, and **Great Namaqualand** in the south. Windhoek became the central town (not becoming the capital until 1891). The coastline contained the isolated British colony of **Walvis Bay;** the rest of the country was in the hands of the German South-West Africa Colonial Company. In 1889 the German government relieved the company of the area because of the company's financial difficulties. Heinrich Goering (Herman's uncle) continued to rule in **German South-West Africa Protectorate [ii].**

Reichskommissars: 24 Apr. 1884–30 Dec. 1886 no fixed rule; 30 Dec. 1886–1889 Heinrich Goering.

452 German South-West Africa Protectorate [ii]. 1889–14 Sept. 1892. *Location:* as **Namibia.** *Capital:* Windhoek (since 1891). Founded as a town in 1870, the name means "place of smoke." Otjimbigwe (until 1891).

History: In 1889 the German government relieved the German South-West Africa Colonial Company of its administration in the area (see **German South-West Africa Protectorate [i]**) and maintained it as a protectorate until 1892 when it became the **German South-West Africa Colony.**

Reichskommissars: 1889–1890 Heinrich Goering; March 1891–14 Sept. 1892 Kurt von François.

453 Ghana. See these **names:**
Ghana Republic (1960–)
Ghana Dominion (1957–1960)
Gold Coast (Self-Rule) (1951–1957)
Gold Coast (1886–1951)
Gold Coast Colony Region (1945–1953)
Gold Coast Northern Territories Civil Protectorate (1907–1957)
Gold Coast Northern Territories (1899–1907)
Ashanti Colony (1901–1957)
Ashanti Protectorate (1896–1901)
Gold Coast Colony (with Lagos) (1874–1886)
Gold Coast Territory [ii] (1866–1874)
Gold Coast Colony (1850–1866)
British Gold Coast Crown Colony (1843–1850)
British Gold Coast (Committee of Merchants) (1828–1843)
Gold Coast Territory [i] (1821–1828)
Gold Coast (British) (1821–1821)
British Gold Coast (Company of Merchants) (1751–1821)
British Gold Coast Settlements (Royal African Company) (1707–1751)
English Gold Coast Settlements (Royal African Company) (1672–1707)
English Gold Coast Settlements (Royal Adventurers) (1662–1672)
English Gold Coast Settlements (East India Company) (1658–1662)
English Gold Coast Settlements (Company of London Merchants) (1651–1658)
English Gold Coast Settlements (Company of Merchants Trading to Guinea) (1632–1651)
English Gold Coast Settlements (1621–1632)
Danish Gold Coast Settlements (1658–1850)
Dutch Gold Coast Settlements (1598–1871)
Portuguese Gold Coast Settlements (1482–1642)

Swedish Gold Coast Settlements (1640–1657)
Prussian Gold Coast Settlements (1701–1720)
Brandenburger Gold Coast Settlements (1682–1701)
Akim (ca. 1500–1899)
Akwamu (1560–1730)
Ashanti Empire (ca. 1680–1896)
Ashanti State (ca. 1570–ca. 1680)
Bono (ca. 1420–1723)
Dagomba (ca. 1440–1896)
Gonja (ca. 1495–ca. 1713)
Twifo-Heman (1480–1730)

454 Ghana Dominion. 6 March 1957–1 July 1960. *Location:* as **Ghana Republic.** *Capital:* Accra. *Other names:* Dominion of Ghana.
History: In 1957 **Gold Coast (Self-Rule),** which included the recently acquired **Togoland British Trust Territory,** became independent as The Dominion of Ghana, the first black dependency of Britain to be freed. In 1960 it became The Republic of Ghana (see **Ghana Republic**).
Governors-General: 6 March 1957–14 May 1957 Sir Charles Arden-Clarke; 14 May 1957–13 Nov. 1957 Kobrina Arku Korsah (acting); 13 Nov. 1957–1 July 1960 Earl of Listowel. *Prime Ministers:* 6 March 1957–1 July 1960 Kwame Nkrumah.

455 Ghana Empire. ca. 350–1240. *Location:* Mali. *Capital:* Kumbi (this was the 11th century capital). *Other names:* Wagadu, Land of Gold, Ghana Kingdom, Aoukar, Ancient Ghana.
History: Ghana was the first great trading empire of Medieval West Africa. Its people were Mande-speaking Soninke tribes and the empire was an enormous trading post and carrier of goods from one part of Africa to another. By the year 800 Ghana was very powerful, its actual name being Wagadu. The "Ghana" was the king himself. There were many capitals, and the empire absorbed vassal state after

vassal state, but by the 11th century the great empire began to decline. The Almoravids in the north were the main cause of Ghana's disintegration. Kumbi was taken in 1076, and a slow death of the empire followed, with the area shrinking as vassal states dropped away. By 1240 it was all over and what was left of the Ghana Empire became part of the greater still **Mali Empire.**
Kings: ca. 350–ca. 350 Kaya Maja; ca. 350–ca. 622 there were 21 kings, unknown by name today; ca. 622–ca. 622 Kanissa'ai; ca. 622–ca. 750 there were 21 kings, unknown by name today; ca. 750–ca. 750 Majan Dyabe Sisse; ca. 750–ca. 1040 [unknown]; ca. 1040–1062 Bassi; 1062–1068 Tunka Menin; 1068–1076 [unknown]; 1076–ca. 1090 Kambine Diaresso; ca. 1090–ca. 1100 Suleiman; ca. 1100–ca. 1120 Banna Bubu; ca. 1120–ca. 1130 Majan Wagadu; ca. 1130–ca. 1140 Gane; ca. 1140–ca. 1160 Musa; ca. 1160–ca. 1180 Birama; ca. 1180–ca. 1200 Diara Kante; ca. 1200–1234 Sumanguru; 1234–1240 [unknown].

456 Ghana Republic. 1 July 1960– .
Location: North West Africa, on the Gold Coast. *Capital:* Accra (name comes from the Akan word "akran," meaning "black ants," which abound here. Accra was formerly a native village). *Other names:* Republic of Ghana.
History: In 1960 **Ghana Dominion** became a republic within the British Commonwealth. Its history has been one of coups and violence.
Presidents: 1 July 1960–24 Feb. 1966 Kwame Nkrumah; 24 Feb. 1966–3 Apr. 1969 Joseph Ankrah (Chairman of the National Liberation Council); 3 Apr. 1969–7 Aug. 1970 Akwasi Afrifa (Chairman of the National Liberation Council); 7 Aug. 1970–31 Aug. 1970 Nii Amaa Ollennu (Acting Chairman of the National Liberation Council); 31 Aug. 1970–13 Jan. 1972 Edward Akufo-Addo; 13 Jan. 1972–5 July 1978 Ignatius Acheampong (Chairman of

the National Redemption Council); 5 July 1978-4 June 1979 Frederick Akuffo (Chairman of the National Redemption Council); 5 June 1979-24 Sept. 1979 Jerry Rawlings (Chairman of the Armed Forces Revolutionary Council); 24 Sept. 1979-31 Dec. 1981 Hilla Limann; 31 Dec. 1981-11 Jan. 1982 Jerry Rawlings (interim Military Leader); 11 Jan. 1982- Jerry Rawlings (Chairman of the Provisional National Defense Council). *Prime Ministers:* 29 Aug. 1969-13 Jan. 1972 Kofi Busia. *Note:* In times of no Prime Minister, the President held that office.

Giuba see **Jubaland Colony**

457 Gobir. ca. 1110-Sept. 1808. *Location:* Niger-Nigeria border. *Capital:* Alkalawa (from 1734); Birnin Lalle (ca. 1720-1734); Goran Rami (unknown dates); Maigali (unknown dates).
History: Gobir took its name from its ancestral home in Yemen, Arabia. It was one of the seven **Hausa States** founded by one of the sons of Bawo, son of Abdullahi, King of Baghdad. Gobir, the northernmost outpost of Hausaland (another way of saying the Hausa States) was a state as early as about 1100. Seemingly apart from things until 1731, it engaged in a war with **Kano Kingdom** until 1743. By 1799 the Gobirawa (people from Gobir) were the most powerful in Hausaland. But soon the Habe dynasty was to be defeated by the Fulanis under Uthman Dan Fodio (see **Fulani Empire**), and after 1808 the rulers of Gobir were Fulani emirs (see **Gobir Emirate**). The Gobirawa fled north, building the town of Tsibiri, from which they harassed the Fulani.
Sultans: (?)-(?) Duma; (?)-(?) Banaturumi; (?)-(?) Sanakafo; (?)-(?) Majigu; (?)-(?) Batutua; (?)-(?) Bawa; (?)-(?) Birtakiskis; (?)-(?) Sirtengi; (?)-(?) Barankimi; (?)-(?) Madaura; (?)-(?) Dangoma; (?)-(?) Zerama; (?)-(?) Biamusu; (?)-(?) Umi; (?)-(?) Shiruma; (?)-(?) Majanjara; (?)-(?)

Kasu; (?)-(?) Chida; (?)-(?) Goji; (?)-(?) Jilabataji; (?)-(?) Ginsarana; (?)-(?) Bawa Nesso; (?)-(?) Badadella; (?)-(?) Chiroma; (?)-(?) Muzakha I; (?)-(?) Muzakha II; (?)-(?) Barankimi; (?)-(?) Ishifi; (?)-(?) Alezzi Kalajuma; (?)-(?) Bachiri; (?)-(?) Muhammadu; (?)-(?) Dalla Gungumi; (?)-(?) Dalla Dawaki; (?)-(?) Chiroma; (?)-(?) Muhammadu; (?)-(?) Maji; (?)-(?) Babba; (?)-(?) Chiroma; (?)-(?) Akal; (?)-(?) Gumsara; (?)-(?) Chiroma; (?)-(?) Maji; (?)-(?) Babba; (?)-(?) Chiroma; ca. 1715 Muhammadu Dan Chiroma; (?)-(?) Barbandoma (or Chuba Dan Muhammadu); (?)-(?) Bachiri (or Akili Dan Chuba); (?)-(?) Yako (or Uban Doro); (?)-(?) Soba Dan Doro; (?)-(?) Nyakum; (?)-(?) ibn Ashe; (?)-1742 Akal; 1742-1770 Babari Dan ibn Ashe; 1770-1777 Dan Gudi Dan Babari; 1777-1777 Gambai; 1777-1795 Bawa Jan Gwarzo; 1795-1801 Yakuba Dan Babari; 1801-1803 Nafata Dan Babari (or Muhamman); 1803-1804 Yunfa Dan Nafata; 1804-Sept. 1808 Salihu.
Note: While this is the most complete list one can compile from available data (mostly oral tradition), its accuracy cannot be substantiated. The early sultans date from the time that the Gobirawa were in Yemen, or en route to Africa, and written records are virtually nonexistent.

458 Gobir Emirate. Sept. 1808-1900. *Location:* Niger-Nigeria border. *Capital:* Alkalawa.
History: In 1808 **Gobir** became an emirate of the **Fulani Empire.** In 1900 it became part of two colonial subdivisions—one French and the other British. The northern part of Gobir became part of **Zinder Autonomous Military Territory** and the southern part became one of the northern sections of **Northern Nigeria Protectorate.**
Sultans: Sept. 1808-1814 Modibbo Dan Fodio; 1814-1817 Gwamki; 1817-1835 Ali; 1836-1858 Mayaki; 1858-1858 Baciri VII; 1858-1883 Bawa Dan Gwamki; 1883-1886 Ibrahim; 1886-

1889 Mainassara Maji; 1889–1890 Almu; 1890–1890 Ibrahim; 1890–1894 Mainassara Maji; 1894–1897 Almu; 1897–Apr. 1898 Ibrahimu Na Mai Fura; Apr. 1898–Jan. 1899 Bakon Dare; Jan. 1899–1907 Umaru Dacili; 1907–14 Nov. 1912 Baturi; 1912–(?) Dan Buddi; (?)–(?) Dan Magaji; (?)–(?) Tumbulki; (?)–(?) Gulbi; ca. 1936–Salau.

459 Gojjam. ca. 1620–1855. *Location:* Ethiopia. *Capital:* Debra Markos. *Other names:* Gojam.
History: A kingdom of Ethiopia which in 1855 went to make up **Ethiopian Empire [ii].**
Kings: ca. 1620–(?) Sarsa Krestos; (?)–ca. 1740 unknown kings; ca. 1740–ca. 1777 Ras Goskol; ca. 1777–1793 Ras Abeto Haylu; 1793–1798 Ras Mared; 1798–1805 Dejaz Saude; 1805–1806 Dejaz Mared Gwalo; 1806–1813 Dejaz Saude; 1813–ca. 1820 Dejaz Walad Rafael; ca. 1820–1828 Dori; 1828–1828 Matantu; 1828–1842 Ras Gosho II; 1842–March 1844 Ras Beru Gugsa; March 1844–Dec. 1844 Merso; Dec. 1844–1852 Ras Gosho II; 1852–1853 Ras Kasa; 1853–1854 Ras Ali II; 1854–1855 Tedla Haylu.

460 Gold Coast. 13 Jan. 1886–8 Feb. 1951. *Location:* as **Gold Coast (Self-Rule).** *Capital:* Accra. *Other names:* Gold Coast Colony.
History: In 1886 **Gold Coast Colony (with Lagos)** split into two colonies — **Gold Coast** and **Lagos Colony.** In 1951 Gold Coast won self-rule (see **Gold Coast [Self-Rule]).** Between those years great changes took place. The original colony of Gold Coast was in the South, and in 1896 **Ashanti Protectorate** was created, becoming **Ashanti Colony** in 1901. The Ashanti areas lay mid country, and in the north were the **Gold Coast Northern Territories,** taken in 1899 and becoming, in 1907, **Gold Coast Northern Territories Civil Protectorate.** From 1945–1953 a separate Gold Coast Colony was cre-

ated within the main country (see **Gold Coast Colony Region).** In 1951 these areas came under the central administration of **Gold Coast (Self-Rule).**
Governors: 13 Jan. 1886–11 Apr. 1887 William Griffith; 11 Apr. 1887–26 Nov. 1887 F.B.P. White (acting); 26 Nov. 1887–30 June 1889 Sir William Griffith; 30 June 1889–18 Feb. 1890 Frederic Hodgson (acting); 18 Feb. 1890–12 June 1891 Sir William Griffith; 12 June 1891–24 Nov. 1891 Frederic Hodgson (acting); 24 Nov. 1891–12 Aug. 1893 Sir William Griffith; 12 Aug. 1893–7 March 1894 Frederic Hodgson (acting); 7 March 1894–7 Apr. 1895 Sir William Griffith; 7 Apr. 1895–19 Apr. 1896 William Maxwell (knighted 1896); 19 Apr. 1896–23 Oct. 1896 Frederic Hodgson (acting); 23 Oct. 1896–6 Dec. 1897 Sir William Maxwell; 6 Dec. 1897–29 May 1898 Frederic Hodgson (acting); 29 May 1898–27 Dec. 1898 Frederic Hodgson; 27 Dec. 1898–13 July 1899 William Low (acting); 13 July 1899–28 June 1900 Sir Frederic Hodgson; 28 June 1900–11 July 1900 William Low (acting); 11 July 1900–29 Aug. 1900 Sir Frederic Hodgson; 29 Aug. 1900–17 Dec. 1900 William Low (acting); 17 Dec. 1900–30 July 1902 Mathew Nathan; 30 July 1902–20 Dec. 1902 Leonard Arthur (acting); 20 Dec. 1902–9 Feb. 1904 Sir Mathew Nathan; 9 Feb. 1904–3 March 1904 Herbert Bryan (acting); 3 March 1904– 10 May 1905 Sir John Rodger; 10 May 1905–12 Nov. 1905 Herbert Bryan (acting); 12 Nov. 1905–2 Apr. 1906 Sir John Rodger; 2 Apr. 1906–2 Sept. 1906 Herbert Bryan (acting); 2 Sept. 1906–9 Oct. 1907 Sir John Rodger; 9 Oct. 1907–28 March 1908 Herbert Bryan (acting); 28 March 1908–30 March 1909 Sir John Rodger; 30 March 1909–29 Aug. 1909 Herbert Bryan (acting); 29 Aug. 1909–1 Sept. 1910 Sir John Rodger; 1 Sept. 1910–21 Nov. 1910 Herbert Bryan (acting); 21 Nov. 1910–5 Feb. 1911 James Thorburn; 5 Feb. 1911–16 June 1911 Herbert Bryan (acting); 16 June 1911–June 1912 James Thor-

burn; 29 June 1912–26 Dec. 1912 Herbert Bryan (acting); 26 Dec. 1912–1 May 1914 Sir Hugh Clifford; 1 May 1914–27 Aug. 1914 Sir William Robertson (acting); 27 Aug. 1914–5 May 1915 Sir Hugh Clifford; 5 May 1915–16 Nov. 1915 Ransford Slater (acting); 16 Nov. 1915–18 Nov. 1916 Sir Hugh Clifford; 18 Nov. 1916–23 Apr. 1917 Ransford Slater (acting); 23 Apr. 1917–1 Apr. 1919 Sir Hugh Clifford; 1 Apr. 1919–8 Oct. 1919 Ransford Slater (acting); 9 Oct. 1919–2 June 1920 Gordon Guggisberg; 2 June 1920–6 Oct. 1920 Ransford Slater (acting); 6 Oct. 1920–11 July 1921 Gordon Guggisberg; 11 July 1921–12 Dec. 1921 R.W.H. Wilkinson (acting); 12 Dec. 1921–2 Apr. 1923 Gordon Guggisberg (knighted 1922); 2 Apr. 1923–17 Aug. 1923 John C. Maxwell (acting); 18 Aug. 1923–1 Oct. 1923 Arthur J. Philbrick (acting); 1 Oct. 1923–31 March 1924 Sir Gordon Guggisberg; 31 March 1924–1 Sept. 1924 John C. Maxwell (acting); 1 Sept. 1924–6 July 1925 Sir Gordon Guggisberg; 6 July 1925–10 Nov. 1925 John C. Maxwell (acting); 10 Nov. 1925–11 Apr. 1926 Sir Gordon Guggisberg; 11 Apr. 1926–27 Sept. 1926 John C. Maxwell (acting); 27 Sept. 1926–24 Apr. 1927 Sir Gordon Guggisberg; 24 Apr. 1927–19 July 1927 John C. Maxwell (acting); 29 July 1927–18 Apr. 1930 Sir Ransford Slater; 18 Apr. 1930–22 Sept. 1930 G.C. du Boulay (acting); 22 Sept. 1930–30 Jan. 1931 Sir Ransford Slater; 30 Jan. 1931–20 Apr. 1931 Geoffrey Northcote (acting); 20 Apr. 1931–8 Dec. 1931 Sir Ransford Slater; 8 Dec. 1931–14 Dec. 1931 G.C. du Boulay (acting); 14 Dec. 1931–5 Apr. 1932 Sir Ransford Slater; 5 Apr. 1932–29 Nov. 1932 Geoffrey Northcote (acting); 30 Nov. 1932–13 May 1934 Sir Shenton Thomas; 13 May 1934–23 Oct. 1934 Geoffrey Northcote (acting); 24 Oct. 1934–24 Oct. 1941 Sir Arnold Hodson; 24 Oct. 1941–29 June 1942 George London (acting); 29 June 1942–2 Aug. 1947 Sir Alan Burns; 2 Aug. 1947–12 Jan. 1948 George London (acting); 12 Jan. 1948–15 Feb. 1949 Sir Gerald Creasy; 15 Feb. 1949–28 March 1949 Sir Robert Scott (acting); 28 March 1949–11 June 1949 Thorleif Mangin (acting); 11 June 1949–11 Aug. 1949 Sir Robert Scott (acting); 11 Aug. 1949–8 Feb. 1951 Sir Arden Clarke.

461 Gold Coast (British). 7 May 1821–17 Oct. 1821. *Location:* as **English Gold Coast Settlements.** *Capital:* Cape Coast Castle.

History: In 1821 the British took over as a crown colony the English-speaking Gold Coast settlements that had been run by the Company of Merchants (see **British Gold Coast [Company of Merchants]**). Later in 1821 these settlements became a subsidiary of the **West African Territories,** ruled from Sierra Leone (see **Gold Coast Territory [i]**).

Governors: 7 May 1821–17 Oct. 1821 John Hope Smith.

462 Gold Coast Colony. 13 Jan. 1850–19 Feb. 1866. *Location:* southern Ghana. *Capital:* Cape Coast Castle. *Other names:* Gold Coast, British Gold Coast.

History: In 1850 the **British Gold Coast Crown Colony** became the Colony of the Gold Coast, an independent British possession. Two months later it grew with the acquisition of the **Danish Gold Coast Settlements.** In 1866 it became part of the **West African Settlements,** as **Gold Coast Territory [ii].**

Governors: 13 Jan. 1850–4 Dec. 1850 Sir William Winniett; 4 Dec. 1850–14 Oct. 1851 James Bannerman (acting); 14 Oct. 1851–June 1853 Stephen Hill; June 1853–Aug. 1853 James Fitzpatrick (acting); Aug. 1853–Feb. 1854 Brodie Cruickshank (acting); Feb. 1854–Dec. 1854 Stephen Hill; Dec. 1854–March 1857 Henry Connor (acting); March 1857–14 Apr. 1858 Sir Benjamin Pine; 14 Apr. 1858–20 Apr. 1860 Henry Bird (acting); 20 Apr. 1860–14 Apr. 1862 Edward Andrews; 14 Apr. 1862–20 Sept. 1862 William Ross (acting); 20 Sept. 1862–1864 Richard Pine. *Lieutenant-Governors:* 1864–1864 William Hackett.

Governors: 1864–1865 Richard Pine; 1865–1865 Rokeby Jones (acting); 1865–Apr. 1865 W.E. Mockler (acting). *Lieutenant-Governors:* Apr. 1865–19 Feb. 1866 Edward Conran.

463 Gold Coast Colony Region. 1945 –1953. *Location:* south Ghana, south of the Ashanti Region. *Capital:* Accra. *Other names:* Gold Coast Colony.

History: In 1945 this area was created as a separate region, but still belonging to the overall British possession of **Gold Coast,** and after 1951 of **Gold Coast (Self-Rule).** A similar position existed with **Ashanti Colony** and **Gold Coast Northern Territories.** This idea was dropped in 1953, although Ashanti and Northern Territories continued to exist until 1957 when **Ghana Dominion** became an independent country.

Chief Commissioners: 1945–1950 Thorleif Mangin; 1950–1953 Arthur Loveridge.

464 Gold Coast Colony (with Lagos). 24 July 1874–13 Jan. 1886. *Location:* south Ghana plus Lagos (in Nigeria). *Capital:* Accra (1877–86); Osu (1874–77); Cape Coast Castle (1874– 74).

History: In 1874 **Gold Coast Territory [ii]** and **Lagos Territory** left the **West African Settlements** which became the **West Africa Settlements.** The two seceding colonies set up as one, with Gold Coast as the dominant partner. This relationship lasted until 1886 when both became separate colonies (see **Lagos Colony** and **Gold Coast).**

Governors: 24 July 1874–7 Apr. 1876 George Strahan. *Lieutenant-Governors:* 7 Apr. 1876–Dec. 1876 Charles Lees; Dec. 1876–5 June 1877 Sanford Freeling. *Governors:* 5 June 1877–13 May 1878 Sanford Freeling. *Lieutenant-Governors:* 13 May 1878–June 1879 Charles Lees. *Governors:* June 1879–1 Dec. 1880 Herbert Ussher. *Lieutenant-Governors:* 1 Dec. 1880–4 March 1881 William Griffith. *Governors:* 4 March 1881–13 May 1882 Sir Samuel Rowe; 13 May 1882–4 Oct. 1882 Alfred Moloney (acting). *Lieutenant-Governors:* 4 Oct. 1882–24 Dec. 1882 William Griffith. *Governors:* 24 Dec. 1882–29 Apr. 1884 Sir Samuel Rowe; 29 Apr. 1884–24 Apr. 1885 William Young; 24 Apr. 1885–13 Jan. 1886 William Griffith (knighted 1887).

465 Gold Coast Northern Territories. 1899–1 Jan. 1907. *Location:* northern segment of Ghana. *Capital:* Tamale. *Other names:* Northern Territories Military Protectorate.

History: In 1899 the British occupied the northernmost part of what later became Ghana. By 1906, when the entire **Gold Coast** was delimited as a colony, the Northern Territories were fully organized as a region. In 1907 the Northern Territories became the **Gold Coast Northern Territories Civil Protectorate,** i.e., no longer under military control.

Chief Commissioners: 1899–1904 Arthur Morris; 1904–1 Jan. 1907 Alan Watherston.

466 Gold Coast Northern Territories Civil Protectorate. 1 Jan. 1907–6 March 1957. *Location:* as **Gold Coast Northern Territories.** *Capital:* Tamale. *Other names:* Gold Coast Northern Territories, Northern Territories.

History: In 1907 the **Gold Coast Northern Territories** went from being a military protectorate to a civil protectorate. In 1957 they ceased to exist as **Ghana Dominion** came into being. The Northern Territories became the basis of the Northern Region of Ghana.

Chief Commissioners: 1 Jan. 1907– 1910 Alan Watherston; 1910–1920 Cecil Armitage; 1920–1924 Arthur Philbrick; 1924–1930 Arthur Walker-Leigh; 1930– 1933 Francis Jackson; 1933–1942 William Jones; 1942–1946 George Gibbs; 1946–1948 William Ingrams; 1948–1950 Edward Jones; 1950–1953 Geoffrey Burden. *Regional Officers:* 1953–1954 Arthur Loveridge; 1954–1957 Sydney MacDonald-Smith.

467 Gold Coast (Self-Rule). 8 Feb. 1951–6 March 1957. *Location:* as **Ghana Republic,** minus the area which was then **Togoland British Trust Territory.** *Capital:* Accra. *Other names:* Gold Coast.

History: In 1951 **Gold Coast** was granted internal autonomy, with powers over **Ashanti Colony** and **Gold Coast Northern Territories.** In 1957 all these were brought together under one administration, that of the independent **Ghana Dominion.**

Governors: 8 Feb. 1951–6 March 1957 Sir Charles Arden-Clarke (until 1951 known as Sir Arden Clarke). *Prime Ministers:* 5 March 1952–6 March 1957 Kwame Nkrumah.

468 Gold Coast Territory [i]. 17 Oct. 1821–25 June 1828. *Location:* as **English Gold Coast Settlements.** *Capital:* Cape Coast Castle.

History: In 1821 the **British Gold Coast Settlements** became part of the **West African Territories** and assumed the name Gold Coast Territory. In 1828 a Committee of Merchants assumed temporary control from the Crown (see **British Gold Coast [Committee of Merchants]**).

Governors: 17 Oct. 1821–27 March 1822 John Hope Smith; 27 March 1822–17 May 1822 Sir Charles Macarthy; 17 May 1822–Dec. 1822 Maj. James Chisholm; Dec. 1822–21 Jan. 1824 Sir Charles Macarthy; 21 Jan. 1824–17 Oct. 1824 Maj. James Chisholm; 17 Oct. 1824–22 March 1825 Maj. Edward Purdon; 22 March 1825–March 1826 Charles Turner; 18 May 1826–15 Nov. 1826 Sir Neil Campbell; 15 Nov. 1826–11 Oct. 1827 Henry Ricketts; 11 Oct. 1827–10 March 1828 Col. Hugh Lumley; 10 March 1828–5 June 1828 Capt. George Hingston; 5 June 1828–25 June 1828 Henry Ricketts.

469 Gold Coast Territory [ii]. 19 Feb. 1866–24 July 1874. *Location:* southern Ghana. *Capital:* Cape Coast Castle. *Other names:* Gold Coast.

History: In 1866 four colonies joined the **West African Settlements** and became territories ruled from Freetown in Sierra Leone, by the Sierra Leone governor, who was also Governor-in-Chief of the West African Settlements. As far as the Gold Coast went, local administrators ruled from Accra. In 1874 **Gold Coast Territory** and **Lagos Territory [i]** broke away together to form **Gold Coast Colony (with Lagos).**

Administrators: 19 Feb. 1866–Feb. 1867 Edward Conran; Feb. 1867–Aug. 1868 Herbert Ussher; Aug. 1868–Nov. 1869 W.H. Simpson (acting); Nov. 1869–July 1871 Herbert Ussher; July 1871–1872 Charles Salmon (acting); 1872–Apr. 1872 Herbert Ussher. *Governors-in-Chief:* Apr. 1872–1872 John Pope Hennessey. *Administrators:* 1872– Nov. 1872 Charles Salmon (acting); Nov. 1872–7 March 1873 Robert Harley. *Governors-in-Chief:* 7 March 1873–17 March 1873 Robert Keate; 17 March 1873–2 Oct. 1873 Robert Harley and Alexander Bravo (acting); 2 Oct. 1873–4 March 1874 Sir Garnet Wolseley. *Administrators:* 4 March 1874–30 March 1874 Col. Maxwell (acting); 30 March 1874–June 1874 William Johnston (acting); June 1874–24 July 1874 George Strahan.

470 Gombe Emirate. 1804–Feb. 1902. *Location:* northeastern Nigeria. *Capital:* Gombe (from 1824. It was renamed Gombe Aba—"Old Gombe" in 1843); from 1913–1919 the capital was Nafada, and from 1919 it has been Doma (re-named Gombe in 1919).

History: Founded in 1804 by Buba Yero, a Fulani chief of the Sokoto Caliphate (see **Fulani Empire**). In 1902 it became part of **Northern Nigeria Protectorate.**

Chiefs: 1804–1841 Buba Yero. *Emirs:* 1841–1844 Suli; 1844–1881 Koiranga; 1881–1888 Zailani; 1888–1895 Hassan; 1895–1898 Tukur; 1898–1922 Umaru; 1922–1935 Haruna; Jan. 1936– Abubakr.

471 Gonder Ethiopia. 14 June 1632–
11 Feb. 1855. *Location:* Ethiopia. *Capital:* Gonder. *Other names:* Ethiopia,
Abyssinia, Ethiopian Empire.

History: In 1632 Fasiladas took over
as emperor from Susneyos, the old
Solomonid emperor (see **Ethiopian
Empire [i]**). This was after much civil
strife, and 1632 saw the beginning of a
new era in Ethiopia. The missionaries
were expelled and the capital was
shifted to the newly built town of
Gonder, which became Africa's second
largest city (after Cairo). This Gon-
derian age petered out in the 1800s as
lack of unity became the biggest draw-
back in the Empire. In 1855 Theodore ascended the throne and began to
unify the Empire (see **Ethiopian Empire [ii]**).

Emperors: 14 June 1632–18 Oct. 1667
Fasiladas (or Alam Sagad); 18 Oct.
1667–19 July 1682 John I (or Yohannes
I, or A'alaf Sagad); 19 July 1682–March
1706 Iyasu I (or Adyam Sagad); March
1706–30 June 1708 Takla Haymanot I;
14 July 1708–14 Oct. 1711 Tewoflos (or
Asrar Sagad); 14 Oct. 1711–19 Feb. 1716
Yostos (or Dsahai Sagad); 19 Feb.
1716–18 May 1721 Dauti III (or Dawit
III, or Adbar Sagad); 18 May 1721–19
Sept. 1730 Bakaffa (or Asma Giyorgis);
19 Sept. 1730–26 June 1755 Iyasu II.
Regents: 19 Sept. 1730–26 June 1755
Menetewab. *Emperors:* 26 June 1755–7
May 1769 Iyoas I (or Adyam Sagad); 7
May 1769–17 Oct. 1769 Yohannes II (or
John II); 17 Oct. 1769–15 Sept. 1777
Takla Haymanot II; 15 Sept. 1777–20
July 1779 Salomon; 20 July 1779–8 Feb.
1784 Takla Giyorgis (or Fehr Sagad); 8
Feb. 1784–24 Apr. 1788 Iyasu III (or
Ba'ala Segab); 24 Apr. 1788–26 July
1789 Takla Giyorgis (or Fehr Sagad);
26 July 1789–Jan. 1794 Hezekiyas; Jan.
1794–15 Apr. 1795 Takla Giyorgis (or
Fehr Sagad); 15 Apr. 1795–Dec. 1795
Ba'eda Maryam II; Dec. 1795–May
1796 Takla Giyorgis (or Fehr Sagad); 21
June 1796–15 July 1797 Walda Salo-
mon; Aug. 1797–4 Jan. 1798 Yonas; 4
Jan. 1798–20 May 1799 Takla Giyorgis

(or Fehr Sagad); 20 May 1799–1799
Walda Salomon; 1799–24 March 1800
Demetros; 24 March 1800–June 1800
Takla Giyorgis (or Fehr Sagad); June
1800–June 1801 Demetros; June 1801–3
June 1818 Egwala Seyon; 3 June 1818–3
June 1821 Iyoas II; 3 June 1821–Apr.
1826 Gigar; Apr. 1826–Apr. 1826 Ba'eda
Maryam III; Apr. 1826–18 June 1830
Gigar; 18 June 1830–18 March 1832
Iyasu IV; 18 March 1832–8 June 1832
Gabra Krestos; 8 June 1832–Oct. 1832
interregnum; Oct. 1832–Aug. 1840
Sahla Dengel; Sept. 1840–Oct. 1841
Yohannes III (or John III); Oct. 1841–
1850 Sahla Dengel; 1850–1851 Yohan-
nes III (or John III); 1851–11 Feb. 1855
Sahla Dengel.

472 Gonja. ca. 1495–ca. 1713. *Location:* Ghana-Ivory Coast. *Capital:*
Pembi.

History: Founded about 1495, Gonja
was conquered about 1713 by **Dagomba.**

Kings: ca. 1495–ca. 1554 Sumayla
Ndewura Dyakpa; ca. 1554–1583 Wadih
(or Naba); 1583–1623 Ma'ura; 1623–
1666 Dyakpa Lanta (or Lata); 1666–
1688 Thaara (or Suleiman); 1688–1709
[unknown]; 1709–ca. 1713 [unknown].

Goosen see **Goshen**

473 Gorée. 10 Feb. 1763–30 Jan.
1779. *Location:* off the coast of Senegal. *Capital:* Saint Louis (Senegal).

History: In 1763 the British returned
Gorée, the islet off the Senegalese
coast, to the French. Their other
possessions (see **Senegal [British] [ii]**)
were renamed **Senegal (Royal African
Company).** In 1779 France took all the
Senegalese possessions owned by Britain and Gorée merged with the new
regime (see **Senegal French Territory**).

Commandants: 12 Sept. 1763–Nov.
1764 Pierre Poncet de la Rivière; March
1765–July 1767 Jean-Georges Le Baillif
des Mesnager; July 1767–March 1768
Claude Le Lardeux de la Gastière;

March 1768–4 Oct. 1768 M. Maizière (acting); 4 Oct. 1768–10 Dec. 1772 Pierre de Rastel de Rocheblaye; 10 Dec. 1772–10 Dec. 1772 Antoine Louis Desmarets de Montchaton (acting); 10 Dec. 1772–Nov. 1774 Charles Boniface; Nov. 1774–Dec. 1777 Joseph Le Brasseur; Dec. 1777–Aug. 1778 Alexandre Armény de Paradis; Aug. 1778–30 Jan. 1779 Charles Boucher (acting).

474 Gorée and Dependencies. 1854–1859. *Location:* off the coast of Senegal. *Capital:* Gorée. *Other names:* Gorée.

History: In 1854 Gorée was detached from **Senegal Colony** and made into a separate colony, which also included the **Gabon Settlements**. A commandant-supérieur had overall control of the colony, and the island of Gorée was ruled by a commandant-particulier under him. In 1859 Gorée was reattached to **Senegal Colony,** and in the following year the **Gabon Settlements** became **Gabon Territory [i].**

Commandants-Supérieurs: 1854–1856 Jérôme Monléon; 1856–1859 Auguste Prôtet. *Commandants-Particuliers of Gorée:* 1854–1856 Timoléon Ropert; 1856–1859 Jean d'Alteyrac; 1859–1859 Georges de Cools. *Note:* for Commandants-Particuliers of **Gabon Settlements** see that entry.

475 Goshen. 24 Oct. 1882–7 Aug. 1883. *Location:* eastern British Bechuanaland, part of Korannaland. *Capital:* Rooigrond. *Other names:* Het Land Goosen, Goosen, Land Goosen (named Goshen from the Bible).

History: A Boer republic, founded on the Rooigrond, it merged with **Stellaland** to form the **United States of Stellaland** in 1883. It was set up on land ceded to the Boers by Bechuana chief Moshete.

Administrators: 24 Oct. 1882–7 Aug. 1883 Gey Van Pettius.

Gouiriko see **Gwiriko**

Gourma see **Gurma**

476 Graaff-Reinet. 6 Feb. 1795–22 Aug. 1796. *Location:* on the Sunday River, Cape of Good Hope Colony, South Africa. *Capital:* Graaff-Reinet (founded in 1786 and named for Governor Van de Graaff and his wife Reinet).

History: Formed in 1785 as an administrative district of the Cape (**Cape of Good Hope Colony**) and ruled by a landdrost (magistrate) and a secretary from the chief town of Graaff-Reinet. In 1795 the Boers of the area rebelled against the liberal, anti-racist laws of the then landdrost Honoratus Maynier, and kicked him out, declaring themselves an independent colony, answerable only to Holland (see also **Swellendam**). Not an independent republic as such, it submitted to the British in 1796, and became a Cape district again (see **British-Occupied Cape Colony [i]**).

Rulers: 6 Feb. 1795–22 Aug. 1796 Adriaan Van Jaarsveld (President of the War Council); 6 Feb. 1795–22 Aug. 1796 Carl Gerotz (National Landdrost).

477 Gran Canária [i]. 6 March 1480–1589. *Location:* Canary Islands. *Capital:* Las Palmas (founded 1478 and named for the palms nearby). *Other names:* Grand Canary.

History: Gran Canária, the major Canary Island, was occupied by the Spanish in 1480. In 1589 it became **Gran Canária Territory [i].**

Governors: 6 March 1480–1491 Pedro de Vera; 1491–1494 Francisco de Maldonaldo; 1494–1495 [unknown]; 1495–1497 Alfonso Fajardo; 1497–1498 [unknown]; 1498–1502 Lope de Valenzuela; 1502–1502 Antonio de Torres; 1502–1503 [unknown]; 1503–1505 Alonso Esudero; 1505–1517 Lope de Sosa y Mesa; 1517–1518 Pedro de Castilla; 1518–1520 Fernán de Guzmán; 1520–1521 Bernardino de Anaya; 1521–1523 Pedro de Castilla; 1523–1526 Diego de Herro; 1526–1529 Martín Cerón; 1529–1531 Bernardo del Nero; 1531–

1532 [unknown]; 1532–1535 Martín Cerón; 1535–1536 Agustín de Zurbarán; 1536–1538 Bernardino de Ledesma; 1538–1540 Juan de Legarte; 1540–1543 Agustín de Zurbarán; 1543–1546 Alonso del Corral; 1546–1549 Juan de Miranda; 1549–1553 Rodrigo de Acuña; 1553–1555 Luís de Vigil; 1555–1557 Rodrigo de Acuña; 1557–1558 Francisco Marquez y Pedrosa; 1558–1559 [unknown]; 1559–1562 Juan Pacheco de Benavides; 1562–1565 Diego del Águila y Toledo; 1565–1568 [unknown]; 1568–1571 Pedro de Herrera; 1571–1575 Juan Alonso de Benavides; 1575–1578 Diego de Melgarejo; 1578–1579 [unknown]; 1579–1584 Martín de Benavides; 1584–1586 Tomás de Cangas; 1586–1589 Álvaro de Acosta.

478 Gran Canária [ii]. 1595–1625. *Location:* as **Gran Canária [i].** *Capital:* Las Palmas. *Other names:* Grand Canary, Gran Canária.

History: In 1595 **Gran Canária Territory [i]** became an individual island again. In 1625 the Captaincy-General was re-imposed on the whole group of islands and Gran Canária became part of **Canary Islands Captaincy-General [ii],** as **Gran Canária Territory [ii].**

Governors: 1595–1599 Alonso de Alvorado y Ulloa; 1599–1601 Antonio Pamachamoso; 1601–1607 Jeronimo de Valderrama y Tovar; 1607–1612 Luís de Mendoza; 1612–1615 Francisco de la Rúa; 1615–1621 Fernando Osorio; 1621–1624 Pedro de Barrionuevo y Melgoza; 1624–1625 Gabriel de Lara.

479 Gran Canária Territory [i]. 1589–1595. *Location:* as **Gran Canária [i].** *Capital:* Las Palmas. *Other names:* Grand Canary Island, Grand Canary, Gran Canária.

History: In 1589 the individuality of **Gran Canária [i],** as with all the Canary Islands (see **Canary Islands Captaincy-General [i]** for further details) was terminated, and each of the islands became a territory, still run by a governor, but answerable to the Captain-

General of the Canary Islands based on Gran Canária. This captain-general served also as governor of Gran Canária Territory. In 1595 Gran Canária, and the other islands, resumed their individual status (see **Gran Canária [ii]**).

Governors-General: 1589–1591 Marqués de Bedmar; 1591–1595 [unknown].

480 Gran Canária Territory [ii]. 1625–1821. *Location:* Canary Islands. *Capital:* Las Palmas. *Other names:* Grand Canary, Gran Canária.

History: see **Tenerife Territory [ii]** for details. In 1821 the island became part of **Canary Islands Province.**

Rulers: ruled by the Captain-General of **Canary Islands Captaincy-General [ii].**

481 Gran Comoro. ca. 1515–1893. *Location:* Comoros. *Capital:* Moroni. *Other names:* Moroni, Angaziya, Grande Comore, Ngaridza.

History: Founded about 1515 as the Sultanate of Ngaridza, the island of Gran Comoro fell under French protection in 1893 as part of the **Mayotte Protectorate.**

Sultans: ca. 1515–end of 16th century 7 Sultans including Tibi; ca. 1600–ca. 1843 [unknown]; ca. 1843–ca. 1850 Sayid Hamza; ca. 1850–1875 Sayid Ahmad; 1875–1909 Sayid Ali.

Grand Bassam see French Ivory Coast [i] and Ivory Coast Territory

Grand Bonny see Bonny

Grand Canary see Gran Canária

Grande Comore see Gran Comoro

Greenville see Mississippi-in-Africa

482 Griqualand East. 26 Dec. 1861–Oct. 1874. *Location:* eastern South Africa, south of Natal. *Capital:* Kokstad (founded in 1862 and named for Adam Kok III). *Other names:* New Griqualand (it is now called Emboland).

History: In 1861 two thousand Griquas left **Adam Kok's Land** under their leader Adam Kok III, and trekked over the Drakensberg Mountains to **Nomansland.** They renamed their new home Griqualand East (cf **Griqualand West**). In 1874 it became part of **British Cape Colony (Self-Rule).**
Captains: 26 Dec. 1861–Oct. 1874 Adam Kok III. *Residents:* 1873–Oct. 1874 Joseph Orpen.

483 Griqualand West. 27 Oct. 1871–17 July 1873. *Location:* the Bechuanaland–South Africa border. *Capital:* Kimberley (founded 1871 and named for the Earl of Kimberley, then colonial secretary).
History: In 1867 diamonds were discovered in **Waterboer's Land. British Cape Colony** and the **South African Republic [ii]** both wanted the area for themselves, naturally, and in 1871 it was made a separate British territory, attached to the Cape. In 1873 it became **Griqualand West Crown Colony.** (See also **Klipdrift Republic.**)
Civil Commissioners: 27 Oct. 1871–10 Jan. 1873 Francis Orpen. *Administrators:* 10 Jan. 1873–17 July 1873 Richard Southey.

484 Griqualand West Crown Colony. 17 July 1873–15 Oct. 1880. *Location:* Bechuanaland–South Africa border. *Capital:* Kimberley.
History: In 1873 **Griqualand West** became a British Crown Colony, and in 1877 it was attached to the Cape (see **British Cape Colony [Self-Rule]**), this move becoming effective in 1880.
Lieutenant-Governors: 17 July 1873–3 Aug. 1875 Richard Southey; 4 Aug. 1875–March 1879 Owen Lanyon; March 1879–15 Oct. 1880 James Rose-Innes, Jr.

Griqualand West Republic see **Klipdrift Republic**

485 Griquatown. 1813–1820. *Location:* the nucleus of **Waterboer's Land.**

Capital: Griquatown (founded 1802 as Klaarwater [Clear Water], named by the Rev. Kramer and the Rev. Anderson on account of the spring there. Originally it was a London Mission Society station, and was renamed in 1813 by the Rev. John Campbell).
History: In the late 18th century, Adam Kok, a Bastaard, and named after his profession (cook), was compelled to leave the Stellenbosch area of the Cape, and headed north, gathering half-breed Bastaards and Griqua Hottentots en route. He died in 1795, and his son, Cornelis Kok I, settled on the Orange River, and Cornelis's two sons Adam Kok II and Cornelis Kok II both settled in the village of Klaarwater, which John Campbell re-named Griquatown in 1813 (see also **Campbell Lands**). Adam Kok II and Barend Barends ruled between them until 1819, when Andries Waterboer took over. Barends went north to become involved with the Matabele, and Adam Kok II went on to form **Adam Kok's Land** (which he named after his son Adam Kok III). Cornelis Kok II went north to **Campbell Lands,** which later became **Cornelis Kok's Land.** Thereafter Griquatown extended its boundaries and became known as **Waterboer's Land.**
Kaptyns (Captains): 1813–1819 Adam Kok II (joint); 1813–1819 Barend Barends (joint); 1819–1820 Andries Waterboer.

Gross Friedrichsburg see **Brandenburger** and **Prussian Gold Coast** entries

486 Guinea. See these **names:**
Guinea Republic (1958–   )
French Guinea Overseas Territory (1946–1958)
French Guinea Colony (1893–1946)
Rivières du Sud Colony (1891–1893)
Rivières du Sud Semi-Autonomous Colony (1889–1891)
Rivières du Sud Territory (1882–1889)

Rivières du Sud Protectorate (1849–1882)
Futa Jallon (ca. 1700-1881)
Samory's Empire (1879–1898)

487 Guinea-Bissau. See these names:
Guinea-Bissau (1973–   )
Portuguese Guinea Overseas Province (1951–1973)
Portuguese Guinea (1879–1951)
Bissau [ii] (1753–1879)
Bissau [i] (1687–1707)
Cacheu (1614–1852)

488 Guinea-Bissau. 24 Sept. 1973– . *Location:* North West Africa. *Capital:* Bissau (established 1687 as a fortified Portuguese post). *Other names:* Republic of Guinea-Bissau, Guinea-Bissau Republic.
History: In 1973, after more than ten years of guerrilla struggle, **Portuguese Guinea Overseas Province** gained independence as The Republic of Guinea-Bissau. Union with **Cape Verde Republic** is probable in the future. The independence of Guinea-Bissau was fully recognized on September 10, 1974.
Governors (Nominal): 24 Sept. 1973–Apr. 1974 José Rodrigues; 2 May 1974–1974 Lt.-Col. San Gouveia; 1974–10 Sept. 1974 Carlos Fabião. *Presidents:* 26 Sept. 1973–14 Nov. 1980 Luís de Almeda Cabral. *Presidents of the Council of the Revolution:* 14 Nov. 1980–14 May 1984 João Vieira. *Chairmen of the Council of State:* 16 May 1984– João Vieira. *Principal Commissioners:* 26 Sept. 1973–7 July 1978 Francisco Mendes; 7 July 1978–28 Sept. 1978 Constantino Teixeira (acting); 28 Sept. 1978–14 Nov. 1980 João Vieira; 14 May 1982–8 March 1984 Victor Saúde Maria. *Note:* Principal Commissioner is the same as Prime Minister. *Note:* in times of no Principal Commissioner, the President or Chairman held that office.

489 Guinea Republic. 2 Oct. 1958– . *Location:* North West Africa.

Capital: Conakry (founded 1884 and named for a local village nearby). *Other names:* République du Guinée, Republic of Guinea, People's Revolutionary Republic of Guinea.
History: The name Guinea comes from the Guinea Coast, which in turn came from the Berber word "aguinaw" meaning "black man." In 1958 **French Guinea Overseas Territory** became independent, the only French colony in North West Africa (see **French West Africa**) to go straight to independence without going through the "training process" of being an autonomous republic within the French Community.
Heads of State: 2 Oct. 1958–12 Nov. 1958 Ahmed Sekou Touré (interim); 12 Nov. 1958–15 Jan. 1961 Ahmed Sekou Touré. *Presidents:* 15 Jan. 1961–26 Mar. 1984 Ahmed Sekou Touré; 27 Mar. 1984–3 Apr. 1984 Louis Lansana Béavogui (interim); 3 Apr. 1984–5 Apr. 1984 Lansana Conté (Head of Military Committee for National Redress); 5 Apr. 1984– Lansana Conté. *Prime Ministers:* 26 Apr. 1972–26 Mar. 1984 Louis Lansana Béavogui; 5 Apr. 1984–18 Dec. 1984 Diara Traoré. *Note:* in times of no Prime Minister, the President held that office.

490 Gulf of Guinea Settlements. 9 Feb. 1839–11 June 1843. *Location:* the coast of Gabon. *Capital:* none.
History: In 1839 the French began settlements along the coast of Gabon, and in 1843 they became the **Gabon Settlements.**
Commanders: 9 Feb. 1839–11 June 1843 Capt. Louis Bouët-Willaumez.

491 Gumel. 1749–1903. *Location:* Kano Province, Northern Nigeria. *Capital:* Gumel (from 1845); Tumbi (until 1845). *Other names:* Gummel, Gumel Emirate, Laute, Lautaye.
History: The name Gumel comes from "Gubele"—Fulani for a "short-horned cow." Founded as an emirate in 1749 by a Kano native named Dan Juma with his Mangawa followers.

About 1755 it became a tributary state of the **Bornu Empire**. It was never part of the **Fulani Empire**. Gumelawa history has been one of wars with **Hadeija**, **Kano** and **Damagaram**, and in 1903 it became part of **Northern Nigeria Protectorate**.

Emirs: 1749–1754 Dan Juma I (or Danyuma); 1754–1760 Adamu Karro; 1760–1777 Dan Juma I (or Danyuma); 1777–1804 Maikota (or Danmaigatiny Uata, or Tanoma); 1804–1811 Kalgo (or Damgalke); 1811–1828 Dan Auwa (or Danyawa); 1828–1843 Muhammad (or Dan Tanoma); 1843–1850 Cheri; 1850–1852 Muhammar Atu; 1852–1861 Cheri; 1861–1872 Abdullahi; 1872–1896 Abubakr; 1896–1915 Ahmadu; 1915–1944 Mamman na Kota; May 1944– Maina Mamman (or Muhammadu).

492 Gurma. 1204–20 Jan. 1895. *Location:* southeast Burkina Faso. *Capital:* Fada N'Gourma (or Fa N'Gurma) (from 1710). *Other names:* Gourma, Fada N'Gourma.

History: Founded in 1204 it was made part of **French West Africa** in 1895, and in the following month part of **Upper Volta Protectorate**.

Kings: 1204–1248 Diaba Lompo; 1248–1292 Tidarpo; 1292–1336 Untani; 1336–1380 Banydoba; 1380–1395 Labi Diebo; 1395–ca. 1425 Tenin; ca. 1425–ca. 1470 Tokurma; ca. 1470–ca. 1520 Gima; ca. 1520–ca. 1553 Gori; ca. 1553–1571 Bogora; 1571–1615 Kampadiboaghi; 1615–ca. 1659 Kampadi; ca. 1659–1684 Tantiari; 1684–1709 Lissoangui; 1709–1736 Yendabri; 1736–1761 Yembirima; 1761–1791 Baghama; 1791–1820 Yanghama; 1820–1849 Yenkirma; 1849–1853 Yentiabri; 1853–1856 Yempabu; 1856–1883 Yempadigu; 1883–1892 Yentuguri; 1892–1911 Batchande; 1911–1952 Kambambori; 1952– Hamtiuri.

493 Gwandu. 1808–March 1903. *Location:* Nigeria. *Capital:* Gwandu (named for the royal farmlands, or "gandu," nearby). *Other names:* Gando, Gandu.

History: In 1808 Uthman Dan Fodio split his **Fulani Empire** into two emirates, **Sokoto** and **Gwandu**. In 1903 Gwandu went the way of the Empire (otherwise known as the Sokoto Caliphate), becoming incorporated into **Northern Nigeria Protectorate**.

Emirs: 1808–1828 Abdullahi Dan Fodio; 1828–1833 Muhammar (or Muhammad I); 1833–1858 Halilu (or Khalil); 1858–1860 Haliru I; 1860–1864 Aliyu; 1864–1868 Abdulkadir; 1868–1875 Almustafa; 1875–1876 Hanuf; 1876–1888 Malik; 1888–1897 Umaru Bakatara; 1897–1898 Abdullahi Bayero; 1898–May 1903 Bayero Aliyu; May 1903–March 1906 Auhammadu (or Muhammad II); March 1906–March 1915 Haliru II; March 1915–Jan. 1918 Muhammadu Bashiru; Jan. 1918–1938 Usman; 1938–12 Jan. 1954 Yahya; 13 Jan. 1954– Harun.

Gwari see **Hausaland**

494 Gwiriko. 1714–1890. *Location:* Burkina Faso (in the bend of the Black Volta River, in the Bobo lands). *Capital:* [unknown]. *Other names:* Gouiriko.

History: This Dyula state was an extension of the Watara Empire of **Kong**, and was founded by Famagan Watara, brother of the founder of **Kong**. It was taken by the French in 1890, eventually forming part of **Upper Volta Protectorate**.

Kings: 1714–1729 Famagan Watara; 1729–1742 Famagan denn Tieba; 1742–1749 Kere Massa; 1749–1809 Magan Oule Watara; 1809–1809 Dramani; 1809–1839 Diori Watara; 1839–1851 Bako Morou Watara; 1851–1854 Laganfiela Moru; 1854–1878 Ali Dian; 1878–1885 Kokoroko Dia; 1885–1892 Sabana; 1892–1897 Tieba Niandane Watara; 1897–1909 Pintieba Watara; 1909–1915 Karamoko.

495 Hadeija. ca. 1460–1805. *Location:* northern Nigeria. *Capital:*

Hadeija. *Other names:* Hadejia.

History: A small kingdom of uncertain origin, it is said to have been founded by Hadiya, a Kanuri hunter from Machinna, who heads a line of 32 Habe kings. Only the last three are known by name. In 1805 it was swallowed up to make the **Hadeija Emirate.**

Rulers: the only known three kings were: (?)–(?) Baude; (?)–(?) Musa; (?)–1805 Abubakr.

496 Hadeija Emirate. 1808–7 Apr. 1906. *Location:* northern Nigeria. *Capital:* Hadeija. *Other names:* Hadejia.

History: In 1805 Umaru, then Sarkin of the little kingdom of **Hadeija** pledged allegiance to Uthman Dan Fodio (see **Fulani Empire**) and joined with the kingdoms of **Auyo,** Garun Gabbas, Gatarwa, Kazura, Fagi and Dawa to form the emirate, an emirate officially established in 1808 by Umaru's brother Moman Kankia. In 1906 it became part of **Northern Nigeria Protectorate.**

Emirs: 1805–1808 Umaru; 1808–1808 Moman Kankia; 1808–1845 Sambo; 1845–1847 Garko; 1847–1848 Abdulkadiri; 1848–1850 Bohari; 1850–1851 Amadu; 1851–1863 Bohari; 1863–1865 Umaru; 1865–1885 Haru; 1885–1906 Muhammadu; 1906–1909 Haruna; 1909–1925 Abdulkadiri; 1925–1950 Usman; June 1950– Haruna.

497 Hafsid Kingdom. 1236–18 Aug. 1534. *Location:* Tunisia plus the present-day area of Constantine in Algeria, plus Tripolitania in Libya. *Capital:* Tunis. *Other names:* Banu Hafs Dynasty.

History: Named for the founder of the House, Abu Hafs Umar, a Berber chieftain, the kingdom was established in 1236 by his grandson Abu Zakkariyya, the Almohad governor of Tunis. Its history is one of continual division, reunification, and fighting with the Abd al-Wadid Kingdom, the Merinid Kingdom and the European powers until in 1534 the Turks took

Tunis (see **Turkish Tunis [i]**). Although the Hafsids continued to rule nominally, their real power was finished from 1534.

Sultans: 1236–Oct. 1249 Abu Zakkariyya Yahya I; Oct. 1249–17 May 1277 Abu Abdallah Muhammad I al-Mustansir; 17 May 1277–Aug. 1279 Abu Zakkariyya Yahya II al-Wathiq; Aug. 1279–28 Jan. 1283 Abu Ishaq Ibrahim I; 28 Jan. 1283–June 1283 Abu Faris (pretender); June 1283–12 July 1284 interregnum; 12 July 1284–4 Nov. 1295 Abu Hafs Umar I; 5 Nov. 1295–18 Aug. 1309 Abu Abdallah Muhammad II Abu Asida; 18 Aug. 1309–4 Sept. 1309 Abu Yahya Abu Bakr al-Shahid; 4 Sept. 1309–14 Nov. 1311 Abu al-Baqa Khalid I; 14 Nov. 1311–Oct. 1317 Abu Yahya Zakkariyya I; Oct. 1317–8 June 1318 Abu Darba; 8 June 1318–19 Oct. 1346 Abu Yahya Abu Bakr; 19 Oct. 1346–15 Sept. 1347 Abu Hafs Umar II; 15 Sept. 1347–10 Apr. 1348 occupied by the Merinids; 10 Apr. 1348–1350 Abu al-Abbas Ahmad al-Fadl; 1350–1357 Abu Ishaq Ibrahim; 1357–1357 occupied by the Merinids; 1357–1369 Abu Isahq Ibrahim; 1369–9 Nov. 1370 Abu al-Baqa Khalid II; 9 Nov. 1370–4 June 1394 Abu al-Abbas Ahmad; 4 June 1394–18 July 1434 Abu Faris Abdul Aziz; 18 July 1434–16 Aug. 1434 interregnum; 16 Aug. 1434–16 Sept. 1435 Abu Abdallah Muhammad IV al-Muntasir; 16 Sept. 1435–1488 Abu Amr Uthman; 1488–1489 Abu Zakkariyya Yahya II; 1489–13 Oct. 1490 Abd al-Mu'min; 13 Oct. 1490–15 May 1494 Abu Yahya Zakkariyya II; 15 May 1494–1526 Abu Abdallah Muhammad V; 1526–1542 Mulay al-Hassan; 1542–Dec. 1569 Ahmad (or Hamida); Dec. 1569–1573 interregnum; 1573–13 Sept. 1574 Mulay Muhammad.

498 Hafsid Tripoli [i]. ca. 1247–1327. *Location:* Tripolitania, Libya. *Capital:* Tripoli. *Other names:* Tripoli (Hafsid).

History: About 1247 the **Almohad Empire** lost Tripoli (see **Almohad Tripoli**) to the Hafsid governors of that town. In 1327 these new rulers turned the town over to the Banu Ammar (see **Tripoli [Banu Ammar]**).

Hafsid Governors: ca. 1247–1279 [unknown]; 1279–1282 Murjim; 1283–(?) Muhammad ibn Isa; (?)–1318 [unknown]; 1318–1327 Muhammad ibn Abu Bakr.

499 Hafsid Tripoli [ii]. 1401–1412. *Location:* Tripolitania, Libya. *Capital:* Tripoli. *Other names:* Tripoli (Hafsid).

History: In 1401 the Hafsids took back Tripoli from the Banu Ammar (see **Tripoli [Banu Ammar]**). In 1412 they lost it to the Egyptian Mamelukes (see **Egyptian Tripoli** and **Circassian Mameluke Empire**).

Rulers: unknown.

500 Hafsid Tripoli [iii]. 1482–26 June 1510. *Location:* Tripolitania, Libya. *Capital:* Tripoli. *Other names:* Tripoli (Hafsid).

History: In 1482 the Hafsids (see **Hafsid Kingdom**) took Tripoli for the last time, this time from the Mamelukes (see **Circassian Mameluke Empire** and **Egyptian Tripoli**). In 1510 it was taken by Spain (see **Tripoli [Spanish]**).

Governors: 1482–1489 Abu Bakr; 1489–1494 Sheikh Ahmad az-Zarraq; 1494–26 June 1510 [unknown].

Hajji Omar's Empire see **Tukolor Empire**

Halphoolaren see **Tukolor Empire**

501 Hammamid Kingdom. 1014–1152. *Location:* Algeria. *Capital:* al-Qalat (built in 1007, the word means "the fortress"). *Other names:* Banu Hammad Dynasty.

History: In 1014 Hammad ibn Buluggin, a Zirid (see **Zirid Kingdom**), declared his independence. Reaching a peak of importance at the end of the 11th century, it fell to the Almohads in 1152 (see **Almohad Empire**).

Kings: 1014–1028 Hammad ibn Bu-luggin; 1028–1055 al-Qa'id; 1055–1055 Muhsin; 1055–1056 interregnum; 1056–1062 Buluggin ibn Muhammad; 1062–1088 al-Nasir ibn Alannas; 1088–1104 al-Mansur ibn al-Nasir; 1104–1104 Badis ibn al-Mansur; 1104–1105 interregnum; 1105–1122 al-Aziz ibn al-Mansur; 1122–1152 Yahya ibn al-Aziz.

502 Harar. 1526–1887. *Location:* east central Ethiopia. *Capital:* Harar (founded in the 7th century) (1526–77, and 1647–1875). *Other names:* Harer, Hararge, Harrar.

History: In 1526 Ahmad Gran, the first emir of the Muslim state of Harar, conquered **Adal [ii]** and took its capital Harar as his own, and named his new state after it. Sir Richard Burton was the first European visitor (in the 1850s). From 1875–1885 the city of Harar was occupied by the Turks, and in 1887 the country was conquered by Menelik II of **Ethiopian Empire [ii]**, and Harar became Harar Province, ruled first by Haile Selassie's father, Ras Makonnen, as governor, and then, in the same position, by the future emperor himself from 1910.

Sultans: 1526–1543 Ahmad Gran ibn Ibrahim; 1543–1567 Nur ibn Mujahid; 1567–1569 Uthman al-Habashi; 1569–1571 Talha ibn al-Abbas; 1571–1573 Nasir ibn Uthman; 1573–1576 Muhammad ibn Nasir; 1576–1576 Mansur ibn Muhammad; 1576–1583 Muhammad ibn Ibrahim; 1583–1647 unknown rulers in the desert; 1647–1653 Ali ibn Daud; 1653–1671 Hashim; 1671–1700 Abdallah; 1700–1721 Talha; 1721–1732 Abu-Bakr; 1732–1733 Khalaf; 1733–1747 Hamid; 1747–1756 Yusuf; 1756–1783 Ahmad ibn Abu-Bakr; 1783–1783 Muhammad; 1783–1794 Abdul-Shakur ibn Yusuf; 1794–1821 Ahmad ibn Muhammad; 1821–1826 Abdurrahman ibn Muhammad; 1826–1834 Abdul Karim ibn Muhammad; 1834–1852 Abu-Bakr ibn Abdul-Mannan; 1852–1856 Ahmad ibn Abu-Bakr; 1856–1875 Muhammad ibn Ali; 1875–1887 Abdallah ibn Muhammad.

503 Hausaland. A term used interchangeably with, but far more often than, Habe Land, Habash Land and Hau-sha Land. The Hausa peoples are, and were, to be found in northern Nigeria and southern Niger. The largest ethnic group in the area, the Hausa formed seven major and seven minor states, called respectively The Hausa Bakwai and The Banza Bakwai (i.e. the seven true Hausa states and the seven bastards). The Hausa Bakwai were Daura, Kano, Zazzau, Gobir, Katsina, Rano and Biram. The Banza Bakwai were Zamfara, Kebbi, Nupe, Gwari, Yauri, Ilorin and Kwararafa.

Haut-Senegal-Niger see **Upper Senegal and Niger**

Haute Volta see **Upper Volta**

504 Heidelberg Republic. 16 Dec. 1880–30 Dec. 1880. *Location:* as Transvaal Province of **South Africa**. *Capital:* Heidelberg (established as a town in 1866, and named for the Heidelberg Catechism used by the Dutch Reformed Church). *Other names:* Republic of Heidelberg, South African Republic.
History: On October 13 (effective December 16), 1880, **Transvaal Colony [i]** became independent of Britain and became the **Heidelberg Republic.** Two weeks later its name reverted to the South African Republic (see **South African Republic [ii]**).
Rulers: 16 Dec. 1880–30 Dec. 1880 Triumvirate of Paul Kruger, Piet Joubert and Marthinus Pretorius.

505 Hereroland. ca. 1730–21 Oct. 1885. *Location:* Namibia. *Capital:* no central government. *Other names:* Herreroland.
History: Founded about 1730, the land of the Hereros was made part of **German South West Africa Protectorate [i]** in 1885.
Chiefs: ca. 1730–(?) [unknown]; (?)–1861 Tjamuaha. *Paramount*

Chiefs: 1861–1890 Maherero; 1890–1917 Samuel Maherero; 1917–1970 Hosea Kutako.

Het Land Goosen see **Goshen** and **United States of Stellaland**

Hogbonu see **Porto-Novo Kingdom [i]**

Hollandia see **Brandenburger** and **Prussian Gold Coast** entries

Hottentot Hollandia see **Cape of Good Hope Colony**

Houeda see **Whydah**

Hova see **Imerina**

506 Ibadan. ca. 1750–1893. *Location:* Western State, Nigeria. *Capital:* Ibadan (name "Eba Odan" means "near the savannah").
History: Founded about 1750 by Yoruba refugees from all over what is now western Nigeria, Ibadan in 1829 became the leading city of the area. There was never a hereditary leader of Ibadan — it was ruled by a "rule-of-the-fittest" system. In 1893 it became part of the **Niger River Delta Protectorate.**
Chiefs: ca. 1750 Maye; (?)–(?) Laborinde; (?)–(?) Lakanle I; (?)–(?) Olyedun; ca. 1800 Lakanle II; (?)–(?) Ohuyole; (?)–(?) Opeagbe; 1855–ca. 1866 Olugboda; ca. 1866–ca. 1870 Ogunmola; ca. 1870–ca. 1872 Oruwusi; ca. 1872–(?) Latosisa; (?)–ca. 1892 vacant; ca. 1892–1893 Fijabi.

Ibani see **Bonny**

Idah see **Igala**

507 Idrisid State. 6 Feb. 789–974. *Location:* northern Morocco and northwestern Algeria. *Capitals:* Hajar an-Nasr (937–74); Fez (807–927, founded between 790 and 808); Walila (until 807).
History: Founded by Idris, a descen-

dent of Ali, as a state free from the persecution of the Abbasids. It became a group of principalities after 828, all of these principalities answerable to the King. In 920 Fez was taken by the Fatimids, to be won back by the Idrisids in 925. Just over a year later the king was defeated by rival Berber tribes and was killed. The Fatimids ruled Fez again, and then in 937 the Idrisids came to power for the third time, this time with a new capital. By 974 the Omayyads were ruling there.

Kings: 6 Feb. 789–June 791 Idris I ibn Abdallah; June 791–Sept. 828 Idris II (or Mulay Idris II); Sept. 828–Apr. 836 Muhammad al-Mustansir; Apr. 836–Feb. 849 Ali I; Feb. 849–863 Yahya I; 863–866 Yahya II; 866–880 Ali II ibn Umar; 880–905 Yahya III al-Miqdam; 905–920 Yahya IV; 920–925 Fatimid rule; 925–927 Hasan al-Hajjam; 927–937 Fatimid rule; 937–948 al-Qasim Gannum; 948–954 Abu'l Aish Ahmad; 954–974 Hasan II.

508 Idutywa Reserve. Aug. 1858–Dec. 1864. *Location:* British Kaffraria, Southern Africa. *Capital:* Idutywa. *Other names:* Idutywa District.

History: Formed as a dependency of the Crown Colony of British Kaffraria (see **British Kaffraria**), it was composed of Bantu fragments of Umhala's clan. A British magistrate ruled. In 1864 it merged into **British Kaffraria Crown Colony.**

Special Magistrates: Aug. 1858–Sept. 1858 John Gawler; Sept. 1858–May 1860 George Colley; May 1860–Sept. 1861 W.G.B. Shepstone; Sept. 1861–Dec. 1864 William B. Chalmers.

509 Ifat. 1285–1415. *Location:* eastern Shoa, Ethiopia-Somalia border. *Capital:* Goncho. *Other names:* Awfat.

History: In 1285 the first Walashma sultan created the state of Ifat by conquering the states of Fatajar, Dawaro and Bali, as well as **Adal [i].** A Muslim state, it continually revolted against Ethiopia, until in 1415 it became part of

Ethiopian Empire [i] as **Adal [ii].**

Sultans: 1285–ca. 1304 Umar ibn Dunyahuz; ca. 1304–ca. 1321 Jaziwi; ca. 1321–ca. 1328 Haqq ud-Din I; ca. 1328–ca. 1330 Hussein; ca. 1330–ca. 1331 Nasir; ca. 1331–ca. 1335 al-Mansur I; ca. 1335–ca. 1337 Jamal ud-Din I; ca. 1337–ca. 1343 Abut; ca. 1343–ca. 1344 Zubair. *Queens:* ca. 1344–ca. 1352 Ma'at Laila. *Sultans:* ca. 1352–ca. 1354 Sabr ud-Din I; ca. 1354–ca. 1360 Qat-Ali; ca. 1360–ca. 1366 Harbi-Ar'ed; ca. 1366–ca. 1373 Haqq ud-Din II; ca. 1373–1415 Sa'd ud-Din Ahmad.

510 Ife. ca. 1000–1900. *Location:* western Nigeria. *Capital:* Ife (formerly called Ile-Ife). *Other names:* Ile-Ife.

History: Traditionally founded by one of the sons of the Yoruba god, Oduduwa, Ife is one of the oldest Yoruba towns (cf. **Ijebu**). It is held by them to be a sacred city, in fact their chief religious center. Ife did not become subject to the **Fulani Empire,** but the slave trade wars of the 1820s and 1830s weakened it. In 1900 it became part of the **Niger River Delta Protectorate.**

Only known Onis (Kings): ca. 1300 Adimu; (?)–(?) Adesoji; Sept. 1930–Aderemi Adesoji.

511 Ifni. 1860–27 Nov. 1912. *Location:* southern Morocco. *Capital:* none.

History: The Spanish had once occupied the post of **Santa Cruz de la Mar Pequeña** on the Moroccan coast, and using this as a precedent persuaded the sultan of Morocco (see **Alawid Morocco**) to give them Ifni. The unoccupied (by Spain) area was made into a protectorate in 1912 (see **Ifni Protectorate**).

Rulers: 1860–27 Nov. 1912 no central administration.

512 Ifni Protectorate. 27 Nov. 1912–1952. *Location:* as **Ifni.** *Capital:* Sidi Ifni ("Ifni" means "rocky desert"). *Other names:* Ifni.

History: In 1912 **Ifni** became a Spanish protectorate. It was occupied by Spanish troops only in 1934, and in 1952 it became part of **Spanish West Africa** — as **Ifni Territory.**
Rulers: 27 Nov. 1912–1934 none; 1934–1952 unknown, if any.

513 Ifni Province. 14 Jan. 1958–4 Jan. 1969. *Location:* as **Ifni.** *Capital:* Sidi Ifni. *Other names:* Ifni.
History: In 1958 **Ifni Territory** left **Spanish West Africa** and became a Spanish province. In 1969 it was given back to the **Kingdom of Morocco.**
Governors: 14 Jan. 1958–1959 Mariano Quirce; 1959–1961 Pedro Alcubierre; 1961–1963 Joaquín Coronado; 1963–1965 Adolfo Campos; 1965–1967 Marino Larrasquito; 1967–4 Jan. 1969 José Rodríguez.

514 Ifni Territory. 1952–14 Jan. 1958. *Location:* as **Ifni.** *Capital:* Sidi Ifni. *Other names:* Ifni.
History: In 1952 **Ifni Protectorate** became a territory of **Spanish West Africa,** an institution it left in 1958 to become **Ifni Province.**
Rulers: 1952–1956 ruled direct by Governor-General of **Spanish Morocco;** 1956–1958 [unknown].

Ifrikiyah, Ifriqa, Ifriqiyah see **Aghlabid Empire, Arab North Africa** and **Omayyad North Africa**

515 Igala. ca. 1525–1901. *Location:* south central Nigeria. *Capital:* Idah. *Other names:* Idah.
History: The Igala people grew up around the present-day town of Idah, which they founded as their capital at the beginning of the 16th century. In 1901 the country became part of the **Northern Nigeria Protectorate.**
Kings: ca. 1525 Abutu Eje; (?)–(?) Ebelejonu; (?)–(?) Agenapoje; ca. 1600 Idoko; (?)–(?) Ayagba; (?)–(?) Akogu; (?)–(?) Ocholi; ca. 1700 Agada; (?)–(?) Amacho; (?)–(?) Itodo; (?)–(?) Ogalla; ca. 1800 Idoko Adegbe; (?)–(?)

Onuche; (?)–1835 Ekalaga; 1835–1856 Amocheje; 1856–1870 Aku Odiba; 1870–1876 Okoliko; 1876–1900 Amaga; 1900–1903 Ocheje Onokpa; 1903–1905 vacant; 1905–1911 Oboni; 1911–1919 Oguche Akpa; 1919–1926 Atabor; 1926–1945 Obaje Ocheje; 1945–1956 Ame; 1957– Alii.

516 Ijebu. (?)–20 May 1892. *Location:* western Nigeria. *Capital:* Ijebu-Ode. *Other names:* Jebu.
History: Traditionally founded by one of the sons of Oduduwa, a Yoruba god, Ijebu was the main go-between for centuries between the Lagos area and its trade with the Yoruba country. The Ijebu are a division of the Yoruba. In 1892 Ijebu became part of the **Niger River Delta Protectorate.**
Only known Kings: ca. 1892 Gbelegbura I; (?)–(?) Ogbagba I; Sept. 1933–ca. 1955 Daniel Adesanya Gbelegbura II; ca. 1955– Sikiru Adetona Ogbagba II.

517 Ikhshid Egypt. 2 Sept. 935–5 Aug. 969. *Location:* Egypt and Syria. *Capital:* al-Fustat.
History: In 935 the governor of **Abbasid Egypt [ii],** Muhammad al-Ikhshid, made himself the independent sovereign of Egypt and Syria. The Abbasids were virtually finished by this time anyway, and in Egypt the Ikhshids ruled until 969, when the Fatimid caliphate took over (see **Fatimid Egypt**).
Kings: 2 Sept. 935–24 July 946 Muhammad al-Ikhshid; 24 July 946–29 Dec. 960 Unujur; 1 Jan. 961–7 Feb. 965 Ali; 8 Feb. 965–23 Apr. 968 Abu al-Misq Kafur; 23 Apr. 968–5 Aug. 969 Ahmad. *Viziers:* 946–8 Feb. 965 Abu al-Misq Kafur.

Île Bonaparte see **Bonaparte**

Île de Bourbon see **Bourbon**

518 Île de France. Apr. 1722–July 1767. *Location:* as **Mauritius** (named Île de France by Guillaume d'Arse).

Capital: Port Louis (from 1736, when it was built); no central capital before 1736. *Other names:* Île Maurice, Mauritius.

History: In 1722 the French East India Company settled the island of Mauritius (see **French Mauritius**), bringing in people from **Réunion,** and being ruled by the Compagnie des Indes (French East India Company). After 1727 the Governor of Île de France (as the French now called it) was also Governor-General of all the French possessions in the Indian Ocean. In 1767 the French Government took it over (see **Île de France Colony**).

Governors: Apr. 1722–1723 Denis de Nyon; 1723–Dec. 1725 Antoine Desforges-Boucher; Dec. 1725–Aug. 1727 Denis de Brousse (acting); Aug. 1727–Aug. 1729 Pierre-Benoît Dumas; Aug. 1729–June 1735 Nicolas de Maupin. *Governors-General:* June 1735–Feb. 1740 Bertrand-François Mahé, Comte de la Bourdonnais; Feb. 1740–Aug. 1740 Didier de Saint Martin (acting); Aug. 1740–March 1746 Bertrand-François Mahé, Comte de la Bourdonnais; March 1746–Feb. 1747 Didier de Saint Martin (acting); Feb. 1747–14 March 1750 Pierre David; 14 March 1750–Jan. 1756 Jean-Baptiste de Lozier; Jan. 1756–Nov. 1759 René de la Villebague; Nov. 1759–July 1767 Antoine Desforges-Boucher.

519 Île de France Colony. July 1767–3 Oct. 1810. *Location:* as **Mauritius.** *Capital:* Port Louis. *Other names:* Mauritius, Île Maurice.

History: In 1767 **Île de France**, then in the hands of the Compagnie des Indes, was made a colony of the French Crown. In 1810 it was taken by Britain (see **British-Occupied Mauritius**).

Governors-General: July 1767–Nov. 1768 Jean Dumas; Nov. 1768–June 1769 Jean Stenauer (acting); June 1769–Aug. 1772 François Desroches; Aug. 1772–Dec. 1776 Charles de Ternay; Dec. 1776–3 May 1779 Antoine de la Brillane; 3 May 1779–30 Jan. 1780

François de Souillac (acting); 30 Jan. 1780–5 Apr. 1785 François de Souillac; 5 Apr. 1785–28 June 1785 Charles de Fresne (acting); 28 June 1785–Nov. 1785 Chevalier de Fleury (acting). *Governors-General of the Isles of France and Bourbon:* Nov. 1785–16 Feb. 1787 François de Souillac; 16 Feb. 1787–Nov. 1789 Joseph d'Entrecasteaux. *Governors-General of the French Establishments to the East of the Cape of Good Hope:* Nov. 1789–Aug. 1790 Thomas de Conway; Aug. 1790–17 June 1792 David de Cossigny; 17 June 1792–28 July 1800 Joseph de Malartic; 29 July 1800–Sept. 1803 François de la Morlière; Sept. 1803–3 Oct. 1810 Charles Décaen.

520 Île de Labourdonnais. 1744–1756. *Location:* as **Seychelles Republic.** *Capital:* none. *Other names:* Îles de Labourdonnais.

History: In 1742 and 1744 Bertrand-François Mahé, Comte de la Bourdonnais, then governor of **Île de France** (later Mauritius) sent Captain Lazare Picault to explore the islands later known as the Seychelles. Until then they had been a favorite hiding-place for pirates in the area (see, for example, **Libertalia**), and the first recorded landings had taken place in 1609 (by the English East India Company). Picard landed finally on Mahé Island (which he named), and he called the group after his superior. In 1756 the French staked a serious claim to the islands and named them **Séchelles.**

Rulers: none.

Ile-Ife see **Ife**

521 Ilha do Cerne. 1507–1598. *Location:* Mauritius. *Capital:* None.

History: Discovered by the Portuguese in 1507 and named Ilha do Cerne ("Island of the Tree-Heart"). Unclaimed until 1598, when the Dutch re-named it Mauritius (see **Dutch Mauritius [i]**).

Rulers: none.

522 Ilorin Emirate. 1831–5 March 1897. *Location:* western Nigeria. *Capital:* Ilorin. *Other names:* Yoruba.

History: Ilorin, meaning perhaps, "town of the elephant," was founded in the late 18th century by Yoruba peoples around their town of Ilorin (see **Ilorin Kingdom**). As a vassal state of **Oyo**, it was ruled by a kakanfo (military commander) named Afonja, who, in 1817, proclaimed the independence of Ilorin. In this he was assisted by a Fulani named Mallam Alimi, and in 1829 Alimi's son became the first Emir of Ilorin Emirate. In 1897 it became part of the **Niger River Delta Protectorate**, in 1900 becoming the only part of Yorubaland to fall under the **Northern Nigeria Protectorate**.

Emirs: 1831–1842 Abdul Salami; 1842–1860 Shi'ta; 1860–1868 Zubeiru; 1868–1891 Shi'ta Aliyu; 1891–1895 Moma; 1895–1915 Suleimanu; 1915–1919 Shu'aibu (or Bawa); 1919–1959 Abdul-Kadiri; 1959– Sulu Gambari.

523 Ilorin Kingdom. (?)–1829. *Location:* Nigeria. *Capital:* Ilorin (founded about 1785). *Other names:* Ilorin.

History: A Yoruba vassal state of **Oyo,** it was conquered by the Fulani in 1810, and in 1829 it became a Fulani emirate (see **Fulani Empire** and **Ilorin Emirate**).

Kings: (?)–1810 [unknown]. *Fulani Governors:* 1810–1818 Afonja; 1818–1829 Mallam Alimi ibn Zubeiru.

524 Imerina. ca. 1300–1810. *Location:* Madagascar. *Capital:* Antananarivo (from 1630); Ambohidrabiby (ca. 1575–1630); Alasora (ca. 1540–ca. 1575); Imerinanjaka (ca. 1500–ca. 1540). *Other names:* Hova Kingdom, Merina Kingdom.

History: The Hova founded their civilization in the Ikopa Valley in the center of Madagascar about 1250. The kingdom was founded about 1300, and by 1810 they had conquered all the other chiefdoms on the big red island,

and therefore became **Madagascar Kingdom.**

Kings: ca. 1300–ca. 1320 Andrianerimerina; ca. 1320–ca. 1500 10 kings unknown by name today. *Queens:* ca. 1500–ca. 1520 Rafohy; ca. 1520–ca. 1540 Rangita. *Kings:* ca. 1540–ca. 1575 Andramanelo; ca. 1575–ca. 1610 Ralambo; ca. 1610–ca. 1630 Andrianjaka; ca. 1630–ca. 1650 Andriantsitakatrandriana; ca. 1650–ca. 1670 Andriantsimitoviaminanandrandehibe; ca. 1670–ca. 1675 Razakatsitakatrandriana; ca. 1675–1710 Andrianamasinavalma; 1710–1794 four kingdoms (see below); 1794–1810 Andrianampoinimerina. *Note:* In 1710 the Kingdom was split into four, with sub kings ruling at the four capitals of Ambohidratimo, Ambohimanga, Antananarivo and Ambohidrabiby. In 1794 Andrianampoinimerina reunited the country.

Inkil see **Bauchi**

525 International Association of the Congo. 22 Apr. 1884–1 July 1885. *Location:* Zaire. *Capital:* none.

History: In 1884 the International Association of the Congo, the private African estate of King Léopold II of the Belgians, which was later to become the **Belgian Congo,** was recognized internationally as a state, covering most of what today is **Zaire.** In 1885 it became the **Congo Free State.**

Kings/Governors: 22 Apr. 1884–1 July 1885 King Léopold II of the Belgians. *Administrators-General:* 22 Apr. 1884–1 July 1885 Francis de Winton. *Administrators:* 22 Apr. 1884–June 1884 Sir Frederic Goldsmid.

Isle of Cloves see **Zanzibar**

526 Italian East Africa. 9 May 1936–5 May 1941. *Location:* Ethiopia, Italian Somaliland and Eritrea. *Capital:* Addis Ababa.

History: On October 3, 1935 Italy invaded Ethiopia, and by 1936 had conquered the **Ethiopian Empire [ii].**

Together with the existing Italian colonies of **Southern Somaliland Crown Colony** (also known as Italian Somaliland) and **Eritrea Colony,** the invaders created Italian East Africa. Ethiopia was divided into four provinces — Amhara, Galla and Sidama, Hara, and Shoa. Vittorio Emanuele ruled through his viceroys. In 1941, with British assistance (notably in the form of Orde Wingate) Haile Selassie regained control of his country, which now became the **Ethiopian Empire [iii].** At the same time the **Eritrea Province** became **British Eritrea** and **Southern Somaliland Crown Colony** became **Somaliland.**

Emperors: 9 May 1936–5 May 1941 Vittorio Emanuele III of Italy. *High Commissioners:* 3 Oct. 1935–27 Nov. 1935 Emilio de Bono; 27 Nov. 1935–22 May 1936 Pietro Badoglio. *Governors-General:* 22 May 1936–21 Dec. 1937 Rodolfo Graziani; 21 Dec. 1937–5 May 1941 Duke of Aosta.

527 Italian Somaliland Colony. 16 March 1905–July 1910. *Location:* northeast Africa. *Capital:* Mogadiscio (Mogadishu). *Other names:* Southern Somaliland Colony, Italian Somaliland.

History: In 1905 the **Benadir Coast Protectorate (Milanese Commercial Society)** became a colony of the Italian state. In 1910 it became a Crown Colony (see **Southern Somaliland Crown Colony**).

Royal Commissioners-General: 16 March 1905–1906 Luigi Mercatelli. *Vice Commissioners-General:* 1906–1906 Alessandro Sapelli (acting). *Governors:* 1906–1907 Giovanni Cerrina-Feroni (acting). *Royal Civil Commissioners:* 1907–1908 Tommaso Carletti. *Governors:* 1908–1908 Tommaso Carletti; 1908–July 1910 Gino Macchioro (acting).

Itebu see **Brass**

Itsekiri see **Warri**

528 Ivory Coast. See these **names:**
Ivory Coast Republic (1960–)
Ivory Coast Autonomous Republic (1958–1960)
Ivory Coast Overseas Territory (1946–1958)
Ivory Coast Colony (1893–1946)
Ivory Coast Protectorate (1889–1893)
French Ivory Coast [ii] (1883–1889)
Ivory Coast Territory (Verdier & Co.) (1878–1883)
Ivory Coast Territory (1860–1878)
French Ivory Coast [i] (1843–1860)
Baule (ca. 1710–ca. 1840)
Denkyira (1550–1701)
Kong (ca. 1710–1888)
Note: The official name of this country is Côte d'Ivoire.

529 Ivory Coast Autonomous Republic. 4 Dec. 1958–7 Aug. 1960. *Location:* as **Ivory Coast Republic.** *Capital:* Abidjan. *Other names:* Autonomous Republic of the Ivory Coast, Ivory Coast, République de la Côte d'Ivoire.

History: In 1958 **Ivory Coast Overseas Territory** became an autonomous republic within the French Community. In 1960 it gained full independence as the **Ivory Coast Republic.**

High Commissioners: 4 Dec. 1958–1960 Ernest de Nattes; 1960–7 Aug. 1960 Yves Guéna. *Prime Ministers:* 4 Dec. 1958–31 Apr. 1959 Auguste Denis (provisional); 2 May 1959–7 Aug. 1960 Félix Houphouët-Boigny.

530 Ivory Coast Colony. 10 March 1893–13 Oct. 1946. *Location:* as **Ivory Coast Republic.** *Capital:* Abidjan (1934–46); Bingerville (1900–34; named for Binger, the lieutenant-governor); Grand Bassam (1893–1900). *Other names:* Côte d'Ivoire, Ivory Coast.

History: In 1893 **Ivory Coast Protectorate** became a colony of France. In 1933 the largest part of the dismembered **Upper Volta Colony** became part of the Ivory Coast, and in 1938 that section was renamed **Upper Ivory Coast.** Upper Volta was re-grouped as a colony in 1947 (as **Upper Volta Overseas Territory**) and meanwhile, in 1946, the Colony of Ivory Coast had itself become an overseas territory (see **Ivory Coast Overseas Territory**).

Lieutenant-Governors: 10 March 1893–1895 Louis-Gustave Binger; 1895–1895 Paul Cousturier (acting); 1895–1896 Joseph Lemaire (acting); 1896–25 Feb. 1896 Pierre Pascal (acting); 25 Feb. 1896–13 May 1896 Eugène Bertin (acting); 13 May 1896–14 May 1896 Jean-Baptiste Castaing (acting); 14 May 1896–19 March 1897 Louis Mouttet (acting); 19 March 1897–1898 Louis Mouttet; 1898–1898 Pierre Bonhomme (acting); 1898–1898 Jean Penel (acting); 1898–1898 Pierre Capest (acting); 1898–11 Sept. 1898 M. Ribes (acting); 11 Sept. 1898–5 Nov. 1902 Henri Roberdeau; 5 Nov. 1902–25 Nov. 1902 Albert Nebout (acting); 25 Nov. 1902–4 May 1903 Joseph Clozel (acting); 4 May 1903–17 July 1904 Joseph Clozel; 17 July 1904–6 Jan. 1905 Émile Merwaert (acting); 6 Jan. 1905–19 Nov. 1905 Joseph Clozel; 19 Nov. 1905–27 Oct. 1906 Albert Nebout (acting); 27 Oct. 1906–25 Aug. 1907 Joseph Clozel; 25 Aug. 1907–25 Apr. 1908 Albert Nebout (acting); 25 Apr. 1908–28 Apr. 1909 Gabriel Angoulvant; 28 Apr. 1909–Aug. 1909 Pierre Brun (acting); Aug. 1909–12 May 1911 Gabriel Angoulvant; 12 May 1911–9 March 1912 Casimir Guyon (acting); 9 March 1912–22 May 1913 Gabriel Angoulvant; 22 May 1913–29 Oct. 1913 Casimir Guyon (acting); 29 Oct. 1913–4 Sept. 1914 Gustave Julien (acting); 4 Sept. 1914–16 June 1916 Gabriel Angoulvant; 16 June 1916–1 Dec. 1916 Maurice Lapalud (acting); 1 Dec. 1916–27 Dec. 1916 Gabriel Angoulvant; 27 Dec. 1916–Jan. 1918 Maurice Lapalud (acting); Jan. 1918–June 1919 Raphaël Antonetti; June 1919–22 Sept. 1919 Maurice Beurnier (acting); 22 Sept. 1919–24 Jan. 1922 Raphaël Antonetti; 24 Jan. 1922–28 Sept. 1922 Pierre Chapon (acting); 28 Sept. 1922–2 Apr. 1924 Raphaël Antonetti; 2 Apr. 1924–2 July 1925 Richard Brunot (acting); 2 July 1925–20 May 1927 Maurice Lapalud; 20 May 1927–March 1928 Maurice Bourgine (acting); March 1928–25 Aug. 1930 Maurice Lapalud; 25 Aug. 1930–28 Oct. 1930 Jules Brévié; 28 Oct. 1930–16 Jan. 1931 Jean-Paul Boutonnet (acting); 16 Jan. 1931–3 March 1931 Dieudonné Reste; 3 March 1931–28 Dec. 1932 Raoul Bourgine (acting); 28 Dec. 1932–7 May 1935 Dieudonné Reste; 7 May 1935–28 June 1935 Alphonse de Pouzois (acting); 28 June 1935–7 March 1936 Adolphe Deitte; 7 March 1936–28 Nov. 1936 Julien Lamy (acting); 28 Nov. 1936–16 July 1938 Gaston Mondon; 16 July 1938–27 Jan. 1939 Louis Bressalles (acting). *Governors:* 27 Jan. 1939–5 March 1940 Horace Crocicchia (acting); 5 March 1940–1 Jan. 1941 Horace Crocicchia; 1 Jan. 1941–29 Sept. 1942 Hubert Deschamps; 29 Sept. 1942–3 Aug. 1943 Georges Rey; 3 Aug. 1943–26 Aug. 1943 Jean-François Toby; 26 Aug. 1943–16 Aug. 1945 André Latrille; 16 Aug. 1945–Apr. 1946 Henri Mauduit; Apr. 1946–13 Oct. 1946 André Latrille.

531 Ivory Coast-Gabon. 4 Aug. 1860–16 Dec. 1883. *Location:* **Ivory Coast Republic** and **Gabon Republic.** *Capital:* Grand Bassam and Libreville. *Other names:* Côte d'Ivoire-Gabon.

History: In 1860 France decided to link **French Ivory Coast [i]** with the **Gabon Settlements,** thus changing their names to **Ivory Coast Territory** and **Gabon Territory [i].** In 1878 Ivory Coast became the official gubernatorial realm of long time resident Arthur Verdier (see **Ivory Coast Territory [Verdier & Co.]**), and in 1883 the "super-colony" of Ivory Coast-Gabon broke up, the result being **French Ivory Coast [ii]** and **Gabon Colony [i].**

Rulers: see **Ivory Coast Territory** and **Gabon Territory [i].**

532 Ivory Coast Overseas Territory. 13 Oct. 1946–4 Dec. 1958. *Location:* as **Ivory Coast Republic.** *Capital:* Abidjan. *Other names:* Ivory Coast, Côte d'Ivoire.

History: In 1946 **Ivory Coast Colony** became an overseas territory of the 4th Republic of France. In 1958 it became **Ivory Coast Autonomous Republic.**

Governors: 13 Oct. 1946–20 Feb. 1947 André Latrille; 20 Feb. 1947–20 May 1947 Oswald Durand (acting); 20 May 1947–29 Jan. 1948 Oswald Durand; 29 Jan. 1948–10 Nov. 1948 Georges Orselli; 10 Nov. 1948–25 Apr. 1952 Laurent Péchoux; 25 Apr. 1952–10 July 1952 Pierre-François Pelieu; 10 July 1952–19 Feb. 1954 Victor Bailly; 19 Feb. 1954–18 Feb. 1956 Pierre Messmer; 18 Feb. 1956–28 May 1956 Pierre Lami (acting); 28 May 1956–23 Feb. 1957 Pierre Lami; 23 Feb. 1957–4 Dec. 1958 Ernest de Nattes.

533 Ivory Coast Protectorate. 10 Jan. 1889–10 March 1893. *Location:* as **Ivory Coast Republic.** *Capital:* Assinie. *Other names:* Assinie, Côte d'Ivoire, French Gold Coast.

History: In 1889 all areas along the coast were brought together under a protectorate, and ruled from Assinie. Expansion began in the hinterland, and in 1893 **Ivory Coast Colony** came into being. (For area before 1889 see **French Ivory Coast [ii]**).

Residents: 10 Jan. 1889–9 Mar. 1890 Marcel Treich-Laplène; 9 Mar. 1890–14 June 1890 Octave Péan (acting); 14 June 1890–1892 Jean Desailles; 1892–1892 Eloi Bricard (acting); 1892–12 Nov. 1892 Julien Voisin (acting); 12 Nov. 1892–10 Mar. 1893 Paul Heckman.

534 Ivory Coast Republic. 7 Aug. 1960– . *Location:* North West Africa, on the Gulf of Guinea. (*Capital:* Abidjan. *Capital designate:* Yamoussoukro). *Other names:* République de Côte d'Ivoire, Côte d'Ivoire, Republic of the Ivory Coast.

History: Named for the ivory trade of the early Portuguese dealers in the area. In 1960 **Ivory Coast Autonomous Republic** became independent.

Presidents: 7 Aug. 1960–27 Nov. 1960 Félix Houphouët-Boigny (interim); 27 Nov. 1960– Félix Houphouët-Boigny.

535 Ivory Coast Territory. 4 Aug. 1860–22 Nov. 1878. *Location:* as **French Ivory Coast [ii]**. *Capital:* Grand Bassam. *Other names:* Grand-Bassam, Côte d'Ivoire.

History: In 1860 **Ivory Coast-Gabon** was initiated as a colony, with the two components becoming territories under French control. In 1878 the government handed over control of the Ivory Coast to the firm called A. Verdier & Co. (see **Ivory Coast Territory [Verdier & Co.]**).

Commandants: 4 Aug. 1860–1862 Charles Liébault; 1862–1863 Joseph Alem; 1863–1863 Jean Noyer; 1863–1864 Jacques Desnouy; 1864–1866 Jean Martin; 1866–1867 Léon Noël; 1867–1869 Alfred Pouzols; 1869–1871 Jean-Louis Vernet. *Residents:* 1871–22 Nov. 1878 Arthur Verdier.

536 Ivory Coast Territory (Verdier & Co.). 22 Nov. 1878–16 Dec. 1883. *Location:* the coastline of what is today the **Ivory Coast Republic.** *Capital:* Grand Bassam. *Other names:* Ivory Coast, Côte d'Ivoire, Grand Bassam.

History: In 1878 the firm of A. Verdier & Co. took over the administration of the **Ivory Coast Territory,** with headquarters at Grand Bassam. In 1883 the country shook off its connection with Gabon (see **Ivory Coast-Gabon**) and became **French Ivory Coast [ii]**.

Residents; 22 Nov. 1878–16 Dec. 1883 Arthur Verdier.

Jama'are see **Jemaari**

537 James Fort (Company of Merchants). 13 June 1750–25 May 1765. *Location:* Gambia. *Capital:* James Fort. *Other names:* Gambia.

History: In 1750, with the effective demise of the Royal African Company (see **James Fort [Royal African Company]**), James Fort fell into the hands of the Company of Merchants Trading in Africa. In 1765 all Gambia settlements fell under **Senegambia Colony** (effective from April 1766) (see also **Bathurst**).

Governors: 13 June 1750–1752 James Alison (acting); 1752–1754 James Skinner; 1754–1755 Robert Lawrie; 1755–1758 Tobias Lisle; 1758–25 May 1765 Joseph Debat.

538 James Fort (French). 27 July 1695–Apr. 1699. *Location:* the mouth of the Gambia River in Gambia. *Capital:* James Fort. *Other names:* French Gambia, Gambia.

History: In 1695 the French took James Fort (see **James Fort [Royal African Company] [i]**) and for four years James Island lay unoccupied. In 1699, at the end of the war between England and France, the Royal African Company resumed its position there (see **James Fort [Royal African Company] [ii]**).

Rulers: none.

539 James Fort (Gambia Adventurers). 18 Nov. 1668–1684. *Location:* as **James Fort (Royal Adventurers).** *Capital:* James Fort. *Other names:* Fort James, James Island, Gambia.

History: In 1668 the Gambia Adventurers sublet from the Royal Adventurers of England (effective from August 1, 1669) the island in the mouth of the Gambia River. In 1684, after twelve years of legal wrangles between the two companies, they both relinquished their claims in favor of the Royal African Company (see **James Fort [Royal African Company]**). The Royal African Company had taken over effective control as far back as 1678.

Agents: 18 Nov. 1668–1672 [unknown]; 1672–1674 Rice Wright; 1674–1677 [unknown]; 1677–1680 Thomas Thurloe; 1680–1681 Thomas Forde; 1681–1684 John Kastell.

540 James Fort (Royal Adventurers). 19 March 1661–18 Nov. 1668.

Location: the mouth of the Gambia River, Gambia. *Capital:* James Fort. *Other names:* James Island, Fort James, Gambia.

History: In 1661 Charles II of England formed the Royal Adventurers of England Trading in Africa, which was designed to enter the slave trade at a roaring pace. St. Andrews Island was taken and re-named James Island (see **Gambia [Dutch Possession]**). Not finding the trade too profitable, this company sublet its operations to the Gambia Adventurers (see **James Fort [Gambia Adventurers]**).

Agents: 19 March 1661–1661 Francis Kerby; 1661–1662 Morgan Facey; 1662–26 Jan. 1664 Stephen Ustick; 26 Jan. 1664–1666 John Ladd; 1666–18 Nov. 1668 [unknown].

541 James Fort (Royal African Company) [i]. 1684–27 July 1695. *Location:* Gambia. *Capital:* James Fort. *Other names:* Fort James, James Island.

History: In 1684 the Royal African Company legally took over the administration of the Gambia settlements of Fort James from the Gambia Adventurers (see **James Fort [Gambia Adventurers]**), even though the Royal African Company had been the real power in the area since 1678. Other establishments were created up the river and along the coast — Macarthy Island, Barrakunda Falls, Bintang, Banyon Point and Juffure. In 1695 the French captured James Fort (see **James Fort [French]**).

Agents: 1684–1688 Alexander Cleeve; 1688–8 June 1693 John Booker; 8 June 1693–1695 William Heath; 1695–27 July 1695 John Hanbury.

542 James Fort (Royal African Company) [ii]. Apr. 1699–13 June 1750. *Location:* as **James Fort (French).** *Capital:* James Fort. *Other names:* Gambia.

History: In 1699, at the close of the French-English War, England regained

James Fort in the mouth of the Gambia River (see **James Fort [French]**). In 1750 the Company of Merchants Trading to Africa took over (see **James Fort [Company of Merchants]**).

Agents: Apr. 1699–1700 Thomas Corker; 1700–1700 Paul Pindar; 1700–1701 Thomas Gresham; 1701–Nov. 1702 Henry Bradshaw; Nov. 1702–7 Dec. 1703 Humphrey Chishull; 7 Dec. 1703–4 Sept. 1704 Thomas Weaver; 4 Sept. 1704–22 June 1706 John Chidley; 22 June 1706–Aug. 1706 Joseph Dakins (acting); Aug. 1706–2 Dec. 1706 John Tozer; 2 Dec. 1706–20 May 1709 John Snow; 20 May 1709–13 Nov. 1713 the island was abandoned; 13 Nov. 1713–Dec. 1714 William Cooke; Dec. 1714–9 Oct. 1717 David Francis; 9 Oct. 1717–4 Feb. 1721 Charles Orfeur. *Governors:* 4 Feb. 1721–6 Oct. 1721 Thomas Whitney; 6 Oct. 1721–13 Apr. 1723 Henry Glynne; 13 Apr. 1723–28 Oct. 1723 Joseph Willey; 28 Oct. 1723–2 Nov. 1725 Robert Plunkett; 2 Nov. 1725–1728 Anthony Rogers; 1728–1728 Richard Hull; 1728–1729 Charles Cornewall; 1729–29 Nov. 1729 Daniel Pepper (acting); 29 Nov. 1729–7 Feb. 1733 Anthony Rogers; 7 Feb. 1733–16 Jan. 1737 Richard Hull; 16 Jan. 1737–1745 Charles Orfeur; 1745–13 June 1750 John Gootheridge.

Jebu see **Ijebu**

543 Jema'a. 1810–1902. *Location:* Zaria Province, Nigeria. *Capital:* Jema'an Darroro.

History: About 1810 Mallam Othman, a Fulani priest, established Jema'a as a vassal state of **Zaria**. In 1902 it became part of Nasarawa Province of **Northern Nigeria Protectorate**. Its capital is now Kafanchan.

Emirs: 1810–1833 Othman; 1833–1837 Abdullahi; 1837–1846 Musa. *Regents:* 1846–1849 Abdarrahman (or Atona). *Emirs:* 1849–1850 Musa; 1850–1869 Adamu; 1869–1881 Muhammadu Adda; 1881–1885 Adamu; 1885–1888 Muhammadu Adda; 1888–1911 Abdul-

lahi (or Machu); 1911–1915 Muhammadu; 1915–1926 Abdullahi; 1926–1960 Muhammadu ibn Muhammadu; 1960–Isa Muhammadu.

544 Jemaari. 1835–1903. *Location:* northern Nigeria. *Capital:* Jemaari (founded 1811). *Other names:* Jama'are, Jamaari.

History: First officially recognized as an emirate in 1835, Jemaari was really founded in 1811 by Hama Wabi, a Fulani flag-bearer. In 1903 it became part of **Northern Nigeria Protectorate.** It was (is) Nigeria's smallest emirate.

Emirs: 1811–1824 Hama Wabi I; 1824– 1854 Sambolei; 1854–1861 Muhammadu Maudo; 1861–1885 Sambo Gabaima; 1885–11 Jan. 1918 Mohama Wabi II; 4 March 1918–1928 Muhammadu Goji Yerima; 1928–Muhammadu Wabi III.

Jibuti see **Djibouti**

Joanna see **Anjouan**

545 Jubaland Colony. 15 July 1924–1 July 1926. *Location:* as Lower Juba Province, southern **Somalia.** *Capital:* Kismayu (or Chisimaio). *Other names:* Oltre Giuba.

History: In 1924 Jubaland was ceded to Italy. In 1926 it became part of **Southern Somaliland Crown Colony.**

High Commissioners/Governors: 15 July 1924–1 July 1926 Corrado Zoli.

Juda see **Whydah**

Jukun see **Kororofa**

546 Kaarta. ca. 1610–1854. *Location:* Mauritania. *Capital:* Kaarta. *Other names:* Bambara Kingdom of Kaarta.

History: For founding of Kaarta in about 1610 see **Segu.** In 1854 Kaarta was taken over by the new **Tukolor Empire.**

Kings: ca. 1610–1640 Nya Ngolo; 1640–1670 Sounsan; 1670–1690 Massa; 1690–1700 Sekolo; 1700–1709 Foro-

Kolo; 1709–1760 Seba-Mana; 1760–1780 Deni ba Bo; 1780–1789 Sira Bo; 1789–1802 Desse-Koro; 1802–1811 Nntin Koro; 1811–1815 Sara-ba; 1815–1818 Moussou Koura Bo; 1818–1833 Bodyan Mori Ba; 1833–1835 period of anarchy; 1835–1844 Nyaralen Gran; 1844–1854 Mamarikan-dyan.

547 Kabyle Algiers. 1520–1525. *Location:* Algeria. *Capital:* Algiers. *Other names:* Algiers (Kabyle).

History: In 1520 Khair ad-Din Barbarossa, the legendary Corsair, lost Algiers to the Kabyles of Algiers (see **Algiers Pashalik [i]**), and went buccaneering in the Mediterranean for five years. In 1525 he returned and re-took Algiers (see **Algiers Pashalik [ii]**). *Rulers:* unknown.

Kacinna see **Katsina**

548 Kaffraria Proper. (?)–1878. *Location:* between the Kei River and Natal on the southeast African coast. *Capital:* Fort Peddie was the main town. *Other names:* Kaffraria, Kaffirland, Transkeian Territories.

History: Kaffraria is a term, like Kaffirland, which took in all of the land along the eastern coast of South Africa, between the Umzinkulu and the Keiskamma Rivers, i.e. those lands inhabited by Xhosas, Pondos and Tembus, between Natal and the Cape. Kaffraria Proper was all this land with the exception of **British Kaffraria**. The following areas comprised Kaffraria Proper, and the dates in which they were annexed by other areas: Alfred — January 1, 1866 to **Natal Colony [ii]**; Fingoland — 1879 to **British Cape Colony (Self-Rule)**; Tembuland — August 26, 1885 to **British Cape Colony (Self-Rule)**; Bomvanaland — 1886 to **British Cape Colony (Self-Rule)**; Kreli's Country — 1886 to **British Cape Colony (Self-Rule)**; Pondoland — September 25, 1894 to **British Cape Colony (Self-Rule)**.

Xhosa Paramount Chiefs: (?)–(?) Mnguni; (?)–(?) Xhosa; (?)–(?) Malan-gana; (?)–(?) Nkosiyamntu; (?)–(?) Tshawe; ca. 1550–ca. 1580 Ngcwangu; ca. 1580–ca. 1610 Sikhomo (or Sikomo); ca. 1610–1640 Togu; 1640–1670 Ngconde; 1670–1702 Tshiwo; 1702–1775 Phalo. *Note:* Phalo's base was **Galekaland.** He had two sons, Galeka and Rarabe (see **Galekaland** and **Queen Adelaide Land** for those branches). *British Residents:* Dec. 1836–Feb. 1839 John Bowker; Feb. 1839–Nov. 1845 Theophilus Shepstone; Nov. 1845–Nov. 1846 John MacLean.

Kalabari see **New Calabar**

549 Kamerun. 1 Jan. 1900–18 Feb. 1916. *Location:* as **Cameroun Republic,** plus (after 1912) a large chunk of **Moyen-Congo.** *Capital:* Buea. *Other names:* German Cameroons Protectorate, Cameroun German Protectorate.

History: In 1900 **German Crown Land of North West Africa** gained a name, a proper name, that of Kamerun. Although the French and British captured most of the huge country in 1914 (see **Cameroun French-British Condominium**) and ruled it jointly until **French Cameroun Territory** and **British Cameroons Territory** came into being, the Germans didn't officially surrender their protectorate until 1916.

Governors: 1 Jan. 1900–17 Jan. 1900 Jesko von Puttkamer (acting); 17 Jan. 1900–31 July 1900 August Köhler (acting); 1 Aug. 1900–6 Sept. 1900 Herr Diehl (acting); 6 Sept. 1900–15 Nov. 1900 Herr von Kamptz (acting); 16 Nov. 1900–3 Feb. 1902 Jesko von Puttkamer (acting); 3 Feb. 1902–5 Oct. 1902 Herr Plehn (acting); 9 Oct. 1902–9 May 1904 Jesko von Puttkamer (acting); 9 May 1904–8 Nov. 1904 Karl Ebermaier (acting); 9 Nov. 1904–31 Jan. 1905 Otto Gleim (acting); 31 Jan. 1905–6 Jan. 1906 Jesko von Puttkamer (acting); 6 Jan. 1906–Nov. 1906 Herr Oberst Müller (acting); Nov. 1906–1 July 1907 Otto Gleim (acting); 1 July 1907–10 Feb. 1909 Theodor Seitz; 10 Feb. 1909–Oct. 1909 Herr Hansen (acting); Oct. 1909–Aug.

1910 Theodor Seitz; Aug. 1910–Sept. 1910 Herr Steinhausen (acting); Sept. 1910–25 Oct. 1910 Herr Hansen (acting); 25 Oct. 1910–Oct. 1911 Otto Gleim; Oct. 1911–29 March 1912 Herr Hansen (acting); 29 March 1912–9 Oct. 1913 Karl Ebermaier; 9 Oct. 1913–1914 Herr Full (acting); 1914–18 Feb. 1916 Karl Ebermaier.

550 Kanem. 784–ca. 1260. *Location:* east of Lake Chad, Chad. *Capital:* Njimi; Kawar (the first capital). *Other names:* Canem.

History: Originally the **Zaghawa Kingdom** prevailed around Lake Chad, then it split into several small states. One tribal division, the Beni Saif, under their leader Dugu (son of Ibrahima, son of Sebu, son of Aisa), founded Kanem on the east side of the lake, with their capital at Njimi. About 784 the Sefawa family began to rule, Dugu being the first king. Humé became a Muslim in 1086. With a key position in the Saharan trade, Kanem flourished and expanded. By the turn of the 13th century Kanem was becoming universally known, and the Kanuri people of Kanem were expanding into **Bornu State.** Kanem reached its peak in the 13th century, and from this time on it really became **Kanem-Bornu.** Old Kanem relapsed into a rebellious state under the Bulala, a tribe who had been there for centuries. They captured Njimi and plagued the new **Kanem-Bornu Empire** for a long time thereafter.

Mais (Kings): 784–835 Dugu; 835–893 Fune; 893–942 Arju (or Aritse); 942–961 Katuri; 961–1019 Boyoma (or Adyoma); 1019–1035 Bulu; 1035–1077 Argi; 1077–1081 Shuwa; 1081–1085 Jil; 1085–1097 Humé ibn Abdul Jalil; 1097–1150 Dunama I ibn Humé; 1150–1176 Biri I; 1176–1194 Bikorom (or Dala, or Abdallah I); 1194–1221 Abdul Jalil (or Jilim); 1221–1259 Dunama Dibbelemi; 1259–1260 Kade.

551 Kanem-Bornu. ca. 1256–ca.

1400. *Location:* around Lake Chad, on the Chad-Nigeria border. *Capital:* Yamia (or Muniyo) (fourth capital); Birni Kimi (third capital); Wudi (second capital); Njimi (first capital). *Other names:* Canem-Bornu, Kanem-Bornu Empire.

History: Dunama Dibbelemi, king of **Kanem,** was the first undisputed ruler of the new Kanem-Bornu Empire. Kashim Biri succeeded him, by which time **Kano Kingdom, Wadai, Adamawa** and all of **Bornu** were under the control of the new empire. The Sefawa Mais (or Kings) continued to rule, as they had in Kanem. Kanem itself now fell into the hands of the Bulala (see **Kanem**). By 1400 the empire became known simply as the Bornu Empire (see **Bornu Empire [i]**).

Emperors: ca. 1256–1259 Dunama Dibbelemi; 1259–1260 Kade; 1260–1288 Kashim Biri (or Abdul Kadim); 1288–1307 Biri II Ibrahim; 1307–1326 Ibrahim I; 1326–1346 Abdullah II; 1346–1350 Selma; 1350–1351 Kure Ghana es-Saghir; 1351–1352 Kure Kura al-Kabir; 1352–1353 Muhammad I; 1353–1377 Idris I Nigalemi; 1377–1386 Daud Nigalemi; 1386–1391 Uthman I; 1391–1392 Uthman II; 1392–1394 Abu Bakr Liyatu; 1394–1398 Umar ibn Idris; 1398–1399 Sa'id; 1399–1400 Kade Afunu.

552 Kangaba Kingdom. ca. 1050–ca. 1237. *Location:* present-day Mali, on the Niger River. *Capital:* Kangaba (1200–37); Dodu (1090–1200); Kiki (1050–90). *Other names:* Kangaba, Mali Kingdom.

History: Reckoned to have been founded around 1050 by Mandingo tribesmen, it was a vassal state of the **Ghana Empire** and grew out of an older Kangaba country in the same area. In 1237 its king, Sundiata Keita, revolted against Ghana and by 1240 had finished the empire off. 1237, or thereabouts, thus marks the beginning of Ghana's successor empire, the **Mali Empire,** which grew out of Kangaba.

Kings: ca. 1050–ca. 1090 Taraore; ca. 1090–ca. 1150 Baraonendana; ca. 1150–ca. 1190 Hamama; ca. 1190–ca. 1200 Di Jigi Bilali; ca. 1200–ca. 1218 Keita Nari fa Majan; ca. 1218–1228 Danagaran Tumo; 1228–1230 Soninke rule; 1230–ca. 1237 Mari Jata I (or Sundiata Keita).

553 KaNgwane. Apr. 1981– . *Location:* on the Transvaal-Swaziland border, Southern Africa. *Capital:* Nyamasane. *Other names:* KaNgwane National State, Swazi, Swazi Territory.

History: The Bantustan (or native homeland) for the Swazis living in **South Africa** (the Ngwani were the race from which the Swazi came). Given a legislative assembly in 1978 and self-government in 1981 it was threatened with a merger with **Swaziland Kingdom** in June 1982, but the Supreme Court overruled South Africa's decision to effect this.

Chief Ministers: Apr. 1981– Enos Mabuza.

554 Kano. (?)–Dec. 998. *Location:* around the present-day town of Kano, Nigeria. *Capital:* Dala Hill.

History: The original settlement of Kano belonged to an early, semi-mythical race of people based around Dala Hill (now a section of Kano City). Dala Hill was founded by a chief named Dala, who came here from origins unknown. In late 998 the land was conquered by the Habe people from the East, who formed a kingdom (see **Kano Kingdom**).

Chiefs: (?)–(?) Dala; (?)–(?) Garageje; (?)–(?) [unknown]; (?)–(?) Buzame; (?)–(?) Barbushe; (?)–(?) [unknown]; (?)–(?) [unknown]; (?)–Dec. 998 Jankare.

555 Kano Emirate. March 1807–3 Feb. 1903. *Location:* Kano, Nigeria. *Capital:* Kano.

History: In 1807 **Kano Kingdom** came to an end when the **Fulani Empire** conquered it and set up an emirate in-stead of a kingdom. In 1903 the British took it over and it became a part of **Northern Nigeria Protectorate**, although continuing as an emirate within Kano Province (created 1903). The modern Kano State of Nigeria (i.e. a state within Nigeria, similar to, say, the state of California within the United States of America) was created in 1968.

Sarkins Kano (Emirs): March 1807–Oct. 1819 Sulimanu; Oct. 1819–Dec. 1845 Ibrahim Dabo; Dec. 1845–Sept. 1855 Osumanu (or Uthman I); Sept. 1855–Nov. 1882 Abdullahi; Nov. 1882–July 1892 Muhammad Bello; July 1892–June 1893 Tukur; July 1893–3 Feb. 1903 Aliyu Babba (or Abu); 3 Apr. 1903–March 1919 Muhammadu Abbas; Sept. 1919–1926 Osumanu II (or Uthman II); 1926–Sept. 1953 Abdullahi Bayero; 1954–1963 Muhammadu Sanusi; 1963–1963 Muhammad Inuwa Abbas; 1963– Ado Bayero.

556 Kano Kingdom. Dec. 998–March 1807. *Location:* Kano Province, northern Nigeria. *Capital:* Kano (from ca. 1100); Sheme (until ca. 1100).

History: Founded late in 998 by Bagauda (one of the grandsons of Bayajida, the legendary ancestor of the Hausa peoples) as one of the seven true Hausa states (see **Hausaland**). Islam was introduced in the 1340s. Its history is one of constant warfare with **Katsina,** its principal rival, and of subjugation to the other kingdoms or empires of the day, most notably **Bornu, Zazzau** and the **Songhai Empire.** In 1807 the **Fulani Empire** conquered Kano, and the kingdom was brought to an end (see **Kano Emirate**). Kano is named for an early inhabitant, a Gaiya smith named Kano.

Sarkis Kano (Kings of Kano): Dec. 998–Jan. 1063 Bagauda (or Yakano); Jan. 1063–Jan. 1095 Warisis; Jan. 1095–Nov. 1133 Gajemasu; Nov. 1133–Oct. 1135 Nawata (joint); Nov. 1133–Oct. 1135 Gawata (joint); Oct. 1135–Dec. 1193 Yusa (or Tsaraki); Dec. 1193–

May 1247 Naguji; May 1247–Jan. 1290 Gujjua; Jan. 1290–July 1306 Shekkarau; July 1306–June 1342 Tsamia (or Barandamasu); June 1342–March 1349 Osumanu (or Zamnagawa); March 1349–Feb. 1385 Yaji I; Feb. 1385–Dec. 1389 Bugaya; Dec. 1389–May 1409 Kanajeji; May 1409–Jan. 1421 Umaru; Jan. 1421–Jan. 1437 Dauda; Jan. 1437–Jan. 1452 Abdullahi Burja; Jan. 1452–Jan. 1452 Dakauta (one night); Jan. 1452–Feb. 1452 Atuma; Feb. 1452–Sept. 1462 Yakubu; Sept. 1462–Aug. 1498 Muhamman Rumfa; Aug. 1498–May 1508 Abdullahi; May 1508–Aug. 1564 Muhamman Kisoki; Aug. 1564–Jan. 1565 Yakufu; Jan. 1565–March 1565 Dauda Abasama I; March 1565–May 1572 Abubakr Kado; May 1572–Jan. 1582 Muhamman Shashere; Jan. 1582–Dec. 1617 Muhamman Zaki; Dec. 1617–Nov. 1622 Muhamma Nazaki; Nov. 1622–Jan. 1648 Kutumbi; Jan. 1648–Jan. 1649 Al-Hajj; Jan. 1649–Dec. 1650 Shekkarau; Dec. 1650–Dec. 1651 Muhamman Kukuna; Dec. 1651–Dec. 1651 Soyaki; Dec. 1651–Sept. 1659 Muhamman Kukuna; Sept. 1659–1670 Bawa; 1670–May 1702 Dadi; May 1702–July 1730 Muhamma Sharefa; July 1730–Feb. 1743 Kumbari; Feb. 1743–May 1752 Alhajji Kabe; May 1752–May 1768 Yaji II; May 1768–Feb. 1776 Babba Zaki; Feb. 1776–Dec. 1780 Dauda Abasama II; Dec. 1780–March 1807 Muhamma Alwali.

557 Karagwe. ca. 1450–1885. *Location:* Tanzania. *Capital:* Bukoba. *Other names:* Karague.

History: About 1450 the Bahinda dynasty came to the fore in Karagwe (see also **Nkore**). In 1885 it had a German protectorate placed over it (see **German East Africa Protectorate [i]**).

Mugabes (Kings): ca. 1450–ca. 1490 Ruhinda Kizarabagabe; ca. 1490–ca. 1520 Ntare I; ca. 1520–ca. 1550 Ruhinda II; ca. 1550–ca. 1575 Ntare II; ca. 1575–ca. 1595 Ruhinda III; ca. 1595–ca. 1620 Ntare III; ca. 1620–ca. 1645 Ruhinda IV; ca. 1645–ca. 1675 Ntare IV; ca. 1675–ca. 1700 Ruhinda V; ca. 1700–ca. 1725 Rusatira; ca. 1725–ca. 1750 Mehiga; ca. 1750–ca. 1774 Kalemera Bwirangenda; ca. 1774–ca. 1794 Ntare V Kiitabanyoro; ca. 1794–ca. 1819 Ruhinda VI Orushongo; ca. 1819–1853 Ndagara I; 1853–1883 Rumanyika I; 1883–1886 Kayenje Kalemera II; 1886–1893 Nyamukuba Ndagara II; 1893–1916 Kanyorozi Ntare VI; 1916–1939 Rumanyika II; 1939–1963 Ruhinda VII.

558 Karamanli Tripoli. 29 July 1711–26 May 1835. *Location:* Tripolitania, Libya. *Capital:* Tripoli. *Other names:* Tripoli, Tarabulus.

History: In 1711 the Karamanlid Dynasty of Turkish governors took over **Tripoli Ottoman Province [i]** and ruled until 1835, when it became **Tripoli Ottoman Province [ii]**.

Sultans: 29 July 1711–4 Nov. 1745 Ahmad I; 4 Nov. 1745–24 July 1754 Muhammad; 24 July 1754–30 July 1793 Ali I; 30 July 1793–20 Jan. 1795 Ali II Burghul; 20 Jan. 1795–11 June 1795 Ahmad II; 11 June 1795–20 Aug. 1832 Yusuf; 20 Aug. 1832–26 May 1835 Ali III.

Karchedon, Kart-Hadasht see **Carthage**

Kasai Republic see **South Kasai Republic**

559 Katagum. 1807–1903. *Location:* northern Nigeria. *Capital:* Azare (from 1916 on); Katagum (1810–1916. Built in 1810); Tashena (until 1810). *Other names:* Katagum Emirate.

History: Founded 1807 by Fulani warrior Mallam Zaki. In 1826 **Bornu Empire [i]** conquered it, but in the same year it was won back. Wars with **Hadeija Emirate** in the 1850s weakened it and in 1903 it surrendered to the British and became part of **Northern Nigeria Protectorate.** In 1916 the capital was moved to Azare.

Sarkins: 1807–1814 Mallam Zaki;

1814–1816 Suleimanu; 1816–1846 Dan-kawa; 1846–1851 Abdurahman; 1851–1868 Kadri (or Abdulkadiri); 1868–1896 Moma Haji; 1896–May 1905 Abdulkadiri II; 1905–1909 Muhammadu; 1909–1947 Abdulkadiri III; 1947–Umaru Faruku.

Katanga see also **Oyo**

560 Katanga Republic. 11 July 1960–15 Jan. 1963. *Location:* southeastern **Zaire**. *Capital:* Elisabethville (established in 1910, and after 1966 called Lubumbashi). *Other names:* Katanga, Shaba.

History: In 1960 the Belgian mining corporations financed and inspired Lunda leader Moise Tshombe to secede Katanga from the newly formed **Congo (Leopoldville)** and independence was declared, with Tshombe as president. In early 1961 Tshombe's followers had murdered Patrice Lumumba, the leftist premier of Congo (Leopoldville). The Congolese army failed to win back Katanga, until then its richest province, but the United Nations put pressure on Tshombe to re-unify in 1963. Katanga is important to world powers only because only the riches in Katanga can pay back the loans made to what is now **Zaire**. Katanga is now officially called the Shaba Province of Zaire.

Presidents: 11 July 1960–15 Jan. 1963 Moise Tshombe.

561 Katsina Emirate. 1806–Apr. 1903. *Location:* northern Nigeria-Niger border. *Capital:* Katsina. *Other names:* Keccina, Ketsina, Katsena.

History: In 1806 **Katsina Kingdom** became a Fulani emirate with the capture of Katsina City by Umaru Dallaji, a Fulani leader. That year many of the nobility and ordinary people of Katsina fled north to what is now Niger, and formed a separate Katsina chiefdom which periodically raided the emirate. In 1903 the emirate became part of **Northern Nigeria Protectorate**. In 1931 Katsina Province was formed from Zaria and Kano Provinces.

Emirs: 1806–1835 Umaru Dallaji; 1835–1844 Sidiku; 1844–1869 Muhamman Bello; 1869–1870 Ahmadu Rufai; 1870–1882 Ibrahim; 1882–1887 Musa; 1887–1904 Abubakr; Jan. 1905–Nov. 1906 Yero; Nov. 1906–1944 Muhammadu Dikko; 5 Aug. 1944–Apr. 1981 Usman Nagogo.

562 Katsina Kingdom. ca. 1015–1806. *Location:* northern Nigeria-Niger border. *Capital:* Katsina (fourth capital); Durbi ta Kusheyi (third capital); Ambuttai (second capital); Durombsi (first capital). *Other names:* Katsena, Kacinna (named for a local princess).

History: Around 1015 the kingdom of Katsina was founded by Kumayo, as one of the Hausa Bakwai (see **Hausaland**), or True Hausa states. Islam came to Katsina about 1450, and in the early 1700s the state reached its peak of power. In 1806 it became a Fulani emirate (see **Katsina Emirate**).

Kings: ca. 1015–ca. 1100 Kumayo; ca. 1100–ca. 1180 Ramba-Ramba; ca. 1180–ca. 1250 Bata tare; ca. 1250–ca. 1300 Jarnanata; ca. 1300–ca. 1350 Sanau; ca. 1350–ca. 1410 Korau; ca. 1410–1452 Ibrahim Yanka Dari; 1452–1492 Yidda Yaki; 1492–1541 Muhammadu Korau; 1541–1543 Ibrahim Sura; 1543–1568 Ali Murabus; 1568–1572 Muhammadu Toya Rero; 1572–1585 Aliyu Karya Giwa; 1585–1589 Usman Tsagarana; 1589–1595 Aliyu Jan Hazo I; 1595–1612 Muhammadu Mai-sa-Maza-Gudu; 1612–1614 Aliyu Jan Hazo II; 1614–1631 Maje Ibrahim; 1631–1634 Abdul Karim; 1634–1635 Ashafa; 1635–1644 Ibrahim Gamda; 1644–1655 Muhammadu Wari; 1655–1667 Suleiman; 1667–1684 Usman No Yi Nawa; 1684–1701 Muhammadu Toya Rero II; 1701–1704 Muhammadu Wari II; 1704–1706 Uban Yari (or Muhammadu Dan Wari); 1706–1715 Karya Giwa II; 1715–1728 Jan Hazo III; 1728–1740 Tsagarana Hassan; 1740–1750 Muhammadu Kabiya (or Mai-Kere); 1750–1751 Tsagarana Yahya; 1751–1758 Karya Giwa III; 1758–1767

Muhammadu Wari III; 1767–1784 Karya Giwa IV; 1784–1801 Agwaragi; 1801–1802 Tsagarana Gwozo; 1802–1804 Bawa Dan Gima; 1804–1805 Mare Mawa Mahmudu; 1805–1806 Magajin Halidu.

563 Kayor. 1549–1885. *Location:* now a province of Senegal. *Capital:* Mbul. *Other names:* Cayor.

History: The Wolof nation originated in **Walo**, north of Kayor, about the year 1100. They were a mixture of tribes. The first two Wolof states were **Walo** and **Dyolof**. Kayor became a vassal state of Dyolof, and in 1549 became independent. A matrilineal society, the first dynasty, the Geedy, produced eleven kings (or "damels"). Then came the Muyoy dynasty, then the Dorobe, the Sonyo, the Gelwar and finally the Wagadu. In 1885 Kayor was annexed to **Senegal Colony.**

Damels: 1549–1549 Detye Fu-N'diogu; 1549–1593 Amari; 1593–1600 Samba; 1600–1610 Khuredya; 1610–1640 Biram Manga; 1640–1647 Dauda Demba; 1647–1664 Dyor; 1664–1681 Birayma Yaasin-Bubu; 1681–1683 Detye Maram N'Galgu; 1683–1684 Faly; 1684–1691 Khuredya Kumba Dyodyo; 1691–1693 Birayma Mbenda-Tyilor; 1693–1693 Dyakhere; 1693–1697 Dethialaw; 1697–1719 Lat Sukaabe; 1719–1748 Isa-Tende; 1748–1749 Isa Bige N'Gone; 1749–1757 M'Bathio Samb; 1757–1758 Birayma Kodu; 1758–1759 Isa Bige N'Gone; 1759–1760 Birayma Yamb; 1760–1763 Isa Bige N'Gone; 1763–1766 Dyor Yaasin Isa; 1766–1777 Kodu Kumba; 1777–1790 Birayma Faatim-Penda; 1790–1809 Amari; 1809–1832 Birayma Fatma; 1832–1855 Isa Ten-Dyor; 1855–1859 Birayma-Fal; 1859–May 1861 Ma-Kodu; May 1861–Dec. 1861 Ma-Dyodyo; 1862–Dec. 1863 Lat-Dyor; Jan. 1864–1868 Ma-Dyodyo; 1868–Dec. 1872 Lat-Dyor; Jan. 1883–Aug. 1883 Amari; 1883–1886 Samba.

564 Kazaure. 1824–1906. *Location:* northern Nigeria. *Capital:* Kazaure (after 1824); Damberta (until 1824). *Other names:* Kazaure Emirate.

History: Kazaure was born as an emirate in 1807 and named for a local hunter by the Fulani founder of the emirate, Dan Tunku. In the year of his death Dan Tunku achieved independence for Kazaure, and the same year (1824) his son moved the capital from Damberta. In 1906 the capital was taken by the British and the emirate became part of **Northern Nigeria Protectorate.**

Emirs: 1807–1824 Dan Tunku; 1824–1857 Dambo; 1857–1886 Muhamman Zangi; 1886–1914 Muhamman Mayaki; 1914–1922 Muhammadu Tura; 1922–1941 Umaru Na'uka; 1941–1969 Adamu ibn Abdulmumini; 1969– al-Hajj Ibrahim Adamu.

565 Kazembe. ca. 1710–1899. *Location:* extreme northern Zambia-Zaire border (as far north as south central Katanga). *Capital:* Kazembe. *Other names:* Kingdom of Kazembe, Cazembe.

History: About 1710 Lunda settlers with Portuguese weapons established a kingdom in the Luapula Valley, which became the strongest and most extensive of the Lunda-Luba kingdoms (see **Luba** and **Lunda**). By 1899 it had been colonized by the British (see **Zambesia**) and the Belgians (see **Congo Free State**).

Kazembes: ca. 1710–ca. 1740 Nganda Bilonda; ca. 1740–ca. 1760 Kaniembo; ca. 1760–ca. 1805 Ilunga; ca. 1805–ca. 1850 Kibangu Keleka; ca. 1850–1854 Mwongo Mfwama; 1854–1862 Cinyanta Munona; 1862–1870 Mwonga Nsemba; 1870–1872 Cinkonkole Kafuti; 1872–1885 Lukwesa Mpanga; 1885–1899 Kaniembo Ntemena.

566 Keana. ca. 1700–1900. *Location:* northern Nigeria. *Capital:* [unknown].

History: Founded around 1700 by Keana, it was taken as part of **Northern**

Nigeria Protectorate by the British in 1900.
Kings: ca. 1700 Keana; (?)–(?) Madafu; (?)–(?) Egwa; (?)–(?) Oshu; (?)–ca. 1789 Azagia I; ca. 1789–ca. 1791 Asiki; ca. 1791–ca. 1795 Alago; ca. 1795–1815 Agadi; 1815–1818 Otaki; 1818–1830 Onyatiko; 1830–1852 Adasho; 1852–1862 Aladoga; 1862–1899 Azagia II; 1899–1900 Ago.

567 Kebbi. 1516–1827. *Location:* northwestern Nigeria. *Capital:* Birnin Kebbi (ca. 1700–1805); Surame (until ca. 1700).
History: In 1516 the Songhai captain Muhammad Kantu made himself ruler of the Kebbawa people who lived between the Niger River and **Zamfara.** Kebbi was one of the Banza Bakwai (see **Hausaland**), and its first capital was at Surame. At the height of its power Kebbi included the states of **Yauri** and **Nupe,** but in 1805 the **Fulani Empire** sacked Birnin Kebbi and forced the submission of the Kebbawa Kingdom by 1813. Resistance to the Fulani continued until in 1827 Samaila established Argungu as his capital (see **Argungu**). The Fulani finally conquered Argungu, as the emirate became known, in 1831.
Kings: 1516–1561 Muhammadu Kantu; 1561–1596 Ahmadu I; 1596–1619 Dawuda; 1619–1621 Ibrahimu I; 1621–1636 Suleimanu I; 1636–1649 Muhammadu; 1649–1662 Maliki Dan Ibrahimu; 1662–1674 Umaru Ciwa; 1674–1676 Muhammadu Kaye; 1676–1684 Ibrahimu II; 1684–1686 Muhammadu na Sifawa; 1686–1696 Ahmadu Dan Amaru; 1696–1700 Tomo; 1700–1717 Muhammadu Dan Giwa; 1717–1750 Somaila; 1750–1754 Muhammadu Dan Tagande; 1754–1775 Abdullahi Toga; 1775–1803 Suleimanu II; 1803–1803 Abubakar Ukar; 1803–1826 Muhammadu Fodi; 1826–1827 Somaila II.
Note: this king list is probably the most sensible of all the Kebbawa king lists.

Keccina see **Katsina**

568 Keffi. ca. 1750–1902. *Location:* northern Nigeria. *Capital:* Keffi (name means "stockade").
History: The Kano-allied kingdom of Keffi is of unknown origin. In 1802 it became a Fulani state, and in 1902 a part of **Northern Nigeria Protectorate.**
Kings: ca. 1750–1802 Kareshi; 1802–1820 Abdu Zanga; 1820–1835 Maizabo; 1835–1859 Jibrilu; 1859–1862 Muhamman; 1862–1877 Ahmadu I; 1877–1894 Sidi Umaru; 1894–1902 Ibrahim; 1902–1921 Abdullahi; 1921–1923 Abubakar; 1923–1928 Abdullahi; 1928–1933 Muhammadu Mayaki; 1933–1948 Abubakar; 7 March 1948– Ahmadu Maikwato.

Keme see **Egypt, 1st Dynasty**

569 Kenedugu. ca. 1650–1 May 1898. *Location:* Mali-Burkina Faso. *Capital:* Sikasso; Bougoula (the first capital, in the very early days). *Other names:* Sikasso, Kenedougou.
History: Nanka Traore founded the small kingdom of Kenedugu in the middle of the 17th century around the town of Bougoula, his people being the Dyula. By 1750 his descendent, Daoula Ba Traore, had established an organized state. Much of the 19th century was taken up by war with the Walata family of **Kong,** and with **Gwiriko.** The French took it over as part of **French Sudan Colony** in 1898.
Faamas (Kings): ca. 1650 Nanka Traore; ca. 1750 Daoula Ba Traore; ca. 1800 Tapri Traore; ca. 1820 Moussa Toroma; ca. 1825–1835 Famorhoba; 1835–1845 Nyanamagha; 1845–1845 Tyemonkonko; 1845–1877 Daoula Ba Traore II; 1877–28 Jan. 1893 Tieba Traore; 28 Jan. 1893–1 May 1898 Babemba Traore.

570 Kenya. See these **names:**
Kenya Republic (1964–   )
Kenya (1963–1964)
Kenya (Self-Rule) (1963–1963)
Kenya Colony and Protectorate (1920–1963)

British East Africa Protectorate (1895–1920)
British East Africa Colony (1888–1895)
   Mombasa (Busaidi) (1837–1895)
   Mombasa (Mazrui) [ii] (1826–1837)
   Mombasa Protectorate (1823–1826)
   Mombasa (Mazrui) [i] (1746–1823)
   Mombasa (Omani) [ii] (1729–1746)
   Mombasa (Portuguese) [ii] (1728–1729)
   Mombasa (Omani) [i] (1698–1728)
   Mombasa (Portuguese) [i] (1593–1698)

571 Kenya. 12 Dec. 1963–12 Dec. 1964. *Location:* as **Kenya Republic.** *Capital:* Nairobi.
History: In 1963 **Kenya (Self-Rule)** became independent within the British Commonwealth, as Kenya. In 1964 it became the Republic of Kenya (see **Kenya Republic).**
Prime Ministers: 12 Dec. 1963–12 Dec. 1964 Jomo Kenyatta. *Governors-General:* 12 Dec. 1963–12 Dec. 1964 Sir Malcolm MacDonald.

572 Kenya Colony and Protectorate. 23 July 1920–1 June 1963. *Location:* as **Kenya Republic.** *Capital:* Nairobi. *Other names:* Kenya.
History: In 1920 most of the **British East Africa Protectorate** was made into a colony and protectorate, the colony inland and the protectorate along the coast. In 1963 it earned self-rule (see **Kenya [Self-Rule]).**
Governors: 23 July 1920–15 Aug. 1922 Sir Edward Northey; 15 Aug. 1922–2 Oct. 1925 Sir Robert Coryndon; 2 Oct. 1925–1930 Sir Edward Grigg; 1930–1930 Henry Moore (acting); 1930–13 Feb. 1931 Sir Edward Grigg; 13 Feb. 1931–1936 Sir Joseph Byrne; 6 Apr. 1937–9 Jan. 1940 Sir Robert Brooke-Popham; 9 Jan. 1940–1942 Sir Henry Moore; 1942–1942 Gilbert Rennie (acting); 1942–11 Dec. 1944 Sir Henry Moore; 11 Dec. 1944–30 Sept. 1952 Sir Philip Mitchell; 30 Sept. 1952–1957 Sir Evelyn Baring; 1957–1958 Richard Turnbull (acting); 1958–23 Oct. 1959 Sir Evelyn Baring; 23 Oct. 1959–1962 Sir Patrick Rennison; 4 Jan. 1963–1 June 1963 Sir Malcolm MacDonald. *Prime Ministers:* Apr. 1962–1 June 1963 Jomo Kenyatta.

573 Kenya Republic. 12 Dec. 1964– . *Location:* East African coast. *Capital:* Nairobi (started about 1897 as a colonial railway settlement, the name comes from a stream nearby, "Enkare Nairobi," meaning "cold water"). *Other names:* Djumhuriya Kenya, Kenya, the Republic of Kenya.
History: In 1964 **Kenya** became a republic.
Presidents: 12 Dec. 1964–22 Aug. 1978 Jomo Kenyatta; 22 Aug. 1978–10 Oct. 1978 Daniel arap Moi (acting); 10 Oct. 1978– Daniel arap Moi.

574 Kenya (Self-Rule). 1 June 1963–12 Dec. 1963. *Location:* as **Kenya Republic.** *Capital:* Nairobi. *Other names:* Kenya.
History: In 1963 **Kenya Colony and Protectorate** won self-rule. In December of that year it became fully independent, as **Kenya.**
Governors: 1 June 1963–12 Dec. 1963 Sir Malcolm MacDonald. *Prime Ministers:* 1 June 1963–12 Dec. 1963 Jomo Kenyatta.

Ketsina see **Katsina**
Kilwa see **Zeng Empire**

575 Kingdom of Morocco. 11 Aug. 1957– . *Location:* North West Africa. *Capital:* Rabat (founded in the 12th century as a "ribat" or military post). *Other names:* Morocco Kingdom, al-Mamlakah al-Maghribiyyah, Maghrib.
History: In 1957 the **Morocco Independent Sultanate** became the Kingdom of Morocco. **Ceuta Presidio** and **Melilla Presidio** are still Spanish enclaves, as are Chafarinas, Velez de la Gomera and Alhucemas, but **Ifni Province** was ceded to Morocco in 1969. In 1976 the Spanish left **Spanish Sahara**

Province and Morocco seized the upper two-thirds of it (Mauritania taking the southern third), taking the rest in 1980 from **Mauritania Republic**.
Kings: 11 Aug. 1957–26 Feb. 1961 Muhammad V; 26 Feb. 1961– Hassan II. *Prime Ministers:* 11 Aug. 1957–15 Apr. 1958 M'barek ben Mustafa el-Bakai; 12 May 1958–3 Dec. 1958 Ahmad Balafrej; 16 Dec. 1958–20 May 1960 Abdullah Ibrahim; 3 May 1961–13 Nov. 1963 Ahmad Reda Guedira; 13 Nov. 1963–7 June 1965 Ahmad Bahmini; 7 July 1967–6 Oct. 1969 Muhammad Benhima; 6 Oct. 1969–6 Aug. 1971 Ahmad Laraki; 6 Aug. 1971–2 Nov. 1972 Muhammad Karim Lamrani; 2 Nov. 1972–22 March 1979 Ahmad Osman; 22 March 1979–19 Nov. 1983 Maati Bouabid; 30 Nov. 1983–30 Sept. 1986 Muhammad Karim Lamrani; 30 Sept. 1986– Azzedine Laraki. *Note:* in times of no Prime Minister, the King held that office.

Kinyarwanda see **Rwanda Republic**

Klein Vrijstaat see **Little Free State**

576 Klipdrift Republic. 1870–13 Dec. 1870. *Location:* the Klipdrift Diamond fields, 20 miles northwest of Kimberley, Cape Province, South Africa. *Capital:* Klipdrift (founded 1870, and re-named in 1873 as Barkly West, for Sir Henry Barkly, governor of the Cape). *Other names:* The Diggers' Republic, Griqualand West Republic, Republic of Griqualand West.
History: In 1870, three years after the first diamond was discovered in the area, the diggers (who had signed a treaty with local Griqua chief Jan Bloem at Nooigedacht) proclaimed a free republic because Pretorius of the **South African Republic [i]** was threatening to annex the area. This forced the British, later in 1870, to march in and take over the republic. This marked the end of the rule of Stafford Parker, a former British able-bodied seaman, and a year later, on October 27, 1871,

the Klipdrift fields merged into the Cape Colony (see **British Cape Colony**) as part of **Griqualand West**.
Presidents: 1870–13 Dec. 1870 Stafford Parker.

Kmt see **Egypt, 1st Dynasty**

Kololo-Rotse Empire see **Barotseland**

577 Kom. ca. 1720–14 July 1884. *Location:* west Cameroun. *Capital:* Laikom.
History: The Ekwu clan traveled extensively before Jina settled in Laikom and founded the Kom dynasty. Jina was the son of Bo, and the rule has passed through the family to the present day. In 1884 Kom became part of the **German Crown Land in North West Africa** (which later became **Kamerun**).
Chiefs: ca. 1720–ca. 1740 Jina; ca. 1740–(?) Kumanbong; (?)–(?) Kwo; (?)–1830 Nkwain; 1830–1855 Tufoyn; 1855–1865 Kumong; 1865–1912 Yu; 1912–1926 Nggam; 1926–1954 Ndi; 1954–1966 Lo'o; 1966– Nsom.

578 Kong. ca. 1710–20 Feb. 1888. *Location:* Ivory Coast. *Capital:* Kong.
History: The Dyula state of Kong was founded in the early 18th century by Shehu Umar Watara, brother of the founder of **Gwiriko**. In 1888 it was conquered by France (see **French Ivory Coast**).
Sheikhs: ca. 1710 Shehu Umar Watara; (?)–(?) [unknown]; (?)–(?) [unknown]; (?)–(?) [unknown]; (?)–(?) [unknown]; (?)–(?) [unknown]; ca. 1815 Bakary Watara; (?)–(?) [unknown]; ca. 1850 Kurakara; (?)–(?) Dabila; ca. 1889–1895 Karamoko; 1895–1962 gBon Culibaly.

579 Kongo. ca. 1350–ca. 1850. *Location:* northern Angola and parts of Zaire and Congo. *Capital:* Mbanza (also called São Salvador). *Other names:* Bakongo, Congo.

History: Named for the Bakongo people, this large kingdom was very powerful by 1400. Nothing is known of Kongo until Diogo Cão (or Cam) discovered the old kingdom in 1483. A good relationship developed between Kongo and Portugal, with the Bakongo becoming Christianized and Europeanized. In the late 1660s the Portuguese abandoned the area (see **Angola Donatária** and **Portuguese West Africa**), long after it had become recognized by the Vatican as a Christian kingdom, and had fallen into ruin. It later (at an uncertain date) became part of **Portuguese West Africa** and part of **Moyen-Congo** and **Congo Free State**. A man calling himself Pedro VII of Kongo died in 1955.

Manis (or Kings): 1350–1483 unknown; 1483–1508 João I (or Nzinga); 1508–1543 Affonso I (or Nzinga Mbemba); 1543–1545 Pedro I (or Nkang Mbemba); 1545–1561 Diogo I; 1561–1562 Affonso II; 1562–1563 Bernardi I; 1563–1582 Henriques I; 1582–1587 Álvaro I; 1587–1609 Jaga Álvaro II; 1609–1615 Bernardi II; 1615–1621 Álvari III; 1621–1624 Pedro II; 1624–1626 García I; 1626–1631 Ambrósio; 1631–1635 Álvaro IV; 1635–1636 Álvaro V; 1636–1641 Álvaro VI; 1641–1661 García II Affonso; 1661–1665 António I; 1665–1666 Álvaro VII; 1666–1666 Álvaro VIII; 1666–1667 Affonso III; 1667–1669 Pedro III; 1669–1674 Álvaro IX (joint); 1669–1674 Pedro III (joint); 1669–1674 Rafael (joint); 1674–1678 Daniel (joint); 1674–1678 Pedro III (joint); 1678–1683 Pedro III; 1683–1709 João II; 1709–1717 João II (joint); 1709–1717 Pedro IV (joint); 1717–1718 Pedro IV; 1718–(?) Pedro V; (?)–ca. 1850 unknown.

580 Kontagora. 1864–1901. *Location:* Niger Province, western Nigeria. *Capital:* Kontagora (founded 1864. Name means "lay down your gourds"). *Other names:* Kontagora Emirate.

History: Created out of Kamberi country in the late 1850s by Fulani chieftain Umaru Nagwamatse, and established as an emirate in 1864, it was brought into **Northern Nigeria Protectorate** in 1901 by the British as Kontagora Province. It is now a division of Niger Province.

Sarkins Sudan: 1864–1876 Umaru Nagwamatse; 1876–1880 Abubakar Modibbo; 1880–1901 Ibrahim Nagamatse; 1901–Apr. 1903 not recognized; Apr. 1903–26 Oct. 1929 Ibrahim Nagwamatse; 26 Oct. 1929–Feb. 1961 Umaru Maidubu; Feb. 1961–1976 Mu'azu; 1976– al-Hajji Saidu Namaska. *Note:* Sarkins Sudan is the plural of Sarkin Sudan (King).

581 Kordofan. ca. 1600–16 Aug. 1821. *Location:* Sudan. *Capital:* al-Ubaid. *Other names:* Kurdufan.

History: The country of Kordofan was independent for 150 years before it became a province of the **Funj Sultanate** in 1748. In 1772 this rule was temporarily thrown off, but re-established in 1784. In 1821 the Egyptians conquered all of the Sudan and Kordofan became a province of **Egyptian Sudan** (see **Kordofan Province**).

Sultans: ca. 1600–ca. 1650 Muhammad I; ca. 1650–ca. 1700 Muhammad II; ca. 1700–(?) Isawi; (?)–1748 Hashim. *Funj Governors:* 1748–1772 Sheikh Muhammad Abu'l Kaylak. *Sultans:* 1772–1784 Hashim. *Funj Governors:* 1784–16 Aug. 1821 Maqdum Musallam.

582 Kordofan Province. 16 Aug. 1821–Dec. 1883. *Location:* Sudan. *Capital:* al-Ubaid. *Other names:* Kurdufan.

History: In 1821 the Egyptians conquered **Kordofan**, and it became a province of the **Egyptian Sudan**. In 1883 the Mahdi (see **Mahdist State**) swallowed it up.

Governors: 16 Aug. 1821–1822 Mehmed Bey; 1822–1825 Halim Bey; 1825–1827 Suleiman Bey Harputli; 1828–1833 Rustum Bey; 1833–1843 [unknown]; 1843–1848 Mustafa Kiridli; 1848–1850 vacant; 1850–1850 Musa Pasha Hamdi; 1850–1857 vacant; 1857–1859 Hassan Ali Pasha Arnavut; 1859–1862 [unknown]; 1862–1865 Hassan Ali Pasha Arnavut; 1865–1873 [unknown]; 1873–1874 Mehmed Sa'id Pasha Wahbi; 1874–1879 [unknown]; 1879–Dec. 1883 Mehmed Sa'id Pasha Wahbi.

583 Kororofa. ca. 1600–1901. *Location:* northern Nigeria/Niger border. *Capital:* Kororofa. *Other names:* Kwararafa, Jukun.

History: A Hausa state formed around the turn of the 17th century and based on descent from a semi-mythical kingdom of the late Middle Ages. In 1901 it was divided between the French **(French West Africa)** and the British **(Northern Nigeria Protectorate).** The people are the Jukun.

Kings: ca. 1600 Agbu Kendja; ca. 1630 Katapka; ca. 1671 Agwabi; (?)–(?) Dawi; (?)–(?) Agigbi; (?)–(?) Nani To; (?)–(?) Dadju; (?)–ca. 1750 Zike; ca. 1750–ca. 1775 Kuwya; ca. 1775–ca. 1800 Matsweu Adi; ca. 1800–1815 Ashu Manu I; 1815–1848 Zikeenya; 1848–1866 Agbu Manu I; 1866–1871 Ashu Manu II; 1871–1902 Agudu Manu; 1903–1915 Agbu Manu II; 1915–1927 Ashu Manu III.

Kotonu see **Cotonou**

584 Koya-Temne. ca. 1505–31 Aug. 1896. *Location:* Sierra Leone. *Capital:* Robanna (after 1720); Port Lokko (1680–1720); Lokko (1560–1680). *Other names:* Temne, Koya, Quiah.

History: Founded about 1505, Koya-Temne was one of the major native political divisions of Sierra Leone before becoming part of **Sierra Leone Colony and Protectorate.**

Kings: ca. 1505–ca. 1550 Farima I; ca. 1550–ca. 1560 Farima II; ca. 1560–1605 Farima III; 1605–1610 Sangrafare (or Pedro); 1610–1630 Borea I; 1630–1664 Borea II; 1664–1680 Felipe II; 1680–1720 Naimbanna I; 1720–1793 Naimbanna II; 1793–1807 Farima IV;

1807–1817 Bai Foki; 1817–1825 Moriba; 1825–1826 Jack Coby (or Kunia Banna); 1826–1840 Fatima; 1840–1859 Moribu Kindo; 1859–1872 Bai Kanta (or Alexander). *Regents:* 1872–1890 Alimani Lahai Bundu. *Kings:* 1890–1898 Bai Kompa (or William Rowe); 1898–1898 Fula Mansa Gbanka. *Sub-Kings of Ko-Fransa:* 1770–1788 Tom I; 1788–1796 Jimmy; 1796–1807 Tom II.

585 Kreli's Country. 19 May 1835–1886. *Location:* as **Galekaland,** i.e. Kaffraria, South Africa. *Capital:* Kentani. *Other names:* Galekaland, Sarili's Country.

History: The name given to **Galekaland** during the reign of the last independent Northern Xhosa chieftain, Kreli (or Sarili), before the British annexation of the country to the Cape (see **British Cape Colony [Self-Rule]**) in 1886. Before this, on June 28, 1881, Kreli had surrendered to the British and had been given land in Elliotdale.

Chiefs: 19 May 1835–1886 Kreli (or Sarili). *Note:* for rulers of the area before 1835, and for chiefs after 1886, see **Galekaland.**

Kurdufan see **Kordofan**

586 Kush. ca. 860 B.C.–ca. 325 A.D. *Location:* Sudan. *Capital:* Meroë (from ca. 590 B.C.–ca. 325 A.D.); Napata (or Marawi) (until ca. 590 B.C.). *Other names:* Cush, Nubia, Ethiopia.

History: The area that is today The Sudan was formerly an Egyptian-occupied country called Old Nubia (as opposed to **Nubia**). The northern division of this country was called Wawat (with headquarters at Aswan) and the southern division was called Kush (with headquarters at Napata). This was the state of affairs for almost five centuries until, by the 11th century B.C., with the decline of Egypt, Kush assumed more and more autonomy until, by about 860 B.C. it became an independent kingdom. The Greeks called it Ethiopia, the Ancient Egyptians called it Kush, and its own particular Nubian-Egyptian culture was maintained throughout its history. Under its king, Kashta, it turned the tables on its northern neighbor by conquering Upper Egypt, and under Kashta's son Piankhi (see **Egypt, 25th Dynasty**), all of Egypt became Kushite. In 671 B.C. this situation ended with the Assyrian invasion of Egypt and the Kushites retired to their home. Kush remained the dominant kingdom in the Sudan until about 325 B.C., when their capital, Meroë, was destroyed by the king of **Axum.**

Kings: ca. 860 B.C. Kashta; (?)–(?) Alara; (?)–(?) Piankhi I; (?)–(?) Kashta II; (?)–(?) Neferkare Shabaha II; (?)–(?) Jedkaure Shebitku; (?)–(?) Hunefertemre; ca. 671 B.C. Urdamen; (?)–(?) Bakare Tanuatamun; (?)–(?) Piankhi II; (?)–(?) Neferankh Asrumeri Amen; (?)–(?) Piankhi III; ca. 653 B.C.–ca. 643 B.C. Hukare Atlanersa; ca. 643 B.C.–ca. 623 B.C. Sekherpereure Senkamanishen; ca. 623 B.C.–ca. 593 B.C. Ankhikare Anlamani; ca. 593 B.C.–ca. 568 B.C. Merkare Aspelta; ca. 568 B.C.–ca. 555 B.C. Wajkare Amtalqa; ca. 555 B.C.–ca. 542 B.C. Sekhemkare Malenaqen; ca. 542 B.C.–ca. 538 B.C. Neferkare Analmaaye; ca. 538 B.C.–ca. 519 B.C. Amaninatakilebte; ca. 519 B.C.–ca. 510 B.C. Karkamani; ca. 510 B.C.–ca. 487 B.C. Setepkare Astabarqamen; ca. 487 B.C.–ca. 468 B.C. Sejertawi Asasunaq; ca. 468 B.C.–ca. 463 B.C. Nasakhma; ca. 463 B.C.–ca. 435 B.C. Heperkare Maluiane; ca. 435 B.C.–ca. 431 B.C. Talakhamane; ca. 431 B.C.–ca. 405 B.C. Neferabre Herinutarekamen; ca. 405 B.C.–ca. 404 B.C. Baskakaren; ca. 404 B.C.–ca. 369 B.C. Sameramen Herusaatef; ca. 369 B.C.–ca. 350 B.C. [unknown]; ca. 350 B.C.–ca. 335 B.C. Ahratan; ca. 335 B.C.–ca. 310 B.C. Ankhkare Nastasen; ca. 310 B.C.–ca. 295 B.C. Amanibakhi; ca. 295 B.C.–ca. 275 B.C. Khnemabre Arkaqamani; ca. 275 B.C.–ca. 260 B.C. Amanislo. *Queen:* ca. 260B.C.–

ca. 250 B.C. Bartare. *Kings:* ca. 250 B.C.–ca. 235 B.C. Amanitekha; ca. 235 B.C.–ca. 218 B.C. Arnekhamani; ca. 218 B.C.–ca. 200 B.C. Arqamani; ca. 200 B.C.–ca. 185 B.C. Tabirqa; ca. 185 B.C.–ca. 170 B.C. [unknown]; ca. 170 B.C.–ca. 160 B.C. Shanakdakhete; ca. 160 B.C.–ca. 145 B.C. [unknown]; ca. 145 B.C.–ca. 120 B.C. Naqrisan; ca. 120 B.C.–ca. 100 B.C. Tanyidamani; ca. 100 B.C.–ca. 80 B.C. [unknown]; ca. 80 B.C.–ca. 65 B.C. [unknown]; ca. 65 B.C.–ca. 33 B.C. Nawidemak; ca. 33 B.C.–ca. 24 B.C. Teriteqas; ca. 24 B.C.–ca. 15 B.C. Akinidad; ca. 15 B.C.–ca. 12 A.D. Natakamani; ca. 12 A.D.–ca. 17 Serkarer; ca. 17–ca. 35 Pisakar; ca. 35–ca. 45 Amanitaraqide; ca. 45–ca. 62 Amanitenmemide. *Queen:* ca. 62–ca. 85 Amanikhatashan. *Kings:* ca. 85–ca. 103 Tarekeniwal; ca. 103–ca. 108 Amanikhalika; ca. 108–ca. 132 Aritenyesbekhe; ca. 132–ca. 137 Aqrakamani; ca. 137–ca. 146 Adeqetali; ca. 146–ca. 165 Takideamani; ca. 165–ca. 184 [unknown]; ca. 184–ca. 194 [unknown]; ca. 194–ca. 209 Teritedakhetey; ca. 209–ca. 228 Aryesbekhe; ca. 228–ca. 246 Teridnide; ca. 246–ca. 246 Aretnide; ca. 246–ca. 266 Teqerideamani; ca. 266–ca. 283 Tamelerdeamani; ca. 283–ca. 300 Yesbekheamani; ca. 300–ca. 308 Lakhideamani; ca. 308–ca. 320 Maleqerabar; ca. 320–ca. 325 Akhedakhetiwal.

587 KwaNdebele. Oct. 1977– . *Location:* north central Transvaal, South Africa. *Capital:* Siyabuswa. *Other names:* KwaNdebele National State, South Ndebele.

History: In 1977 KwaNdebele achieved self-rule. The homeland for the Southern Matabele (or Ndebele), its future independence is not certain.

Chief Ministers: Oct. 1977– Simon Sikosana.

Kwararafa see **Kororofa**

588 KwaZulu. 1 Apr. 1972– . *Location:* northern Natal, South Africa

Capital: Ulundi; formerly Nongoma. *Other names:* KwaZulu National State.

History: A Bantustan (or homeland) for the Zulu people, it is composed of more than 30 discontinuous exclaves throughout Natal. Formerly the Zulu Territorial Authority, it became self-governing in 1977.

Chief Ministers: 1 Apr. 1972– Gatsha Buthelezi.

Kyrene see **Pentapolis**

589 Lafia. 1780–1900. *Location:* central Nigeria. *Capital:* Lafia (1804 onwards. Formerly called Lafian Beri-Beri, the name Lafia means "comfortably settled"); Anane (1780–1804).

History: Established in 1780 as a political entity by expatriates from **Bornu** led by Dunama, it never became a Fulani emirate, but maintained its independence until 1900, when it became part of **Northern Nigeria Protectorate.**

Chiefs: 1780–1809 Dunama. *Emirs:* 1809–1814 Musa Dan Jaji; 1814–1819 Umar I; 1819–1844 Laminu; 1844–1849 Musa Gana; 1849–1866 Abdullahi Dalla; 1866–1868 Ari; 1868–1873 Umar II; 1873–1881 Abdullahi Dalla Bahagu; 1881–1903 Mohamman Agwe I; 1903–1918 Musa; 1918–1926 Abdullahi; 1926–1933 Muhammadu Angulu; 1933–1949 Mohamman Agwe II; 1949–1952 Makwangiji Na'ali (acting); 1952– Yusufu Musa.

590 Lafiagi. 1824–1900. *Location:* west central Nigeria. *Capital:* Lafiagi (built 1810). *Other names:* Lafiaji, Lafiagi Emirate.

History: The name means "a small hill" in Nupe, and it was founded as a town by Mallam Maliki, a Fulani chief. In 1824 the Emirate was founded. In 1900 it became part of **Northern Nigeria Protectorate.**

Chiefs: 1810–1824 Mallam Maliki. *Emirs:* 1824–1833 Manzuma; 1833–1834 Aliyu; 1834–1845 Abdulkadiri; 1845–1853 Aliyu; 1853–1868 Abdulkadiri; 1868–1882 Ibrahim Halilu; 1882–1891 Aliyu; 1891–1892 Abdurrahim; 1892–

1915 Ahmadu; 1915–1945 Muhamman Bello; 1945–1949 Abubakr Kawu. *Chiefs:* 1949–1951 Maliki; 1951–1961 Abubakr Ceceko; 1961– Umaru Oke-Ode.

Lagid Egypt see **Egypt of the Ptolemies**

591 Lagos. 6 Aug. 1861–22 Aug. 1862. *Location:* Lagos Island (in Nigeria), plus Iddo Island, plus Badagry, Palma and Leckie. *Capital:* Lagos.

History: In 1861 the Kingdom of Lagos (see **Lagos Kingdom**) came to an end as Britain claimed it. The administrator took over the consulship of the **Bight of Benin** as well. In 1862 **Lagos Settlement** came into being.

Governors: 6 Aug. 1861–22 Jan. 1862 William McCoskry (acting); 22 Jan. 1862–22 Aug. 1862 Henry Freeman.

592 Lagos Colony. 13 Jan. 1886–16 Feb. 1906. *Location:* Lagos, Nigeria. *Capital:* Lagos. *Other names:* Lagos.

History: In 1886 **Lagos Territory [ii]** became a separate colony of the British Empire. On October 18, 1887 a protectorate was established in the Lagos hinterland (see **Lagos Protectorate**). In 1906 the Colony of Lagos was incorporated into **Southern Nigeria Colony and Protectorate.**

Governors: 13 Jan. 1886–1889 Alfred Moloney (knighted 1890); 1889–1890 George Denton (acting); 1890–1891 Sir Alfred Moloney; 1891–1897 Gilbert Carter (knighted 1893); 1897–1899 Henry McCallum (knighted 1898); 1899–1902 Sir William MacGregor; 1902–1903 Henry Reeve (acting); 1903–Aug. 1904 Henry Reeve; Aug. 1904–16 Feb. 1906 Walter Egerton (knighted 1905).

593 Lagos Kingdom. ca. 1700–6 Aug. 1861. *Location:* southern Nigeria. *Capital:* Lagos (named for the lagoons nearby by the Portuguese).

History: The Yoruba settled the island of Lagos, but it was a vassal state

of **Benin,** under which Lagos acted as a western province. By the early 1800s it was a major slave-trading center, and independent from **Benin,** but in 1861 it was taken over by the British, as **Lagos.**
Obas (Kings): ca. 1700 Ashikpa; (?)–(?) Ado; (?)–(?) Gabaro; (?)–(?) Akinshemoyin; ca. 1805–ca. 1808 Kekere; ca. 1808–1811 Olugun Kutere; 1811–1821 Adele I; 1821–ca. 1832 Oshinlokun; ca. 1832–1833 Idewu Ogulari; 1833–1834 Adele I; 1834–1841 Oluwole; 1841–July 1845 Akitoye I; July 1845–Feb. 1852 Kosoko; Feb. 1852–1853 Akitoye I; 1853–1885 Docemo (or Dosumu); 1885–1900 Oyekan I; 1900–1920 Eshugbayi Eleko; 1920–1931 Samusi Olusi; 1931–1932 Eshugbayi Eleko; 1932–1 Oct. 1949 Falolu; 1 Oct. 1949–1964 Alaiyeluwa Oba Adeniji Adele II; Feb. 1965– Adeyinka Oyekan II.

594 Lagos Protectorate. 18 Oct. 1887–27 Dec. 1899. *Location:* on the mainland, behind Lagos Island, Nigeria. *Capital:* ruled from Lagos.
History: In 1887 the British established a protectorate over the Lagos hinterland. In 1899 (effective January 1, 1900) the Protectorate came to form part of **Southern Nigeria Protectorate**).
Rulers: ruled from Lagos.

595 Lagos Settlement. 22 Aug. 1862–19 Feb. 1866. *Location:* Lagos, Nigeria. *Capital:* Lagos. *Other names:* Lagos.
History: In 1862 **Lagos** became Lagos Settlement. In 1866 it became a territory of the **West African Settlements** (see **Lagos Territory [i]**).
Governors: 22 Aug. 1862–1863 Henry Freeman; 1863–1864 W.R. Mullinar (acting); 1864–Apr. 1865 John Glover (acting); Apr. 1865–19 Feb. 1866 John Glover.

596 Lagos Territory [i]. 19 Feb. 1866–24 July 1874. *Location:* Lagos, Nigeria. *Capital:* Lagos. *Other names:* Lagos.

History: In 1866 **Lagos Settlements** became a territory of the **West African Settlements.** In 1874 it and **Gold Coast Territory [ii]** broke away from the Federation and set up as a single colony called **Gold Coast Colony (with Lagos)** (see also **Gold Coast Territory [ii]**).
Administrators: 19 Feb. 1866–Feb. 1866 Charles Patey; Feb. 1866–1870 John Glover; 1870–1870 Miles Cooper (acting); 1870–1870 John Glover; 1870–1871 W.H. Simpson (acting); 1871–1872 J. Gerrard (acting); 1872–1872 Henry Fowley (acting); 1872–1873 George Berkeley; 1873–1873 Charles Lees (acting); 1873–1874 George Strahan; 1874–24 July 1874 John Shaw (acting).

597 Lagos Territory [ii]. 24 July 1874–13 Jan. 1886. *Location:* Lagos, Nigeria. *Capital:* Lagos. *Other names:* Lagos.
History: In 1874 **Lagos Territory [i]** became Lagos Territory [ii] (see **Lagos Territory [i]** for details). In 1886 Gold Coast and Lagos split up into separate colonies, **Lagos Colony** coming into being.
Administrators: 24 July 1874–1875 Charles Lees; 1875–1878 John Dumaresq (acting); 1878–1878 F. Simpson (acting); 1878–1878 Malcolm Brown (acting); 1878–1880 Alfred Moloney (acting). *Lieutenant-Governors:* 1880–1880 Brandford Griffith. *Administrators:* 1880–1883 C.D. Turton (acting). *Deputy-Governors:* 1883–1883 Alfred Moloney; 1883–1883 Fred Evans; 1883–1884 Brandford Griffith; 1884–1884 Murray Rumsey; 1884–1885 Knapp Burrow; 1885–13 Jan. 1886 C. Pike.

Land Goosen see **Goshen**

Land of Gold see **Ghana Empire**

Land of Punt see **Punt**

Landeen see **Gazaland**

598 Lapai. 1825–24 June 1898. *Lo-*

cation: Niger State, northern Nigeria. *Capital:* Lapai (after 1936 the capital became Badeggi-Lapai).

History: In 1825 Lapai was created a separate emirate of the **Fulani Empire**, in the place of the Gwari people who had lived there in the kingdom of **Payi** (hence the name Lapai). In 1898 it became part of the **Niger River Delta Protectorate,** and in 1900 it became part of **Northern Nigeria Protectorate.**

Emirs: 1825–1832 Dauda Maza; 1832–1835 Yamusa; 1835–1838 Baji; 1838–1874 Jantabu; 1874–1875 Atiku; 1875–1893 Bawa; 1893–1907 Abdulkadiri; 1907–1923 Ibrahim; 1923–Apr. 1937 Aliyu Gana; 1937–Nov. 1954 Umaru; 1954– Muhammadu Kobo.

599 Las Palmas de Gran Canária Province. 1927–8 May 1983. *Location:* Gran Canária, Fuerteventura, Lanzarote, Alegrancia, Graciosa, Lobos— these islands in the Canary Islands. *Capital:* Las Palmas.

History: In 1927 **Canary Islands Protectorate** was split into two separate provinces of Spain (see also **Santa Cruz de Tenerife Province** for further details). In 1983 the two, Las Palmas and Santa Cruz de Tenerife, joined to form **Canary Islands (Self-Rule).**

Rulers: [unknown].

Lautaye, Laute see **Gumel**

600 Lebowa. 2 Oct. 1972– . *Location:* central Transvaal, South Africa. *Capital:* Lebowakgomo. *Other names:* Lebowa National State.

History: Lebowa is the Bantustan (National Homeland) for the Northern Sotho ("lebowa" means "north") including the Pedi. It achieved self-government in 1972, but still remains part of **South Africa.**

Chief Ministers: 2 Oct. 1972–8 May 1973 Maurice Matlala; 8 May 1973– Cedric Phatudi.

601 Lesotho. See these **names:**
Lesotho (1966–)

Basutoland (Self-Rule) (1964–1966)
Basutoland High Commission Territory (1884–1964)
Basutoland Territory (1871–1884)
Basutoland Crown Protectorate (1868–1871)
Basutoland Protectorate (1843–1868)
Basutoland Kingdom (1822–1843)

602 Lesotho. 4 Oct. 1966– . *Location:* Southern Africa. *Capital:* Maseru (means "the place of red sandstone"). *Other names:* the Kingdom of Lesotho.

History: In 1966 **Basutoland (Self-Rule)** gained its independence as the Kingdom of Lesotho.

Motlotlehis (Kings): 4 Oct. 1966–2 Feb. 1970 Moshoeshoe II (Constantine Sereng Seeiso); 4 Dec. 1970– Moshoeshoe II (Constantine Sereng Seeiso). *Queens Regent:* 2 Feb. 1970–4 Dec. 1970 Mamaohato. *Tona Kholas (Prime Ministers):* 4 Oct. 1966–19 Jan. 1986 Chief Leabua Jonathan; 27 Jan. 1986– Joshua Letsie. *Chairmen of Military Council:* 24 Jan. 1986– Justinus Lekhanya.

603 Liberia. See these **names:**
Liberia Republic (1847–)
Liberia Commonwealth (1839–1847)
Liberia Colony (1824–1839)
Cape Mesurado Colony (1821–1824)
Maryland-in-Liberia (1854–1857)
Maryland Colony (1834–1854)
Bassa Cove (1835–1839)
Edina (1832–1837)
Mississippi-in-Africa (1835–1842)
Port Cresson (1832–1835)
New Georgia (1824–1839)
Petit Dieppe (1364–1413)

604 Liberia Colony. 15 Aug. 1824–1 Apr. 1839. *Location:* around Monrovia, Liberia. *Capital:* Monrovia. *Other names:* the Colony of Liberia, Liberia.

History: The Colony was declared in 1824 upon expansion from the original colony of Cape Mesurado (see **Cape Mesurado Colony**), the original colony later becoming Monrovia (or rather where Monrovia is today). In 1839, upon expansion, and the taking in of other colonies, **Liberia Commonwealth** came into being.

Colonial Agents: 15 Aug. 1824–22 Aug. 1824 Jehudi Ashmun (acting); 22 Aug. 1824–26 March 1828 Jehudi Ashmun; 26 March 1828–8 Nov. 1828 Lott Carey (acting); 8 Nov. 1828–22 Dec. 1828 Colston Waring (acting); 22 Dec. 1828–19 Apr. 1829 Richard Randall; 19 Apr. 1829–14 Sept. 1829 Joseph Mechlin, Jr. (acting); 14 Sept. 1829–27 Feb. 1830 Joseph Mechlin, Jr.; 27 Feb. 1830–12 Apr. 1830 John Anderson (acting); 12 Apr. 1830–4 Dec. 1830 Anthony Williams (acting); 4 Dec. 1830–24 Sept. 1833 Joseph Mechlin, Jr.; 24 Sept. 1833–1 Jan. 1834 George McGill (acting); 1 Jan. 1834–10 May 1835 John Pinney; 10 May 1835–12 Aug. 1835 Nathaniel Brander (acting); 12 Aug. 1835–25 Sept. 1836 Ezekiel Skinner; 25 Sept. 1836–1 Apr. 1839 Anthony Williams (acting).

605 Liberia Commonwealth. 1 Apr. 1839–26 July 1847. *Location:* as **Liberia Republic.** *Capital:* Monrovia (named in 1824 by Robert Goodloe Harper, a local resident, for President James Monroe of the U.S.A.). *Other names:* Commonwealth of Liberia, Liberia.

History: In 1839 **Liberia Colony** became a commonwealth as a result of expansion, giving self-rule to the country. The Commonwealth consisted of the counties of Grand Bassa and Montserrado, which in turn consisted of the settlements of Monrovia, New Georgia, Caldwell, Millsburg, Bexley, Marshall, Bassa Cove and Edina. In 1847 the country threw off American colonial rule forever and became **Liberia Republic.**

Governors: 1 Apr. 1839–3 Sept. 1841 Thomas Buchanan; 3 Sept. 1841–20 Jan. 1842 Joseph Roberts (acting); 20 Jan. 1842–26 July 1847 Joseph Roberts.

606 Liberia Republic. 26 July 1847– . *Location:* North West Africa.

Capital: Monrovia (built on the site of the original **Cape Mesurado Colony,** and named Monrovia by Robert Goodloe Harper in 1824, for President James Monroe of the U.S.A.). *Other names:* Republic of Liberia, Liberia, Second Republic of Liberia (after 1980).

History: In 1847 The Commonwealth of Liberia (see **Liberia Commonwealth**) became an independent republic. In 1857 **Maryland-in-Liberia** became part of the Republic, and in 1880 the Kingdom of Medina was incorporated.

Presidents: 26 July 1847–Oct. 1847 Samuel Benedict (President of the Convention); Oct. 1847–3 Jan. 1848 Joseph Roberts (President-elect/Governor); 3 Jan. 1848–2 Jan. 1856 Joseph Roberts; 2 Jan. 1856–4 Jan. 1864 Stephen Benson; 4 Jan. 1864–6 Jan. 1868 Daniel Warner; 6 Jan. 1868–4 Jan. 1870 James Payne; 4 Jan. 1870–26 Oct. 1871 Edward Roye; 26 Oct. 1871–1 Jan. 1872 James Smith; 1 Jan. 1872–24 Feb. 1876 Joseph Roberts; 24 Feb. 1876–1 Jan. 1878 James Payne; 1 Jan. 1878–20 Jan. 1883 Anthony Gardner; 20 Jan. 1883–4 Apr. 1884 Alfred Russell; 4 Apr. 1884–4 Jan. 1892 Hilary Johnson; 4 Jan. 1892–12 Nov. 1896 Joseph Cheeseman; 12 Nov. 1896–10 Dec. 1900 William Coleman; 10 Dec. 1900–4 Jan. 1904 Garretson Gibson; 4 Jan. 1904–1 Jan. 1912 Arthur Barclay; 1 Jan. 1912–5 Jan. 1920 Daniel Howard; 5 Jan. 1920–3 Dec. 1930 Charles King; 3 Dec. 1930–1 Jan. 1944 Edwin Barclay; 1 Jan. 1944–23 July 1971 William Tubman; 23 July 1971–12 Apr. 1980 William Tolbert; 12 Apr. 1980–26 July 1984 Samuel Doe (Chairman and Head of State); 26 July 1984–6 Jan. 1986 Samuel Doe (President of the Interim National Assembly); 6 Jan. 1986– Samuel Doe.

607 Libertalia. ca. 1680–ca. 1691. *Location:* southeastern coast of Madagascar. *Capital:* unknown. *Other names:* Libertatia, Republic of Libertalia, Republic of Libertatia.

History: The following account is

vague and without accurate dates. The whole story of Libertalia (or Libertatia — even the name is uncertain) is shrouded not so much in mystery as in legend. Historians never wrote about the pirate republic, it was only story tellers who did so. Even the location of the pirates' stronghold is debated — some say it was on the southeastern coast of Madagascar, some say on the northwest, and yet others say on the island of **Anjouan** in the Comoros. Most important is the name of the place — Libertalia or Libertatia. Around 1672 a French seaman, Captain Misson, and an ex-Vatican priest, Lieutenant Caraccioli, formed a pirate crew on board a captured ship, the "Victoire." With their oyster the whole world, they plied their trade from the Caribbean to Africa, and wound up in Madagascar and the Comoros. They holed up in **Anjouan** for a while, fighting in local wars. Caraccioli was now captain of his own ship, and he and Misson founded a republic in Madagascar, calling it Libertalia. Soon they were joined by Captain Thomas Tew, another pirate. Soon their colony, and the Red Sea pirate trade, increased. A government was set up, but after a raid by local natives during which Caraccioli was killed, and after the loss of Tew's ship, Misson and Tew left for the Americas, Misson drowning en route. Tew was to die several years later.

Lords Conservator: Capt. Misson. *Admirals:* Capt. Thomas Tew. *Secretaries of State:* Capt. Caraccioli.

608 Libya. See these **names:**
Libyan Arab Jamahiriyya (1977–)
Libyan Arab People's Republic (1976–1977)
Libyan Republic (1969–1976)
Libyan Kingdom (1951–1969)
British Tripolitania (1942–1951)
French Fezzan (1943–1951)
Cyrenaica (Autonomous) (1949–1951)
British Cyrenaica (1942–1949)
Libya (Italian Colony) (1934–1943)

Libya (1929–1934)
Tripolitania Colony (1919–1929)
Cirenaica Colony (1919–1929)
Tripolitania Protectorate (1911–1919)
Cirenaica Protectorate (1912–1919)
Tripolitanian Republic (1918–1923)
Tripoli Ottoman Province [ii] (1835–1911)
Fezzan Pashalik (1842–1912)
Karamanli Tripoli (1711–1835)
Fezzan (ca. 1566–1842)
Tripoli Ottoman Province [i] (1551–1711)
Tripoli (Knights of Malta) (1530–1551)
Tripoli (Spanish) (1510–1530)
Hafsid Tripoli [iii] (1482–1510)
Egyptian Tripoli (1412–1482)
Hafsid Tripoli [ii] (1401–1412)
Tripoli (Banu Ammar) (1327–1401)
Hafsid Tripoli [i] (ca. 1247–1327)
Almohad Tripoli (1160–ca. 1247)
Norman Tripolitania (1148–1160)
Zirid Tripoli (977–1148)
Fatimid Tripoli (909–977)
Aghlabid Tripoli (800–909)
Phazania Kingdom (ca. 430–666)
Tripolitania Roman Province (297–442)
Pentapolis Territory (331 B.C.–75 B.C.)
Pentapolis (631 B.C.–331 B.C.)

609 Libya. 24 Jan. 1929–1 Jan. 1934. *Location:* as modern day Libya, although not as extensive in the southern region. *Capital:* Tripoli. *Other names:* Italian Libya, the Fourth Shore.

History: In 1929 **Tripolitania Colony** and **Cirenaica Colony** were brought together under one roof to form Libya, although Cirenaica was ruled by a separate authority. In 1934 Libya became a colony (see **Libya Italian Colony**).

Governors-General: 24 Jan. 1929–31 Dec. 1933 Pietro Badoglio. *Vice Governors of Cirenaica:* 24 Jan. 1929–13 March 1930 Domenico Siciliani; 13 March 1930–30 May 1934 Rodolfo Graziani; 1 June 1934–1 Jan. 1935 Guglielmo Nasi.

610 Libya (Italian Colony). 1 Jan. 1934–29 Jan. 1943. *Location:* Libya. *Capital:* Tripoli. *Other names:* Libya, Italian Libya.

History: In 1934 **Libya**, an Italian possession, became a colony. On October 25, 1938 it was declared a part of Italy (effective from January 9, 1939), but in 1943 the Cirenaica area (i.e. the eastern area) was lost to the Allies, and in 1943 so were Tripolitania (i.e. the western area) and Fezzan (i.e. the southern area). The result was: **British Cyrenaica, British Tripolitania** and **French Fezzan.**

Governors-General: 1 Jan. 1934–28 June 1940 Italo Balbo; 28 June 1940–30 June 1940 Giuseppe Bruni; 30 June 1940–11 Feb. 1941 Rodolfo Graziani; 11 Feb. 1941–19 July 1941 Italo Garibaldi; 19 July 1941–29 Jan. 1943 Ettore Bastico. *Vice-Governors of Cirenaica:* 1 Jan. 1934–23 Apr. 1935 Guglielmo Nasi.

611 Libyan Arab Jamahiriyya. 2 March 1977– . *Location:* North Africa. *Capital:* Tripoli (known as Oea in ancient times, along with Sabratha and Leptis Magna it formed the African Tripolis, or three cities). *Other names:* Libya, People's Socialist Libyan Arab Jamahiriyya.

History: In 1977 the **Libyan Arab People's Republic** became the People's Socialist Libyan Arab Jamahiriyya, a socialist centralized republic (jamahiriyya means "republic").

Secretaries-General: 2 March 1977–1 March 1979 Muammar al-Qaddafi; 1 March 1979–7 Jan. 1981 Abdul Ali al-Obeidi; 7 Jan. 1981–16 Feb. 1984 Muhammad az-Zaruq Rajab; 16 Feb. 1984–1 March 1987 Miftah al-Istah; 1 March 1987– Umar Mustafa al-Muntasir. *National Leaders:* 1 March 1979– Muammar al-Qaddafi.

612 Libyan Arab People's Republic. 5 Jan. 1976–2 March 1977. *Location:* as **Libyan Arab Jamahiriyya.** *Capital:* Tripoli. *Other names:* Libya.

History: In 1976 Colonel Qaddafi, leader of the **Libyan Republic** changed the name of the country to the Libyan Arab People's Republic. In 1977 it changed again, to the **Libyan Arab Jamahiriyya.**

Secretaries-General: 5 Jan. 1976–2 March 1977 Muammar al-Qaddafi. *Prime Ministers:* 5 Jan. 1976–2 March 1977 Abdal-Salem Jallud.

613 Libyan Kingdom. 24 Dec. 1951–1 Sept. 1969. *Location:* North Africa. *Capital:* Tripoli. *Other names:* Kingdom of Libya, United Kingdom of Libya, Federal Kingdom of Libya.

History: In 1949 **British Cyrenaica** became an autonomous state, **Cyrenaica (Autonomous)** headed by the Sanussi leader Idris. The locals called the place The Kingdom of Libya and called the emir the King. Idris formed a Libyan government, however, on March 29, 1951 in readiness for the moment later in the year when foreign forces left Libya altogether, that is as occupying forces. The three components which made up this new Kingdom of Libya were: **Cyrenaica (Autonomous), British Tripolitania** and **French Fezzan.** From 1951 to 1963 the three provinces of Cyrenaica, Tripolitania and Fezzan were granted autonomy under a federal kingdom, but the provinces were abolished in 1963 and the country became a unitary state. In 1969 Colonel Muammar al-Qaddafi, at the head of a military junta, seized power, creating the **Libyan Republic.**

Kings: 24 Dec. 1951–1 Sept. 1969 Idris al-Mahdi es-Sanussi (or Idris I). *Prime Ministers:* 24 Dec. 1951–15 Feb. 1954 Mahmoud Bey Muntasir; 19 Feb. 1954–11 Apr. 1954 Muhammad al-Saqisli; 12 Apr. 1954–23 May 1957 Mustafa Ben Halim; 26 May 1957–16 Oct. 1960 Abdul Majid Kubar; 16 Oct. 1960–21 March 1963 Muhammad Ben Othaman; 21 March 1963–24 Jan. 1964 Muhiaddin Fekini; 24 Jan. 1964–21 March 1965 Mahmoud Bey Muntasir; 21 March 1965–28 June 1967 Hussein

Maziq; 29 June 1967–25 Oct. 1967 Abdul Qadir Badri; 25 Oct. 1967–4 Sept. 1968 Abd al-Hamid al-Bakkush; 4 Sept. 1968–1 Sept. 1969 Wanis al-Qaddafi.

614 Libyan Republic. 1 Sept. 1969–5 Jan. 1976. *Location:* North Africa. *Capital:* Tripoli. *Other names:* The Republic of Libya; Libyan Arab Republic, Libi, Libya.

History: In 1969 Colonel Qaddafi, at the head of a military junta, seized power in the Kingdom of Libya (see **Libyan Kingdom**) and usurped King Idris. A republic was created, commonly called Libya. In 1976 it became the **Libyan Arab People's Republic,** but before this happened, in 1974 Libya and **Tunisia Republic** joined to form the **Arab Islamic Republic.** It lasted two days.

Military Revolutionary Leaders: 1 Sept. 1969–13 Sept. 1969 Muammar al-Qaddafi. *Chairmen of Revolutionary Command Council:* 13 Sept. 1969–5 Jan. 1976 Muammar al-Qaddafi. *Prime Ministers:* 8 Sept. 1969–16 Jan. 1970 Suleiman al-Maghrebi; 16 July 1972–5 Jan. 1976 Abdal-Salam Jallud. *Note:* in times of no Prime Minister, the Chairman held that office.

Lijdenburg see **Lydenburg**

615 Lijdenrust. 1886–1887. *Location:* southwest Africa. *Capital:* Grootfontein. *Other names:* Lydenrust.

History: In 1886 the Republic of **Upingtonia** changed its name to Lijdenrust when British support was not forthcoming and German protection was. German protection didn't amount to much and the hostiles became too much for the young republic which ceased to exist in 1887.

Presidents: 1886–1887 G.D.P. Prinsloo.

616 Little Free State. 10 March 1886–2 May 1891. *Location:* southwest of Swaziland, in eastern Transvaal.

Capital: it was too small to have a capital, as such. *Other names:* Klein Vrijstaat, The Republic of Klein Vrijstaat.

History: In 1886 Umbandine of Swaziland ceded a very small area in the southwest of his kingdom to F.I. Maritz and J.F. Ferreira, two Transvaal officials. The Republic of Klein Vrijstaat (population 72) was proclaimed, intended by the Boers as a first foothold in Swaziland. In 1891 it became Ward 1 of the District of Piet Retief in the **South Africa Republic.**

Rulers: 10 March 1886–2 May 1891 ruled by a triumvirate.

617 Little Popo. ca. 1750–19 July 1883. *Location:* Togo. *Capital:* Little Popo. *Other names:* Anecho.

History: Founded about 1750, Little Popo became a French protectorate in 1883 (see **Little Popo French Protectorate**).

Kings: ca. 1750–ca. 1775 Quam Dessu; ca. 1775–ca. 1800 Foli Arlonko; ca. 1800–1820 Aholin; 1820–1859 Akuete Zankli Lawson I. *Regents:* 1859–1868 Late Adjromitan. *Kings:* 1869–19 July 1883 Alexandre Boevi Lawson II.

618 Little Popo French Protectorate. 19 July 1883–24 Dec. 1885. *Location:* Togo. *Capital:* Little Popo. *Other names:* Anecho Protectorate.

History: In 1883 France placed a protectorate on **Little Popo.** In 1885 it went to become part of **Togoland Colony,** hence part of the German Empire.

Kings: 19 July 1883–1906 Georges Betnui Lawson III; 1906–1918 Jackson Kpavuvu Lawson IV; 1918–1922 vacant; 1922–1948 Frederick Boevi Lawson V; 1948–1955 Glin Lawson VI.

Lotse Empire see **Barotseland**

619 Louisbourg. 11 Feb. 1774–27 May 1786. *Location:* The Bay of Antongil, northeast Madagascar. *Capital:* Louisbourg (named for Louis XV of France).

History: In 1774 Maritius Beynow-

ski, a Pole recently escaped from Siberia, was commissioned by France to found a settlement here. France refused him a protectorate however, and in 1777 he received monies from the new United States of America government and proclaimed himself king of the whole northeast coast of Madagascar. He was killed by the French in 1786.
Kings: 11 Feb. 1774–27 May 1786 Maritius Beynowski.

Lounda see **Lunda**

620 Lower Congo-Gabon Colony. 5 July 1902–29 Dec. 1903. *Location:* **Congo People's Republic** and **Gabon Republic.** *Capital:* Brazzaville. *Other names:* Moyen-Congo-Gabon Colony.
History: In French Equatorial Africa (see **French Congo**) it was difficult in the early days to establish a satisfactory administrative system due to the constantly shifting and expanding boundaries of the French territories. In 1902 **Moyen-Congo-Gabon** was made into a colony comprising **Moyen-Congo District** and **Gabon Territory [iv].** Both were ruled by the **French Congo,** the commissioner-general delegating the government of Lower Congo-Gabon to the lieutenant-governor of Moyen-Congo, who was therefore immediate power in the two segments of this short-lived "super-colony." In 1903 it dissolved and two separate colonies were created from it: **Moyen-Congo Colony [ii]** and **Gabon Colony [iii].**
Rulers: see Moyen-Congo District for list of lieutenant-governors.

621 Lower Egypt. ca. 5000 BC.–ca. 3100 B.C. *Location:* the part of current Egypt north of Cairo, i.e. the Nile Delta area. *Capital:* Buto (latterly); Behdet (formerly). *Other names:* Northern Egypt.
History: **Lower Egypt** and **Upper Egypt** were the two kingdoms which developed in pre-dynastic times in Egypt. Horus, the falcon, was the chief god. Lower Egypt was the country of the Red Crown (Upper Egypt having the White Crown). Around 3100 B.C. Menes of Upper Egypt conquered the Northern Kingdom and united the two into **Egypt, 1st Dynasty.**
Kings: (?)–(?) Tiu; (?)–(?) Thes; (?)–(?) Askiu; (?)–(?) Waznar.

Lozi Empire see **Barotseland**

Luanda see **Dutch West Africa**

622 Luba Empire [i]. ca. 1585–ca. 1620. *Location:* southern Zaire. *Capital:* Mwibele. *Other names:* Luba Kingdom, Empire of Luba, Luba, Kingdom of Luba.
History: About 1560 a powerful warrior, Kongolo, invaded the area and subjected the several local chiefdoms, thus creating the first Luba Empire. He was joined by Ilunga Mbili, a hunter, who later returned to his homeland. A son, Ilunga Kalala, was born to Ilunga Mbili's wife (she was Kongolo's half sister), and when he came of age he developed into a great warrior and extended Kongolo's kingdom. Kongolo, jealous of the young man's success, and afraid of his power, attempted to have him killed. Kalala defeated Kongolo in war and established the second Luba Empire (see **Luba Empire [ii]**).
Emperors: ca. 1585–ca. 1620 Kongolo.

623 Luba Empire [ii]. ca. 1620–ca. 1885. *Location:* as **Luba Empire [i].** *Capital:* Munza. *Other names:* Luba, Empire of Luba.
History: About 1620 Ilunga Kalala toppled the first Luba Empire (see **Luba Empire [i]**) and established the second. Several other Luba kingdoms (vassals of Luba) were established in the area around this time (e.g. Kalundwe, Kikonja, Kaniok). Also out of Luba came the **Lunda Empire,** which far outstripped its parent in the northeast, and **Kazembe,** which arose in

what is now northern **Zambia** around
1710. About 1885 the Luba Empire was
incorporated into the **Congo Free
State.**
Emperors: ca. 1620–ca. 1640 Ilunga
Kalala; ca. 1640–ca. 1650 Kasongo
Mwine Kibanza; ca. 1650–ca. 1670
Ngoi Sanza; ca. 1670–ca. 1685 Kasongo
Kabundulu; ca. 1685–ca. 1700 Kumwimba Mputu; ca. 1700–ca. 1715 Kasongo Bonswe; ca. 1715–ca. 1740 Mwine
Kombe Dai; ca. 1740–ca. 1742 Kadilo;
ca. 1742–ca. 1749 Kekenya; ca. 1749–
ca. 1769 Kaumbo; ca. 1769–ca. 1780
Miketo; ca. 1780–ca. 1810 Ilunga Sunga;
ca. 1810–ca. 1840 Kumwimba Ngombe;
ca. 1840–ca. 1840 Ndai Mujinga; ca.
1840–ca. 1870 Ilunga Kabala; ca.
1870–ca. 1880 Muloba; ca. 1880–ca.
1882 Kitamba; ca. 1882–1885 Kasongo
Kalombo. *Kings:* 1885–1891 Dai Mande;
1891–Oct. 1917 Kasongo Nyembo.

624 Lunda Empire. ca. 1620–25
May 1891. *Location:* southern Zaire.
Capital: Musumba. *Other names:*
Lounda, Lunda Kingdom, Kingdom of
Lunda, Lunda, Empire of Lunda,
Mwata Yamvo Empire.
History: The biggest of the Luba
states, it was created when a Luba
nobleman, Cibinda Ilunga, married a
princess of the **Lunda Kingdom** and
became its king. By 1680 the Lunda
Empire, as it now was, had expanded
enormously, and the Mwata Yamvo (as
the emperor became known) developed
a reputation which spread over most of
Africa. In 1891 the Lunda Empire
became part of the **Congo Free State.**
Emperors: ca. 1620–ca. 1630 Cibinda
Ilunga; ca. 1630–ca. 1660 Yavu Ilunga.
Mwata Yamvos: ca. 1660–ca. 1687
Yavu a Nawej; ca. 1687–ca. 1719 Mbal
Iyavu; ca. 1719–ca. 1720 Mukaz Mun-
ying Kabalond; ca. 1720–ca. 1748 Muteba Kat Kateng; ca. 1748–ca. 1766
Mukaz Waranankong; ca. 1766–ca.
1773 Nawej Mufa Muchimbunj; ca.
1773–ca. 1802 Chikombi Iyavu; ca.
1802–1852 Nawej Ditend; 1852–1857
Mulaji Namwan; 1857–1873 Muteba

Chikombu; 1873–1874 Mbala Kmong
Isot; 1874–1883 Mbumb Muteba Kat;
1883–1884 Chimbindu Kasang; 1884–
1884 Kangapu Nawej; 1884–1886 Mu-
dib; 1886–1887 Mutand Mukaz; 1887–
Nov. 1887 Mbala Kalong; Nov. 1887–
1903 Mushidi; 1903–1920 Muteba III;
1920–1951 Kamba; 1951–1963 Ditend
Yavu; 1963–1965 Musidi; 1965–1975
Muteba IV; 1975–   Mbumba.

625 Lunda Kingdom. ca. 1500–ca.
1620. *Location:* southern Zaire. *Capi-
tal:* Musumba. *Other names:* Lunda,
Lounda.
History: Of unknown extraction, the
Lunda Kingdom was introduced to
Luba (see **Luba Empire**) culture by
Cibinda Ilunga who, about 1620, came
to Lunda and married its princess (see
Lunda Empire, which it became).
Kings: ca. 1500–ca. 1516 Mwaaka.
Mwata Yamvos: ca. 1516–ca. 1550 Yala
Maaku; ca. 1550–ca. 1590 Kunde; ca.
1590–ca. 1600 Luedji; ca. 1600–ca. 1620
Nkonda Matit. *Note:* the Mwata
Yamvo was the "great ruler."

626 Lydenburg Republic. 17 Dec.
1856–4 Apr. 1860. *Location:* east cen-
tral Transvaal. *Capital:* Lydenburg.
Other names: Republiek Lijdenburg,
Lijdenburg, Lydenburg.
History: In 1856 **Lydenburg Ter-
ritory** extended to take in the old area
of **Ohrigstad,** and Lydenburg was
officially declared a republic. In 1858 it
extended ever further by incorporating
the Republic of Utrecht (see **Utrecht
Republic),** and in 1860 the completed
Lydenburg merged into the **South
African Republic [i],** to make a unified
Boer Transvaal area.
Commandants-General: 17 Dec.
1856–1859 Willem Joubert; 1859–4
Apr. 1860 Joseph Van Dyck.

627 Lydenburg Territory. 1846–17
Dec. 1856. *Location:* east central Transvaal, South Africa. *Capital:* Lydenburg (formed in 1849 and named for
the "lyden" or "sufferings" of the

pioneers). *Other names:* Lydenburg, Lijdenburg.

History: In 1849 the Republic of **Ohrigstad** was abandoned due to plague and tsetse fly. The survivors left for the South to form a new territory around the town of Lydenburg. In 1856 this territory became **Lydenburg Republic.**

Commandants-General: 1846–1850 Andries Pretorius (acting); Jan. 1851–17 Dec. 1856 Willem Joubert.

Lydenrust see **Lijdenrust**

628 Machico Donatária. 1418–1580. *Location:* Madeira Island, Madeira. *Capital:* Machico.

History: see **Porto Santo Donatária** for details of history. In 1580 it became part of **Madeira Colony.**

Rulers: unknown.

Macina see **Masina**

629 Madagascar. See these **names:**
Madagascar Democratic Republic (1975–)
Malagasy Republic (1960–1975)
Madagascar Semi-Autonomous Republic (1958–1960)
Madagascar Overseas Territory (1946–1958)
Madagascar British Military Territory (1942–1946)
Madagascar Colony (1896–1942)
Madagascar Protectorate (1890–1896)
French-Controlled Madagascar (1885–1890)
Nossi-Bé Colony (1878–1896)
Nossi-Bé Dependent Colony (1843–1878)
Nossi-Bé Territory (1840–1843)
Diego Suarez Colony (1886–1896)
Sainte Marie de Madagascar Territory [ii] (1878–1896)
Sainte Marie de Madagascar Colony (1853–1878)
Sainte Marie de Madagascar Dependent Colony (1843–1853)
Sainte Marie de Madagascar Territory [i] (1818–1843)
Sainte Marie de Madagascar (1750–1818)
Fort-Dauphin Colony (1642–1674)
Libertalia (ca. 1680–ca. 1691)
Louisbourg (1774–1786)
Madagascar Kingdom (1810–1896)
Imerina (ca. 1300–1810)

630 Madagascar British Military Territory. 25 Sept. 1942–13 Oct. 1946. *Location:* as **Madagascar Colony.** *Capital:* Tananarive. *Other names:* Madagascar.

History: In 1942 Britain took the island of Madagascar (see **Madagascar Colony**), but the French governor-general continued to rule until 1946 when it was given back to France (the Fourth Republic), which made it an overseas territory of France (see **Madagascar Overseas Territory**).

Governors-General: 25 Sept. 1942–7 Jan. 1943 M. Bech (acting); 7 Jan. 1943–3 May 1943 Paul de Gentilhomme; 3 May 1943–1944 Pierre de Saint-Mart; 1944–27 March 1946 Paul de Saint-Mart; 27 March 1946–19 May 1946 Robert Boudry (acting); 19 May 1946–13 Oct. 1946 Jules de Coppet. *Occupied Territories Administrators:* 25 Sept. 1942–1943 Anthony Sillery.

631 Madagascar Colony. 6 Aug. 1896–25 Sept. 1942. *Location:* as **Madagascar Democratic Republic.** *Capital:* Tananarive (Antananarivo).

History: In 1896 a colony was created from the **Madagascar Protectorate.** In 1942 the British took temporary control (see **Madagascar British Military Territory**).

Queens: 6 Aug. 1896–28 Feb. 1897 Ranavalona III. *Residents-General:* 6 Aug. 1896–28 Sept. 1896 Hippolyte Laroche. *Governors-General:* 28 Sept. 1896–21 Apr. 1899 Gen. Joseph Galliéni; 21 Apr. 1899–3 July 1900 Gen. Pennequin (acting); 3 July 1900–11 May 1905 Gen. Joseph Galliéni; 11 May 1905–3 Dec. 1905 Charles Louis Lepreux (acting); 23 Dec. 1905–13 Dec.

1909 Jean Augagneur; 13 Dec. 1909–16 Jan. 1910 Hubert Garbit (acting); 16 Jan. 1910–31 Oct. 1910 Henri Core (acting); 31 Oct. 1910–5 Aug. 1914 Albert Picquié; 5 Aug. 1914–13 Oct. 1914 Hubert Garbit (acting); 13 Oct. 1914–24 July 1917 Hubert Garbit; 24 July 1917–1 Aug. 1918 Martial Merlin; 1 Aug. 1918–12 July 1919 Abraham Schrameck; 12 July 1919–22 June 1920 Casimir Guyon (acting); 22 June 1920–13 March 1923 Hubert Garbit; 13 March 1923–20 Feb. 1924 Charles Brunet (acting); 20 Feb. 1924–24 Jan. 1926 Marcel Olivier; 24 Jan. 1926–18 March 1927 Hugues Berthier (acting); 18 March 1927–30 Jan. 1929 Marcel Olivier; 30 Jan. 1929–1 May 1930 Hugues Berthier (acting); 1 May 1930–19 June 1931 Léon Cayla; 19 June 1931–29 Jan. 1932 Louis Bonvin (acting); 29 Jan. 1932–12 Oct. 1933 Léon Cayla; 12 Oct. 1933 29 Oct. 1934 Joseph Bernard (acting); 29 Oct. 1934–31 March 1936 Léon Cayla; 31 March 1936–17 Apr. 1937 Léonce Jore (acting); 17 Apr. 1937–22 Apr. 1939 Léon Cayla; 22 Apr. 1939–10 June 1939 Léon Reallon (acting); 10 June 1939–30 July 1940 Jules de Coppet; 30 July 1940–11 Apr. 1941 Léon Cayla; 11 Apr. 1941–25 Sept. 1942 Armand Annet.

632 Madagascar Democratic Republic. 21 Dec. 1975– . *Location:* off the east coast of Africa, in the Indian Ocean. *Capital:* Antananarivo (founded in the 17th century). *Other names:* Madagascar, Democratic Republic of Madagascar, Repoblika Demokratika n'i Madagaskar.
History: In 1975 the **Malagasy Republic** became the Democratic Republic of Madagascar.
Presidents: 21 Dec. 1975– Didier Ratsiraka. *Prime Ministers:* 21 Dec. 1975–30 July 1976 Joel Rakotomalala; 12 Aug. 1976–14 Aug. 1977 Justin Rakotoniaina; 14 Aug. 1977–Dec. 1987 Desiré Rakotoarijaona; Dec. 1987–Feb. 1988 Victor Ramahatra (acting); Feb. 1988– Victor Ramahatra.

633 Madagascar Kingdom. 1810–6 Aug. 1896. *Location:* as Madagascar. *Capital:* Antananarivo. *Other names:* Madagascar, Kingdom of Madagascar.
History: Between 1800 and 1830 the dominant native kingdom of **Imerina** extended its control over most of the island of Madagascar, with its central headquarters in Antananarivo. Thus it took in the other kingdoms of Antemoro, Sakalava, Betsimisaraka, Zafi-Raminia, Menaba and Boina, all aided by Britain in an attempt to keep the French from gaining the island. The French maintained only the island bases of **Sainte-Marie** and **Nossi-Bé**, but by 1885 they controlled all of Madagascar (see **French-Controlled Madagascar**). In 1896 the kingdom came to an end, the monarch remaining as a figurehead. This was the beginning of the **Madagascar Colony.**
Kings: 1810–27 July 1828 Radama I. *Queens:* 28 July 1828–16 Aug. 1861 Ranavalona I. *Kings:* 23 Aug. 1861–12 May 1863 Radama II. *Queens:* 12 May 1863–30 March 1868 Rasoaherina; 1 Apr. 1868–13 July 1883 Ranavalona II; 13 July 1883–6 Aug. 1896 Ranavalona III. *Prime Ministers:* 14 July 1864–6 Aug. 1896 Rainilaiarivony. *Note:* in times of no Prime Minister, the monarch fulfilled that function.

634 Madagascar Overseas Territory. 13 Oct. 1946–14 Oct. 1958. *Location:* as **Madagascar Colony.** *Capital:* Tananarive.
History: In 1946 **Madagascar British Military Territory** became French again, an overseas territory of the Fourth Republic. In 1958 it voted to become a semi-autonomous republic within the French Community (see **Madagascar Semi-Autonomous Republic**).
High Commissioners: 13 Oct. 1946–Dec. 1947 Jules de Coppet; Feb. 1948–3 Feb. 1950 Pierre de Chevigné; 3 Feb. 1950–1953 Isaac Bargues; 1953–14 Oct. 1958 Jean-Louis Soucadaux.

635 Madagascar Protectorate. 5 Aug. 1890–6 Aug. 1896. *Location:* Madagascar. *Capital:* Tananarive. *History:* In 1890 **French-Controlled Madagascar** became an official French protectorate. In 1896 it became **Madagascar Colony,** thus ending the de facto and real rule of the local kingdoms, and incorporating the other French colonies on or around the island (see **Diego Suarez, Nossi Be** and **Sainte Marie**). *Queens:* 5 Aug. 1890–6 Aug. 1896 Ranavalona III. *Residents-General:* 5 Aug. 1890–11 Oct. 1891 Maurice Bompard; 11 Oct. 1891–Oct. 1892 M. Lacoste (acting); Oct. 1892–1894 Arthur Larrouy; 1894–1 Dec. 1895 Charles Le Myre de Villiers; 1 Dec. 1895–6 Aug. 1896 Hippolyte Laroche.

636 Madagascar Semi-Autonomous Republic. 14 Oct. 1958–26 June 1960. *Location:* as **Madagascar Colony.** *Capital:* Tananarive (Antananarivo). *Other names:* Madagascar, Malagasy Republic. *History:* In 1958 **Madagascar Overseas Territory** became a semi-autonomous republic within the French Community. In 1960 it became fully independent as **Malagasy Republic.** *High Commissioners:* 14 Oct. 1958–26 June 1960 Jean-Louis Soucadaux. *Presidents:* 27 Apr. 1959–26 June 1960 Philibert Tsiranana.

637 Madeira. See these **names:**
Madeira Overseas District (1834–)
Madeira Colony (1580–1834)
Funchal Donatária (1418–1580)
Machico Donatária (1418–1580)
Porto Santo Donatária (1418–1580)

638 Madeira Colony. 1580–1834. *Location:* an archipelago of several islands, two inhabited, 360 miles off the coast of North West Africa. *Capital:* Funchal. *Other names:* Madeira, Ilhas de Madeira. *History:* In 1580 the three donatárias, **Funchal Donatária, Machico**

Donatária (these two on the island of Madeira) and **Pôrto Santo Donatária** (its own island), were united as a Portuguese colony. In 1834 Madeira became a metropolitan district of Portugal (see **Madeira Overseas District**). Between 1801–02, and 1807–14 Britain occupied the islands, but nominal Portuguese rule continued during that time.

Governors-General: 1580–1581 [unknown]; 1581–1585 João Leitão; 1585–1591 Tristão da Veiga; 1591–1595 António de Barreido; 1595–1600 Diogo de Azambuja e Melo; 1600–1603 Cristóvão de Sousa; 1603–1609 João d'Eça; 1609–1614 Manuel Coutinho; 1614–1618 Jorge da Câmara; 1618–1622 Pedro da Silva; 1622–1624 Francisco Henriques; 1624–1625 [unknown]; 1625–1626 Fernão de Saldanha; 1626–1628 Jerónimo Fernando; 1628–1634 Francisco de Sousa; 1634–1636 João de Meneses; 1636–1640 Luis Pinto; 1640–1642 [unknown]; 1642–1645 Nunho Freire; 1645–1648 Manuel Mascarenhas; 1648–1651 Manuel da Silva; 1651–1655 Bartolomeu de Vasconcelos; 1655–1660 Pedro da Silva da Cunha; 1660–1665 Diogo Furtado; 1665–1668 Francisco de Mascarenhas; 1668–1669 [unknown]; 1669–1672 Pires de Sousa e Meneses; 1672–1676 João de Saldanha e Albuquerque; 1676–1680 Alexandre de Moura e Albuquerque; 1680–1684 João de Brito; 1684–1688 Pedro Brandão; 1688–1690 Lourenço de Almada; 1690–1694 Rodrigo da Costa; 1694–1698 Pantaleão de Sá e Melo; 1698–1701 António de Melo; 1701–1704 João de Ataíde e Azevedo; 1704–1712 Duarte Pereira; 1712–1715 Pedro Álvares da Cunha; 1715–1718 João da Gama; 1718–1724 Jorge de Sousa e Meneses; 1724–1727 Francisco Freire; 1727–1734 Filipe Mascarenhas; 1734–1737 João Branco; 1737–1747 Francisco Gurjão; 1747–1751 João do Nascimento; 1751–1754 Álvaro de Távora; 1754–1757 Manuel de Saldanha e Albuquerque; 1757–1759 Gaspar Brandão; 1759–1767 José de Sá; 1767–1777 João Pereira;

1777–1781 João Coutinho; 1781–1798 Diogo Coutinho; 1798–1800 [unknown]; 1800–1803 José da Câmara; 1803–1807 Ascenso Freire; 1807–1813 Pedro de Antas e Meneses; 1813–1814 Luis de Gouveia e Almeida; 1814–1815 [unknown]; 1815–1819 Florencio de Melo; 1819–1821 Sebastião Botelho; 1821–1822 Rodrigo de Melo; 1822–1823 António de Noronha; 1823–1827 Manuel de Portugal e Castro; 1827–1828 José Valdês; 1828–1830 José Monteiro; 1830–1834 Álvaro de Sousa e Macedo.

639 Madeira Overseas Province. 1834– . *Location:* Madeira, in the North Atlantic Ocean. *Capital:* Funchal. *Other names:* Funchal District, Funchal Islands, Ilhas de Madeira.

History: In 1834 **Madeira Colony** became an overseas district of Portugal. There are two inhabited islands, Madeira and Porto Santo, and two uninhabited groups—the Desertas and the Selvagens. The Desertas comprise three islets 11 miles southeast of Madeira: Chão, Bugio and Deserta Grande, and a rock, Sail Rock. The Selvagens (or Salvage Islands) comprise three rocks located 156 miles south of Madeira.

Rulers: [unknown].

640 Mahdist State. 6 Jan. 1884–2 Sept. 1898. *Location:* as **Sudan Republic.** *Capital:* Omdurman. *Other names:* al-Mahdiyah.

History: In 1881 Muhammad Ahmad proclaimed himself The Mahdi (the awaited redeemer of Islam) in **Egyptian Sudan,** and set about a holy war against foreign rule, with the aim of re-establishing basic Islamic principles. By the beginning of 1884 it can be said that Sudan was truly Mahdist, and by the death of Gordon at Khartoum on January 26, 1885 the Mahdist State enveloped most of what is today the **Sudan Republic.** The Mahdi died soon afterward, his ideals becoming lost in the power of the new political state. In 1898 the British and Egyptians con-

quered the area, and **Sudan** became the name of the country for the next few months.

Mahdis: 29 June 1881–21 June 1885 Muhammad Ahmad ("The Mahdi"); 21 June 1885–2 Sept. 1898 Abdallah ibn-Muhammad al-Taashi ("The Khalifa").

Mahoré see **Mayotte**

Makdishu see **Mogadishu**

Makuria see **Mukurra**

641 Malagasy Republic. 26 June 1960–21 Dec. 1975. *Location:* as **Madagascar Democratic Republic.** *Capital:* Antananarivo. *Other names:* République Malgache, Republic of Madagascar, Madagascar Republic, Madagascar.

History: In 1960 **Madagascar Semi-Autonomous Republic** gained its independence from France, and in 1975 it changed its name to **Madagascar Democratic Republic.**

Presidents: 26 June 1960–18 May 1972 Philibert Tsiranana; 18 May 1972–8 Oct. 1972 Philibert Tsiranana (Titular Head of State); 18 May 1972–8 Oct. 1972 General Gabriel Ramanantsoa (Head of the National Army); 8 Oct. 1972–5 Feb. 1975 Gabriel Ramanantsoa; 5 Feb. 1975–11 Feb. 1975 Richard Ratsimandrava; 11 Feb. 1975–15 June 1975 Gilles Andriamahazo (Head of the National Military Directorate); 15 June 1975–21 Dec. 1975 Didier Ratsiraka (President of the Supreme Revolutionary Council).

642 Malawi. See these **names:**
Malawi Republic (1966–   )
Malawi (1964–1966)
Nyasaland (Self-Rule) (1963–1964)
Nyasaland Protectorate (1907–1963)
British Central Africa Protectorate (1893–1907)
Nyasaland (1891–1893)
Shiré River Protectorate (1889–1891)

643 Malawi. 6 July 1964–6 July

1966. *Location:* as **Malawi Republic.**
Capital: Zomba (named for Mount
Zomba, on whose slopes the town lies).
History: In 1964 **Nyasaland (Self-
Rule)** became independent as Malawi
(the name means "land of flames"). In
1966 it declared itself a republic (see
Malawi Republic).
Prime Ministers: 6 July 1964–6 July
1966 Hastings Banda. *Governors-General:* 6 July 1964–6 July 1966 Sir Glyn
Jones.

644 Malawi Republic. 6 July
1966– . *Location:* the extreme north
of Southern Africa. *Capital:* Lilongwe
(established as a town in 1947, chosen
as the new capital in 1964, and was the
capital from January 1, 1975); Zomba
(until January 1, 1975). *Other names:*
The Republic of Malawi, Malaŵi.
History: In 1966 **Malawi** became a
republic within the British Commonwealth.
Presidents: 6 July 1966–6 July 1971
Dr. Hastings Banda; 6 July 1971– Dr.
Hastings Banda (President for Life).

645 Mali. See these **names:**
Mali Republic (1960–)
Sudanese Republic (1960–1960)
Mali Federation (1960–1960)
Mali Autonomous Federation (1959–
1960)
Sudanese Republic Territory (1959–
1960)
Sudanese Republic (Autonomous)
(1958–1959)
French Sudan Overseas Territory
(1946–1958)
French Sudan (1920–1946)
Upper Senegal and Niger Colony
(1904–1920)
Senegambia and Niger Territories
(1902–1904)
Upper Senegal and Niger Territory
(1899–1902)
French Sudan Colony (1895–1899)
French Sudan Civil Territory (1893–
1895)
French Sudan Military Territory
(1892–1893)

French Sudan Territory (1890–1892)
Upper Senegal Protectorate (1881–
1890)
Upper Senegal Territory (1880–1881)
Beledugu (ca. 1670–1870)
Ghana Empire (ca. 350–1240)
Kangaba Kingdom (ca. 1050–ca.
1237)
Mali Empire (ca. 1237–1464)
Masina (ca. 1400–1862)
Segu (ca. 1600–1861)
Songhai Empire (1464–1640)
Songhai Kingdom (ca. 500–1464)
Timbuktu (1591–1780)
Tukolor Empire (1854–1891)

646 Mali Autonomous Federation.
4 Apr. 1959–20 June 1960. *Location:* as
Mali Federation. *Capital:* Dakar.
Other names: Mali Federation, Autonomous Mali Federation, Sudan Federation.
History: On January 17, 1959 (implemented April 4) **Senegal Autonomous Republic** and **Sudanese Republic
(Autonomous)** got together to form the
Mali Federation, an autonomous body
within the French Community, composed of two component territories
therefore: **Senegal** and **Sudanese Republic Territory.** In 1960 the whole
federation became independent from
France (see **Mali Federation**). Two
other countries were to have joined but
backed out at the last moment—**Upper
Volta Autonomous Republic** and
Dahomey Autonomous Republic.
Presidents: 4 Apr. 1959–20 June 1960
Modibo Keita. *Vice-Presidents:* 4 Apr.
1959–20 June 1960 Mamadou Dia.
Heads of the Federal Assembly: 4 Apr.
1959–20 June 1960 Léopold Senghor.

647 Mali Empire. ca. 1237–1464.
Location: West Africa, from the coast
of Senegal to the Niger River. *Capital:*
Djeriba (or Niani). *Other names:* Empire of Mali, Mali (name means "where
the king lives"), Malinke Empire, Mandingo Empire.
History: About 1237 Sundiata Keita,

the king of **Kangaba Kingdom** conquered the **Ghana Empire,** thus establishing the new Mandingo empire of Mali. A Mandingo himself, Sundiata Keita ruled until 1255, when his successor adopted the title of Mansa (Emperor). Under Mansa Musa it reached its peak. By the beginning of the 15th century revolts and invasions began to take their toll and the empire began to crumble. It was replaced as the power in the area by the **Songhai Empire,** although nominal Mansas continued to rule.
Military Commanders: ca. 1237–1255 Mari Jata I (or Sundiata Keita). *Mansas:* 1255–1270 Uli; 1270–1274 Wati; 1274–1274 Khalifa; 1274–1285 Abu Bakr I; 1285–1300 Sakura (usurper); 1300–1305 Qu; 1305–1310 Muhammad; 1310–1312 Abu Bakr II; 1312–1337 Musa I (or Kankan Musa); 1337–1341 Magha I; 1341–1360 Suleiman; 1360–1360 Qasa; 1360–1374 Mari Jata II; 1374–1387 Musa II; 1387–1388 Magha II; 1388–1390 Sandaki (usurper); 1390–ca. 1420 Magha III; ca. 1420–ca. 1460 Musa III; ca. 1460–ca. 1480 Mule; ca. 1480–1496 Muhammad II; 1497–1536 Muhammad III; 1536–1590 [unknown]; 1590–ca. 1610 Nyani Mansa Muhammad; ca. 1610–ca. 1670 [unknown]; ca. 1670–(?) Mama Magha.

648 Mali Federation. 20 June 1960–20 Aug. 1960. *Location:* Mali and Senegal. *Capital:* Dakar (originally a coastal village, the name comes from the Wolof word "dakhar" meaning "the tamarind tree"). *Other names:* Sudan Federation.
History: In 1960 the **Mali Autonomous Federation** became independent from France, taking into independence its two component parts—**Senegal** and **Sudanese Republic Territory.** Later in the year Senegal seceded and the two countries became **Senegal Republic** and **Sudanese Republic.**
Presidents: 20 June 1960–20 Aug. 1960 Modibo Keita. *Vice-Presidents:*

20 June 1960–20 Aug. 1960 Mamadou Dia. *Heads of the Federal Assembly:* 20 June 1960–20 Aug. 1960 Léopold Senghor.

Mali Kingdom see **Kangaba Kingdom**

649 Mali Republic. 22 Sept. 1960– . *Location:* North West Africa. *Capital:* Bamako (originally a local settlement and occupied by the French in 1880). *Other names:* République du Mali, Republic of Mali, Mali.
History: In 1960 the **Sudanese Republic** became the Republic of Mali, named after the old **Mali Empire** (the name meaning "where the king resides").
Presidents: 22 Sept. 1960–19 Nov. 1968 Modibo Keita; 19 Nov. 1968–6 Dec. 1968 Yoro Diakité and Moussa Traoré (Military Leaders); 6 Dec. 1968–19 Sept. 1969 Moussa Traoré (Chairman of Military Committee of National Liberation); 19 Sept. 1969–Moussa Traoré. *Prime Ministers:* 6 Dec. 1968–19 Sept. 1969 Yoro Diakité; 6 June 1986– Mamadou Dembele. *Note:* in times of no Prime Minister, the President held that office.

Malinke Empire see **Mali Empire**

Mameluke Egypt see **Bahrite** and **Circassian Mameluke** entries

Mamprusi see **Mossi States**

650 Mandara. ca. 1500–1902. *Location:* Cameroun. *Capital:* Mora (from 1894); Dulo (ca. 1580–1894). *Other names:* Wandala.
History: The Kingdom of Mandara was founded around 1500 and in 1902 was taken over by the Germans as part of **Kamerun.**
Kings: ca. 1500–(?) Sukda; (?)–(?) [unknown]; (?)–(?) Ti-Maya; ca. 1600–ca. 1619 Sankré; ca. 1619–(?) Aldawa Nanda; (?)–(?) [unknown]; (?)–ca. 1715 Naldawa Nazariza. *Sultans:*

ca. 1715–ca. 1737 Mai Bukar Aji; ca. 1737–1757 Mahmadi Makia; 1757–1773 Ti-Kse Bldi; 1773–1828 Bukar D'Gjiama; 1828–1842 Hiassae; 1842–1894 Bukar Narbanha; 1895–1911 Umar Adjara; 1911–1915 Bukar Afade; 1915–1922 Umar Adjara; 1922–May 1924 Amada; May 1924–March 1926 Kola Adama; March 1926–18 March 1942 Bukar Afade; 18 March 1942– Hamidu Umar.

Mandingo Empire see **Mali Empire**

Mandinka Empire see **Samory's Empire**

Maqdishu see **Mogadishu**

Maqurrah see **Mukurra**

Marinid see **Merinid**

651 Maryland Colony. 12 Feb. 1834–8 June 1854. *Location:* present-day Maryland County, Liberia (i.e. on Cape Palmas). *Capital:* Harper (founded 1834). *Other names:* Maryland-in-Africa, Maryland, Maryland-in-Liberia.
History: Founded in 1834 by James Hall of the Maryland State Colonization Society, it became in 1854 an independent republic, **Maryland-in-Liberia.**
Governors: 12 Feb. 1834–Feb. 1836 Dr. James Hall; Feb. 1836–1 July 1836 Oliver Holmes, Jr.; 1 July 1836–28 Sept. 1836 ruled by a three-man committee; 28 Sept. 1836–1848 John Russwurm; 1848–1848 Dr. Samuel F. McGill (acting); 1848–9 June 1851 John Russwurm; 9 June 1851–6 June 1854 Dr. Samuel F. McGill (acting).

652 Maryland-in-Liberia. 8 June 1854–19 Feb. 1857. *Location:* present-day Maryland County, Liberia. *Capital:* Harper (formerly called Cape Palmas, and renamed for Robert Good-loe Harper, a local citizen and supporter). *Other names:* The Republic of Maryland-in-Liberia, Maryland-in-Africa.
History: In 1854 **Maryland Colony** became an independent republic, calling itself Maryland-in-Liberia. In 1857 it became part of **Liberia Republic,** as Maryland County.
Governors: 8 June 1854–Dec. 1855 William A. Prout; Dec. 1855–June 1856 Boston Drayton (acting); June 1856–19 Feb. 1857 Boston Drayton.

653 Mascara. 22 Nov. 1832–Dec. 1847. *Location:* northern Algeria. *Capital:* no capital from 1843–47; Tiaret (1835–43. Also Tahart, the name means "the lioness." The town is now called Tagdemt); Mascara (until 1835. Mascara means "mother of soldiers" and was founded as a Turkish military garrison in 1701). *Other names:* Mascaran Emirate, Mascara Emirate.
History: In 1832 Abdelkedir (Abd al-Qadir), the legendary Algerian leader, formed his own state, a real political state, in the armpit of the French (see **French Possessions in North Africa**). He harassed the French to such an extent that in 1837 France signed the Treaty of Tafna with him, which gave Abdelkedir control of the entire interior of the provinces of Oran and the Titteri. The town of Mascara had been laid to ruins by the French in 1835 and Abdelkedir moved his capital to the fortress of Tiaret. In 1840 the French moved against him in force and took Tiaret in 1843. From that time Abdelkedir was mostly in Morocco. In 1847 he was forced to surrender, and the Emirate of Mascara (the first modern state in Algeria) became part of **French Algeria Military Province.**
Emirs: 22 Nov. 1832–Dec. 1847 Abdelkedir (or Abd al-Qadir).

654 Mashonaland Protectorate. 29 Oct. 1889–23 Jan. 1894. *Location:* Zimbabwe. *Capital:* Fort Salisbury (from September 10, 1890).
History: In 1889 the area of Mashonaland was made into a British protec-

torate, courtesy of the British South Africa Company. In 1894 **Matabeleland** another conquest, was added to it, and the joint area became known as **South Zambesia**.

Rulers: 29 Oct. 1889–29 June 1890 no fixed rule; 29 June 1890–17 Sept. 1891 Archibald Colquhoun (acting Resident-Commissioner); 18 Sept. 1891–8 Oct. 1893 Dr. Leander Starr Jameson (Chief Magistrate); 8 Oct. 1893–23 Jan. 1894 Andrew Duncan (Acting Chief Magistrate).

655 Masina. ca. 1400–1862. *Location:* Mali. *Capital:* Hamdallahi (from 1819). *Other names:* Macina.

History: Founded about 1400 by the Fulanis, Masina was conquered by the **Tukolor Empire** in 1862.

Kings: ca. 1400–1404 Majan Dyallo; 1404–1424 Birahim I; 1424–1433 Ali I; 1433–1466 Kanta; 1466–1480 Ali II; 1480–1510 Nguia; 1510–1539 Sawadi; 1539–1540 Ilo; 1540–1543 Amadi Sire; 1543–1544 Hammadi I; 1544–1551 Bubu I; 1551–1559 Ibrahim; 1559–1583 Bubu II; 1583–ca. 1595 Hammadi II; ca. 1595–1599 Moroccan rule; 1599–1603 Hammadi II; 1603–1613 Bubu III; 1613–1625 Birahim II; 1625–1627 Silamaran; 1627–1663 Hammadi III; 1663–1663 Hammadi IV; 1663–1673 Ali III; 1673–1675 Gallo; 1675–1696 Gurori I; 1696–1706 Gueladio; 1706–1761 Guidado; 1761–1780 Hammadi V; 1780–1801 Ya Gallo; 1801–1810 Gurori II; 1810–1814 [unknown]. *Sheikhs:* 1814–1844 Hamadu I; 1844–1852 Hamadu II; 1852–1862 Hamadu III; 1862–1863 under Tukolor military government. *Tukolor Regents:* 1863–1864 Sidi al-Bakka; 1864–1864 Sheikh Abidin al-Bakha'i. *Sheikhs:* 1864–1871 Badi Tali; 1871–1872 Badi Sidi; 1872–1873 Ahmadu. *Tukolor Regents:* 1873–1874 Sheikh Abidin al-Bakha'i.

656 Masmouda Pirates' Republic. ca. 1602–1614. *Location:* on the Moroccan coast. *Capital:* Masmouda. *Other names:* Masmudah, Masmouda.

History: Founded by buccaneer Captain Henry Mainwaring, it took its name from the Berber tribe, the Masmudah. In 1614 it was incorporated into **Sa'did Morocco**.

Rulers: unknown.

657 Massawa Protectorate. 6 Feb. 1885–1 Jan. 1890. *Location:* central Eritrean coast, Ethiopia. *Capital:* Massawa. *Other names:* Mitsiwa.

History: In 1885 Massawa was taken by the Italians. That and **Assab** were combined in 1890 with the Danakil area to form **Eritrea Colony**.

Commandants: 6 Feb. 1885–15 Dec. 1885 Tancredi Saletta; 15 Dec. 1885–18 March 1887 Carlo Gene; 18 March 1887–Oct. 1887 Tancredi Saletta; Nov. 1887–1888 Alessandro di San Marzano; 1888–20 Dec. 1889 Antonio Baldissera; 20 Dec. 1889–1 Jan. 1890 Baldassare Orero.

658 Matabeleland. Nov. 1837–Jan. 1894. *Location:* Zimbabwe. *Capital:* Bulawayo (from 1881. Founded in 1838); Inyati (1837–70). *Other names:* Ndebeleland, Moselekatze's Land, Mzilikazi's Land, Matabele Empire.

History: In 1836–37 the all-conquering Zulu refugee, Mzilikazi (or Moselekatze), and his cross-sectional band of warriors were defeated by the Boers and forced across the Limpopo into what is now Zimbabwe. Here they formed the Matabele Empire which covered all of what is today Zimbabwe. Mzilikazi, leader of the Northern Khumalo branch of the Zulu, died in 1868, and, after two years of succession disputes, his son, Lobengula, came to the throne. On Feb. 11, 1888 Matabeleland came under British domination as **Zambesia** was roughly hewn, and the Matabele fell under a British protectorate until 1894 when the tribe was finally conquered, being added to **Mashonaland Protectorate** to form **South Zambesia**. *Note:* The Matabele were an offshoot of the Zulus. Mzilikazi had served under Chaka (see

Zululand), and had been condemned to death. He fled north with a large part of the Zulu army, and in 1817 he settled north of the Vaal River, near what is now Pretoria. By 1836 they were a very important tribe. The name means "Men of the long shields."
Chiefs of the Northern Khumalo: (?)–(?) Zazalita; (?)–(?) Langa; (?)–(?) Mangete; (?)–1818 Mashobane; 1818–Nov. 1837 Mzilikazi (or Moselekatze). *Matabele Kings:* Nov. 1837–9 Sept. 1868 Mzilikazi (or Moselekatze). *Regents:* 9 Sept. 1868–24 Jan. 1870 Nombate. *Matabele Kings:* 24 Jan. 1870–Jan. 1894 Lobengula.

659 Mauretania [i]. (?)–ca. 100 B.C. *Location:* northern Morocco and northern Algeria. *Capital:* Iol.
History: Of ancient origin Mauretania was inhabited for centuries by tribes known to the Romans as Massaesyli or Mauri. Around 100 B.C. it was split into two—**Mauretania West** and **Mauretania East.**
Only known King: ca. 206 B.C. Baqa.

660 Mauretania [ii]. 38 B.C.–33 B.C. *Location:* northern Morocco and northern Algeria. *Capital:* Iol.
History: In 38 B.C. Bocchus III united **Mauretania West** and **Mauretania East.** Five years later he gave his united kingdom to the Romans as a gift (see **Mauretania [Roman]**).
Kings: 38 B.C.–33 B.C. Bocchus III.

661 Mauretania Caesariensis. 42 A.D.–ca. 395. *Location:* northern Algeria. *Capital:* Caesarea Mauretaniae (from about 300); Caesarea (now Cherchel) (until ca. 300).
History: In 42 A.D. **Mauretania (Roman)** was split into two sections—Caesariensis (meaning "of Caesar") and Tingitana (meaning "of Tingis") (see **Mauretania Tingitana**). Later, out of a part of Caesariensis was formed **Mauretania Sitifensis**, in 297. About 395 the rest of Caesariensis came under

the Roman Prefecture of Italy (Subdivision: Diocese of Africa).
Rulers: 42–ca. 395 [unknown].

662 Mauretania East. ca. 100 B.C.–38 B.C. *Location:* northern Algeria. *Capital:* Iol. *Other names:* East Mauretania.
History: About 100 B.C. **Mauretania [i]** was divided into Mauretania East and **Mauretania West.** In 38 B.C. it was re-united by Bocchus III into **Mauretania [ii].**
Kings: ca. 100 B.C.–85 B.C. Bocchus I; 85 B.C.–82 B.C. Volux; 82 B.C.–ca. 51 B.C. Bogud; ca. 51 B.C.–38 B.C. Bocchus III. *Note:* for Bocchus II see **Mauretania West.**

663 Mauretania (Roman). 33 B.C.–42 A.D. *Location:* northern Morocco and northern Algeria. *Capital:* Caesarea (after 25 B.C.); Iol (until 25 B.C.).
History: In 33 B.C. **Mauretania [ii]** was given to the Romans by Bocchus III, and the Romans allowed the Mauretanians to continue to rule it. In 42 A.D. the Romans occupied it and divided it into **Mauretania Tingitana** (the old **Mauretania West)** and **Mauretania Caesariensis** (the old **Mauretania East).**
Caretaker Kings: 33 B.C.–25 B.C. Bocchus III; 25 B.C.–23 A.D. Caius Julius Juba II; 23 A.D.–40 A.D. Ptolemaeus; 40 A.D.–42 A.D. Aedemon.

664 Mauretania Sitifensis. 297–435. *Location:* eastern Algeria. *Capital:* Sitifis (now Setif).
History: Formed out of the eastern part of **Mauretania Caesariensis** by Diocletian in 297 A.D., Sitifensis went to the Vandals by agreement in 435 (see **Vandal North Africa**).
Rulers: 297–435 [unknown].

665 Mauretania Tingitana. 42 A.D.–ca. 395. *Location:* northern Morocco. *Capital:* Tingis (now Tangier).
History: In 42 A.D. **Mauretania**

(Roman) was formally annexed by the Romans and divided into Mauretania Tingitana in the west and **Mauretania Caesariensis** in the east. About the year 300 the Romans gave up a lot of Tingitana to the Baquate tribe, and around 395 the rest came under the Roman Prefecture of Gaul (Subdivision: The Diocese of Spain).
Rulers: 42–ca. 395 [unknown].

666 Mauretania West. ca. 100 B.C.–38 B.C. *Location:* northern Morocco. *Capital:* Tingis. *Other names:* West Mauretania.
History: About 100 B.C. **Mauretania [i]** was split into Mauretania West and **Mauretania East.** In 38 B.C. Bocchus III re-united the two to re-form Mauretania (see **Mauretania [ii]**).
Kings: ca. 100 B.C.–ca. 85 B.C. Iphthas; ca. 85 B.C.–ca. 70 B.C. Askalis; ca. 70 B.C.–ca. 56 B.C. Bocchus II; ca. 56 B.C.–ca. 51 B.C. Sosus; ca. 51 B.C.–38 B.C. Bogud II. *Note:* for Bocchus I and Bocchus III see **Mauretania East.**

667 Mauritania. See these **names:**
Mauritania Republic (1960–)
Mauritania Autonomous Republic (1958–1960)
Mauritania Overseas Territory (1949–1958)
Mauritania Colony (1921–1949)
Mauritania Civil Territory (1904–1921)
Mauritania Protectorate (1903–1904)
Trarza Protectorate (1902–1903)
Adrar (ca. 1800–1909)
Brakna (ca. 1650–1904)
Kaarta (ca. 1610–1854)
Tagant (ca. 1580–1905)
Trarza (ca. 1640–1902)

668 Mauritania Autonomous Republic. 28 Nov. 1958–28 Nov. 1960. *Location:* as **Mauritania Republic.** *Capital:* Saint Louis (Senegal). *Other names:* Autonomous Republic of Mauritania, Mauritania Islamic Republic, Mauritania, Islamic Republic

of Mauritania.
History: In 1958 **Mauritania Overseas Territory** became an autonomous republic within the French Community. In 1960 it became fully independent, as **Mauritania Republic.**
High Commissioners: 28 Nov. 1958–Feb. 1959 Henri Bernard; Feb. 1959–28 Nov. 1960 Pierre Anthonioz. *Chairmen of Executive Council:* 28 Nov. 1958–23 June 1959 Mokhtar Ould Daddah. *Prime Ministers:* 23 June 1959–28 Nov. 1960 Mokhtar Ould Daddah.

669 Mauritania Civil Territory. 18 Oct. 1904–1 Jan. 1921. *Location:* as **Mauritania Republic.** *Capital:* Saint Louis (Senegal). *Other names:* Mauritania.
History: In 1904 **Mauritania Protectorate** became a civil territory of France. In 1920 (effective from January 1, 1921) it became **Mauritania Colony.**
Commandants: 18 Oct. 1904–12 May 1905 Xavier Coppolani; 12 May 1905–27 May 1905 Capt. Frerejean (acting); 27 May 1905–Sept. 1907 Bernard Capdebosq; Sept. 1907–1909 Col. Henri Gouraud; 1909–1909 Col. Claudel (acting); 1909–1 Jan. 1910 Col. Aubert (acting); 1 Jan. 1910–1 March 1912 Col. Henri Patey; 1 March 1912–Apr. 1914 Col. Charles Mouret; Apr. 1914–17 Nov. 1916 Louis Obissier; 17 Nov. 1916–11 Dec. 1920 Henri Gaden. *Lieutenant-Governors:* 11 Dec. 1920–1 Jan. 1921 Henri Gaden.

670 Mauritania Colony. 1 Jan. 1921–7 Aug. 1949. *Location:* as **Mauritania Republic.** *Capital:* Saint Louis (Senegal). *Other names:* Mauritania, Mauritanie.
History: In 1920 (effective from January 1, 1921) **Mauritania Civil Territory** became a colony. In 1949 it became **Mauritania Overseas Territory.**
Lieutenant-Governors: 1 Jan. 1921–Dec. 1927 Henri Gaden; 13 Jan. 1928–27 Jan. 1928 Alphonse Choteau; 27

Jan. 1928–Oct. 1928 René Chazal (acting); Oct. 1928–21 Nov. 1929 Alphonse Choteau; 21 Nov. 1929–19 June 1931 René Chazal; 19 June 1931–22 June 1933 Gabriel Descemet; 22 June 1933–7 Apr. 1934 Louis Antonin (acting); 7 Apr. 1934–5 July 1934 Gabriel Descemet; 5 July 1934–Aug. 1934 Adolphe Deitte; Aug. 1934–1 Sept. 1934 Jean-Baptiste Chazelas (acting); 1 Sept. 1934–15 Apr. 1935 Richard Brunot; 15 Apr. 1935–10 Sept. 1935 Jean-Baptiste Chazelas (acting); 10 Sept. 1935–1 Sept. 1936 Jules de Coppet; 1 Sept. 1936–24 Oct. 1936 Jean-Louis Beyriès (acting); 24 Oct. 1936–7 Aug. 1938 Oswald Durand (acting); 7 Aug. 1938–Nov. 1938 Charles Dumas (acting); Nov. 1938–28 Aug. 1941 Jean-Louis Beyriès (acting); 28 Aug. 1941–4 May 1944 Jean-Louis Beyriès; 4 May 1944–31 July 1945 Christian Laigret; 31 July 1945–30 Apr. 1946 René Babin (acting); 30 Apr. 1946–19 July 1947 Georges Poirier (acting); 19 July 1947–31 Dec. 1947 Lucien Geay; 1 Jan. 1948–7 Aug. 1949 Henri de Mauduit.

671 Mauritania Overseas Territory. 7 Aug. 1949–28 Nov. 1958. *Location:* as **Mauritania Republic.** *Capital:* Saint Louis (Senegal). *Other names:* Mauritania.

History: In 1949 **Mauritania Colony** became an overseas territory of the French Fourth Republic. In 1958 it became the **Mauritania Autonomous State.**

Lieutenant-Governors: 7 Aug. 1949–21 Sept. 1950 Édouard Terrac (acting). *Governors:* 21 Sept. 1950–25 Apr. 1952 Jacques Rogué; 25 Apr. 1952–6 Apr. 1954 Pierre Messmer; 6 Apr. 1954–23 June 1955 Albert Mouragues; 23 June 1955–14 May 1956 Jean-Paul Parisot; 14 May 1956–5 Oct. 1958 Albert Mouragues. *High Commissioners:* 5 Oct. 1958–28 Nov. 1958 Henri Bernard. *Chairmen of Executive Council:* 21 May 1957–28 Nov. 1958 Mokhtar Ould Daddah.

672 Mauritania Protectorate. 12 May 1903–18 Oct. 1904. *Location:* as **Mauritania Republic.** *Capital:* Saint Louis (Senegal). *Other names:* Mauritania.

History: In 1905 a protectorate was established over most of what is today **Mauritania Republic,** by the French commandant Coppolani. It was really an extension of **Trarza Protectorate** which had been created the year before, and by 1903–1904 most of the other kingdoms and emirates in the area had been brought into the Mauritania Protectorate. In 1904 it became **Mauritania Civil Territory.**

Commandants: 12 May 1903–18 Oct. 1904 Xavier Coppolani.

673 Mauritania Republic. 28 Nov. 1960– . North West Africa. *Capital:* Nouakchott (developed as a city and as the capital after independence). *Other names:* Republic of Mauritania, Islamic Republic of Mauritania, Mauritania, Mauritania Islamic Republic.

History: Mauritania (meaning "land of the Moors") became independent from France in 1960. Prior to this it was an autonomous republic within the French Community (see **Mauritania Autonomous Republic**). It held southern Spanish Sahara (see **Saharan Arab Democratic Republic** for details) from February 28, 1976 until 1980.

Presidents: 20 Aug. 1961–10 July 1978 Mokhtar Ould Daddah; 10 July 1978–3 June 1979 Mustafa Ould Saleck (Leader of the Military Committee for National Salvation); 3 June 1979–4 Jan. 1980 Muhammad Mahmoud Ould Ahmad Louly; 4 Jan. 1980–12 Dec. 1984 Muhammad Ould Haidalla; 12 Dec. 1984– Maaouya Ould Sidi Ahmad Taya. *Prime Ministers:* 28 Nov. 1960–20 Aug. 1961 Mokhtar Ould Daddah; 6 Apr. 1979–27 May 1979 Ahmad Ould Bouceif; 27 May 1979–31 May 1979 Ahmad Salem Ould Sidi (interim); 31 May 1979–4 Jan. 1980 Muhammad Ould Haidalla; 12 Dec. 1980–25 Apr. 1981 Sidi Ahmad Ould Bneijara; 26

Apr. 1981-8 March 1984 Maaouya Ould Sidi Ahmad Taya. *Note:* in times of no Prime Minister, the President held that office.

674 Mauritius. See these **names:**
Mauritius (1968–)
Mauritius Colony (1814–1968)
British-Occupied Mauritius (1810–1814)
Île de France Colony (1767–1810)
Île de France (1722–1767)
French Mauritius (1715–1722)
Dutch Mauritius Colony [ii] (1664–1710)
Dutch Mauritius [ii] (1658–1664)
Dutch Mauritius Colony [i] (1638–1658)
Dutch Mauritius [i] (1598–1638)
Ilha do Cerne (1507–1598)
Rodrigues Dependency (1814–)
Rodrigues Colony (1638–1814)
Diego Ruy's Island (1507–1638)

675 Mauritius. 12 March 1968– . *Location:* east of Madagascar in the Indian Ocean (including **Rodrigues**). *Capital:* Port Louis. *History:* In 1968 **Mauritius Colony** became independent from Britain. *Prime Ministers:* 12 March 1968-11 June 1982 Sir Seewoosagur Ramgoolam; 11 June 1982– Aneerood Jugnauth. *Governors-General:* 12 March 1968-3 Sept. 1968 Sir John Rennie; 3 Sept. 1968-Aug. 1970 Sir Len Williams; Aug. 1970-Oct. 1970 Sir Abdul Raman Osman (acting); Oct. 1970-Dec. 1971 Sir Len Williams; Dec. 1971-Feb. 1972 Sir Abdul Raman Osman (acting); Feb. 1972-27 Dec. 1972 Sir Len Williams; 27 Dec. 1972-31 Oct. 1977 Sir Abdul Raman Osman; 31 Oct. 1977-24 March 1978 Henry Garrioch (acting); 24 March 1978-26 Apr. 1979 Sir Abdul Raman Osman; 26 Apr. 1979-17 Jan. 1986 Dayendranath Burrenchobay; 17 Jan. 1986– Sir Veerasamy Ringadoo.

676 Mauritius Colony. 30 May 1814–12 March 1968. *Location:* as **Mauritius.** *Capital:* Port Louis. *Other names:* Mauritius.

History: In 1814 Britain was officially ceded **British-Occupied Mauritius.** In 1968 the island finally became independent as **Mauritius.**

Governors: 30 May 1814–1817 Sir Robert Farquhar; 1817–1818 Gage Hall (acting); 1818–1819 John Dalrymple (acting); 1819–1820 Ralph Darling (acting); 1820–1823 Sir Robert Farquhar; 1823–1828 Sir Lowry Cole; 1828–1833 Sir Charles Colville; 1833–1840 Sir William Nicolay; 1840–1842 Sir Lionel Smith; 1842–1849 Sir William Gomm; 1849–1850 Sir George Anderson; 1850–1851 [unknown]; 1851–1857 Sir James Higginson; 1857–1863 Sir William Stevenson; 1863–Dec. 1870 Sir Henry Barkly; Dec. 1870–1871 [unknown]; 1871–1874 Baron Stanmore; 1874–1879 Sir Arthur Phayre; 1879–1880 Sir George Bowen; 1880–1882 Sir Frederick Broome; 1882–1883 [unknown]; 1883–1887 Sir John Pope Hennessey; 1887–1888 Francis Fleming (acting); 1888–1889 Sir John Pope Hennessey; 1889–1892 Sir Charles Lees; 1892–1894 Sir Hubert Jerningham; 1894–1894 Charles King-Harman (acting); 1894–1897 Sir Hubert Jerningham; 1897–1903 Sir Charles Bruce; 1903–20 Aug. 1904 [unknown]; 20 Aug. 1904–1911 Cavendish Boyle; 1911–13 Nov. 1911 George Smith (acting); 13 Nov. 1911–1914 John Chancellor (knighted 1913); 1914–1914 John Middleton (acting); 1914–18 May 1916 Sir John Chancellor; 18 May 1916–1921 Sir Hesketh Bell; 1921–1921 Edward Denham (acting); 1921–19 Feb. 1925 Sir Hesketh Bell; 19 Feb. 1925–30 Aug. 1930 Herbert Read; 30 Aug. 1930–21 Oct. 1937 Wilfred Jackson (knighted 1931); 21 Oct. 1937–5 July 1942 Sir Bede Clifford; 5 July 1942–May 1949 Sir Donald Mackenzie-Kennedy; May 1949–26 Sept. 1949 [unknown] (acting); 26 Sept. 1949–30 July 1953 Sir Hilary Blood; 30 July 1953–22 Apr. 1954 [unknown] (acting); 22 Apr. 1954–25 Oct. 1959 Sir Robert Scott; 3 Nov. 1959–17 Sept. 1962 Sir Colville Deverell; 17 Sept. 1962–12

March 1968 Sir John Rennie. *Chief Ministers:* 26 Sept. 1961–12 March 1964 Sir Seewoosagur Ramgoolam. *Prime Ministers:* 12 March 1964–12 March 1968 Sir Seewoosagur Ramgoolam.

677 Mayotte. ca. 1515–25 March 1841. *Location:* Comoros, in the Indian Ocean. *Capital:* Chingoni (latterly); Msamboro (formerly). *Other names:* Mayuta, Mahoré, Mayotte Sultanate.

History: The Kingdom of Mayotte, founded about 1515, had several encounters with French pirates, as did all of the Comoros Islands prior to the French protectorate (see **Anjouan, Moheli, Andruna, Gran Comoro**). That protectorate (see **Mayotte Protectorate**) came about in 1841, six years after **Anjouan** had occupied it.

Sultans: ca. 1515–ca. 1530 Hassan I; ca. 1530–ca. 1550 Muhammad; ca. 1550–ca. 1590 Isa. *Queens-Regent:* ca. 1590–ca. 1595 Amina. *Regents:* ca. 1595–ca. 1620 Bwana Fuma ibn Ali. *Sultans:* ca. 1620–ca. 1640 Ali I; ca. 1640–ca. 1680 Umar; ca. 1680–ca. 1700 Ali II. *Queens-Regent:* ca. 1700–ca. 1714 Aisa; ca. 1714–ca. 1720 Monavo Fani. *Sultans:* ca. 1720–1727 Abu Bakr; 1727–1752 Salim I; 1752–1790 Bwana Kombo I; 1790–1807 Salim II; 1807–1817 Salih; 1817–1829 Ahmad; 1829–1832 Bwana Kombo II; 1832–19 Nov. 1835 Andrianametaka. *Anjouan Qadis in Charge:* 19 Nov. 1835–ca. 1838 Umar; ca. 1838–25 March 1841 Adriantsuli.

678 Mayotte Department. 9 Feb. 1976– . *Location:* in the Comoros. *Capital:* Dzaoudzi. *Other names:* The Territorial Collectivity of Mayotte, Mahoré.

History: The **Comoros** became independent in 1975. On December 22, 1974 and on February 9, 1976 the island of Mayotte voted to remain a French territory, an overseas dependency of France. However, the **Comoros Republic** claims it as an integral part of their country.

Commissioners of the Republic (or Prefects): 9 Feb. 1976–1978 Jean-Marie Cousirou; 1978–1980 Jean Rigotard; 1980–1981 Philip Kessler; 6 Jan. 1982–Jan. 1983 Christian Pellerin; Jan. 1983–1985 Yves Bonnet; 1985– François Bonelle. *Presidents of the General Council:* Jan. 1983– Younoussa Bamana.

679 Mayotte Protectorate. 25 March 1841–5 Sept. 1887. *Location:* one of the Comoros Islands in the Indian Ocean. *Capital:* Chingoni.

History: In 1841 Andriantsuli, the local king, ceded **Mayotte** to the French, who occupied it in 1843. The neighboring islands in the archipelago became part of the new French protectorate: **Andruna** in 1852, **Anjouan** in 1866, **Mohéli** in 1886, and **Moroni** in 1893. By the time of the inclusion of Moroni, Mayotte Protectorate had become known as the **Comoros Protectorate** (in 1887).

Commandants: 29 Aug. 1843–16 June 1844 Paul Rang; 16 June 1844–22 Oct. 1844 Capt. A. Thiebault (acting); 22 Oct. 1844–5 Jan. 1846 Auguste Lebrun; 5 Jan. 1846–11 Dec. 1849 Pierre Passot. *Commissioners:* 11 Dec. 1849–13 June 1851 Stanislas Livet; 13 June 1851–18 Oct. 1853 Philibert Bonfils; 18 Oct. 1853–12 Dec. 1855 André Brisset; 12 Dec. 1855–12 Dec. 1857 André-César Vérand; 12 Dec. 1857–14 Aug. 1860 Charles Morel; 14 Aug. 1860–10 Dec. 1864 Charles Gabrié; 10 Dec. 1864–8 July 1868 Joseph Colomb; 8 July 1868–15 Apr. 1869 Joseph Hayes (acting); 15 Apr. 1869–21 May 1869 L.G. Leguay (acting); 21 May 1869–4 March 1871 Joseph Colomb; 4 March 1871–19 Dec. 1871 Jules Ventre de la Touloubre (acting); 19 Dec. 1871–1 March 1875 Jules Ventre de la Touloubre; 1 March 1875–16 Sept. 1875 Claude Fontaine (acting); 16 Sept. 1875–26 Dec. 1875 François Perriez (acting); 26 Dec. 1875–2 Jan. 1878 Jules Ventre de la Touloubre; 2 Jan. 1878–15 Jan. 1879 M.J. Roblin (acting); 15 Jan. 1879–7 Sept. 1879

Charles-Henri Vassal; 7 Sept. 1879-16 Dec. 1879 Charles Rayet (acting); 16 Dec. 1879-17 Apr. 1880 Numa Sasias (acting); 17 Apr. 1880-4 June 1882 François Perriez; 4 June 1882-21 Feb. 1883 Édouard Marie (acting); 21 Feb. 1883-3 March 1885 François Perriez; 3 March 1885-19 Aug. 1887 Philotée Gerville-Réache; 19 Aug. 1887-5 Sept. 1887 Paul Celeron de Blainville.

Mbire Empire see **Mwene Mutapa Empire**

680 Melilla. 1497-1556. *Location:* Melilla, Morocco. *Capital:* Melilla.

History: A town of antiquity (named Rusaddir), Melilla was a Berber city in 1497 when it fell to the Spanish. It became the property of the family of the Duke of Medina Sidonia and remained thus until 1556 when the Spanish Crown took it over (see **Melilla [Spanish]**). In 1508 Velez de la Gomera was brought under Spanish rule and placed in the administration of Melilla.

Rulers: unknown.

681 Melilla Comandancia. 27 Nov. 1912-7 Apr. 1956. *Location:* northern Morocco. *Capital:* Melilla. *Other names:* Melilla.

History: In 1912 **Melilla District** became a comandancia of **Spanish Morocco,** and to all intents and purposes remained autonomous, ruled by a commander answerable to the Governor-General of Spanish Morocco. In 1956, with the departure of the Spanish (and the French) from Morocco, Spain maintained Melilla as a presidio (or plaza) of Spain. It is represented in the Spanish cortes by the Mayor of Melilla.

Rulers: ruled by the Governor-General of Spanish Morocco through a commander in Melilla.

682 Melilla District. 1847-27 Nov. 1912. *Location:* Melilla, Morocco. *Capital:* Melilla. *Other names:* Melilla.

History: In 1847, upon the establishment of the **Spanish Captaincy-General of North Africa, Melilla (Spanish)** became a district of the Captaincy-General. Like **Ceuta District** it had its own governor, as before, except that the Governor of Ceuta became the Captain-General of North Africa. In 1912, on the establishment of **Spanish Morocco,** Melilla became a comandancia (see **Melilla Comandancia).**

Governors: 1847-1848 Manuel Arcaya; 1848-1850 Ignacio Chacón; 1850-1854 José de Castro y Méndez; 1854-1856 Manuel del Villar; 1856-1858 José Morcillo Ezquerra; 1858-1860 Manuel del Villar; 1860-1861 Luis de la Breche; 1861-1862 Felipe del Espinar; 1862-1863 Manuel Álvarez Maldonaldo; 1863-1864 Tomás O'Ryan y Vázquez; 1864-1866 Bartolomé Benavides y Campuzano; 1866-1868 José Salcedo y González; 1868-1871 Pedro Beaumont y Peralta; 1871-1873 Bernardo Alemañy y Perote; 1873-1879 Andrés Cuadra y Bourman; 1879-1880 Manuel Macías y Casado; 1880-1880 Angel Navascués; 1880-1881 Evaristo García y Reyna; 1881-1886 Manuel Macías y Casado; 1886-1887 Teodoro Camino y Alcobendas; 1887-1888 Mariano de la Iglesia y Guillén; 1888-1888 Juan Villalonga y Soler; 1888-1889 Rafael Assin y Bazán; 1889-1891 José Mirelis y González; 1891-1893 Juan Garcia y Margallo; 1893-1894 Manuel Macías y Casado; 1894-1894 Juan Arolas y Esplugues; 1894-1895 Rafael Cerero; 1895-1898 José Alcántara Pérez; 1898-1899 Fernando Alameda y Liancourt; 1899-1904 Venancio Hernández y Fernández; 1904-1905 Manuel Serrano y Ruíz; 1905-1905 Enrique Segura y Campoy; 1905-1910 José Marina Vega; 1910-27 Nov. 1912 José García Aldave.

683 Melilla (Spanish). 1556-1847. *Location:* Melilla, Morocco. *Capital:* Melilla. *Other names:* Melilla.

History: In 1556 **Melilla,** since 1497 in the hands of the family of the Duke of Medina Sidonia, was taken by the Spanish Crown. In 1508 Velez de la Gomera had been, and in 1673 Alhucemas was to be, brought under Spanish rule, and both were placed under the administration of Melilla. In 1847 the **Spanish Captaincy-General of North Africa** was created, and Melilla became a territory of that body (see **Melilla Territory.**

Governors: 1556–1559 Alonso de Urrea; 1559–1561 [unknown]; 1561–1568 Pedro de Córdoba; 1568–1571 Francisco de Córdoba; 1571–1595 Antonio de Tejada; 1595–1596 Jerónimo de los Barrios; 1596–1601 Martín Dávalos y Padilla; 1601–1603 [unknown]; 1603–1611 Pedro de Heredia; 1611–1612 [unknown]; 1612–1617 Domingo de Dieguez; 1617–1618 Gaspar de Mondragón; 1618–1619 Domingo de Ochoa; 1619–1620 Diego de Leyva; 1620–1622 Francisco Rodríguez de Sanabria; 1622–1624 Francisco Ruíz; 1624–1625 [unknown]; 1625–1632 Luis de Sotomayor; 1632–1633 Pedro Moreo; 1633–1635 Tomás Mejía de Escobedo; 1635–1637 [unknown]; 1637–1648 Gabriel de Penalosa y Estrada; 1648–1649 [unknown]; 1649–1649 Luis de Sotomayor; 1649–1650 Jordán Jerez; 1650–1651 [unknown]; 1651–1655 Pedro Palacio y Guevara; 1655–1656 Diego de Arce; 1656–1669 Luis de Velázquez y Angulo; 1669–1672 Francisco Osorio y Astorga; 1672–1674 Diego de Arce; 1674–1675 [unknown]; 1675–1680 José Frias; 1680–1683 Diego Toscano y Brito; 1683–1684 [unknown]; 1684–1686 Diego Pacheco y Arce; 1686–1687 [unknown]; 1687–1687 Francisco López Moreno; 1687–1688 Antonio Domínguez de Durán; 1688–1691 Bernabé Ramos y Miranda; 1691–1692 [unknown]; 1692–1697 Antonio de Zúñiga y la Cerda; 1697–1703 Domingo Canal y Soldevila; 1703–1704 [unknown]; 1704–1707 Blas de Trincheria; 1707–1711 Diego de Flores; 1711–1714 Juan Jerónimo Ungo de Velasco; 1714–1715 Patricio Gómez de la Hoz; 1715–1716 Conde de Desallois; 1716–1719 Pedro Borrás; 1719–1719 Francisco Ibáñez y Rubalcava; 1719–1730 Alonso de Guevara y Vasconcelos; 1730–1732 Juan Andrés del Thoso; 1732–1757 Antonio Villalba y Angulo; 1757–1758 Francisco de Alba; 1758–1767 Narciso Vázquez y Nicuesa; 1767–1772 Miguel Fernández de Saavedra; 1772–1777 José Carrión y Andrade; 1777–1779 Bernardo Tortosa; 1779–1780 [unknown]; 1780–1782 Antonio Manso; 1782–1786 José Granados; 1786–1788 José Naranjo; 1788–1798 José Rivera; 1798–1800 Fernando Moyano; 1800–1814 Ramón Conti; 1814–1821 Jacinto Díaz Capilla; 1821–1823 Antonio Mateos y Malpartida; 1823–1824 Juan Pérez del Hacho y Oliván; 1824–1826 Luis Cappa y Rioseco; 1826–1829 Manuel García; 1829–1830 Juan Serrano y Reyna; 1830–1835 Luis Cappa y Rioseco; 1835–1838 Rafael Delgado y Moreno; 1838–1839 [unknown]; 1839–1847 Demetrio María de Benito y Hernández.

Memphusi see **Mamprusi** (which refers directly to **Mossi States)**

Menaba see **Madagascar Kingdom**

Merina see **Imerina**

684 Merinid Empire. 1268–23 May 1465. *Location:* Morocco. *Capital:* Fez (from 1248). *Other names:* Marinid Empire, Marinid Kingdom, Merinid Kingdom.

History: The Merinids were the third Berber dynasty to rule all of Morocco. A tribe of the Zanatah group, they had been in existence since about 1150, in eastern Morocco, and in 1248 they captured Fez, making it their capital instead of their old headquarters at Taza. They made several attempts to recapture Spanish possessions in Spain, and toward the end of the empire it fell into anarchy, and was taken over by the Wattasid Empire.

Kings: 1196–1218 Abu Muhammad Abdul Haqq I; 1218–1240 Uthman I; 1240–12 Nov. 1244 Muhammad I; 12 Nov. 1244–30 July 1258 Abu Yahya Abu-Bakr; 30 July 1258–20 March 1286

Abu Yusuf Yakub; 20 March 1286–10 May 1307 Abu Yakub Yusuf; 10 May 1307–23 July 1308 Abu Thabit Amir; 23 July 1308–Nov. 1310 Abu'l Rabi Suleiman; Nov. 1310–Sept. 1331 Abu Said Uthman II; Sept. 1331–Sept. 1348 Abu'l Hassan Ali I; Sept. 1348–3 Dec. 1358 Abu Inan Faris; 3 Dec. 1358–July 1359 Muhammad II as-Said; Aug. 1359–1 Oct. 1361 Abu Salim Ali II; 1 Oct. 1361–Nov. 1361 Abu Umar Tashufin; Nov. 1361–29 Dec. 1361 Abdul Halim; 29 Dec. 1361–30 Aug. 1366 Abu Zayyan Muhammad III; 30 Aug. 1366–23 Oct. 1372 Abu'l Faris Abdul Aziz I; 23 Oct. 1372–18 June 1374 Abu Zayyan Muhammad IV; 18 June 1374–1384 Abu'l Abbas Ahmad; 1384–28 Sept. 1386 Musa; 28 Sept. 1386–9 Nov. 1386 Abu Zayyan Muhammad V; 20 Nov. 1386–1393 Abu'l Abbas Ahmad; 1393–1396 Abu'l Faris Abdul Aziz I; 1396–1398 Abdallah; 1398–1420 Abu Said Uthman III; 1420–1428 interregnum; 1428–23 May 1465 Abu Muhammad Abdul Haqq II.

Messau see **Misau**

Mining Republic, Mining State see **South Kasai Republic**

685 Mirambo. ca. 1858–1895. *Location:* Tanzania. *Capital:* Unyanyembe. *Other names:* Nyamwezi, Unyamwezi.
History: An East African sultanate, it became part of **German East Africa Protectorate [ii]** in 1895.
Sultans: ca. 1858–ca. 1860 Fundakira; ca. 1860–ca. 1865 Msavila; ca. 1865–1876 Kiyungu; 1876–1893 Isike. *Queens:* 1893–1893 Mugalula. *Sultans:* 1894–1898 Kutagamoto; 1898–1898 Koswika.

686 Misau Emirate. 1831–1903. *Location:* northern Nigeria. *Capital:* Misau. *Other names:* Missau, Messau.
History: Founded in 1831 by Mamman Manga, son of a Fulani warrior, and enlarged in the 1870s, in 1903 it was conquered by the British and became

part of **Northern Nigeria Protectorate.**
Emirs: 1831–1833 Mamman Manga (or Moma Manga); 1833–1850 Amadu; 1850–1861 Usman; 1861–1886 Mamman Sali (or Moma Sali); 1886–1900 Hama Manga; 1900–1903 Amadu; 1903–Oct. 1926 Mamman al-Hajji (or Moma Alhaji); Oct. 1926– Ahmadu Waziri. *Premiers:* 14 Feb. 1918–Oct. 1926 Ahmadu Waziri.

687 Mississippi-in-Africa. 1835–1842. *Location:* on the Sinoe River, Liberia. *Capital:* Greenville (called Sino until 1838 and re-named for James Green, a colonization advocate). *Other names:* Greenville, Mississippi, Colony of Sinoe, Sinoe Colony.
History: In 1835 the Mississippi and Louisiana State Colonization Societies founded this colony in what is now Liberia for freed slaves from the American state of Mississippi only. In 1842 it was admitted to the **Liberia Commonwealth,** as Sinoe County.
Rulers: 1835–June 1837 no chief executive; June 1837–10 Sept. 1838 Josiah Finley (Governor); 10 Sept. 1838–1842 no chief executive.

Mitsiwah see **Massawa**

Moçambique see **Mozambique**

688 Mogadishu Republic. ca. 1238–ca. 1400. *Location:* Mogadishu, Somalia. *Capital:* Mogadishu. *Other names:* Maqdishu, Mogadiscio, Aristocratic Republic of Mogadishu, Republic of Mogadishu, Makdishu.
History: This is about the only stage of Mogadishu's history worth recording, in other words the period during which it had the initiative to rise above the simple and uneventful daily life of that most excruciatingly boring of historical subjects—an East African sultanate, which is what the city-state of Mogadishu became after its little republican flame had gone out.
Heads of the Republic: ca. 1238–(?) Sheikh Muhammad; (?)–ca. 1300

[unknown]; ca. 1300–ca. 1331 Sheikh Abubakr; ca. 1331–(?) Tewfik; (?)–(?) Rahman; (?)–ca. 1390 Yusuf; ca. 1390–ca. 1400 Fahr ad-Din.

689 Mohéli. (?)–1886. *Location:* Comoros Islands. *Capital:* Fomboni. *Other names:* Moili, Mwali, Mohéli Sultanate, Mohilla.
History: Of uncertain origin, the Sultanate of Mohéli became a part of the **Mayotte Protectorate** in 1886.
Sultans: 1828–1842 Andriamane-taha. *Queens:* 1842–1868 Jumbe Fatimah. *Sultans:* 1868–1871 Muhammad; 1871–1888 Marjani; 1888–1912 Salima Masimba.

690 Mombasa (Busaidi). 1837–1 July 1895. *Location:* Mombasa, Kenya. *Capital:* Mombasa. *Other names:* Mombasa.
History: The al-Bu Sa'id family of Oman in Arabia extended their territories to include most of East Africa north of Lourenço Marques and south of the Horn of Africa (see also **Zanzibar Sultanate**). In 1837 Mombasa came under the rule of Zanzibar and in 1895 it became part of **British East Africa Colony**.
Governors: 1837–1860 Abdallah ibn Hamish; 1860–1873 Mubarrak ibn Rashid; 1873–1 July 1895 Rashid ibn Hamish.

691 Mombasa (Mazrui) [i]. 1746–Dec. 1823. *Location:* Kenya. *Capital:* Mombasa. *Other names:* Mombasa, Mvita.
History: In 1746 the Omani governor of Mombasa, Ali ibn Othman, a member of the Mazrui family, declared himself sultan of the newly independent sultanate of Mombasa. In 1823 the country became **Mombasa Protectorate.**
Sultans: 1746–1755 Ali ibn Othman; 1755–1773 Masud ibn Nasir; 1773–1782 Abdallah ibn Muhammad; 1782–1811 Ahmad ibn Muhammad; 1811–Dec. 1823 Abdallah ibn Muhammad.

692 Mombasa (Mazrui) [ii]. 1826–1837. *Location:* Kenya. *Capital:* Mombasa. *Other names:* Mombasa.
History: In 1826 the al-Busaidi dynasty of Oman (who later ruled in **Zanzibar**) attacked Mombasa, took it over and installed a governor in what was **Mombasa Protectorate**. In 1837 the Busaidis actually occupied Mombasa (see **Mombasa [Busaidi]**).
Governors: 1826–March 1835 Salem ibn Ahmad (or Muhammad Asmani al-Mazrui); March 1835–1836 Nasr ibn Ahmad; 1836–1837 Rashid ibn Salem; 1837–1837 Khamis ibn Rashid.

693 Mombasa (Omani) [i]. 12 Dec. 1698–12 March 1728. *Location:* Kenya. *Capital:* Mombasa. *Other names:* Mombasa, Mvita.
History: In 1698 the Omani Imam Sa'if ibn Sultan stormed Mombasa, the great port on the coast of what is today Kenya (see **Mombasa [Portuguese] [i]**) and expelled the Portuguese. The area was much extended, and in 1728 the Portuguese re-captured it (see **Mombasa [Portuguese] [ii]**).
Military Commanders: 12 Dec. 1698–Dec. 1698 Imam Sa'if ibn Sultan; Dec. 1698–12 March 1728 Nasr ibn Abdallah al-Mazrui.

694 Mombasa (Omani) [ii]. 21 Sept. 1729–1746. *Location:* Kenya. *Capital:* Mombasa. *Other names:* Mombasa, Mvita.
History: In 1729 the Portuguese were defeated in Mombasa (see **Mombasa [Portuguese] [ii]**) and left the Kenya-Tanzania coast forever. The Omani governors resumed their rule until 1746 when the governor was murdered and his brother assumed the title of Sultan and declared his independence from Oman (see **Mombasa [Mazrui] [i]**).
Governors: 21 Sept. 1729–1735 [unknown]; 1735–1739 Sa'id al-Hadermi; 1739–1746 Muhammad ibn Othman al-Mazrui; 1746–1746 Ali ibn Othman al-Mazrui.

695 Mombasa (Portuguese) [i].
1593–12 Dec. 1698. *Location:* as **Mombasa (Portuguese) [ii].** *Capital:* Mombasa. *Other names:* Mombasa, Mvita. *History:* In 1593 Portugal captured Mombasa. In 1698 they lost this quite unimportant territory to the Omanis (see **Mombasa [Omani] [i]**).
Capitães-Mores: 1593–1596 Mateus de Vasconcelos; 1596–1598 António de Andrade; 1598–1606 Rui Soares de Melo; 1606–1609 Gaspar Pereira; 1609–1610 Pedro de Abreu; 1610–1614 Manuel Pereira; 1614–1620 Simão Pereira; 1620–1625 Francisco Pereira; 1625–1626 João Semedo; 1626–1629 Marçal de Macedo; 1629–15 Aug. 1631 Pedro de Gambôa; 15 Aug. 1631–1635 Pedro Botelho; 1635–1639 Francisco de Seixas e Cabreira; 1639–1642 Martim Manuel; 1642–1643 [unknown]; 1643–1646 Manuel Coutinho; 1646–1648 Diogo da Silva; 1648–1651 António de Meneses; 1651–1653 Francisco de Seixas e Cabreira; 1653–1658 [unknown]; 1658–1663 José da Silva; 1663–1667 Manuel de Campos; 1667–1670 João Cota; 1670–1671 vacant; 1671–1673 José da Costa; 1673–1676 Manuel de Campos; 1676–1679 Francisco de Faria; 1679–(?) Manuel Franco; (?)–1682 Pedro Henriques; 1682–1686 Leonardo da Costa; 1686–1688 João Portugal; 1688–1693 Duarte de Melo; 1693–1694 Pascual Sarmento; 1694–1696 João Leão; 1696–1697 António de Melo; 1697–1698 Príncipe de Faza; 1698–12 Dec. 1698 Leonardo Souto-Maior. *Note:* Capitães-Mores is the plural of Capitão-Mor (Captain-Major).

696 Mombasa (Portuguese) [ii]. 12 March 1728–21 Sept. 1729. *Location:* Mombasa, Kenya. *Capital:* Mombasa. *Other names:* Mombasa, Mvita. *History:* In 1728 the Portuguese recaptured Mombasa (see **Mombasa [Omani] [i]**). In 1729 the Omanis recaptured it (see **Mombasa [Omani] [ii]**).
Capitães-Mores: 12 March 1728–21 Sept. 1729 Álvaro de Melo e Castro. *Note:* Capitães-Mores is the plural of Capitão-Mor (Captain-Major).

697 Mombasa Protectorate. Dec. 1823–1826. *Location:* Kenya. *Capital:* Mombasa. *Other names:* Mombasa. *History:* In 1823 Admiral William Owen of the British Navy established a protectorate over Mombasa (see **Mombasa [Mazrui] [i]**), the area being disputed by the Sultan of Muscat and the Sultan of Mombasa. In 1826 Owen was ushered out by the Sultan of Mombasa (see **Mombasa [Mazrui] [ii]**).
Sultans: Dec. 1823–1825 Abdallah ibn Ahmad; 1825–1826 Suleiman ibn Ali. *Governors:* Dec. 1823–13 Feb. 1824 Adm. William Owen; 13 Feb. 1824–29 May 1824 J.J. Reitz; Sept. 1824–1826 Lt. Emery.

Monomatapa see **Mwene Mutapa Empire**

Morisco Republic see **Bou Regreg**

698 Morocco. See these **names:**
Kingdom of Morocco (1957–)
Morocco (Independent Sultanate) (1956–1957)
French Morocco (1912–1956)
Spanish Morocco (1912–1956)
French-Occupied Morocco (1907–1912)
Ceuta Comandancia (1912–1956)
Ceuta District (1847–1912)
Ceuta (Spanish) (1640–1847)
Ceuta (Portuguese) (1415–1640)
Melilla Comandancia (1912–1956)
Melilla District (1847–1912)
Melilla (Spanish) (1556–1847)
Melilla (1497–1556)
Spanish Captaincy-General of North Africa (1847–1912)
Rif Republic (1923–1926)
Tangier International Zone (1923–1956)
British Tangier (1662–1684)
Portuguese Tangier (1471–1662)
Ifni Province (1958–1969)
Ifni Territory (1952–1958)
Ifni Protectorate (1912–1952)
Ifni (1860–1912)

Bou Regreg (1627–1641)
Barbary — explanation and referral entry
Masmouda Pirates' Republic (ca. 1602–ca. 1614)
Santa Cruz de la Mar Pequeña (1478–1524)
 Alawid Morocco (1659–1907)
 Sa'did Morocco (1549–1659)
 Wattasid Empire (1465–1549)
 Merinid Empire (1268–1465)
 Almohad Empire (1147–1268)
 Almoravid Empire (1031–1147)
 Tangier Emirate (1421–1471)
 Idrisid State (789–974)
 Mauretania Tingitana (42–ca. 395)
Mauretania West (ca. 100 B.C.–38 B.C.)

699 Morocco (Independent Sultanate). 2 March 1956–11 Aug. 1957. *Location:* as the **Kingdom of Morocco,** but without Ifni or Spanish Sahara. *Capital:* Rabat. *Other names:* Independent Sultanate of Morocco.

History: In 1956 France (on March 2) and Spain (on April 7) yielded their protectorates (see **French Morocco** and **Spanish Morocco**) to the Sultan, who declared an independent state. Spain kept **Ifni Province, Ceuta Presidio** and **Melilla Presidio,** as well as the Northern Moroccan islands of Alhucemas, Chafarinas, and Velez de la Gomera — all as exclaves of Spain. On October 20, 1956 Tangier, till then an international zone (see **Tangier International Zone**) was given back to Morocco. The following year the Sultan became King (see **Kingdom of Morocco**).

Sultans: 2 March 1956–11 Aug. 1957 Sidi Muhammad V (Sidi Muhammad ben Yusuf). *Prime Ministers:* 2 March 1956–11 Aug. 1957 M'barek ben Mustafa el-Bakai.

Moroni see **Gran Comoro**

Moselekatze's Land see **Matabeleland**

700 Mossi States. The Southern Mossi chiefdoms were: Mamprusi (or Memphusi), **Dagomba** and Nanumba — all in modern Ghana.

The Northern Mossi chiefdoms were: Tenkodogo, Zandoma, **Gurma, Wagadugu** and **Yatenga** — all in modern Burkina Faso.

About the year 1100 a Dagomba king called Nedega, who ruled at Gambaga, appeared in the Volta area. His daughter Yenenga married a Mandingo hunter called Riala. Ouidiraogo, their son, founded the Mossi Empire at Tenkodogo. Rawa, his son, founded the kingdom of Zandana which, later, under his grandson Yadega, became the state of **Yatenga.** In the East, Rawa's brother, Diaba, founded **Gurma,** while Oubri (flourished probably around 1350), one of their nephews, founded **Wagadugu.** Separately these states existed as kingdoms (or chiefdoms) within the family-related Mossi Empire. This division, by 1900 (and after 3 years of French colonial rule) had been reduced to **Gurma, Wagadugu** and **Yatenga.** Small kingdoms within Wagadugu were Boussouma and Yako. Small kingdoms within Yatenga were Rotenga, Zitenga and Riziam. There were 34 rulers (emperors) of the Mossi Empire.

701 Moyen-Congo. 27 Apr. 1886–29 June 1886. *Location:* as **Moyen-Congo Territory.** *Capital:* Brazzaville. *Other names:* Congo Français, French Congo, Middle Congo.

History: In Apr. 1886 Pierre Savorgnan de Brazza became the Commissioner-General of the **French Equatorial African Protectorate.** For the next two months the Moyen-Congo area, formerly the **Moyen-Congo Protectorate,** was reorganized into a colony, which it became in June 1886 (see **Moyen-Congo Colony [i]**).

Rulers: 27 Apr. 1886–29 June 1886 Direct rule by the Commissioner-General of the French Equatorial African Protectorate.

702 Moyen-Congo Colony [i]. 29 June 1886–11 Dec. 1888. *Location:* as **Moyen-Congo Territory.** *Capital:* Brazzaville. *Other names:* Middle Congo, Lower Congo, Moyen-Congo, French Congo, Congo Français.
History: In 1886 **Moyen-Congo** became a colony. In 1888 it became part of **Moyen-Congo-Gabon** as **Moyen-Congo Territory.**
Rulers: 29 June 1886–11 Dec. 1888 Direct rule by the Commissioner-General of the French Equatorial African Protectorate.

703 Moyen-Congo Colony [ii]. 29 Dec. 1903–30 June 1934. *Location:* as **Congo People's Republic.** *Capital:* Brazzaville. *Other names:* Moyen-Congo, Middle Congo, French Congo, Congo Français.
History: In 1903 **Moyen-Congo District** became a colony again. From 1911–1916 a large part of Moyen-Congo was in German hands, as part of **Kamerun.** In 1934 the colony became **Moyen-Congo Region,** part of **French Equatorial Africa Colony.**
Lieutenant-Governors: 29 Dec. 1903–5 Apr. 1906 Émile Gentil; 5 Apr. 1906–16 Jan. 1908 Adolphe Cureau; 16 Jan. 1908–17 Nov. 1908 Édouard Dubosc-Taret (acting); 17 Nov. 1908–27 June 1910 Adolphe Cureau; 27 June 1910–28 July 1911 Édouard Dubosc-Taret (acting); 28 July 1911–16 Apr. 1916 Lucien Fourneau; 16 Apr. 1916–17 July 1917 Jules Carde; 17 July 1917–2 Apr. 1919 Jules Le Prince (acting); 2 Apr. 1919–16 May 1919 Edmond Cadier; 16 May 1919–21 Aug. 1919 Jean Marchand (acting); 21 Aug. 1919–17 Aug. 1922 Matteo Alfassa; 17 Aug. 1922–24 Apr. 1923 Georges Thomann (acting); 24 Apr. 1923–21 July 1925 Jean Marchand (acting); 21 July 1925–1 Dec. 1929 ruled direct by Governor-General of French Equatorial Africa; 1 Dec. 1929–4 Dec. 1930 Marcel Marchessou (acting); 4 Dec. 1930–May 1931 Pierre Bonnefont (acting); May 1931–1932 Charles-Max Masson de Saint-Félix; 1932–21 Nov. 1932 Émile Buhot-Launay; 21 Nov. 1932–30 June 1934 ruled direct by Governor-General of French Equatorial Africa.

704 Moyen-Congo District. 5 July 1902–29 Dec. 1903. *Location:* as **Congo People's Republic.** *Capital:* Brazzaville. *Other names:* Middle Congo, Lower Congo, French Congo, Congo Français, Moyen-Congo, District of Moyen-Congo.
History: In 1902 the colony of **Lower Congo-Gabon** came into being and **Moyen-Congo Territory,** until then part of **Moyen-Congo-Gabon,** became the District of Moyen-Congo, part of the new colony. In 1903 it became a separate colony, **Moyen-Congo Colony [ii].**
Lieutenant-Governors: 5 July 1902–11 July 1902 Jean-Baptiste Lemaire; 11 July 1902–29 Dec. 1903 Émile Gentil.

705 Moyen-Congo-Gabon. 11 Dec. 1888–5 July 1902. *Location:* **Congo People's Republic** and **Gabon Republic.** *Capital:* Brazzaville. *Other names:* Lower Congo-Gabon.
History: In 1888 it was found to be most effective to combine **Moyen-Congo Colony [i]** with **Gabon Colony [ii]** to form a large territory called Moyen-Congo-Gabon, with headquarters at Brazzaville. The two components were renamed **Moyen-Congo Territory** and **Gabon Territory [iii].** In 1902 this "super-territory" became a colony (see **Lower Congo-Gabon Colony**).
Rulers: see *both* Moyen-Congo Territory *and* Gabon Territory [iii] for exact dates.

706 Moyen-Congo Overseas Territory [i]. 31 Dec. 1937–13 Oct. 1946. *Location:* as **Congo People's Republic.** *Capital:* Brazzaville. *Other names:* Middle Congo, Moyen-Congo, French Congo, Congo Français, Térritoire du Moyen-Congo.
History: In 1937 **Moyen-Congo Region** became an overseas territory of

France, still part of the greater colony of **French Equatorial Africa Colony.** In 1946 it became an overseas territory of the Fourth Republic in France (see **Moyen-Congo Overseas Territory [ii]).** *Lieutenant-Governors:* 31 Dec. 1937–10 Feb. 1941 Direct rule by the Governor-General of French Equatorial Africa Colony; 10 Feb. 1941–21 Feb. 1942 Gabriel Fortune; 21 Feb. 1942–19 July 1942 Jean Capagorry (acting); 19 July 1942–20 Aug. 1945 Gabriel Fortune; 20 Aug. 1945–30 Apr. 1946 Direct rule by the Governor-General of French Equatorial Africa Colony; 30 Apr. 1946–16 May 1946 Christian Laigret (acting); 16 May 1946–13 Oct. 1946 Direct rule by the Governor-General of French Equatorial Africa Colony.

707 Moyen-Congo Overseas Territory [ii]. 13 Oct. 1946–28 Nov. 1958. *Location:* as **Congo People's Republic.** *Capital:* Brazzaville. *Other names:* Middle Congo, Moyen-Congo, French Congo, Congo Français, Térritoire du Moyen-Congo.

History: In 1946 **Moyen-Congo Overseas Territory [i]** became an overseas territory of the Fourth Republic of France, and still remained a part of **French Equatorial Africa Colony.** In 1958 it achieved self-rule as **Congo Autonomous Republic.**

Lieutenant-Governors: 13 Oct. 1946–6 Nov. 1946 Direct rule by the Governor-General of French Equatorial Africa Colony; 6 Nov. 1946–31 Dec. 1947 Numa Sadoul; 31 Dec. 1947–1 March 1950 Jacques Fourneau; 1 March 1950–25 Apr. 1952 Paul Le Layec; 25 Apr. 1952–15 July 1953 Jean-Georges Chambon; 15 July 1953–19 Feb. 1954 Ernest-Eugène Rouys (acting); 19 Feb. 1954–2 Nov. 1956 Ernest-Eugène Rouys; 2 Nov. 1956–29 Jan. 1958 Jean-Michel Soupault; 29 Jan. 1958–28 Nov. 1958 Charles Dériaud (acting). *Prime Ministers:* 26 July 1958–28 Nov. 1958 Jacques Opangoult.

708 Moyen-Congo Protectorate. 5 Feb. 1883–27 Apr. 1886. *Location:* as **Moyen-Congo Territory.** *Capital:* Brazzaville. *Other names:* French Congo, Middle Congo, Congo Français. *History:* In 1883 the Moyen-Congo Protectorate was established to protect French interests in the area. In 1886 it became simply **Moyen-Congo.** See also **Portuguese Congo** for sidebar interest.

Commissioners: 5 Feb. 1883–27 Apr. 1886 Pierre Savorgnan de Brazza.

709 Moyen-Congo Region. 30 June 1934–31 Dec. 1937. *Location:* as **Congo People's Republic.** *Capital:* Brazzaville. *Other names:* Middle Congo, Moyen-Congo, French Congo, Congo Français, Région du Moyen-Congo, Region of Moyen-Congo.

History: In 1934 the **French Equatorial Africa Colony** was formed, and **Moyen-Congo Colony [ii]** became part of it, as the Region of Moyen-Congo. In 1937, still part of the AEF, it became **Moyen-Congo Overseas Territory [i].**

Rulers: 30 June 1934–31 Dec. 1937 Direct rule by the Governor-General of French Equatorial Africa Colony.

710 Moyen-Congo Territory. 11 Dec. 1888–5 July 1902. *Location:* the coastal areas of what is today **Congo People's Republic.** *Capital:* Brazzaville. *Other names:* Middle Congo, Moyen-Congo, French Congo, Congo Français, Lower Congo.

History: In 1888 **Moyen-Congo Colony [i]** became a part of **Moyen-Congo-Gabon** and was reduced to a territory. In 1902 its over-colony changed its name to **Lower Congo-Gabon,** and the territory then became **Moyen-Congo District.**

Lieutenant-Governors: 11 Dec. 1888–12 Aug. 1889 Direct rule by the Commissioner-General of the French Equatorial African Protectorate; 12 Aug. 1889–27 Apr. 1894 Fortuné de Chavannes; 27 Apr. 1894–1 May 1899 Albert Dolisie; 1 May 1899–5 July 1902 Jean-Baptiste Lemaire.

711 Mozambique. See these **names:**
Mozambique People's Republic
(1975–)
Mozambique Overseas Province
(1951–1975)
Mozambique Colony (1836–1951)
Mozambique, The Zambezi and
Sofala Colony (1752–1836)
Mozambique, Sofala, Rios de
Cuama and Monomatapa Colony
(1609–1752)
Mozambique Captaincy-General
(1569–1609)
Sofala and Mozambique Captaincy
(1507–1569)
Sofala Captaincy (1501–1507)
Gazaland (1824–1895)

712 Mozambique Captaincy-General. 1569–1609. *Location:* Mozambique. *Capital:* Mozambique. *Other names:* Mozambique.
History: In 1569, growing in importance and development, **Sofala and Mozambique Captaincy** became a captaincy-general, and the name "Mozambique" became the principal one from that time. In 1609 it became a colony, as **Mozambique, Sofala, Ríos de Cuama and Monomatapa Colony.**
Captains-General: 1569–June 1573 Francisco Barreto; June 1573–1577 Vasco Homem (acting); 1577–1577 Fernando Monroi (acting); 1577–1577 Simão da Silveira (acting); 1577–1582 Pedro de Castro; 1582–1586 Nunho Pereira; 1586–1589 Jorge de Meneses; 1589–1590 Lourenço de Brito; 1590–1595 Pedro de Sousa; 1595–1598 Nunho da Cunha e Ataíde; 1598–1601 Álvaro Abranches; 1601–1604 Vasco de Mascarenhas; 1604–1607 Sebastião de Macedo; 1607–1609 Estévão de Ataíde.

713 Mozambique Colony. March 1836–11 June 1951. *Location:* Mozambique. *Capital:* Lourenço Marques (from 1897); Mozambique (until 1897). *Other names:* Portuguese West Africa, Moçambique, Mozambique.
History: In 1836 **Mozambique, The**

Zambesi and Sofala Colony became simply Mozambique Colony. In 1951 it became an overseas province of Portugal (see **Mozambique Overseas Province**).
Governors-General: March 1836–March 1837 provisional rule; March 1837–Oct. 1837 António de Melo; Oct. 1837–March 1838 Marquês de Aracaty; March 1838–25 March 1840 Council of Government; 25 March 1840–May 1841 Joaquim Marinho; May 1841–15 Feb. 1843 João Xavier; 15 Feb. 1843–May 1847 Rodrigo de Abreu e Lima; May 1847–Oct. 1851 Domingos do Vale; Oct. 1851–Apr. 1854 Joaquim de Magalhães; Apr. 1854–Sept. 1857 Vasco de Carvalho e Meneses; Sept. 1857–Feb. 1864 João de Almeida; Feb. 1864–Apr. 1864 Council of Government; Apr. 1864–Oct. 1867 António de Canto e Castro; Oct. 1867–Sept. 1868 António de Lacerda; Sept. 1868–Feb. 1869 Council of Government; Feb. 1869–Apr. 1869 António de Almeida; Apr. 1869–Dec. 1869 Fernão Leal; Dec. 1869–June 1870 Council of Government; June 1870–Aug. 1870 Inácio Alves (acting); Aug. 1870–Dec. 1873 José do Amaral; Dec. 1873–Aug. 1874 Council of Government; Aug. 1874–Dec. 1877 José de Carvalho e Meneses; Dec. 1877–Jan. 1880 Francisco da Cunha; Jan. 1880–Aug. 1881 Augusto Sarmento; Aug. 1881–Feb. 1882 Carlos de Arcos; Feb. 1882–Apr. 1882 Joao d'Ávila (acting); Apr. 1882–Apr. 1885 Agostinho Coelho; Apr. 1885–July 1885 Council of Government; July 1885– March 1889 Augusto de Castilho Barreto e Noronha; March 1889–July 1889 José d'Almeida (acting); July 1889–July 1890 José Ferreira; July 1890–2 July 1891 Joaquim Machado; 2 July 1891–May 1893 Rafael de Andrade; May 1893–13 Jan. 1894 Francisco da Silva; 13 Jan. 1894–July 1894 João Correia e Lança (acting); July 1894–Jan. 1895 Fernão de Magalhães e Meneses; Jan. 1895–Dec. 1895 António Enes; Jan. 1896–March 1896 João Correia eLança (acting); March 1896–Nov.

1897 Joaquim de Albuquerque; Nov. 1897–Aug. 1898 Baltasar Cabral; Aug. 1898–Dec. 1898 Carlos Alberto Schultz Xavier; Dec. 1898–March 1900 Álvaro Ferreira; March 1900–May 1900 Julio da Costa; May 1900–Oct. 1900 Joaquim Machado; Oct. 1900–Dec. 1902 Manuel Gorjão; Dec. 1902–Feb. 1905 Tomás Rosado; Feb. 1905–Oct. 1906 João de Sequeira; Oct. 1906–Nov. 1910 Alfredo de Andrade; Nov. 1910–May 1911 José Ribeiro; May 1911–Feb. 1912 José de Azevedo e Silva; Feb. 1912–March 1913 José de Magalhães; March 1913–Apr. 1914 Augusto dos Santos; Apr. 1914–May 1915 Joaquim Machado; May 1915–Oct. 1915 Alfredo Coelho; Oct. 1915–Apr. 1918 Álvaro de Castro; Apr. 1918–Apr. 1919 Pedro do Amorim; Apr. 1919–March 1921 Manuel da Fonseca. *High Commissioners/Governors-General:* March 1921–Sept. 1923 Manuel Camacho; Sept. 1923–Sept. 1924 Manuel da Fonseca (acting). *Governors-General/ High Commissioners:* Sept. 1924–May 1926 Victor Hugo de Azevedo Coutinho; May 1926–Nov. 1926 Ivens Ferraz (acting). *High Commissioners/ Governors-General:* Nov. 1926–Apr. 1938 José Cabral. *Governors-General/ High Commissioners:* Apr. 1938–1940 José de Oliveira; 1941–1946 José de Bettencourt; 1946–May 1947 [unknown] (acting); May 1947–Dec. 1948 Luis de Sousa e Vasconcelos e Funchal; Dec. 1948–11 June 1951 Gabriel Teixeira.

714 Mozambique Overseas Province. 11 June 1951–25 June 1975. *Location:* Mozambique. *Capital:* Lourenço Marques. *Other names:* Portuguese East Africa, Mozambique, Moçambique.
History: In 1951 **Mozambique Colony** became an overseas province of Portugal. From 1964 onwards the Mozambique Liberation Front (FRELIMO) waged a guerrilla war for independence, and in 1975 achieved it, as **Mozambique.**
Governors-General/High Commis-

sioners: 11 June 1951–1958 Gabriel Teixeira; 1958–1961 Pedro de Barros; 1961–1964 Manuel Rodrigues; 1964–1969 José da Costa Almeida; 1969–Oct. 1971 Eduardo Arantes e Oliveira; Oct. 1971–1973 Manuel dos Santos; 1973–17 Aug. 1974 Henriques de Melo; 17 Aug. 1974–12 Sept. 1974 Ferro Ribeiro (acting); 12 Sept. 1974–25 June 1975 Victor Crespo. *Prime Ministers:* 20 Sept. 1974–25 June 1975 Joaquim Chissano.

715 Mozambique People's Republic. 25 June 1975– . *Location:* southeast coast of Africa. *Capital:* Maputo (until February 3, 1976 called Lourenço Marques. Named for a Portuguese trader, Marques, in 1544, the town developed around a fortress built in 1787, and became a city in 1887). *Other names:* Mozambique, People's Republic of Mozambique, Moçambique.
History: In 1975 **Mozambique Overseas Province** gained its independence after much fighting between Portugal and Frelimo (Mozambique Liberation Front).
Presidents: 25 June 1975–19 Oct. 1986 Samora Machel; 19 Oct. 1986– Joaquim Chissano. *Prime Ministers:* 17 July 1986– Mario Machungo. *Note:* in times of no Prime Minister, the President held that office.

716 Mozambique, Sofala, Ríos de Cuama and Monomatapa Colony. 1609–1752. *Location:* Mozambique. *Capital:* Mozambique. *Other names:* Portuguese East Africa, Mozambique, Moçambique.
History: In 1609 **Mozambique Captaincy-General** became a colony. In 1752 it was freed of its subordinate position to Goa, in India, and became an individual colony, with the name **Mozambique, The Zambesi and Sofala Colony.**
Governors: 1609–1611 Nunho Pereira; 1611–1612 Estévão de Ataíde; 1612–1612 Diogo de Madeira (acting); 1612–1614 João de Azevedo; 1614–1618

Rui Sampaio; 1618–1623 Nunho Pereira; 1623–1623 Nunho da Cunha; 1623–1624 Lopo de Almeida; 1624–1627 Diogo de Meneses; 1627–1631 Nunho Pereira; 1631–1632 Cristóvão de Brito e Vasconcelos (acting); 1632–1633 Diogo de Meneses; 1633–1634 Filipe de Mascarenhas; 1634–1639 Lourenço de Souto-Maior; 1639–1640 Diogo de Vasconcelos; 1640–1641 António de Brito Pacheco; 1641–1642 Francisco da Silveira; 1642–1646 Júlio Moniz da Silva; 1646–1648 Fernão Baião; 1648–1651 Álvaro de Távora; 1651–1652 Francisco de Mascarenhas; 1652–1657 Francisco de Lima; 1657–1661 Manuel de Sampaio; 1661–1664 Manuel de Mascarenhas; 1664–1667 Antonio de Melo e Castro; 1667–1670 Inácio de Carvalho; 1670–1673 João Freire; 1673–1674 Simão da Silva; 1674–1674 André da Fonseca; 1674–1676 Manuel da Silva (acting); 1676–1682 João Freire; 1682–1686 Caetano de Melo e Castro; 1686–1689 Miguel de Almeida; 1689–1692 Manuel Pinto; 1692–1693 Tomé Correia; 1693–1694 Francisco de Mesquita (acting); 1694–1695 Estévão da Costa; 1695–1696 Franciso da Costa; 1696–1699 Luís Sampaio; 1699–1703 Jácome Sarmento; 1703–1706 João de Almeida; 1706–1707 Luís de Brito Freire; 1707–1712 Luís de Camara; 1712–1714 João de Almeida; 1714–1715 Francisco de Mascarenhas; 1715–1719 Francisco de Souto-Maior; 1719–1721 Francisco de Alarção e Souto-Maior; 1721–1723 Álvaro de Melo e Castro; 1723–1726 António Sequeira e Faria; 1726–1730 António Fróis; 1730–1733 António de Melo; 1733–1736 José Leal; 1736–1739 Nicolau de Almeida; 1739–1743 Lourenço de Noronha; 1743–1746 Pedro da Gama e Castro; 1746–1750 Caetano de Sá; 1750–1752 Francisco de Melo e Castro.

717 Mozambique, The Zambesi and Sofala Colony. 1752–March 1836. *Location:* Mozambique. *Capital:* Mozambique. *Other names:* Mozambique, Portuguese East Africa.

History: In 1752 Mozambique threw off Goa rule in India. Prior to this it was **Mozambique, Sofala, Ríos de Cuama and Monomatapa Colony.** It then became an autonomous colony of Portugal, and in 1836 it became **Mozambique Colony.**

Governors: 1752–March 1758 Francisco de Melo e Castro; March 1758–Apr. 1758 João de Melo; Apr. 1758–28 May 1759 David Marquês Pereira; 28 May 1759–1763 Pedro de Saldanha e Albuquerque; 1763–1765 João Barba; 1765–June 1779 Baltasar do Lago; June 1779–1780 provisional administration; 1780–1781 José de Vasconcelos e Almeida; 1781–4 Jan. 1782 Vicente de Maia e Vasconcelos (acting); 4 Jan. 1782–21 Aug. 1782 Pedro de Saldanha e Albuquerque; 21 Aug. 1782–1786 a junta was in power; 1786–1793 António de Melo e Castro; 1793–1797 Diogo Coutinho; 1797–Sept. 1801 Francisco Meneses da Costa; Sept. 1801–Aug. 1805 Isidro de Almeida Sousa e Sá; Aug. 1805–Dec. 1807 Francisco do Amaral Cardoso; Dec. 1807–14 Aug. 1809 a junta was in power; 14 Aug. 1809–Aug. 1812 António de Melo e Castro de Mendonça; Aug. 1812–Feb. 1817 Marcos de Abreu e Meneses; Feb. 1817–Sept. 1818 João de Albuquerque; Sept. 1818–Nov. 1819 a junta was in power; Nov. 1819–June 1821 João Brito-Sanches; June 1821–June 1824 two juntas were in power; June 1824–Jan. 1825 João da Silva; Jan. 1825–Aug. 1829 Xavier Botelho; Aug. 1829–Jan. 1832 Paulo de Brito; Jan. 1832–March 1834 a junta was in power; March 1834–March 1836 José Pegado.

Mpondoland see **Pondoland**

718 Mukurra. ca. 340–ca. 675. *Location:* Sudan. *Capital:* Old Dunqulah. *Other names:* Maqurrah, Makuria.

History: One of the major kingdoms of the Dark Ages Nilotic Sudan, Mukurra was converted to Christianity about 550. About 675 the state swal-

lowed up **Nubia** and the new kingdom became known as **Dongola**.
Rulers: unknown.

719 Muri [i]. 1833–1892. *Location:* northern Nigeria. *Capital:* Muri (Hammaruwa). *Other names:* Muri Emirate, Hammaruwa Kingdom.
History: By 1817 the **Fulani Empire** had taken most of the Muri territory and Hamman Ruwa, the Fulani Captain, was created governor of the area. In 1833 he gained independence for Muri as an emirate. In 1892 the perennial enemy, the Jukun (see **Kororofa**) attacked again, and the Emir of Muri enlisted the aid of a French adventurer named Mizon, who, due to his rather vague connection with the French Army, succeeded in placing a perfectly legal French protectorate over the emirate, with himself as governor (see **Muri Protectorate**).
Governors: 1817–1833 Hamman Ruwa. *Emirs:* 1833–1836 Ibrahim; 1836–1836 Hamman; 1836–1848 Ibrahim; 1848–1861 Hamman; 1861–1869 Hamadu; 1869–1873 Burba; 1873–1874 Abubakar; 1874–1892 Muhammadu Nya.

720 Muri [ii]. 1893–Sept. 1901. *Location:* as **Muri [i]**. *Capital:* Jalingo. *Other names:* Hammaruwa Kingdom.
History: In 1893 the Muriwa kicked Mizon out of **Muri Protectorate**, and so re-established their independent kingdom with a new capital at Jalingo. In 1901 it became part of **Northern Nigeria Protectorate** as the Lau Division of Muri Province. The town of Lau was the capital from 1901–1910, while Mutum Biyu was the capital from 1910–1917. Since 1917 Jalingo has been the capital of the emirate.
Emirs: 1893–June 1896 Muhammadu Nya; 1897–1903 Hassan; 1903–1953 Muhammadu Mafindi; 1953– Muhammadu Tukur.

721 Muri Protectorate. 1892–1893.
Location: as **Muri [i]** and **Muri [ii]**.
Capital: Muri (Hammaruwa).
History: In 1892 the Frenchman Capt. Louis Mizon established a proper protectorate over **Muri [i]**. In 1893 he was expelled and **Muri [ii]** continued the progress of the emirate.
Emirs: 1892–1893 Muhammadu Nya.
Governors: 1892–1893 Louis Mizon.

Muwahhid Dynasty see **Almohad Empire**

Mvita see **Mombasa**

Mwali see **Mohéli**

Mwata Yamvo Empire see **Lunda Empire**

722 Mwene Mutapa Empire. ca. 1330–ca. 1888. *Location:* Zimbabwe/Mozambique. *Capital:* Mount Fura (from ca. 1445); Zimbabwe (until ca. 1445). *Other names:* Mbire Empire, Monomatapa, Monomotapa, Mwenemutapa, Empire of the Mwene Mutapa.
History: About 1330 a kingdom grew up, probably in succession to one in the ancient city of Zimbabwe (or Great Zimbabwe), between the Zambesi and Limpopo Rivers, and founded by Mbire. His great-great-grandson, Nyatsimba, acquired the title "Mwene Mutapa" ("Ravager of the Lands"), and was the first great conqueror and expander of the state into an empire. From the 1530s the Portuguese influence grew stronger and stronger, and legends about the Mwene Mutapa grew wilder and wilder (they are still legion today). In 1629 the Mwene Mutapa of the day attempted to throw the Portuguese out, but they deposed him and installed a successor. Colonial rule was beginning and the power of the Mwene Mutapa sagged until by the end of the 17th century it was virtually eclipsed by the crescent power of **Rozwi**. Technically the state continued to exist as a small chiefdom in the north of what is

now **Zimbabwe,** until it became incorporated into **Zambesia.**

Kings: ca. 1530–(?) Mbire; (?)–(?) [unknown]; (?)–(?) [unknown]; (?)–(?) [unknown]. *Mwene Mutapas:* ca. 1430–ca. 1450 Nyatsimba Mutota; ca. 1450–1480 Matope Nyanhehwe Nebedza; 1480–1480 Mavura Maobwe; 1480–1490 Nyahuma Mukombero; 1490–1494 Changamire; 1494–1530 Chikuyo Chisamarengu; 1530–1550 Neshangwe Munembire; 1550–1560 Chivere Nyasoro; 1560–1589 Negomo Chisamhuru; 1589–1623 Gatsi Rusere; 1623–1629 Nyambu Kapararidze; 1629–1652 Mavura Mhande Felipe; 1652–1663 Siti Kazurukamusapa; 1663–1692 Kamharapasu Mukombwe; 1692–1694 Nyakambira; 1694–1707 Nyamaende Mhande; 1707–1711 Nyenyedzi Zenda; 1711–1719 Boroma Dangwarangwa; 1719–1735 Samatambira Nyamhandu I; 1735–1740 Nyatsutsu; 1740–1759 Dehwe Mapunzagutu; 1759–1785 Changara; 1785–1790 Nyamhandu II; 1790–1810 Chiwayo; 1810–1835 Nyasoro; 1835–1868 Kataruza; 1868–1870 Kandeya; 1870–1887 Dzuda; 1887–1917 Chioko.

Mzilikazi's Land see **Matabeleland**

723 Namibia. See these **names:**
Namibia (1968–   )
Ovamboland Homeland (1968–   )
South West Africa United Nations Supervised Territory (1966–1968)
South West Africa United Nations Mandate (1946–1966)
South West Africa Mandate (1921–1946)
South West Africa Protectorate (1915–1921)
German South West Africa Colony (1892–1915)
German South West Africa Protectorate [ii] (1889–1892)
German South West Africa Protectorate [i] (1884–1889)
Walvis Bay Protectorate (1878–1885)
Rehoboth (1870–1885)
Oorlam Territory (1838–1886)
Witbooi Territory (ca. 1838–1893)
Hereroland (ca. 1730–1885)

724 Namibia. 12 June 1968–   . *Location:* on the west coast of Southern Africa, between **South Africa** and **Angola,** but excluding the exclave of Walvis Bay, which belongs to South Africa. *Capital:* Windhoek. *Other names:* South West Africa.

History: In 1968 the United Nations changed the name of **South-West Africa United Nations Supervised Territory** to Namibia (from the Namib Desert—a name meaning "area where nothing lives"), in what looks like the final stage of this country's development before independence from **South Africa.** S.W.A.P.O. (the South West Africa People's Organization of Namibia), formerly the Ovambo People's Organization, and consisting mainly of Ovambos (the largest ethnic group in the country) came to the fore in demanding self-determination. Led by Sam Nujoma and Hendrik Witbooi, S.W.A.P.O. (founded in 1958) engaged in political discussion and guerrilla warfare to achieve their aims, but **South Africa** refused to deal with them. In 1977 **Walvis Bay** was reincorporated into **South Africa,** and this port (lying in the center of the Namibian coastline) added another obstacle to settlement of the independence question. In 1977 an Administrator-General was sent out by **South Africa.** The occupation of Namibia by **South Africa** is a fact, and continues to be looked upon as illegal by most of the world, including the United Nations. Keen to alleviate world hostility, on Dec. 22, 1988 **South Africa** did agree to recognize Namibia's independence within the following year or two. Another question is that of the Bantustans, or Native Homelands. On October 2, 1968 **South Africa** created a "model" homeland for the Ovambos, and called it **Ovamboland,** giving it some degree of self-rule. However, the "model" turned out to be inaccessible to the world. On May 1, 1973 it achieved self-government, but the inaccessibility remained. Complete independence for **Ovamboland Homeland** is on the cards (independence of a sort achieved by **Transkei, Ciskei, Bophuthatswana** and **Venda**), and it is a matter of time to see whether that happens before the country of Namibia itself becomes independent. There are nine other Bantustans in Namibia now: Kavangoland, created October 10, 1972 in northeastern Namibia, with the capital at Rundu, is a homeland for the Kavango peoples (or Okavango). It is a strip of land three miles wide along the Okavango River. East Caprivi is a Bantustan for the Mafwe and the Masubia peoples, and is on the Caprivi Strip in northeastern Namibia. It was created in March 1972 and its capital is Ngwese. Kaokoland is in the Kaokoveld in northwestern Namibia, and its capital is Ohopoho. It is the homeland for the Himba and the Tjimba-Herero peoples. Damaraland is in the Namib Desert and is the homeland for the Damaras. Its capital is Weltwitschia. Hereroland is in the Kalahari Desert and is the Bantustan for the Hereros. Namaland is in the south and has as its capital, Gibeon. It is the homeland for the Namas (the former Namaquas). Bushmanland is also in the Kalahari Desert and is the homeland for the Bushmen or San peoples. Tswanaland is a fabricated homeland for a fabricated group of tribes—the "Tswanas." Essentially it is a convenient dumping ground for a lot of "inconvenient" natives. Finally, Rehoboth Gebiet, in central Namibia, has its capital at Rehoboth. This is the Bantustan for the Basters (Bastaards), and is the traditional home of these people (see also **Rehoboth,** their old homeland from 1870–1885).

Administrators: 12 June 1968–1 Nov. 1968 Wenzel du Plessis; 1 Nov. 1968–1 Nov. 1971 Johannes Van de Wath; 1 Nov. 1971–1 Sept. 1977 Barend Van der Walt. *Administrators-General:* 1 Sept. 1977–2 Aug. 1979 Marthinus Steyn;

2 Aug. 1979–4 Sept. 1980 Gerrit Van Niekerk Viljoen; 4 Sept. 1980–1 Feb. 1983 Danie Hough; 1 Feb. 1983–1 July 1985 Willie Van Niekerk; 1 July 1985– Louis Pienaar. *Commissioners-General:* 1 May 1970– Jannie de Wet. *Local Government:* 17 June 1985– provisional, with rapidly alternating ministers. *Chiefs of the Hereros:* 12 June 1968–26 July 1970 Hosea Kutako; 26 July 1970– Clemens Kapuuo. *U.N. Commissioners:* 13 June 1967–(?) Constantine Stavropoulos (acting); 18 Dec. 1973–1 Jan. 1977 Sean MacBride; 1 Jan. 1977–1 Apr. 1982 Martti Ahtisaari; 1 Apr. 1982–31 June 1987 Brajesh Chandra Mishra; 31 June 1987–21 Dec. 1988 Bernt Carlsson.

Nanumba see **Mossi States**

Napoleonic Egypt see **French Egypt**

725 Natal Colony [i]. 12 May 1843–31 May 1844. *Location:* as Natal Province, **South Africa.** *Capital:* Pietermaritzburg. *Other names:* Natal.

History: In 1843 **Natalia** was taken as a colony by Britain. In 1844 it was annexed by **British Cape Colony** as **Natal District.**

Special Commissioners: 12 May 1843–31 May 1844 Henry Cloete.

726 Natal Colony [ii]. 12 July 1856–10 May 1893. *Location:* eastern South Africa, i.e. as Natal Province of **South Africa.** *Capital:* Pietermaritzburg (founded 1839 and named for Piet Retief and Gerrit Maritz). *Other names:* Natal.

History: In 1856 **Natal District,** part of **British Cape Colony,** was reconstituted a separate British Crown Colony as Natal Colony. On January 1, 1866 it extended its borders to include the district of Alfred, and in 1893 it became self-governing (see **Natal Colony [Self-Rule]**).

Lieutenant-Governors: 12 July 1856–5 Nov. 1856 Henry Cooper; 5

Nov. 1856–31 Dec. 1864 John Scott; 31 Dec. 1864–26 July 1865 John Thomas (acting Administrator); 26 July 1865–24 May 1867 John Bisset (acting Administrator); 24 May 1867–19 July 1872 Robert Keate; 19 July 1872–30 Apr. 1873 Anthony Musgrave; 30 Apr. 1873–22 July 1873 Thomas Milles (Officer Administering); 22 July 1873–1 Apr. 1875 Sir Benjamin Pine; 1 Apr. 1875–3 Sept. 1875 Sir Garnet Wolseley (Officer Administering); 3 Sept. 1875–20 Apr. 1880 Sir Henry Bulwer; 20 Apr. 1880–5 May 1880 William Bellairs (Officer Administering); 5 May 1880–2 July 1880 Henry Clifford (Officer Administering). *Governors:* 2 July 1880–17 Aug. 1880 Sir George Colley; 17 Aug. 1880–14 Sept. 1880 Henry Alexander (Officer Administering); 14 Sept. 1880–27 Feb. 1881 Sir George Colley; 28 Feb. 1881–3 Apr. 1881 Sir Evelyn Wood (Officer Administering); 3 Apr. 1881–9 Aug. 1881 Redvers Buller (Officer Administering); 9 Aug. 1881–22 Dec. 1881 Sir Evelyn Wood (Officer Administering); 22 Dec. 1881–6 March 1882 Charles Mitchell (Officer Administering); 6 March 1882–23 Oct. 1885 Sir Henry Bulwer; 18 Feb. 1886–5 June 1889 Sir Arthur Havelock; 1 Dec. 1889– 10 May 1893 Sir Charles Mitchell.

727 Natal Colony (Self-Rule). 10 May 1893–30 May 1910. *Location:* as **Natal Colony [ii].** *Capital:* Pietermaritzburg. *Other names:* Natal.

History: In 1893 **Natal Colony [ii]** became self-ruling, and in 1897 it extended its boundaries by adding **British Zululand.** In 1902 it added parts of southern **Transvaal Colony [ii],** and in 1910 was one of the four self-ruling colonies to form the **Union of South Africa.** Natal then became the Province of Natal.

Governors: 10 May 1893–13 July 1893 Sir Charles Mitchell; 13 July 1893–27 Sept. 1893 Seymour Haden (Officer Administering); 28 Sept. 1893–6 March 1901 Sir Walter Hely-Hutchinson; 13 May 1901–7 June 1907 Sir Henry McCallum; 2 Sept. 1907–23 Dec. 1909 Sir Mathew Nathan; 17 Jan. 1910–30 May 1910 3rd Baron Methuen. *Chief Ministers:* 4 July 1893–14 Feb. 1897 Sir John Robinson; 15 Feb. 1897–4 Oct. 1897 Harry Escombe; 5 Oct. 1897–8 June 1899 Henry Binns (knighted 1898); 9 June 1899–17 Aug. 1903 Sir Albert Hime; 18 Aug. 1903–16 May 1905 George Sutton; 16 May 1905–22 Nov. 1906 Charles Smythe; 28 Nov. 1906–30 May 1910 Frederick Moor.

728 Natal District. 31 May 1844–12 July 1856. *Location:* Natal Province of **South Africa.** *Capital:* Pietermaritzburg.

History: In 1844 the young **Natal Colony [i]** became a district of **British Cape Colony.** Some Boers accepted British rule, others left for the Transvaal. Southern Zululand and **Pondoland** were restored to their original owners, and in 1856 Natal District became **Natal Colony [ii],** a separate British Crown Colony.

Lieutenant-Governors: 31 May 1844–4 Dec. 1845 Direct Cape Rule; 4 Dec. 1845–1 Aug. 1849 Martin West; 2 Aug. 1849–19 Apr. 1850 Edmond Boys; 19 Apr. 1850–12 Oct. 1852 Benjamin Pine; 12 Oct. 1852–31 Jan. 1853 Edmond Boys; 1 Feb. 1853–22 March 1853 Major W.R. Preston (acting); 22 March 1853–3 March 1855 Benjamin Pine; 3 March 1855–12 July 1855 Henry Cooper.

729 Natalia. 20 Oct. 1838–12 May 1843. *Location:* present-day Natal Province of **South Africa,** but larger. *Capital:* Pietermaritzburg. *Other names:* Natalia Republic, Natal Republic, Republic of Natal.

History: In 1838 the **Free Province of New Holland in South East Africa** became a republic, as Natalia. Later that year it acquired the British settlement of **Port Natal [ii]** and in 1839 southern Zululand and the land of the Mpondos (later **Pondoland**). In 1843 it was taken over by the British as a colony, **Natal Colony [i].**

Military Leaders: 20 Oct. 1838–23 Nov. 1838 Andries Pretorius. *Commandants-General:* 23 Nov. 1838–9 Aug. 1842 Andries Pretorius; 9 Aug. 1842–12 May 1843 Gerrit Rudolf.

Ndebeleland see **Matabeleland**

730 Ndongo. ca. 1358–ca. 1675. *Location:* southern Angola. *Capital:* Mbanza Kabassa. *Other names:* Dongo.

History: In the 14th century the Ngola peoples came from Central Africa and settled in southern Angola. The latter part of the history of Ndongo is one of war with the Portuguese, and in the late 17th century it became part of the Portuguese Imperial system (see **Portuguese West Africa**).

The only known rulers of Ndongo are: *Chiefs:* ca. 1358 Ngola-a-Nzinga. *Kings:* ca. 1619–1624 Ngola Nzinga Mbandi. *Queens:* 1624–1663 Jinga (or Anna de Souza Nzina).

Nembe see **Brass**

New Africa see **Africa Nova**

731 New Calabar. ca. 1550–5 June 1885. *Location:* Niger Delta, Nigeria. *Capital:* Elem Kalabari. *Other names:* Calabar, Kalabari, Calbaria, Awome.

History: There were two Calabars— New Calabar and Old Calabar (so-called after the mid–17th century to avoid confusion with New Calabar). Originally there were two states on the Nigerian coast: Efik, at the mouth of the Cross River, and Kalabari, 150 miles to the west on the Niger Delta. Kalabari was named for the founder of the tribe, but it is not known how the name Calabar came to be applied to the Efik state. However, by about 1650 Old Calabar was the name given to the Cross River state and New Calabar to the Niger Delta state. New Calabar (or Kalabari) was founded at an unknown date, legend says by Kalabari. Over the years it became the main slave-trading

state on the Niger Coast, and then, like **Bonny** and **Brass**, a dealer in palm oil. In 1885 it became part of the **Oil Rivers Protectorate.**

Kings: ca. 1550–ca. 1575 Kalabari; ca. 1575–ca. 1590 Owoma; ca. 1590–ca. 1600 Opukoroye; ca. 1600–ca. 1620 Owerri Daba; ca. 1620–ca. 1655 Igbessa; ca. 1655–ca. 1680 Kamalo (or King Robert); ca. 1680–ca. 1720 Mangi Suku; ca. 1720–ca. 1726 Igonibaw; ca. 1726–ca. 1733 Ngbesa; ca. 1733–ca. 1740 Omuye; ca. 1740–ca. 1745 Bokoye; ca. 1745–ca. 1750 Daba; ca. 1750–ca. 1770 Kalagba; ca. 1770–ca. 1790 Amakiri; ca. 1790–ca. 1835 Amakuru (or Amakiri II); ca. 1835–Apr. 1863 Karibo (or Amakiri III); Apr. 1863–ca. 1900 Abe (or Amakiri IV, or Prince Will).

732 New Georgia. 1824–1 Apr. 1839. *Location:* on Stockton Creek, Liberia. *Capital:* [unknown].

History: In 1824 the U.S. Government settled New Georgia with Congo Recaptives (slaves rescued by the Americans in mid-ocean). In 1839 it became part of **Liberia Commonwealth.**

Rulers: [unknown].

New Griqualand see **Griqualand East**

New Oyo see **Oyo**

733 New Republic. 16 Aug. 1884–11 Sept. 1887. *Location:* northwest Zululand (north Natal), South Africa. *Capital:* Vrijheid (or Vryheid) (means "freedom"). *Other names:* Nieuwe Republiek, Republiek Vrijheid, Vrijheid Republic.

History: In 1884, in return for helping to place Dinuzulu on the Zulu throne, Transvaal Boers (including Louis Botha) took half of Zululand and, incorporating the districts of Vrijheid, Utrecht and Wakkerstrom, created the New Republic. By 1885 they were claiming three-quarters of

Zululand, and on October 22, 1886 Britain recognized the New Republic, but with considerably withdrawn boundaries. In 1887 it became incorporated with the **South Africa Republic,** as the District of Vrijheid.
Presidents: 16 Aug. 1884–11 Sept. 1887 Lukas Meyer.

Ngaridza see **Gran Comoro**

Nieuwe Republiek see **New Republic**

734 Niger. See these **names:**
Niger Republic (1960–)
Niger Autonomous Republic (1958–1960)
Niger Overseas Territory (1946–1958)
Niger Colony (1922–1946)
Niger Civil Territory (1920–1922)
Niger Military Territory (1910–1920)
Zinder Autonomous Military Territory (1900–1910)
  Biram (ca. 1100–1805)
  Damagaram (1731–1899)
  Gobir (ca. 1110–1808)
  Gobir Emirate (1808–1900)
  Kororofa (ca. 1600–1901)

735 Niger Autonomous Republic. 19 Dec. 1958–3 Aug. 1960. *Location:* as **Niger Republic.** *Capital:* Niamey. *Other names:* Niger, République du Niger, Autonomous Republic of Niger. *History:* In 1958 **Niger Overseas Territory** became self-governing. In 1960 it gained full independence as **Niger Republic.** *High Commissioners:* 19 Dec. 1958–3 Aug. 1960 Don-Jean Colombani. *Chairmen of Government Council:* 19 Dec. 1958–3 Aug. 1960 Hamani Diori.

736 Niger Civil Territory. 4 Dec. 1920–13 Oct. 1922. *Location:* as **Niger Republic.** *Capital:* Zinder. *Other names:* Niger, Térritoire Civil du Niger. *History:* In 1920 **Niger Military Territory,** then part of the **French Sudan,** became a civil territory in preparation for becoming **Niger Colony,** which it

did in 1922. *Commissioners:* 4 Dec. 1920–1921 Lucien Rueff; 1921–13 Oct. 1922 Jules Brévié.

737 Niger Coast Protectorate. 13 May 1893–27 Dec. 1899. *Location:* southern Nigeria, excluding **Lagos Colony.** In other words, the same area as **Oil Rivers Protectorate.** *Capital:* Old Calabar.
History: In 1893 the **Oil Rivers Protectorate** became the Niger Coast Protectorate, i.e. a stretch of land across the Niger Delta protected by Britain. In 1899 it became the bulk of the **Southern Nigeria Protectorate.**
Commissioners/Consuls-General: 13 May 1893–1893 Ralph Moor (acting); 1893–1896 Sir Claude MacDonald; 1896–Nov. 1896 Ralph Moor; Nov. 1896–4 Jan. 1897 Mr. Phillips (acting); Feb. 1897–27 Dec. 1899 Ralph Moor (knighted 1897).

738 Niger Colony. 13 Oct. 1922–13 Oct. 1946. *Location:* as **Niger Republic.** *Capital:* Niamey (from 1926); Zinder (1922–26). *Other names:* Niger.
History: In 1922 **Niger Civil Territory** became a French colony. In 1946 it became **Niger Overseas Territory.**
Lieutenant-Governors: 13 Oct. 1922–1923 Jules Brévié; 1923–1925 Léonce Jore (acting); 1925–9 Oct. 1929 Jules Brévié; 9 Oct. 1929–21 Nov. 1929 Jean-Baptiste Fayout (acting); 21 Nov. 1929–30 Oct. 1930 Alphonse Choteau; 30 Oct. 1930–9 Sept. 1931 Louis Placide Blacher; 9 Sept. 1931–25 May 1933 Théophile Tellier; 25 May 1933–May 1934 Maurice Bourgine; May 1934–16 March 1935 Léon Pêtre; 16 March 1935–Aug. 1936 Joseph Court; Aug. 1936–Dec. 1936 Auguste Calvel (acting). *Governors:* Dec. 1936–29 Apr. 1938 Joseph Court; 29 Apr. 1938–18 Feb. 1939 Jean-Baptiste Chazelas (acting); 18 Feb. 1939–7 Nov. 1940 Jean Rapenne; 7 Nov. 1940–8 Dec. 1940 Léon Solomiac (acting); 8 Dec. 1940–4 March 1942 Maurice Falvy; 4 March

1942–30 Apr. 1946 Jean-François Toby; 30 Apr. 1946–13 Oct. 1946 Jacques Gosselin (acting).

739 Niger Districts Protectorate. 5 June 1885–10 July 1886. *Location:* northern Nigeria. *Capital:* Lokoja.

History: Sir George Goldie's United Africa Company, formed in 1879, created a large protectorate over a good deal of northern Nigeria in 1885. In 1885 his company was chartered as the Royal Niger Company, and the name of the area under his control became the **Niger River Delta Protectorate.**

Directors: 5 June 1885–10 July 1886 Sir George Goldie.

740 Niger Military Territory. 22 June 1910–4 Dec. 1920. *Location:* Niger. *Capital:* Zinder (1911–20); Niamey (1910–11). *Other names:* Niger, Térritoire Militaire du Niger.

History: In 1910 **Zinder Autonomous Military Territory,** part of **Upper Senegal–Niger** became the Military Territory of Niger. In 1920 it became **Niger Civil Territory.** By 1910 Upper Senegal–Niger had been pushed as far administratively as possible and it was deemed necessary to create Niger.

Commandants: 22 June 1910–27 Sept. 1911 Paul Venel; 27 Sept. 1911–1912 Col. Hocquart; 1912–24 Feb. 1913 Charles de Maugras (acting). *Commissioners:* 24 Feb. 1913–4 Dec. 1913 Charles de Maugras (acting); 4 Dec. 1913–15 Nov. 1915 Paul Venel; 15 Nov. 1915–24 Jan. 1918 Charles Mourin; 24 Jan. 1918–Aug. 1919 Félix Méchet; Aug. 1919–1920 Claude Lefebvre; 1920–5 July 1920 Maurice Renauld (acting); 5 July 1920–4 Dec. 1920 Lucien Rueff.

741 Niger Overseas Territory. 13 Oct. 1946–19 Dec. 1958. *Location:* as **Niger Republic.** *Capital:* Niamey. *Other names:* Niger.

History: In 1946 **Niger Colony** became an overseas territory of the Fourth French Republic. In 1958 it won self-rule (see **Niger Autonomous Republic).**

Governors: 13 Oct. 1946–20 Nov. 1946 Jean-François Toby (acting); 20 Nov. 1946–24 Nov. 1948 Jean-François Toby; 24 Nov. 1948–25 Feb. 1949 Lucien Geay (acting); 25 Feb. 1949–29 March 1950 Ignace Colombani (acting); 29 March 1950–11 Feb. 1952 Jean-François Toby; 11 Feb. 1952–23 Feb. 1953 Fernand Casimir (acting); 23 Feb. 1953–21 Dec. 1954 Jean-François Toby; 21 Dec. 1954–3 Nov. 1956 Jean-Paul Ramadier; 3 Nov. 1956–29 Jan. 1958 Paul Bordier; 29 Jan. 1958–25 Aug. 1958 Louis Rollet (acting). *High Commissioners:* 25 Aug. 1958–19 Dec. 1958 Don-Jean Colombani. *Prime Ministers:* 1957–14 Dec. 1958 Djibo Bakari; 14 Dec. 1958–19 Dec. 1958 Hamani Diori.

742 Niger Republic. 3 Aug. 1960– . *Location:* North West Africa. *Capital:* Niamey (origin of name uncertain and there are several legends concerning it). *Other names:* République du Niger, Republic of Niger.

History: In 1960 **Niger Autonomous Republic** became independent as the Republic of Niger, named for the Niger River (from "gher n-gheren" which in Tamashak means "river among rivers").

Presidents: 3 Aug. 1960–9 Nov. 1960 Hamani Diori (interim); 9 Nov. 1960–15 Apr. 1974 Hamani Diori; 17 Apr. 1974–10 Nov. 1987 Seyni Kountché; 10 Nov. 1987– Ali Seibou. *Prime Ministers:* 24 Jan. 1983–14 Nov. 1983 Oumarou Mamane; 14 Nov. 1983– Hamid Algabid. *Note:* in times of no Prime Minister, the President held that office.

743 Niger River Delta Protectorate. 10 July 1886–9 Aug. 1899. *Location:* northern Nigeria. *Capital:* Lokoja (founded 1860 by William Balfour Baikie). *Other names:* Royal Niger Company.

History: Sir George Goldie arrived in North West Africa in 1877, and in 1879 he combined all the British commercial interests on the Niger into The United African Company. In 1885 he established the **Niger Districts Protectorate,** which the following year became the Niger River Delta Protectorate. Goldie's company made treaties, fought battles, and generally was responsible for bringing British rule over northern Nigeria. In 1899 the British Government revoked the charter and took over the area for itself (see **Northern Nigeria Protectorate).**

Governors: 10 July 1886–25 Feb. 1895 1st Baron Aberdare; 25 Feb. 1895–9 Aug. 1899 Sir George Goldie. *Vice-Governors:* 10 July 1886–25 Feb. 1895 Sir George Goldie.

744 Nigeria. See these **names:**
Nigeria Federal Republic (1963–   )
Nigeria (1960–1963)
Nigeria Federation (1954–1960)
Nigeria Colony and Protectorate (1914–1954)
  Biafra (1967–1970)
  Nigeria Eastern Region (1939–1960)
  Nigeria Western Region (1939–1960)
  Nigeria Southern Provinces (1914–1939)
    Nigeria Northern Region (1914–1962)
    Southern Nigeria Colony and Protectorate (1906–1914)
      Northern Nigeria Protectorate (1899–1914)
      Southern Nigeria Protectorate (1899–1906)
        Niger Coast Protectorate (1893–1899)
          Oil Rivers Protectorate (1885–1893)
          Bights of Biafra and Benin (1867–1885)
            Bight of Biafra (1849–1867)
            Bight of Benin (1852–1861)
            Lagos Protectorate (1887–1899)
            Lagos Colony (1886–1906)
            Lagos Territory [ii] (1874–1886)
            Lagos Territory [i] (1866–1874)
            Lagos Settlement (1862–1866)
            Lagos (1861–1862)
          Niger River Delta Protectorate (1886–1899)

Niger Districts Protectorate (1885–1886)
Muri Protectorate (1892–1893)
Abeokuta (ca. 1830–1893)
Abuja (1828–1902)
Agaie (1832–1898)
Argungu (1827–1902)
Bauchi Emirate (1805–1902)
Bedde (1825–1902)
Benin (1170–1897)
Biu (ca. 1535–1899)
Bonny (ca. 1450–1885)
Bornu State (ca. 850–ca. 1260)
Brass (ca. 1450–1885)
Daniski (1447–1806)
Daura-Baure (ca. 1825–1903)
Daura Emirate (1805–1903)
Daura Kingdom (ca. 700–1805)
Daura-Zango (1825–1903)
Doma (1232–1901)
East Nupe (1796–1805)
Egba United Government (1893–1914)
Fika (1806–1899)
Fulani Empire (1804–1903)
Gombe Emirate (1804–1902)
Gumel (1749–1903)
Gwandu (1808–1893)
Hadeija (ca. 1460–1805)
Hadeija Emirate (1808–1906)
Hausaland — explanation and referral entry
Ibadan (ca. 1750–1893)
Ife (ca. 1000–1900)
Igala (ca. 1528–1901)
Ijebu ([?]–1892)
Ilorin Emirate (1831–1897)
Ilorin Kingdom ([?]–1829)
Jema'a (1810–1902)
Jemaari (1835–1903)
Kano ([?]–998)
Kano Emirate (1807–1903)
Kano Kingdom (998–1807)
Katagum (1807–1903)
Katsina Emirate (1806–1903)
Katsina Kingdom (ca. 1015–1806)
Kazaure (1824–1906)
Keana (ca. 1700–1900)
Kebbi (1516–1827)
Keffi (ca. 1750–1902)
Kontagora (1864–1901)
Lafia (1780–1900)

Lafiagi (1824–1900)
Lagos Kingdom (ca. 1700–1861)
Lapai (1825–1898)
Misau Emirate (1831–1903)
Muri [ii] (1893–1901)
Muri [i] (1833–1892)
New Calabar (ca. 1550–1885)
Nupe Emirate (1835–1901)
Nupe Kingdom [ii] (1805–1835)
Nupe Kingdom [i] (1531–1796)
Opobo (1870–1884)
Oyo (ca. 1400–1900)
Potiskum (ca. 1809–1901)
Rabih's Empire (1893–1901)
Warri (ca. 1475–1884)
Wase (Basharawa) (ca. 1790–1820)
Wase (Fulani) (1820–1898)
West Nupe (1796–1805)
Yauri (ca. 1400–1901)
Zamfara (ca. 1200–1902)
Zaria (ca. 1578–1835)
Zaria Emirate (1835–1902)
Zazzau (ca. 1010–1578)

745 Nigeria. 1 Oct. 1960–1 Oct. 1963. *Location:* as **Nigeria Federal Republic.** *Capital:* Lagos.

History: In 1960 **Nigeria Federation** became independent as Nigeria. In 1963 it became **Nigeria Federal Republic.**

Governors-General: 1 Oct. 1960–16 Nov. 1960 Sir James Robertson; 16 Nov. 1960–1 Oct. 1963 Nnamdi Azikiwe. *Premiers:* 1 Oct. 1960–1 Oct. 1963 Sir Abubaka Tafawa Balewa.

746 Nigeria Colony and Protectorate. 1 Jan. 1914–1 Oct. 1954. *Location:* as **Nigeria.** *Capital:* Lagos. *Other names:* Nigeria.

History: In 1914 Lord Lugard united **Southern Nigeria Colony and Protectorate** and **Northern Nigeria Protectorate** to form the British colony and protectorate of Nigeria. The southern and northern regions continued to be administered separately (see **Nigeria Southern Provinces** and **Nigeria Northern Region**), both answerable to Lagos. In 1939 Southern Provinces split into two, **Nigeria Eastern Region** and **Nigeria Western Region,** still admin-

istered separately. In 1954 a measure of self-rule came to Nigeria (see **Nigeria Federation**). *Note:* The name Nigeria was chosen for the new colony in 1914 on the suggestion of Lady Lugard (she was Flora Shaw at the time), rather than other proposed names like Niger Sudan, Negretia and Goldesia.

Governors-General: 1 Jan. 1914–July 1919 Sir Frederick Lugard. *Governors:* 8 Aug. 1919–1921 Sir Hugh Clifford; 1921–1921 Donald Cameron (acting); 1921–May 1925 Sir Hugh Clifford; May 1925–13 Nov. 1925 [unknown] (acting); 13 Nov. 1925–1930 Sir Graeme Thompson; 1930–17 June 1931 [unknown] (acting); 17 June 1931–1935 Sir Donald Cameron; 1935–1 Nov. 1935 John Maybin (acting); 1 Nov. 1935–1 July 1940 Sir Bernard Bourdillon; 1 July 1940–1 July 1940 Sir John Shuckburgh (never took office); 1 July 1940–1942 Sir Bernard Bourdillon; 1942–1942 Sir Alan Burns (acting); 1942–18 Dec. 1943 Sir Bernard Bourdillon; 18 Dec. 1943–1947 Sir Arthur Richards; 1947–5 Feb. 1948 [unknown] (acting); 5 Feb. 1948–1952 Sir John MacPherson; 1952–1952 Arthur Benson (acting); 1952–1 Oct. 1954 Sir John MacPherson. *Chief Ministers:* May 1952–1 Oct. 1954 Nnamdi Azikiwe.

747 Nigeria Eastern Region. 1939–1 Oct. 1960. *Location:* southeastern Nigeria. *Capital:* Enugu. *Other names:* Eastern Nigeria.

History: In 1939 **Nigeria Southern Provinces** was divided into two— Nigeria Eastern Region and **Nigeria Western Region,** in order to make the demarcated lines more compatible with ethnic groupings. Both of these regions were administratively answerable to the Nigerian capital in Lagos. In 1960 with independence, these regions ceased to exist as colonial divisions.

Chief Commissioners: 1939–1943 George Shute; 1943–1948 Frederick Carr; 1948–1951 James Pyke-Nott. *Lieutenant-Governors:* 1951–1952 James Pyke-Nott; 1952–1954 Clement

Pleass (knighted 1953). *Governors:* 1954–1956 Sir Clement Pleass; 1956–1 Oct. 1960 Sir Robert Stapledon. *Premiers:* 1 Oct. 1954–1959 Nnamdi Azikiwe; Jan. 1960–1 Oct. 1960 Michael Okpara.

748 Nigeria Federal Republic. 1 Oct. 1963– . *Location:* North West Africa. *Capital:* Lagos (not for long — a Federal Capital Territory has been allocated in the center of Nigeria). (Lagos was originally called "eko," meaning "war camp." The Portuguese called it "Lago de Curamo," then "Onin," then "Lagos" for a harbor in Portugal.) *Other names:* Federal Republic of Nigeria, Nigeria.

History: In 1963 **Nigeria** became a federal republic within the British Commonwealth. From 1967–1970 Eastern Nigeria broke away to form **Biafra.** *Presidents:* 1 Oct. 1963–15 Jan. 1966 Nnamdi Azikiwe; 15 Jan. 1966–29 July 1966 Johnson Aguiyi-Ironsi (Head of Military Council); 29 July 1966–29 July 1975 Yokubu Gowon (Head of Military Council); 29 July 1975–13 Feb. 1976 Murtala Ramat Muhammad (Head of State); 13 Feb. 1976–1 Oct. 1979 Olusegun Obasanjo (Head of Military Government); 1 Oct. 1979–31 Dec. 1983 Alhajji Shehu Shagari; 3 Jan. 1984–27 Aug. 1985 Muhammad Buhari (Chairman of the Supreme Military Council); 30 Aug. 1985– Ibrahim Babangida. *Prime Ministers:* 1 Oct. 1963–15 Jan. 1966 Sir Abubaka Tafawa Balewa (Premier); 15 Jan. 1966–17 Jan. 1966 Mallam Dipchairina (acting); 15 Feb. 1976–31 Dec. 1983 Shehu Musa Yar Adua.

749 Nigeria Federation. 1 Oct. 1954–1 Oct. 1960. *Location:* as **Nigeria Federal Republic.** *Capital:* Lagos. *Other names:* The Federation of Nigeria.

History: In 1954 **Nigeria Colony and Protectorate** and **Cameroons British Trust Territory** merged to form the partially autonomous Federation of Nigeria. In 1960 the whole country

became independent as **Nigeria** (see also **Nigeria Western Region, Nigeria Eastern Region** and **Nigeria Northern Region**).

Governors-General: 1 Oct. 1954–15 June 1955 Sir John MacPherson; 15 June 1955–1 Oct. 1960 Sir James Robertson. *Premiers:* 2 Sept. 1957–1 Oct. 1960 Sir Abubaka Tafawa Balewa. *Presidents:* 12 Dec. 1959–1 Oct. 1960 Nnamdi Azikiwe.

750 Nigeria Northern Region. 1 Jan. 1914–1962. *Location:* northern Nigeria. *Capital:* Kaduna (1917–1962. "Kaduna" means "crocodile" in Hausa, and the town was built in 1913); Zungeru (1914–1917). *Other names:* Northern Region.

History: In 1914, on Amalgamation (see **Nigeria Southern Provinces** for details), the Northern Region of Nigeria continued to be ruled separately, subject to Lagos. This was the only division of **Nigeria** which continued to exist after independence in 1960.

Lieutenant-Governors: 1 Jan. 1914–1917 Charles Temple; 1917–1921 Herbert Goldsmith; 1921–1925 William Gowers; 1925–1930 Richmond Palmer; 1930–1932 Cyril Alexander. *Chief Commissioners:* 1932–1937 George Browne; 1937–1943 Theodore Adams; 1943–1947 John Patterson; 1947–1951 Eric Thompstone. *Lieutenant-Governors:* 1951–1952 Eric Thompstone; 1952–1954 Bryan Sharwood-Smith (knighted 1953). *Governors:* 1954–2 Dec. 1957 Sir Bryan Sharwood-Smith; 2 Dec. 1957–1962 Sir Gawain Bell. *Premiers:* 1 Oct. 1954–1962 Alhaji Ahmadu Bello.

751 Nigeria Southern Provinces. 1 Jan. 1914–1939. *Location:* southern Nigeria. *Capital:* Enugu (from 1928); Calabar (until 1928). *Other names:* Southern Provinces, Southern Region.

History: In 1914, with the amalgamation of all colonies and protectorates in the area into **Nigeria Colony and Protectorate,** the Southern Provinces and **Nigeria Northern Region** continued to

be administered separately, albeit both answerable to Lagos. In 1939 the Southern Provinces split into two— **Nigeria Western Region** and **Nigeria Eastern Region.**
Lieutenant-Governors: 1 Jan. 1914–1920 Alexander Boyle; 1921–1925 Harry Moorhouse; 1925–1929 Upton Ruxton; 1929–1930 Cyril Alexander; 1930–1935 Walter Buchanan-Smith. *Chief Commissioners:* 1935–1939 William Hunt.

752 Nigeria Western Region. 1939–1 Oct. 1960. *Location:* southwestern Nigeria. *Capital:* Ibadan. *Other names:* Western Nigeria.
History: In 1939 **Nigeria Southern Provinces** split into two regions (see **Nigeria Eastern Region** for details). In 1960 they ceased to exist as **Nigeria** came into being.
Chief Commissioners: 1939–1946 Gerald Whiteley; 1946–1951 Theodore Hoskins-Abrahall. *Lieutenant-Governors:* 1951–1951 Theodore Hoskins-Abrahall; 1951–1954 Hugo Marshall. *Governors:* 1954–1 Oct. 1960 Sir John Rankine. *Premiers:* 1 Oct. 1954–Dec. 1959 Obafemi Awolowo; Dec. 1959–1 Oct. 1960 Samuel Akintola.

753 Nile Provisional Government. March 1969–1970. *Location:* southern Sudan. *Capital:* none. *Other names:* NPG.
History: (See also **Southern Sudan Provisional Government.**) In 1962 William Deng, Joseph Oduho, Aggrey Jaden and Father Lohure Saturnino created the Sudan African Closed Districts National Union, which in 1963 changed its name to the Sudan African National Union (SANU). This was the first major liberation movement for the Southern Sudan. In 1965 SANU split over the issue of compromise with the Khartoum government, and SANU-Inside (headed by William Deng) and SANU-in-Exile (headed by Oduho and Saturnino) came into being. SANU-Inside continued, within the Sudan, until the murder of Deng in 1968, while

SANU-in-Exile re-grouped and formed the Azania Liberation Front in 1965 (Azania meaning "black Africa"). Meanwhile Aggrey Jaden had formed the Sudan African Liberation Front in 1965 and later in the year merged SALF with ALF. Also formed, in 1963, was the Southern guerrilla organization Anya Nya, headed by Joseph Lagu, which operated in the southern provinces. In 1967 the **Southern Sudan Provisional Government (SSPG)** was formed, with Aggrey Jaden as president. In 1969 this was replaced by the Nile Provisional Government, formed in Uganda. Its leaders were Gordon Mayen and Maro Morgan. Also in 1969 was formed the South Sudan Liberation Movement, by Joseph Lagu, who succeeded in bringing together most of the southern political factions by 1971, including the **Anyidi Revolutionary Government,** which had been formed in 1969 as the likely successor to the Nile Provisional Government. On February 28, 1972 the SSLM was the main spokesman at the Addis Ababa Conference between Khartoum and the South, and as a result a certain autonomy was granted to the Southern Provinces, a Southern Region High Executive Committee being set up. Some elements continued to fight for complete independence for the Southern region.
Presidents: March 1969–1970 Gordon Mayen.

Nimby see **Brass**

Nkole see **Nkore**

754 Nkore. ca. 1430–1896. *Location:* southwest Uganda. *Capital:* Mbarara. *Other names:* Nkole, Ankole, Ankhole.
History: About 1430 the Bahinda dynasty from **Karagwe** began to rule in Nkore, one of the old Ugandan chiefdoms (others were **Buganda, Bunyoro,** the many tribes forming Busoga, as well as Bukedi, Toro, Kitara, Buduu,

Acholi, Bugisu). In 1896 it was placed under a protectorate, falling under the enveloping **Uganda Protectorate.** In 1967 the kingdom was abolished. The Nkole people consist of nine parts Iru and one part Hima.

Mugabes (Kings): ca. 1430–ca. 1446 Ruhinda; ca. 1446–ca. 1475 Nkuba; ca. 1475–ca. 1503 Nyaika; ca. 1503–ca. 1531 Nyabugaro Ntare I; ca. 1531–ca. 1559 Rushango; ca. 1559–ca. 1587 Ntare II Kagwejegyerera; ca. 1587–ca. 1615 Ntare III Rugamaba; ca. 1615–ca. 1643 Kasasira; ca. 1643–ca. 1671 Kitera (joint); ca. 1643–ca. 1671 Kumongye (joint); ca. 1671–ca. 1699 Mirindi; ca. 1699–ca. 1727 Ntare IV Kitabanyoro; ca. 1727–ca. 1755 Macwa; ca. 1755–ca. 1783 Rwabirere (joint); ca. 1755–ca. 1783 Karara I (joint); ca. 1755–ca. 1783 Karaiga (joint); ca. 1755–ca. 1783 Kahaya I (joint); ca. 1783–ca. 1811 Nyakashaija (joint); ca. 1783–ca. 1811 Bwarenga (joint); ca. 1783–ca. 1811 Rwebishengye (joint); ca. 1811–ca. 1839 Kayunga (joint); ca. 1811–ca. 1839 Gasiyonga I (joint); ca. 1839–ca. 1867 Mutambuka; ca. 1867–1895 Ntare V; 1895–1944 Kahaya II; 1944–8 Sept. 1967 Gasiyonga II.

Nobatae, Nobatia see **Nubia**

Noman's Land see **Griqualand East**

755 Norman Tripolitania. 1148–22 Jan. 1160. *Location:* Tripoli and the eastern Tunisia coast. *Capital:* Tripoli.

History: In 1148 the Normans from Sicily conquered the area of the Gulf of Libya, but during the period 1158–60 lost it to the newly arriving **Almohad Empire.** The fall of Tripoli marked the end of Norman rule in North Africa.

Kings: 1148–26 Feb. 1154 Roger II of Sicily; 26 Feb. 1154–22 Jan. 1160 William I of Sicily.

North Bechuanaland see **Bechuanaland**

756 North Zambesia. 23 Jan. 1894–3 May 1895. *Location:* as **Zambia.** *Capital:* Fort Salisbury (South Zambesia).

History: In 1894, on the splitting up of **Zambesia** into North Zambesia (all land of British occupation north of the Zambesi River), and **South Zambesia,** stage one in the evolution of the Rhodesias was complete, i.e. the setting up of two Rhodesias (see **Zambesia** for fuller details of the area prior to 1894). In 1895 the situation was simplified further by North and South Zambesia joining to form the **Rhodesia Protectorate.**

Rulers: 23 Jan. 1894–3 May 1895 Direct rule from South Zambesia.

757 North Eastern Rhodesia. 29 Jan. 1900–17 Aug. 1911. *Location:* Zambia. *Capital:* Fort Jameson (now known as Chipata) (named for Dr. Leander Starr Jameson [later Sir Starr Jameson] and established in 1899).

History: In 1900, on the dividing of the **Rhodesia Protectorate** (see that entry for fuller details) this area, with the same administrators as were under the protectorate, became officially North Eastern Rhodesia. In 1911 it became part of **Northern Rhodesia.**

Administrators: 29 Jan. 1900–31 May 1900 Robert Codrington (Deputy); 31 May 1900–24 Apr. 1907 Robert Codrington; 24 Apr. 1907–Jan. 1909 Lawrence Wallace (acting); Jan. 1909–16 May 1911 Leicester Beaufort; 16 May 1911–17 Aug. 1911 Hugh Marshall (acting).

North West Madagascar Territory see **Nossi-Bé Territory**

758 North Western Rhodesia. 29 Jan. 1900–17 Aug. 1911. *Location:* Zambia. *Capital:* Lealui.

History: In 1900 the **Rhodesia Protectorate** came to an end, being split into three parts by the BSAC (British South Africa Company), who administered all of Northern Rhodesia until 1924, and all of Southern Rhodesia till 1923. The three parts created were

North Western Rhodesia, **North Eastern Rhodesia** and **Southern Rhodesia.** The northern areas had been delimited and administered as North East and North West Rhodesia while part of **Rhodesia Protectorate** (see that entry for list of those rulers), but it wasn't until 1900 that the geographical splits took place. In 1911 North Western Rhodesia and North Eastern Rhodesia became one area — **Northern Rhodesia.**

Residents in Barotseland: 29 Jan. 1900–18 Sept. 1907 Robert Coryndon. *Administrators:* 18 Sept. 1900–8 Apr. 1907 Robert Coryndon; 8 Apr. 1907–20 Oct. 1907 Hugh Hole (acting); 20 Oct. 1907–Feb. 1908 John Carden (acting); Feb. 1908–16 Dec. 1908 Robert Codrington; Jan. 1909–17 Aug. 1911 Lawrence Wallace (acting).

Northern Egypt see **Lower Egypt**

759 Northern Nigeria Protectorate. 27 Dec. 1899–1 Jan. 1914. *Location:* northern Nigeria. *Capital:* Zungeru (from Sept. 1902); Jebba (1900–02); Lokoja (1899–1902).

History: Operationally from January 1, 1900 the area which is today **Nigeria Federal Republic** was split into two British protectorates — Northern Nigeria Protectorate and **Southern Nigeria Protectorate,** as well as the then-existing **Lagos Colony.** By March 15, 1903 conquest of northern Nigeria was complete, and in 1906 Lagos and Southern Nigeria united. In 1914 all areas united, including Northern Nigeria Protectorate, to form **Nigeria Colony and Protectorate.**

High Commissioners: 1 Jan. 1900–May 1906 Frederick Lugard (knighted 1901); July 1906–Apr. 1907 Sir William Wallace (acting); Apr. 1907–1908 Sir Percy Girouard. *Governors:* 1908–28 Sept. 1909 Sir Percy Girouard; 28 Sept. 1909–1912 Sir Hesketh Bell; 1912–1 Jan. 1914 Sir Frederick Lugard.

760 Northern Rhodesia. 17 Aug. 1911–1 Apr. 1924. *Location:* as **Zambia.**

Capital: Livingstone (now called Maramba) (named for Dr. Livingstone, the explorer).

History: In 1911 the two districts of **North Western Rhodesia** and **North Eastern Rhodesia** became one — Northern Rhodesia, still ruled by the British South Africa Company (BSAC). In 1924 the country became a British protectorate (see **Northern Rhodesia Protectorate**).

Administrators: 17 Aug. 1911–17 March 1921 Lawrence Wallace (knighted 1918); 17 March 1921–20 Sept. 1923 Sir Drummond Chaplin; 20 Sept. 1923–1 Apr. 1924 Richard Goode (acting).

761 Northern Rhodesia Protectorate. 1 Apr. 1924–22 Jan. 1964. *Location:* as **Zambia.** *Capital:* Lusaka (1935–64); Livingstone (1924–35).

History: In 1924 **Northern Rhodesia,** until then in the hands of the British South Africa Company (BSAC), became a British protectorate. In 1964 the country acquired self-rule (see **Northern Rhodesia [Self-Rule]**).

Governors: 1 Apr. 1924–25 July 1927 Sir Herbert Stanley; 25 July 1927–31 Aug. 1927 Richard Goode (acting); 31 Aug. 1927–1931 Sir James Maxwell; 1931–1931 Donald Mackenzie-Kennedy (acting); 1931–30 Nov. 1932 Sir James Maxwell; 1 Dec. 1932–20 March 1934 Sir Ronald Storrs; 20 March 1934–31 Aug. 1938 Sir Hubert Young; 1 Sept. 1938–9 Apr. 1941 Sir John Maybin; 9 Apr. 1941–15 Oct. 1941 William Logan (acting); 16 Oct. 1941–15 Oct. 1947 Sir John Waddington; 16 Oct. 1947–18 Feb. 1948 Richard Stanley (acting); 19 Feb. 1948–8 March 1954 Sir Gilbert Rennie; 8 March 1954–24 May 1954 Alexander Williams (acting); 25 May 1954–22 Apr. 1959 Sir Arthur Benson; 22 Apr. 1959–22 Jan. 1964 Sir Evelyn Hone.

762 Northern Rhodesia (Self-Rule). 22 Jan. 1964–24 Oct. 1964. *Location:* as **Zambia.** *Capital:* Lusaka. *Other names:*

Northern Rhodesia.

History: In early 1964 **Northern Rhodesia Protectorate** became self-governing, and later in the year it achieved independence from Britain, as **Zambia**.

Governors: 22 Jan. 1964–24 Oct. 1964 Sir Evelyn Hone. *Prime Ministers:* 22 Jan. 1964–24 Oct. 1964 Kenneth Kaunda.

763 Nossi-Bé Colony. 1878–6 Aug. 1896. *Location:* as **Nossi-Bé Territory**. *Capital:* Hellville. *Other names:* Nosy-Bé, Nossi-Vey.

History: In 1878 **Nossi-Bé Dependent Colony** became an independent colony, that is a colony of France dependent on no other colony. In 1896, when the whole of Madagascar became a colony (see **Madagascar Colony**), Nossi-Bé was merged into it.

Governors: 1878–1883 Alphonse Seignac-Lesseps; 1883–1886 Alexandre Le Maître; 1886–1888 Léon Clément-Thomas; 1888–1889 Furcy Augustin Armanet; 1889–6 Aug. 1896 Joseph François.

764 Nossi-Bé Dependent Colony. 25 March 1843–1878. *Location:* as **Nossi-Bé Territory**. *Capital:* Hellville. *Other names:* Nosy-Bé, Nossi-Vey.

History: In 1843 **Nossi-Bé Territory**, then under **Réunion** administration, was transferred to **Mayotte** as a dependent colony. In 1878 it became a separate colony (see **Nossi-Bé Colony**).

Governors: 25 March 1843–1845 Charles Morel; 1845–1848 Henri-Martin Lamy; 1848–1851 Jean-Ernest Marchaisse; 1851–1851 Alexandre Berg; 1851–1852 Jean Lapeyre-Bellair; 1852–1853 Thomas Dupuis; 1853–1854 André Brisset; 1854–1855 Louis Arnoux; 1855–1856 Joseph Septans; 1856–1858 Thomas Dupuis; 1858–1860 Paul-Gustave Sachet; 1860–1861 Justin Dupérier; 1861–1865 Vincent Derussat; 1865–1866 Pierre Lucas; 1866–1868 Joseph Hayes; 1868–1869 Louis Chériner; 1869–1870 Aimé Champy; 1870–1871 Jules Ventre de la Touloubre; 1871–1872 Jean-Baptiste Barnier; 1872–1873 Marie-Alexandre Leclos; 1873–1874 Honoré Léchelle; 1874–1875 Claude Fontaine; 1875–1876 Joseph Carle; 1876–1876 Arthur-Paul Feutray; 1876–1878 François Ferriez.

765 Nossi-Bé Territory. 14 July 1940–25 March 1843. *Location:* off the northwest coast of Madagascar. *Capital:* Hellville (named for Admiral de Hell, French Commander in the Indian Ocean, and named by Pierre Passot). *Other names:* North-West Madagascar Territory, Nosy-Bé (means "great island").

History: In 1840 the Sakalava ruler of the northwest portion of Madagascar ceded the island of Nossi-Bé to France. It was used as a naval station, and was placed under the administration of **Réunion**. In 1843 it became **Nossi-Bé Dependent Colony**, under the administration of **Mayotte Protectorate**.

Governors: 3 Feb. 1841–1842 François Gouhot; 1842–1842 Capt. Pierre Passot; 1842–25 March 1843 Charles Morel.

Nosy Boraha see **Sainte Marie de Madagascar**

766 Nubia. ca. 325–ca. 675. *Location:* northern Sudan. *Capital:* Pachoras (or Bukharas) (today called Faras). *Other names:* Nobatae, Nobatia.

History: The Nobatae, or X-Group, a Nilotic Sudanese group, ruled Nubia from about 325 after Meroë was destroyed (see **Kush**). The Nobatae were converted to Christianity about 540. Engulfed by **Mukurra** about 675, the two states became **Dongola**. The name Nubia continued until 1821 when the Egyptians conquered the area (see **Egyptian Sudan**).

Rulers: unknown.

767 Numidia. 201 B.C.–46 B.C.

Location: Algeria. *Capital:* Cirta (or Kirtha — from the Phoenician, meaning "a city." It was renamed Constantine in 313 A.D.).

History: Numidia was the Roman name for the country that is now Algeria. From before the 6th century B.C. it was inhabited by a variety of semi-nomadic tribes, but in 201 B.C. it was united as a country by Masinissa, of the Massyli tribe living near Cirta. Masinissa, an ally of **Carthage**, went over to the Roman side in 206 B.C., and by 201 B.C. he ruled the Roman client kingdom of Numidia. On his death the Romans split his kingdom among his three sons, and this division stayed in force until 112 B.C. when Jugurtha reunified the kingdom for seven years before the Romans won back control. Numidian territory was heavily reduced. In 49 B.C. Juba attempted to throw off Roman rule, but was defeated in 46 B.C. and Julius Caesar formed **Africa Nova** from it as a Roman province.

Kings: 201 B.C.–148 B.C. Masinissa; 148 B.C.–118 B.C. Micipsa (joint); 148 B.C.–118 B.C. Gulussa (joint); 148 B.C.–118 B.C. Mastanabal (joint); 118 B.C.–112 B.C. Adherbal (joint); 118 B.C.–117 B.C. Hiempsal I (joint); 118 B.C.–105 B.C. Jugurtha (joint until 112 B.C.); 105 B.C.–ca. 88 B.C. Gauda; ca. 88 B.C.–ca. 62 B.C. Hiempsal II; ca. 62 B.C.–46 B.C. Juba I.

Nupe East see **East Nupe**

768 Nupe Emirate. 1835–1901. *Location:* northern Nigeria. *Capital:* Bida (from 1857); Raba (until 1857).

History: In 1835 **Nupe Kingdom [ii]** became a Fulani emirate, and in 1901 it was incorporated into **Northern Nigeria Protectorate** as Bida Emirate within Niger Province.

Emirs: 1835–1841 Uthman Zaki; 1841–1847 Masaba; 1847–1856 Umar Bahaushe; 1856–1859 Uthman Zaki; 1859–1873 Masaba; 1873–1884 Umar Majigi; 1884–1895 Malik; 1895–1901 Abu-Bakr; 1901–Feb. 1916 Muhammad; 1916–1926 Bello; 1926–1935 Sa'id; 1935–1962 Muhammad Ndayako; 1962– Uthman Sarki.

769 Nupe Kingdom [i]. 1531–1796. *Location:* Niger Province, Nigeria. *Capital:* Bedeghi (1776–96); Biaghi (1766–76); Bedeghi (1760–66); Biaghi (1741–60); Labuji (1717–41); Jebba (ca. 1660–1717); Pategi (ca. 1580–ca. 1660); Gbara (now Jimunli) (ca. 1550–ca. 1580); Bida-Nupiko (1531–ca. 1550).

History: Tsoede, the illegitimate son of Attah of Idah, founded the kingdom of Nupe in 1531. In 1796 the kingdom temporarily split up into two separate kingdoms, **West Nupe** and **East Nupe.**

Etsus (Kings): 1531–1591 Tsoede (or Edegi, or Choede); 1591–1600 Shaba (or Tsoacha); 1600–1625 Zaulla (or Zavunla, or Zagulla); 1625–1670 Jiga (or Jia, or Jigba); 1670–1679 Mamman Wari; 1679–1700 Abdu Waliyi; 1700–1710 Aliyu; 1710–1713 Ganamace (or Sachi Gana Machi); 1713–1717 Ibrahima; 1717–1721 Idrisu I (or Ederisu); 1721–1742 Tsado (or Chado, or Abdullahi); 1742–1746 Abu Bakr Kolo; 1746–1759 Jibrin (or Jibrilu); 1759–1767 Ma'azu; 1767–1777 Majiya I (or Zubeiru); 1777–1778 Iliyasu; 1778–1795 Ma'azu; 1795–1795 Alikolo Tankari; 1795–1796 Mamma.

770 Nupe Kingdom [ii]. 1805–1835. *Location:* Nigeria. *Capital:* Zugurma (1830–35); Adama Lulu (1810–30); Raba (1805–10). *Other names:* Nupe.

History: In 1805 **East Nupe** and **West Nupe** were reunited. In 1835 Nupe became a part of the **Fulani Empire** as **Nupe Emirate.**

Kings: 1805–1810 Majiya II; 1810–1830 Idrisu II; 1830–1834 Majiya II; 1834–1835 Tsado.

Nupe West see **West Nupe**

Nyamwezi see **Mirambo**

771 Nyasaland. 14 May 1891–22

Feb. 1893. *Location:* as **Malawi Republic.** *Capital:* Zomba (established 1885).

History: In 1891 the **Shiré River Protectorate** was expanded and became Nyasaland. In 1893 the name was changed to **British Central Africa Protectorate.**

Commissioners/Consuls-General: 14 May 1891–22 Feb. 1893 Harry Johnston.

772 Nyasaland Protectorate. 6 July 1907–9 May 1963. *Location:* as **Malawi Republic.** *Capital:* Zomba.

History: In 1907 the term **British Central Africa Protectorate** was superseded by the more popular Nyasaland to describe the area now called **Malawi.** From 1953–63 it was, with **Northern Rhodesia Protectorate** and **Southern Rhodesia Colony** part of the **Federation of Rhodesia and Nyasaland.** In 1963 Nyasaland achieved self-rule (see **Nyasaland [Self-Rule]**).

Governors: 6 July 1907–30 Sept. 1907 Francis Pearce (acting); 1 Oct. 1907–1 May 1908 Sir William Manning (acting); 1 May 1908–1 Apr. 1910 Sir Alfred Sharpe; 1 Apr. 1910–3 July 1910 Francis Pearce (acting); 4 July 1910–6 Feb. 1911 Henry Wallis (acting); 6 Feb. 1911–23 Sept. 1913 Sir William Manning; 23 Sept. 1913–1921 George Smith (knighted 1914); 1921–1921 Richard Rankine (acting); 1921–12 Apr. 1923 Sir George Smith; 12 Apr. 1923–27 March 1924 Richard Rankine (acting); 27 March 1924–30 May 1929 Sir Charles Bowring; 30 May 1929–7 Nov. 1929 Wilfred Davidson-Houston (acting); 7 Nov. 1929–22 Nov. 1932 Shenton Thomas (knighted 1931); 22 Nov. 1932–9 Apr. 1934 Sir Hubert Young; 9 Apr. 1934–21 Sept. 1934 Kenneth Hall (acting); 21 Sept. 1934–14 Jan. 1939 Sir Harold Kittermaster; 20 March 1939–8 Aug. 1942 Sir Donald Mackenzie-Kennedy; 8 Aug. 1942–27 March 1947 Sir Edmund Richards; 27 March 1947–30 March 1948 ruled by acting-governors; 30 March 1948–31 May 1951 Geoffrey Colby (knighted 1949); 31 May 1951–11 Nov. 1954 ruled by acting-governors; 11 Nov. 1954–10 Apr. 1956 Sir Geoffrey Colby; 10 Apr. 1956–10 Apr. 1961 Sir Robert Armitage; 10 Apr. 1961–9 May 1963 Sir Glyn Jones. *Prime Ministers:* 1 Feb. 1963–9 May 1963 Hastings Banda.

773 Nyasaland (Self-Rule). 9 May 1963–6 July 1964. *Location:* as **Malawi Republic.** *Capital:* Zomba. *Other names:* Nyasaland.

History: On February 1, 1963 (effective from May 9) the **Nyasaland Protectorate** was granted self-rule, and in 1964 became independent as **Malawi.**

Governors: 9 May 1963–6 July 1964 Sir Glyn Jones. *Prime Ministers:* 9 May 1963–6 July 1964 Hastings Banda.

Nzwani see **Anjouan**

774 Obock Colony. 24 June 1884–1896. *Location:* **Djibouti** coast. *Capital:* Djibouti (from 1892); Obock (1884–92). *Other names:* Obok.

History: In 1884 the **French Coast of the Somalis** was finally occupied by the French and renamed Obock Colony. The whole coast was gradually placed under protectorate (e.g. Tadjouna) until in 1896 the area was renamed again, as **French Somaliland.**

Commandants: 24 June 1884–7 Sept. 1887 Léonce Lagarde. *Governors:* 7 Sept. 1887–1896 Léonce Lagarde.

775 Ohrigstad. 11 Aug. 1845–1846. *Location:* eastern Transvaal, South Africa. *Capital:* Andries-Ohrigstad (founded in 1845). *Other names:* The Republic of Ohrigstad, Ohrigstad Republic, Andries-Ohrigstad.

History: Hendrik Potgieter left Potchefstroom in 1845 after Britain took over Natal, and headed northwest, buying a new area from the Pedi tribe, and building a new republic around the town of Andries-Ohrigstad, named after the head of a Dutch trading company. In 1846 Potgieter left to found **Zoutpansberg,** and shortly thereafter the small republic of Ohrigstad came to an end, plagued by fever and tsetse fly, the inhabitants repairing south to found the territory of Lydenburg (see **Lydenburg Territory**).

Head Commandants: 1 Aug. 1845–1846 Hendrik Potgieter; 1846–1846 [unknown].

776 Oil Rivers Protectorate. 5 June 1885–13 May 1893. *Location:* as **Niger Coast Protectorate.** *Capital:* Old Calabar.

History: Between 1884 and 1897 Britain announced a string of protectorates along the **Bights of Biafra and Benin,** over the Niger Delta states of **Brass, Bonny, Opobo,** Aboh, Old Calabar and **Benin.** By 1885 the British were calling the whole area The Oil River States because of the palm oil trade in the area. In 1893 it became the **Niger Coast Protectorate.**

Consuls-General: 5 Jan. 1885–1 Jan. 1891 Edward Hyde Hewett. *Vice-Consuls:* 1 Jan. 1891–3 Aug. 1891 Capt. Synge. *Commissioners/Consuls-General:* 3 Aug. 1891–1893 Claude MacDonald (knighted 1892); 1893–13 May 1893 Ralph Moor (acting).

Okoloba see **Bonny**

Old Africa see **Africa Vetus**

Old Oyo see **Oyo**

Oltre Giuba see **Jubaland Colony**

Omar al-Hajj's Empire see **Tukolor Empire**

777 Omayyad Egypt. July 658–9 Aug. 750. *Location:* Egypt. *Capital:* al-Fustat. *Other names:* Egypt, Umayyad Egypt.

History: In 658 the first Omayyad governor took office (before this, see **Egypt [Arab]**), and for the next ninety-two years the Omayyad caliph in Damascus ruled Egypt through this governor and his successors. In 750 the Caliphate became Abbasid (see **Abbasid Egypt**). Arabic replaced Greek as the national language in 706.

Governors: July 658–Jan. 664 Amr ibn al Asi; Jan. 664–Feb. 664 Abdallah ibn Amr; Feb. 664–665 Otba ibn Abi Sufyan; 665–20 May 667 Okbar ibn Amr; 20 May 667–9 Apr. 682 Maslama ibn Mukhallad; 9 Apr. 682–14 May 682 Muhammad ibn Maslama; 14 May 682–Apr. 684 Sa'id ibn Yezid; Apr. 684–11 Feb. 685 Abd ar-Rahman ibn Ghadam; 11 Feb. 685–1 July 703 Abd al-Aziz ibn Marwan; 1 July 703–30 Jan. 709 Abdallah ibn Abd al-Malik; 30 Jan. 709–14 Nov. 714 Kurra ibn Sharik; 14 Nov. 714–Nov. 717 Abd al-Malik ibn Rifa'a; Nov. 717–1 Apr. 720 Ayyub ibn Shurahbil; 1 Apr. 720–May 721 Bishr ibn Safwan; May 721–724 Handhala ibn Safwan; 724–2 May 724 Muhammad ibn Abd al-Malik; 2 May 724–27 Apr. 727 al-Hurr ibn Yusuf; 27 Apr. 727–16 May 727 Hafs ibn al-Walid; 16 May 727–30 May 727 Abd al-Malik ibn Rifa'a; 30 May 727–July 735 al-Walid ibn Rifa'a; July 735–12 Jan. 737 Abd ar-Rahman ibn Khalid; 12 Jan. 737–2 July 742 Handhala ibn Safwan; 2 July 742–21 March 745 Hafs ibn al-Walid; 21 March 745–7 Apr. 745 Hassan ibn Atahiya; 7 Apr. 745–4 Oct. 745 Hafs ibn al-Walid; 4 Oct. 745–19 March 748 al-Hawthara ibn Suheyl; 19 March 748–March 750 al-Mughira ibn Obeydallah; March 750–9 Aug. 750 Abd al-Malik ibn Marwar.

778 Omayyad North Africa. 703–9 July 800. *Location:* Algeria, Tunisia and Libya. *Capital:* al-Qayrawan. *Other names:* Ifriqiyah, Ifrikiya, Ifriqa.

History: In 703 the Omayyad Caliphate conquered **Byzantine North Africa [iii].** In 800 it fell to the **Aghlabid Empire.**

Governors: 703–715 Abdarrahman Musa; 715–718 Muhammad ibn Yazid; 718–720 Ismail; 720–721 Yazid; 721–721 Muhammad ibn Aus al-Ansari; 721–

729 Bisr; 729–734 Ubayda; 734–741 Ubayd Allah; 741–742 Kultum; 742–747 Hanzala; 747–755 Abdarrahman; 755–755 Ilyas; 755–758 Habib; 758–July 758 Asim Warfaguma; July 758–Aug. 761 Abdarrahman; Aug. 761–765 Muhammad; 765–765 Isa; 765–765 Ali; 765–766 al-Aghlab; 766–767 al-Hassan; 768–772 Abu Gafar Hazarmard Umar; 772–24 March 787 Abu Halid Yazid; 24 March 787–788 Daud; 788–2 Feb. 791 Abu Hatim Rawh; 2 Feb. 791–794 Nasr; 794–795 al-Fadl; 795–796 Hartama; 796–800 Muhammad ibn Muqatil; 800–800 Tammam; 800–9 July 800 Muhammad ibn Muqatil.

779 Oorlam Territory. 1838–1886. *Location:* Namibia. *Capital:* Windhoek.

History: The Oorlam Khoikhoi were one branch of the Oorlam peoples who controlled a section of what is today **Namibia** prior to the German takeover in 1884. Jager Afrikaner's son, Junker, arrived in Windhoek in 1838, and his family became the predominant one in the country. In 1885 Jan Jonker ceded territory to the Germans and in 1886 accepted a protectorate (see **German South West Africa Protectorate [i]**).

Rulers: 1800–1823 Jager Afrikaner; 1823–1861 Junker Afrikaner; 1861–1863 Christiaan Afrikaner; 1863–1889 Jan Jonker Afrikaner.

780 Opobo. 1870–19 Dec. 1884. *Location:* Uyo Province of Southern Nigeria. *Capital:* Opobo (named for Opobo, a great ruler of **Bonny.** Named by Jaja). *Other names:* Opubu, Ekwanga, Egwanga.

History: In 1870 Jubo Jubogha, a **Bonny** nobleman, came to the slave-trading village of Egwanga and set up the Kingdom of Opobo. Known as Jaja (or Chief Jaja) by the Europeans, Jubo destroyed the economic power of **Bonny** and turned Opobo into the chief oil-trading state along the Niger Delta. In 1884 Opobo was taken over by the British (see **Bights of Biafra and Benin**).

Jaja was deposed in 1887.

Kings: 1870–19 Dec. 1884 Jubo Jubogha (or Chief Jaja).

781 Oran (Spanish) [i]. 1509–1708. *Location:* around Oran, on the Algerian coast. *Capital:* Oran. *Other names:* Oran, Spanish Oran, Wahran.

History: In 1509 the Spanish occupied the town of Oran. In 1708 the Turks took it (see **Oran [Turkish]**), and in 1732 the Spanish re-took it (see **Oran [Spanish] [ii]**).

Governors: 1509–1509 Conde de Oliveto; 1509–1510 Rui Díaz de Rojas; 1510–1512 Diego de Córdoba; 1512–1517 Martín de Argote; 1517–1522 Diego, Marqués de Comares; 1522–1523 Luis, Marqués de Comares; 1523–1525 Luís de Cárdenas; 1525–1531 Luís, Marqués de Comares; 1531–1534 Pedro de Godoy; 1534–1558 Martín, Conde de Alcandete; 1558–1564 Alonso, Conde de Alcandete; 1564–1565 Andrés Ponce de Leon; 1565–1567 Hernán de Guzmán; 1567–1571 Marqués de Navarrés; 1571–1573 Felipe de Borja; 1573–1574 Diego, Conde de Comares; 1574–1575 Luís de Bocanegra; 1575–1585 Marqués de Cortes; 1585–1589 Pedro de Padilla; 1589–1594 Diego, Conde de Comares; 1594–1596 Gabriel de Zúñiga; 1596–1604 Francisco, Conde de Alcandete; 1604–1607 Conde de Teba; 1607–1608 Diego de Toledo y Guzmán; 1608–1616 Conde de Aguilar de Inestrillas; 1616–1625 Duque de Maqueda; 1625–1628 Marqués de Velada; 1628–1632 Visconde de Santa Clara de Avellido; 1632–1639 Marqués de Flores Dávila; 1639–1643 Marqués del Viso; 1643–1647 Marqués de Viana; 1647–1652 Marqués de Flores Dávila; 1652–1660 Marqués de San Román; 1660–1666 Duque de San Lúcar; 1666–1672 Marqués de los Vélez; 1672–1675 Diego de Portugal; 1675–1678 Iñigo de Toledo y Osorio; 1678–1681 Marqués de Algava; 1681–1682 Conde de la Monclova; 1682–1683 Conde de Cifuentes; 1683–1685 Marqués de Osera; 1685–1687 Marqués de Santa Cruz de Paniagua; 1687–1687

Conde de Bracamonte; 1687–1691 Conde de Guaro; 1691–1692 Comte de Charny; 1692–1697 Duque de Cansano; 1697–1701 Marqués de Casasola; 1701–1704 Juan Francisco de Araña; 1704–1707 Carlo Carafa; 1707–1708 Marqués de Valdecañas.

782 Oran (Spanish) [ii]. 1732–1792. *Location:* as **Oran (Spanish) [i].** *Capital:* Oran. *Other names:* Orán, Spanish Oran, Wahran.

History: In 1732 the Spaniards retook Oran (see **Oran [Turkish] [i]**), and held it until 1792. In 1790 it was devastated by an earthquake. In 1792 it was returned to the Turks, who settled a Jewish community there (see **Oran [Turkish] [ii]**).

Governors: 1732–1733 Marqués de Santa Cruz de Mercenado; 1733–1733 Marqués de Villadarias; 1733–1738 José Vallejo; 1738–1742 José de Aramburu; 1742–1748 Alexandre de la Mothe; 1748–1752 Marqués de la Real Corona; 1752–1758 Juan Antonio de Escoiquiz; 1758–1765 Juan Zermeño; 1765–1767 Cristóbal de Córdoba; 1767–1770 Conde de Bolognino; 1770–1774 Eugenio de Alvarado y Perales Hurtado y Colomo; 1774–1778 Pedro Zermeño; 1778–1779 Luís de Carvajal; 1779–1785 Pedro Guelfi; 1785–1789 Luis de las Casas y Aragorri; 1789–1790 Marqués de Campo Santo; 1790–1791 Conde de Cumbre Hermosa; 1791–1792 Juan de Courten.

783 Oran (Turkish) [i]. 1708–1732. *Location:* north Algeria. *Capital:* Oran. *Other names:* Wahran.

History: In 1708 the Turks took Oran from the Spanish (see **Oran [Spanish] [i]**). In 1732 they lost it to the Spanish again (see **Oran [Spanish] [ii]**).

Governors: 1708–1717 Saban Bey; 1717–1732 [unknown].

784 Oran (Turkish) [ii]. 1792–1831. *Location:* north Algeria. *Capital:* Oran. *Other names:* Wahran.

History: In 1792 the Ottoman Empire re-took the port and hinterland of Oran

from Spain (see **Oran [Spanish] [i]**). In 1831 Oran was taken by the French and became part of their **French Possessions in North Africa.**

Governors: 1792–(?) Mehmed Bey al-Kabir; (?)–ca. 1800 Osman Bey; ca. 1800–(?) Mustafa Bey al-Manzalah; (?)–ca. 1804 Mehmed Bey Makkalas; ca. 1804–(?) [unknown]; (?)–1831 Hassan Bey.

785 Orange Free State. 10 Apr. 1854–21 May 1900. *Location:* as Orange Free State Province of **South Africa.** *Capital:* Bloemfontein. *Other names:* Oranje Vrij Staat, Orange River Free State, Orange River Republic.

History: In 1854 the **Orange River State** became the Orange Free State, expanding its boundaries in 1861, 1866 and 1871. In 1900, during the Boer War, Britain took it again, as the **Orange River Colony.**

Presidents: 10 Apr. 1854–15 May 1854 Josias Hoffman (Leader of Provisional Government of Seven); 15 May 1854–10 Feb. 1855 Josias Hoffman; 10 Feb. 1855–27 Aug. 1855 Jacobus Venter (Chairman of Provisional Government of Four); 27 Aug. 1855–25 June 1859 Jacobus Boshof; 25 June 1859–15 Dec. 1859 Elias Snyman (acting); 15 Dec. 1859–8 Feb. 1860 Jacobus Venter; 8 Feb. 1860–15 Apr. 1863 Marthinus Pretorius; 15 Apr. 1863–20 June 1863 Joseph Allison (acting); 20 June 1863–5 Nov. 1863 Jacobus Venter (acting); 5 Nov. 1863–31 Aug. 1872 Jan Brand; 31 Aug. 1872–4 Oct. 1872 Friedrich Höhne (acting); 4 Oct. 1872–16 June 1873 Committee comprising William Collins, Friedrich Schnehage and Gerhardus du Toit; 16 June 1873–16 July 1888 Jan Brand (knighted 1882); 16 July 1888–10 Jan. 1889 Pieter Blignaut (acting); 11 Jan. 1889–17 Nov. 1895 Francis Reitz; 17 Nov. 1895–21 Feb. 1896 Pieter Blignaut (acting); 21 Feb. 1896–21 May 1900 Marthinus Steyn.

786 Orange River Colony. 21 May 1900–6 Dec. 1906. *Location:* as Orange

Free State Province of **South Africa.**
Capital: Bloemfontein.

History: In 1900 Britain took over the **Orange Free State** as the Orange River Colony. Marthinus Steyn, former President of the Free State, spent 1900–1906 in Europe, returning to the colony to head the National Political Party of the colony. Self-rule was granted on Dec. 6, 1906 (see **Orange River Colony [Self-Rule]**).

Governors: Jan. 1901–21 June 1902 Sir Hamilton Goold-Adams (acting); 21 June 1902–1 Apr. 1905 Viscount Milner; 2 Apr. 1905–6 Dec. 1906 2nd Earl of Selborne. *Presidents:* 21 May 1900–30 May 1902 Marthinus Steyn; 30 May 1902–31 May 1902 Christiaan De Wet (acting).

787 Orange River Colony (Self-Rule). 6 Dec. 1906–30 May 1910. *Location:* as **Orange River Colony.** *Capital:* Bloemfontein. *Other names:* Orange Free State.

History: In 1906 the **Orange River Colony** became self-ruling, and became known locally as The Orange Free State. In 1910 it became the Orange Free State Province of the **Union of South Africa.**

Governors: 6 Dec. 1906–7 June 1907 2nd Earl of Selborne; 7 June 1907–30 May 1910 Sir Hamilton Goold-Adams. *Prime Ministers:* 25 Nov. 1907–30 May 1910 Abraham Fischer. *Party Presidents:* 6 Dec. 1906–30 May 1910 Marthinus Steyn.

788 Orange River Sovereignty. 3 Feb. 1848–23 Feb. 1854. *Location:* as Orange Free State Province of **South Africa.**

Capital: Bloemfontein. *Other names:* Orange River Territory.

History: In 1848 Sir Harry Smith finally annexed to Britain all land between the Orange and Vaal Rivers, leaving it in the hands of a British resident. This area included **Transorangia** and **Winburg,** and he called it the Orange River Sovereignty. In 1854 its

independence was achieved, as the **Orange River State.**

Residents: 8 March 1845–23 July 1852 Henry Warden; 23 July 1852–23 Feb. 1854 Henry Green. *Special Commissioners:* 6 Apr. 1853–23 Feb. 1854 Sir George Clerk.

789 Orange River State. 23 Feb. 1854–10 Apr. 1854. *Location:* as **Orange Free State.** *Capital:* Bloemfontein.

History: In early 1854 **Orange River Sovereignty** became independent from Britain, as the Orange River State. A few months later it changed its name to **Orange Free State.**

Leaders of the Provisional Government of Seven: 23 Feb. 1854–10 Apr. 1854 Josias Hoffman.

790 Ottoman Egypt [i]. 22 Jan. 1517–25 July 1798. *Location:* northeast Africa. *Capital:* Cairo. *Other names:* Egypt.

History: In 1517 the Sultan of Turkey conquered Egypt (see **Circassian Mameluke Empire**), and a pasha was installed to supervise the Mameluke beys who continued to rule the country as effective administrators. In 1798 Egypt (the northern and administrative part anyway) was taken by Napoleon (see **French Egypt**).

Pashas: 25 Aug. 1517–29 Sept. 1522 Kha'ir Bey; 1 Oct. 1522–27 May 1523 Mustafa; 28 May 1523–June 1523 Qasim; 19 Aug. 1523–Feb. 1524 Ahmad; Feb. 1524–24 March 1525 Qasim; Apr. 1525–14 June 1525 Ibrahim; 15 June 1525–22 Jan. 1535 Suleiman (or Khadim); 23 Jan. 1535–10 Dec. 1536 Khusru; 11 Dec. 1536–8 June 1538 Suleiman; 9 June 1538–11 Apr. 1549 Daud; 12 Apr. 1549–Dec. 1553 Ali Semiz; Dec. 1553–31 May 1556 Muhammad (or Dukagin); 1 June 1556–8 May 1559 Iskander; 9 May 1559–25 Aug. 1560 Ali Khadim; 26 Aug. 1560–26 Jan. 1564 Lala Shahin; 1 Feb. 1564–20 Apr. 1566 Ali Sufi; 21 Apr. 1566–26 Dec. 1567 Mahmud; 27 Dec. 1567–13 Dec.

1568 Sinan; 14 Dec. 1568–24 June 1571 Tsherkes Iskander; 25 June 1571–2 May 1573 Sinan; 3 May 1573–13 Jan. 1575 Hussein; 14 Jan. 1575–28 June 1580 Masih (or Khadim); 29 June 1580–16 June 1583 Hassan (or Khadim); 17 June 1583–7 Oct. 1585 Ibrahim; 8 Oct. 1585–30 May 1587 Sinan (or Defter); 31 May 1587–30 Apr. 1591 Uways; 2 May 1591–10 May 1595 Hafiz Ahmad; 11 May 1595–30 March 1596 Kurd; 1 Apr. 1596–16 July 1598 Sayyid Muhammad; 17 July 1598–30 July 1601 Khidr; 31 July 1601–14 Sept. 1603 Yawuz Ali; 15 Sept. 1603–24 Sept. 1604 Ibrahim al-Hajj; 25 Sept. 1604–16 July 1605 Muhammad (or Gurji); 17 July 1605–27 May 1607 Hassan ibn Hussein; 29 May 1607–July 1611 Muhammad (or Oghuz); July 1611–29 Apr. 1615 Muhammad (or Sufi); 30 Apr. 1615–8 Feb. 1618 Ahmad; 9 Feb. 1618–1 Nov. 1618 Mustafa Lefkeli; 2 Nov. 1618–6 Aug. 1619 Ja'far; 6 Aug. 1619–16 Aug. 1620 Mustafa; 17 Aug. 1620–5 March 1622 Hussein (or Miri); 7 March 1622–16 July 1622 Muhammad (or Babar); 17 July 1622–5 July 1623 Ibrahim; 6 July 1623–12 Oct. 1623 Mustafa (or Qara); 13 Oct. 1623–12 Feb. 1624 Ali (or Tshetshedji); 13 Feb. 1624–16 May 1626 Mustafa (or Qara); 17 May 1626–8 Sept. 1628 Bairam; 8 Sept. 1628–15 Oct. 1630 Muhammad (or Tabany-Yasy); 16 Oct. 1630–11 July 1631 Musa; 12 July 1631–13 March 1633 Khalil; 14 March 1633–17 Oct. 1635 Ahmad (or Baqirdji); 21 Oct. 1635–5 Oct. 1637 Hussein (or Deli); 6 Oct. 1637–29 Aug. 1640 Muhammad (or Juwan Qapiji Sultanzade); 30 Aug. 1640–3 Oct. 1642 Mustafa (or Naqqash); 4 Oct. 1642–22 Apr. 1644 Maqsud; 22 Apr. 1644–15 Apr. 1646 Ayyub; 16 Apr. 1646–2 Dec. 1647 Muhammad (or Haydar Agha Zade); 2 Dec. 1647–20 Dec. 1647–Mustafa (or Mustari); 20 Dec. 1647–28 Feb. 1649 Muhammad (or Sharaf); 1 March 1649–Feb. 1651 Ahmad (or Tarkhunji); Feb. 1651–9 Sept. 1652 Abd ar-Rahman (or Khadim); 10 Sept. 1652–28 May 1656 Muhammad (or Khasseki); 29 May 1656–

20 June 1657 Mustafa (or Khaliji-Zade Damad); 21 June 1657–30 June 1660 Muhammad (or Shahsuwar-Zade-Ghazi); 1 July 1660–22 May 1660 Mustafa (or Gurji); 23 May 1660–1 Apr. 1664 Ibrahim (or Defterdar); 2 Apr. 1664–20 Feb. 1667 Umar (or Silahdar); 21 Feb. 1667–14 Nov. 1668 Ibrahim (or Sufi); 14 Nov. 1668–29 Dec. 1669 Ali (or Qaraqash); 30 Dec. 1669–9 June 1673 Ibrahim; 10 June 1673–28 July 1675 Hussein (or Jambalat-Zade); 29 July 1675–11 May 1676 Ahmad (or Defterdar); 12 May 1676–18 June 1680 Abd ar-Rahman; 19 June 1680–29 Apr. 1683 Uthman; 1 May 1683–31 March 1687 Hamza; 1 Apr. 1687–14 Nov. 1687 Hassan; 15 Nov. 1687–15 Oct. 1689 Hassan (or Damad); 16 Oct. 1689–12 Apr. 1691 Ahmad (or Mufattish Kiaya); 12 Apr. 1691–30 July 1695 Ali (or Khaznadar); 1 Aug. 1695–30 Sept. 1697 Ismail; 1 Oct. 1697–9 Oct. 1699 Hussein (or Firari); 9 Oct. 1699–6 May 1704 Muhammad (or Qara); 7 May 1704–7 Oct. 1704 Suleiman; 7 Oct. 1704–31 Aug. 1706 Muhammad (or Rami); 1 Sept. 1706–Sept. 1707 Ali; Sept. 1707–28 Oct. 1709 Hassan (or Damad); 28 Oct. 1709–Aug. 1710 Ibrahim; Aug. 1710–30 July 1711 Khalil (or Khosej); 1 Aug. 1711–30 Aug. 1714 Wali; 1 Sept. 1714–29 June 1717 Abdi; 1 July 1717–9 Sept. 1720 Ali (or Kiaya); 10 Sept. 1720–30 Apr. 1721 Rajab; 1 May 1721–30 Sept. 1725 Muhammad (or Nishanji); 1 Oct. 1725–Feb. 1726 Ali Muraly; Feb. 1726–29 Sept. 1727 Muhammad (Nishanji); 30 Sept. 1727–Oct. 1727 Abdi; Oct. 1727–10 July 1729 Abu Bakr; 11 July 1729–30 June 1733 Abdallah (or Heupruluzade); 1 July 1733–1734 Muhammad (or Silahdar); 1734–1734 Uthman; 1734–Dec. 1734 Abu Bakr; Dec. 1734–1741 Ali (or Hakimzade); 1741–3 July 1743 Yahya; 3 July 1743–28 Feb. 1744 Muhammad Sa'id; 1 March 1744–31 Aug. 1748 Muhammad (or Raghib); 1 Sept. 1748–Jan. 1752 Ahmad (or al-Hajj); Jan. 1752–Dec. 1752 Muhammad Melek; Dec. 1752–Oct. 1755 Hassan ash-

Sharawi; Oct. 1755–Dec. 1756 Ali (or Hakimzade); Dec. 1756–29 Apr. 1757 Sa'id ad-Din; 30 Apr. 1757–1760 Muhammad Sa'id; 1760–Dec. 1762 Mustafa (or Bahir Keuse); Dec. 1762–Jan. 1765 Ahmad; Jan. 1765–1766 Bakr; 1766–Apr. 1767 Hamza (or Silahdar Mahir); Apr. 1767–Apr. 1767 Muhammad Melek; Apr. 1767–1768 Muhammad (or Ruqim); 1768–1768 Muhammad (or Diwitdar). *Governors:* 1768–13 Apr. 1773 Ali Bey al-Kabir; 13 Apr. 1773–10 June 1775 Abu'dh Dhahab (or Mehmed Bey); 26 June 1775–Aug. 1777 Murad Bey; Aug. 1777–Feb. 1778 Ismail Bey; Feb. 1778–1786 Murad Bey; 1786–1790 Ismail Bey; 1790–25 July 1798 Murad Bey (joint); 1790–25 July 1798 Ibrahim Bey (joint).

791 Ottoman Egypt [ii]. 27 June 1801–15 Sept. 1882. *Location:* Egypt. *Capital:* Cairo. *Other names:* Egypt.

History: In June 1801 the French surrendered Cairo (see **French Egypt**) and Ottoman rule resumed (see also **Ottoman Egypt [i]**). By September the French had left Egypt. In 1811 the Viceroy, Muhammad Ali (or Mahomet Ali) created an autonomous state in Egypt, virtually independent of Constantinople, with himself as Vali (or viceroy). On May 3, 1833 Turkey recognized Egypt's independence of action, and on Feb. 13, 1841 Muhammad Ali gained Egypt as an hereditary possession, this becoming an hereditary vice-royalty in 1866, a move which gave Egypt almost total independence from the Porte. The Vali became a Khedive. On Nov. 17, 1869 the Suez Canal was opened, and in 1882 Egypt became a British sphere of influence because the Khedive refused to pay his taxes to Turkey, and Britain helped out (see **British-Occupied Egypt**).

Governors: 27 June 1801–10 Aug. 1801 Nasih Pasha; 10 Aug. 1801–Jan. 1802 Kucuk Hussein Pasha; Jan. 1802-3 May 1803 Khusrau Pasha; 3 May 1803–June 1803 Taher Pasha (usurper); June 1803–July 1803 Khur-shid Pasha; July 1803–31 Jan. 1804 Ali Pasha Jazairl. *Valis:* March 1804–2 Nov. 1805 Khurshid Pasha; 2 Nov. 1805-1 Sept. 1848 Muhammad Ali; 1 Sept. 1848–10 Nov. 1848 Ibrahim. *Diwan Presidents:* 10 Nov. 1848–30 Nov. 1848 Sa'ib Pasha. *Valis:* 30 Nov. 1848–13 July 1854 Abbas I; 14 July 1854–18 Jan. 1863 Muhammad Sa'id; 18 Jan. 1863–25 June 1879 Ismail (Khedive from 1866); 25 June 1879–15 Sept. 1882 Tewfiq (Khedive). *Prime Ministers:* 15 Aug. 1878–18 Feb. 1879 Nubar Pasha; 2 Feb. 1882–25 May 1882 Mahmud Sami. *War Ministers:* 25 May 1882–17 June 1882 Ahmad Arabi. *Prime Ministers:* 17 June 1882–28 Aug. 1882 Ragib Pasha; 28 Aug. 1882–15 Sept. 1882 Cherif Pasha. *British Agents/Consuls-General:* 11 Sept. 1882–15 Sept. 1882 Sir Evelyn Baring. *Note:* in times of no Prime Minister, the Vali fulfilled that function.

Ouadaï, Ouaddaï see **Wadai**

Ouagadougou see **Wagadugu**

Ouahigouya see **Yatenga**

Oualo see **Walo**

Oubangui-Chari see **Ubangi-Shari**

Ouidah see **Whydah**

Ouolof see **Dyolof**

Ouwere, Ouwerre see **Warri**

792 Ovamboland Homeland. 2 Oct. 1968– . *Location:* northern **Namibia**. *Capital:* Oshakati. *Other names:* Owambo, Amboland.

History: Established as the first Bantustan (native homeland) in **Namibia** by the South African government, it is not recognized internationally as a self-governing state. It is meant to be the homeland for the Ovambo (or Ambo) people. Set up in 1968, it achieved self-government on May 1, 1973, and complete independence depends on the future of **Namibia**.

Chief Ministers: 2 Oct. 1968–14 Jan. 1972 Uushona Shiimi; 14 Jan. 1972–16 Aug. 1975 Chief Filemon Elifas; 16 Aug. 1975–July 1980 Cornelius Njoba. *Note:* After 1980, when the post of Chief Minister was abolished, the government fell completely back into the hands of **South Africa**.

793 Oyo. ca. 1400–1900. *Location:* Oyo State, Nigeria. *Capital:* New Oyo (from about 1840); Old Oyo (from about 1550 until about 1840). *Other names:* Oyo Empire, New Oyo, Old Oyo, Katanga (sic).

History: Founded by a farming section of the Yoruba tribe, the people of Oyo became cavalrymen, and their Alafins (or Kings) began to expand the area into an empire. In the 1550s Orompotu established the old city of Oyo, which by the 1830s had broken up. At this stage Atiba became the founder of both a new dynasty and the new town of Oyo. In 1900 Oyo was incorporated into **Northern Nigeria Protectorate**.

Alafins: ca. 1400–(?) Oranyan (son of Oduduwa); (?)–(?) Ajaka; (?)–(?) Sango; (?)–(?) Ajika; (?)–(?) Aganju; (?)–(?) Kori; (?)–(?) Oluaso; ca. 1520–(?) Onigbogi; (?)–(?) Ofinran; (?)–(?) Egunoju; ca. 1555–ca. 1580 Orompotu; ca. 1580–ca. 1590 Ajiboyede; ca. 1590–1614 Abipa; 1614–ca. 1640 Obalokun; ca. 1640–ca. 1652 Oluodo; ca. 1652–ca. 1690 Ajagbo; ca. 1690–ca. 1692 Odarawu; ca. 1692–(?) Kanran; (?)–(?) Jayin; (?)–(?) an interregnum existed; (?)–ca. 1724 Ayibi; ca. 1724–ca. 1725 Osiyago; ca. 1725–ca. 1735 Ojigi; ca. 1735–ca. 1740 Gberu; ca. 1740–1746 Amuniwaiye; 1746–1754 Onisile; 1754–1754 Labisi; 1754–1754 Agboluje; 1754–1770 Majeogbe; 1770–Apr. 1789 Abiodun; May 1789–1796 Aole; 1796–1796 Awonbioju; 1796–1796 Adebo; 1796–1797 Maku; 1797–1802 an interregnum existed; 1802–1830 Majotu; 1830–1833 Amodo; 1833–1835 Oluewu; ca. 1836–1859 Atiba; 1859–1875 Adelu; 1875–

1905 Adeyemi I; 1905–1911 Lawani; 1911–1943 Ladigbolu I; 1943–1946 Adeniran; 1946–1955 vacant; 1956–1970 Ladigbolu II; 1970–19 Nov. 1970 an interregnum existed; 19 Nov. 1970–Lamidi Adeyemi II.

794 Pentapolis. 631 B.C.–331 B.C. *Location:* eastern Libya. *Capital:* Cyrene (or Kyrene). *Other names:* Cyrene Colony, Kyrene.

History: In 631 B.C. the people of Thera (present Santorini), an island in the Aegean, were told by the Delphic Oracle to found this new land. After opposition from the natives, they established themselves at the Five Towns (or Pentapolis) of Cyrene, Barca, Apollonia, Berenice and Arsinoë. In 331 B.C. it was incorporated into **Alexandrian Egypt**, as **Pentapolis Territory**.

Kings: 631 B.C.–(?) Battus I; ca. 599 B.C.–ca. 580 B.C. Arsecilaus I; ca. 580 B.C.–ca. 554 B.C. Battus II; ca. 554 B.C.–ca. 550 B.C. Arsecilaus II; ca. 550 B.C.–ca. 550 B.C. Learchus (usurper); ca. 550 B.C.–ca. 525 B.C. Battus III; ca. 525 B.C.–ca. 515 B.C. Arsecilaus III; ca. 515 B.C.–ca. 465 B.C. Battus IV: ca. 465 B.C.–ca. 460 B.C. Arsecilaus IV; ca. 460 B.C.–331 B.C. democratic rule.

795 Pentapolis Territory. 331 B.C.–75 B.C. *Location:* eastern Libya. *Capital:* Cyrene. *Other names:* Kyrene Territory.

History: In 331 B.C. **Pentapolis** became part of Alexander the Great's empire, and in 323 B.C. part of **Alexandrian Egypt**'s successor state, the **Egyptian Satrapy**. In 305 B.C. Pentapolis, still a territory, became the eastern outpost of **Egypt of the Ptolemies**. In 75 B.C. it became the Roman province of Cyrenaica (see **Cyrenaica Roman Province**).

Emperors: 331 B.C.–13 June 323 B.C. Alexander the Great. *Governors:* 323 B.C.–322 B.C. Thibron of Sparta. *Satraps:* 322 B.C.–313 B.C. Ptolemy (later called Ptolemy Soter). *Strategoi:* 313 B.C.–308 B.C. Ophellas. *Kings:* 308 B.C.–258 B.C. Magas; 258 B.C.–257 B.C. Demetrios. *Queens:* 258 B.C.–246 B.C. Berenice. *Kings:* 246 B.C.–240 B.C. Ptolemy III Euergetes of Egypt; 240 B.C.–240 B.C. Ekdelos (joint usurper); 240 B.C.–240 B.C. Demophanes (joint usurper); 240 B.C.–222 B.C. Ptolemy III Euergetes of Egypt; 222 B.C.–205 B.C. Ptolemy IV Eupator of Egypt; 205 B.C.–204 B.C. Philemon; 204 B.C.–200 B.C. [unknown]; 200 B.C.–149 B.C. under rule from Numidia; 149 B.C.–116 B.C. Ptolemy VIII Euergetes (or Physcon) of Egypt; 116 B.C.–110 B.C. Ptolemaios Aspion. *Tyrants:* 110 B.C.–110 B.C. Nikostratos; 110 B.C.–110 B.C. Leandros. *Kings:* 110 B.C.–96 B.C. Ptolemaios Aspion; 96 B.C.–75 B.C. under Roman rule. *Note:* Strategoi is the plural of Strategos (General).

796 Persian Egypt. 616–628. *Location:* Egypt. *Capital:* Alexandria. *Other names:* Egypt.

History: In 616 the Persians conquered **Byzantine Egypt [i]** and ruled it through a traitorous patriarch for 12 years until kicked out by a combination of Roman Emperor Heraclius and the Arabs (see **Byzantine Egypt [ii]**).

Patriarch-Prefects: 616–628 Benjamin.

797 Petit Dieppe. 1364–1413. *Location:* Buchanan and Greenville areas of Liberia. *Capital:* unknown. *Other names:* French Gold Coast Settlements, French Gold Coast.

History: In 1364 a settlement of Norman merchants from Dieppe was established in this area. Very little is known about the whole affair, and some historians doubt the authenticity of it all.

Rulers: unknown.

Pewenet see **Punt**

798 Phazania Kingdom. ca. 430–

666. *Location:* Libya. *Capital:* Murzuq (name means "sand sea"). *Other names:* Fezzan.

History: Part of the territory of the Garamantes, Phazania was thus part of the land conquered by the Romans in 19 B.C. and named Phazania. About 430 A.D., after the Vandals took most of North Africa (see **Vandal North Africa**), Phazania gained its independence under a Berauna dynasty. In 666 the Arabs conquered it and it became part of the Arab world (see **Arab North Africa [ii]**).

Rulers: unknown.

Philippolis see **Adam Kok's Land**

Plantation Island see **Shenge**

799 Pondoland. 7 Oct. 1844–29 Oct. 1867. *Location:* Kaffraria, South Africa. *Capital:* Port St. Johns. *Other names:* Mpondoland.

History: In 1844 Faku was recognized by the British as ruler of Pondoland. In 1867, on his death, Pondoland split into two parts, **Pondoland East** and **Pondoland West.**

Chiefs: ca. 1552 Kondwana; (?)–(?) Ncindise; (?)–(?) Cabe; (?)–(?) Cilwayo; (?)–(?) Dayeni; (?)–(?) Tahle; (?)–(?) Nyawuza; (?)–(?) Ncqungushe; 1824–29 Oct. 1867 Faku.

800 Pondoland East. 29 Oct. 1867–25 Sept. 1894. *Location:* Pondoland. *Capital:* Quakeni (about 8 miles from Lusikisiki). *Other names:* East Pondoland.

History: See **Pondoland West** for details of history.

Chiefs: 29 Oct. 1867–28 Oct. 1887 Mqikela; 28 Oct. 1887–15 Feb. 1888 vacant; 15 Feb. 1888–25 Sept. 1894 Sigcau.

801 Pondoland West. 29 Oct. 1867–25 Sept. 1894. *Location:* Pondoland. *Capital:* Nyandeni (in the Libode District). *Other names:* West Pondoland.

History: In 1867, on the death of

Faku, **Pondoland** split into two, East and West Pondoland (see also **Pondoland East**). In 1894 the two separate countries were annexed to the Cape (see **British Cape Colony [Self-Rule]**) under the name of **British Pondoland**.

Chiefs: 29 Oct. 1867–29 Aug. 1876 Ndamase; 29 Aug. 1876–25 Sept. 1894 Nqiliso.

802 Port Cresson. Dec. 1832–June 1835. *Location:* near **Bassa Cove**, Liberia. *Capital:* Port Cresson (named for colonizer Elliott Cresson). *Other names:* Bassa Cove.

History: Founded by Black Quakers of the New York and Pennsylvania Colonization Societies sometime in December 1832, it was destroyed in 1835 in a raid by Joe Harris, the local Bassa leader. A little while later it was re-formed as **Bassa Cove**.

Chief Magistrates: Dec. 1832–June 1835 Edward Hankinson.

803 Port Natal [i]. 7 Aug. 1824–30 Apr. 1828. *Location:* around Durban, Natal Province, South Africa. *Capital:* Port Natal.

History: Vasco da Gama discovered and named Natal on Christmas Day, 1497. From 1686 to 1725 the Dutch expressed some interest in the area, but in the early 19th century Chaka, the Zulu king, conquered all of present Natal. In 1824 he ceded an area around Port Natal, 100 miles by 30, to Lieutenant Francis Farewell, who claimed the area for Britain. Farewell and his companions colonized the area, but in 1828 the settlement broke up due to the instability of the country following the assassination of Chaka. A few European settlers remained, then in 1835 Allan Gardiner founded **Port Natal [ii]**.

Commanders: 7 Aug. 1824–30 Apr. 1828 Lt. Francis Farewell.

804 Port Natal [ii]. 6 May 1835–4 Feb. 1838. *Location:* southern Natal, **South Africa**. *Capital:* Durban (laid out June 23, 1835 and named for Sir Benjamin D'Urban, the Governor of **British Cape Colony**).

History: In 1835 Allan Gardiner, a sailor turned missionary, settled a new population in Port Natal (see **Port Natal [i]**), renaming the town Durban. Dingaan, the Zulu king, ceded all of southern Natal to Gardiner, who intended it to be a Cape district. This swallowed up the area which had once been Francis Farewell's domain (see **Port Natal [i]**) and in 1838 it became **Port Natal [iii]**.

Administrators: 6 May 1835–4 Feb. 1838 Allan Gardiner.

805 Port Natal [iii]. Nov. 1838–24 Dec. 1839. *Location:* Natal coast, South Africa. *Capital:* Port Natal. *Other names:* Fort Victoria, Victoria.

History: In early 1838 **Port Natal [ii]** ceased to function and Allan Gardiner left the colony, only a few farmers remaining. In November 1838 the Military Secretary to Sir George Napier (Governor of the Cape—see **British Cape Colony**), Major Samuel Charters, arrived to take possession of the port for the Cape. He built a stockade, Fort Victoria, and in January 1839 he left for the Cape. The British pulled out in December 1839 and the land became part of the **Free Province of New Holland**, which in turn became **Natalia**.

Military Administrators: Nov. 1838–Jan. 1839 Samuel Charters; Jan. 1839–24 Dec. 1839 Henry Jervis.

806 Porto-Novo Colony. 22 June 1893–22 June 1894. *Location:* around Porto-Novo, Benin. *Capital:* Porto-Novo.

History: In 1893 **Porto-Novo Protectorate [ii]** became a colony. In 1894 it merged into **Dahomey Colony**.

Lieutenant-Governors: 22 June 1893–22 June 1894 Victor Ballot. *Kings:* 22 June 1893–22 June 1894 Tofa (ruled until 1908).

807 Porto-Novo Kingdom [i]. 1688–25 Feb. 1863. *Location:* Benin. *Capital:* Hueta. *Other names:* Hogbonu, Ajashe, Adjatshe, Adjatché.

History: From the same stock as **Abomey,** the Porto-Novo Kingdom was created in 1688, and was called Hogbonu (later Ajashe). It became a leading slave-trade state, and in 1863 became **Porto-Novo Protectorate [i].**

Kings: 1688–1729 Té-Agbanlin I; 1729–1739 Hiakpon; 1739–1746 Lokpon. *Queens:* 1746–1752 Hude. *Kings:* 1752–1757 Messe; 1757–1761 Huyi; 1761–1765 Gbeyon; 1765–1775 interregnum; 1775–1783 Ayikpe; 1783–1794 Ayaton; 1794–1807 Huffon; 1807–1816 Ajohan; 1816–1818 Toyi; 1818–1828 Hueze; 1828–1836 Toyon; 1836–1848 Meyi; 1848–25 Feb. 1863 Sodji.

808 Porto-Novo Kingdom [ii]. 2 Jan. 1865–14 Apr. 1882. *Location:* as **Porto-Novo Kingdom [i].** *Capital:* Porto-Novo. *Other names:* Porto-Novo, Ajashe, Adjatshe, Adjatché.

History: In 1865 the **Porto-Novo Protectorate [i]** came to an end, and the kingdom was left to its own devices, until 1882, when the French re-instituted a protectorate over it (see **Porto-Novo Protectorate [ii]**).

Kings: 2 Jan. 1865–1872 Mikpon; 1872–1874 Messi; 1874–7 Feb. 1908 Tofa; 7 Feb. 1908–1913 Gbedissin; 1913–1929 Hudji; 1929–1930 Toli; 1930–1940 Gbehinto; 1941– Gbesso Toyi.

809 Porto-Novo Protectorate [i]. 25 Feb. 1863–2 Jan. 1865. *Location:* as **Porto-Novo Kingdom [i].** *Capital:* Porto-Novo. *Other names:* Porto-Novo.

History: In 1863 **Porto-Novo Kingdom [i]** became a French protectorate, much to the consternation of the British. In 1865 this came to an end and the kingdom was re-established as the sole monarchy of the area (see **Porto-Novo Kingdom [ii]**).

Agents: 25 Feb. 1863–2 Jan. 1865 Marius Daumas. *Kings:* 25 Feb. 1863–1864 Sodji; 1864–2 Jan. 1865 Mikpon.

810 Porto-Novo Protectorate [ii]. 14 Apr. 1882–22 June 1893. *Location:* around Porto-Novo, Benin. *Capital:* Porto-Novo.

History: In 1882 the French re-established a protectorate over **Porto-Novo Kingdom [ii].** In 1893 it became **Porto-Novo Colony.** (See also **Porto-Novo Kingdom [i], Porto-Novo Protectorate [i]** and **Cotonou.**)

Kings: 14 Apr. 1882–22 June 1893 Tofa. *Residents:* June 1882–1883 Bonaventure Colonna de Lecca; 1883–1883 Henri Guilman; 1883–1884 Daniel Germa; 1884–July 1884 Léopold Maignot; July 1884–1886 Charles Disnematin-Dorat; 1886–1886 Émmanuel Roget; 1886–1887 Jean-Marie Bayol; 1887–16 June 1887 Gentian Péréton; 16 June 1887–11 July 1888 Victor Ballot. *Administrators:* 11 July 1888–1889 Paul de Beeckmann. *Residents:* 1889–19 Oct. 1889 Louis Tautain; 19 Oct. 1889–22 Dec. 1891 Victor Ballot. *Lieutenant-Governors:* 22 Dec. 1891–22 June 1893 Victor Ballot. *Note:* from 1883 these administrators were also the administrators of Cotonou. *Note:* Disnematin-Dorat was also Military Commandant of Cotonou. *Note:* Roget was also Commandant of Cotonou.

811 Porto Santo Donatária. 1418–1580. *Location:* Porto Santo Island, Madeira. *Capital:* Vila de Porto Santo ("Vila" for short).

History: In 1418 the Madeiras were discovered by Gonçalves Zarco, a Portuguese navigator. In 1420 settlement began of Porto Santo, **Machico Donatária** and **Funchal Donatária.** Wine and sugar were the main thrusts of the economy. The big island of Madeira was split into two donatárias (lands granted to a noble family by the Crown): Funchal and Machico, while the small island of Porto Santo was its own donatária. In 1580 the Portuguese Crown cancelled the donatárias and made the island group a colony (see

Madeira Colony).
Rulers: unknown.

812 Portuguese Congo. 26 Feb. 1884–26 June 1884. *Location:* Congo (Brazzaville) (at the mouth of the Congo River). *Capital:* none. *Other names:* Congo Portugues.
History: In 1884 the Portuguese overstepped their bounds and set up an area of interest within the French sphere of influence. A few months later they were persuaded to move out. (See also **Moyen-Congo Protectorate.**)
Rulers: unknown, if any.

813 Portuguese Gold Coast Settlements. 19 Jan. 1482–9 Jan. 1642. *Location:* the coast of Ghana. *Capital:* São Jorge da Mina (El Mina) (until 1637). *Other names:* São Jorge da Mina.
History: In 1482 the Portuguese came to the Gold Coast, with their base at São Jorge da Mina (Saint George of Mina). In 1637 their headquarters were taken by the Dutch (see **Dutch Gold Coast Settlements**) and by 1642 all the Portuguese territory in the area had been ceded to the Dutch.
Capitães-Mores: 19 Jan. 1482–1484 Diogo de Azambuja; ca. 1486 Alvaro Vaz Pestano; ca. 1487 João Fogaça; ca. 1493 Lopo Soares de Albergaria; ca. 1502 Nuno Vaz de Castelo Branco; ca. 1504 António de Miranda de Azevedo; 1504–1505 Diogo Lopes de Sequeira; 1505–(?) Martinho da Silva; ca. 1508–1509 Capitão Bobadilha; 1509–ca. 1510 Manuel de Gois; (?)–1513 Afonso Caldeira; ca. 1517–1519 Fernão Lopes Correia; 1519–1522 Duarte Pacheco Pereira; 1522–1524 Afonso de Albuquerque; 1524–1525 João de Barros; 1525–1529 [unknown]; 1529–(?) Estevão de Gama; 1536–1539 Manuel de Albuquerque; 1539–1541 António de Miranda; 1541–1541 Fernão Cardoso; 1541–(?) Lopo de Sousa Coutinho; 1545–(?) Diogo Soares de Albergaria; 1548–1550 Lopo de Sousa Coutinho; 1550–1552 Diogo Soares de Albergaria; 1552–ca. 1555 Rui de Melo; ca. 1557–(?) Afonso Gonçalves Botofago; (?)–1562 Rui Gomes de Azevedo; 1562–(?) Manuel De Mesquita Perestrelo; 1564–(?) Martim Afonso; 1570–(?) António de Sá; ca. 1574–(?) Mendio da Mota; ca. 1579–(?) Vasco Fernandes Pimentel; (?)–1584 João Rodrigues Peçanha; 1594–(?) Bernardinho Ribeiro Pacheco; 1586–ca. 1595 João Róis Coutinho; ca. 1595–ca. 1596 Duarte Lobo da Gama; ca. 1596–1608 Cristóvão da Gama; 1608–1613 Duarte de Lima; 1613–1613 João do Castro; 1613–ca. 1615 Pedro da Silva; 1616–1624 Manuel da Cunha e Teive; 1624–ca. 1625 Francisco de Souto-Maior; (?)–(?) Luis Tomé de Castro; (?)–1629 João da Sera de Morais; ca. 1632–1634 Pedro de Mascarenhas; 1634–9 Jan. 1642 António da Rocha Magalhães. *Note:* Capitães-Mores is the plural of Capitão-Mor (Captain-Major).

814 Portuguese Guinea. 1879–11 June 1951. *Location:* as **Guinea-Bissau.** *Capital:* Bissau (from 1941); Bolama (1879–1941). *Other names:* Portuguese Guinea Colony.
History: In 1879 **Bissau** and the erstwhile **Cacheu,** as well as neighboring areas in what is today **Guinea-Bissau,** were released from subjection to Cape Verde and transformed into a colony. In 1951 it became **Portuguese Guinea Overseas Province.**
Governors: 1879–1881 Agostinho Coelho; 1881–1884 Pedro de Gouveia; 1884–1885 [unknown]; 1885–1886 Francisco Barbosa; 1886–1887 José de Brito; 1887–30 May 1887 Eusébio Castella do Vale; 30 May 1887–4 Sept. 1888 Francisco da Silva; 4 Sept. 1888–1890 Joaquim Correia e Lança; 1890–30 Apr. 1891 Augusto dos Santos; 30 Apr. 1891–1895 Luís de Vasconcelos e Sá; 1895–26 May 1895 Eduardo Oliveira; 26 May 1895–1897 Pedro de Gouveia; 1897–1898 Álvaro da Cunha (acting); 1898–1899 Albano Ramalho; 1899–1900 Álvaro da Cunha (acting); 1900–1903 Joaquim Biker; 1903–1904 Alfredo Martins; 1904–João Valente;

1904–1906 Carlos Pessanha; 1906–1909 João Muzanty; 1909–23 Oct. 1910 Francelino Pimentel; 23 Oct. 1910–Aug. 1913 Carlos Pereira; Aug. 1913–1914 José Sequeira; 1914–1915 José Duque; 1915–1917 José Sequeira; 1917–1917 Manuel Coelho; 1917–1918 Carlos Ferreira; 1918–1919 José Duque; 1919–1919 José Marinho; 1919–1920 Henrique Guerra; 1920–1921 [unknown]; 1921–1926 José Caroço; 1926–1927 [unknown]; 1927–1931 António de Magalhães; 1931–1932 João Zilhão; 1932–1940 Luís António Viegas; 1940–1941 [unknown]; 1941–25 Apr. 1945 Ricardo Vaz Monteiro; 25 Apr. 1945–1950 Manuel Rodrigues; 1950–1951 [unknown]; 1951–11 June 1951 Raimundo Serrão.

815 Portuguese Guinea Overseas Province. 11 June 1951–24 Sept. 1973. *Location:* as **Guinea-Bissau.** *Capital:* Bissau.

History: In 1951 **Portuguese Guinea** became an overseas province of Portugal. In 1973 it gained independence as **Guinea-Bissau.**

Governors: 11 June 1951–1953 Raimundo Serrão; 1953–1956 Diogo de Melo e Alvim; 1956–1958 Álvaro Távares; 1958–1962 António Correia; 1962–1965 Vasco Rodrigues; 1965–24 May 1968 Arnaldo Schultz; 24 May 1968–July 1973 António de Spínola; 30 Aug. 1973–24 Sept. 1973 José Rodrigues.

816 Portuguese Tangier. 28 Aug. 1471–29 Jan. 1662. *Location:* northern Morocco. *Capital:* Tangier. *Other names:* Tangier.

History: In 1471 the Portuguese took **Tangier Emirate,** and in 1662 ceded it to the British (see **British Tangier**).

Governors: 28 Aug. 1471–148? Ruis de Melo; 148?–1486 Conde de Oliveira; 1486–1489 Conde de Tarouca; 1489–1501 [unknown]; 1501–1508 Conde de Tarouca; 1508–151? [unknown]; 151?–1522 Conde de Monsanto; 1522–1531

Duarte de Meneses; 1531–1552 João de Meneses; 1552–1553 Luís de Loureiro; 1553–1562 Bernardim de Carvalho; 1562–1564 [unknown]; 1564–1566 Lourenço de Távora; 1566–1572 [unknown]; 1572–1573 Ruis de Carvalho; 1573–1574 [unknown]; 1574–1578 Duarte de Meneses; 1578–15?? Pedro da Silva; 15??–1605 [unknown]; 1605–1610 Nuño de Mendonça; 1610–1614 Affonso de Noronha; 1614–1 July 1617 Conde de Tarouca; 1 July 1617–1621 Pedro Manuel; 1621–1624 Marques de Montalvão; 1624–1628 Conde de Linhares; 1628–1637 Conde de la Torre; 1637–1643 Conde de Sarzedas; 1643–1653 [unknown]; 1653–1656 Rodrigo de Lencastre; 1656–1661 Conde de Ericeira; 1661–29 Jan. 1662 Luis de Almeida.

817 Portuguese West Africa. 1589–14 Feb. 1885. *Location:* most of what is today Angola, but without Cabinda. *Capital:* Luanda (but for the period 1641–48 see **Dutch West Africa**).

History: In 1589 **Angola Donatária** was returned to the Portuguese Crown. During the 17th century the territory held by the Portuguese was increased, e.g. Benguela was colonized in 1617, and the kingdoms of **Ndongo,** Ovimbundu, **Kongo,** and others were subjugated. In 1641 the Dutch captured all the Portuguese coastal possessions (including the capital, Luanda), and held them for seven years, having forced the Portuguese into the interior (see **Dutch West Africa**). In 1885 the Berlin Conference recognized Portuguese West Africa as a colony (see **Portuguese West Africa Colony**), and granted the exclave of Cabinda as part of that colony.

Governors: 1589–1591 Luís Serrão; 1591–June 1592 André Pereira; June 1592–1593 Francisco de Almeida; 1593–1594 Jerónimo de Almeida; 1594–1602 João de Mendonça; 1602–1603 João Coutinho; 1603–1606 Manuel Pereira; 1606–Sept. 1607 [unknown]; Sept. 1607–1611 Manuel Forjaz; 1611–1615 Bento Cardoso; 1615–1617 Manuel

Pereira; 1617–1621 Luís de Vasconcelos; 1621–1623 João de Sousa; 1623–1623 Pedro Coelho; 1623–1624 Simão de Mascarenhas; 1624–4 Sept. 1630 Fernão de Sousa; 4 Sept. 1630–1635 Manuel Coutinho; 1635–18 Oct. 1639 Francisco da Cunha; 18 Oct. 1639–Oct. 1645 Pedro de Meneses; Oct. 1645–1646 Francisco de Souto-Maior; 1646–24 Aug. 1648 a triumvirate junta was in power; 24 Aug. 1648–1651 Salvador de Sá e Benavides; March 1652–1653 Rodrigo Henriques; 1653–Oct. 1654 Bartolomeu da Cunha (acting); Oct. 1654–18 Apr. 1658 Luís Chicorro; 18 Apr. 1658–1661 João Vieira; 1661–Sept. 1666 André de Negreiros; Sept. 1666–Feb. 1667 Tristão da Cunha; Feb. 1667–Aug. 1669 juntas were in power; Aug. 1669–1676 Francisco de Távora; 1676–1680 Pires de Sousa e Meneses; 1680–1684 João da Silva e Sousa; 1684–1688 Luís da Silva; 1688–1691 João de Lencastre; 1691–1694 Gonçalo de Meneses; 1694–1697 Henrique de Magalhães; 1697–1701 Luís de Meneses; 1701–1703 Bernardino Távares; 1703–1705 a junta was in power; 1705–1709 Lourenço de Almada; 1709–1713 António Castro e Ribafria; 1713–1717 João de Noronha; 1717–1722 Henrique de Figueiredo e Alarcão; 1722–1725 António de Carvalho; 1725–1726 José da Costa (acting); 1726–1732 Paulo de Albuquerque; 1732–1738 Rodrigo de Meneses; 1738–1748 João de Magalhães; 1748–1749 Fonseca Coutinho (acting); 1749–1753 Marquês de Lovradio; 1753–1758 António da Cunha; 1758–1764 António de Vasconcelos; 1764–1772 Francisco de Sousa Coutinho; 1772–1779 António de Lencastre; 1779–1782 João da Câmara; 1782–1784 juntas were in power; 1784–1790 Barão de Moçâmedes; 1790–1797 Manuel Vasconcelos; 1797–1802 Miguel de Melo; 1802–1806 Fernando de Noronha; 1806–1807 [unknown]; 1807–1810 António da Gama; 1810–1816 José Barbosa; 1816–1819 Luís da Mota Feo e Torres; 1819–1821 Manuel de Albuquerque; 1821–1822 Joaquim de Lima; 1822–1823 a junta was in power; 1823–

1823 Cristóvão Dias; 1823–1829 Nicolau Branco; 1829–1834 Barão de Santa Comba Dão; 1834–1836 a junta was in power; 1836–1836 Domingos de Oliveira Daun. *Governors-General:* 1837–1839 Manuel Vidal; 1839–1839 António de Noronha; 1839–1842 Manuel Malheiro (acting); 1842–1843 José Leite; 1843–1844 [unknown]; 1844–1845 Lourenço Possolo; 1845–1848 Pedro da Cunha; 1848–1851 Adrião Pinto; 1851–1853 António de Sousa; 1853–1853 António Graça; 1853–1854 Visconde de Pinheiro; 1854–1860 José do Amaral; 1860–1861 Carlos Franco; 1861–1862 Sebastião de Calheiros e Meneses; 1862–1865 José Baptista de Andrade; 1865–1868 Francisco Cardoso; 1868–1869 [unknown]; 1869–1870 José do Amaral; 1870–1873 José da Ponte e Horta; 1873–1876 José Baptista de Andrade; 1876–1878 Caetano de Almeida e Albuquerque; 1878–1880 Vasco de Carvalho e Meneses; 1880–1882 António Dantas; 1882–14 Feb. 1885 Francisco do Amaral.

818 Portuguese West Africa Colony. 14 Feb. 1885–15 Aug. 1914. *Location:* as **Angola People's Republic** (including the exclave of Cabinda from February 14, 1885). *Capital:* Luanda. **Other names:** Portuguese West Africa.

History: In 1885, at the Berlin Conference, **Portuguese West Africa** was recognized internationally as a colony of Portugal. Also, the exclave of Cabinda (or Kabinda), just across the mouth of the Congo River (on the border of what is today **Zaire-Congo People's Republic**) was awarded to Portuguese West Africa. In 1914 the area became **Angola Colony.**

Governors-General: 14 Feb. 1885–1886 Francisco do Amaral; 1886–25 Aug. 1892 Guilherme Capelo; 25 Aug. 1892–Sept. 1893 Jaime Godins (acting); Sept. 1893–1896 Álvaro Ferreira; 1896–1897 Guilherme Capelo; 1897–1900 António Curto; 1900–1903 Francisco Moncada; 1903–1904 Eduardo da Costa; 1904–1904 Custódio de Borja;

1904–1906 António Curto (acting); 1906–1907 Eduardo da Costa; 1907–1909 Henrique Couceiro; 1909–1909 Álvaro Ferreira (acting); 1909–1910 José Roçadas; 1910–1911 Caetano Gonçalves (acting); 1911–1912 Manuel Coelho; 1912–15 Aug. 1914 José Norton de Matos.

819 Potchefstroom. Nov. 1838–17 Jan. 1852. *Location:* western Transvaal, South Africa. *Capital:* Potchefstroom (founded 1838 – the oldest town in the Transvaal). *Other names:* The Republic of Potchefstroom.

History: Formerly Matabele country under Mzilikaze, they were driven out of that area in 1838 by Boers led by Hendrik Potgieter who felt frustrated in **Winburg.** The new republic was named for Potgieter, Scherl and Stockenstroom, the three Boer leaders, and was the first Boer republic north of the Vaal River. In 1852 it became recognized as independent – as the **Dutch African Republic.**

Head Commandants: Nov. 1838–1845 Hendrik Potgieter; 1845–Jan. 1851 Andries Pretorius. *Commandants:* 1847–17 Jan. 1852 Gert Kruger. *Commandants-General:* Jan. 1851–17 Jan. 1852 Andries Pretorius.

820 Potiskum. ca. 1809–1901. *Location:* northern Nigeria. *Capital:* Potiskum.

History: About 1809, in the middle of the troubles created by the **Fulani Empire,** a chief of the Ngizim tribe founded the town of Potiskum, extending the area under his control and ruling his own people and the local Karekare tribe. In 1901 it became part of **Northern Nigeria Protectorate,** and in 1909 the town of Potiskum became the center for the newly formed Fika Province.

Mois (Kings): ca. 1809–(?) Bauya; (?)–(?) Awani; (?)–(?) Dungari; (?)–(?) Dowi; (?)–1836 Muzgai; 1836–1839 Jaji; 1839–1859 Nego; 1859–1886 Numainda; 1886–1895 Gubbo; 1895–1901 Bundi; 1901–1915 Agudum.

821 Príncipe Donatária. 1500–1753. *Location:* São Tomé and Príncipe. *Capital:* Santo António.

History: In 1500 the island of Príncipe (see **Príncipe Island**) was created a donatária, i.e. a parcel of land given to a Portuguese family or families of high rank and standing by the Portuguese Crown. In 1753 it became a part of **São Tomé and Príncipe Portuguese Possessions.**

Rulers: unknown.

822 Príncipe Island. 1470–1500. *Location:* São Tomé and Príncipe. *Capital:* none. *Other names:* Prince Island.

History: Discovered by the Portuguese in 1470, Príncipe (cf **São Tomé Island**) was made into a donatária in 1500 (see **Príncipe Donatária**).

Rulers: none.

Proconsular Africa see **Africa Proconsularis**

823 Prussian Gold Coast Settlements. 1701–1720. *Location:* as **Brandenburger Gold Coast Settlements.** *Capital:* Gross-Friedrichsburg. *Other names:* Gross-Friedrichsburg, Hollandia.

History: In 1701 Brandenburg became the main part of Prussia, and the **Brandenburger Gold Coast Settlements** became the Prussian Gold Coast Settlements. After 1716 they were effectively abandoned, and in 1720 sold to the Dutch (see **Dutch Gold Coast Settlements**).

Governors: 1701–1704 Adriaan Grobbe; 1704–1706 Johann Münz; 1706–1709 Heinrich Lamy; 1709–1710 Frans de Lange; 1710–1716 Nicolas Dubois; 1716–1716 Anton Van der Meden; 1716–1720 the settlements were abandoned by the Prussians.

Ptolemaic Egypt see **Egypt of the Ptolemies**

Puerto de Isabel see **Fernando Po (Spanish)**

824 Punt. ca. 3500 B.C.–(?) B.C. *Location:* Somalia (?) (possibly in the area of the Red Sea). *Capital:* unknown. *Other names:* Land of Punt, Pwnt, Pwani, Punue, Pewenet, Puanet.

History: A semi-mythical land visited by certain Egyptian pharaohs in the ancient days (Punt was the Egyptian name for the country). When it began and when it ended is unknown. The whole country may not have existed.

Rulers: unknown.

825 Qwaqwa. 1 Nov. 1974– . *Location:* Orange Free State–Lesotho border, South Africa. *Capital:* Phuthaditjhaba. *Other names:* Qwaqwa National State, Qwa Qwa, Basotho-Qwaqwa.

History: Qwaqwa is the Bantustan (National Homeland) created for the Southern Sotho tribes of the Kwena and Tlokwa. Formerly it was called Witzieshoek. In 1974 it achieved self-rule within the state of **South Africa.**

Chief Ministers: 1 Nov. 1974–19 May 1975 Wessels Mota; 19 May 1975–Tsiame Kenneth Mopeli.

826 Queen Adelaide Land. 10 Dec. 1835–17 Dec. 1847. *Location:* present-day **Ciskei,** i.e. the area of South Africa between the Keiskamma and Kei Rivers. *Capital:* Grahamstown. *Other names:* Eastern Cape Province.

History: This was the disannexed **Queen Adelaide Province** and was ruled from 1835–1847 by the lieutenant-governors of the Eastern Districts of the Cape Colony (see **British Cape Colony**), in 1847 becoming **British Kaffraria Colony.**

Lieutenant-Governors: 10 Dec. 1835–13 Sept. 1836 Col. Harry Smith (acting); 13 Sept. 1836–9 Aug. 1838 Sir Andries Stockenstroom; 9 Aug. 1838–31 Aug. 1839 John Hare (acting); 31 Aug. 1839–Sept. 1846 John Hare; Sept. 1846–9 Apr. 1847 Direct rule from British Cape Colony; 9 Apr. 1847–4 Nov. 1847 Sir Henry Young; 4 Nov. 1847–17 Dec. 1847 Direct rule from British Cape Colony.

Note: The Xhosa rulers of the area were the Rarabe offshoot of the main Xhosa line, and are listed below:

Kings: 1760–1785 Rarabe; 1785–1797 Ndlambe (Regent); 1797–13 Nov. 1829 Ngqika (or Gaika); 13 Nov. 1829–1 June 1878 Sandile. *Note:* for Xhosa rulers in Kaffraria before Rarabe, see **Kaffraria Proper.**

827 Queen Adelaide Province. 10 May 1835–5 Dec. 1835. *Location:* as **Queen Adelaide Land,** which it became. *Capital:* King William's Town (founded by Sir Benjamin D'Urban in 1835 and named for William IV of The United Kingdom).

History: In 1835 Sir Benjamin D'Urban and Colonel Harry Smith annexed the area as a natural extension of the Cape's eastern boundary, forcing out the Xhosa natives, and naming it Queen Adelaide Province, in honor of the wife of King William IV of The United Kingdom. Later in the same year D'Urban and Smith disannexed it and re-admitted the Xhosa, the land being ruled thenceforth by the lieutenant-governors of the Eastern Districts of **British Cape Colony** (see **Queen Adelaide Land**).

Administrators: 10 May 1835–5 Dec. 1835 Col. Harry Smith.

Quiah see **Koya-Temne**

Qusantina see **Constantine**

828 Rabih's Empire. 1893–23 Aug. 1901. *Location:* Nigeria, east of Lake Chad. *Capital:* Dikwa (the capital before 1893, or rather Rabih's base of operations, was Logone [1892–93]). *Other names:* Rabeh's Empire, Empire of Rabih.

History: A Sudanese general, Rabih az-Zubayr ibn Fadl Allah, arrived in the Lake Chad area about 1879 with 400 followers, on the run from the Egyptians. By raiding towns he grew in power until he had several thousand

troops. In 1893 he occupied the **Bornu Empire** and his own empire dates properly from that time. He established his capital in the town of Dikwa and took over much of the **Fulani Empire**. In 1900 he and his forces met the French at Kusseri and he was killed. For a short while he was succeeded by his son, Fadl Allah, but his vast holdings became part of either **French West Africa** or **Northern Nigeria Protectorate**.
Emperors: 1893–22 Apr. 1900 Rabih az-Zubayr ibn Fadl Allah; 22 Apr. 1900–23 Aug. 1901 Fadl Allah.

Rano see **Hausaland**

Regnum Organa see **Bornu Empire**

829 Rehoboth. 1870–15 Sept. 1885. *Location:* central Namibia (Great Namaqualand). *Capital:* Rehoboth. *Other names:* Baster Gebiet, Rehoboth Republic, Land of the Bastaards.
History: In 1870 the Bastaards (or Basters) settled in their own land. A people of mixed races, usually of Afrikaaners who had "married" Nama women, they came from Cape Colony (see **British Cape Colony**) and settled in Rehoboth.
Kaptyns (Captains): 1870–15 Sept. 1885 Hermanus Van Wyk.

830 Republic of Egypt. 18 June 1953–1 Feb. 1958. *Location:* as **Arab Republic of Egypt**. *Capital:* Cairo. *Other names:* Egypt Republic, Egyptian Republic.
History: In 1952 the military ousted King Farouk and the **Egyptian Kingdom** came to an effective end. The real end came in 1953 when a republic was declared with Naguib as the first ruler. The Suez Crisis began in 1956 when Nasser nationalized the Canal and closed it to international traffic. In 1958 Egypt and Syria joined together to form the **United Arab Republic**.
Presidents: 18 June 1953–14 Nov. 1954 Muhammad Naguib; 17 Nov. 1954–1 Feb. 1958 Gamal Abdel Nasser.

Prime Ministers: 25 Feb. 1954–27 Feb. 1954 Gamal Abdel Nasser; 18 Apr. 1954–17 Nov. 1954 Gamal Abdel Nasser. *Note:* in times of no Prime Minister, the President held that office.

831 Réunion. See these **names:**
Réunion Department (1946–   )
Réunion Colony (1848–1946)
Bourbon [ii] (1815–1848)
Bourbon (British) (1810–1815)
Bonaparte (1801–1810)
Réunion (1793–1801)
Bourbon Colony (1764–1793)
Bourbon [i] (1649–1764)
Santa Apollonia (French) (1642–1649)
Santa Apollonia (French Possession) (1638–1642)
Santa Apollonia (1513–1638)
Diva Morgabin (1502–1513)

832 Réunion. 1793–1801. *Location:* in the Indian Ocean. *Capital:* Saint Denis. *Other names:* Réunion des Patrioles.
History: In 1793, with the fall of the House of Bourbon in France, the Île de Bourbon (see **Bourbon Colony**) changed its name to Réunion. In 1801 it became Île Bonaparte (see **Bonaparte**).
Governors: 1793–1794 Jean-Baptiste Vigoureux du Plessis; 1794–1801 Philippe Jacob de Cordemoy.

833 Réunion Colony. 1848–19 March 1946. *Location:* as **Réunion,** in the Indian Ocean. *Capital:* Saint Denis. *Other names:* Réunion.
History: In 1848 **Bourbon [ii]** became Réunion again. In 1946 it became **Réunion Departement**.
Governors: 1848–1850 Joseph-Napoléon Sarda-Garriga; 1850–1852 Louis Doret; 1852–1858 Louis Hubert-Delisle; 1858–1864 Rodolphe Darricau; 1864–1869 Marc Dupré; 1869–1875 Louis de Lormel; 1875–1879 Pierre Faron; 1879–1886 Pierre Cuinier; 1886–1888 Étienne Richaud; 1888–1893 Louis Manès; 1893–1896 Henri Danel; 1896–1901 Laurent Beauchamp; 1901–1906

Paul Samary; 1906–1908 Adrien Bonhoure; 1908–1910 Lucien Guy; 1910–1910 Philippe Jullien; 1910–1913 François Rodier; 1913–1920 Pierre Duprat; 1920–1923 Frédéric Estèbe; 1923–1925 Maurice Lapalud; 1925–1934 Jules Repiquet; 1934–1936 Alphonse Choteau; 1936–1938 Léon Truitard; 1938–1940 Joseph Court; 1940–1942 Pierre Aubert; 1942–19 March 1946 André Capagorry.

834 Réunion Department. 19 March 1946– . *Location:* Reunion. *Capital:* Saint Denis. *Other names:* Département d'Outremer Réunion.

History: In 1946 **Réunion Colony** became an overseas department of France.

Prefects: 19 March 1946–1947 André Capagorry; 1947–1950 Paul Demange; 1950–1953 Roland Béchoff; 1953–1956 Pierre Philip; 1956–1962 Jean-François Perreau-Pradier; 1963–1966 Alfred Diefenbacher; 1966–1969 Jean Vaudeville; 1969–1972 Paul Cousserau; 1972–1975 Claude Vieillescazes; 1975–1976 Robert Lamy; 1976–Nov. 1982 Bernard Landouzy. *Government Commissioners:* Nov. 1982–1983 Michel Levallois; 1983– Michel Blangy.

835 Rhodesia. 24 Oct. 1964–11 Nov. 1965. *Location:* as **Southern Rhodesia.** *Capital:* Salisbury. *Other names:* Rhodesia Colony.

History: In 1964 **Zambia** became independent. Prior to this it had been **Northern Rhodesia Protectorate.** This left a colony with the name of Southern Rhodesia (see **Southern Rhodesia Colony**), the "Southern" part of the name thus becoming redundant. Hence, from 1964, it became known simply as Rhodesia. In 1965 Prime Minister Ian Smith made a Unilateral Declaration of Independence (UDI) (see **Rhodesia Independent State**).

Governors: 24 Oct. 1964–11 Nov. 1965 Sir Humphrey Gibbs. *Prime Ministers:* 24 Oct. 1964–11 Nov. 1965 Ian Smith.

836 Rhodesia Independent State. 11 Nov. 1965–2 March 1970. *Location:* as **Southern Rhodesia.** *Capital:* Salisbury. *Other names:* Rhodesia.

History: In 1965 **Rhodesia** became independent following a UDI (unilateral declaration of independence) made by its Prime Minister Ian Smith. Britain regarded the state as illegal, and although a governor remained in theory until 1969, Rhodesia's effective independence from Britain can be dated from 1965. In 1970 a new constitution was accepted in Rhodesia, making the country a republic (see **Rhodesia Republic**).

Prime Ministers: 11 Nov. 1965–2 March 1970 Ian Smith. *Officers Administering:* 17 Nov. 1965–24 June 1969 Clifford Dupont. *Presidents:* 24 June 1969–2 March 1970 Clifford Dupont (acting). *Nominal Governors:* 11 Nov. 1965–21 Aug. 1969 Sir Humphrey Gibbs.

837 Rhodesia Protectorate. 3 May 1895–29 Jan. 1900. *Location:* present-day **Zambia** and **Zimbabwe.** *Capital:* Salisbury (until 1897 this city was known as Fort Salisbury). *Other names:* Rhodesia.

History: In 1895 the term "Rhodesia" was first used, named for Cecil Rhodes, the main British colonizing force in the area, the only man after whom two countries have been named (North and South Rhodesia). [Note: it was decided, for no apparent reason, to pronounce the name as Rho*des*ia, with the stress on the second syllable, rather than *Rho*desia, with the stress on the first.] The Rhodesia Protectorate lasted for five years until, in 1900 it was split into three — **North Western Rhodesia, North Eastern Rhodesia,** and **Southern Rhodesia.** Prior to 1895 the area had been in a state of conquest, the British South Africa Company bringing to an end the native states of **Barotseland** in the north, and in the south the states of **Mashonaland** and **Matabeleland.** From 1894–1895 these areas were known as

North Zambesia and **South Zambesia.**
Rhodesia Protectorate was ruled from
Salisbury in the south by a variety of
administrators, although the territory
north of the Zambesi (later **Zambia**),
was administered locally by Administrators of North Eastern and North
Western Rhodesia (these administrators were subject to Salisbury until
1900).
Administrators: 3 May 1895–June
1895 Dr. Leander Starr Jameson; June
1895–2 May 1896 Joseph Vintcent (act-
ing); 2 May 1896–23 July 1897 Earl
Grey; 24 July 1897–4 Dec. 1898 William
Milton (acting). *Administrators of
Mashonaland/Senior Administrators
of Southern Rhodesia:* 5 Dec. 1898–29
Jan. 1900 William Milton. *Acting-
Administrators of Mashonaland:* 5
Dec. 1898–Jan. 1899 Sir Thomas Scan-
len; 22 June 1899–5 Dec. 1899 Capt.
Arthur Lawley. *Administrators of
Matabeleland:* Nov. 1896–Feb. 1897
Capt. Arthur Lawley (acting); Feb.
1897–4 Dec. 1898 Capt. Arthur Lawley
(Deputy); 5 Dec. 1898–29 Jan. 1900
Capt. Arthur Lawley. *Residents in
Barotseland:* 8 Apr. 1897–29 Jan. 1900
Robert Coryndon. *Administrators of
North-Eastern Rhodesia:* 1 July 1895–
June 1897 Patrick Forbes; June 1897–10
July 1898 Henry Daly (acting); 11 July
1898–29 Jan. 1900 Robert Codrington
(Deputy).

838 Rhodesia Republic. 2 March
1970–21 Apr. 1979. *Location:* as **Southern Rhodesia.** *Capital:* Salisbury.
History: On June 20, 1969 (effective
from March 2, 1970) **Rhodesia Independent State** became a self-declared
republic. In 1979 it became **Zimbabwe-
Rhodesia.**
Presidents: 2 March 1970–16 Apr.
1970 Clifford Dupont (acting); 16 Apr.
1970–14 Jan. 1976 Clifford Dupont; 14
Jan. 1976–21 March 1978 John Wrat-
hall. *Presidents of the Council of State:*
21 March 1978–1 Aug. 1978 John Wrat-
hall; 1 Aug. 1978–2 Nov. 1978 Henry
Everard (acting); 2 Nov. 1978–21 Apr.

1979 Jade Pithey (acting). *Prime Ministers:* 2 March 1970–21 Apr. 1979 Ian
Smith.

839 Ribeira Grande. 1495–1587. *Location:* northern Cape Verde Islands.
Capital: Cidade da Ribeira Grande.
Other names: Ribeira Grande Donatária.
History: In 1495 the various islands
of the Cape Verde Archipelago were
taken over by the Portuguese Crown.
Before that they had been in the hands
of Portuguese nobles (see **Cape Verde
Islands**). They were given as donatárias, or captaincies, to individuals
with enough money to run them. The
main one was Ribeira Grande, and the
others were grouped together as **Cape
Verde Dominion** (see also **Cape Verde
Colony** for further details). In 1587 all
of these donatárias were grouped together as **Cape Verde Colony.**
Capitães-Mores/Corregedores:
1550–1555 Jorge Pimentel; 1555–1558
Manuel de Andrade; 1558–1562 Luis de
Evangelho; 1562–1565 Bernardo de
Alpoim; 1565–1569 Manuel de Andrade; 1569–1578 António Tinoco;
1578–1583 Gaspar de Andrade; 1583–
1587 Diogo Magro. *Note:* Capitães-
Mores is the plural of Capitão-Mor
(Captain-Major). *Note:* Corregedores
is the plural of Corregedor (Magistrate). *Note:* unknown rulers before
1550.

Rif see also **Spanish Morocco**

840 Rif Republic. Feb. 1923–27 May
1926. *Location:* northern Morocco, in
the area called The Rif. *Capital:* Ajdir.
Other names: Jumhuriyya Rifiya, Republic of the Rif.
History: In 1923 Berber warlord and
bandit chief Abdel Krim (Abd al-Qrim)
formed a republic within **Spanish
Morocco,** and succeeded in maintaining this "republic" for five years until
halted by a massive combined French-
Spanish operation. By this time he had
awakened much sympathy throughout

the world for his cause, which was to kick the foreigners out of his country. On May 27, 1926 he was forced to surrender, and was exiled to **Reunion** in the Indian Ocean. This was the end of the Rif Republic.

Presidents/Princes of the Rif: Feb. 1923–27 May 1926 Abdel Krim. *Prime Ministers:* Feb. 1923–27 May 1926 Ben Hajj Hatmi.

841 Rio de Oro Dependent Protectorate. 6 Apr. 1887–27 Nov. 1912. *Location:* Spanish Sahara. *Capital:* Villa Cisneros. *Other names:* Spanish Sahara Protectorate, Spanish West Africa.

History: In 1887 **Rio de Oro Protectorate** became a dependent protectorate, answerable to the **Canary Islands.** In 1912 it became **Spanish West Africa.** It wasn't until 1903 that Rio de Oro was effectively settled.

Rulers: 6 Apr. 1887–1903 Direct administration from the Canary Islands; 1903–27 Nov. 1912 Francisco Bens Argandoña.

842 Rio de Oro Protectorate. 9 Jan. 1885–6 Apr. 1887. *Location:* the coast of Spanish Sahara. *Capital:* none. *Other names:* Spanish West Africa.

History: In 1885 the **Rio de Oro Settlements** became a protectorate of Spain. In 1887, with the onset of direct rule from the **Canary Islands,** it became **Rio de Oro Dependent Protectorate.**

Rulers: no local administration.

843 Rio de Oro Settlements. 1860–9 Jan. 1885. *Location:* Spanish Sahara coast. *Capital:* none. *Other names:* Spanish West Africa.

History: In 1860 the Spanish acquired rights to **Ifni** and the stretch of coast which became Rio de Oro—these courtesy of Morocco (see **Alawid Morocco**). In 1885 Spain declared a protectorate over Rio de Oro (see **Rio de Oro Protectorate**).

Rulers: 1860–9 Jan. 1885 No central administration.

844 Rio Muni Colony. 27 June 1900–1926. *Location:* the mainland of **Equatorial Guinea.** *Capital:* ruled from Santa Isabel, on Fernando Po.

History: In 1900 **Rio Muni Protectorate** became a Spanish colony. In 1926 Rio Muni, the island of Fernando Po (see **Fernando Po [Spanish] [ii]**), and the island of Annobon (see **Annobon [Spanish Possession]**) were united to form the colony called **Spanish Guinea.**

Rulers: ruled from Fernando Po (Spanish) [ii].

845 Rio Muni Protectorate. 9 Jan. 1885–27 June 1900. *Location:* as **Rio Muni Colony.** *Capital:* none.

History: In 1885 the Spanish infiltrated the mainland of what later became **Equatorial Guinea.** In 1900 it was delimited as a colony (see **Rio Muni Colony**). The main people in this territory were (are) the Fang, and the name "Rio Muni" refers to the estuary into which the larger rivers of the area flow.

Rulers: none.

846 Rivières du Sud Colony. 17 Dec. 1891–10 March 1893. *Location:* as **Guinea Republic.** *Capital:* Conakry. *Other names:* South Rivers Colony.

History: In 1891 the **Rivières du Sud Semi-Autonomous Colony** became fully autonomous as The Colony of Rivières du Sud. In 1893 it became **French Guinea.**

Lieutenant-Governors: 17 Dec. 1891–22 July 1892 Noël Ballay; 22 July 1892–10 March 1893 Paul Cousturier (acting).

847 Rivières du Sud Protectorate. 5 Aug. 1849–12 Oct. 1882. *Location:* the coast of **Guinea Republic.** *Capital:* Saint Louis (Senegal). *Other names:* South Rivers.

History: In 1849 the French established a protectorate over the

coastal area of Guinea, which they called Rivières du Sud. In 1880 they took Tomba Island and in 1881 **Futa Jalon.** Various settlements were made and in 1882 the area became **Rivières du Sud Territory.**
Rulers: Ruled direct by the Governors of Senegal Colony at Saint Louis.

848 Rivières du Sud Semi-Autonomous Colony. 1 Aug. 1889–17 Dec. 1891. *Location:* as **Guinea Republic.** *Capital:* Saint Louis (Senegal); Conakry (local Headquarters). *Other names:* South Rivers.
History: In 1889 **Rivières du Sud Territory** became partially autonomous from Senegal, and in 1891 it became fully so, as **Rivières du Sud Colony.**
Lieutenant-Governors: 1 Aug. 1889–1890 Jean-Marie Bayol; 1890–17 Dec. 1891 Noël Ballay.

849 Rivières du Sud Territory. 12 Oct. 1882–1 Aug. 1889. *Location:* the coast of **Guinea Republic.** *Capital:* Saint Louis (Senegal), with Conakry as local headquarters from 1884. *Other names:* South Rivers.
History: In 1882 the **Rivières du Sud Protectorate** became a territory, still under control from Saint Louis in **Senegal Colony,** but this time with a lieutenant-governor. In 1889 it became a partially autonomous colony (see **Rivières du Sud Semi-Autonomous Colony).**
Lieutenant-Governors: 12 Oct. 1882–1 Aug. 1889 Jean-Marie Bayol.

Riziam see **Mossi States**

850 Rodrigues Colony. 1638–1814. *Location:* in the Indian Ocean, to the east of **Mauritius.** *Capital:* Port Mathurin.
History: In 1638 **Diego Ruy's Island** was colonized by the French. In 1814 it was awarded to the British (see **Rodrigues Dependency).**
Rulers: [unknown].

851 Rodrigues Dependency. 1814– . *Location:* as **Rodrigues Colony.** *Capital:* Port Mathurin.
History: In 1814 **Rodrigues Colony** became a British dependency of **Mauritius.**
Rulers: ruled from Port Louis, Mauritius.

Roha Empire see **Zagwe Ethiopia**

852 Roman Egypt. 30 B.C.–330 A.D. *Location:* Egypt. *Capital:* Alexandria. *Other names:* Egypt.
History: With Cleopatra's death in 30 B.C. (see **Egypt of the Ptolemies),** Roman rule began in Egypt. The country was Octavian's own personal property, administered as a province of Rome, by a prefect. In 330 A.D. Constantine made it a diocese of the Roman Church (see **Egyptian Diocese of Rome).**
Prefects: 30 B.C.–26 B.C. Cornelius Gallus; 26 B.C.–25 B.C. Petronius; 25 B.C.–24 B.C. Aelius Gallus; 24 B.C.–13 B.C. Petronius; 13 B.C.–7 B.C. Rubrius Barbarus; 7 B.C.–23 Sept. 1 A.D. Turranius; 23 Sept. 1 A.D.–(?) Maximus; (?)–(?) Aquila; 17–21 Vitrasius Pollio; 21–ca. 31 Galerius; ca. 31–ca. 32 Vitrasius Pollio; ca. 32–32 Julius Severus; 32–37 Avillius Flaccus; 37–37 Aemilius Rectus; 37–38 Seius Strabo; 38–28 Apr. 39 Naevius Sertorius Macro; 28 Apr. 39–42 Vitrasius Pollio; 42–ca. 47 Aemilius Rectus; ca. 47–48 Julius Postumus; 48–5 Apr. 54 Vergilius Capito; 5 Apr. 54–55 Lusius; 55–56 Metius Modestus; 56–60 Claudius Balbillus; 60–67 Julius Vestinus; 67–28 Sept. 68 Caecina Tuscus; 28 Sept. 68–71 Julius Alexander; 71–(?) Julius Lupus; (?)–2 Feb. 82 Paulinus; 2 Feb. 82–86 Stettius Africanus; 86–10 Apr. 90 Septimus Vegetus; 10 Apr. 90–14 March 95 Mettius Rufus; 14 March 95–98 Petronius Secundus; 98–29 Aug. 103 Pompeius Planta; 29 Aug. 103–105 Vibius Maximus; 105–109 Minicius Italus; 109–116 Sulpicius Simius; 116–117 Rutilius Lupus; 117–23 Apr. 118

Marcius Turbo; 23 Apr. 118–18 Feb. 121 Rhammius Martialis; 18 Feb. 121–20 March 126 Haterius Nepos; 20 March 126–25 Feb. 134 Flavius Titianus; 25 Feb. 134–(?) Petronius Mamertinus; (?)–30 March 139 Valerius Eudaemon; 30 March 139–12 Jan. 148 Avidius Heliodorus; 12 Jan. 148–150 Petronius Honoratus; 150–29 Aug. 154 Munatius Felix; 29 Aug. 154–ca. 159 Sempronius Liberalis; ca. 159–ca. 160 Volusius Maecianus; ca. 160–163 Valerius Proculus; 163–6 Jan. 165 Annius Syriacus; 6 Jan. 165–10 May 166 Domitius Honoratus; 10 May 166–ca. 167 Flavius Titianus; ca. 167–26 Oct. 175 Bassaeus Rufus; 26 Oct. 175–177 Calvisius Statianus; 177–180 Pactumeius Magnus; 180–181 Maenius Flavianus; 181–(?) Flavius Priscus; (?)–(?) Marcus Aurelius Papirius Dionysius; 6 March 193–195 Mantennius Sabinus; 195–11 July 197 Ulpius Primianus; 11 July 197–202 Aemilius Saturninus; 202–202 Maecius Laetus; 202–16 March 215 Subatianus Aquila; 16 March 215–5 June 216 Septimius Heracleitus; 5 June 216–218 Valerius Datus; 218–13 Aug. 219 Basilianus; 13 Aug. 219–June 232 Geminius Chrestus; June 232–(?) Maevius Honorianus; (?)–(?) Julianus; (?)–(?) Epagathus; 17 July 250–(?) Appius Sabinus; (?)–(?) Aemilianus; (?)–(?) Firmus; (?)–(?) Celerinus; (?)–(?) [unknown]; (?)–(?) [unknown]; (?)–(?) [unknown]; ca. 302–28 Feb. 303 Pompeius; 28 Feb. 303–307 Culcianus; 307–17 Aug. 323 Satrius Arrianus; 17 Aug. 323–330 Sabinianus.

Rostemid Kingdom see **Rustumid Emirate**

Rotenga see **Mossi States**

Royal Niger Company see **Niger River Delta Protectorate**

853 Rozwi. ca. 1480–1838. *Location:* Zimbabwe, and parts of Botswana. *Capital:* Dhlo Dhlo. *Other names:* Borozwi, Rozvi, Varozvi, Changamire.

History: A Karanga empire established about 1480 by Changamire I (son of Matope of **Mwene Mutapa**). A later Changamire (Dunbo) overthrew the Portuguese in his area of the Zambesi, and his name became the title of the ruler of Rozwi (i.e. "the Changamire"). The mfecane, or turmoil created in southeast Africa by the Zulu migrations, caused the demise of the Rozwi Empire, and it was swallowed up by **Matabeleland** in 1838.

Kings: ca. 1480–1494 Changamire I; 1494–1530 Changamire II; 1530–ca. 1660 [unknown]; ca. 1660–1695 Changamire Dunbo; ca. 1695–ca. 1700 [unknown]; ca. 1700–1710 Changamire Negamo; (?)–(?) Chirisamuru; ca. 1825 Changamire Baswi; ca. 1828–1831 Changamire Chirisamaru II; 1831–1866 Changamire Tohwechipi.

854 Ruanda. ca. 1350–1890. *Location:* Rwanda. *Capital:* Kigali. *Other names:* Rwanda.

History: The Tutsi, or Watusi, skilled warriors, came to the Ruanda-Urundi area in the mid-14th century, and peacefully assumed dominance over the Hutu population. They ruled until 1899 when the **German East Africa Protectorate [i]** was placed over them, as it had been over **Burundi,** although the Germans never really controlled it. After World War I it was assigned to Belgium as part of **Ruanda-Urundi.**

Mwamis (Kings): ca. 1350–ca. 1386 Ndahiro Ruyange; ca. 1386–ca. 1410 Ndoba; ca. 1410–ca. 1434 Samembe; ca. 1434–ca. 1458 Nsoro Samukondo; ca. 1458–ca. 1482 Ruganza Bwimba; ca. 1482–ca. 1506 Cyilima Rugwe; ca. 1506–ca. 1528 Kigeri I Mukobanya; ca. 1528–ca. 1552 Mibambwe I Mutabaazi; ca. 1552–ca. 1576 Yuhi I Gahima; ca. 1576–ca. 1600 Ndahiro II Cyaamatare; ca. 1600–ca. 1624 Ruganza II Ndoori; ca. 1624–ca. 1648 Mutara I Seemugeshi; ca. 1648–ca. 1672 Kigeri II Nyamuheshera; ca. 1672–ca. 1696 Mibambwe II Gisanura; ca. 1696–ca. 1720

Yuhi II Mazimpaka; ca. 1720–ca. 1744 Karemeera Rwaaka; ca. 1744–ca. 1768 Cyilima II Rujugira; ca. 1768–ca. 1792 Kigeri III Ndabarasa; ca. 1792–ca. 1797 Mibambwe III Seentaabyo; ca. 1797–ca. 1830 Yuhi III Gahandiro; ca. 1830–1853 Mutara II Rwoogera; 1853–1895 Kigeri IV Rwabugiri; 1895–Nov. 1896 Mibambwe IV Rutulindwa; Nov. 1896–1931 Yuhi IV Musinga; 16 Nov. 1931–25 July 1959 Mutara III Rudahigwa; 1959–28 Jan. 1961 Kigeri V Ndahundirwa.

855 Ruanda-Urundi Mandate. 20 Oct. 1924–21 Aug. 1925. *Location:* East Africa (**Rwanda** and **Burundi**). *Capital:* Bujumbura (Usumbura).

History: In 1924 **Ruanda-Urundi Territory** became a League of Nations mandate (this from August 23, 1923, effective from October 20, 1924). In 1925 it became a mandated territory (see **Ruanda-Urundi Mandated Territory**).

Residents-General: 20 Oct. 1924–21 Aug. 1925 Pierre Ryckmans. *Kings of Ruanda:* 20 Oct. 1924–21 Aug. 1925 Yuhi IV Musinga. *Kings of Burundi:* 20 Oct. 1924–21 Aug. 1925 Mwambutso II.

856 Ruanda-Urundi Mandated Territory. 21 Aug. 1925–3 Dec. 1946. *Location:* as **Ruanda-Urundi Trust Territory.** *Capital:* Bujumbura (or Usumbura).

History: In 1925 the **Ruanda-Urundi Mandate** became a mandated territory (a subtly different constitution), being split administratively into Ruanda and Urundi. In 1946 the country became a United Nations Trust Territory (see **Ruanda-Urundi Trust Territory**).

Residents-General: 21 Aug. 1925–1928 Pierre Ryckmans. *Vice Governors-General:* 1928–30 June 1932 Charles Voisin; 30 June 1932–3 Dec. 1946 Pierre Jungers. *Kings of Ruanda:* 21 Aug. 1925–1931 Yuhi IV Musinga; 1931–3 Dec. 1946 Mutara III Rudahigwa. *Kings of Burundi:* 21 Aug. 1925–3 Dec. 1946 Mwambutsa II.

857 Ruandi-Urundi Territory. 30 May 1919–20 Oct. 1924. *Location:* as **Ruanda-Urundi Trust Territory.** *Capital:* Leopoldville (Belgian Congo) (1923–24); Boma (Belgian Congo) (1919–23).

History: In 1919 **Belgian Ruanda-Urundi** was given to Belgium officially, and was governed through the **Belgian Congo.** In 1924 it became **Ruanda-Urundi Mandate.**

Residents-General: 1920–1922 Alfred Marcorati; 1922–20 Oct. 1924 Pierre Ryckmans. *Kings of Ruanda:* 30 May 1919–20 Oct. 1924 Yuhi IV Musinga. *Kings of Burundi:* 30 May 1919–20 Oct. 1924 Mwambutsa II.

858 Ruanda-Urundi Trust Territory. 3 Dec. 1946–1 July 1962. *Location:* East Africa (**Rwanda** and **Burundi**). *Capital:* Bujumbura. *Other names:* Ruanda-Urundi United Nations Trust Territory, Ruanda-Urundi.

History: In 1946 **Ruanda-Urundi Mandated Territory** became a United Nations Trust Territory, still ruled by Belgium through the **Belgian Congo.** In 1959 two individual component parts were created within the Trust Territory, viz Rwanda and Burundi, and these were granted autonomy in 1961 as **Rwanda Autonomous Republic** and **Burundi Autonomous Kingdom,** but still ruled over by Belgium. In 1962 complete independence came to both, as **Rwanda Republic** and **Burundi Kingdom.**

Vice Governors-General: 11 Dec. 1946–1952 Léon Pétillon; 1952–1955 Alfred Claeys-Boúúaert; 1955–1959 Jean-Paul Harroy. *Residents-General:* 1959–1 July 1962 Jean-Paul Harroy. *Kings of Ruanda:* 3 Dec. 1946–25 July 1959 Mutara III Rudahigwa; 9 Oct. 1959–28 Jan. 1961 Kigeri V Ndahundirwa. *Kings of Burundi:* 3 Dec. 1946–1 July 1962 Mwambutsa II. *Presidents of Rwanda:* 28 Jan. 1961–1 July 1962 Grégoire Kayibanda. *Prime Ministers of Rwanda:* 10 Oct. 1960–28 Jan. 1961 Joseph Gitera. *Prime Ministers of*

Burundi: 26 Jan. 1961–28 Sept. 1961 Joseph Cimpaye.

Rusaddir see **Melilla**

859 Rustumid Emirate. 776–31 July 911. *Location:* Tahert, Algeria (near present-day Tiaret). *Capital:* Wargla (from 909); Tahert (until 909). *Other names:* Tahert, Tahart, Rostemid Kingdom, Banu Rustum.

History: A city-state in northwestern Algeria, Tahert was the center of the heterodox Kharijite doctrine for over a hundred years, and was ruled by Abd al-Rahman ibn Rustum and his descendants as the Rustumids. With the **Aghlabid Empire** in the east and the **Idrisid State** in the west, it was finally destroyed by the Kutama mountain tribes led by Abu Abdallah al-Shi'i.

Emirs: 776–784 Abd al-Rahman ibn Rustum; 784–823 Abd al-Wahhab; 823–871 Abu Sa'id al-Aflah; 871–871 Abu Bakr; 871–894 Abu al-Yaqzan Muhammad; 894–907 Abu Hatim Yusuf; 907–909 Yaqub ibn al-Aflah; 909–909 Abu Suleiman; 909–31 July 911 Yaqub ibn al-Aflah.

860 Rwanda and Burundi. See these names:
Rwanda Republic (1962–   )
Rwanda Autonomous Republic (1961–1962)
Burundi Republic (1966–   )
Burundi Kingdom (1962–1966)
Burundi Autonomous Kingdom (1961–1962)
Ruanda-Urundi Trust Territory (1946–1962)
Ruanda-Urundi Mandated Territory (1925–1946)
Ruanda-Urundi Mandate (1924–1925)
Ruanda-Urundi Territory (1919–1924)
Belgian Ruanda-Urundi (1916–1919)
Burundi (ca. 1675–1903)
Ruanda (ca. 1350–1890)

861 Rwanda Autonomous Repub-

lic. 28 Jan. 1961–1 July 1962. *Location:* as **Rwanda Republic.** *Capital:* Kigali. *Other names:* Rwanda, Ruanda, Democratic and Sovereign Republic of Rwanda, Autonomous Republic of Rwanda.

History: In 1961 the Rwanda Provisional Government proclaimed a republic within the **Ruanda-Urundi Trust Territory.** The Tutsi minority had reigned nominally since foreign occupation, and in 1959 the Hutu majority revolted and overthrew the monarchy, abolishing it on proclamation of the republic in 1961. The UN did not recognize the new, 1961, self-declared republic of Rwanda, but under their aegis elections were held later that year. In 1962, with the dismemberment of the Trust Territory, **Rwanda Republic** came into being. (See also **Burundi Autonomous Kingdom.**)

Presidents: 28 Jan. 1961–26 Oct. 1961 Dominique Mbonyumutwa; 26 Oct. 1961–1 July 1962 Grégoire Kayibanda. *Governors of Ruanda-Urundi:* 28 Jan. 1961–1 July 1962 Jean-Paul Harroy.

862 Rwanda Republic. 1 July 1962–   . *Location:* east central Africa. *Capital:* Kigali. *Other names:* Rwanda, Republic of Rwanda, Kinyarwanda.

History: By 1962, when **Ruanda-Urundi Trust Territory** gained its independence, its two components were **Rwanda Autonomous Republic** and **Burundi Autonomous Kingdom.** These became Rwanda Republic and **Burundi Kingdom.**

Presidents: 1 July 1962–5 July 1973 Grégoire Kayibanda; 5 July 1973– Juvenal Habyarimana.

863 Sa'did Morocco. 28 Jan. 1549–1659. *Location:* Morocco. *Capital:* Marrakesh (from 1524); Sous (before 1524).

History: In 1511 Mulay Ahmad, the sheikh of the Sharifian Sa'adi tribe, was declared leader of a jihad to expel the Portuguese who had settled under the weak **Wattasid Empire.** In 1524 they

captured Marrakesh and set up a rival
government to the Banu Wattas, and in
1548 seized Fez. It had little support as
the new rule in Morocco; by the early
17th century it was in decline, and being
ruled by different factions from Fez
and Marrakesh. In 1659 the Alawids
took it over (see **Alawid Morocco**).

Sheikhs: 1511–1517 Muhammad al-
Qa'im; 1517–1525 Ahmad I al-Araj;
1525–28 Jan. 1549 Muhammad II al-
Mahdi. *Sultans:* 28 Jan. 1549–23 Oct.
1557 Muhammad II al-Mahdi; 23 Oct.
1557–21 Jan. 1574 Abdallah al-Ghalib;
31 March 1574–1576 Muhammad III al-
Mutawakkil; 1576–4 Aug. 1578 Abdul
Malik I al-Ghazi; 15 Aug. 1578–19 Aug.
1603 Ahmad II al-Mansur; 19 Aug.
1603–1610 Zaydan an-Nasir; 1610–1613
Muhammad IV al-Mamun (from
Fez);1610–1626 Zaydan an-Nasir (from
Marrakesh); 1613–1624 Abdallah II
(from Fez); 1624–1626 Abdul Malik III
(from Fez); 1626–1628 Zaydan an-Nasir;
1628–10 March 1631 Abdul Malik II; 10
March 1631–21 Feb. 1636 al-Walid; 21
Feb. 1636–1655 Muhammad V al-As-
gher; 1655–1659 Ahmad III al-Abbas.

**864 Saharan Arab Democratic Re-
public.** 28 Feb. 1976– . *Location:* Between Morocco and Mauritania. *Capital:* based at Tindouf, Algeria. *Other
names:* Western Sahara, Sahrawi Arab
Democratic Republic, Arab Democratic Republic, SADR.

History: Morocco had laid claims to
Spanish Sahara for a long time based
on the fact that 11th century tribes in
the area had given their allegiance to
Morocco. The Spanish acquired rights
here in 1860 from Morocco (see **Rio de
Oro Settlements**), and in 1885 established a protectorate over the coastal
region (see **Rio de Oro Protectorate**).
(See also **Rio de Oro Dependent Protectorate**.) In 1912 it became (with **Ifni**)
part of **Spanish West Africa**, and by
1934 the interior was colonized. In 1958
Spanish Sahara became a province of
Spain (see **Spanish Sahara Province**),
and in 1973 the world's largest phos-

phate deposit was discovered here.
Spain determined to evacuate, and on
November 6, 1975, 350,000 unarmed
Moroccans entered Spanish Sahara in
the "Green March." On November 14,
1975 the area became jointly controlled
by Spain, Morocco and Mauritania,
and in 1976 Western Sahara came into
being as the Spanish left. On that day,
POLISARIO (the Popular Front for
the Liberation of Seguia el-Hamra and
Rio de Oro) declared a provisional
government-in-exile of the Saharan
Arab Democratic Republic, with
headquarters in Algeria (they had
formerly been in Mauritania). In fact,
Morocco and Mauritania divided the
country between them on April 14,
1976, Morocco gaining the upper two-
thirds (i.e. all of Seguia el-Hamra and
half of Rio de Oro) and the phos-
phates, while Mauritania gained the
southern portion of Rio de Oro (Tiris
el-Gharbia). **Polisario** (founded in 1973
to gain independence from Spain) proved such an able guerrilla organization
that both Mauritania's and Morocco's
economies were shattered by the con-
flict. More nations began to recognize the Saharan Arab Democratic
Republic; on August 5, 1979 Mauritania withdrew from Western Sahara,
and the Moroccans promptly stepped
into Tiris el-Gharbia and renamed it
Oued Eddahab (the Arabic form of Rio
de Oro), thereby annexing all of
Western Sahara as a territory of
Morocco. It was split into four
provinces—Boujdour,   Essmara,
Laayoune and Oued Eddahab. Inevitably the SADR will become a
recognized country.

Heads of State: 16 Oct. 1982– Muhammad Abdelaziz. *Prime Ministers:* 5
March 1976–4 Nov. 1982 Muhammad
Lamine Ould Ahmed; 4 Nov. 1982–18
Dec. 1985 Mahfud Ali Beida; 18 Dec.
1985– Muhammad Lamine Ould Ahmed.

865 Saint Helena. See these **names:**
Saint Helena Colony (1834–)

Saint Helena (East India Company) [ii] (1821–1834)
Saint Helena British Crown Colony (1815–1821)
Saint Helena (East India Company) [i] (1659–1815)
Saint Helena (Dutch) (1645–1651)

866 Saint Helena British Crown Colony. 15 Oct. 1815–5 May 1821. *Location:* as **Saint Helena Colony.** *Capital:* Jamestown. *Other names:* St. Helena, Saint Helena.

History: In 1815 Napoleon was deported to Saint Helena (see **Saint Helena [East India Company] [i]**) and the British Crown assumed direct responsibility for the colony as long as their notorious prisoner was there. Napoleon lived at Longwood, 2½ miles southwest of Jamestown for six years until he died in 1821, whereupon the East India Company resumed control of the island's affairs (see **Saint Helena [East India Company] [ii]**).

Governors: 15 Oct. 1815–1816 Mark Wilks; 1816–5 May 1821 Hudson Lowe.

867 Saint Helena Colony. 22 Apr. 1834– . *Location:* an island in the South Atlantic Ocean, 1200 miles west of Africa. *Capital:* Jamestown. *Other names:* St. Helena, Saint Helena.

History: In 1834 **Saint Helena (East India Company) [ii]** became a direct British colony, rather than ruled by the East India Company. It is still a colony. It has as dependencies **Ascension** and **Tristan da Cunha.**

Governors: 22 Apr. 1834–1836 Charles Dallas; 1836–1842 George Middlemore; 1842–1846 Hamelin Trelawney; 1846–1851 Patrick Ross; 1851–1856 Thomas Browne; 1856–1863 Edward Hay; 1863–1870 Charles Elliot; 1870–1873 Charles Patey; 1873–1884 Hudson Janisch; 1884–1887 Grant Blunt; 1887–1897 William Grey-Wilson; 1897–1903 Robert Sterndale; 1903–1911 Henry Gallwey (knighted 1910 and after 1911 known as Sir Henry Galway); 1911–1920 Harry Cordeaux; 1920–1925 Rob-

ert Peel; 1925–1932 Charles Harper; 1932–1938 Steuart Davis; 1938–18 March 1941 Guy Pilling; 18 March 1941–31 May 1947 William Gray; 31 May 1947–11 Jan. 1954 George Joy; 11 Jan. 1954–12 Feb. 1958 James Harford; 12 Feb. 1958–27 Feb. 1962 Robert Alford; 27 Feb. 1962–1968 Sir John Field; 1968–1972 Sir Dermot Murphy; 1972–1977 Sir Thomas Oates; 1977–1981 G.C. Guy; 1981–3 Aug. 1984 John Massingham; 3 Aug. 1984– Francis Baker.

868 Saint Helena (Dutch). 1645–1651. *Location:* as **Saint Helena Colony.** *Capital:* none. *Other names:* St. Helena, Saint Helena.

History: In 1645 the Dutch may have made the first attempt at settling this island which had been discovered and named by Portuguese navigator João de Nova Castela on May 21, 1502 (named for the mother of Emperor Constantine of Rome). However the settlement proved fruitless and it was left to the British East India Company to make the first real permanent settlement, in 1659 (see **Saint Helena [East India Company] [i]**).

Rulers: none.

869 Saint Helena (East India Company) [i]. 1659–15 Oct. 1815. *Location:* as **Saint Helena Colony.** *Capital:* Jamestown (built 1659 and named for the Duke of York [later James II]). *Other names:* St. Helena, Saint Helena.

History: In 1659 the British East India Company took possession of Saint Helena, which had been abandoned by the Dutch eight years before (see **Saint Helena [Dutch]**). In 1815, when Napoleon was exiled to the island, the British took over administration of Saint Helena for six years (see **Saint Helena British Crown Colony**).

Governors: 1659–1661 John Dutton; 1661–1671 Robert Stringer; 1671–1672 Richard Coney; 1672–1673 Anthony Beale; 1673–1673 Richard Munden;

1673–1674 Richard Kedgwin; 1674–1678 Gregory Field; 1678–1690 John Blackmore; 1690–1693 Joshua Johnson; 1693–1697 Richard Kelinge; 1697–1707 Stephen Poirier; 1707–1708 Thomas Goodwin; 1708–1711 John Roberts; 1711–1714 Benjamin Boucher; 1714–1719 Isaac Pyke; 1719–1723 Edward Johnson; 1723–1727 John Smith; 1727–1731 Edward Byfield; 1731–1738 Isaac Pyke; 1738–1739 John Goodwin; 1739–1741 Robert Jenkins; 1741–1741 Thomas Lambert; 1741–1743 George Powel; 1743–1747 David Dunbar; 1747–1764 Charles Hutchison; 1764–1782 John Skottowe; 1782–1788 Daniel Corneille; 1788–1800 Robert Brooke; 1800–1801 Francis Robson; 1801–1808 Robert Patton; 1808–1813 Alexander Beatson; 1813–15 Oct. 1815 Mark Wilks.

870 Saint Helena (East India Company) [ii]. 5 May 1821–22 Apr. 1834. *Location:* as **Saint Helena Colony.** *Capital:* Jamestown. *Other names:* St. Helena, Saint Helena.

History: In 1821 Napoleon died in exile on Saint Helena. For six years it had been administered directly by Britain (see **Saint Helena British Crown Colony**). In 1821, then, the East India Company resumed control of the island (see also **Saint Helena [East India Company] [i]**). In 1834 the Crown took it over for good (see **Saint Helena Colony**).

Governors: 5 May 1821–1823 Hudson Lowe; 1823–1828 Alexander Walker; 1828–22 Apr. 1834 Charles Dallas.

Saint Mary see **Bathurst Colony**

Saint Thomas see **São Tomé**

871 Sainte Marie de Madagascar. 30 July 1750–15 Oct. 1818. *Location:* off the northeastern coast of Madagascar. *Capital:* none. *Other names:* Sainte Marie.

History: A little island off the northeast coast of Madagascar, it was ceded to France in 1750 by the local ruler, but remained virtually unoccupied until 1818, when it became a colony (see **Sainte Marie de Madagascar Colony**).

Administrators: 30 July 1750–July 1754 M. Gosse; July 1754–15 Oct. 1818 no fixed central administration.

872 Sainte Marie de Madagascar Colony. 1853–1878. *Location:* as **Sainte Marie de Madagascar.** *Capital:* Ambodifototra. *Other names:* Sainte-Marie.

History: In 1853 **Sainte Marie de Madagascar Dependent Colony** became an independent colony. In 1878 it was back under the administration of **Réunion,** as **Sainte Marie de Madagascar Territory [ii].**

Commandants: 1853–1855 Jean-Pierre Durand; 1855–1858 Jean-Baptiste Raffenel; 1858–1868 Jean-Paul de la Grange; 1868–1874 Louis Blandinières; 1874–1878 Charles-Henri Vassal.

873 Sainte Marie de Madagascar Dependent Colony. 25 March 1843–1853. *Location:* as **Sainte Marie de Madagascar.** *Capital:* Ambodifototra. *Other names:* Sainte-Marie.

History: In 1843 **Sainte Marie de Madagascar Territory [i],** until then ruled by **Réunion,** became a dependent colony of **Mayotte.** In 1853 it became **Sainte Marie de Madagascar Colony.**

Commandants: 25 March 1843–1849 Raimond Vergès; 1849–1850 Pierre-Balthasar Mermier; 1850–1851 André Brisset; 1851–1853 Pierre-Balthasar Mermier; 1853–1853 Félix Grébert.

874 Sainte Marie de Madagascar Territory [i]. 15 Oct. 1818–25 March 1843. *Location:* as **Sainte Marie de Madagascar.** *Capital:* Ambodifototra. *Other names:* Sainte-Marie.

History: In 1819 the French moved into **Sainte Marie de Madagascar,** and the territory was placed under the administration of **Réunion.** In 1843 it became **Sainte Marie de Madagascar**

Dependent Colony, under the administration of **Mayotte.**
Commandants: 1819–15 Apr. 1821 Jean-Louis Carayon; 15 Apr. 1821–2 Apr. 1823 Jean-Baptiste Roux; 2 Apr. 1823–29 Apr. 1823 François Albrand; 29 Apr. 1823–Oct. 1826 Hercule Blévec; Oct. 1826–May 1827 Capt. Giraud (acting); May 1827–1829 Hercule Blévec; 1829–1830 Jean-Louis Carayon; 1830–1841 direct rule from Bourbon [ii]; 1841–25 March 1843 Raimond Vergès.

875 Sainte Marie de Madagascar Territory [ii]. 1878–6 Aug. 1896. *Location:* as **Sainte Marie de Madagascar** (now Nossi Boraha). *Capital:* Ambodifototra (local headquarters); Saint Denis (on Réunion). *Other names:* Sainte Marie, Nosy Boraha.
History: In 1878 **Sainte Marie de Madagascar Colony** fell back under the jurisdiction of **Réunion.** In 1896 it was taken in by France (as with **Diego Suarez** and **Nossi-Bé**) as part of **Madagascar Colony.**
Rulers: ruled direct from **Réunion Colony.**

Sakalava see **Madagascar Kingdom**

Salé-Rabat see **Bou Regreg**

876 Samory's Empire. 1879–29 Sept. 1898. *Location:* Guinea. *Capital:* Bissandugu. *Other names:* Mandinka Empire.
History: In 1847 the 17-year-old Samory Touré from Sanankoro in present-day Guinea became a trader, later serving in the army of a Mandinka war-leader. In 1879 he formed his empire (otherwise called the Mandinka Empire) by conquest. From 1882 until his capture in 1898 he resisted the French, and died in exile on Gabon in 1900. His empire became part of **French West Africa.**
Emperors: 1879–29 Sept. 1898 Samory Touré.

877 Santa Apollonia. 9 Feb. 1513–
1638. *Location:* Reunion. *Capital:* none.
History: In 1513 **Diva Morgabin** was re-named Santa Apollonia, still a Portuguese possession. In 1638 it was taken by the French (see **Santa Apollonia [French Possession]**).
Rulers: none.

878 Santa Apollonia (French). 1642–1649. *Location:* as **Réunion.** *Capital:* no official capital.
History: In 1642 **Santa Apollonia (French Possession)** was officially claimed by Jacques Pronis of France. He deported a dozen French mutineers to the island from **Fort-Dauphin Colony** in Madagascar, and these convicts became the first settlers on what was to become **Réunion.** In 1645 these convicts were returned to France, and in 1649 France annexed the island officially, as Bourbon (see **Bourbon [i]**).
Rulers: unknown.

879 Santa Apollonia (French Possession). 1638–1642. *Location:* as **Réunion.** *Capital:* none.
History: In 1638 Frenchman François Cauche hoisted the French flag on **Santa Apollonia,** previously a Portuguese-claimed island. In 1642 it became inhabited for the first time (see **Santa Apollonia [French]**).
Rulers: none.

880 Santa Cruz de la Mar Pequeña. 1478–1524. *Location:* somewhere on the coast of Morocco opposite the Canary Islands, probably in the area of Ifni. *Capital:* unknown exactly, but probably Santa Cruz. *Other names:* Santa Cruz de Mar Pequeña.
History: In 1478 the Spanish occupied a post here and for almost 50 years they used it as a slave-dealing entrepôt. It was abandoned in 1524.
Rulers: unknown.

881 Santa Cruz de Tenerife Province. 1927–8 May 1983. *Location:* Tenerife, La Palma, Gomero, Hierro—

these islands in the Canary Islands. *Capital:* Santa Cruz de Tenerife.

History: In 1927 **Canary Islands Protectorate** was split up into two provinces of Metropolitan Spain, Santa Cruz de Tenerife and **Las Palmas de Gran Canária Province.** This was due to the rivalry between the ports of Las Palmas and Tenerife. In 1983 the Canary Islands as a whole became an autonomous province of Spain (see **Canary Islands [Self-Rule]**). *Rulers:* [unknown].

São Jorge de Mina see **Portuguese Gold Coast Settlements**

São Paulo de Loanda see **Angola Donatária**

882 São Tomé. 1522–1753. *Location:* as **São Tomé Island.** *Capital:* São Tomé.

History: In 1522 the Portuguese Crown assumed control of the island of São Tomé. Before that it had been a donatária (see **São Tomé Donatária**), as was Príncipe (see **Príncipe Donatária**). From 1641–1644 the Dutch occupied São Tomé (but not Príncipe), but the Portuguese administration continued. In 1753 São Tomé joined with Príncipe Donatária to form **São Tomé and Príncipe Portuguese Possessions.**

Capitães-Mores: 1522–(?) Vasco Estevens; 1531–ca. 1535 Henrique Pereira; ca. 1535–1541 [unknown]; 1541–1545 Diogo Pereira; 1545–1546 [unknown]; 1546–ca. 1554 Francisco de Paiva; ca. 1554–ca. 1558 [unknown]; ca. 1558–(?) Pedro Botelho; 1560–1564 Cristóvão de Sousa; 1564–1569 Francisco de Gouveia; 1569–1571 Francisco Teles; 1571–1575 Diogo Salema; 1575–ca. 1582 António Maciel; ca. 1582–ca. 1584 [unknown]; ca. 1584–1586 Francisco de Figueiredo. *Governors:* 1586–1587 Francisco de Figueiredo; 1587–1591 Miguel de Moura; 1591–1592 Duarte da Silva; 1592–1593 Francisco de Vila Nova (acting); 1593–1597 Fernando de Meneses; 1597–ca. 1598 Vasco de Carvalho; ca. 1598–1601 João da Cunha (acting); 1601–1604 António Monteiro (acting); 1604–(?) Pedro de Andrade; (?)–1609 João da Cunha (acting); 1609–1609 Fernando de Noronha; 1609–1609 João da Cunha (acting); 1609–1611 Constantino Távares; João da Cunha (acting); 1611–1611 Francisco Teles de Meneses; 1611–1613 Luís de Abreu; 1613–1614 Feliciano Carvalho; 1614–1616 Luís de Abreu; 1616–1620 Miguel Baharem; 1620–1621 Pedro da Cunha; 1621–1623 Félix Pereira; 1623–1627 Jerónimo de Melo Fernando; 1627–1628 André Maracote; 1628–1632 Lourenço de Távora (acting); 1632–1632 Francisco Barreto de Meneses; 1632–1636 Lourenço de Távora (acting); 1636–1636 António de Carvalho; 1636–1640 Lourenço de Távora (acting); 1640–1640 Manuel Carneiro; 1640–1641 Miguel de Melo e Albuquerque (acting); 1641–1642 Paulo da Ponte (acting); 1642–ca. 1650 Lourenço de Távora; ca. 1650–1656 [unknown]; 1656–ca. 1657 Cristóvão do Rego; ca. 1657–ca. 1661 [unknown]; ca. 1661–(?) Pedro da Silva; 1669–1671 Paulo de Noronha; 1671–1673 ruled by a Chamber Senate; 1673–1677 Julião de Campos Barreto; 1677–1680 Bernardim Freire de Andrade; 1680–1683 Jacinto de Figueiredo e Abreu; 1683–1686 João da Cunha (acting); 1686–1686 António Lemos; 1686–1689 Bento de Sousa Lima; 1689–1693 António de Lacerda; 1693–1694 António de Barredo; 1695–1696 José Sodré; 1696–1697 João Matos; 1697–1702 Manuel da Camara; 1702–1709 José da Castro; 1709–1710 Vicente Pinheiro; 1710–1715 ruled by a junta; 1715–1716 Bartolomeu Ponte; 1716–1717 ruled by a Chamber Senate; 1717–1720 António Mendonça; 1720–1722 ruled by a junta; 1722–1727 José da Camara; 1727–1734 Serafim Sarmento; 1734–1736 Lope Coutinho; 1736–1741 José Souto-Maior; 1741–1741 António de Castelo Branco; 1741–1744 ruled by a Chamber Senate; 1744–1744 Francisco da Conceição; 1744–1745 Francisco de Alva Brandão (acting);

1745–1747 ruled by a Chamber Senate; 1747–1748 Francisco das Chagas; 1748–1751 ruled by a Chamber Senate; 1751–1751 António Neves; 1751–1753 ruled by a Chamber Senate. *Note:* Capitães-Mores is the plural of Capitão-Mor (Captain-Major).

883 São Tomé and Príncipe. See these **names:**
São Tomé and Príncipe Democratic Republic (1975–)
São Tomé and Príncipe Autonomous Republic (1974–1975)
São Tomé and Príncipe Overseas Province (1951–1974)
São Tomé and Príncipe Portuguese Possessions (1753–1951)
São Tomé (1522–1753)
São Tomé Donatária (1485–1522)
São Tomé Island (1470–1485)
Príncipe Donatária (1500–1753)
Príncipe Island (1470–1500)

884 São Tomé and Príncipe Autonomous Republic. 21 Dec. 1974–13 July 1975. *Location:* as **São Tomé and Príncipe Democratic Republic.** *Capital:* São Tomé. *Other names:* São Tomé and Príncipe.
History: In 1974, after agitation by the MLSTP (Movement for the Liberation of São Tomé and Príncipe) led by Dr. Manuel Pinto da Costa, the islands were granted autonomy. Some autonomy had been granted in 1973, when the local government had been recognized by the Organization of African Unity, but not until 1974, when a transitional government was set up in São Tomé and Príncipe did complete independence become a soon-to-happen reality. It happened in 1975 (see **São Tomé and Príncipe Democratic Republic**).
High Commissioners: 21 Dec. 1974–13 July 1975 Pires Veloso. *Prime Ministers:* 21 Dec. 1974–13 July 1975 Leonel d'Alva.

885 São Tomé and Príncipe Democratic Republic. 12 July 1975–   . *Loca-*

tion: off the coast of West Africa, on the Equator, in the Bight of Biafra. *Capital:* São Tomé. *Other names:* Saint Thomas, São Tomé and Príncipe, Democratic Republic of São Tomé and Príncipe.
History: In 1975 **São Tomé and Príncipe Autonomous Republic** gained its independence. The republic has two principal islands — São Tomé (Capital — São Tomé. São Tomé is also the capital of the Republic) and Príncipe (Capital — Santo António).
Presidents: 12 July 1975– Manuel Pinto da Costa. *Prime Ministers:* 12 July 1975–Apr. 1979 Miguel Trovoada. *Note:* in times of no Prime Minister, the President held that office.

886 São Tomé and Príncipe Overseas Province. 11 June 1951–21 Dec. 1974. *Location:* as **São Tomé and Príncipe Democratic Republic.** *Capital:* São Tomé. *Other names:* São Tomé.
History: In 1951 **São Tomé and Príncipe Portuguese Possessions** became an overseas province of Portugal. In 1973 a certain amount of autonomy was granted to the islands by Portugal, largely as a result of the agitation by the MLSTP (Movement for the Liberation of São Tomé and Príncipe) led by Dr. Manuel Pinto da Costa. In 1974 real autonomy came about (see **São Tomé and Príncipe Autonomous Republic**).
Governors: 11 June 1951–28 June 1952 Mario Castro (acting); 28 June 1952–18 Apr. 1953 Guilherme Pinto; 18 Apr. 1953–19 May 1953 Fernando Rodrigues (acting); 19 May 1953–July 1953 Affonso de Sousa (acting); July 1953–Aug. 1954 Francisco Barata; Aug. 1954–15 June 1955 Luís Faria; 15 June 1955–5 Dec. 1956 José Machado (acting); 5 Dec. 1956–13 Oct. 1957 Octávio Gonçalves; 13 Oct. 1957–Aug. 1963 Manuel Amaral; Aug. 1963–30 Oct. 1963 Alberto Campos (acting); 30 Oct. 1963–1972 António Sebastião. *High Commissioners:* 1973–21 Dec. 1974 João Gonçalves. *Leaders of MLSTP:* 1973–21 Dec. 1974 Manuel Pinto da Costa.

887 São Tomé and Príncipe Portuguese Possessions. 1753–11 June 1951. *Location:* as **São Tomé and Príncipe Democratic Republic.** *Capital:* São Tomé. *Other names:* São Tomé and Príncipe.

History: In 1753 the donatária of Príncipe (see **Príncipe Donatária**) and the Portuguese Crown possession of **São Tomé** merged into one government. In 1951 it became **São Tomé and Príncipe Overseas Province.**

Governors: 1753–1755 ruled by a Chamber Senate; 1755–1755 Lopo Coutinho; 1755–1758 ruled by a Chamber Senate; 1758–1761 Luís da Mota e Melo; 1761–1767 ruled by a Chamber Senate; 1767–1768 Lourenço Palha; 1768–1770 ruled by a Chamber Senate; 1770–1778 Vincente Ferreira; 1778–1782 João de Azambuja; 1782–1788 Cristóvão de Sá; 1788–1797 João Leote; 1797–1797 Inácio Coutinho; 1797–1797 Manuel de Carvalho (acting); 1797–1798 Varela Borca (acting); 1798–1799 Manuel da Mota; 1799–1799 Francisco de Vide; 1799–1802 João Baptista de Silva; 1802–1805 Gabriel de Castro; 1805–1817 Luís Lisboa; 1817–1824 Felipe de Freitas; 1824–1830 João de Brito; 1830–1834 Joaquim da Fonseca; 1834–1836 Provisional Government in power; 1836–1837 Fernando de Noronha (acting); 1837–1838 Leandro da Costa; 1838–1839 José de Urbanski; 1839–1843 José da Costa; 1843–2 March 1843 Leandro da Costa; 2 March 1843–1 May 1846 José Marquês; 1 May 1846–30 Sept. 1847 ruled by a Chamber Senate; 30 Sept. 1847–20 Nov. 1847 Carlos de Morais e Almeida; 20 Nov. 1847–20 July 1848 ruled by a Chamber Senate; 20 July 1848–12 Dec. 1849 José Pessôa; 12 Dec. 1849–9 March 1851 Leandro da Costa; 9 March 1851–20 March 1853 José Marquês; 20 March 1853–28 July 1855 Francisco da Pina Rolo; 28 July 1855–March 1857 Adriana Passálaqua; March 1857–15 Jan. 1858 ruled by a Chamber Senate; 15 Jan. 1858–May 1858 Francisco Correia; May 1858–1859 ruled by a Chamber Senate; 1859–21 Nov. 1860 Luis Pereira e Horta; 21 Nov. 1860–8 July 1862 José de Melo; 8 July 1862–17 Nov. 1862 ruled by a Chamber Senate; 17 Nov. 1862–30 March 1863 José da Costa Moura; 30 March 1863–8 Jan. 1864 João Baptista Brunachy; 8 Jan. 1864–2 Aug. 1865 Estanislau de Assunção e Almeida; 2 Aug. 1865–30 July 1867 João Baptista Brunachy; 30 July 1867–30 Sept. 1867 António da Fonseca; 30 Sept. 1867–30 May 1869 Estanislau de Assunção e Almeida; 30 May 1869–7 Oct. 1872 Pedro Lopes; 7 Oct. 1872–28 Oct. 1873 João de Carvalho; 28 Oct. 1873–1 Nov. 1876 Gregório Ribeiro; 1 Nov. 1876–28 Sept. 1879 Manuel de Assunção e Almeida; 28 Sept. 1879–28 Nov. 1879 Francisco Ferreira do Amaral; 28 Nov. 1879–3 Jan. 1880 Custódio de Borja (acting); 3 Jan. 1880–30 Dec. 1881 Vicente de Melo e Almada; 30 Dec. 1881–26 Jan. 1882 Augusto Leão (acting); 26 Jan. 1882–24 May 1884 Francisco da Silva; 24 May 1884–8 Aug. 1885 Custódio de Borja; 8 Aug. 1885–19 Sept. 1885 Augusto Cabral (acting); 19 Sept. 1885–25 Sept. 1885 Custódio de Borja; 25 Sept. 1885–25 Feb. 1886 Augusto Cabral (acting); 25 Feb. 1886–25 Aug. 1886 Custódio de Borja; 25 Aug. 1886–9 March 1890 Augusto Sarmento; 9 March 1890–26 June 1891 Firmeno da Costa; 26 June 1891–8 Dec. 1894 Francisco de Miranda; 8 Dec. 1894–8 Apr. 1895 Jaime Godins (acting); 8 Apr. 1895–5 Apr. 1897 Cipriano Jardim; 5 Apr. 1897–5 Apr. 1899 Joaquim da Graça Correia e Lança; 5 Apr. 1899–3 Jan. 1901 Amáncio Cabral; 3 Jan. 1901–8 May 1901 Francisco Vieira (acting); 8 May 1901–8 Oct. 1902 Joaquim de Brito; 8 Oct. 1902–7 June 1903 João Guimarães; 7 June 1903–14 Dec. 1903 João Ferreira; 14 Dec. 1903–13 Apr. 1907 Francisco de Paula Cid; 13 Apr. 1907–24 June 1907 Vitor Lemos e Melo (acting); 24 June 1907–24 Oct. 1908 Pedro Berquó; 24 Oct. 1908–13 March 1909 Vitor Lemos e Melo (acting); 13 March 1909–13 June 1910 José da

Fonseca; 13 June 1910–21 July 1910 Jaime do Rego; 21 July 1910–7 Aug. 1910 Henrique de Oliveira (acting); 7 Aug. 1910–11 Nov. 1910 Fernando de Carvalho; 12 Nov. 1910–28 Nov. 1910 Carlos Pimentel e Melo (acting); 28 Nov. 1910–14 June 1911 António Guedes; 14 June 1911–24 Dec. 1911 Jaime do Rego; 24 Dec. 1911–13 May 1913 Mariano Martins; 13 May 1913–31 May 1915 Pedro Machado; 31 May 1915–6 June 1915 José de Sousa e Faroo; 6 June 1915–28 July 1918 Rafael Oliveira (acting); 28 July 1918–11 June 1919 João Ferreira; 11 June 1919–25 Sept. 1920 Avelino Leite; 25 Sept. 1920–22 Oct. 1920 José Velez (acting); 22 Oct. 1920–2 July 1921 Eduardo de Lemos (acting); 2 July 1921–23 Jan. 1924 António Pereira; 23 Jan. 1924–8 July 1926 Eugénio Branco; 8 July 1926–31 Aug. 1928 José Rato; 31 Aug. 1928–30 Jan. 1929 Sebastião Barbosa (acting); 30 Jan. 1929–31 Oct. 1929 Francisco Penteado; 31 Oct. 1929–17 Dec. 1933 Luís Fernandes; 17 Dec. 1933–8 May 1941 Ricardo Vaz Monteiro; 8 May 1941–5 Apr. 1945 Amadeu de Figueiredo; 5 Apr. 1945–July 1948 Carlos Gorgulho; July 1948–8 Oct. 1950 Affonso de Sousa (acting); 8 Oct. 1950–11 June 1951 Mario Castro (acting).

888 São Tomé Donatária. 1485–1522. *Location:* as São Tomé. *Capital:* São Tomé. *Other names:* São Tomé.

History: In 1485 **São Tomé Island,** discovered only fifteen years previously by the Portuguese, was made into a donatária by the Crown. São Tomé is much larger than Príncipe, its neighbor (see **Príncipe Island** and **Príncipe Donatária**). In 1522 the Crown took possession of São Tomé (see **São Tomé**).

Capitães-Mores: 1485–1490 João de Paiva; 1490–1493 João Pereira; 1493–1499 Álvaro Souto-Maior; 1499–ca. 1510 Fernão de Melo; ca. 1510–(?) [unknown]; ca. 1516–(?) Diogo de Alcáçova; ca. 1517–1522 João de Melo.

Note: Capitães-Mores is the plural of Capitão-Mor (Captain-Major).

889 São Tomé Island. 1470–1485. *Location:* São Tomé and Príncipe. *Capital:* none. *Other names:* Saint Thomas.

History: In 1470 the island of São Tomé was discovered by the Portuguese (cf **Príncipe Island**). In 1485 it became a donatária (see **São Tomé Donatária**).

Rulers: none.

Sarili's Country see **Kreli's Country**

890 Séchelles. 1756–1770. *Location:* as **Seychelles Republic.** *Capital:* none. *Other names:* Seychelles, Îles de Séchelles.

History: In 1756 France made the first formal claim to the group of islands known later as The Seychelles (see **Île de Labourdonnais**). In 1770 it became a French colony (see **Séchelles French Colony**).

Rulers: none.

891 Séchelles French Colony. 1770–1794. *Location:* as **Seychelles Republic.** *Capital:* Mahé. *Other names:* Les Séchelles, The Seychelles, Séchelles French Colony.

History: In 1770 **Séchelles** became a French colony. In 1794 the islands were captured by the British (see **British Occupied Séchelles**).

Commandants: 1770–1772 M. de Launay; 1772–1775 M. Anselme; 1775–1778 M. Le Roux de Kermeseven; 1778–1781 M. Saint-Amant de Romainville; 1781–1783 M. Berthelot de la Coste; 1783–1786 Capt. François de Souillac; 1786–1789 M. Motais de Narbonne; 1789–1792 Louis de Malavois; 1792–1794 Charles Esnouf.

892 Segu. ca. 1600–10 March 1861. *Location:* Mali. *Capital:* Segu-koro (1750 onwards); Ngoi (1736–50); Segu-koro (ca. 1600–1736). *Other names:* Ségou, Bambara Kingdom of Segu.

History: Segu and **Kaarta** were the two Bambara states founded in the early 17th century by two brothers— Barama-Ngolo and Nya Ngolo (the latter founding Kaarta). Segu expanded and in 1861 was swallowed up in the **Tukolor Empire.** From 1861–90 the dynasty continued to rule in exile, and in 1890 Mari, the last ruler, was killed by the French.

Kings: ca. 1600–1620 Barama-Ngolo; 1620–1640 Soma; 1640–1660 Fa Sine; 1660–1710 Mamari Biton; 1710–1711 Bakari; 1711–1736 De-Koro; 1736–1740 Tonmassa Dembele (or Tonmansa); 1740–1744 Kanou-ba-Nyouma Bari; 1744–1748 Kafadyougou; 1748–1750 a period of anarchy; 1750–1787 Ngolo Dyara; 1787–1808 Man-nsor; 1808–1827 Da Kaba; 1827–1839 Tye-Folo; 1839– 1840 Nyene-Mba I; 1840–1843 a period of anarchy; 1843–1849 Ben; 1849–1851 Kon-Maran; 1851–1854 Demba; 1854– 1856 Touro-Koro Mari; 1856–10 March 1861 Ali; 13 Apr. 1861–1870 Kege Mari; 1870–1878 Nyene-Mba II; 1878–1878 Mamuru; 1878–1883 Massatana; 1883– 1887 Karanoko; 1887–29 May 1890 Mari Dyara.

893 Sekonyela's Land. 1822–Sept. 1853. *Location:* Caledon River Valley, South Africa. *Capital:* Joalaboholo. *Other names:* Sikonyela's Land, Batlokoa Lands.

History: As a result of Zulu King Chaka's movements in the early 1820s, all the tribes in the area were pushed out and forced to move on. This caused havoc in South Africa and was called the "Mefacane" or "hammering." **Basutoland Kingdom** was formed as a result, as was the area of land ruled by Sekonyela, son of King Mokotjo of the Batlokoa ("The people of the Wild Cat") and his Mantateesi. Deadly rival to Moshoeshoe of Basutoland, Sekonyela was eventually driven out by Moshoeshoe and finally granted land in the Herschel District of the Cape (see **British Cape Colony**) by Sir George Clerk of the British Government. In 1853 this land was swallowed up into the Cape.

Kings: 1822–July 1856 Sekonyela; July 1856–1881 Lelingoanna (joint); July 1856–1881 Lehana (joint).

Senaar see **Funj Sultanate**

894 Senegal. See these **names:**
Senegal Republic (1960–)
Senegal (1959–1960)
Senegal Autonomous Republic (1958–1959)
Senegal Overseas Territory (1946–1958)
Senegal Colony and Protectorate (1904–1946)
Senegal Colony (1817–1904)
Goree and Dependencies (1854–1859)
Senegal (British) [iii] (1809–1817)
Senegal French Territory (1779–1809)
Senegambia Colony (1765–1779)
Senegal (Royal African Company) (1763–1765)
Goree (1763–1779)
Senegal (British) [ii] (1758–1763)
Senegal French Colony (Compagnie des Indes) (1718–1758)
Senegal French Colony (Royal Company of Senegal) (1696–1718)
Senegal French Settlements (Compagnie du Guinee) [ii] (1693–1696)
Senegal (British) [i] (1693–1693)
Senegal French Settlements (Compagnie du Guinee) [i] (1684–1693)
Senegal French Settlements (Compagnie d'Afrique) (1682–1684)
Senegal French Settlements (Compagnie du Senegal) (1672–1682)
Senegal French Settlements (Colbert's West Indian Company) (1664–1672)
Senegal French Settlements (Compagnie du Cap Vert et du Senegal) (1658–1664)
Senegal French Settlements (Compagnie Normande) (1626–1658)
Baol (ca. 1550–1877)
Dyolof (ca. 1350–1889)
Futa Toro (1513–1877)
Kayor (1549–1885)
Walo (1186–1855)

895 Senegal. 4 Apr. 1959–20 Aug. 1960. *Location:* as **Senegal Republic.** *Capital:* Dakar.

History: In 1959 **Senegal Autonomous Republic** and the **Autonomous Sudanese Republic** joined together to form the **Mali Autonomous Federation** (this was on January 17, 1959, effective from April 4, 1959). The Federation was composed of two territories, viz Senegal and **Sudanese Republic Territory.** In June 1960 this Federation gained total independence from France, as the **Mali Federation,** and the two component territories retained their names (as above) until August 1960 when the Federation fell apart. The two countries became, respectively, **Senegal Republic** (which is what it is known as today) and the **Sudanese Republic** (which the following month became **Mali Republic** which is what it is known today).

High Commissioners: 4 Apr. 1959–20 June 1960 Pierre Lami. *Prime Ministers:* 4 Apr. 1959–20 June 1960 Mamadou Dia.

896 Senegal Autonomous Republic. 25 Nov. 1958–4 Apr. 1959. *Location:* as **Senegal Republic.** *Capital:* Dakar. *Other names:* Senegal, République du Sénégal, Autonomous Republic of Senegal.

History: In 1958 **Senegal Overseas Territory** became an autonomous republic within the French Community. In April 1959 this state became part of the **Mali Autonomous Federation,** and as such became known simply as **Senegal.**

High Commissioners: 25 Nov. 1958–4 Apr. 1959 Pierre Lami. *Presidents of Council:* 25 Nov. 1958–4 Apr. 1959 Mamadou Dia.

897 Senegal (British) [i]. Jan. 1693–July 1693. *Location:* as **Senegal French Settlements.** *Capital:* none. *Other names:* Senegal.

History: In January 1693 the British captured Senegal (see **Senegal French**

Settlements (Compagnie du Guinée [i]) for the first time. Later that year it was won back by the French (see **Senegal French Settlements (Compagnie du Guinée [ii]).**

Rulers: none.

898 Senegal (British) [ii]. 30 Apr. 1758–10 Feb. 1763. *Location:* the coast of Senegal. *Capital:* Saint Louis. *Other names:* Senegal.

History: In 1758 the British took all of the French possessions in Senegal from the Compagnie des Indes (see **Senegal French Colony [Compagnie des Indes]).** In 1763 Gorée was returned (and only Gorée) to the French, and the remainder of the colony was renamed **Senegal (Royal African Company).**

Governors: 30 Apr. 1758–10 Feb. 1763 Richard Worge.

899 Senegal (British) [iii]. 13 July 1809–25 Jan. 1817. *Location:* Senegal coastline and islands. *Capital:* Freetown (Sierra Leone). *Other names:* Senegal.

History: In 1809 the British took **Senegal French Territory.** France regained it in 1817. That latter date finally brought an end to the seemingly incessant power struggle between France and Britain in this area of the world. In 1817 France created **Senegal Colony.**

Governors: 13 July 1809–1811 Charles Maxwell; 1811–1814 Charles Macarthy; 1814–19 Apr. 1816 Thomas Brereton; 19 Apr. 1816–25 Jan. 1817 [unknown] (acting).

900 Senegal Colony. 25 Jan. 1817–13 Feb. 1904. *Location:* Senegal. *Capital:* Saint Louis. *Other names:* Senegal.

History: In 1817 France regained her Senegal possessions entirely from Britain (see **Senegal [British] [iii]).** During the colony's life it expanded into the hinterland, especially during and after the administration of Governor Faidherbe. In 1895 Senegal became the base administrative area of **French West Africa** and until 1902 was ruled by the

Governor-General of that Federation. In 1904 **Senegal Colony and Protectorate** came into being. Note: From 1854–59 Gorée was detached as a separate colony (see **Gorée and Dependencies**). *Commandants:* 17 June 1817–Dec. 1817 Julien Schmaltz; Dec. 1817–13 March 1819 Capt. Fleuriau (acting); 13 March 1819–14 Aug. 1820 Julien Schmaltz; 14 Aug. 1820–1 March 1821 Louis Lecoupé de Montereau; 1 March 1821–18 May 1827 Jacques-François Roger; 18 May 1827–7 Jan. 1828 M. Gerbidon (acting). *Governors:* 7 Jan. 1828–11 May 1829 Jean Guillaume Jubelin; 11 May 1829–24 May 1831 Pierre Brou; 24 May 1831–18 Oct. 1833 Thomas Renault de Saint-Germain; 18 Oct. 1833–13 Nov. 1833 M. Cadest (acting); 13 Nov. 1833–10 May 1834 Germain Quernel; 10 May 1834–1 July 1836 Louis Pujol; 1 July 1836–Dec. 1836 Louis Malavois; Dec. 1836–13 Sept. 1837 Louis Guillet (acting); 13 Sept. 1837–12 Apr. 1839 Julien Soret; 12 Apr. 1839–19 May 1841 Guillaume Charmasson de Puy-Laval; 19 May 1841–7 May 1842 Jean-Baptiste Montagniès de la Roque; 7 May 1842–5 Feb. 1843 Édouard Pageot des Noutières; 5 Feb. 1843–8 Dec. 1843 Louis Bouët-Willaumez; 8 Dec. 1843–July 1844 M. Laborel (acting); July 1844–11 Dec. 1845 Pierre Thomas (acting); 11 Dec. 1845–20 March 1846 François Ollivier; 20 March 1846–30 Aug. 1846 M. Hoube (acting); 30 Aug. 1846–24 Aug. 1847 Ernest Bourdon de Grammont; 24 Aug. 1847–7 Sept. 1847 M. Caille (acting); 7 Sept. 1847–Nov. 1847 Léandre Berlin-Duchâteau (acting); Nov. 1847–1848 Auguste Baudin; 1848–1848 Léandre Berlin-Duchâteau (acting); 1848–11 Oct. 1850 Auguste Baudin; 11 Oct. 1850–Apr. 1853 Auguste Prôtet; Apr. 1853–31 Jan. 1854 M. Verand (acting); 31 Jan. 1854–16 Dec. 1854 Auguste Prôtet; 16 Dec. 1854–4 Sept. 1858 Louis Faidherbe; 4 Sept. 1858–12 Feb. 1859 A. Robin (acting); 12 Feb. 1859–1 June 1861 Louis Faidherbe; 1 June 1861–1 Dec. 1861 Léopold Stéphan (acting); 1 Dec. 1861–13 May 1863 Jean-Bernard Jauréguiberry; 13 May 1863–14 July 1863 Jean Pinet-Laprade (acting); 14 July 1863–1 May 1865 Louis Faidherbe; 1 May 1865–12 Dec. 1865 Jean Pinet-Laprade (acting); 12 Dec. 1865–18 Aug. 1869 Jean Pinet-Laprade; 18 Aug. 1869–17 Oct. 1869 Ferdinand Tredos (acting); 17 Oct. 1869–18 June 1876 François Victorien Valière; 18 June 1876–Apr. 1880 Col. Louis Brière de l'Isle; Apr. 1880–4 Aug. 1881 Louis de Lanneau; 4 Aug. 1881–Oct. 1881 Marie Auguste Deville de Perrière (acting); Oct. 1881–28 June 1882 Henri Canard; 28 June 1882–15 Nov. 1882 Aristide Marie Vallon; 15 Nov. 1882–28 June 1883 René Servatius; 28 June 1883–25 July 1883 Adolphe Le Boucher (acting); 25 July 1883–15 Apr. 1884 Henry Bourdiaux (acting); 15 Apr. 1884–14 Apr. 1886 Alphonse Seignac-Lesseps; 14 Apr. 1886–29 Apr. 1888 Jules Genouille; 29 Apr. 1888–22 Sept. 1890 Léon Clément-Thomas; 22 Sept. 1890–19 May 1895 Henri de la Mothe; 19 May 1895–28 June 1895 Louis Mouttet (acting); 28 June 1895–28 Sept. 1895 Jean-Baptiste Barthélemy Chaudié. *Governors-General of French West Africa:* 28 Sept. 1895–1 Nov. 1900 Jean-Baptiste Barthélemy Chaudié; 1 Nov. 1900–26 Jan. 1902 Noël Ballay; 26 Jan. 1902–15 March 1902 Pierre Capest (acting); 15 March 1902–11 Nov. 1902 Ernest Roume (acting). *Lieutenant-Governors:* 11 Nov. 1902–13 Feb. 1904 Lucien Guy.

901 Senegal Colony and Protectorate. 13 Feb. 1904–13 Oct. 1946. *Location:* Senegal. *Capital:* Dakar. *Other names:* Senegal.

History: In 1904 **Senegal Colony** became Senegal Colony and Protectorate because it had taken under French protection so much of the hinterland. In 1946 it became an overseas territory of the Fourth Republic of France (see **Senegal Overseas Territory**).

Lieutenant-Governors: 13 Feb. 1904–

26 Aug. 1907 Lucien Guy; 26 Aug. 1907–15 Dec. 1907 Joost Van Vollenhouven (acting). *Governors-General of French West Africa:* 15 Dec. 1907–10 June 1908 Martial Merlin (acting). *Lieutenant-Governors:* 17 Dec. 1908–23 Feb. 1909 Maurice Gourbeil; 23 Feb. 1909–2 May 1909 Antoine Gaudard (acting); 2 May 1909–7 July 1909 Jean Peuvergne; 7 July 1909–13 Nov. 1909 Antoine Gaudard (acting); 13 Nov. 1909–5 Feb. 1911 Jean Peuvergne; 5 Feb. 1911–13 May 1914 Henri Core; 13 May 1914–Dec. 1916 Raphaël Antonetti; 20 March 1917–23 Sept. 1920 Fernand Lévecque; 23 Sept. 1920–17 Sept. 1921 Théophile Pascal (acting); 17 Sept. 1921–24 July 1925 Pierre Didelot; 24 July 1925–23 May 1926 Théodore Maillet (acting); 23 May 1926–23 Oct. 1926 Joseph Cadier (acting); 23 Oct. 1926–12 March 1929 Léonce Jore; 12 March 1929–4 July 1930 Maurice Beurnier; 4 July 1930–15 Aug. 1931 Théodore Maillet; 15 Aug. 1931–14 Oct. 1931 Benoît Louis Rebonne (acting); 14 Oct. 1931–22 May 1933 Maurice Beurnier; 22 May 1933–24 Dec. 1933 Léon Solomiac (acting); 24 Dec. 1933–Dec. 1936 Maurice Beurnier. *Governors:* Dec. 1936–25 Oct. 1938 Louis Lefebvre; 25 Oct. 1938–30 Dec. 1940 Georges Parisot; 1 Jan. 1941–22 Dec. 1942 Georges Rey; 22 Dec. 1942–2 Dec. 1943 Hubert Deschamps; 2 Dec. 1943–June 1945 Charles Dagain; June 1945–Apr. 1946 Pierre Maestracci; Apr. 1946–13 Oct. 1946 Oswald Durand.

902 Senegal French Colony (Compagnie des Indes). 15 Dec. 1718–30 Apr. 1758. *Location:* Senegal. *Capital:* Saint Louis. *Other names:* Senegal, Sénégal (Compagnie des Indes Orientales).

History: In 1718 **Senegal French Colony (Royal Company of Senegal)** was taken over by the French East India Company. In 1758 the British took over all the French possessions in the Senegal area (see **Senegal [British] [ii]**).

Directors: 15 Dec. 1718–May 1720

André Bruë; May 1720–Apr. 1723 Nicolas Després de Saint-Robert; Apr. 1723–1725 Julien Dubellay; 1725–1726 Nicolas Després de Saint-Robert; 1726–1726 Arnaud Plumet; 1726–1733 Jean Levens de la Roquette; 1733–7 March 1733 M. Lejuge; 7 March 1733–1736 Sebastien Devaulx (acting); 1736–1738 Sebastien Devaulx; 1738–1746 Pierre David; 1746–30 Apr. 1758 Jean-Baptiste Estoupan de la Bruë.

903 Senegal French Colony (Royal Company of Senegal). March 1696–15 Dec. 1718. *Location:* Senegal. *Capital:* Saint Louis. *Other names:* Senegal.

History: In 1696 **Senegal French Settlements (Compagnie du Guinée) [ii]** was taken by the Royal Company of Senegal and became a colony. In 1718 the Compagnie des Indes took over (see **Senegal French Colony [Compagnie des Indes]**).

Directors: March 1696–4 Apr. 1697 Jean Bourguignon (acting); 4 Apr. 1697–1702 André Bruë; 1702–1706 Joseph LeMaître; 1706–1710 Michel Jajolet de la Courbe; 1710–1711 Guillaume de Mustellier; 1711–2 May 1713 Pierre de Richebourg; 2 May 1713–20 Apr. 1714 [unknown]; 20 Apr. 1714–15 Dec. 1718 André Bruë.

904 Senegal French Settlements (Colbert's West India Company). 28 May 1664–9 Apr. 1672. *Location:* Senegal. *Capital:* Saint Louis. *Other names:* Senegal.

History: In 1664 the Cape Verde and Senegal Company (see **Senegal French Settlements [Compagnie du Cap Vert et du Sénégal]**) changed hands, going to Colbert's Compagnie des Indes Occidentales. In 1672 the Compagnie d'Afrique took over management of Senegal (see **Senegal French Settlements [Compagnie d'Afrique]**).

Governors: 28 May 1664–1668 M. Jacquet; 1668–9 Apr. 1672 M. de Richemont.

905 Senegal French Settlements

(Compagnie d'Afrique). 1682–12 Sept. 1684. *Location:* Senegal. *Capital:* Saint Louis. *Other names:* Senegal.

History: In 1682 the Senegal Company (see **Senegal French Settlements [Compagnie du Sénégal]**) lost the area to the African Company. In 1684 it changed hands again, this time going to the Guinea Company of Senegal (see **Senegal French Settlements [Compagnie du Guinée] [i]**).

Directors: 1682–12 Sept. 1684 Denis Basset.

906 Senegal French Settlements (Compagnie du Cap Vert et du Sénégal). 1658–28 May 1664. *Location:* around the mouth of the Senegal River, Senegal. *Capital:* Saint Louis (from 1659). *Other names:* Senegal.

History: In 1658 the Senegal Settlements changed hands, from the Compagnie Normande (see **Senegal French Settlements [Compagnie Normande]**) to those of the Cape Verde and Senegal Company. In 1664 they changed hands once again (see **Senegal French Settlements [Colbert's West India Company]**).

Governors: 1658–1661 M. Raguenet; 1661–28 May 1664 M. de Boulay.

907 Senegal French Settlements (Compagnie du Guinée) [i]. 12 Sept. 1684–Jan. 1693. *Location:* Senegal. *Capital:* Saint Louis. *Other names:* Senegal.

History: In 1684 the Company of Guinea took over the mainland area of what is today the coast of Senegal. (See **Senegal French Settlements [Compagnie d'Afrique].**) In 1693 the British took Senegal (see **Senegal [British] [i]**).

Directors: 12 Sept. 1684–1689 Louis Moreau de Chambonneau; 1689–1690 Michel Jajolet de la Courbe; 1690–Jan. 1693 Louis Moreau de Chambonneau.

908 Senegal French Settlements (Compagnie du Guinée) [ii]. July 1693–March 1696. *Location:* as Senegal. *Capital:* Saint Louis. *Other names:* Senegal.

History: In the middle of 1693 the French re-took Senegal from the British (see **Senegal [British] [i]**). In 1696 the rule was transferred from the Compagnie du Guinée to the Royal Senegal Company (see **Senegal French Colony [Royal Company of Senegal]**).

Directors: July 1693–March 1696 Jean Bourguignon.

909 Senegal French Settlements (Compagnie du Sénégal). 9 Apr. 1672–1682. *Location:* as Senegal. *Capital:* Saint Louis. *Other names:* Senegal.

History: In 1672 the **Senegal French Settlements (Colbert's West India Company)** were taken over by the Senegal Company. In 1682 they transferred to the African Company (see **Senegal French Settlements [Compagnie d'Afrique]**). On November 1, 1677 Gorée was taken from the Dutch and attached to Senegal (see also **Gorée**).

Governors: 1672–1673 M. de Richemont (acting). *Directors:* 1674–1682 Jacques Fuméchon.

910 Senegal French Settlements (Compagnie Normande). 1626–1658. *Location:* around the mouth of the Senegal River, Senegal. *Capital:* no fixed central administrative capital. *Other names:* Senegal.

History: The first explorers to the area of the mouth of the Senegal River were the Portuguese, but the French established settlements here in 1626, under the command of the Normandy Company. These settlements were not permanent, neither were those under the successor company, the Cape Verde and Senegal Company (see **Senegal French Settlements [Compagnie du Cap Vert et du Sénégal]**).

Governors: 1626–1631 Thomas Lambert; 1631–1641 Jacques Fuméchon; 1641–1648 Jean Caullier; 1649–1650 M. de Soussy; 1651–1658 M. Mésineau.

911 Senegal French Territory. 30 Jan. 1779–13 July 1809. *Location:* Senegal coastline and islands. *Capital:* Saint Louis. *Other names:* Senegal.

History: In 1779 the French took back their Senegalese possessions (see **Senegambia Colony**) and later that year took the British settlements on the Gambia River (see **French Gambia**), bringing an end to the **Senegambia Colony** (actually that colony did not cease to exist until the Treaty of Paris in 1783). This made the French the possessors (from 1779– 1783) of the entire Senegambia coastline, and (from 1783–1809) of all the Senegal possessions. In 1809 they lost everything to the British again (see **Senegal [British] [iii]**).

Commandants: 30 Jan. 1779–31 Jan. 1779 Charles Boucher (acting); 31 Jan. 1779–March 1779 Duc de Lauzun; March 1779–7 March 1781 Jacques-Joseph Eyriès; 7 March 1781–July 1782 J.B. Bertrand (acting); July 1782–Feb. 1784 Anne-Guilin Dumontêt; Feb. 1784–Feb. 1786 Louis Le Gardeur de Repentigny; Feb. 1786–June 1786 Stanislas de Boufflers; June 1786–Feb. 1787 François Blanchot de Verly (acting); Feb. 1787–Dec. 1787 Stanislas de Boufflers; Dec. 1787–1790 François Blanchot de Verly; 1790–May 1792 Charles Boucher (acting); May 1792–Jan. 1801 François Blanchot de Verly; Jan. 1801–2 July 1801 M. Charbonnes (acting); 2 July 1801–27 Oct. 1802 Louis Lasserre; 27 Oct. 1802–Sept. 1807 François Blanchot de Verly; Sept. 1807–13 July 1809 Pierre Levasseur.

912 Senegal Overseas Territory. 13 Oct. 1946–25 Nov. 1958. *Location:* Senegal. *Capital:* Dakar. *Other names:* Senegal.

History: In 1946 **Senegal Colony and Protectorate** became an overseas territory of the Fourth Republic of France. In 1958 it gained autonomy within the French Community, as **Senegal Autonomous Republic.**

Governors: 13 Oct. 1946–20 May 1947 Oswald Durand; 20 May 1947–19 Oct. 1950 Laurent Wiltord; 19 Oct. 1950–25 Apr. 1952 Victor Bailly; 25 Apr. 1952–1954 Lucien Geay; 1954–19 Feb. 1954 Daniel Goujon; 19 Feb. 1954–31 Oct. 1955 Maxime Jourdain; 31 Oct. 1955–10 Feb. 1957 Don-Jean Colombani; 10 Feb. 1957–25 Nov. 1958 Pierre Lami.

913 Senegal Republic. 20 Aug. 1960– . *Location:* North West Africa. *Capital:* Dakar. *Other names:* Republic of Senegal, Senegalese Republic, République Sénégalaise, République du Sénégal.

History: In 1960 the **Mali Federation** broke up, and **Senegal Republic** and **Sudanese Republic** resulted. Senegal was formally proclaimed on Sept. 5, 1960. In 1982 Senegal and **The Gambia** joined politically to form **Senegambia.**

Presidents: 20 Aug. 1960–6 Sept. 1960 Léopold Senghor (interim); 6 Sept. 1960–31 Dec. 1980 Léopold Senghor; 1 Jan. 1981– Abdou Diouf. *Prime Ministers:* 20 Aug. 1960–17 Dec. 1962 Mamadou Dia; 28 Feb. 1970–31 Dec. 1980 Abdou Diouf; 1 Jan. 1981–3 Apr. 1983 Habib Thiam; 3 Apr. 1983–29 Apr. 1983 Moustapha Niasse (interim). *Note:* in times of no Prime Minister, the President held that office.

914 Senegal (Royal African Company). 10 Feb. 1763–25 May 1765. *Location:* the coast and parts of the mainland of Senegal. *Capital:* Saint Louis. *Other names:* Senegal.

History: In 1763 **Senegal (British) [i]** divested itself of **Gorée** and returned it to the French. The remaining coastal territory was governed by the Royal African Company; in 1765 this area and British posts on the Gambia River merged as the first British Crown Colony in Africa—**Senegambia Colony.**

Governors: 10 Feb. 1763–25 May 1765 John Barnes.

915 Senegambia. 1 Feb. 1982– . *Location:* **Senegal Republic** and the **Gambia Republic.** *Capital:* Dakar. *Other names:* La Conféderation de

Sénégambie, Senegambia Confederation, Confederation of Senegambia.
History: On Nov. 14 and Dec. 17, 1981 **Senegal Republic** and the **Gambia Republic** signed long-planned agreements which came into force on Feb. 1, 1982, forming them into a political confederation, adopting joint defense and monetary policies, but retaining individual sovereignty. Although the two countries speak a different language, the peoples are closely related.
Presidents: 1 Feb. 1982– Abdou Diouf. *Vice-Presidents:* 1 Feb. 1982– Sir Dawda Jawara.

916 Senegambia Colony. 25 May 1765–11 Feb. 1779. *Location:* Senegal (minus Gorée) and the British posts in Gambia. *Capital:* Saint Louis (Senegal); James Island (local Gambia headquarters). *Other names:* Province of Senegambia.
History: In 1765 **Senegal (Royal African Company)** was merged with the British posts (see **James Fort**) on the Gambia River, and all these areas were re-constituted as the Colony of Senegambia, the first British Crown Colony in Africa (Gambia passing to the Crown effectively in April 1766). In 1779 the French re-took their former Senegalese possessions and, with **Gorée, Senegal French Territory** was created. In 1779 the French took the British Gambia possessions too, and they were abandoned (see **French Gambia**). The Colony of Senegambia officially came to an end at the Treaty of Paris in 1783, by which Britain regained the **Gambia Settlements** and France secured **Senegal French Territory,** but in reality the Senegambia terminated in 1779.
Governors: 25 May 1765–Nov. 1775 Charles O'Hara; Nov. 1775–8 Apr. 1777 Matthias MacNamara; 8 Apr. 1777–18 Aug. 1778 John Clarke; 18 Aug. 1778–11 Feb. 1779 William Lacy (never assumed office); 18 Aug. 1778–11 Feb. 1779 George Fall (acting). *Gambia Superintendents of Trade:* 25 May 1765–1766 Joseph Debat. *Gambia*

Lieutenant-Governors: 1766–24 Jan. 1774 Joseph Debat; 24 Jan. 1774–Aug. 1774 William Myres; Aug. 1774–Nov. 1775 Matthias MacNamara; Nov. 1775–Dec. 1775 Thomas Sharpless (acting); Dec. 1775–8 Aug. 1776 Joseph Wall; 8 Aug. 1776–1776 George Fall (acting); 1776–18 Aug. 1778 William Lacy (acting); 18 Aug. 1778–11 Feb. 1779 George Fall (acting) (also acting Governor of the Colony).

917 Senegambia and Niger Territories. 1 Oct. 1902–18 Oct. 1904. *Location:* as **Mali Republic.** *Capital:* Kayès. *Other names:* Senegambia-Niger, Sénégambie-Niger. *History:* In 1902 **Upper Senegal and Niger Territory** became Senegambia and Niger Territories, still subject to Senegal. In 1904 it became **Upper Senegal and Niger Colony.**
Delegates: 1 Oct. 1902–18 Oct. 1904 Amédée Merlaud-Ponty.

Sennaar, Sennar see **Funj Sultanate**

918 Seychelles. See these **names:**
Seychelles Republic (1976–   )
Seychelles (Self-Rule) (1975–1976)
Seychelles Crown Colony (1903–1975)
Seychelles Dependent Colony (1814–1903)
Seychelles Colony (1810–1814)
British-Occupied Séchelles (1794–1810)
Séchelles French Colony (1770–1794)
Séchelles (1756–1770)
Île de Labourdonnais (1744–1756)

919 Seychelles Colony. 1810–30 May 1814. *Location:* as **Seychelles Republic.** *Capital:* Mahé. *Other names:* Séchelles.
History: In 1810 Britain formally annexed **British Occupied Séchelles.** In 1814 it was ceded to Britain formally as **Seychelles Dependent Colony.**
Civil Agents/Commissioners: 1810–1811 Jean-Baptiste Quéau de Quincy

(acting); 1811–1812 Bartholomew Sullivan; 1812–30 May 1814 Bibye Lasage.

920 Seychelles Crown Colony. Aug. 1903–1 Oct. 1975. *Location:* as **Seychelles Republic.** *Capital:* Victoria. *Other names:* The Seychelles.
History: In 1903 **Seychelles Dependent Colony,** i.e. dependent on **Mauritius,** became a separate British Crown Colony. In 1908 Coetivy was transferred from Mauritius; in 1922 the Farquhar Islands were, too. In 1965 the Governor of the Seychelles became also the High Commissioner for the British Indian Ocean Territory (a group of islands further east in the Indian Ocean, to which Seychelles lost some islands). In 1967 and 1970 self-rule measures were given to the Seychelles, and in 1975 it became self-governing (see **Seychelles [Self-Rule]**).
Governors: Aug. 1903–1904 Sir Ernest Sweet-Escott; 1904–1912 Sir Walter Davidson; 1912–1918 Sir Charles O'Brien; 1918–1921 Sir Eustace Twistleton-Wykeham-Fiennes; 1921–1927 Sir Joseph Byrne; 1927–1928 Sir Malcolm Stevenson; 1928–1934 Montagu Honey (knighted 1932); 1934–1936 Sir Gordon Lethem; 1936–5 Jan. 1942 Sir Arthur Grimble; 5 Jan. 1942–July 1947 Sir William Logan; July 1947–14 May 1951 Sir Percy Selwyn-Clarke; 14 May 1951–18 Oct. 1953 Frederick Crawford; 18 Oct. 1953–1958 Sir William Addis; 1958–7 Nov. 1961 Sir John Thorp; 7 Nov. 1961–1967 Earl of Oxford and Asquith; 1967–1969 Sir Hugh Norman-Walker; 1969–1973 Sir Bruce Greatbatch; 1973–1 Oct. 1975 Sir Colin Allen. *Chief Ministers:* 1970–1 Oct. 1975 James Mancham.

921 Seychelles Dependent Colony. 30 May 1814–Aug. 1903. *Location:* as **Seychelles Republic.** *Capital:* Victoria. *Other names:* Seychelles, The Seychelles, Seychelles Territory. *History:* In 1814 the **Seychelles Colony** (new English spelling—see **Séchelles**) was formally ceded to Britain under the jurisdiction of Mauritius (see **British-Occupied Mauritius**). In 1903 it became a separate British Crown Colony (see **Seychelles Crown Colony**).
Civil Agents/Commissioners: 30 May 1814–1815 Bibye Lasage; 1815–1822 Edward Madge. *Civil Agents:* 1822–1837 George Harrison; 1837–1839 Arthur Wilson. *Civil Commissioners:* 1839–1850 Charles Mylius; 1850–1852 Robert Keate; 1852–1862 George Wade; 1862–1868 Swinburne Ward. *Chief Civil Commissioners:* 1868–1874 William Franklyn; 1874–1879 Charles Salmon; 1879–1880 Arthur Havelock; 1880–1882 Francis Blunt; 1882–1888 Arthur Barkly. *Administrators:* 1888–1895 Thomas Griffith; 1895–1899 Henry Stewart; 1899–Aug. 1903 Ernest Sweet-Escott.

922 Seychelles Republic. 29 June 1976– . *Location:* 115 islands, northeast of Madagascar in the Indian Ocean. *Capital:* Victoria (on Mahé Island). *Other names:* The Seychelles, Seychelles, Republic of the Seychelles, Republic of Seychelles.
History: In 1976 **Seychelles (Self-Rule)** became independent within the Commonwealth.
Presidents: 29 June 1976–5 June 1977 James Mancham; 5 June 1977– France-Albert René. *Prime Ministers:* 29 June 1976–5 June 1977 France-Albert René. *Note:* in times of no Prime Minister, the President held that office.

923 Seychelles (Self-Rule). 1 Oct. 1975–29 June 1976. *Location:* as **Seychelles Republic.** *Capital:* Victoria. *Other names:* Seychelles.
History: In 1975 **Seychelles Crown Colony** achieved absolute self-rule. In 1976 it won independence from Britain, as **Seychelles Republic.**
High Commissioners: 1 Oct. 1975–29 June 1976 Sir Colin Allen. *Prime Ministers:* 1 Oct. 1975–29 June 1976 James Mancham.

Shaba see **Katanga Republic**

Shangana see **Gazaland**

924 Shenge. 1810–1888. *Location:* off the Sierra Leone coast. *Capital:* Shenge. *Other names:* Plantation Island.

History: Founded in 1810 by the Caulkers, Shenge lasted as a political unit until 1888 when it became part of **Sierra Leone Territory [iii].**

Kings: 1810–1831 George Stephen Caulker I; 1831–1842 Thomas Stephen Caulker; 1842–1849 vacant; 1849–15 Aug. 1871 Thomas Stephen Caulker; 15 Aug. 1871–1881 George Stephen Caulker II. *Regents:* 1881–1888 Thomas Neale Caulker.

Shewa see **Shoa**

925 Shiré River Protectorate. 21 Sept. 1889–14 May 1891. *Location:* Malawi. *Capital:* Zomba. *Other names:* Shiré Heights Protectorate.

History: In 1889 a protectorate was proclaimed by Britain over the Shiré River, then the local area most populated with British. In 1891 it expanded to become **Nyasaland.**

Commissioners: 21 Sept. 1889–14 May 1891 Harry Johnston.

926 Shoa [i]. ca. 1470–1856. *Location:* central Ethiopia. *Capital:* Ankober (from 1813); Qundi (1808–13); Doqait (1745–1808); [unknown] (ca. 1470–1745). *Other names:* Shewa.

History: Shoa became the center of **Ethiopian Empire [ii]** in 1856 when its king became emperor (see also **Shoa [ii]**).

Neguses (or Kings): ca. 1470–1510 Malak Sagad; 1510–(?) vacant; (?)–1580 Negasse I; 1580–1625 Gabriel; 1625–1703 Negasse II; 1703–1718 Asfa Wossen; 1718–1745 Abbiye; 1745–1775 Ammehayes; 1775–1808 Asfa Wossen II; 1808–1813 Ras Wossen Seged; 1813–1847 Ras Sahle Selassie; 1847–1855 Hayla Melekot; 1855–1856 Lij Kasa

(or Tewodoros II, or Theodore II).

927 Shoa [ii]. 1886–3 Nov. 1889. *Location:* Ethiopia. *Capital:* Addis Ababa (from 1887); Ankober (1886–87). *Other names:* Shewa.

History: In 1886 Menelik II regained his kingdom (see **Shoa [i]**), and in 1889 he became emperor of **Ethiopian Empire [ii].**

Kings: 1886–3 Nov. 1889 Menelik II (or Sahle Mariam).

Siante see **Ashanti**

928 Sierra Leone. See these **names:**
Sierra Leone Republic (1971–   )
Sierra Leone Dominion (1961–1971)
Sierra Leone Colony and Protectorate (1895–1961)
Sierra Leone Colony [ii] (1888–1895)
Sierra Leone Territory [iii] (1874–1888)
Sierra Leone Territory [ii] (1866–1874)
Sierra Leone Crown Colony [ii] (1850–1866)
Sierra Leone Territory [i] (1821–1850)
Sierra Leone Crown Colony [i] (1808–1821)
Sierra Leone Colony [i] (1799–1808)
Sierra Leone (1791–1799)
Freedom Province (1787–1789)
Aku (ca. 1826–1880)
Banana Island (ca. 1770–1820)
Bumpe (1820–1888)
Koya-Temne (ca. 1505–1896)
Shenge (1810–1888)

929 Sierra Leone. Jan. 1791–5 July 1799. *Location:* as Freetown, Sierra Leone. *Capital:* Freetown (from 1792); Granville Town (1791–92). *Other names:* Freetown (from 1792).

History: In 1791 the Sierra Leone Company was formed, with the same ideals as that of Granville Sharp, who had sponsored **Freedom Province.** The new company formed a new settlement on the ashes of Freedom Province, with the remaining settlers from that prov-

ince. In 1792 it was boosted by the arrival of Nova Scotian blacks from Canada. Also in 1792 Freetown was built. In 1799 the country became **Sierra Leone Colony [i].**
Agents: Jan. 1791–June 1791 Mr. Falconbridge; June 1791–March 1792 [unknown]. *Superintendents:* March 1792–July 1792 John Clarkson. *Governors:* July 1792–31 Dec. 1792 John Clarkson; 31 Dec. 1792–March 1794 William Dawes; March 1794–6 May 1795 Zachary Macaulay; 6 May 1795–March 1796 William Dawes; March 1796–Apr. 1799 Zachary Macaulay; Apr. 1799–May 1799 John Gray; May 1799–5 July 1799 Thomas Ludlum.

930 Sierra Leone Colony [i]. 5 July 1799–1 Jan. 1808. *Location:* the coast of Sierra Leone. *Capital:* Freetown. *Other names:* Sierra Leone.
History: In 1799 **Sierra Leone** became a colony, still governed by the Sierra Leone Company. In 1808 the area became a Crown Colony (see **Sierra Leone Crown Colony [i]**).
Governors: 5 July 1799–1800 Thomas Ludlum; 1800–Jan. 1801 John Gray; Jan. 1801–Feb. 1803 William Dawes; Feb. 1803–1803 William Day; 1803–1805 Thomas Ludlum; 1805–4 Nov. 1805 William Day; 1806–1 Jan. 1808 Thomas Ludlum.

931 Sierra Leone Colony [ii]. 28 Nov. 1888–24 Aug. 1895. *Location:* the coastal section of Sierra Leone. *Capital:* Freetown. *Other names:* Sierra Leone.
History: In 1888 **Sierra Leone Territory [iii]** became a colony after breaking away from the **West Africa Settlements.** In 1895, with the establishment of the protectorate in the hinterland, the **Sierra Leone Colony and Protectorate** was set up.
Governors: 28 Nov. 1888–1889 James Hay (knighted 1889); 1889–1889 Lt.-Col. Patchett and Maj. Foster (acting); 1889–1890 J.M. Maltby (acting); 1890–1891 Sir James Hay; 1891–1892 J.J. Crooks (acting); 1892–1892 W.H.Q. Jones (acting); 1892–1893 Sir Francis Fleming; 1893–1893 W.H.Q. Jones (acting); 1893–1894 Sir Francis Fleming; 1894–1894 W.H.Q. Jones (acting); 1894–1895 Frederic Cardew; 1895–24 Aug. 1895 Lt.-Col. Caulfield (acting).

932 Sierra Leone Colony and Protectorate. 24 Aug. 1895–27 Apr. 1961. *Location:* as **Sierra Leone Dominion.** *Capital:* Freetown. *Other names:* Sierra Leone.
History: In 1895 the colony of Sierra Leone (see **Sierra Leone Colony [ii]**) was amalgamated with a protectorate established over the hinterland of the country. In 1961 the whole country became independent, as **Sierra Leone Dominion.**
Governors: 24 Aug. 1895–1897 Frederic Cardew (knighted 1897); 1897–1897 J.C. Gore (acting); 1897–1897 Lt.-Col. Caulfield (acting); 1897–1899 Sir Frederic Cardew; 1899–1899 Mathew Nathan (acting); 1899–1900 Sir Frederic Cardew; 1900–11 Dec. 1900 Lt.-Col. Caulfield (acting); 11 Dec. 1900–3 Oct. 1904 Sir Charles King-Harman; 3 Oct. 1904–1910 Leslie Probyn (knighted 1909); 1910–1913 Sir Edward Merewether; 1913–1913 Claud Hollis (acting); 1913–1915 Sir Edward Merewether; 1915–9 March 1916 [unknown]; 9 March 1916–1921 Richard Wilkinson; 1921–1921 James Maxwell (acting); 1921–4 May 1922 Richard Wilkinson; 4 May 1922–24 Sept. 1927 Ransford Slater (knighted 1924); 24 Sept. 1927–1929 Sir Joseph Byrne; 1929–1930 Mark Young (acting); 1930–23 May 1931 Sir Joseph Byrne; 23 May 1931–17 July 1934 Arnold Hodson (knighted 1932); 17 July 1934–21 May 1937 Henry Moore (knighted 1935); 21 May 1937–5 July 1941 Douglas Jardine (knighted 1938); 5 July 1941–4 Sept. 1947 Sir Hubert Stevenson; 4 Sept. 1947–Dec. 1952 Sir George Beresford-Stooke; Dec. 1952–1 Sept. 1956 Sir Robert Hall; 1 Sept. 1956–27 Apr. 1961 Maurice Dorman (knighted 1957). *Chief Ministers:* 1954–

1958 Milton Margai. *Prime Ministers:* 1958–27 Apr. 1961 Milton Margai.

933 Sierra Leone Crown Colony [i]. 1 Jan. 1808–17 Oct. 1821. *Location:* the coast of Sierra Leone. *Capital:* Freetown. *Other names:* Sierra Leone.
History: In 1808 **Sierra Leone Colony [i]** became a Crown Colony. In 1821 it became part of the **West African Territories**, as **Sierra Leone Territory [i].**
Govenors: 1 Jan. 1808–21 July 1808 Thomas Ludlum (acting); 21 July 1808–12 Feb. 1810 Thomas Thompson; 12 Feb. 1810–May 1811 Edward Columbine; May 1811–1 July 1811 Robert Bones (acting); 1 July 1811–July 1814 Charles Maxwell; July 1814–Dec. 1814 Charles Macarthy (acting); Dec. 1814–Jan. 1815 J. Mailing (acting); Jan. 1815–March 1815 R. Purdie (acting); March 1815–June 1815 William Appleton (acting); June 1815–July 1815 Capt. H.B. Hyde (acting); July 1815–1 Jan. 1816 Charles Macarthy (acting); 1 Jan. 1816–July 1820 Charles Macarthy (knighted 1820); July 1820–1821 Alexander Grant (acting); 1821–1821 Lt.-Col. Burke (acting); 1821–17 Oct. 1821 Alexander Grant (acting).

934 Sierra Leone Crown Colony [ii]. 13 Jan. 1850–19 Feb. 1866. *Location:* as **Sierra Leone Territory (ii)**. *Capital:* Freetown. *Other names:* Sierra Leone.
History: In 1850 the **West African Territories** came to an end, and **Sierra Leone Territory [i]** became a Crown Colony for the second time. In 1866 it became a territory again (see **Sierra Leone Territory [ii]**), as part of the **West African Settlements**.
Governors: 13 Jan. 1850–1852 Norman MacDonald; 1852–1854 Arthur Kennedy; 1854–1854 Robert Dougan (acting); 1854–1855 Stephen Hill; 1855–1855 Robert Dougan; 1855–1859 Stephen Hill; 1859–1860 Alexander Fitzjames (acting); 1860–1861 Stephen Hill; 1861–1862 William Hill and Lt.-Col. Smith (acting); 1862–1865 Samuel Blackall; 1865–19 Feb. 1866 Col. Chamberlayne (acting).

935 Sierra Leone Dominion. 27 Apr. 1961–19 Apr. 1971. *Location:* North West Africa. *Capital:* Freetown. *Other names:* Dominion of Sierra Leone, Sierra Leone.
History: In 1961 **Sierra Leone Colony and Protectorate** became an independent member of the British Commonwealth. In 1971 it became **Sierra Leone Republic**, still in the Commonwealth.
Prime Ministers: 27 Apr. 1961–28 Apr. 1964 Sir Milton Margai; 29 Apr. 1964–17 March 1967 Albert Margai (knighted 1965); 17 March 1967–21 March 1967 Siaka P. Stevens (never served); 21 March 1967–23 March 1967 David Lansana; 23 March 1967–27 March 1967 Ambrose Genda (Chairman of National Reformation Council—never served); 20 Apr. 1968–26 Apr. 1968 Anti-Corruption Revolutionary Movement in power, led by Patrick Conteh; 26 Apr. 1968–Sept. 1970 Siaka P. Stevens; Sept. 1970–Sept. 1970 Sheku Bochari Kawusu Conteh (acting); Sept. 1970–19 Apr. 1971 Siaka P. Stevens. *Governors-General:* 27 Apr. 1961–7 July 1962 Sir Maurice Dorman; 7 July 1962–1962 Sir Henry Lightfoot-Boston (acting); 1962–21 March 1967 Sir Henry Lightfoot-Boston; 27 March 1967–19 Apr. 1968 Andrew Juxon-Smith (also Chairman of National Reformation Council); 22 Apr. 1968–31 March 1971 Banja Tejan-Sie (acting); 31 March 1971–19 Apr. 1971 Christopher Okoro Cole (acting). *Note:* in times of no Prime Minister, the Governor-General held that office.

936 Sierra Leone Republic. 19 Apr. 1971– . *Location:* North West Africa. *Capital:* Freetown. *Other names:* Republic of Sierra Leone.
History: In 1971 **Sierra Leone Dominion** was proclaimed a republic.
Presidents: 19 Apr. 1971–21 Apr. 1971 Christopher Okoro Cole (acting); 21

Apr. 1971–28 Nov. 1985 Siaka P. Stevens; 28 Nov. 1985– Joseph Saidu Momoh. *Prime Ministers:* 19 Apr. 1971–21 Apr. 1971 Siaka P. Stevens; 21 Apr. 1971–8 July 1975 Sorie Koroma; 8 July 1975–14 June 1978 Christian Kamara-Taylor. *Note:* in times of no Prime Minister, the President held that office.

937 Sierra Leone Territory [i]. 17 Oct. 1821–13 Jan. 1850. *Location:* as **Sierra Leone Crown Colony [i].** *Capital:* Freetown. *Other names:* Sierra Leone.

History: In 1821 on the formation of the **West African Territories, Sierra Leone Crown Colony [i]** became the dominant territory of that bund — as a territory. In 1850, on the dissolution of the Territories, Sierra Leone became **Sierra Leone Crown Colony [ii].**

Governors: 17 Oct. 1821–Nov. 1821 Alexander Grant (acting); Nov. 1821– 21 Jan. 1824 Sir Charles Macarthy; 21 Jan. 1824–5 Feb. 1825 Daniel Hamilton (acting); 5 Feb. 1825–7 March 1826 Sir Charles Turner; 8 March 1826–1826 Kenneth Macaulay (acting); 1826–Aug. 1826 Samuel Smart (acting); Aug. 1826– Dec. 1827 Sir Neil Campbell. *Lieutenant-Governors:* Dec. 1827–May 1828 Hugh Lumley; May 1828–9 June 1828 Dixon Denham; 9 June 1828–1828 Hugh Lumley; 1828–Nov. 1828 Samuel Smart (acting); Nov. 1828–1829 Henry Ricketts (acting); 1829–1830 Augustine Evans (acting); 1830–1830 Alexander Fraser (acting); 1830–July 1833 Alexander Findlay; July 1833–Dec. 1833 Michael Melville (acting); Dec. 1833–1834 Octavius Temple; 1834–Feb. 1835 Thomas Cole (acting); Feb. 1835–1837 Henry Campbell; 1837–1837 Thomas Cole (acting). *Governors:* 1837–1840 Richard Doherty; 1840–Apr. 1841 John Jeremie; Apr. 1841–Sept. 1841 J. Carr (acting); Sept. 1841–Jan. 1842 William Fergusson (acting); Jan. 1842–July 1844 George MacDonald; July 1844–1845 William Fergusson; 1845–13 Jan. 1850 Norman MacDonald.

938 Sierra Leone Territory [ii]. 19 Feb. 1866–17 Dec. 1874. *Location:* as **Sierra Leone Colony.** *Capital:* Freetown. *Other names:* Sierra Leone.

History: In 1866 **Sierra Leone Crown Colony** became part of the **West African Settlements.** In 1874 it became **Sierra Leone Territory [iii]** (see for further details).

Rulers: as the Governors of Sierra Leone were also the Governors-General of the **West African Settlements,** see that entry for list of Governors.

939 Sierra Leone Territory [iii]. 17 Dec. 1874–28 Nov. 1888. *Location:* as **Sierra Leone Colony.** *Capital:* Freetown. *Other names:* Sierra Leone.

History: In 1874, with the change of structure of the **West African Settlements,** i.e. its change of name to **West Africa Settlements** and all that that implied (see that entry for details), **Sierra Leone Territory [ii]** became Sierra Leone Territory [iii]; in short, it maintained its status as one of the settlements, but under a subtly new umbrella-name. In 1888, on the dissolution of the **West Africa Settlements,** Sierra Leone became a separate colony (see **Sierra Leone Colony [ii]**).

Rulers: as the Governors of Sierra Leone were also the Governors-General of the **West Africa Settlements,** see that entry for list of Governors.

Sikasso see **Kenedugu**

Sikonyela's Land see **Sekonyela's Land**

Sinoe see **Mississippi-in-Africa**

940 Sofala and Mozambique Captaincy. 8 Sept. 1507–1569. *Location:* the coast of Mozambique. *Capital:* Mozambique (1554–69); Sofala (1512–54); Kilwa (1507–1512. Kilwa is located in what is today Kenya). *Other names:* Portuguese East Africa, Mozambique, Sofala, Moçambique.

History: In 1507, with the opening up

of the coast of Mozambique, **Sofala Captaincy** became the Captaincy of Sofala and Mozambique. Posts began to be built up the Zambesi River, such as Tete and Sena. In 1569 **Mozambique Captaincy-General** came into existence.
Capitães-Mores: 8 Sept. 1507–Feb. 1508 Vasco de Abreu; Feb. 1508–1509 Rui Patalim (acting); 1509–24 June 1512 António de Saldanha; 24 June 1512–June 1515 Simão de Azevedo; June 1515–July 1515 Sancho de Tovar (acting); July 1515–June 1518 Cristóvão de Távora; June 1518–July 1521 Sancho de Tovar; July 1521–1525 Diogo de Sepúlveda; 1525–1528 Lopo de Almeida; 1528–1531 António de Meneses; 1531–1538 Vicente Pegado; 1538–1541 Aleixo Chicorro; 1541–1548 João de Sepúlveda; 1548–1551 Fernão de Távora; 1551–1553 Diogo de Mesquita; 1553–1557 Diogo de Sousa; 1557–1560 Sebastião de Sá; 1560–1564 Pantaleão de Sá; 1564–1567 Jerónimo Barreto; 1567–1569 Pedro Rolim. *Note:* Capitães-Mores is the plural of Capitão-Mor (Captain-Major).

941 Sofala Captaincy. 1501–8 Sept. 1507. *Location:* Sofala, Mozambique. *Capital:* Kilwa (Kenya): Sofala (local headquarters). *Other names:* Sofala, Portuguese East Africa.
History: On March 2, 1498 Vasco da Gama landed on the coast of what is today Mozambique. In 1501 a Portuguese administration was commenced at Sofala, and a fort built in 1505. In 1507, with the opening up of the coast, **Sofala and Mozambique Captaincy** came into being, still subject to Goa in India.
Capitães-Mores: 1501–4 May 1505 Sancho de Tovar; 4 May 1505–March 1506 Pedro de Nhuya; March 1506–Dec. 1506 Manuel Fernandes; Dec. 1506–8 Sept. 1507 Nunho Vaz Pereira. *Note:* Capitães-Mores is the plural of Capitão-Mor (Captain-Major).

Sokoto Caliphate see **Fulani Empire**

942 Somalia. See these **names:**
Somalia Democratic Republic (1969–)
Somalia (1960–1969)
Somalia State (1960–1960)
Somaliland Italian Trusteeship (1949–1960)
Somaliland (1941–1949)
Southern Somaliland Crown Colony (1910–1941)
Italian Somaliland Colony (1905–1910)
Benadir Coast Protectorate (Milanese Commercial Society) (1898–1905)
Benadir Coast Protectorate (Royal Commission) (1896–1898)
Benadir Coast Protectorate (Filonardi Company) (1893–1896)
Benadir Coast Protectorate (1889–1893)
Jubaland Colony (1924–1926)
British Somaliland Protectorate (1887–1960)
British Somaliland (1884–1887)
Egyptian Somaliland (1877–1884)
Adal [ii] (1415–1526)
Adal [i] (ca. 900–1285)
Mogadishu Republic (ca. 1238–ca. 1400)
Punt (ca. 3500 B.C.–[?] B.C.)

943 Somalia. 1 July 1960–21 Oct. 1969. *Location:* as **Somalia Democratic Republic.** *Capital:* Mogadishu. *Other names:* Somali Republic.
History: In 1960 **British Somaliland** was granted independence (see **Somalia State**) and five days later **Somaliland Italian Trusteeship** was united with it to form Somalia. In 1969 Somalia became the **Somalia Democratic Republic.**
Presidents: 1 July 1960–10 June 1967 Aden Abdullah Osman Daar; 10 June 1967–15 Oct. 1969 Abdi Rashid Shermarke; 15 Oct. 1969–21 Oct. 1969 office vacant. *Prime Ministers:* 1 July 1960–12 July 1960 Muhammad Ibrahim Egal; 12 July 1960–14 June 1964 Abdi Rashid Shermarke; 14 June 1964–27 Sept. 1964 Abdi Rizak Hajji Hussein (acting); 27 Sept. 1964–10 June 1967 Abdi Rizak Hajji Hussein; 10 June 1967–21 Oct.

1969 Muhammad Ibrahim Egal.

944 Somalia Democratic Republic.
21 Oct. 1969– . *Location:* northeast
Africa. *Capital:* Mogadishu (or Maqdishu, Mogadisho, Mogadiscio)
(founded about 950 by Arabs). *Other
names:* Somalia, Jamhuuriyada Demu-
qraadiga Soomaaliyeed.
History: In 1969 **Somalia** became a
democratic republic after a coup.
Somalis dream of a "Greater Somalia,"
taking in not only Somalia but the
Ogaden region of Ethiopia, the southern part of Djibouti, and the eastern
strip of Kenya; in short all the Somali-
populated areas.
*Presidents of the Supreme Revolu-
tionary Council:* 21 Oct. 1969–1 July
1976 Muhammad Siyad Barre. *Secretaries-General:* 1 July 1976– Muhammad Siyad Barre. *Prime Ministers:* 30
Jan. 1987– Muhammad Ali Saman-
tar.

945 Somalia State. 26 June 1960–1
July 1960. *Location:* as **British Somali-
land Protectorate.** *Capital:* Hargeysa
(Hargeisa). *Other names:* Somalia, The
State of Somalia.
History: On June 26, 1960 **British
Somaliland Protectorate** became in-
dependent as The State of Somalia.
Five days later **Somaliland Italian
Trusteeship** became independent, at its
very moment of independence joining
with the week-old Somalia State to
form **Somalia** on July 1.
Prime Ministers: 26 June 1960–1 July
1960 Muhammad Ibrahim Egal.

946 Somaliland. 26 Feb. 1941–21
Nov. 1949. *Location:* as **Italian Somali-
land Colony.** *Capital:* Mogadiscio
(Mogadishu). *Other names:* British-
Occupied Italian Somaliland.
History: In 1941 the British took
Southern Somaliland Crown Colony
and placed a governor in charge of this
Italian colony. This marked the end of
real Italian rule in East Africa (see
Italian East Africa). In 1949 the British

gave it back to Italy on a trusteeship
basis (see **Somaliland Italian Trusteeship**). Because the land was so bleak of
prospect this was looked on as a pun-
ishment.
Governors: 26 Feb. 1941–9 March
1941 Carlo de Simone. *British Military
Administration Governors:* 26 Feb.
1941–1941 Reginald H. Smith; 1941–
1943 William E.H. Scupham; 1943–
1948 Dennis Wickham; 1948–1948 Eric
de Candole; 1948–21 Nov. 1949 Geoffrey Gamble.

947 Somaliland Italian Trusteeship.
21 Nov. 1949–1 July 1960. *Location:* as
Italian Somaliland Colony. *Capital:*
Mogadiscio (Mogadishu). *Other
names:* Italian Somaliland, Somaliland
Italian U.N. Trusteeship.
History: In 1949 **Somaliland** became
an Italian U.N. Trusteeship (effective
from April 1, 1950), or trust territory.
Thus Italy regained control of its
former colony, but only because no one
else wanted it. In 1960 it became independent and joined **Somalia State** to
form **Somalia.**
Administrators: 21 Nov. 1949–1953
Giovanni Fornari; 1953–1955 Enrico
Martino; 1955–1958 Enrico Anzilotti;
1958–1 July 1960 Mario di Stefani.
Prime Ministers: 1956–1 July 1960 Abdullahi Issa Muhammad.

948 Songhai Empire. 1464–1640.
Location: most of the western Sahara,
mainly **Mali.** *Capital:* Dendi (from
1591); Gao (until 1591). *Other names:*
Songhay Empire.
History: The Songhai people came
from the middle Niger region, and
about 500 A.D. established the **Songhai Kingdom,** with a line of kings
called "dias." At the turn of the 7th century they came to **Gao,** their capital remaining as Kukya. In 1010 the 15th dia,
Kossoi, was converted to Islam, and
moved his capital to Gao. The town of
Gao, then the state of Gao, went to
form the nucleus of what became the
Songhai Empire. In 1325 Gao became

part of the **Mali Empire**. In 1335 the last of the dias died, and a new era of "sunnis" or "shihs" began. In 1375 the second sunni, Suleiman-Mar, won back independence from the Mali Empire, and in 1464 Sunni Ali became king of Gao and Songhai lands, entering into a phase of expansion which began the Songhai Empire. The empire reached its height under the first of the ten Askia kings, Askia the Great. In 1582 Morocco invaded with firearms, and in 1591 the key cities of **Gao** and **Timbuktu** were taken. The Songhai Empire was virtually finished, and the emperor fled to Dendi, where he and his successors continued to rule in exile. Only guerrilla raids by groups of Songhais kept the name of the Empire alive. The Moroccans left in 1618, but by about 1640 the former empire was reduced to a group of small, weak states in the southeastern section of the former empire.

Emperors: 1464–6 Nov. 1492 Sunni Ali (or Sonni Ali); 6 Nov. 1492–1493 Baru; 3 March 1493–26 Aug. 1528 Askia the Great (formerly Muhammad Touray); 26 Aug. 1528–12 Apr. 1531 Musa; 12 Apr. 1531–22 Apr. 1537 Muhammad Bunkan; 22 Apr. 1537–2 March 1538 Askia the Great; 2 March 1538–1539 Ismail; 1539–25 March 1549 Ishaq I; 25 March 1549–Aug. 1582 Dawud; Aug. 1582–15 Dec. 1586 Muhammad II (or Al-Hajj); 15 Dec. 1586–9 Apr. 1588 Muhammad Bani; 9 Apr. 1588–14 Apr. 1591 Ishaq II; 14 Apr. 1591–1591 Muhammad Gao; 1591–1599 Nuh; 1599–1612 Harun; 1612–1618 al-Amin; 1618–1635 Dawud II; 1635–1640 Ismail.

949 Songhai Kingdom. ca. 500–1464. *Location:* Mali. *Capital:* Gao (from 1010); Kukya (ca. 500–1010). *Other names:* Sonrhai Kingdom.

History: About 500 A.D. the Songhai people established their kingdom (see **Songhai Empire** for fuller details). In 1464 it became the **Songhai Empire**.

Dias (Kings): ca. 500–ca. 837 un-

known; ca. 837–ca. 849 Alayaman; ca. 849–861 Za Koi; 861–873 Takoi; 873–885 Akoi; 885–897 Ku; 897–909 Ali Fai; 909–921 Biyai Komai; 921–933 Biyai Bei; 933–945 Karai; 945–957 Yama Karaonia; 957–969 Yama Dombo; 969–981 Yama Danka Kibao; 981–993 Kukorai; 993–1005 Kenken; 1005–1025 Za Kosoi; 1025–1044 Kosai Dariya; 1044–1063 Hen Kon Wanko Dam; 1063–1082 Biyai Koi Kimi; 1082–1101 Nintasanai; 1101–1120 Biyai Kaina Kimba; 1120–1139 Kaina Shinyunbo; 1139–1158 Tib; 1158–1177 Yama Dao; 1177–1196 Fadazu; 1196–1215 Ali Koro; 1215–1235 Bir Foloko; 1235–1255 Yosiboi; 1255–1275 Duro; 1275–1295 Zenko Baro; 1295–1325 Bisi Baro; 1325–1332 Bada. *Sunnis (Sheikhs):* 1333–1340 Ali Konon; 1340–1347 Salman Nari; 1347–1354 Ibrahim Kabay; 1354–1362 Uthman Kanafa; 1362–1370 Bar Kaina Ankabi; 1370–1378 Musa; 1378–1386 Bukar Zonko; 1386–1394 Bukar Dalla Boyonbo; 1394–1402 Mar Kirai; 1402–1410 Muhammad Dao; 1410–1418 Muhammad Konkiya; 1418–1426 Muhammad Fari; 1426–1434 Karbifo; 1434–1442 Mar Fai Kolli-Djimo; 1442–1449 Mar Arkena; 1449–1456 Mar Arandan; 1456–1464 Suleiman Daman.

Soudain Français see **French Sudan**

950 South Africa. See these **names:**
South Africa (1961–   )
Union of South Africa (Self-Rule) (1931–1961)
Union of South Africa (1910–1931)
British Cape Colony (Self-Rule) (1872–1910)
Natal Colony (Self-Rule) (1893–1910)
Orange River Colony (Self-Rule) (1906–1910)
Transvaal Colony (Self-Rule) (1906–1910)
Transkei (1976–   )
Bophuthatswana (1977–   )
Venda (1979–   )
Ciskei (1981–   )
KwaNdebele (1977–   )
KaNgwane (1981–   )

Lebowa (1972–   )
GazaNkulu (1973–   )
KwaZulu (1972–   )
QwaQwa (1974–   )
British Cape Colony (1814–1872)
Natal Colony [ii] (1856–1893)
Orange River Colony (1900–1906)
Transvaal Colony [ii] (1900–1906)
British-Occupied Cape Colony [ii] (1806–1814)
Dutch Cape Colony (1803–1806)
British-Occupied Cape Colony [i] (1795–1803)
Cape of Good Hope Colony (1652–1795)
Natal District (1844–1856)
Natal Colony [i] (1843–1844)
Natalia (1838–1843)
Free Province of New Holland in South East Africa (1836–1838)
Port Natal [iii] (1838–1839)
Port Natal [ii] (1835–1838)
Port Natal [i] (1824–1828)
Orange Free State (1854–1900)
Orange River State (1854–1854)
Orange River Sovereignty (1848–1854)
Transorangia (1824–1848)
South Africa Republic (1884–1900)
Transvaal State (1881–1884)
South African Republic [ii] (1880–1881)
Heidelberg Republic (1880–1880)
Transvaal Colony [i] (1877–1880)
South African Republic [i] (1856–1877)
Dutch African Republic (1852–1856)
Potchefstroom (1838–1852)
Winburg Republic (1837–1848)
Lydenburg Republic (1856–1860)
Lydenburg Territory (1846–1856)
Ohrigstad (1845–1846)
Griqualand West Crown Colony (1873–1880)
Griqualand West (1871–1873)
Klipdrift Republic (1870–1870)
New Republic (1884–1887)
Little Free State (1886–1891)
United States of Stellaland (1883–1885)
Stellaland (1882–1883)
Goshen (1882–1883)

Zoutpansberg (1849–1858)
British Kaffraria Crown Colony (1860–1866)
British Kaffraria Colony (1847–1860)
Queen Adelaide Land (1835–1847)
Queen Adelaide Province (1835–1835)
British Pondoland (1894–1910)
Swellendam (1795–1795)
Graaff-Reinet (1795–1796)
Utrecht Republic (1856–1858)
Utrecht Settlement (1852–1856)
Lijdenrust (1886–1887)
Upingtonia (1885–1886)
British Zululand (1887–1897)
Zululand Province (1879–1887)
Idutywa Reserve (1858–1864)
Sekonyela's Land (1822–1853)
Kreli's Country (1835–1886)
Galekaland (1750–1835)
Kaffraria Proper ([?]–1878)
Pondoland East (1867–1894)
Pondoland West (1867–1894)
Pondoland (1844–1867)
Zululand (1817–1879)
Waterboer's Land (1820–1871)
Cornelis Kok's Land (1824–1857)
Adam Kok's Land (1826–1861)
Griqualand East (1861–1874)
Griquatown (1813–1820)
Campbell Lands (1813–1824)
Tembuland (1750–1885)
Fingoland (1835–1875)

951 South Africa. 31 May 1961–   .
Location: Southern Africa. *Capital:* Pretoria (administrative); Cape Town (legislative); Bloemfontein (judicial). *Other names:* Republiek Van Zuid-Afrika, The Republic of South Africa, Azania (African name).

History: Formerly the **Union of South Africa (Self-Rule),** comprising the four provinces of Cape of Good Hope, Natal, Transvaal and Orange Free State. (See also **Walvis Bay** and **Namibia.**) The self-governing Union of South Africa became independent of Britain technically in 1931, but it wasn't until 1961 that the South Africans could safely say that the British had gone, and a republic was declared.

State Presidents: 31 May 1961–1 June 1967 Charles Swart; 1 June 1967–6 Dec. 1967 Theophilus Dönges (never inaugurated); 1 June 1967–10 Apr. 1968 Tom Naude (acting); 10 Apr. 1968–21 Feb. 1975 Jim Fouché; 19 Apr. 1975–21 Aug. 1978 Nicolaas Diederichs; 29 Sept. 1978–4 June 1979 John Vorster; 4 June 1979–19 June 1979 Marais Viljoen (interim); 19 June 1979–14 Sept. 1984 Marais Viljoen; 14 Sept. 1984– Pieter W. Botha (Executive State President). *Prime Ministers:* 31 May 1961–6 Sept. 1966 Hendrik Verwoerd; 6 Sept. 1966–13 Sept. 1966 Theophilus Dönges (acting); 13 Sept. 1966–28 Sept. 1978 John Vorster; 28 Sept. 1978–14 Sept. 1984 Pieter W. Botha. *Note:* in 1984 P.W. Botha combined the offices of State President and Prime Minister to make Executive State President, with himself in that role.

952 South Africa Republic. 2 Feb. 1884–1 Sept. 1900. *Location:* Transvaal. *Capital:* Pretoria. *Other names:* Zuid-Afrikaansche Republiek, South African Republic, Z.A.R., S.A.R.

History: In 1884 **Transvaal State** became the South Africa Republic under British suzerainty. In 1900 it was taken over by Britain as the **Transvaal Colony,** being officially awarded to Britain after the South African War, in 1902. *Presidents:* 2 Feb. 1884–July 1884 Piet Joubert (acting); July 1884–Aug. 1900 Paul Kruger; Aug. 1900–1 Sept. 1900 Schalk Burger (acting).

953 South African Republic [i]. 16 Dec. 1856–12 Apr. 1877. *Location:* as **Transvaal State.** *Capital:* Pretoria (from 3 Apr. 1860); Potchefstroom (until 3 Apr. 1860). *Other names:* Zuid-Afrikaansche Republiek, Z.A.R., S.A.R.

History: In 1856 the **Dutch African Republic** became the South African Republic. In 1858 **Zoutpansberg** joined the S.A.R., as did **Lydenburg Republic** in 1860, all to form a united Transvaal area under Boer Republican rule. In

1877 Britain annexed the S.A.R., calling it the Colony of Transvaal (see **Transvaal Colony [i]**). *Presidents:* 16 Dec. 1856–1 Jan. 1857 Marthinus Pretorius (acting); 1 Jan. 1857–6 Feb. 1860 Marthinus Pretorius; 6 Feb. 1860–9 Oct. 1860 Johannes Grobelaar (acting); 9 Oct. 1860–20 Jan. 1863 Stephanus Schoeman (acting); 2 Apr. 1862–24 Oct. 1863 Willem van Rensburg (acting); 24 Oct. 1863–10 May 1864 Willem van Rensburg; 10 May 1864–16 Nov. 1871 Marthinus Pretorius; 16 Nov. 1871–1 July 1872 Daniel Erasmus (acting); 1 July 1872–Feb. 1875 Thomas Burgers; Feb. 1875–Apr. 1876 Piet Joubert (acting); Apr. 1876–12 Apr. 1877 Thomas Burgers.

954 South African Republic [ii]. 30 Dec. 1880–5 Apr. 1881. *Location:* Transvaal Province of **South Africa.** *Capital:* Pretoria. *Other names:* Zuid-Afrikaansche Republiek, Z.A.R., S.A.R.

History: At the end of 1880 **Heidelberg Republic,** itself only two weeks old, became the South African Republic again, a name it had had from 1856–1877 (see **South African Republic [i]**). In 1881 it became **Transvaal State.** *Rulers:* 30 Dec. 1880–5 Apr. 1881 Triumvirate of Paul Kruger, Piet Joubert and Marthinus Pretorius.

955 South Kasai Republic. 8 Aug. 1960–27 Aug. 1960. *Location:* south central Zaire. *Capital:* Bakwanga (founded 1909, and renamed Mbuji Mayi in 1966). *Other names:* Kasai Republic, Kasai, Mining State, Mining Republic.

History: In 1960, immediately after independence of the **Belgian Congo** as **Congo (Léopoldville),** Albert Kalonji broke away to form a separate government in Kasai (Kasai was named for the river, and ultimately for the Kasai tribe). Later in August he and Moise Tshombe of **Katanga Republic** joined in a federation. Bakwanga was captured by Congolese troops on August

27, which brought an effective end to the Mining Republic, although it maintained a form of identity until 1962.

Presidents: 8 Aug. 1960–23 Aug. 1960 Albert Kalonji (Provisional President); 23 Aug. 1960–27 Aug. 1960 Albert Kalonji.

South Ndebele see **KwaNdebele**

South Rivers see **Rivières du Sud**

956 South West Africa Mandate. 1 Jan. 1921–11 Dec. 1946. *Location:* as **Namibia.** *Capital:* Windhoek. *Other names:* South West Africa.

History: In 1921 **South West Africa Protectorate** became a League of Nations Class C Mandate. A Class C Mandate authorized the occupying power to exercise full control over the territory as an integral part of its own state. In 1946 it became **South West Africa United Nations Mandate.**

Administrators: 1 Jan. 1921–31 March 1926 Gysbert Hofmeyer; 1 Apr. 1926–1 Apr. 1933 Albertus Werth; 1 Apr. 1933–1 Apr. 1943 David Conradie; 1 Apr. 1943–11 Dec. 1946 Petrus Hoogenhout.

957 South West Africa Protectorate. 15 July 1915–1 Jan. 1921. *Location:* as **Namibia.** *Capital:* Windhoek. *Other names:* South West Africa.

History: It was South Africa which conquered the Germans in **German South West Africa Colony.** It fell under South African military administration and in 1921 it was awarded to the **Union of South Africa** as a League of Nations Mandate (see **South West Africa Mandate**).

Military Governors: 15 July 1915–30 Oct. 1915 General P.S. Beves. *Administrators:* 31 Oct. 1915–1 Oct. 1920 Sir Howard Gorges; 1 Oct. 1920–1 Jan. 1921 Gysbert Hofmeyer.

958 South West Africa United Nations Mandate. 11 Dec. 1946–27 Oct. 1966. *Location:* as **Namibia.** *Capital:* Windhoek. *Other names:* South West

Africa.

History: In 1946, when United Nations Trusteeships were being awarded to former Mandates, South Africa refused one for **South West Africa Mandate,** continuing to rule their acquired territory as before, except this time with a technical UN mandate. South Africa wanted to annex the area, but the UN refused permission for this. In 1966 the UN took away the mandate by United Nations General Assembly Resolution #2145, saying that South Africa hadn't fulfilled its obligations in South West Africa, and it became **South West Africa United Nations Supervised Territory.**

Administrators: 11 Dec. 1946–6 Dec. 1951 Petrus Hoogenhout; 6 Dec. 1951–1 Dec. 1953 Albertus van Rhijn; 1 Dec. 1953–1 Dec. 1963 Daniel Viljoen; 1 Dec. 1963–27 Oct. 1966 Wenzel du Plessis.

959 South West Africa United Nations Supervised Territory. 27 Oct. 1966–12 June 1968. *Location:* as **Namibia.** *Capital:* Windhoek. *Other names:* South West Africa.

History: In 1966 the United Nations terminated the Mandate over which South West Africa was ruled by South Africa (see **South West Africa United Nations Mandate**). On May 19, 1967 the UN established an 11-member UN Council for South West Africa to administer the territory until independence (set then for June 1968), but the South Africans would not allow the council entry into South West Africa. South Africa refused to accept the termination of the mandate. In 1968 the UN changed the name of the area to **Namibia.**

Administrators: 27 Oct. 1966–12 June 1968 Wenzel du Plessis. *Chiefs of the Hereros:* 27 Oct. 1966–12 June 1968 Hosea Kutako.

960 South Zambesia. 23 Jan. 1894–3 May 1895. *Location:* as **Zimbabwe.** *Capital:* Salisbury (founded September 12, 1890 as Fort Salisbury, and named for Lord Salisbury, the British Prime Minister).

History: In 1894 **Matabeleland** (which, from February 11, 1888 was supposed to have been a British Protectorate called Matabeleland Protectorate — except that the Matabele didn't accept, recognize and in most cases even know this protectorate existed) definitely became a British territory, and was annexed by the British South Africa Company (BSAC), as part of **Mashonaland Protectorate.** Naturally the Matabele couldn't be part of Mashonaland, so the name was changed to South Zambesia, while north of the Zambesi River the land became **North Zambesia.** In 1895 North Zambesia and South Zambesia merged to form **Rhodesia Protectorate.**

Chief Magistrates: 23 Jan. 1894–May 1894 Andrew Duncan (acting); May 1894–9 Sept. 1894 Dr. Leander Starr Jameson. *Administrators:* 9 Sept. 1894–28 Oct. 1894 Dr. Leander Starr Jameson; 28 Oct. 1894–1 Apr. 1895 Francis Rhodes (acting); 1 Apr. 1895–3 May 1895 Dr. Leander Starr Jameson.

Southern Egypt see **Upper Egypt**

961 Southern Nigeria Colony and Protectorate. 16 Feb. 1906–1 Jan. 1914. *Location:* southern Nigeria. *Capital:* Lagos.

History: In 1906 the **Southern Nigeria Protectorate** and **Lagos Colony** united to form the British Colony and Protectorate of Southern Nigeria. In 1914 this combined with **Northern Nigeria Protectorate** to form **Nigeria Colony and Protectorate.**

Governors: 16 Feb. 1906–1907 Sir Walter Egerton; 1907–1907 James Thorburn (acting); 1907–1912 Sir Walter Egerton; 1912–1 Jan. 1914 Sir Frederick Lugard.

962 Southern Nigeria Protectorate. 27 Dec. 1899–16 Feb. 1906. *Location:* southern Nigeria, excluding **Lagos Colony.** *Capital:* Old Calabar (after 1904 called Calabar).

History: In 1899 the **Niger Coast Protectorate** became the Southern Nigeria Protectorate, operational from January 1, 1900. In 1906 the separate British colony of Lagos (see **Lagos Colony**) joined to this to form the **Southern Nigeria Colony and Protectorate.**

High Commissioners: 1 Jan. 1900–1900 Sir Ralph Moor; 1900–1900 Henry Gallwey (after 1911 Galway) (acting); 1900–Aug. 1904 Sir Ralph Moor; Aug. 1904–16 Feb. 1906 Walter Egerton (knighted 1905).

963 Southern Rhodesia. 29 Jan. 1900–21 Sept. 1923. *Location:* as **Southern Rhodesia Colony.** *Capital:* Salisbury. *Other names:* Southern Rhodesia Protectorate (from 1911).

History: In 1900 the **Rhodesia Protectorate** split into three separate units. Two of these, **North Western Rhodesia** and **North Eastern Rhodesia** went to form present-day **Zambia,** while the third became Southern Rhodesia. In 1911 this became a protectorate of Britain; actually this was just a confirmation of what had been a protectorate since 1900 — nothing changed in the country, it was still ruled by the British South Africa Company, as it had been since 1890 and as it would be until it became **Southern Rhodesia Colony** in 1923.

Administrator of Mashonaland/ Senior Administrator of Southern Rhodesia: 29 Jan. 1900–24 Jan. 1901 William Milton. *Administrators:* 24 Jan. 1901–31 Oct. 1914 William Milton; 2 Nov. 1914–24 Dec. 1914 Sir Francis Newton (acting); 24 Dec. 1914–15 Oct. 1919 Drummond Chaplin (knighted 1917); 15 Oct. 1919–14 Dec. 1919 Clarkson Tredgold (acting); 14 Dec. 1919–10 Sept. 1920 Sir Drummond Chaplin; 10 Sept. 1920–10 Dec. 1920 Ernest Montagu (acting); 10 Dec. 1920–15 Nov. 1922 Sir Drummond Chaplin; 15 Nov. 1922–10 May 1923 Ernest Montagu (acting); 10 May 1923–21 Sept. 1923

Sir Drummond Chaplin. *Administrators of Matabeleland:* 29 Jan. 1900–March 1901 Capt. Arthur Lawley.

964 Southern Rhodesia Colony. 21 Sept. 1923–24 Oct. 1964. *Location:* to the north of **South Africa.** *Capital:* Salisbury. *Other names:* Southern Rhodesia.

History: In 1923 **Southern Rhodesia Protectorate** became a British colony. In 1964, with the independence of the other Rhodesia, i.e. **Northern Rhodesia Protectorate** (which became **Zambia**), the term **Rhodesia** now applied only to the southern colony. From 1953–63 it formed part of the **Federation of Rhodesia and Nyasaland.**

Governors: 21 Sept. 1923–23 Sept. 1923 Percy Fynn (acting); 23 Sept. 1923–1 Oct. 1923 office vacant; 1 Oct. 1923–Feb. 1926 Sir John Chancellor; Feb. 1926–Sept. 1926 Murray Bissett (acting); Sept. 1926–30 May 1928 Sir John Chancellor; 30 May 1928–15 June 1928 office vacant; 15 June 1928–24 Nov. 1928 Murray Bissett (acting); 24 Nov. 1928–30 June 1934 Sir Cecil Rodwell; 1 July 1934–8 Jan. 1935 Alexander Russell (acting); 8 Jan. 1935–6 Jan. 1942 Sir Herbert Stanley; 8 Jan. 1942–10 Dec. 1942 Sir Alexander Russell (acting); 10 Dec. 1942–26 Oct. 1944 Sir Evelyn Baring; 26 Oct. 1944–20 Feb. 1945 Sir Robert Hudson (acting); 20 Feb. 1945–2 Feb. 1946 Sir Campbell Tait; 2 Feb. 1946–19 July 1946 Sir Alexander Russell (acting); 19 July 1946–14 Jan. 1947 Sir Robert Hudson (acting); 14 Jan. 1947–17 Oct. 1950 Sir John Kennedy; 17 Oct. 1950–13 Nov. 1950 Walter Thomas (acting); 13 Nov. 1950–21 Nov. 1953 Sir John Kennedy; 21 Nov. 1953–26 Nov. 1954 Sir Robert Tredgold (acting); 26 Nov. 1954–28 Dec. 1959 Sir Peveril William-Powlett; 28 Dec. 1959–24 Oct. 1964 Humphrey Gibbs (knighted 1960). *Premiers:* 1 Oct. 1923–28 Aug. 1927 Sir Charles Coghlan; 2 Sept. 1927–5 July 1933 Howard Moffatt. *Prime Ministers:* 5 July 1933–

6 Sept. 1933 George Mitchell; 12 Sept. 1933–7 Sept. 1953 Godfrey Huggins (knighted 1941); 7 Sept. 1953–8 Feb. 1958 Garfield Todd; 8 Feb. 1958–15 Dec. 1962 Sir Edgar Whitehead; 16 Dec. 1962–13 Apr. 1964 Winston Field; 13 Apr. 1964–24 Oct. 1964 Ian Smith.

965 Southern Somaliland Crown Colony. July 1910–26 Feb. 1941. *Location:* as **Italian Somaliland Crown Colony.** *Capital:* Mogadiscio (Mogadishu). *Other names:* Italian Somaliland Crown Colony.

History: In 1910 **Italian Somaliland Colony** became a Crown Colony of Italy. In 1926 **Jubaland Colony** became part of the country, and in 1935 the country itself became part of **Italian East Africa.** When that conglomerate fell apart at the hands of the British, Southern (or Italian) Somaliland became simply **Somaliland.**

Governors: July 1910–1916 Giacomo de Martino; 1916–21 June 1920 Giovanni Cerrina-Ferroni; 21 June 1920–8 Dec. 1923 Carlo Ricci; 8 Dec. 1923–1 June 1928 Cesare de Val Cismon; 1 June 1928–1 July 1931 Guido Corni; 1 July 1931–7 March 1935 Maurizio Rava; 7 March 1935–22 May 1936 Rodolfo Graziani; 22 May 1936–24 May 1936 Angelo de Rubeis (acting); 24 May 1936–15 Dec. 1937 Ruggero Santini; 15 Dec. 1937–11 June 1940 Francesco Saverio Caroselli; 11 June 1940–31 Dec. 1940 Gustavo Pesenti; 31 Dec. 1940–26 Feb. 1941 Carlo de Simone.

966 Southern Sudan Provisional Government. 1967–March 1969. *Location:* Southern Sudan (i.e. the provinces of Equatoria, Upper Nile and Bahr al-Ghazal). *Capital:* no central capital. *Other names:* SSPG.

History: The problem in the Sudan reflects the basic problem throughout most of Africa. Before the Europeans came, Africa was divided into tribes, that is tribes with a religion, language and culture. Often these tribes formed kingdoms, and even empires, and when other chiefdoms were subjugated the trouble started. Sooner or later those kingdoms, and especially empires, dissolved, and new ones took their place. This was the natural ebb and flow of African history, crude power usurping feebler power. When the Europeans arrived they carved Africa up between them. All was well (?) under colonial rule, but upon independence (and in many cases before it) a new kind of trouble started. Provisional governments-in-exile sprang up (see **Angola, Algeria, Saharan Arab Democratic Republic** for example), countries broke away from the newly formed republics (see **Katanga, Stanleyville, South Kasai, Namibia, Eritrea, Biafra**) spurred on by a desire for ethnic unity rather than a unity created artificially by the European powers a century or so before. The **Sudan Republic** and its predecessor the **Sudan Democratic Republic** developed its own cancer of this sort in its three southernmost provinces. Black, African (Azanian), non-Muslims wanted to be free of Islam and Khartoum, and a ragged, poverty-stricken, beaten-up army called the Anyanya (formed in 1963) has been struggling (as have other groups since 1956) to have its own country in the south. The SSPG replaced the Azania Liberation Front (founded 1965) and was itself replaced in 1969 by the **Nile Provisional Government**. In 1972 the Addis Ababa Agreement gave the South a certain autonomy.

Presidents: 1967–March 1969 Aggrey Jaden.

Soutpansberg see **Zoutpansberg**

967 Spanish Captaincy-General of North Africa. 1847–27 Nov. 1912. *Location:* Morocco. *Capital:* Ceuta.

History: In 1847 the Captaincy-General of North Africa was created in order to bring all the Spanish enclaves along the North African coast under one administration. These enclaves were: **Ceuta (Spanish), Melilla (Spanish),** Velez de la Gomera, Alhucemas and Chafarinas. The governor of Ceuta became the Captain-General of the whole lot. In 1912, with the establishment of **Spanish Morocco,** the Captaincy-General merged into it.

Captains-General: 1847–1851 Antonio Ros de Olano; 1851–1854 Salvador de la Puente Pita; 1854–1857 Mariano Rebigliato; 1857–1858 Carlos Tobía; 1858–1858 Manuel Gasset Mercader; 1858–1864 Ramón Gómez Pulido; 1864–1865 Manuel Álvarez Maldonaldo; 1865–1866 Ramón Gómez Pulido; 1866–1866 Antonio Peláez Campomanes; 1866–1868 José Oribe Sans; 1868–1868 Antonio del Rey y Caballero; 1868–1870 Joaquín Cristón y Gasatín; 1870–1872 Enrique Serrano Dolz; 1872–1873 Carlos Sáenz Delcourt; 1873–1873 Manuel Keller y García; 1873–1875 Fulgencio Gávila y Solá; 1875–1876 Pedro Sartorius y Tapia; 1876–1877 Fernando del Piño Villamil; 1877–1877 Juan García Torres; 1877–1878 Victoriano López Pinto; 1878–1879 José María Velasco Postigo; 1879–1881 José Aizpuru y Lorriez Fontecha; 1881–1883 José Merello y Calvo; 1883–1883 José Pascual de Bonanza; 1883–1889 Juan López Pinto y Marín Reyna; 1889–1891 Narciso de Fuentes y Sánchez; 1891–1894 Miguel Correa y García; 1894–1898 Rafael Correa y García; 1898–1901 Jacinto de León y Barreda; 1901–1903 Manuel de Aguilar y Diosdado; 1903–1907 Francisco Fernandez Bernal; 1907–1908 Fernando Álvarez de Sotomayor y Flórez; 1908–1910 José García Aldave; 1910–27 Nov. 1912 Felipe Alfau y Mendoza.

968 Spanish Guinea. 1926–1938. *Location:* as **Equatorial Guinea.** *Capital:* Santa Isabel.

History: In 1926 **Rio Muni Colony** and **Fernando Po (Spanish) [ii]** were united as Spanish Guinea. In 1938 the area became the **Spanish Territories of the Gulf of Guinea.**

Governors: 1926–1931 Miguel de Prado; 1931–1932 Gustavo de Sostoa y Sthamer; 1932–1933 [unknown]; 1933–1934 Estanislao García; 1934–1935 Angel Feltrer; 1935–1936 Luis Saéz; 1936–1937 [unknown]; 1937–1937 Manuel de Mendívil y Elío; 1937–1938 Juan Fontán y Lobé.

969 Spanish Guinea Overseas Province. 30 July 1959–15 Dec. 1963. *Location:* as **Equatorial Guinea.** *Capital:* Santa Isabel. *Other names:* Spanish Guinea.

History: In 1959 the **Spanish Territories of the Gulf of Guinea** became an overseas province of Spain. In 1963 it changed its name to **Equatorial Africa (Self-Rule).**

Governors: 30 July 1959–1962 Faustino González; 1962–15 Dec. 1963 Francisco Rodriguez.

970 Spanish Morocco. 27 Nov. 1912–7 Apr. 1956. *Location:* northern Morocco and the southern — Tarfaya — region. *Capital:* Tetuán. *Other names:* Rif, er-Rif.

History: The Algeciras Act of April 8, 1906 gave France and Spain main control in Morocco, and a certain territory was granted to Spain as a protectorate in 1912, basically an extension in land from the territory of the **Spanish Captaincy-General of North Africa,** but also including the far south of Morocco. Subsequent agreements decreased the size of this area to the advantage of **French Morocco.** After 1934 the Spanish High Commissioner had jurisdiction for some years over **Spanish West Africa** (also known as the Southern Protectorate of Morocco, and previously called **Rio de Oro**). In 1956 Spain, following on the heels of France, gave her protectorate lands back to Morocco (which had become independent of France in March). Spain still holds enclaves in Morocco — Alhucemas, Chafarinas, Velez de la Gomera, **Ceuta Presidio** and **Melilla Presidio,** and until 1969, **Ifni.** The last Spanish troops left Morocco proper on August 31, 1961.

High Commissioners: 3 Apr. 1913–15 Aug. 1913 Felipe Alfau y Mendoza; 17 Aug. 1913–9 July 1915 José Marina y Vega; 9 July 1915–18 Nov. 1918 Francisco Gomez y Jordana; 27 Jan. 1919–13 July 1922 Dámaso Berenguer y Fuste; 15 July 1922–22 Jan. 1923 Ricardo Burguete y Lana; 22 Jan. 1923–16 Feb. 1923 Miguel Villanueva (never took office); 16 Feb. 1923–14 Sept. 1923 Luis Silvela y Casado; 25 Sept. 1923–2 Oct. 1924 Luis Aizpuru; 16 Oct. 1924–2 Nov. 1925 Miguel Primo de Rivera y Orbaneja; 2 Nov. 1925–1928 José Sanjurjo, Marques de Malmusi; 1928–19 Apr. 1931 Francisco Gomez Jordana y Sousa; 19 Apr. 1931–20 June 1931 José Sanjurjo, Marques de Malmusi; 20 June 1931–May 1933 Luciano Ferrer; May 1933–23 Jan. 1934 Juan Moles; 23 Jan. 1934–March 1936 Manuel Avello; March 1936–July 1936 Juan Moles; July 1936–1936 Alvarez Buylla; 1936–1936 Saenz de Buruaga; 1936–1936 Francisco Franco Bahamonde; 1936–Aug. 1937 Luis Orgaz y Yoldi; Aug. 1937–1939 Juan Beigbeder y Atienza; Feb. 1940–12 May 1941 Carlos Asensio; 12 May 1941–4 March 1945 Luis Orgaz y Yoldi; 4 March 1945–March 1951 José Iglesias; March 1951–7 Apr. 1956 Rafael Valiño y Marcen. *Khalifas (Sultan's Representatives):* 19 Apr. 1913–9 Nov. 1923 Mulay al-Mahdi; 9 Nov. 1923–8 Nov. 1925 vacant; 8 Nov. 1925–7 Apr. 1956 Mulay Hassan ben al-Mahdi.

Spanish Sahara Protectorate see **Rio de Oro Dependent Protectorate**

971 Spanish Sahara Province. 10 Jan. 1958–28 Feb. 1976. *Location:* North West Africa. *Capital:* El-Aaiún. *Other names:* Spanish Sahara, Sahara Español.

History: In 1958 Spanish Sahara (formerly **Rio de Oro**) left **Spanish West Africa,** and combined with Seguia el-Hamra to form a separate Spanish province. Four days later **Ifni**

Territory did the same, and **Spanish West Africa** died as an entity a few months later. **Ifni Province** became part of the **Kingdom of Morocco** in 1969 and in 1976 Spain gave up Spanish Sahara Province, leaving it to be ripped apart by Morocco and Mauritania.

Governors-General: 10 Jan. 1958–1958 José Vázquez; 1958–1961 Mariano Alonso; 1961–1964 Pedro Alcubierre; 1964–1965 Joaquín Coronado; 1965–1967 Angel Larrando; 1967–4 March 1971 José Tejero; 4 March 1971–1975 Fernando de Santiago y Diaz de Mendívil; 1975–28 Feb. 1976 Federico de Salazar y Nieto.

972 Spanish Territories of the Gulf of Guinea. 1938–30 July 1959. *Location:* as **Equatorial Guinea**. *Capital:* Santa Isabel. *Other names:* Spanish Guinea.

History: In 1938 **Spanish Guinea** became known officially as the Spanish Territories of the Gulf of Guinea. In 1959 it became **Spanish Guinea Overseas Province**.

Governors: 1938–1941 Juan Fontán y Lobé; 1941–1943 Mariano Alonso; 1943–1949 Juan Rubío; 1949–30 July 1959 Faustino González.

973 Spanish Tunis [i]. 20 July 1535–1539. *Location:* Tunisia. *Capital:* Tunis. *Other names:* Tunis (Spanish).

History: In 1535 the Spanish took Tunis from the Turks (see **Turkish Tunis [i]**). The Hafsid Sultan continued to reign as a vassal of the Spanish. In 1539 the Turks took Tunis again (see **Turkish Tunis [ii]**).

Sultans: 20 July 1535–1539 Mulay al-Hassan.

974 Spanish Tunis [ii]. 1573–13 Sept. 1574. *Location:* Tunisia. *Capital:* Tunis. *Other names:* Tunis.

History: In 1573 Don John of Austria and his Spanish fleet, fresh from their two-year-old triumph at Lepanto, captured Tunis from the Turks (see **Turkish Tunis [ii]**). In 1574 Don John

lost it to the Turks (see **Tunis Pashalik**).

Military Overlords: 1573–13 Sept. 1574 Don John of Austria. *Hafsid Sultans (Vassals):* 1573–13 Sept. 1574 Mulay Muhammad.

975 Spanish West Africa. 27 Nov. 1912–10 Apr. 1958. *Location:* southern Morocco, i.e. **Rio do Oro** plus **Ifni** (the latter only after 1952). *Capital:* Villa Cisneros. *Other names:* Africa Occidental Española, Southern Protectorate of Morocco, Spanish Sahara, Rio de Oro.

History: In 1912 **Rio de Oro Dependent Protectorate**, until then a part of the **Canary Islands,** became Spanish West Africa, or The Southern Protectorate of Morocco. On that day **Ifni** became **Ifni Protectorate,** which in 1952 was to become part of Spanish West Africa—as **Ifni Territory.** In January 1958 the two component parts of Spanish West Africa left to become new entities—Ifni and Rio de Oro became provinces of Spain (see **Ifni Province** and **Spanish Sahara Province**). A few months later a dead Spanish West Africa lay down and came to an official end.

Governors-General: 27 Nov. 1912–1925 Francisco Bens Argandoña; 1925–1932 Guillermo de la Peña Cusi; 1932–1933 Eduardo Navarro; 1933–1934 Jose Gonzales Deleito; 1934–1939 Antonio de Oro Pulido; 1939–1949 José López; 1949–1952 Francisco Rosalen y Burguet; 1952–1954 Venancio Gil; 1954–1957 Ramon de Santallana; 1957–10 Apr. 1958 Enrique Quirce.

976 Stanleyville People's Republic. 7 Sept. 1964–1 July 1965. *Location:* Kisangani, Zaire. *Capital:* Stanleyville (established 1883 and first known as Falls Station, it was named for Henry M. Stanley, pioneer of the Belgian Congo, and in 1966 renamed Kisangani). *Other names:* Congolese People's Republic, République Populaire du Congo.

History: In 1964 rebels took over Stanleyville with the intention of overthrowing Moise Tshombe's government in the **Congo Democratic Republic.** Less than a year later the rebel government died out and the two became **Congo (Kinshasa).**
Presidents: 7 Sept. 1964–1 July 1965 Christophe Gbenye.

977 Stanleyville Republic. 13 Dec. 1960–5 Aug. 1961. *Location:* around Kisangani, Zaire. *Capital:* Stanleyville (founded in 1883 and first called Falls Station. Renamed for Sir Henry Stanley, and after 1966 renamed Kisangani).
History: In 1960 Antoine Gizenga, the former premier of **Congo (Leopoldville),** broke away and formed his own government at Stanleyville. It lasted almost a year until being taken back into the newly formed **Congo (Kinshasa).**
Prime Ministers: 13 Dec. 1960–5 Aug. 1961 Antoine Gizenga.

978 Stellaland. 26 July 1882–7 Aug. 1883. *Location:* eastern British Bechuanaland, part of Korannaland. *Capital:* Vrijburg. *Other names:* Republic of Stellaland (named for a comet seen at the time—"stella" is Latin for "star").
History: In 1882 the Boers technically invaded British territory, and set up the Republic of Stellaland, to be followed soon after by **Goshen.** In 1883 the two republics merged, as the **United States of Stellaland.**
Administrators: 26 July 1882–7 Aug. 1883 Gerrit Van Niekerk.

979 Sudan. See these **names:**
Sudan Republic (1985–)
Sudan Democratic Republic (1956–1985)
Sudan (Self-Rule) (1952–1956)
Anglo-Egyptian Sudan (1899–1952)
Sudan (1898–1899)
Mahdist State (1884–1898)
Anyidi Revolutionary Government (1969–1970)
Nile Provisional Government (1969–1970)
Southern Sudan Provisional Government (1967–1969)
Bahr al-Ghazal Province (1869–1894)
Equatoria Province (1871–1889)
Kordofan Province (1821–1883)
Darfur Sultanate [ii] (1899–1916)
Darfur Province (1874–1883)
Darfur Sultanate [i] (1603–1874)
Egyptian Sudan (1821–1884)
Funj Sultanate (1504–1821)
Kordofan (ca. 1600–1821)
Alwah ([?]–1504)
Dongola (ca. 675–1323)
Mukurra (ca. 340–ca. 675)
Nubia (ca. 325–ca. 675)
Kush (ca. 860 B.C.–ca. 325 A.D.)

980 Sudan. 2 Sept. 1898–19 Jan. 1899. *Location:* as **Sudan Republic.** *Capital:* Khartoum. *Other names:* The Sudan.
History: In 1898 the **Mahdist State** was brought to an end by British and Egyptian forces under Lord Kitchener. In 1899 the **Anglo-Egyptian Sudan** was officially proclaimed.
Military Governors: 2 Sept. 1898–19 Jan. 1899 Lord Kitchener.

981 Sudan Democratic Republic. 1 Jan. 1956–15 Dec. 1985. *Location:* as **Sudan Republic.** *Capital:* Khartoum. *Other names:* Sudan, The Sudan, is-Sudan, Democratic Republic of the Sudan.
History: In 1956 **Sudan (Self-Rule)** became independent. In 1985 the Sudan Democratic Republic became the **Sudan Republic** with disastrous consequences, political, economic and libertarian, to the man on the street.
Presidents: 17 Nov. 1958–15 Nov. 1964 Ibrahim Abboud; 15 Nov. 1964–10 June 1965 office vacant; 10 June 1965–25 May 1969 Ismail al-Azhari; 25 May 1969–19 July 1971 Ja'far al-Numayri (Chairman of the Revolutionary Council); 19 July 1971–22 July 1971 Babakr an-Nur (Communist President—never

took office); 22 July 1971–6 Apr. 1985 Ja'far al-Numayri; 9 Apr. 1985–15 Dec. 1985 Abd ar-Rahman Siwar ad-Dahab (Chairman of the Transitional Military Council). *Prime Ministers:* 1 Jan. 1956–5 July 1956 Ismael al-Azhari; 5 July 1956–17 Nov. 1958 Abdallah Khalil; 1 Nov. 1964–14 June 1965 Sirr al-Khatim al-Khalifah; 14 June 1965–27 July 1966 Muhammad Mahjub; 27 July 1966–16 May 1967 Sadiq al-Mahdi; 16 May 1967–25 May 1969 Muhammad Mahjub; 25 May 1969–28 Oct. 1969 Abu Bakr Awadullah; 9 Aug. 1976–10 Sept. 1977 Rashid Bakr; 22 Apr. 1985–15 Dec. 1985 al-Gizouli Dafalla. *Note:* in times of no Prime Minister, the President held that office.

Sudan Federation see **Mali Federation**

982 Sudan Republic. 15 Dec. 1985– . *Location:* northeast Africa, south of Egypt. *Capital:* Khartoum (built as a Turkish camp in 1821, the name means "elephant's tusk." By 1823 it was a city.). *Other names:* Jumhuriyat is-Sudan ad-Dimuqratiyah, is-Sudan, The Sudan, Sudan.
History: In 1985, several months after the coup which ousted Numayri, the **Sudan Democratic Republic** lost the word "Democratic," actually as well as semantically. The principal political internal problem in The Sudan is the Southern Region's desire to be independent, or at least autonomous. Since 1967 this has been a thorn in the side of the government in Khartoum (see **Southern Sudan Provisional Government**).
Presidents: 15 Dec. 1985–6 May 1986 Abd er-Rahman Siwar ad-Dahab. *Chairmen of the Supreme Council:* 6 May 1986– Ahmad al-Mirghani. *Prime Ministers:* 15 Dec. 1985–6 May 1986 al-Gizouli Dafalla; 6 May 1986– Sadiq al-Mahdi.

983 Sudan (Self-Rule). 22 Oct. 1952–1 Jan. 1956. *Location:* as **Sudan Republic.** *Capital:* Khartoum. *Other names:* Sudan, is-Sudan.
History: In 1952 self-rule came to the **Anglo-Egyptian Sudan.** In 1956 it became fully independent as **Sudan Democratic Republic.**
Governors-General: 22 Oct. 1952–Dec. 1954 Sir Robert Howe; 11 March 1955–12 Dec. 1955 Sir Knox Helm. *Prime Ministers:* 22 Oct. 1952–Nov. 1953 Sayid Abderrahman ibn al-Mahdi; 9 Jan. 1954–1 Jan. 1956 Ismail al-Azhari.

984 Sudanese Republic. 20 Aug. 1960–22 Sept. 1960. *Location:* as **Mali Republic.** *Capital:* Bamako. *Other names:* République Soudainaise, Republic of Sudan.
History: In 1960 the **Mali Federation** came to an end, and the two component parts, **Sudanese Republic Territory** and **Senegal** went their own ways to become the Sudanese Republic and **Senegal Republic.** Later in 1960 the Sudanese Republic became **Mali Republic.**
Presidents: 20 Aug. 1960–22 Sept. 1960 Modibo Keita.

985 Sudanese Republic (Autonomous). 24 Nov. 1958–4 Apr. 1959. *Location:* as **Mali Republic.** *Capital:* Bamako. *Other names:* République Soudainaise.
History: In 1958 **French Sudan Overseas Territory** became an autonomous republic within the French Community. In 1959 it became part of the Mali Federation (see **Mali Autonomous Federation** and **Sudanese Republic Territory**).
High Commissioners: 24 Nov. 1958–4 Apr. 1959 Jean-Charles Sicurani. *Presidents:* March 1959–4 Apr. 1959 Modibo Keita. *Prime Ministers:* 24 Nov. 1958–4 Apr. 1959 Jean-Marie Koné.

986 Sudanese Republic Territory. 4 Apr. 1959–20 Aug. 1960. *Location:* as **Mali Republic.** *Capital:* Bamako.

History: On January 17, 1959 (effective from April 4, 1959), the **Mali Federation** (see also **Mali Autonomous Federation**) came into being, composed of Sudanese Republic Territory (formerly **Sudanese Republic [Autonomous]**) and **Senegal** (formerly **Senegal Autonomous Republic**). Both of these countries retained their republic status, but merged into the one ruling body of the Federation. In June 1960 independence took place (see **Sudanese Republic**).

High Commissioners: 4 Apr. 1959–20 June 1960 Jean-Charles Sicurani. *Prime Ministers:* 16 Apr. 1959–20 June 1960 Modibo Keita.

Swazi Territory see **KaNgwane**

987 Swaziland. See these **names:**
Swaziland Kingdom (1968–)
Swaziland (Self-Rule) (1967–1968)
Swaziland [ii] (1964–1967)
Swaziland High Commission Territory (1906–1964)
Swaziland Protectorate (1893–1906)
Swaziland [i] (1818–1893)

988 Swaziland [i]. 1818–13 Nov. 1893. *Location:* **Swaziland Kingdom.** *Capital:* Elangeni.
History: A Nguni clan originally called Ngwane, related to the Zulus, the Swazi were pursued to what is now Swaziland from the Pongola River by the Zulus between 1818 and 1820. The Ngwane chieftaincy had been in existence for over 200 years, and the first king of Swaziland, Sobhuza I, represented the continual chain of monarchy. He tried to live in peace, and his son Mswati (or Mswazi), after whom the country is named, was a more aggressive king, and cultivated friendship with the Boers. On the death of Mswati the Boers took an active interest in Swaziland, supporting Mbandzeni in his claim to the Paramount Chieftaincy. In 1893 the Queen Regent applied to Britain for protection, which happened under Transvaal direction (i.e. it was protected from the Transvaal) (see **Swaziland Protectorate**).
Paramount Chiefs: 1818–1836 Sobhuza I; 1836–1868 Mswati (or Mswazi); 1868–1874 Ludvonga; 1874–6 Oct. 1889 Mbandzeni (or Umbandzeni); 23 Oct. 1889–13 Nov. 1893 Boon (or Bunu, or Ubanu, or Ngwane).

989 Swaziland [ii]. 1 Aug. 1964–25 Apr. 1967. *Location:* as **Swaziland Kingdom.** *Capital:* Mbabane. *Other names:* Swaziland.
History: In 1964 **Swaziland High Commission Territory** became known as simply Swaziland, and achieved limited self-rule. In 1967 it became fully self-governing (see **Swaziland [Self-Rule]**).
Kings: 1 Aug. 1964–25 Apr. 1967 Sobhuza II. *Commissioners:* 1 Aug. 1964–25 Apr. 1967 Francis Loyd (knighted 1965).

990 Swaziland High Commission Territory. 1 Dec. 1906–1 Aug. 1964. *Location:* as **Swaziland Kingdom.** *Capital:* Mbabane. *Other names:* Swaziland Protectorate.
History: In 1906 the **Swaziland Protectorate** became a High Commission Territory, directly dependent on the High Commissioner for South Africa (see **Union of South Africa** and **Union of South Africa [Self-Rule]** for list of High Commissioners). In 1907 the first Resident Commissioner was appointed for Swaziland, and in 1964 the High Commission Territories (see also **Bechuanaland High Commission Territory** and **Basutoland High Commission Territory**) came to an end and Swaziland was granted limited self-rule (see **Swaziland [ii]**).
Administrators: 1 Dec. 1906–1907 Enraght Mooney. *Resident Commissioners:* 1907–1916 Robert Coryndon; 1916–Oct. 1928 Montagu Honey; Oct. 1928–1 Apr. 1935 Thomas A. Dickson; 1 Apr. 1935–Oct. 1935 [unknown] (acting); Oct. 1935–Nov. 1937 Allan Marwick; Nov. 1937–30 Sept. 1942 Charles

Bruton; 30 Sept. 1942–25 Aug. 1946 Eric Featherstone; 25 Aug. 1946–1950 Edward Beetham; 1950–1956 David Morgan; 1956–1963 Brian Marwick. *Commissioners:* 1963–1964 Sir Brian Marwick; 1964–1 Aug. 1964 Francis Loyd. *Paramount Chiefs:* 1 Dec. 1906–4 Sept. 1921 Sobhuza II. *Ngwenyamas (Kings):* 4 Sept. 1921–1 Aug. 1964 Sobhuza II.

991 Swaziland Kingdom. 6 Sept. 1968– . *Location:* Southern Africa. *Capital:* Mbabane. *Other names:* Swaziland.

History: In 1968 **Swaziland (Self-Rule)** gained total independence and became the independent Kingdom of Swaziland, even though the kingdom had been recognized by the British in 1961.

Ngwenyamas (Kings): 6 Sept. 1968–21 Aug. 1982 Sobhuza II. *Queens-Regent:* 21 Aug. 1982–10 Aug. 1983 Dzeliwe Shongwe; 10 Aug. 1983–25 Apr. 1986 Ntombi Thwala. *Ngwenyamas (Kings):* 25 Apr. 1986– Mswati III. *Prime Ministers:* 6 Sept. 1968–17 March 1976 Makhosini Dhlamini; 17 Mar. 1976–25 Oct. 1979 Maphevu Dhlamini; 25 Oct. 1979–23 Nov. 1979 Ben Nsibandze (acting); 23 Nov. 1979–23 March 1983 Mandabala Fred Dhlamini; 23 March 1983–6 Oct. 1986 Bhekimpi Dhlamini; 6 Oct. 1986– Sotsha Ernest Dhlamini.

992 Swaziland Protectorate. 13 Nov. 1893–1 Dec. 1906. *Location:* Swaziland. *Capital:* Bremersdorf (founded 1890 by a trader named Bremer). *Other names:* Swaziland.

History: In 1893 Britain established a protectorate over **Swaziland,** but did not send a resident, ruling it through the **Transvaal Colony [ii].** In 1906 it became **Swaziland High Commission Territory.**

Paramount Chiefs: 13 Nov. 1893–1899 Ubanu. *Kings:* 1899–1899 Isitoso. *Paramount Chiefs:* 1899–1 Dec. 1906 Sobhuza II. *Administrators:* 19 Feb.

1895–1902 T. Krogh; 1902–1 Dec. 1906 Enraght Mooney.

993 Swaziland (Self-Rule). 25 Apr. 1967–6 Sept. 1968. *Location:* as **Swaziland Kingdom.** *Capital:* Mbabane. *Other names:* Swaziland.

History: In 1967 **Swaziland [ii]** became self-governing and the kingdom (recognized by the British since 1961) was granted self-rule. In 1968 it became fully independent as The Kingdom of Swaziland, a member of the British Commonwealth (see **Swaziland Kingdom**).

Commissioners: 25 Apr. 1967–6 Sept. 1968 Sir Francis Loyd. *Ngwenyamas (Kings):* 25 Apr. 1967–6 Sept. 1968 Sobhuza II. *Prime Ministers:* 25 Apr. 1967–6 Sept. 1968 Makhosini Dhlamini.

994 Swedish Gold Coast Settlements. 22 Apr. 1650–20 Apr. 1663. *Location:* the coast of Ghana. *Capital:* Fort Frederiksborg.

History: In 1640 the Swedes arrived on the Gold Coast, and by 1650 had started a colony with bases at Butri and Carlsborg (later Cape Coast Castle). Later on Anamabo, Osu, Takoradi, Apollonia and Fort Frederiksborg (later Christiansborg) came under their control, but by 1663 their posts had all fallen to the Danes (see **Danish Gold Coast Settlements**).

Directors: 22 Apr. 1650–1656 Hendrik Carlof. *Governors:* 1656–Feb. 1658 J. Philippus von Krusenstierna. *Commanders:* (?)–20 Apr. 1663 Tonnies Voss.

995 Swellendam. 18 June 1795–Nov. 1795. *Location:* in the Bree River Valley, Cape of Good Hope Colony, South Africa. *Capital:* Swellendam (founded in 1743 and named for the Cape governor Hendrik Swellengrebel and his wife, née Damme).

History: In 1795, following the lead of **Graaff-Reinet,** the Cape Town–ruled administrative district of Swellendam revolted against the rule of the local landdrost (magistrate) and declared an independent colony, answerable to the Dutch government in Europe. Often referred to by historians as an independent republic, it submitted to the British when they took over the Cape in 1795, and was reincorporated into the Cape Colony (see **Cape of Good Hope Colony** and **British-Occupied Cape Colony [i]**).

National Commandants: 18 June 1795–Nov. 1795 Petrus Jacobus Delport. *Presidents of the National Assembly:* 18 June 1795–Nov. 1795 Hermanus Steyn.

Table Bay see **Cape of Good Hope Colony**

996 Tagant. ca. 1580–1905. *Location:* Mauritania. *Capital:* Tagant. *Other names:* Tagant Emirate, Emirate of Tagant.

History: Founded in the late 16th century, the Muslim dynasty of Idu Aysh, descendants of the Almoravids, created the Emirate of Tagant, which in 1905 was incorporated by the French into **Mauritania Civil Territory**.

Emirs: ca. 1580–ca. 1595 Ould Rizg; ca. 1595–ca. 1730 [unknown]; ca. 1730–ca. 1785 Sheikh Muhammad Shayin; ca. 1785–ca. 1820 Muhammad al-Bakr; ca. 1820–ca. 1831 Su'aidi Ahmad; ca. 1831–1836 Muhammad Sayin; 1836–1 Apr. 1905 Bakar; 1 Apr. 1905–1905 Uthman; 1905–Aug. 1918 not recognized as an emirate; Aug. 1918– Abdarrahman.

Tahart, Tahert see **Rustumid Emirate**

Tambookieland see **Tembuland**

Tanga see **Tangier** (which refers also to the main **Morocco** heading)

997 Tanganyika. 9 Dec. 1961–9 Dec. 1962. *Location:* as **German East Africa,** minus **Ruanda-Urundi**. *Capital:* Dar es-Salaam. *Other names:* Tanganyika Dominion, Dominion of Tanganyika.

History: In 1961 **Tanganyika (Self-Rule)** became independent as Tanganyika. The following year it became **Tanganyika Republic.**

Governors-General: 9 Dec. 1961–9 Dec. 1962 Sir Richard Turnbull. *Prime Ministers:* 9 Dec. 1961–22 Jan. 1962 Julius Nyerere; 22 Jan. 1962–9 Dec. 1962 Rashidi Kawawa. *Presidents:* 2 Nov. 1962–9 Dec. 1962 Julius Nyerere.

998 Tanganyika and Zanzibar United Republic. 26 Apr. 1964–29 Oct. 1964. *Location:* as **Tanzania**. *Capital:* Dar es-Salaam. *Other names:* The United Republic of Tanganyika and Zanzibar.

History: In 1964 **Tanganyika Republic** and **Zanzibar Republic** united. Later that year the name changed to **Tanzania**. Internal self-government was maintained for Zanzibar as part of the deal.

Presidents: 27 Apr. 1964–29 Oct. 1964 Julius Nyerere. *Presidents of Zanzibar:* 27 Apr. 1964–29 Oct. 1964 Abeid Amani Karume.

999 Tanganyika Mandate. 10 Jan. 1920–11 Dec. 1946. *Location:* as **Tanganyika**. *Capital:* Dar es-Salaam. *Other names:* Tanganyika (name invented by Sir Cosmo Parkinson).

History: In 1920 the League of Nations awarded **British-Occupied German East Africa** to Britain as a mandate. In 1946 it became **Tanganyika Territory.**

Administrators: 10 Jan. 1920–22 July 1920 Sir Horace Byatt. *Governors:* 22 July 1920–1924 Sir Horace Byatt; 1924–5 March 1925 John Scott (acting); 5 March 1925–1929 Sir Donald Cameron; 1929–1929 Douglas Jardine (acting); 1929–Jan. 1931 Sir Donald Cameron; Jan. 1931–1933 Sir Stewart Symes; 19 Feb. 1934–8 July 1938 Sir Harold MacMichael; 8 July 1938–19 June 1941 Sir Mark Young; 19 June 1941–28 Apr. 1945 Sir Wilfred Jackson; 28 Apr. 1945–11 Dec. 1946 Sir William Battershill.

1000 Tanganyika Republic. 9 Dec. 1962–26 Apr. 1964. *Location:* as **Tanganyika.** *Capital:* Dar es-Salaam. *Other names:* The Republic of Tanganyika.

History: In 1962 **Tanganyika** became a republic, and in 1964 it joined with **Zanzibar Republic** to form **Tanganyika and Zanzibar United Republic.**

Presidents: 9 Dec. 1962–26 Apr. 1964 Julius Nyerere.

1001 Tanganyika (Self-Rule). 1 May 1961–9 Dec. 1961. *Location:* as **Tanganyika.** *Capital:* Dar es-Salaam. *Other names:* Tanganyika.

History: In 1961 **Tanganyika Territory** was granted self-rule. Later in the year it became independent, as **Tanganyika.**

Governors-General: 1 May 1961–9 Dec. 1961 Sir Richard Turnbull. *Prime Ministers:* 1 May 1961–9 Dec. 1961 Julius Nyerere.

1002 Tanganyika Territory. 11 Dec. 1946–1 May 1961. *Location:* as **Tanganyika.** *Capital:* Dar es-Salaam. *Other names:* Tanganyika United Nations Trust Territory, Tanganyika U.N. Trusteeship.

History: In 1946 the **Tanganyika Mandate** became a United Nations Trust Territory. In 1961 it won self-rule (see **Tanganyika [Self-Rule]**).

Governors: 11 Dec. 1946–18 June 1949 Sir William Battershill; 18 June 1949–15 July 1958 Sir Edward Twining; 15 July 1958–1 May 1961 Sir Richard Turnbull. *Chief Ministers:* 2 Sept. 1960–1 May 1961 Julius Nyerere.

1003 Tangier Emirate. 1421–28 Aug. 1471. *Location:* Tangier, Morocco and environs. *Capital:* Tangier. *Other names:* Tanga, Tangier.

History: In 1421 the Merinid governor of Tangier (see **Merinid Kingdom**) became an independent emir. Until then Tangier had belonged to the Merinids. In 1471 the Portuguese took Tangier (see **Portuguese Tangier**).

Emirs: 1421–1437 Salih ibn Salih; 1437–28 Aug. 1471 Abu'l Hassan Ali al-Mandari.

1004 Tangier International Zone. 1923–29 Oct. 1956. *Location:* northern Morocco. *Capital:* Tangier. *Other names:* Tanger, Tangiers.

History: In 1923 the city of Tangier, until then an integral part of **French Morocco,** became an international zone, ruled over by an internationally elected administration representing Britain, Spain, France, Portugal, Italy, the Netherlands, Belgium, Sweden and (later) the U.S.A. Although prior to 1923 it had enjoyed a special status as a city, it was not until 1923 that the rule of the city became international. In 1956 it reverted to **Morocco (Independent Sultanate).** During World War II Spain took control of it.

Administrators: 1923–1926 unknown; 1926–1929 Paul Alberge; 1929–14 June 1940 Joseph Le Fur; 14 June 1940–3 Nov. 1940 [unknown]. *Spanish Military Commanders:* 3 Nov. 1940–1941 Col. José Yuste; 1941–18 Nov. 1942 Col. Uriarte; 18 Nov. 1942–Oct. 1945 Col. Pothous. *Administrators:* Oct. 1945–18 March 1948 Luis Correia; 18 March 1948–Aug. 1948 [unknown]; Aug. 1948–1951 H.L.F.C. Van Vredenbusch; 1951–Dec. 1954 José Archer; 4 Jan. 1955–29 Oct. 1956 Robert d'Hallebast. *Sultan's Representatives:* 1923–1941 al-Hajj Muhammad at-Tazi Bu Ashran; 1941–1945 vacant; 1945–1954 al-Hajj Muhammad at-Tazi Bu Ashran; 1954–8 July 1956 Si Ahmad at-Tazi.

1005 Tanzania. See these **names:**
Tanzania (1964–)
Tanganyika and Zanzibar United Republic (1964–1964)
Zanzibar Republic (1964–1964)
Zanzibar Independent Sultanate (1963–1964)
Zanzibar (Self-Rule) (1963–1963)
Zanzibar Protectorate (1890–1963)
Zanzibar Sultanate (1862–1890)

Zanzibar (Omani) (1698–1862)
Tanganyika Republic (1962–1964)
Tanganyika (1961–1962)
Tanganyika (Self-Rule) (1961–1961)
Tanganyika Territory (1946–1961)
Tanganyika Mandate (1920–1946)
British-Occupied German East
Africa (1916–1920)
German East Africa Protectorate [ii]
(1891–1918)
German East Africa Protectorate [i]
(1885–1891)
Zeng Empire (980–1515)
Karagwe (ca. 1450–1885)
Mirambo (ca. 1858–1895)

1006 Tanzania. 29 Oct. 1964– .
Location: East Africa. *Capital:* Dar es-
Salaam (not for long. Dodoma is ex-
pected to be the capital by 1990.) (Dar
es-Salaam means "haven of peace.").
Other names: United Republic of Tanzania, Jamhuriya na Muungano wa
Tanzania.
History: In October 1964 **Tanganyika and Zanzibar United Republic**
became the United Republic of Tanzania.
Presidents: 29 Oct. 1964–5 Nov. 1985
Julius Nyerere; 5 Nov. 1985– Ali Has-
san Mwinyi. *Presidents of Zanzibar:* 29
Oct. 1964–7 Apr. 1972 Abeid Amani
Karume; 12 Apr. 1972–27 Jan. 1984
Aboud Jumbe; 19 Apr. 1984–17 Oct.
1985 Ali Hassan Mwinyi; 17 Oct.
1985– Idris Abdul Wakil. *Prime Min-
isters:* 17 Feb. 1972–13 Feb. 1977 Rashidi Kawawa; 13 Feb. 1977–5 Nov.
1980 Edward M. Sokoine; 7 Nov. 1980–
24 Feb. 1983 Cleopa David Msuya; 24
Feb. 1983–12 Apr. 1984 Edward M.
Sokoine; 24 Apr. 1984–6 Nov. 1985
Salim Ahmed Salim; 6 Nov. 1985–
Joseph Warioba.

Tarabalus see **Tripoli** and **Tripolitania**

Tawanaland see **Batwanaland**

Tchad see **Chad**

Tekoror see **Tukolor**

1007 Tembuland. 1750–14 July 1885.
Location: Transkei, South Africa.
Capital: Umtata. *Other names:* Tam-
bookieland, Thembuland, Amathem-
buland.
History: A branch of the Southern
Nguni, the Tembu formed a kingdom
in 1750. In 1885 it went to Britain as
part of **British Cape Colony (Self-
Rule).**
Kings: ca. 1750–1800 Ndaba; 1800–
1830 Ngubencuka. *Regents:* 1830–1845
Fadana. *Kings:* 1845–1849 Mthikrakra.
Regents: 1849–1863 Joyi. *Kings:* 1863–
1884 Nyangelizwe; 1884–1920 Dalin-
dyebo. *Regents:* 1920–1924 Silimela.
Kings: 1924–1926 Jangilizwe (or
Sampu); 1926– Sabata.

Temne see **Koya-Temne**

1008 Tenerife [i]. 1495–1589. *Location:* Canary Islands. *Capital:* La
Laguna (founded 1496 and named for
the old [extinct] lagoon). *Other names:*
Teneriffe (origin of name uncertain:
possible "Tener" and "Yfe" meaning
"Snow Mountain").
History: In 1495 Tenerife was conquered by Spain, and became one of
the two most important of the Canary
Islands (see also **Gran Canária**). In 1496
the Governor of Tenerife became, for a
few years, the Governor-General of all
the Canaries, but as each island continued to function under its own governor, this system neither lasted long nor
worked dramatically well. However, in
1589, a Captain-General was appointed
to rule over all the Canaries, each
island thus becoming a territory (see
Canary Islands Captaincy-General).
(See also **Tenerife Territory [i]**).
Governors: 1495–1525 Alonso de
Lugo; 1525–1538 Pedro de Lugo; 1538–
1540 Alfonso Dávila; 1540–1543 Juan
Verdugo; 1543–1546 Jerónimo de Sotomayor; 1546–1548 Diego de Figueroa;
1548–1550 Juan Bautista de Ayora;
1550–1551 Duque de Estrada; 1551–1554

Juan de Miranda; 1554–1557 Juan de Cepeda; 1557–1558 [unknown]; 1558–1559 Hernando de Cañizares; 1559–1561 [unknown] (possibly the last name of "Plaza"); 1561–1562 Alfonso de Llarena; 1562–1565 Armenteros de Paz; 1565–1567 Juan de Guevara; 1567–1570 Eugenio de Salazar; 1570–1573 Juan del Campo; 1573–1577 Juan de Fonseca; 1577–1579 Juan de Leiva; 1579–1582 Juan de Fonseca; 1582–1584 Lázaro de León; 1584–1589 Juan de la Fuente.

1009 Tenerife [ii]. 1595–1625. *Location:* as **Tenerife [i].** *Capital:* La Laguna. *Other names:* Teneriffe.

History: In 1595, on the dissolution of the **Canary Islands Captaincy-General, Tenerife Territory [i]** became autonomous again (or rather it resumed its individual status as a colony). In 1625, however, the Captaincy-General was brought back, this time to stay (see **Canary Islands Captaincy-General [ii]**) and Tenerife became a territory once more (see **Tenerife Territory [ii]**).

Governors: 1595–1597 Tomás de Cangas; 1597–1601 Pedro de la Vega; 1601–1603 Luís Gudiel y Ortiz; 1603–1608 Francisco de Benavides; 1609–1615 Juan de Espinosa; 1615–1618 Melchor de Pereda; 1618–1621 Diego Bazán; 1621–1624 Rodrigo de Bohorques; 1624–1625 Diego Bracamonte.

1010 Tenerife Territory [i]. 1589–1595. *Location:* as **Tenerife [i].** *Capital:* La Laguna. *Other names:* Teneriffe.

History: In 1589, on the institution of the **Canary Islands Captaincy-General, Tenerife [i]** became a territory of that body. In 1595 it became **Tenerife [ii].**

Governors: 1589–1595 Tomás de Cangas.

1011 Tenerife Territory [ii]. 1625–1821. *Location:* Tenerife, Canary Islands. *Capital:* Santa Cruz de Tenerife. *Other names:* Tenerife.

History: In 1625, when the **Canary Islands Captaincy-General [ii]** was established over all the Canaries, **Tenerife [ii],** until then a colony in its own right (cf **Gran Canaria [ii]**), became a mere territory, subject to the Captain-General residing in Las Palmas on **Gran Canaria Territory [ii].** In 1821 it, and **Gran Canaria Territory [ii],** and all the other islands in the group, became part of **Canary Islands Province.**

Rulers: ruled by the Captain-General of Canary Islands Captaincy-General [ii].

Tenkodogo see **Mossi States**

Territory of the Afars and Issas see **Afars and Issas Territory**

Thembuland see **Tembuland**

1012 Timbuktu. 30 May 1591–1780. *Location:* Mali. *Capital:* Timbuktu. *Other names:* Tombouctou, Timbuctu, Timbuctoo.

History: Tin Buktu (Place of Buktu — an old woman), the most mysterious town in Africa. Founded by Tuaregs as a camp about 1100, it became the terminus of one of the major Trans-Saharan caravan routes, and between the 15th and 17th centuries a center of Islam in Africa. It became part of the **Ghana Empire,** the **Mali Empire, Yatenga** for a while in the 1300s, then the Tuaregs ruled it until November 29, 1468 when the **Songhai Empire** took it over. Timbuktu had always been more than just a town. It was a small state, with the city as the capital. Its fame spread to the rest of the world comparatively quickly (and not just because of the euphony of its name). By 1375 it was to be found on a Spanish map. Under the Songhais, Timbuktu reached its height, but in 1591 it was taken by the Moroccans, as was a lot of what is today Mali. Timbuktu became the capital of these marauding Moroccans, and was ruled by a Moroccan pasha who, more and more as the years went by, became

independent from his masters in Marrakesh. The decline of Timbuktu was
evident by 1780 when the Bambara
tribes made a second and more permanent conquest of the city. In 1800 the
Tuaregs took it over; 1813–1814 saw it
in the hands of **Masina:** 1814–1826 in
the hands of the Tuaregs once more;
then from 1826–1844 in the hands of
Masina again. From 1844–1862 the
Tuaregs regained control of Timbuktu,
the **Tukolor Empire** taking it from
them. In 1864 it fell to the Tuaregs for
the last time. In July 1893 it became
part of the French Empire (see **French
Sudan Military Territory**).

Pashas: 17 Aug. 1591–1594 Mahmud
I; 1594–1597 al-Mansur I; 1597–1599
Mahmud Taba II; 1599–1600 Ammar I;
1600–1604 Suleiman; 1604–11 Oct. 1612
Mahmud Longo III; 11 Oct. 1612–13
March 1617 Ali I; 13 March 1617–June
1618 Ahmad I; June 1618–Jan. 1619
Haddu; Jan. 1619–4 Nov. 1621 Muham-
mad I; 4 Nov. 1621–1622 Hammu I;
1622–1627 Yusuf I; 1627–1628 Ibrahim
I; 1628–July 1632 Ali II; July 1632–17
Oct. 1632 Ali III; 17 Oct. 1632–1634
Sa'ud I; 1634–1635 Abdarrahman I;
1635–1637 Sa'id I; 1637–1642 Masud;
1642–1646 Muhammad II; 1646–1647
Ahmad II; 1647–1647 Hamid; 1648–
1651 Yahya I; 1651–1654 Hammadi I;
1654–1654 Muhammad III; 1655–1657
Muhammad IV; 1657–1659 Muhammad V; 1659–1659 Allal; 1659–1660 al-
Hajj al-Mukhtar; 1660–1661 Hammu
II; 1661–1662 Ali IV; 1662–1662 Ali V;
1662–1665 Ammar II; 1665–1665
Muhammad VI; 1666–1666 Nasir I;
1666–1667 Abdarrahman II; 1667–1670
Nasir II; 1670–1670 Muhammad VII;
1671–1671 Muhammad VIII; 1672–1675
Ali VI; 1675–1678 Sa'id; 1678–1678 Abdallah I; 1679–1679 Dun-Nun I; 1680–
1680 Muhammad IX; 1681–1681 Dun-
Nun I; 1682–1682 Muhammad VIII;
1683–1683 Ba-Haddu Salim; 1683–1683
al-Fa Benkano; 1683–1683 Zenka;
1684–1684 Muhammad IX; 1684–1684
Ali VII; 1685–1685 al-Mubarrak I;
1686–1686 Sa'ud II; 1686–1686 al-Has-

san; 1687–1687 Abdallah II; 1688–1688
al-Abbas; 1688–1688 al-Mansur II;
1689–1689 Ahmad III; 1690–1690 Sa'ud
II; 1691–1691 Sanibar I; 1691–1693
Ibrahim II; 1693–1693 Baba Saiyid I;
1693–1693 al-Mubarrak I; 1693–1694
Ibrahim II; 1694–1694 Dun-Nun I;
1694–1694 Ahmad IV; 1694–1695 Sanibar I; 1695–1696 Abdallah III; 1696–
1696 Hammadi II; 1696–1697 al-Mubarrak II; 1697–1697 Muhammad X;
1697–1697 Ali VIII; 1697–1697 Yahya
II; 1697–1698 Abdallah IV; 1698–1699
al-Mansur II; 1699–1700 Hammadi II;
1700–1700 Abdallah IV; 1700–1701
Yusuf II; 1701–1701 Muhammad XI;
1702–1702 Ahmad V; 1702–1703 Ali IX;
1703–1703 Santa'a; 1703–1703 Mami I;
1703–1704 Muhammad XI; 1704–1704
Muhammad X; 1704–1705 Abdallah
IV; 1705–1705 Sa'id III; 1705–1706
Mami I; 1706–1706 al-Mubarrak III;
1706–1707 Nasir II; 1707–1707 Abdallah IV; 1707–1708 Ali X; 1708–1708
Muhammad XII; 1708–1709 Hammadi
III; 1709–1709 Yahya III; 1709–1710
Yahya IV; 1710–1711 Babakar I; 1711–
1711 Yusuf II; 1711–1712 Abdelkadir;
1712–1712 Abdallah IV; 1712–1712 Ali
IX; 1712–1713 al-Mansur III; 1713–1713
Mami I; 1713–1713 Ali X; 1713–1714 Abdallah V; 1714–1714 Ammar III;
1714–1714 Ba-Haddu II; 1714–1715 Abdallah V; 1715–1715 Ba-Haddu II;
1715–1716 Muhammad XII; 1716–1716
Ali XI; 1716–1716 Abdallah V; 1716–
1719 al-Mansur II; 1719–1721 Ba-Haddu
II; 1721–1722 Abdal Jaffar I; 1722–1725
Abdallah V; 1725–1726 Mahmud IV;
1726–1726 Abdarrahman III; 1726–
1727 Abdallah V; 1727–1729 Ba-Haddu
II; 1729–1729 Yusuf II; 1729–1731 Abdallah V; 1731–1732 Muhammad XIII;
1732–1733 al-Hassan II; 1733–1734
Muhammad XII; 1734–1735 Sa'id IV;
1735–1736 Hammadi IV; 1736–1737
Sa'id IV; 1737–1737 Hammadi IV;
1737–1738 Muhammad XII; 1738–1738
al-Fah Ibrahim III; 1738–1738 Hammadi V; 1738–1738 al-Fah Ibrahim IV;
1738–1739 Sa'id V; 1739–1740 Yahya V;
1740–1741 Baba Saiyid II; 1741–1741 al-

Hassan III; 1741–1742 Sa'id V; 1742–1743 Sa'id VI; 1743–1745 Sa'id V; 1745–1746 Baba Saiyid II; 1746–1748 al-Fah Mahmud; 1748–1748 Abdal Jaffar II; 1748–ca. 1749 Babakar II; ca. 1749–ca. 1750 Sa'id VI; ca. 1750–(?) Ali XII; (?)–(?) Ali XIII; (?)–(?) Ba-Haddu III; (?)–1780 Baba Ali.

Tlemcen, Tlemsen see **Abd-al-Wadid Kingdom**

Tocolor see **Tukolor**

1013 Togo. See these **names:**
Togo (1960–)
Togo Autonomous Republic (1956–1960)
Togo Associated Territory (1946–1956)
Togoland British Trust Territory (1946–1956)
Togoland British Mandated Territory (1923–1946)
Togoland French Mandate (1920–1946)
Togoland British Mandate (1920–1923)
French Togoland (1916–1920)
British Togoland (1916–1920)
Togoland French-British Condominium (1914–1916)
Togoland Colony (1905–1914)
Togoland Protectorate (1884–1905)
Little Popo French Protectorate (1883–1885)
Little Popo (ca. 1750–1883)

1014 Togo. 27 Apr. 1960– . *Location:* North West Africa. *Capital:* Lomé. *Other names:* Republic of Togo, République Togolaise, Togolese Republic.
History: In 1960 **Togo Autonomous Republic** became independent as Togo ("water's edge" in Ewe) Republic.
Heads of State: 27 Aug. 1960–12 Apr. 1961 Sylvanus Olimpio. *Presidents:* 12 Apr. 1961–13 Jan. 1963 Sylvanus Olimpio. *Chairmen:* 13 Jan. 1963–5 May 1963 Émanuel Bodjolle. *Presidents:* 16 Jan. 1963–5 May 1963

Nicolas Grunitzky (acting); 5 May 1963–13 Jan. 1967 Nicolas Grunitzky; 13 Jan. 1967–14 Apr. 1967 Kléber Dadjo; 14 Apr. 1967–18 Apr. 1967 Étienne Éyadema (Chairman of National Reconciliation Committee); 18 Apr. 1967– Étienne Éyadema (after May 1974 known as Gnassingbe Éyadema).

1015 Togo Associated Territory. 13 Dec. 1946–30 Aug. 1956. *Location:* as **Togo.** *Capital:* Lomé. *Other names:* Togoland Trust Territory, Togoland Trusteeship, Togoland French UN Trusteeship, Associated Territory of Togo, French Togoland, Togoland UN Trust Territory.
History: In 1946 **Togoland French Mandate** became a United Nations trusteeship in France's care. France called it the Associated Territory of Togo. In 1956 it was granted a large measure of self-rule (see **Togo Autonomous Republic**).
Commissioners: 13 Dec. 1946–8 March 1948 Jean Noutary; 8 March 1948–20 Sept. 1951 Jean Cédile; 20 Sept. 1951–25 Apr. 1952 Yves Digo; 25 Apr. 1952–3 Feb. 1955 Laurent Péchoux; 3 Feb. 1955–6 Aug. 1955 Jean-Louis Bérard (acting); 6 Aug. 1955–30 Aug. 1956 Jean-Louis Bérard.

1016 Togo Autonomous Republic. 30 Aug. 1956–27 Apr. 1960. *Location:* as **Togo.** *Capital:* Lomé. *Other names:* Autonomous Republic of Togo.
History: In 1956 **Togo Associated Territory** was given partial autonomy in preparation for its independence in 1960 as **Togo.**
Commissioners: 30 Aug. 1956–23 March 1957 Jean-Louis Bérard; 23 March 1957–June 1957 Joseph Rigal (acting). *High Commissioners:* June 1957–27 Apr. 1960 Georges-Léon Spénale. *Chief Ministers:* 12 Sept. 1956–27 Apr. 1958 Nicolas Grunitzky. *Prime Ministers:* 27 Apr. 1958–16 May 1958 Nicolas Grunitzky; 16 May 1958– 27 Apr. 1960 Sylvanus Olimpio.

1017 Togoland British Mandate. 30 Sept. 1920–11 Oct. 1923. *Location:* southeastern Ghana. *Capital:* Ho. *Other names:* Togo, West Togo, British Togoland.
History: In 1920 **British Togoland** became an official League of Nations mandate. In 1923 it was handed over to the **Gold Coast** to be administered from there (see **Togoland British Mandated Territory**).
Administrators: 30 Sept. 1920–11 Oct. 1923 Francis Jackson.

1018 Togoland British Mandated Territory. 11 Oct. 1923–13 Dec. 1946. *Location:* southeastern Ghana. *Capital:* Ho. *Other names:* Togo, West Togo, British Togoland.
History: In 1923 **Togoland British Mandate** became a territory of the **Gold Coast** and was ruled from Accra. In 1946 it became a United Nations Truth Territory, still administered by Britain from Accra in the Gold Coast (see **Togoland British Trust Territory**).
Rulers: 11 Oct. 1923–13 Dec. 1946 Ruled direct from Accra in the Gold Coast.

1019 Togoland British Trust Territory. 13 Dec. 1946–13 Dec. 1956. *Location:* southeast Ghana. *Capital:* Ho (founded in the early 18th century). *Other names:* Togo, British Togoland, West Togo.
History: In 1946 **Togoland British Mandated Territory** became a United Nations Trust territory, still ruled from Accra in the **Gold Coast**. In 1956 it became part of **Gold Coast (Self-Rule)**, which a few months later became the Dominion of Ghana (see **Ghana Dominion**).
Rulers: 13 Dec. 1946–13 Dec. 1956 Ruled direct from Accra in Gold Coast and Gold Coast (Self-Rule).

1020 Togoland Colony. 1 Jan. 1905–31 Aug. 1914. *Location:* as **Togoland Protectorate.** *Capital:* Lomé. *Other names:* German Togoland, Togoland, Togo.
History: In 1905 **Togoland Protectorate** became a colony of Germany. In 1914 Britain and France occupied it (see **Togoland French-British Condominium**).
Governors: 1 Jan. 1905–11 May 1905 Waldemar Horn; 11 May 1905–7 Nov. 1910 Julius Zech; 7 Nov. 1910–31 March 1911 vacant; 31 March 1911–19 June 1912 Edmund Brückner; 19 June 1912–31 Aug. 1914 Adolf Frederick, the Herzog of Mecklenburg.

1021 Togoland French-British Condominium. 31 Aug. 1914–27 Dec. 1916. *Location:* as **Togo** plus the Volta Region of **Ghana Republic.** *Capital:* Lomé. *Other names:* Togo.
History: In 1914 the Germans surrendered their **Togoland Colony** to the French and British forces, who set up a joint condominium until 1916 when they partitioned the country (see **British Togoland** and **French Togoland**).
Military Administrators: 31 Aug. 1914–27 Dec. 1916 Gaston Fourn.

1022 Togoland French Mandate. 30 Sept. 1920–13 Dec. 1946. *Location:* as **Togo.** *Capital:* Lomé. *Other names:* French Togoland, Togoland French League of Nations Mandate.
History: In 1920 **French Togoland** became an official League of Nations Mandate (cf **Togoland British Mandate**). In 1946 it became a United Nations Trusteeship (see **Togo Associated Territory**).
Governors: 30 Sept. 1920–1921 Alfred-Louis Woelfel. *Commissioners:* 1921–2 Jan. 1922 Alfred-Louis Woelfel; 2 Jan. 1922–22 Dec. 1922 Auguste Bonnecarrère (acting); 22 Dec. 1922–24 Apr. 1923 Auguste Bonnecarrère; 24 Apr. 1923–9 Oct. 1923 Léon Bauche (acting); 9 Oct. 1923–25 Feb. 1925 Auguste Bonnecarrère; 25 Feb. 1925–21 Nov. 1925 Léon Bauche (acting); 21 Nov. 1925–18 Sept. 1927 Auguste Bonnecarrère; 18 Sept. 1927–13 Jan. 1928 Bernard Sladous (acting); 13 Jan.

1928–Feb. 1929 Léon Pêtre (acting); Feb. 1929–28 May 1930 Auguste Bonnecarrère; 28 May 1930–Dec. 1930 Maurice Bourgine (acting); Dec. 1930–27 Dec. 1931 Auguste Bonnecarrère; 27 Dec. 1931–18 Oct. 1933 Robert de Guise; 18 Oct. 1933–7 May 1934 Léon Pêtre (acting); 7 May 1934–31 Dec. 1934 Maurice Bourgine. *Administrators:* 1 Jan. 1935–25 Sept. 1936 Léon Geismar; 25 Sept. 1936–1937 Michel Montagné. *Commissioners:* 1937–21 Sept. 1938 Michel Montagné (acting); 21 Sept. 1938–Apr. 1939 Marc Antoine Gradassi (acting); Apr. 1939–1 Jan. 1941 Michel Montagné; 1 Jan. 1941–28 Aug. 1941 Léonce Delpech (acting); 28 Aug. 1941–19 Nov. 1941 Léonce Delpech; 19 Nov. 1941–12 Apr. 1942 Jean-François de Saint-Alary (acting); 12 Apr. 1942–31 Aug. 1943 Pierre Saliceti; 31 Aug. 1943–10 Jan. 1944 Albert Mercadier (acting); 10 Jan. 1944–4 Nov. 1944 Jean Noutary (acting); 4 Nov. 1944–31 March 1945 Jean Noutary; 31 March 1945–July 1945 Henri-François Gaudillot (acting); July 1945–13 Dec. 1946 Jean Noutary.

1023 Togoland Protectorate. 5 July 1884–1 Jan. 1905. *Location:* as **French Togoland** and **British Togoland** combined. *Capital:* Lomé (1897–1905); Sebe (1887–97); Bagida (1884–87). *Other names:* Togoland, German Togoland.
History: The Germans arrived at the Togo coast in 1880, and in 1884 the Imperial flag went up to signify a protectorate. In 1905 this became a colony (see **Togoland Colony**).
Reichskommissars: 5 July 1884–6 July 1884 Gustav Nachtigal. *Provisional Consuls:* 6 July 1884–26 June 1885 Heinrich Randad. *Reichskommissars:* 26 June 1885–May 1887 Ernst Falkenthal; July 1887–17 Oct. 1888 Jesko von Puttkamer (acting); 17 Oct. 1888–14 June 1891 Eugen von Zimmerer; 14 June 1891–4 June 1892 vacant; 4 June 1892–1893 Jesko von Puttkamer. *Landeshauptmänner:* 1893–18

Nov. 1895 Jesko von Puttkamer; 18 Nov. 1895–1898 August Köhler. *Governors:* 1898–19 Jan. 1902 August Köhler; 20 Jan. 1902–1 Dec. 1902 vacant; 1 Dec. 1902–1 Jan. 1905 Waldemar Horn.

Tombouctou see **Timbuktu**

Toucouleur see **Tukolor**

1024 Transkei. 26 Oct. 1976– . *Location:* southeast **South Africa.** *Capital:* Umtata (founded in the 1870s and named for the Umtata River). *Other names:* Republic of Transkei, Iriphabliki Yetranskei.
History: In 1976 the Transkei ("beyond the Kei River") became the first Bantustan, or native homeland, in **South Africa** to gain its independence from the Republic of South Africa, although, like the other Bantustans, it is recognized by South Africa and the other native homelands alone. It is divided into three separate pieces of land, originally the basic areas of the Xhosa peoples, and it became self-governing in May 1963, with D. Potgieter as the South African Commissioner-General in charge until independence, and on December 11, 1963 Chief Kaiser Matanzima was elected Chief Minister, a post he held until October 26, 1976.
Presidents: 26 Oct. 1976–1 Dec. 1978 Botha Sigcau; 20 Feb. 1979–20 Feb. 1986 Chief Kaiser Matanzima; 20 Feb. 1986– Nyangelizwe Ndamase. *Prime Ministers:* 26 Oct. 1976–20 Feb. 1979 Chief Kaiser Matanzima; 20 Feb. 1979–24 Sept. 1987 George Matanzima; 24 Sept. 1987–5 Oct. 1987 Major-General Bantu Holomisa (military usurper); 5 Oct. 1987–30 Dec. 1987 Stella Sigcau; 30 Dec. 1987– Major-General Bantu Holomisa (head of military council).

Transkeian Territories see **Kaffraria Proper**

1025 Transorangia. 1824–3 Feb. 1848. *Location:* the southern part of today's Orange Free State Province of

South Africa, between the Orange and the Vet Rivers. *Capital:* Bloemfontein.

History: In 1824 independent Boer trekkers from the Cape (see **British Cape Colony**) began crossing the Orange River to settle here. In 1836 Great Trek Boers arrived and in 1845 Harry Smith established the first white rule, at Bloemfontein, in the form of a resident. In 1848, Smith, then Sir Harry Smith, finally annexed Transorangia and **Winburg** together as the **Orange River Sovereignty.**

Residents: Jan. 1846–3 Feb. 1848 Henry Warden.

1026 Transvaal Colony [i]. 12 Apr. 1877–16 Dec. 1880. *Location:* as modern-day Transvaal Province of **South Africa.** *Capital:* Pretoria. *Other names:* Transvaal.

History: In 1877 Britain annexed the **South African Republic [i]** and called it The Colony of Transvaal. In 1880 the Boers received permission for independence and for a short while the state became known as the **Heidelberg Republic.**

Administrators: 12 Apr. 1877–4 March 1879 Sir Theophilus Shepstone; 4 March 1879–16 Dec. 1880 Owen Lanyon (knighted 1880). *High Commissioners of South-East Africa:* 28 June 1879–29 Sept. 1879 Sir Garnet Wolseley. *Governors/High Commissioners of South-East Africa:* 29 Sept. 1879–16 Dec. 1880 Sir Garnet Wolseley.

1027 Transvaal Colony [ii]. 1 Sept. 1900–6 Dec. 1906. *Location:* as Transvaal Province, **South Africa.** *Capital:* Pretoria. *Other names:* Transvaal.

History: In 1900 Britain re-annexed the **South Africa Republic,** calling it once again The Colony of Transvaal. This became legal and official at the end of the South African War on May 31, 1902, and in 1906 it achieved self-rule (see **Transvaal Colony [Self-Rule]**).

Presidents: 1 Sept. 1900–31 May 1902 Schalk Burger (acting). *Governors:* 21 June 1902–29 Sept. 1902 Viscount

Milner; 29 Sept. 1902–3 Dec. 1905 Sir Arthur Lawley (acting); 4 Dec. 1905–2 Oct. 1906 Sir Richard Solomon (acting); 2 Oct. 1906–6 Dec. 1906 2nd Earl of Selborne.

1028 Transvaal Colony (Self-Rule). 6 Dec. 1906–30 May 1910. *Location:* as **Transvaal Colony [ii].** *Capital:* Pretoria (founded in 1855 and named for Andries Pretorius by his son, and originally called Pretoria Philadelphia). *Other names:* Transvaal.

History: In 1906 **Transvaal Colony [ii]** achieved self-rule. In 1910 it became Transvaal Province of the **Union of South Africa.**

Governors: 6 Dec. 1906–30 May 1910 2nd Earl of Selborne. *Prime Ministers:* 4 Feb. 1907–30 May 1910 Louis Botha.

1029 Transvaal State. 5 Apr. 1881–2 Feb. 1884. *Location:* Transvaal, South Africa. *Capital:* Pretoria.

History: In 1881 **South African Republic [ii]** became the Transvaal State. In 1884 it was renamed **South Africa Republic** (i.e. no "n" on the end of Africa).

Presidents: 5 Apr. 1881–16 Apr. 1883 A Triumvirate ruled, composed of Paul Kruger, Piet Joubert and Marthinus Pretorius; 16 Apr. 1883–8 May 1883 Paul Kruger (President-elect); 8 May 1883–Sept. 1883 Paul Kruger; Sept. 1883–2 Feb. 1884 Piet Joubert (acting).

1030 Trarza. ca. 1640–15 Dec. 1902. *Location:* Mauritania. *Capital:* Trarza.

History: The dynasty of Ulad Ahmad ibn Daman ruled the state of Trarza until it was taken over by the French in 1902 as a protectorate (see **Trarza Protectorate**).

Sultans: ca. 1640–ca. 1660 Ahmad ibn Daman; ca. 1660–1703 Addi I; 1703–1727 Ali Sandura; 1727–ca. 1758 Umar I; ca. 1758–(?) Mukhtar Ould Amar; (?)–(?) Muhammad Babana; (?)–(?) Addi II; (?)–(?) Mukhtar II; (?)–(?) Muhammad II; (?)–ca. 1800 Ali

Kuri; ca. 1800–(?) Aleit; (?)–(?) Umar Kumba II; (?)–(?) Muhammad III; (?)–(?) Mukhtar III; (?)–1833 Umar III; 1833–1860 Muhammad IV al-Habib; 1860–July 1871 Sidi Mbairika; July 1871–1873 Ahmad Salum; 1873–Oct. 1886 Sidi Ali Diombot; Oct. 1886–Dec. 1886 Sheikh Muhammad Fadl; Dec. 1886–1891 Umar Salum; 1891–1903 Ould Sidi Ahmad Salum; 1903–1903 Muhammad Salum Ould Brahim; 1903–1917 Sheikh Sa'd Bu (or Sidi Ould Deid); 1917–1932 Sheikh al-Khalifa (or Sidi Buya). *Viziers:* 1873–1898 Hayarum. *Note:* although there were other viziers, Hayarum is the only noteworthy one.

1031 Trarza Protectorate. 15 Dec. 1902–12 May 1903. *Location:* Mauritania. *Capital:* Saint Louis (Senegal).

History: In 1902 Coppolani, the French commandant, established a protectorate over **Trarza.** In 1903 it merged into **Mauritania Protectorate.**

Commandants: 15 Dec. 1902–12 May 1903 Xavier Coppolani.

1032 Tripoli (Banu Ammar). 1327–1401. *Location:* Tripolitania, Libya. *Capital:* Tripoli. *Other names:* Tripoli.

History: In 1327 the Banu Ammar Dynasty was founded in Tripoli with permission from the **Hafsid Kingdom** (see also **Hafsid Tripoli [i]**). In 1401 it was re-taken by the **Hafsid Kingdom** of Tunisia (see **Hafsid Tripoli [ii]**).

Sultans: 1327–1327 Thabit I ibn Ammar; 1327–1348 Muhammad; 1348–1355 Thabit II; 1355–1371 [unknown]; 1371–1392 Abu Bakr; 1392–1397 Ali ibn Ammar; 1397–1401 Yahya (joint); 1397–1401 Abdul Wahid (joint).

1033 Tripoli (Knights of Malta). 1530–14 Aug. 1551. *Location:* western Libya. *Capital:* Tripoli.

History: In 1530 the Grand Master of the Knights of Malta received from the Spanish (see **Tripoli [Spanish]**) the area of Tripolitania. It was governed for twenty-one years by one of the Grand

Master's representatives, and in 1551 was taken by the Ottoman Empire (see **Tripoli Ottoman Province [i]**).

Governors: 1530–ca. 1533 Gaspard de Sanguesse; ca. 1533–ca. 1538 Georg Schilling; ca. 1538–1542 Fernand de Brancamont; 1542–1551 Christopher de Solefertan; 1551–14 Aug. 1551 Fray Gaspar de Valier.

1034 Tripoli Ottoman Province [i]. 14 Aug. 1551–29 July 1711. *Location:* western Libya. *Capital:* Tripoli. *Other names:* Tripolitania, Tarabulus.

History: In 1551 the Turks conquered Tripoli from the Grand Masters of the Knights of Malta (see **Tripoli [Knights of Malta]**). In 1711 they awarded it to the Karamanli Dynasty (see **Karamanli Tripoli**).

Aghas: 14 Aug. 1551–1553 Murad. *Pashas:* 1553–1565 Dragut; 1565–1568 Eulj Ali (or Lucciali); 1569–1580 Jafar; 1580–1581 Murad; 1582–1584 Kaid Ramadan; 1584–1588 Mustafa; 1588–1595 Hussein; 1595–1600 Ibrahim; 1600–1606 Iskender; 1606–1607 Selim; 1607–1609 Ali; 1609–1609 Ahmad. *Deys:* 1610–1620 Suleiman; 1620–1631 Mustafa Sherif. *Pashas:* 1631–1631 Kasim. *Deys:* 1631–1631 Ramadan Agha; 1631–7 Nov. 1649 Mehmed Saqizli; 7 Nov. 1649–1672 Osman Saqizli; 1672–28 Nov. 1672 Osman Reis as-Suhali; 28 Nov. 1672–26 Apr. 1673 Bali Javush. *Pashas:* 26 Apr. 1673–1675 Arnavut Halil. *Deys:* 1675–May 1675 Mustafa Pehlevan; May 1675–3 Apr. 1676 Ibrahim Misirli-Oglu; 5 Apr. 1676–7 Apr. 1676 Ibrahim Jelebi; 7 Apr. 1676–4 Apr. 1677 Mustafa Kapudan; 4 Apr. 1677–27 Apr. 1678 Baba Osman. *Beys:* 27 Apr. 1678–9 Sept. 1679 Ak Mehmed. *Deys:* 9 Sept. 1679–11 June 1683 Hassan Abaza; 11 June 1683–13 June 1683 Yulk Mahmud; 13 June 1683–18 June 1684 Ali Jezairli; 18 June 1684–8 Feb. 1687 Hajji Abdallah Izmirli; May 1687–Nov. 1687 Ibrahim Terzi; Nov. 1687–19 May 1701 Mehmed Imam Kerdeki; 19 May 1701–11 Aug. 1701 Osman; 11 Aug. 1701–29 July 1702 Mustafa Galibuli;

29 July 1702–Oct. 1706 Mehmed Imam. *Pashas:* Oct. 1706–Nov. 1709 Halil. *Deys:* Nov. 1709–23 Nov. 1710 Ibrahim Alayali; 23 Nov. 1710–20 Jan. 1711 Ismail Hoja; 20 Jan. 1711–20 Jan. 1711 Hajji Rejeb; 20 Jan. 1711–4 July 1711 Mehmed Hussein Javush Bey; 4 July 1711–29 July 1711 Abu Umays Mahmud.

1035 Tripoli Ottoman Province [ii]. 26 May 1835–5 Nov. 1911. *Location:* western Libya. *Capital:* Tripoli. *Other names:* Tripolitania.

History: In 1835 the Karamanli dynasty came to an end (see **Karamanli Tripoli**) as the ruling house of Tripoli, and the Ottoman Empire resumed direct control, ruling through a governor (or Pasha). In 1911 the Italians conquered Libya and took Tripoli from the Turks (see **Tripolitania Protectorate**).

Pashas: 27 June 1835–7 Sept. 1835 Mustafa Negib; 7 Sept. 1835–Apr. 1837 Mehmed Reis; Apr. 1837–1838 Tahir; 1838–3 Aug. 1838 Hassan; 3 Aug. 1838–July 1842 Ali Asker; July 1842–Apr. 1847 Mehmed Emin; Apr. 1847–Oct. 1848 Ragib; Oct. 1848–1849 Hajji Ahmed Izzet; 1849–Oct. 1852 Mustafa Asim; Oct. 1852–1855 Mustafa Nuri; 1855–1858 Osman Nazhar; 1858–Aug. 1860 Ahmed Izzet; Aug. 1860–Apr. 1867 Mahmud Nedim Bey; Apr. 1867–July 1867 Hassan (acting); July 1867–May 1870 Ali Reza; May 1870–June 1870 Mustafa (acting); June 1870–Sept. 1871 Mehmed Halid; Sept. 1871–1872 Mehmed Rashid; 1872–6 June 1873 Ali Reza; 6 June 1873–1874 Samih; 1874–1875 Mustafa Asim; 1875–1876 Mustafa; 1876–1878 Mehmed Jelaleddin; 1878–1878 Savfet; 1878–July 1879 Sabri; July 1879–May 1880 Ahmed Izzet; May 1880–Oct. 1881 Mehmed Nazif; Oct. 1881–June 1896 Ahmed Rasim; June 1896–March 1899 Nemik Bey; March 1899–July 1900 Hashim Bey; July 1900–Dec. 1903 Hafiz Mehmed; Dec. 1903–May 1904 Hassan Husni (or Hussein Effendi); May 1904–Aug. 1904 Abderrahman Bey (acting);

Aug. 1904–1908 Rejeb; 1908–Aug. 1909 Ahmed Fawzi; Aug. 1909–Aug. 1910 Hassan Husni (or Hussein Effendi); Aug. 1910–5 Nov. 1911 Ibrahim.

1036 Tripoli (Spanish). 26 June 1510–1530. *Location:* western Libya. *Capital:* Tripoli. *Other names:* Tripolitania, Tarabalus.

History: In 1510 the Spanish in Sicily conquered Tripoli from the Hafsid Kingdom (see **Hafsid Tripoli [iii]**), which had ruled the area for almost 300 years. In 1530 the Spaniards handed Tripoli to the Knights of Malta (see **Tripoli [Knights of Malta]**).

Governors: 26 June 1510–1510 Pedro de Navarra; 1510–1511 Jayme de Requesens; 1511–1520 Guillem de Moncada; 1520–1530 [unknown].

1037 Tripolitania Colony. 17 May 1919–24 Jan. 1929. *Location:* western Libya. *Capital:* Tripoli.

History: In 1919 the Italians made their **Tripolitania Protectorate** into a colony. In 1929 they re-united it and **Cirenaica Colony** into **Libya**, a single possession.

Governors: 1 Aug. 1919–6 July 1920 Vittorio Menzinger; 6 July 1920–16 July 1921 Luigi Mercatelli; 16 July 1921–3 July 1925 Giuseppe Volpi di Misurata; 3 July 1925–1927 Emilio de Bono; 1927–1927 Ernesto Queirolo (acting); 1927–18 Dec. 1928 Emilio de Bono. *Emirs:* July 1922–1923 Idris al-Mahdi as-Sanusi.

1038 Tripolitania Protectorate. 5 Nov. 1911–17 May 1919. *Location:* western Libya. *Capital:* Tripoli. *Other names:* Tripoli Italian Protectorate.

History: In 1911 Italy took **Tripoli Ottoman Province,** and a year later had taken all of Libya (see **Cirenaica Protectorate** for further details). Tripolitania Protectorate was set up, and in 1919 it became **Tripolitania Colony.** From 1915–1919 the same governor ruled both protectorates.

Governors: 5 Nov. 1911–11 Oct. 1911

Raffaele Borea Ricci d'Olmo; 11 Oct. 1911–1912 Carlo Caneva; 1912–2 June 1913 Ottavio Ragni; 2 June 1913–1914 Vincenzo Garioni; 1914–1915 Luigi Druetti; 1915–1915 Giulio Cesare Tassoni; 1915–5 Aug. 1918 Giovan-Battista Ameglio; 5 Aug. 1918–17 May 1919 Vincenzo Garioni. *Ottoman Pashas Residing:* 5 Nov. 1911–1912 Bekir Samih Bey. *Ottoman Governors-General:* 1915–1917 Suleiman al-Baruni; 1917–1918 Nuri Bey; 1918–1918 Ishak Bey; 1918–1918 Osman Fuad Pasha.

1039 Tripolitania Roman Province. 297–442. *Location:* western Libya. *Capital:* Leptis Magna.
History: Created in 297 out of **Africa Roman Province [i]**, as were **Byzacena Roman Province** and **Africa Roman Province [ii]**. In 442 Tripolitania went to the Vandals (see **Vandal North Africa**).
Rulers: 297–442 [unknown].

1040 Tripolitanian Republic. 16 Nov. 1918–1923. *Location:* Tripolitania, Libya. *Capital:* Aziziyah. *Other names:* Jumhuriyya at-Tarabulusiyah, Republic of Tripolitania.
History: In 1918 local Libyans formed their own short-lived republic in Tripolitania. During 1923 it merged into the newly formed **Tripolitania Colony.**
Chairmen: 16 Nov. 1918–Nov. 1920 Suleiman al-Baruni; Nov. 1920–1923 Ahmad al-Muraiyid.

1041 Tristan d'Acunha. 1506–14 Aug. 1816. *Location:* as **Tristan da Cunha.** *Capital:* none. *Other names:* Tristão da Cunha.
History: Discovered in 1506 by Portuguese navigator Admiral Tristão da Cunha, the island group was claimed by Portugal. There were three unsuccessful attempts at colonization, two in the 1600s and one in 1810. In 1816 Britain took possession of the islands (see **Tristan da Cunha**).
Rulers: none.

1042 Tristan da Cunha. See these names:
Tristan da Cunha Dependency (1938–)
Tristan da Cunha (1816–1938)
Tristan d'Acunha (1506–1816)

1043 Tristan da Cunha. 14 Aug. 1816–1938. *Location:* South Atlantic Ocean, halfway between **South Africa** and South America. *Capital:* Edinburgh.
History: Three small islands, Tristan, Nightingale and Inaccessible, lying in the Southern Atlantic, became a British possession in 1816. Before that, as **Tristan d'Acunha** they had been a vaguely Portuguese possession, but it was the British garrisoning troops on the main island of Tristan who determined their ownership. The garrison was withdrawn in 1817 and one settler and his family remained. By 1886 there were 97 inhabitants. In 1938 the three islands, and their associated island, Gough Island, were made dependencies of **Saint Helena Colony** (see **Tristan da Cunha Dependency**).
Commandants: Nov. 1816–May 1817 Capt. Abraham Cloete.

1044 Tristan da Cunha Dependency. 1938– . *Location:* as **Tristan da Cunha.** *Capital:* Edinburgh. *Other names:* Tristan da Cunha.
History: In 1938 **Tristan da Cunha** became a dependency of **Saint Helena Colony.** On October 9, 1961 a volcano erupted on Tristan, the main island in the group, and the inhabitants were evacuated to Britain. They returned in November 1963.
Rulers: ruled from Saint Helena Colony.

1045 Tukolor Empire. 1854–1 Jan. 1891. *Location:* Mali. *Capital:* Bandiagara (from 1884); Timbuctu (until 1884). *Other names:* Empire of al-Hajj Umar, Toucouleur, Tocolor, Tekoror, Halphoolaren, Omar al-Hajj's Empire, Umar al-Hajj's Empire, Hajji Omar's

Empire, al-Hajji Umar Empire.

History: In 1854 Umar al-Hajj began his jihad (holy war), conquering the Bamabara states of **Segu** and **Kaarta,** and forming an empire. The Tukolor were (and are) a tribe of Fulbe-speaking Islamic peoples from the Senegal region, and this empire passed from father to son. In 1891 the French put the son to flight, captured the empire, and incorporated it into what became **French West Africa,** or to be more specific it became a section of **French Sudan Military Territory.**

Emperors: 1854–1864 Umar al-Hajj; 1864–1870 Mustafa; 1870–1872 Ahmadu; 1872–1873 Alamami (acting); 1873–1874 Muntaga; 1874–1 Jan. 1891 Ahmadu.

1046 Tulunid Egypt. 15 Sept. 868–10 Jan. 905. *Location:* Egypt. *Capital:* al-Qata'i (from 870); al-Fustat (868–70).

History: In 868 the Tulunids broke away from the Abbasid Caliphate in Baghdad (see **Abbasid Egypt [i]**), and formed an independent state of Egypt (and Syria). Ahmad ibn Tulun was a Turk who arrived in Egypt in 868 as vice-governor for the Abbasids, and immediately formed his own dynasty. His successors were weaklings, and in 905 the state came again under Abbasid control (see **Abbasid Egypt [ii]**).

Sultans: 15 Sept. 868–20 May 884 Ahmad ibn Tulun; 20 May 884–Jan. 896 Khumarawayh; Jan. 896–26 July 896 Jaysh; 26 July 896–30 Dec. 904 Harun; 30 Dec. 904–10 Jan. 905 Shayban.

1047 Tunis Pashalik. 13 Sept. 1574–9 July 1705. *Location:* Tunisia. *Capital:* Tunis. *Other names:* Tunis Regency, Tunis.

History: In 1574 Spanish forces left Tunis (see **Spanish Tunis [ii]**), and the North African state became a Turkish pashalik. The pasha was the head of government, and late in the 16th century the deys took power. In the 17th century the beys took over from the

deys. The Muradids were the real rulers during the 17th century, but in 1702 the agha of the spahis, Ibrahim, became bey and in 1704, dey and pasha. In 1705 Husain ibn Ali became bey, and began the Husainid dynasty in Tunis (see **Tunis Regency**).

Pashas: 13 Sept. 1574–1576 Sinan; 1576–1587 Kilik Ali. *Deys:* 1587–1590 Ibrahim Ruzili; 1590–1 Oct. 1610 Uthman; 1 Oct. 1610–Dec. 1637 Yusuf. *Beys:* 1612–1631 Murad; 1631–1659 Hammuda Pasha; 1659–19 Aug. 1675 Murad II; 19 Aug. 1675–1696 Muhammad; 1696–1699 Ramdan; 1699–1702 Murad III; 1702–1704 Ibrahim ash-Sharif. *Deys:* 1704–9 July 1705 Ibrahim.

1048 Tunis Regency. 9 July 1705–12 May 1881. *Location:* Tunis. *Capital:* Tunis. *Other names:* Husainid Tunis, Husaynid Tunis.

History: In 1705 the Muradid Beys of Tunis (see **Tunis Pashalik**) came to an end, and the Husainids succeeded, the country still being a dominion of the Ottoman Empire, but now being styled a regency. In 1881 the French took Algeria, and the bey continued to rule until Tunisia was made a republic (see **Tunisia Protectorate, Tunisia** and **Tunisia Republic**).

Beys: 9 July 1705–4 Sept. 1735 Husain I; 4 Sept. 1735–1756 Ali I; 1756–March 1759 Muhammad I; March 1759–26 May 1782 Ali II; 26 May 1782–15 Sept. 1814 Hammuda; 15 Sept. 1814–19 Dec. 1814 Uthman; 20 Dec. 1814–23 March 1824 Mahmud; 23 March 1824–1835 Husain II; 1835–10 Oct. 1837 Mustafa; 10 Oct. 1837–29 May 1855 Ahmad I; 29 May 1855–23 Sept. 1859 Muhammad II; 23 Sept. 1859–12 May 1881 Muhammad III as-Sadiq.

1049 Tunisia. See these **names:**
Tunisia Republic (1957–   )
Tunisia (1956–1957)
Arab Islamic Republic (1974–1974)
Tunisia Protectorate (1881–1956)
Tunis Regency (1705–1881)

Tunis Pashalik (1574–1705)
Spanish Tunis [ii] (1573–1574)
Turkish Tunis [ii] (1539–1573)
Spanish Tunis [i] (1535–1539)
Turkish Tunis [i] (1534–1535)
Hafsid Kingdom (1236–1534)
Almohad Tunis (1159–1236)
Banu Khurasan Tunis (1059–1159)
Zirid Kingdom (973–1159)
Fatimid North Africa (910–973)
Berber Tunisia (909–910)
Aghlabid Empire (800–909)
Omayyad North Africa (703–800)
Byzantine North Africa [iii] (697–703)
Arab North Africa [ii] (667–697)
Byzantine North Africa [ii] (649–667)
Arab North Africa [i] (647–649)
Byzantine North Africa [i] (534–647)
Vandal North Africa (430–534)
Africa (Roman Province) [ii] (297–439)
Africa (Roman Province [i] (29 B.C.–297 A.D.)
Africa Vetus (146 B.C.–29 B.C.)
Africa Proconsularis (320–442)
Byzacena Roman Province (297–442)
Carthage (ca. 550 B.C.–146 B.C.)

1050 Tunisia. 20 March 1956–25 July 1957. *Location:* North Africa. *Capital:* Tunis.
History: In 1956 **Tunisia Protectorate,** a long-time French possession, became independent, and the following year the **Tunisia Republic** was proclaimed.
Beys: 20 March 1956–25 July 1957 Muhammad VIII al-Amin. *Prime Ministers:* 20 March 1956–10 Apr. 1956 Tahar ibn Ammar; 10 Apr. 1956–25 July 1957 Habib Bourguiba.

1051 Tunisia Protectorate. 12 May 1881–20 March 1956. *Location:* as **Tunisia.** *Capital:* Tunis. *Other names:* Tunis, Tunisie.
History: In 1881 the **Tunis Regency** came to an end and French rule began.

By June 8, 1883 French control of the whole of what is today Tunisia was effected. On June 3, 1955 internal autonomy was granted to the Tunisians, and in 1956 full independence came (see **Tunisia**).
Residents-General: 13 May 1881–18 Feb. 1882 Théodore Rouston; 18 Feb. 1882–Nov. 1886 Paul Cambon; Nov. 1886–Nov. 1892 Justin Massicault; Nov. 1892–14 Nov. 1894 Maurice Rouvier; 14 Nov. 1894–Nov. 1900 René Millet; Nov. 1900–27 Dec. 1901 Benoît de Merkel (acting); 27 Dec. 1901–29 Dec. 1906 Eugène Pichon; 7 Feb. 1907–26 Oct. 1918 Gabriel Alapetite; 26 Oct. 1918–23 Nov. 1920 Pierre Flandin; Jan. 1921–18 Feb. 1929 Lucien Saint; 18 Feb. 1929–29 July 1933 François Manceron; 29 July 1933–21 March 1936 Marcel Peyrouton; 17 Apr. 1936–18 Oct. 1938 Armand Guillon; 22 Nov. 1938–3 June 1940 Eirik Labonne; 3 June 1940–22 July 1940 Marcel Peyrouton; 26 July 1940–10 May 1943 Jean-Pierre Estéva; 10 May 1943–22 Feb. 1947 Charles Mast; 22 Feb. 1947–13 June 1950 Jean Mons; 13 June 1950–Dec. 1951 Louis Périllier; 13 Jan. 1952–2 Sept. 1953 Jean de Hauteclocque; 2 Sept. 1953–5 Nov. 1954 Pierre Voizard; 5 Nov. 1954–13 Sept. 1955 Comte Boyer de la Tour du Moulin; 13 Sept. 1955–20 March 1956 Roger Seydoux Fornier de Clausonne.
Beys: 12 May 1881–28 Oct. 1882 Muhammad III as-Sadiq; 28 Oct. 1882–11 June 1902 Ali Muddat; 11 June 1902–11 May 1906 Muhammad IV al-Hadi; 11 May 1906–10 July 1922 Muhammad V an-Nasir; 10 July 1922–11 Feb. 1929 Muhammad VI al-Habib; 11 Feb. 1929–19 July 1942 Ahmad II; 19 July 1942–14 May 1943 Muhammad VII al-Muncif; 15 May 1943–20 March 1956 Muhammad VIII al-Amin. *Prime Ministers:* 1922–26 Oct. 1926 Si Mustafa Dingizli; 26 Oct. 1926–2 March 1932 Si Halil bu Hajib ibn Salim; 2 March 1932–Dec. 1942 Sidi Muhammad al-Hadi al-Ahwa; Jan. 1943–20 Aug. 1947 Salah Eddine ibn Muhammad Baccouche; 20 Aug. 1947–17 March 1950 Mustafa Kaak; 17

March 1950–28 March 1952 Muhammad Chenik; 28 March 1952–2 March 1954 Salah Eddine ibn Muhammad Baccouche; 2 March 1954–16 June 1954 Muhammad as-Salih; 6 July 1954–2 Aug. 1954 Georges Dupoizat (acting); 2 Aug. 1954–20 March 1956 Tahar ben Ammar.

1052 Tunisia Republic. 25 July 1957– . *Location:* North Africa, between Libya and Algeria. *Capital:* Tunis (founded about 1000 B.C., and origin of name is unknown). *Other names:* The Republic of Tunisia, al-Jumhuriyya at-Tunisiyah, Tuunis.

History: In 1957 **Tunisia** became a republic. In 1974, for a short while, it joined with the **Libyan Republic** to form the **Arab Islamic Republic.**

Presidents: 25 July 1957–18 March 1975 Habib Bourguiba; 18 March 1975–7 Nov. 1987 Habib Bourguiba (President for Life); 7 Nov. 1987– Zine Ben Ali. *Prime Ministers:* 6 Nov. 1969–2 Nov. 1970 Bahi Ladgham; 2 Nov. 1970–26 Feb. 1980 Hedi Nouira; 1 March 1980–23 Apr. 1980 Muhammad Mzali (acting); 23 Apr. 1980–8 July 1986 Muhammad Mzali; 8 July 1986–2 Oct. 1987 Rachid Sfar; 2 Oct. 1987–7 Nov. 1987 Zine Ben Ali; 7 Nov. 1987– Hedi Baccouche. *Note:* in times of no Prime Minister, the President held that office.

1053 Turkish Tunis [i]. 18 Aug. 1534–20 July 1535. *Location:* Tunis and parts of Tunisia. *Capital:* Tunis. *Other names:* Tunis.

History: In 1534 Khair ad-Din, the Turkish corsair also known as Red Beard or Barbarossa, conquered Tunis from the **Hafsid Kingdom** and deposed the Hafsid Dynasty (which continued as a dynasty in exile). Khair-ad-Din took most of what is today **Tunisia Republic.** The piracy of the new rulers of Tunis worried Europe and the Spaniards took Tunis the following year (see **Spanish Tunis**).

Beylerbeg (Bey of Beys): 18 Aug.

1534–20 July 1535 Khair ad-Din (or Barbarossa).

1054 Turkish Tunis [ii]. 1539–1573. *Location:* Tunisia. *Capital:* Tunis. *Other names:* Tunis (Turkish).

History: In 1539 the Turks recaptured Tunis (see **Spanish Tunis [i]**) and then in 1573 the Spaniards re-took it (see **Spanish Tunis [ii]**). During the first 30 years of Turkish Tunis [ii] the Hafsid sultan ruled as a vassal to Turkey.

Sultans: 1539–1542 Mulay al-Hassan; 1542–Dec. 1569 Ahmad (or Hamida); Dec. 1569–1573 direct Ottoman rule.

Twanaland see **Batwanaland**

1055 Twifo-Heman. 1480–1560. *Location:* as **Akwamu.** *Capital:* Aseremankese. *Other names:* Twifu-Heman.

History: In 1480 Agyen Kokobo founded the Akan state of Twifo-Heman. In 1560 it became the state of **Akwamu.**

Chiefs: 1480–1500 Agyen Kokobo; 1500–1520 Ofusu Kwabi; 1520–1540 Oduro; 1540–1560 Ado.

1056 Ubangi-Bomu Territory. 1893–13 July 1894. *Location:* Central African Republic. *Capital:* none.

History: The first territory carved out by the French in today's Central African Republic. In 1894 it began to be administered and was expanded as **Ubangi-Shari Colony [i].**

Rulers: unknown, if any.

1057 Ubangi-Shari-Chad Colony. 11 Feb. 1906–12 Apr. 1916. *Location:* present-day southern Chad and all of Central African Republic. *Capital:* Bangui. *Other names:* Oubangui-Chari-Tchad, Ubangi Shari and Chad Colony.

History: In 1906 **Ubangi-Shari Colony [i]** and **Chad Protectorate** joined to produce the greater colony of Ubangi-Shari-Chad, the two components becoming **Ubangi-Shari Territory** and **Chad Territory.** In 1916 the colony

came to an end, although the Lieutenant-Governor of the new **Ubangi-Shari Colony [ii]** continued to be responsible (through a Military Commandant) for the new **Chad**.
Lieutenant-Governors: 4 Apr. 1906–28 Feb. 1909 Émile Merwart; 28 Feb. 1909–5 Aug. 1910 Lucien Fourneau (acting); 5 Aug. 1910–10 June 1911 Paul Adam (acting); 10 June 1911–24 Nov. 1913 Frédéric Estèbe; 24 Nov. 1913–12 Apr. 1916 Pierre Adam.

1058 Ubangi-Shari Colony [i]. 13 July 1894–11 Feb. 1906. *Location:* as **Central African Republic.** *Capital:* Abiras. *Other names:* Oubangui-Chari, Upper Ubangi Protectorate.
History: In 1894 the French expanded from Gabon and the Congo into the forks of the two rivers, the Ubangi and the Shari, and created the colony of Ubangi-Shari (see also **Ubangi-Bomu Territory**). In 1906 the area became **Ubangi-Shari Territory** within **Ubangi-Shari-Chad Colony.**
Commissioners: 13 July 1894–20 Oct. 1894 Col. E. Décazes; 20 Oct. 1894–1897 Victor Liotard. *Lieutenant-Governors:* 1897–1899 Victor Liotard. *Commissioners:* 1900–May 1904 Adolphe Cureau. *Governors-Delegate:* May 1904–22 Aug. 1905 Alphonse Iaeck (acting); 22 Aug. 1905–11 Feb. 1906 Victor Emanuel Merlet (acting).

1059 Ubangi-Shari Colony [ii]. 12 Apr. 1916–30 June 1934. *Location:* as **Central African Republic.** *Capital:* Bangui. *Other names:* Ubangi-Shari, Oubangui-Chari.
History: In 1916 the greater colony of **Ubangi-Shari-Chad** broke up into the colonies of Ubangi-Shari and **Chad**. In 1934 **Ubangi-Shari Region** came into being, as it became part of **French Equatorial Africa Colony.**
Lieutenant-Governors: 12 Apr. 1916–12 Oct. 1916 Pierre Adam; 12 Oct. 1916–17 July 1917 Victor Emmanuel Merlet; 17 July 1917–16 May 1919 Auguste Lamblin (acting); 16 May

1919–31 Aug. 1920 Auguste Lamblin; 31 Aug. 1920–Dec. 1921 Henri Dirat (acting); Dec. 1921–17 Aug. 1923 Auguste Lamblin; 17 Aug. 1923–Nov. 1924 Pierre François (acting); Nov. 1924–1 July 1926 Auguste Lamblin; 1 July 1926–July 1928 Georges-David Prouteaux (acting); July 1928–22 Oct. 1929 Auguste Lamblin; 22 Oct. 1929–30 Oct. 1930 Georges-David Prouteaux (acting); 30 Oct. 1930–8 March 1933 Adolphe Deitte; 8 March 1933–Jan. 1934 Pierre Bonnefont (acting); Jan. 1934–30 June 1934 Adolphe Deitte.

1060 Ubangi-Shari Overseas Territory [i]. 31 Dec. 1937–13 Oct. 1946. *Location:* as **Central African Republic.** *Capital:* Bangui. *Other names:* Ubangi-Shari, Oubangui-Chari, Térritoire d'Oubangui-Chari.
History: In 1937 **Ubangi-Shari Region** became an overseas territory. In 1946 it continued as such, but of the Fourth Republic of France (see **Ubangi-Shari Territory [ii]**), and still part of **French Equatorial Africa Colony.**
Governors: 31 Dec. 1937–28 March 1939 Charles Max Masson de Saint-Félix; 28 March 1939–15 July 1941 Pierre de Saint-Mart (acting); 15 July 1941–30 May 1942 Pierre de Saint-Mart; 30 May 1942–30 July 1942 André Latrille; 30 July 1942–3 Apr. 1946 Henri Sautot; 3 Apr. 1946–24 May 1946 Jean Chalvet; 24 May 1946–13 Oct. 1946 Henri LaCour (acting).

1061 Ubangi-Shari Overseas Territory [ii]. 13 Oct. 1946–1 Dec. 1958. *Location:* as **Central African Republic.** *Capital:* Bangui. *Other names:* Ubangi-Shari, Oubangui-Chari.
History: In 1946 **Ubangi-Shari Overseas Territory [i]** became an overseas territory of the Fourth Republic of France. In 1958 it gained self-rule as the **Central African Republic (Autonomous)** upon the dissolution of **French Equatorial Africa Colony.**
Governors: 13 Oct. 1946–5 Apr. 1948 Jean Chalvet; 5 Apr. 1948–30 Nov.

1948 Jean Mauberna (acting); 1 Dec. 1948–27 Jan. 1949 Auguste Éven (acting); 27 Jan. 1949–4 Jan. 1950 Pierre Delteil; 4 Jan. 1950–10 March 1950 Auguste Éven (acting); 10 March 1950–9 July 1951 Ignace Colombani; 9 July 1951–19 Oct. 1951 Pierre Raynier (acting); 19 Oct. 1951–16 Feb. 1954 Louis Grimald; 16 Feb. 1954–29 Jan. 1958 Louis Sanmarco; 29 Jan. 1958–1 Dec. 1958 Paul Bordier.

1062 Ubangi-Shari Region. 30 June 1934–31 Dec. 1937. *Location:* as **Central African Republic.** *Capital:* Bangui. *Other names:* Ubangi-Shari, Oubangui-Chari.
History: In 1934 **Ubangi-Shari Colony [ii]** became a region of the greater colony of the A.E.F. (see **French Equatorial Africa Colony**). In 1937 it became **Ubangi-Shari Overseas Territory [i]**, still part of the A.E.F. Colony.
Lieutenant-Governors: 30 June 1934–17 Aug. 1934 Adolphe Deitte. *Governors-Delegate:* 17 Aug. 1934–21 May 1935 Adolphe Deitte; 21 May 1935–30 May 1935 Richard Brunot; 30 May 1935–Dec. 1935 Pierre Bonnefont (acting); Dec. 1935–24 Oct. 1936 Richard Brunot. *Governors:* 24 Oct. 1936–31 Dec. 1937 Charles-Max Masson de Saint-Félix.

1063 Ubangi-Shari Territory. 11 Feb. 1906–12 Apr. 1916. *Location:* as **Central African Republic.** *Capital:* Bangui. *Other names:* Oubangui-Chari, Ubangi-Shari.
History: In 1906 **Ubangi-Shari Colony [i]** became a territory within the greater colony of **Ubangi-Shari-Chad Colony,** the other component of this colony being **Chad Territory.** In 1916 Ubangi-Shari-Chad Colony dissolved and both territories became separate again (see **Chad** and **Ubangi-Shari Colony [ii]**).
Governors-Delegate: 11 Feb. 1906–16 Feb. 1906 Victor Emmanuel Merlet (acting); 16 Feb. 1906–4 Apr. 1906 Louis

Lamy. *Lieutenant-Governors:* 4 Apr. 1906–28 Feb. 1909 Émile Merwart; 28 Feb. 1909–5 Aug. 1910 Lucien Fourneau (acting); 5 Aug. 1910–10 June 1911 Paul Adam (acting); 10 June 1911–24 Nov. 1913 Frédéric Estèbe; 24 Nov. 1913–12 Apr. 1916 Pierre Adam.

Ubani see **Bonny**

1064 Uganda. See these **names:**
Uganda Republic (1967–)
Uganda Commonwealth (1963–1967)
Uganda Dominion (1962–1963)
Uganda (Self-Rule) (1962–1962)
Uganda Protectorate (1894–1962)
Uganda (1890–1894)
Buganda (1395–1890)
Bunyoro (ca. 1400–1896)
Nkore (ca. 1430–1896)

1065 Uganda. 26 Dec. 1890–18 June 1894. *Location:* central East Africa. *Capital:* Kampala. *Other names:* Buganda.
History: On December 18, 1890 Frederick Lugard occupied the area of Uganda for the British East Africa Company, and the following week a British Protectorate was declared over the local kingdom of **Buganda.** Done by international agreement, this marked the start of Britain's long involvement with Uganda. In 1894 the whole area became **Uganda Protectorate.**
Military Administrator: 26 Dec. 1890–17 March 1893 Capt. Frederick Lugard. *Commissioners:* 17 March 1893–30 May 1893 Sir Gerald Portal; 30 May 1893–4 Nov. 1893 Capt. MacDonald (acting); 4 Nov. 1893–10 May 1894 Henry Colville; 10 May 1894–18 June 1894 Frederick Jackson (acting).

1066 Uganda Commonwealth. 9 Oct. 1963–8 Sept. 1967. *Location:* as **Uganda Republic.** *Capital:* Kampala. *Other names:* Uganda, The Commonwealth of Uganda.
History: In 1963 the Dominion of Uganda (see **Uganda Dominion**) became the Commonwealth of Uganda.

On April 15, 1966 the country became a republic, but civil unrest prevented its ratification until 1967, when the country officially became **Uganda Republic**. *Presidents:* 9 Oct. 1963–2 March 1966 Sir Edward Mutesa II, King of Buganda; 2 March 1966–15 Apr. 1966 Milton Obote (acting); 15 Apr. 1966–8 Sept. 1967 Milton Obote. *Prime Ministers:* 9 Oct. 1963–2 March 1966 Milton Obote. *Note:* in times of no Prime Minister, the President held that office.

1067 Uganda Dominion. 9 Oct. 1962–9 Oct. 1963. *Location:* as **Uganda Republic**. *Capital:* Kampala. *Other names:* Uganda, The Dominion of Uganda.
History: In 1962 **Uganda (Self-Rule)** became totally independent within the British Commonwealth, as the Dominion of Uganda. In 1963 it became the Commonwealth of Uganda (see **Uganda Commonwealth**).
Governors-General: 9 Oct. 1962–9 Oct. 1963 Sir Walter Coutts. *Prime Ministers:* 9 Oct. 1962–9 Oct. 1963 Milton Obote.

1068 Uganda Protectorate. 18 June 1894–1 March 1962. *Location:* as **Uganda Republic**. *Capital:* Kampala (1958–62); Entebbe (1905–58) (founded in 1893); Kampala (1894–1905).
History: On April 11, 1894 **Uganda** was declared a British protectorate (in force from June 18). On June 30, 1896 **Bunyoro** came into the protectorate, and on July 3, 1896 so did Busoga. In 1962 Uganda won self-rule (see **Uganda [Self-Rule]**).
Commissioners: 18 June 1894–24 Aug. 1894 Frederick Jackson (acting); 24 Aug. 1894–1897 Ernest Berkeley; 1897–1897 Frederick Jackson (acting); 1897–July 1899 Ernest Berkeley; July 1899–Nov. 1901 Sir Harry Johnston; Nov. 1901–1905 James Sadler; 1905–18 Oct. 1907 Hesketh Bell. *Governors:* 18 Oct. 1907–31 Jan. 1910 Hesketh Bell (knighted 1908); 1 Feb. 1910–3 Apr. 1911

Harry Cordeaux (never took office); 3 Apr. 1911–10 Feb. 1918 Federick Jackson (knighted 1913); 10 Feb. 1918–15 Aug. 1922 Robert Coryndon (knighted 1919); 15 Aug. 1922–1924 Sir Geoffrey Archer; 1924–1924 John Sturrock (acting); 1924–18 May 1925 Sir Geoffrey Archer; 18 May 1925–23 Nov. 1932 William Gowers (knighted 1926); 23 Nov. 1932–17 Oct. 1935 Sir Bernard Bourdillon; 17 Oct. 1935–7 July 1940 Philip Mitchell (knighted 1937); 7 July 1940–31 Dec. 1944 Sir Charles Dundas; 1 Jan. 1945–17 Jan. 1952 Sir John Hall; 17 Jan. 1952–26 Feb. 1957 Sir Andrew Cohen; 26 Feb. 1957–19 Oct. 1961 Sir Frederick Crawford; 19 Oct. 1961–1 March 1962 Sir Walter Coutts. *Chief Ministers:* 2 July 1961–1 March 1962 Benedicte Kiwanuka.

1069 Uganda Republic. 8 Sept. 1967– . *Location:* central East Africa. *Capital:* Kampala (means "hill of the impala"; it was selected as the capital by Lugard in 1890). *Other names:* The Republic of Uganda, Uganda.
History: In 1967 **Uganda Commonwealth** became an official republic within the British Commonwealth, and the traditional kingdoms (i.e. **Buganda, Nkore** and **Bunyoro**) were abolished.
Presidents: 8 Sept. 1967–25 Jan. 1971 Milton Obote; 25 Jan. 1971–20 Feb. 1971 Idi Amin (Leader of Revolutionary Council); 20 Feb. 1971–25 June 1976 Idi Amin; 25 June 1976–11 Apr. 1979 Idi Amin (President for Life); 13 Apr. 1979–20 June 1979 Yusufu Lule; 20 June 1979–12 May 1980 Godfrey Binaisa; 18 May 1980–17 Sept. 1980 Paulo Muwanga (Chairman of the Military Commission); 17 Sept. 1980–27 July 1985 Milton Obote; 29 July 1985–27 Jan. 1986 Tito Okello (Chairman of Military Council); 29 Jan. 1986– Yoweri Museveni (Head of State and Chairman of the National Resistance Council). *Prime Ministers:* 13 Dec. 1980–27 July 1985 Erifasi Otema Allimadi; 1 Aug. 1985–25 Aug. 1985 Paulo Muwanga; 25 Aug. 1985–

30 Jan. 1986 Abraham Waligo; 30 Jan. 1986– Samson Kisekka.

1070 Uganda (Self-Rule). 1 March 1962–9 Oct. 1962. *Location:* as **Uganda Republic.** *Capital:* Kampala. *Other names:* Uganda.
History: In early 1962 **Uganda Protectorate** achieved self-rule. In October it became (too early?) independent as the Dominion of Uganda (see **Uganda Dominion**).
Governors-General: 1 March 1962–9 Oct. 1962 Sir Walter Coutts. *Prime Ministers:* 1 March 1962–25 Apr. 1962 Benedicte Kiwanuka; 25 Apr. 1962–9 Oct. 1962 Milton Obote.

Umar al-Hajj's Empire see **Tukolor Empire**

Umayyad see **Omayyad**

1071 Union of South Africa. 31 May 1910–11 Dec. 1931. *Location:* as **South Africa.** *Capital:* Cape Town (legislative); Pretoria (administrative). *Other names:* South Africa, Dominion of South Africa.
History: In 1910 the colonies of Transvaal, Orange River Colony, Natal and Cape Colony (see **Transvaal Colony [Self-Rule], Orange River Colony [Self-Rule], Natal Colony [Self-Rule],** and **British Cape Colony [Self-Rule]**) were united to form the Union of South Africa, ruled over by a British-appointed Governor-General and a South African Prime Minister and Government. On July 1, 1910 it became a dominion of the British Empire and in 1931 a fully self-governing dominion (see **Union of South Africa [Self-Rule]**).
Governors-General/High Commissioners: 31 May 1910–17 July 1912 Viscount Gladstone; 17 July 1912–11 Nov. 1912 Sir Reginald Harte (acting HC); 17 July 1912–11 Nov. 1912 Lord de Villiers (acting GG); 11 Nov. 1912–11 July 1914 Viscount Gladstone; 11 July 1914–8 Sept. 1914 Sir James Murray (acting HC); 11 July 1914–2 Sept. 1914 Lord de Villiers (acting GG); 8 Sept. 1914–17 July 1920 Viscount Buxton; 17 July 1920–20 Nov. 1920 Sir James Rose-Innes (acting GG); 3 Sept. 1920–20 Nov. 1920 Beresford Carter (acting HC); 20 Nov. 1920–5 Dec. 1923 Prince Arthur of Connaught; 5 Dec. 1923–21 Jan. 1924 Sir James Rose-Innes (acting GG); 10 Dec. 1923–21 Jan. 1924 Sir Rudolph Bentinck (acting HC); 21 Jan. 1924–21 Dec. 1930 Earl of Athlone. *Governors-General:* 21 Dec. 1930–26 Jan. 1931 Jacob de Villiers (acting); 26 Jan. 1931–11 Dec. 1931 Earl of Clarendon. *High Commissioners:* 6 Apr. 1931–11 Dec. 1931 Sir Herbert Stanley. *Prime Ministers:* 15 Sept. 1910–1918 Louis Botha; 1918–1919 François Malan; 1919–27 Aug. 1919 Louis Botha; 3 Sept. 1919–23 June 1924 Jan Smuts; 30 June 1924–11 Dec. 1931 James (J.B.M.) Hertzog.

1072 Union of South Africa (Self-Rule). 11 Dec. 1931–30 May 1961. *Location:* South Africa. *Capital:* Cape Town (legislative); Pretoria (administrative). *Other names:* South Africa.
History: In 1931 the **Union of South Africa** became independent of Great Britain. The British Governor-General and High Commissioner remained until 1961, when connections with Britain were severed and the country became a republic (see **South Africa**).
Prime Ministers: 11 Dec. 1931–5 Sept. 1939 James (J.B.M.) Hertzog; 5 Sept. 1939–26 May 1948 Jan Smuts; 3 June 1948–29 Oct. 1954 Daniel Malan; 29 Oct. 1954–30 Nov. 1954 Nicolaas C. Havenga (acting); 2 Dec. 1954–24 Aug. 1958 Johannes Strijdom; 3 Sept. 1958–30 May 1961 Hendrik Verwoerd. *Presidents:* 18 May 1961–30 May 1961 Charles Swart. *Governors-General:* 11 Dec. 1931–17 March 1937 Earl of Clarendon; 17 March 1937–5 Apr. 1937 John Curlewis (acting); 5 Apr. 1937–28 Aug. 1943 Sir Patrick Duncan; 28 Aug. 1943–31 Dec. 1945 Nicolaas de Wet (acting); 31 Dec. 1945–20 Sept. 1950 Brand Van Zyl; 1 Jan. 1951–25 Nov. 1959 Ernest

Jansen; 12 Jan. 1960–18 May 1961 Charles Swart. *Officer Administering:* 18 May 1961–30 May 1961 L.C. Steyn. *High Commissioners:* 11 Dec. 1931–1 Aug. 1933 Sir Herbert Stanley; 1 Aug. 1933–1 Dec. 1933 Edward Evans (acting); 1 Dec. 1933–6 Jan. 1935 Sir Herbert Stanley; 7 Jan. 1935–3 Jan. 1940 Sir William Clark; 3 Jan. 1940–24 May 1941 Sir Walter Huggard (acting); 24 May 1941–13 May 1944 Lord Harlech; 13 May 1944–23 June 1944 Harold Priestman (acting); 23 June 1944–27 Oct. 1944 Sir Walter Huggard; 27 Oct. 1944–1 Oct. 1951 Sir Evelyn Baring; 2 Oct. 1951–2 Feb. 1955 Sir John le Rougelet; 4 March 1955–Dec. 1958 Sir Percivale Liesching; 15 Jan. 1959–30 May 1961 Sir John Maud.

1073 United Arab Republic. 1 Feb. 1958–2 Sept. 1971. *Location:* as **Arab Republic of Egypt.** *Capital:* Cairo. *Other names:* U.A.R., Egypt.

History: In 1958 the **Republic of Egypt** and Syria united politically as the U.A.R., and Egypt and Yemen formed the United Arab States (dissolved in 1961). In 1961 Syria withdrew from the U.A.R., but Egypt kept the name until 1971 when Sadat changed it to the **Arab Republic of Egypt.** In 1967, during the Six-Day war with Israel, Egypt lost Sinai, not to regain it until 1979.

Presidents: 1 Feb. 1958–28 Sept. 1970 Gamal Abdel Nasser; 29 Sept. 1970–15 Oct. 1970 Muhammad Anwar as-Sadat (interim); 15 Oct. 1970–2 Sept. 1971 Muhammad Anwar as-Sadat. *Prime Ministers:* 24 Sept. 1962–29 Sept. 1965 Ali Sabry; 29 Sept. 1965–10 Sept. 1966 Zahariah Mohieddin; 10 Sept. 1966–19 June 1967 Sidqi Suleiman; 20 June 1970–2 Sept. 1971 Mahmoud Fawzi. *Note:* in times of no Prime Minister, the President held that office.

1074 United States of Stellaland. 7 Aug. 1883–30 Sept. 1885. *Location:* **Stellaland** and **Goshen** combined. *Capital:* Vrijburg. *Other names:* Het Land Goosen, Stellaland, Bechuanaland Republic, Republic of Bechuanaland.

History: The combination of the two Boer republics, **Stellaland** and **Goshen,** both on Korannaland, which straddled the "Missionary Road" to the interior of Africa, led to both **Transvaal State** (after 1884 called **South Africa Republic**) and **British Cape Colony (Self-Rule)** claiming them. The London Convention split the United States of Stellaland down the middle, Britain winning control of the road. Britain had formed **Bechuanaland Protectorate [i]** earlier in the same year, under which the western part of the United States of Stellaland fell, and the **South Africa Republic** got the rest. This was all finalized by Sept. 1885, when it merged into other areas (notably **Bechuanaland Protectorate [ii]**) in this rapid process typical of the time and place.

Administrators: 7 Aug. 1883–30 Sept. 1885 Gerrit Van Niekerk.

Unyamwezi see **Mirambo**

Unyoro see **Bunyoro**

1075 Upingtonia. 20 Oct. 1885–1886. *Location:* as **Lijdenrust.** *Capital:* Grootfontein.

History: A Boer republic founded in 1885 by 46 Thirstland trekkers and named for Sir Thomas Upington, the Prime Minister of the Cape, in the hope that **British Cape Colony (Self-Rule)** would support the fledgling republic. It didn't, so in 1886 Upingtonia accepted Bismarck's offer of German protection and was renamed **Lijdenrust.**

Presidents: 20 Oct. 1885–1886 G.D.P. Prinsloo.

1076 Upper Egypt. ca. 5000 B.C.–ca. 3100 B.C. *Location:* the part of current Egypt south of Cairo, but not as far south as Lake Aswan. *Capital:* Nekhen (ca. 3400 B.C.–ca. 3100 B.C.) (later called Hierakonpolis); Naqadah (ca. 5000 B.C.–ca. 3400 B.C.). *Other names:* Southern Egypt.

History: Around 3100 B.C. King

Menes of Upper Egypt united his country with **Lower Egypt,** to form **Egypt, 1st Dynasty.**
Kings: ca. 4500 B.C. Merimde; ca. 4000 B.C. Badari; ca. 3700 B.C. Amra; ca. 3200 B.C. Girza; ca. 3150-ca. 3100 B.C. Menes (or Narmer, Meni or Min).

1077 Upper Ivory Coast. 1 Jan. 1938-4 Sept. 1947. *Location:* southern **Burkina Faso.** *Capital:* Ouagadougou.
History: In 1938 the part of **Upper Volta Colony** which went to the **Ivory Coast Protectorate** in 1932 was constituted a single administrative district, although it had been referred to as Upper Ivory Coast since 1932. In 1947 it was dismantled and placed back into the **Upper Volta Overseas Territory.**
Rulers: 1 Jan. 1938-29 July 1940 Edmond Louveau (Résident-Supérieur); 29 July 1940-13 Oct. 1946 ruled directly by the Ivory Coast Colony; 13 Oct. 1946-4 Sept. 1947 ruled directly by Ivory Coast Overseas Territory.

Upper River see **Upper Senegal**

1078 Upper Senegal and Niger Colony. 18 Oct. 1904-4 Dec. 1920. *Location:* as **Mali Republic.** *Capital:* Bamako (1908-20); Kayès (1904-08). *Other names:* Upper Senegal-Niger, Haut-Sénégal-Niger.
History: In 1904 **Senegambia and Niger Territories** became the Colony of Upper Senegal and Niger, thus ending five years of being subject to Senegal (see **Senegal Colony**). In 1920 it became **French Sudan.**
Lieutenant-Governors: 18 Oct. 1904-1 Sept. 1906 Amédée Merlaud-Ponty; 1 Sept. 1906-1 Jan. 1907 Jean Peuvergne (acting); 1 Jan. 1907-28 Aug. 1907 Amédée Merlaud-Ponty; 28 Aug. 1907-1908 Jean Peuvergne; May 1909-17 Dec. 1909 Joseph Clozel; 17 Dec. 1909-14 Aug. 1910 Henri Lejeune (acting); 14 Aug. 1910-13 Jan. 1912 Joseph Clozel; 13 Jan. 1912-Aug. 1912 Philippe Henry (acting); Aug. 1912-12 Dec. 1912 Joseph Clozel; 12 Dec. 1912-Aug. 1913

Philippe Henry (acting); Aug. 1913-16 June 1915 Joseph Clozel; 16 June 1915-1 July 1915 Philippe Henry (acting); 1 July 1915-28 July 1916 Louis Thiébaud (acting); 28 July 1916-20 Apr. 1917 Raphaël Antonetti; 20 Apr. 1917-21 May 1917 Albert Nébout (acting); 21 May 1917-20 Feb. 1918 Louis Periquet (acting); 20 Feb. 1918-20 Aug. 1919 Auguste Brunet; 20 Aug. 1919-March 1920 Marcel Olivier; March 1920-10 Aug. 1920 Jean Terasson de Fougères (acting); 10 Aug. 1920-4 Dec. 1920 Théodore Maillet (acting).

1079 Upper Senegal and Niger Territory. 17 Oct. 1899-1 Oct. 1902. *Location:* as **Mali Republic.** *Capital:* Kayès. *Other names:* Upper Senegal-Middle Niger, Haut-Sénégal-Niger, Upper Senegal-Middle Niger Territories.
History: In 1899 **French Sudan Colony** became subject to Senegal (see **Senegal Colony**), as a territory, named Upper Senegal-Niger. In 1902 it became **Senegambia and Niger Territories.**
Delegates: 17 Oct. 1899-1 Oct. 1902 Amédée Merlaud-Ponty.

1080 Upper Senegal Protectorate. 21 March 1881-18 Aug. 1890. *Location:* as **Mali Republic,** but not as extensive. *Capital:* Kayès. *Other names:* Upper River Protectorate, Upper River.
History: In 1881 **Upper Senegal Territory** became a protectorate of the French government. In 1890 it became **French Sudan Territory.**
Commandants-Superior: 21 March 1881-3 Sept. 1883 Gustave Borgnis-Desbordes; 3 Sept. 1883-18 June 1884 Charles Boilève; 18 June 1884-4 Sept. 1884 Antoine Combes (acting); 4 Sept. 1884-Sept. 1885 Antoine Combes; Sept. 1885-Aug. 1886 Henri Frey; Aug. 1886-28 Oct. 1888 Joseph Galliéni; 28 Oct. 1888-18 Aug. 1890 Louis Archinard.

1081 Upper Senegal Territory. 6 Sept. 1880-21 March 1881. *Location:* as **Mali Republic,** but not as extensive.

Capital: Kayès. *Other names:* Upper River Territory, Upper River.

History: In 1880 a commandant-supérieur was appointed by the French government to look after French interests in the area of what is today Mali. The area had been opened up by Louis Faidherbe, the great administrator of Senegal from the 1850s. In 1881 the Territory of Upper Senegal became **Upper Senegal Protectorate**.

Commandants-Superior: 6 Sept. 1880–21 March 1881 Gustave Borgnis-Desbordes.

Upper Ubangi Protectorate see **Ubangi-Shari Colony [i]**

1082 Upper Volta Autonomous Republic. 11 Dec. 1958–5 Aug. 1960. *Location:* as **Burkina Faso**. *Capital:* Ouagadougou. *Other names:* Haute Volta, Voltaic Republic, Autonomous Republic of Upper Volta.

History: In 1958 France granted autonomy within the French Community to **Upper Volta Overseas Territory**. In 1960 it became fully independent as **Upper Volta Republic**.

High Commissioners: 11 Dec. 1958–Feb. 1959 Max Berthet; Feb. 1959–5 Aug. 1960 Paul Masson. *Prime Ministers:* 11 Dec. 1958–11 Dec. 1959 Maurice Yaméogo. *Presidents:* 11 Dec. 1959–5 Aug. 1960 Maurice Yaméogo.

1083 Upper Volta Colony. 1 March 1919–1 Jan. 1933. *Location:* as **Burkina Faso**. *Capital:* Ouagadougou. *Other names:* Haute Volta, Upper Volta.

History: In 1919 a chunk of **Upper Senegal and Niger Colony** was carved out and called the Colony of Upper Volta, and consisted of the areas Bobo Dioulasso, Ouagadougou (Wagadugu), Gurma (Fada N'Gourma), Say, Ouahigouya, Dedougou, Gaoua and Dori. Later in 1919 a Governor was appointed and on September 5, 1932 the Colony was dismembered (to take effect on January 1, 1933), being split up between **French Sudan** (which got

Ouahigouya and parts of Dori and Dedougou), **Niger Colony** (which got Fada [formerly Gurma, or Fada N'Gourma] and the other part of Dori) and **Ivory Coast Protectorate** (which got the rest in a lump called **Upper Ivory Coast** or Haute Côte d'Ivoire). In 1947 **Upper Volta Overseas Territory** came into being.

Lieutenant-Governors: 9 Nov. 1919–6 Aug. 1921 Édouard Hesling (appointed 16 May 1919); 6 Aug. 1921–26 May 1922 Louis Fousset (acting); 26 May 1922–9 May 1924 Édouard Hesling; 9 May 1924–10 Dec. 1924 Louis Fousset (acting); 10 Dec. 1924–May 1926 Édouard Hesling; May 1926–Nov. 1926 Louis Fousset (acting); Nov. 1926–7 Aug. 1927 Édouard Hesling; 7 Aug. 1927–13 Jan. 1928 Robert Arnaud (acting); 13 Jan. 1928–10 Jan. 1929 Albéric Fournier; 10 Jan. 1929–1 Dec. 1929 Louis Fousset (acting); 1 Dec. 1929–20 Jan. 1930 Henri Chessé (acting); 20 Jan. 1930–1 Aug. 1930 Albéric Fournier; 1 Aug. 1930–20 Jan. 1931 François Bernard (acting); 20 Jan. 1931–22 Dec. 1932 Albéric Fournier; 22 Dec. 1932–31 Dec. 1932 Gabriel Descemet. *Administrators:* 31 Dec. 1932–1 Jan. 1933 Henri Chessé.

1084 Upper Volta Overseas Territory. 4 Sept. 1947–11 Dec. 1958. *Location:* as **Burkina Faso**. *Capital:* Ouagadougou (founded about 1050 as a native capital). *Other names:* Haute Volta, Upper Volta.

History: In 1947 the old colony of Upper Volta (see **Upper Volta Colony**) was re-established as the Overseas Territory of Upper Volta. In 1958 it became **Upper Volta Autonomous Republic**.

Administrators: 4 Sept. 1947–29 Apr. 1948 Gaston Mourgues (acting). *Governors:* 29 Apr. 1948–22 March 1950 Albert Mouragues; 22 March 1950–Oct. 1950 Lucien Geay (acting); Oct. 1950–25 Apr. 1952 Albert Mouragues; 25 Apr. 1952–Oct. 1952 Roland Pré (acting); Oct. 1952–23 Feb. 1953

Albert Mouragues; 23 Feb. 1953–3 Nov. 1956 Salvador-Jean Etcheber; 3 Nov. 1956–15 July 1958 Yvon Bourges; 15 July 1958–11 Dec. 1958 Max Berthet (acting). *Prime Ministers:* 27 Apr. 1958–11 Dec. 1958 Maurice Yaméogo.

1085 Upper Volta Protectorate. 20 Feb. 1895–1 March 1919. *Location:* as **Burkina Faso.** *Capital:* Ouagadougou. *Other names:* Haute-Volta.
History: In 1895 the French placed a protectorate over the Volta region. It was ruled by the military until 1904 when it was administered by **Senegambia and Niger Territories** which became **Upper Senegal and Niger Colony.** In 1919 Upper Volta became a colony (see **Upper Volta Colony**).
Commandants: 20 Feb. 1895–June 1898 Georges Destenave; June 1898–18 Oct. 1904 Col. Crane; 18 Oct. 1904–1 March 1919 see rulers of Senegambia and Niger Territories & Upper Senegal and Niger Colony.

1086 Upper Volta Republic. 5 Aug. 1960–4 Aug. 1984. *Location:* as **Burkina Faso.** *Capital:* Ouagadougou. *Other names:* Haute-Volta, République du Haute-Volta, Republic of Upper Volta, Voltaic Republic.
History: In 1960 **Upper Volta Autonomous Republic** became truly independent. In 1984 it changed its name to **Burkina Faso.**
Presidents: 8 Dec. 1960–3 Jan. 1966 Maurice Yaméogo; 3 Jan. 1966–13 Feb. 1971 Sangoulé Lamizama (Chief of State); 13 Feb. 1971–25 Nov. 1980 Sangoulé Lamizama; 25 Nov. 1980–7 Nov. 1982 Saye Zerbo (Head of the Military Committee of Recovery); 7 Nov. 1982–4 Aug. 1983 Jean-Baptiste Ouedraogo (Chairman of the Provisional Committee of Popular Salvation); 4 Aug. 1983–4 Aug. 1984 Thomas Sankara (Chairman of National Revolutionary Council). *Prime Ministers:* 5 Aug. 1960–8 Dec. 1960 Maurice Yaméogo; 16 July 1978–25 Nov. 1980 Joseph Conombo; 10 Jan. 1983–17 May 1983

Thomas Sankara. *Note:* in times of no Prime Minister, the President held that office.

Urundi see **Burundi**

1087 Utrecht Republic. Feb. 1856–May 1858. *Location:* along the Buffalo River in northern Natal. *Capital:* Utrecht. *Other names:* Republic of Utrecht.
History: In 1856 **Utrecht Settlement** became a republic. In 1858 it became part of **Lydenburg Republic.**
Landdrosts (Magistrates): Feb. 1856–May 1858 J.C. Steyn. *Commandants:* Feb. 1856–May 1858 J.C. Klopper.

1088 Utrecht Settlement. 1852–Feb. 1856. *Location:* as **Utrecht Republic.** *Capital:* Utrecht (formed 1852 and named after the Dutch town). *Other names:* Utrecht.
History: In 1852 a Boer settlement was founded and named Utrecht. In 1856 it became a republic (see **Utrecht Republic**).
Landdrosts (Magistrates): 1852–1855 A.T. Spies; 1855–Feb. 1856 J.C. Steyn. *Commandants:* 1852–Feb. 1856 J.C. Klopper.

Valvisch Bay see **Walvis Bay**

1089 Vandal North Africa. 430–Apr. 534. *Location:* North Africa (Tunisia, Algeria, Libya). *Capital:* Carthage (from 439).
History: In 429 the Vandals crossed from Europe and took **Africa Proconsularis** from the Romans. In 534–535 it yielded to **Byzantine North Africa [i],** the Byzantines expelling the Vandals.
Emperors: 430–25 Jan. 477 Geiserich; 25 Jan. 477–23 Dec. 484 Hunerich; 23 Dec. 484–3 Sept. 496 Gundamund; 3 Sept. 496–6 May 523 Thrasamund; 6 May 523–19 May 530 Hilderich; 19 May 530–15 May 534 Gelimer.

Varozvi see **Rozwi**

Vatua see **Gazaland**

1090 Venda. 13 Sept. 1979– . *Location:* South Africa. *Capital:* Thohoyandou. *Other names:* Vhavenda, Republic of Venda, Republiek van Venda, Riphapubliki ya Venda.

History: Venda (the name means "world" or "land") is the Bantustan, or homeland, of the Vhavenda tribe. It is split into two entirely separate units, and was the third homeland to achieve independence from **South Africa** (see also **Transkei**, **Bophuthatswana** and **Ciskei**), but this independence is not recognized internationally. It had achieved self-government on February 1, 1973 with Patrick Mphephu as Chief Minister, and Mphephu has continued to rule the country ever since.

Presidents: 13 Sept. 1979– Patrick Mphephu. *Note:* Mphephu is also Prime Minister.

Victoria see also **Port Natal [iii]**

1091 Victoria Colony. 1858–19 July 1884. *Location:* Ambas Bay, Cameroun. *Capital:* Victoria.

History: Founded as a British colony in 1858, Victoria was established by Baptist missionaries and in 1884, with the onset of the Germans in the area (see **German Crown Lands of North West Africa**), the British Crown placed a protectorate over the little colony (see **Ambas Bay British Protectorate**).

Rulers: 1858–19 July 1884 [unknown].

Voltaic Republic see **Upper Volta**

Vrijheid Republiek see **New Republic**

1092 Wadai. ca. 1500–3 June 1909. *Location:* the Ouaddaï Prefecture of Eastern Chad. *Capital:* Abéché. *Other names:* Ouaddaï, Ouadaï, Waday.

History: There have been three states of Wadai. The first was pre–1500. In the 14th century Wadai became a quasi-independent state of Maba peoples, subject to **Darfur**. Nothing else is known of this state, but it was apparently destroyed at the end of the 15th century. Wadai #2 grew out of this, and in the 16th century the Tunjur tribe conquered it. In 1611 Abd al-Krim, a Maba, threw them out, and in 1635 he became the first Muslim kolak of Wadai (kolak = king). This marks the beginning of the third Wadai. Civil wars, conquest and slave-trading form the basis of Wadai's history after 1635, and in 1909 France invaded, annexing it to **Chad Territory**. Direct French military rule did not cease until 1935, when a new kolak was installed but with very limited powers over the prefecture of Ouaddaï.

Maliks (Kings): before 1500 unknown; ca. 1500 Karama; (?)–(?) Gamal ad-Din; (?)–(?) Durdur; (?)–(?) al-Kamin. *Sultans:* (?)–(?) Muhammad Tunjur; (?)–(?) Yakub al-Mwakir; (?)–(?) Hamid; (?)–1635 Daud. *Kolaks (Kings):* 1635–1655 Abd al-Krim; 1655–1678 Sharuf (or Kharut al-Khabir); 1678–1681 Sharif (or Kharif); 1681–1707 Yakob Arous; 1707–1747 Kharut as-Sarhir; 1747–1795 Muhammad Jawda (or Joda); 1795–1803 Salih Deret; 1803–1813 Abd al-Karim (or Sabun); 1813–1829 Yusuf Kharifain; 1829–1829 Ragib; 1829–1834 Abd al-Aziz; 1834–1843 Adam; 1843–1858 Muhammad Sharif; 1858–1874 Ali; 1874–1898 Yusuf II; 1898–1901 Ibrahim; 1901–Dec. 1901 Abu-Ghazali; 1902–3 June 1909 Muhammad Doud Mourrah; 1909–5 June 1912 Acyl (or Asil); 5 June 1912–1935 direct French rule; 1935–1945 Muhammad Urada; 1945–1960 Ali Silek.

Wagadu see **Ghana Empire**

1093 Wagadugu. ca. 1495–13 Sept. 1896. *Location:* Burkina Faso. *Capital:* Dazuli (from 1620); Lumbila (1590–1620); La (1520–90); Lugusi (1517–20); Guilongou (ca. 1495–1517). *Other names:* Ouagadougou.

History: A **Mossi** kingdom, which grew out of Oubritenga, and founded by Oubri about 1495. Son of Naba Zoungourana and a Ninisi woman called Poughtoenga, he was the first of a long line of moro nabas of Wagadugu. In 1896 the country was occupied by France and in 1897 it became part of the French protectorate of Upper Volta (see **Upper Volta Protectorate**).

Moro Nabas: ca. 1495–ca. 1517 Oubri (or Wubri); ca. 1517–ca. 1520 Soarba; ca. 1520–ca. 1525 Naskyemde; ca. 1525–ca. 1535 Nasbire; ca. 1535–ca. 1550 Nyingnyemdo; ca. 1550–ca. 1570 Koudoumie; ca. 1570–ca. 1590 Kouda; ca. 1590–ca. 1599 Dawema; ca. 1599–(?) Zwetembusma; (?)–(?) Nyadfo; (?)–(?) Nattia; (?)–(?) Namega; (?)–(?) Kida; (?)–(?) Kemba; (?)–(?) Kolera; ca. 1690 Zana; (?)–(?) Giliga; (?)–1729 Ubra; 1729–1737 Muatiba; 1737–1744 Warga; 1744–1784 Zombre; 1784–(?) Kom I; (?)–1795 Sagha I; 1795–1825 Doulougou; 1825–1842 Sawadogho; 1842–(?) Karfo; (?)–ca. 1854 Baogo; 1854–1871 Koutou; 1871–1889 Sanem; 1889–21 Jan. 1897 Wobgho (or Boukhary Koutou); 28 Jan. 1897–16 Feb. 1905 Sigiri; 27 Feb. 1905–12 Feb. 1942 Kom II; 23 March 1942–12 Nov. 1957 Sagha II; 28 Nov. 1957–1971 Kougri.

Wahiguya see **Yatenga**

Wahran see **Oran**

Walfisch Bay see **Walvis Bay**

1094 Walo. 1186–1855. *Location:* Senegal. *Capital:* [unknown].

History: Founded in 1186, the kingdom of Walo lasted 700 years before becoming part of **Senegal Colony.**

Kings: 1186–1202 N'Dya-N'Dya; 1202–1211 Mbang Waad; 1211–1225 Barka Mbody; 1225–1242 Tyaaka Mbar; 1242–1251 [unknown]; 1251–1271 Amadu Faaduma; 1271–1278 Yerim Mbanyik; 1278–1287 Tyukli; 1287–1304 Naatago Tany; 1304–1316 Fara Yerim; 1316–1331 Mbay Yerim; 1331–1336 Dembaane Yerim; 1336–1343 N'dyak Kumba Sam Dyakekh; 1343–1348 Fara Khet; 1348–1355 N'dyak Kumba-gi tyi Ngelogan; 1355–1367 N'dyak Kumba-

Nan Sango; 1367–1380 N'dyak Ko N'Dyay Mbanyik; 1380–1381 Mbany Naatago; 1381–1398 Meumbody N'dyak; 1398–1415 Yerim Mbanyik Konegil; 1415–1485 Yerim Kode; 1485–1488 Fara Toko; 1488–1496 Fara Penda Teg Rel; 1496–1503 Tyaaka Daro Khot; 1503–1508 Naatago Fara N'dyak; 1508–1519 Naatago Yerim; 1519–1531 Fara Penda Dyeng; 1531–1542 Tani Fara N'dyak; 1542–1549 Fara Koy Dyon; 1549–1552 Fara Koy Dyop; 1552–1556 Fara Penda Langan Dyam; 1556–1563 Fara Ko Ndaama; 1563–1565 Fara Aysa Naalem; 1565–1576 Naatago Kbaari Daaro; 1576–1640 Beur Tyaaka Loggar; 1640–1674 Yerim Mbanyik Aram Bakar; 1674–1708 Naatago Aram Bakar; 1708–1733 N'dyak Aram Bakar Teedyek; 1733–1734 Yerim N'date Bubu; 1734–1735 Meu Mbody Kumba Khedy; 1735–1735 Yerim Mbanyik Anta Dyop; 1735–1736 Yerim Khode Fara Mbuno; 1736–1780 N'dyak Khuri Dyop; 1780–1792 Fara Penda Teg Rel; 1792–1801 N'dyak Kumba Khuri Yay; 1801–1806 Saayodo Yaasin Mbody; 1806–1812 Kruli Mbaaba; 1812–1821 Amar Faatim Borso; 1821–1823 Yerim Mbanyik Teg; 1823–1837 Fara Penda Adam Sal; 1837–1840 Kherfi Khari Daano; 1840–1855 Mbeu Mbody Maalik.

1095 Walvis Bay Protectorate. 12 March 1878–7 Aug. 1885. *Location:* on the coast of Namibia. *Capital:* Walvis Bay. *Other names:* Walvis Bay, Valvisch Bay, Whale Bay, Walfisch Bay, Walvisbaai.

History: In 1878 Britain established a protectorate over Walvis Bay, the largest port in what is today **Namibia,** and the immediate coastal strip of 434 square miles. In 1885 this lonely exclave became part of **British Cape Colony (Self-Rule).** In 1910, it became part of the **Union of South Africa.** In 1922 it was assigned to **South West Africa Mandate** for administrative purposes, and in August 1977 it was re-incorporated into **South Africa.**

Residents: June 1878–Nov. 1880 Maj. D. Erskine; Nov. 1880–7 Aug. 1885 Maj. Benjamin Musgrave.

Wandala see **Mandara**

1096 Warri. ca. 1475–1884. *Location:* Benue Provinces, southern Nigeria. *Capital:* Warri. *Other names:* Itsekiri Kingdom, Itsekiri, Ouwerre, Ouwere.

History: Founded by Prince Ginuwa from **Benin** (60 miles to the north), the town of Warri became the capital of this Itsekiri kingdom. After a certain success in the slave-trade, then the palm-oil trade, Warri fell apart and was taken over by the British in 1884 (see **Bights of Biafra and Benin**).

Obas (Kings): ca. 1475–ca. 1500 Ginuwa I; ca. 1500–ca. 1580 [unknown]; ca. 1580–ca. 1600 Dom Domingo; ca. 1600–ca. 1644 [unknown]; ca. 1644–(?) António de Mingo; (?)–ca. 1780 [unknown]; ca. 1780–ca. 1792 Manuel Otobia (or Aitogbuwa); ca. 1792–ca. 1805 Sebastian Otobia (or Erejuwa); ca. 1805–1848 João (or Akengbuwa). *Queens-Regent:* 1848–1853 Dola. *Regents:* 1853–ca. 1858 Eri. *Governors of the River:* ca. 1858–Feb. 1870 Diare; Feb. 1870–1879 Chanomi; 1879–1883 Olomu; 1884–1894 Nana Olomu (or Eriomulu); 1894–1937 vacant; 1937– Ginuwa II.

1097 Wase (Basharawa). ca. 1790–1820. *Location:* Wase, northern Nigeria. *Capital:* the capital of this chiefdom was on the site of what is today the town of Wase. *Other names:* Bashar.

History: From Konkiok in **Bornu** came the Basharawa to settle on a small hill near the present-day town of Gaduk. Later they moved to what is today Wase Town. The Jukun tribe took them over at about this time, but shortly thereafter the Fulani conquered them and built the town of Wase (see **Wase [Fulani]**). The Besharawa were relocated to the west, to Wase Tofa, which

was their capital from 1820–24, and then, about 1824, to Ganua. About 1835 they moved again, this time to Gworam, near Bashar. In 1839 they moved to Bashar, and in 1898, along with **Wase (Fulani)**, became part of the **Niger Delta Protectorate**.

Chiefs: ca. 1790–ca. 1805 Tokta; ca. 1805–1820 Yamusa; 1820–ca. 1824 Karu; ca. 1824–1835 Yamusa; 1835–1838 Karu; 1838–ca. 1880 Abubakr; ca. 1880–1892 interregnum; 1892–1892 Usmanu (never took office); 1892–1898 Abubakar.

1098 Wase (Fulani). 1820–1898. *Location:* northern Nigeria. *Capital:* Wase (built 1820).

History: In 1820 the Fulani attacked Wase (see **Wase [Basharawa]**) and conquered it. From then on it was a vassal state of **Bauchi**, and the Basharawa went off to live in Wase Tofa, a town not far away, where they remained firmly in the control of the Fulani. In 1898 the Fulani chiefdom was taken over by the Royal Niger Company (see **Niger River Delta Protectorate**), and in 1902 it became an official emirate.

Madakins: 1820–1828 Hassan. *Sarkins:* 1828–1848 Abdullahi I; 1848–1866 Hamman I; 1866–1869 Hamman II; 1869–1874 Suleimanu; 1874–1877 Muhammadu I; 1877–1898 Muhammadu II; 1898–1909 Muhammadu III (or Yaki); 1909–1919 Abdullahi II; 1919–1928 Muhammadu IV; 1929–1947 Abubakr; 1948– Abdullahi Maikano III.

1099 Waterboer's Land. 1820–27 Oct. 1871. *Location:* as **Griqualand West Crown Colony.** *Capital:* Griquatown. *Other names:* Griqualand West.

History: In 1820 Andries Waterboer became the captain of **Griquatown,** the area immediately becoming known as Waterboer's Land. He extended his boundaries by treaty in 1838. In 1855 the territory of Albania came within his rule and in 1860 Nicolaas Waterboer gained all of **Cornelis Kok's Land,** which Cornelis Kok had given to Adam

Kok III in 1857. From 1867–70 Waterboer was the claimant to whom the
Keate Award of 1871 officially gave the
diamond lands. In 1871 Waterboer
asked for, and received, British protection as **Griqualand West.**
  Kaptyns (Captains): 1820–13 Dec.
1852 Andries Waterboer; 23 Dec. 1852–
27 Oct. 1871 Nicolaas Waterboer.

  1100 Wattasid Empire. 23 May
1465–28 Jan. 1549. *Location:* northern
Morocco. *Capital:* Fez (from 1472);
Asila (1465–72). *Other names:* Banu
Wattas Dynasty, Bani Wattas Dynasty.
  History: Around 1428 the viziers
became virtual rulers of Morocco
under the Merinids (see **Merinid Empire**) and in 1459 they set up their own
dynasty—the Wattasids, which by 1465
had replaced the Merinids as the official
ruling power in the Western Maghrib.
A weak dynasty however, it controlled
only northern Morocco, and throughout the dynasty's reign the Portuguese
settled various towns on the coast of
Morocco. These were: Alcazarseguer
in 1458, Anfa in 1469, Arzila in 1471,
Tangier in 1471 (see **Portuguese Tangier**), Massa in 1488, Agadir in 1505,
Safi in 1508, Azemmour in 1513, Maza-
gan in 1514, Mehdia in 1515 and Agouz
in 1519. The legitimacy of the Banu
Wattas was never fully recognized and
by 1511 the Sa'did Dynasty was already
taking over (see **Sa'did Morocco**).
  Sultans: 23 May 1465–1505 Muhammad ash-Sheikh; 1505–1524 Muhammad II al-Bartuqali; 1524–1545 Ahmad
al-Wattasi; 1545–1547 Muhammad III
al-Qasri; 1547–28 Jan. 1549 Ahmad
al-Wattasi.

  Wenburg see **Winburg**

  1101 West Africa Settlements. 17
Dec. 1874–28 Nov. 1888. *Location:*
Gambia and Sierra Leone. *Capital:*
Freetown. *Other names:* British West
Africa Settlements.
  History: In July 1874 **Gold Coast
Territory [ii]** and **Lagos Territory [i]**
broke away from the **West African Set-
tlements,** leaving only **Gambia Ter-
ritory [ii]** and **Sierra Leone Territory
[ii]** as members. Later that year the
name of the larger body changed to
West Africa Settlements, now with
only two corporate members—**Gambia
Territory [iii]** and **Sierra Leone Ter-
ritory [iii].** As with the **West African
Settlements,** the Governor of Sierra
Leone was also the Governor-in-Chief
of the **West Africa Settlements.** In 1888
it ceased to exist, Sierra Leone and
Gambia having left the month before.
  Governors-in-Chief: 17 Dec. 1874–
1875 George French (acting); 1875–1875
Cornelius Kortright; 1875–1876 Dr.
Samuel Rowe; 1876–1877 Cornelius
Kortright; 1877–1877 Horatio Huggins
(acting); 1877–1880 Dr. Samuel Rowe
(knighted 1880); 1880–1881 William
Streeten (acting); 1881–1881 Sir Samuel
Rowe; 1881–1881 Franas Pinkett (acting); 1881–1883 Arthur Havelock;
1883–1883 Franas Pinkett (acting);
1883–1884 Arthur Havelock; 1884–1884
Arthur Tarleton (acting); 1884–1885
Franas Pinkett (acting); 1885–1886 Sir
Samuel Rowe; 1886–1887 James Hay
(acting); 1887–1888 Sir Samuel Rowe;
1888–1888 J.M. Maltby (acting); 1888–
28 Nov. 1888 James Hay (acting).

  1102 West African Settlements. 19
Feb. 1866–17 Dec. 1874. *Location:*
Gambia, Sierra Leone, Gold Coast,
Lagos. *Capital:* Freetown. *Other
names:* British West African Settle-
ments.
  History: In 1866 the West African
Settlements were formed, ruled by the
Governor of Sierra Leone. In 1874
Gold Coast Territory [ii] and **Lagos
Territory [i]** broke away to form **Gold
Coast Colony (with Lagos),** which left
only **Sierra Leone Territory [iii]** and
Gambia Territory [iii] to be part of the
new **West Africa Settlements.**
  Governors-in-Chief: 19 Feb. 1866–
1867 Samuel Blackall; 1867–1867 Gus-
tavus Yonge (acting); 1867–1868 Sam-
uel Blackall; 1868–1869 Sir Arthur

Kennedy; 1869–1869 John Kendall (acting); 1869–1871 Sir Arthur Kennedy; 1871–1871 John Kendall (acting); 1871–1871 Capt. Sheppard (acting); 1871–Jan. 1872 Sir Arthur Kennedy; Jan. 1872–Feb. 1872 John Kendall (acting); Feb. 1872–7 March 1873 John Pope Hennessey; 7 March 1873–17 March 1873 Robert Keate; 17 March 1873–2 Oct. 1873 Robert Harley and Alexander Bravo (acting); 2 Oct. 1873–4 March 1874 Sir Garnet Wolseley; 4 March 1874–17 Dec. 1874 George Berkeley.

1103 West African Territories. 17 Oct. 1821–13 Jan. 1850. *Location:* North West Africa. *Capital:* Freetown (Sierra Leone). *Other names:* West African Settlements, British West Africa.

History: In 1821 all British forts and settlements in North West Africa were put under the rule of a Governor-in-Chief based in Freetown. The constituent parts of the new organization all became territories, and were as follows: (1) **Gambia Territory [i],** which became in 1829 **Bathurst Settlement and Dependencies in the Gambia,** and then in 1843 separated from West African Territories and became a separate colony (see **Gambia Colony [i]**); (2) **Gold Coast Territory [i]** which separated in 1828 to be run by a Committee of Merchants (although the links between that government and that of Sierra Leone were still strong). In 1843 **British Gold Coast (Committee of Merchants)** became the property of the British Crown once more (see **British Gold Coast Crown Colony**); (3) **Sierra Leone Territory [i],** which was a territory of West African Territories from 1821–1850, the only one in fact which lasted. The West African Territories was the precursor of the **West African Settlements** which was to come about a decade or so later.

Rulers: 17 Oct. 1821–13 Jan. 1850 For Governors-in-Chief see Governors of Sierra Leone Territory [i].

West Mauretania see **Mauretania West**

1104 West Nupe. 1796–1805. *Location:* around the town of Jima, Niger Province, Nigeria. *Capital:* Raba. *Other names:* Nupe West.

History: In 1796 the two grandsons of the King of **Nupe Kingdom [i],** Jimada and Majiya (their grandfather was Iliyasu), began a civil war which created two states out of the old Kingdom of Nupe—West Nupe and **East Nupe.** With the death of Jimada, the country was re-united under Majiya (see **Nupe Kingdom [ii]**).

Kings: 1796–1805 Majiya.

West Pondoland see **Pondoland West**

Western Nigeria see **Nigeria Western Region**

1105 Western Sahara. See these names:

Saharan Arab Democratic Republic (1976–)

Spanish Sahara Province (1958–1976)

Spanish West Africa (1912–1958)

Rio de Oro Dependent Protectorate (1887–1912)

Rio de Oro Protectorate (1885–1887)

Rio de Oro Settlements (1860–1885)

Whale Bay see **Walvis Bay**

1106 Whydah French Protectorate. 30 Nov. 1891–22 June 1894. *Location:* Benin. *Capital:* Savi. *Other names:* Ouidah, Houeda, Juda, Ajuda.

History: In 1891 France declared a protectorate over **Whydah Kingdom,** effective from December 3, 1892. In 1894 Whydah became part of **Dahomey Colony,** which is roughly today's **Benin Republic.**

Kings: 30 Nov. 1891–22 June 1894 Nugbododhone.

1107 Whydah Kingdom. ca. 1580–

30 Nov. 1891. *Location:* Benin. *Capital:* Savi. *Other names:* Ajuda, Houeda, Juda, Ouidah.

History: Founded about 1580 by refugees from **Allada,** Whydah grew into a slave-trading kingdom as did all those kingdoms in what is today **Benin Republic.** From 1727 Whydah was subjugated by **Abomey Kingdom** and ruled through an Abomey governor in collaboration with the Whydah king. In 1891 the French placed a protectorate over Whydah (see **Whydah French Protectorate).**

Kings: ca. 1580–ca. 1620 Haholo; ca. 1620–ca. 1640 Kpassé; ca. 1640–(?) [unknown]; (?)–(?) [unknown]; ca. 1669–(?) Ayohuan; ca. 1690–1703 Agbangia; 1703–1708 Amah; 1708–Feb. 1727 Huffon. *Nominal Kings:* Feb. 1727–1741 Huffon; 1741–(?) [unknown]; (?)–Dec. 1774 [unknown]; Dec. 1774–1775 Agbamy. *Abomey Governors:* Feb. 1727–1744 Dassu; 1744–ca. 1765 Dedele; ca. 1765–(?) Sekplon; (?)–(?) Bassoh; (?)–(?) [unknown]; 1868–1879 Adjossogbé; 1879–ca. 1882 Zinhumme; ca. 1882–ca. 1884 Seklocka; ca. 1884–ca. 1887 Aguessi Dagba; ca. 1887–ca. 1890 Jagba; ca. 1890–1898 Nugbododhone.

1108 Winburg Republic. 17 Jan. 1837–3 Feb. 1848. *Location:* Orange Free State. *Capital:* Winburg (founded 1841). *Other names:* Winburg, Wenburg.

History: In 1837 the Boers established their first major settlement here, in a section of land ceded them by the Sotho. They then founded the Republic of Winburg. In 1848 it became part of **Orange River Sovereignty.**

Commandants-General: 17 Jan. 1837–1 Sept. 1838 Hendrik Potgieter; 1 Sept. 1838–3 Feb. 1848 Andries Pretorius.

1109 Witbooi Territory. ca. 1838–12 Apr. 1893. *Location:* Namibia. *Capital:* Gibeon.

History: Another branch of the Oorlams (see **Oorlam Territory),** the Witbooi family was allied to the Afrikaner family, but ruled in a different territory. In 1893 they signed a treaty of protection with the Germans (see **German South West Africa Protectorate [ii]).**

Rulers: 1798–1875 Kido Witbooi; 1875–1888 Moses Witbooi; 1888–1889 Paul Visser; 1889–1905 Hendrick Witbooi.

Wolof Empire see **Dyolof**

X-Group see **Nubia**

Yako see **Mossi States**

1110 Yatenga. 1540–1895. *Location:* Burkina Faso. *Capital:* Ouahigouya (after 1757); Gourcy (before 1757). *Other names:* Yatenga, Wahiguya, Ouahigouya.

History: Founded by Yadega (from **Wagadugu),** this northern Mossi Kingdom (see **Mossi States)** was set up on land which was once part of Zandoma. In 1895 it became a French protectorate as part of **French West Africa,** or more specifically of **French Sudan Colony.**

Nabas: ca. 1540 Yadega; (?)–(?) Yaulumfao; (?)–(?) Kurita; (?)–(?) Geda; (?)–(?) Tonugum; (?)–(?) Possinga; (?)–(?) Nassege; (?)–(?) Vante; (?)–(?) Bonga; (?)–(?) Sugunum; (?)–(?) Kissun; (?)–(?) Zangayella; (?)–(?) Lanlassé; (?)–(?) Nassodoba; ca. 1650 Lambwegha; (?)–(?) Niago; (?)–(?) Parima; (?)–(?) Kumpaugum; (?)–(?) Nabassere; (?)–(?) Tusuru; (?)–(?) Sini; (?)–1754 Piga I; 1754–1754 Kango; 1754–1757 Wabgho; 1757–1787 Kango; 1787–1803 Sagha; 1803–1806 Kaogho; 1806–1822 Tougouri; 1822–1825 Kom; 1825–1831 Ragongo; 1831–1831 Ridimba; 1831–1834 Diogore; 1834–1850 Totebalobo; 1850–1851 interregnum; 1851–1877 Yemde; 1877–1879 Sanem; 1879–1884 Noboga; 1884–1885 Piga II; 1885–May 1894 Baogho; June 1894–27 Jan. 1899 Boulli; 4 Feb. 1899–1902 Ligidi; 1902–1914 Kobgha; 1914–1954

Tougouri II; 1954–1960 Sigiri; 1960–
Kom II.

1111 Yauri. ca. 1400–1901. *Location:* Sokoto Province, northern Nigeria. *Capital:* Yelwa (from 1888); Ikum Island (1850–88); Bin Yauri (or Ireshe, or Ireshe Bino) (until 1850).
History: The date of the founding of the kingdom of Yauri is very speculative and lost in the mists of African time. 1400 seems as good a date as any, and better than 950 which is the date traditionally given. It is one of the Banza Bakwai (see **Hausaland**), i.e. the seven illegitimate Hausa States, as opposed to the Hausa Bakwai. It may have been founded by Katsina hunters, or by Songhai warriors, but the Gunagwa tribe seem to be the progenitors. Long a tributary state of **Kebbi,** it pledged allegiance to the emir of **Gwandu,** one of the main **Fulani Empire** overlords, and the king became an emir, thus continuing the dynasty. In 1850 there was a civil war, and in 1901 Yauri became part of **Northern Nigeria Protectorate.**
Kings: ca. 1400 Tafarilu; (?)–(?) Kamuwa; (?)–(?) Buyanga; (?)–(?) Sakazu; (?)–(?) Yauri; (?)–(?) Kisagare; (?)–(?) Jerabana I; ca. 1575 Gimba; (?)–(?) Gimba II; (?)–(?) Kasafogi; ca. 1615 Jerabana II; (?)–(?) Gimba III; (?)–(?) Kasagurbi; ca. 1650 Kana; (?)–(?) Jan Rina; (?)–(?) Dutsi; (?)–(?) Lafiya I; (?)–(?) Kada; (?)–(?) Gamdi; (?)–(?) Dan Ibrahimu; (?)–(?) Muhammadu; (?)–(?) Lafiya II; (?)–(?) Yanazu; (?)–(?) Umaru Gamdi; (?)–(?) Suleimanu Jerabana; (?)–(?) Aliyu Lafiya; (?)–(?) Ahmadu Jerabana; (?)–(?) Shu'aibu Madara; ca. 1790–1799 Mustafa Gazari; March 1799–ca. 1810 Albishir (or Dan Ayi). *Emirs:* ca. 1810–Nov. 1829 Albishir (or Dan Ayi); Nov. 1829–June 1835 Ibrahimu (or Dogon Sharki); June 1835–March 1844 Jibrilu (or Gajere); March 1844–Sept. 1848 Abubakar Jatau; Sept. 1848–Sept. 1850 Jibrilu (or Gajere); Sept. 1850–Jan. 1871 Yakuba (or Dan Gajere) (joint until 1869); Sept. 1850–Jan. 1869 Suleimanu Dan Addo (joint); Jan. 1871–Jan. 1888 Abdullahi Gallo; Jan. 1888–Feb. 1904 Abdullahi Abarshi; Feb. 1904–1915 Jibrilu; 1915–March 1923 Aliyu; March 1923–1955 Abdullahi; 1955– Muhammad Tukur.

Yola see **Adamawa**

Yoruba, Yorubaland see **Ilorin Emirate**

Zafi-Rominia see **Madagascar Kingdom**

1112 Zaghawa Kingdom. (?)–ca. 1350. *Location:* Chad. *Capital:* Njimi.
History: A group of Arab clans in northern Chad and part of Darfur (i.e. present-day Sudan) founded this kingdom. Of nomadic Berber origins they controlled much of the Trans-Saharan trade in the Middle Ages. They helped found the kingdom of **Kanem,** as well as **Gobir.** They expanded seriously in the 11th century, and reached their height in the 13th century. Their language was (is) close to that of the Teda and about 25,000 Zaghawa exist today.
Rulers: unknown.

1113 Zagwe Ethiopia. 1117–1268. *Location:* Ethiopia. *Capital:* Roha. *Other names:* Ethiopia, Roha Empire.
History: In 1117 the Zagwe dynasty took possession of Ethiopia. In 1268 it became part of the **Ethiopian Empire [i].**
Emperors: 1117–1133 Marari; 1133–1172 Yemrehana Krestos; 1172–1212 Gebra Maskal Lalibela; 1212–1260 Na'akueto La'ab; 1260–1268 Yetbarak.

1114 Zaire. See these **names:**
Zaire (1971–)
Congo (Kinshasa) (1965–1971)
Congo Democratic Republic (1964–1965)
Congo (Leopoldville) (1960–1964)
Stanleyville People's Republic (1964–

1965)
   Stanleyville Republic (1960–1961)
   South Kasai Republic (1960–1960)
   Katanga Republic (1960–1963)
   Belgian Congo (1908–1960)
   Congo State (Belgian) (1908–1908)
   Congo Free State (1885–1908)
   International Association of the Congo (1884–1885)
   Kongo (ca. 1350–ca. 1850)
   Luba Empire [i] (ca. 1585–ca. 1620)
   Luba Empire [ii] (ca. 1620–ca. 1885)
   Lunda Kingdom (ca. 1500–ca. 1620)
   Lunda Empire (ca. 1620–1891)

1115 Zaire. 21 Oct. 1971– . *Location:* Central Africa. *Capital:* Kinshasa (named for a village once on the site of Leopoldville). *Other names:* Republic of Zaire, Zaïre, République du Zaïre.

History: In 1971 **Congo (Kinshasa)** became Zaire, thus ending the confusion of names in the Congo Basin (see also **Congo [Brazzaville]** and **Congo People's Republic**). Zaire was so renamed in 1971 for the Zaire River (also re-named from The Congo), but whereas the new name of the state caught on instantly worldwide, the new name of the river was used only in Zaire. "Zaire" means "great river," specifically The Congo.

Presidents: 21 Oct. 1971– Joseph Desiré Mobutu (or Mobutu Sese Seko). *First State Commissioners:* 6 July 1977–6 March 1979 Mpinga Kasenda; 6 March 1979–27 Aug. 1980 Bo-Boliko Lokonga; 27 Apr. 1980–23 Apr. 1981 Nguza Karl-I-Bond; 23 Apr. 1981–5 Nov. 1982 N'Singa Udjuu; 5 Nov. 1982–31 Oct. 1986 Kengo wa Dondo; 22 Jan. 1987– Mabi Mulumba. *Note [i]:* First State Commissioner is equivalent to Prime Minister. *Note [ii]:* In times of no First State Commissioner, the President held that office.

Zakzak see **Zazzau**

1116 Zambesia. 30 Oct. 1888–23 Jan. 1894. *Location:* as **Zambia.** *Capital:* Fort Salisbury (from September 10,

1890).

History: In 1888, when the British South Africa Company (BSAC) under Cecil Rhodes began infiltrating the areas which are now **Zambia** and **Zimbabwe,** there were only native states there. **Barotseland** was the principal state in the Zambia area then, and the British began calling the land "Zambesia." After 1889 the term came to be applied only to the regions north of the Zambesi River, because in the south the native kingdom of **Mashonaland** had become a British protectorate known as **Mashonaland Protectorate.** So, although **Mashonaland Protectorate** was merely a part of Zambesia, it was such a big part of southern Zambesia that, in the minds of the people it equaled the British territory south of the Zambesia River. Hence the reapplication of the term after 1889. In 1894 things changed drastically. Another kingdom south of the Zambesi was conquered—**Matabeleland**—and this added to Mashonaland Protectorate created a new country—**South Zambesia,** while all land north of the Zambesi now became **North Zambesia.**

Rulers: No fixed rule in Zambesia between 1888 and 1894 except in **Mashonaland Protectorate.**

1117 Zambia. See these **names:**
Zambia (1964–)
Northern Rhodesia (Self-Rule) (1964–1964)
Northern Rhodesia Protectorate (1924–1964)
   Northern Rhodesia (1911–1924)
   North Eastern Rhodesia (1900–1911)
   North Western Rhodesia (1900–1911)
   Rhodesia Protectorate (1895–1900)
   North Zambia (1894–1895)
   Zambesia (1888–1894)
Federation of Rhodesia and Nyasaland (1953–1963)
   Kazembe Kingdom (ca. 1710–1899)
   Barotseland (ca. 1550–1891)

1118 Zambia. 24 Oct. 1964– . *Location:* north of the Zambesi River in

Southern Africa. *Capital:* Lusaka (founded in 1905 and named for Lusaakas, the headman of a nearby village). *Other names:* The Republic of Zambia (named for the Zambesi River).

History: On October 24, 1964 **Northern Rhodesia (Self-Rule),** which included Barotseland, became the independent republic of Zambia, a free nation within the British Commonwealth. *Presidents:* 24 Oct. 1964– Kenneth Kaunda. *Prime Ministers:* 28 Aug. 1973–27 May 1975 Mainza Chona; 27 May 1975–20 July 1977 Elijah Mudenda; 20 July 1977–16 June 1978 Mainza Chona; 16 June 1978–18 Feb. 1981 Daniel Lisulo; 18 Feb. 1981–24 Apr. 1985 Nalumino Mundia; 24 Apr. 1985– Kebby Musokotwane. *Note:* in times of no Prime Minister, the President held that office.

1119 Zamfara. ca. 1200–1902. *Location:* nothern Nigeria/southern Niger border. *Capital:* Anka (from ca. 1820); Ruwan Gora (ca. 1810–ca. 1820); Sabon Gari (ca. 1805–ca. 1810); Kiawa (ca. 1756–ca. 1805); Birnin Zamfara (ca. 1300–ca. 1756); Dutsi (until ca. 1300).

History: Named for a princess called Fara, the Zamfarawa (Men of Fara) settled in Dutsi about 1200. About 1756 they were driven out of the area by the Gobirawa (see **Gobir**), and for the next fifty years regularly changed capitals, finally settling at Anka as vassals of the **Fulani Empire.** In 1902 their kingdom was divided between **Zinder Autonomous Military Territory** and **Northern Nigeria Protectorate.**

Sarkins: ca. 1200 Dakka I; (?)–(?) Jatau; (?)–(?) Jimir Dakka; (?)–(?) Kokai Kokai; (?)–(?) Dudufani I. *Queens:* (?)–(?) Algoje. *Sarkins:* ca. 1300 Bakurukuru; (?)–(?) Bakawa; (?)–(?) Gimshikki; (?)–(?) Karafau; (?)–(?) Gatamma; (?)–(?) Kudandam; (?)–(?) Bardau; (?)–(?) Gubarau; (?)–(?) Tasgarin Burum; (?)–(?) Durkusa; (?)–(?) Mowashi; (?)–(?) Kigaya; (?)–(?) Tabarau; (?)–(?) Dudufani II; ca. 1550 Burum I (twin sarkin); (?)–(?)

Burum II (twin sarkin); (?)–(?) Taritu; (?)–(?) Fati I (twin sarkin); (?)–(?) Fati II (twin sarkin); ca. 1625 Zartai; (?)–(?) Dakka II; (?)–(?) Tasau; (?)–(?) Zaude; (?)–(?) Aliyu; (?)–(?) Hamidu Karima; (?)–(?) Abdu na Makaki; (?)–(?) Suleimana; (?)–(?) Muhammadu na Makaki; (?)–(?) Abdu na Tamane; (?)–(?) Maliki (or Malu); ca. 1715 Babba I; (?)–(?) Yakubu I; (?)–(?) Jimirra (or Jirau); (?)–(?) Falkari (or Fashane); ca. 1734 Babba II; (?)–(?) Yakubu II; ca. 1756 Maroki; ca. 1805 Abarshi; (?)–(?) Fari; (?)–(?) Dan Bako; (?)–(?) Dan Gado; ca. 1825 Tukudu; (?)–1829 Abdu Fari; 1829–1853 Abubakar; 1853–1877 Muhammadu Dan Gigala; 1877–1896 Hassan; 1896–1899 Muhammadu Farin Gani; 1899–1904 Abdullahi Gade; 1904–1916 Abdu Kakkabi; 1916–1928 Muhammadu Katar; 1928–1946 Muhammadu Fari; 1946– Ahmadu Barmo.

Zandoma see **Mossi States**

Zang see **Zeng**

Zango see **Daura-Zango**

1120 Zanzibar Independent Sultanate. 10 Dec. 1963–12 Jan. 1964. *Location:* as **Zanzibar Republic.** *Capital:* Zanzibar. *Other names:* Zanzibar, Zanzibar Sultanate.

History: In 1963 **Zanzibar (Self-Rule)** became an independent sultanate within the British Commonwealth. Early the following year the Sultan was deposed and **Zanzibar Republic** was declared.

Sultans: 10 Dec. 1963–12 Jan. 1964 Sayid Jamshid ibn Abdullah. *Prime Ministers:* 10 Dec. 1963–12 Jan. 1964 Muhammad Shamte.

1121 Zanzibar (Omani). 1698–10 March 1862. *Location:* Zanzibar, Tanzania. *Capital:* Zanzibar. *Other names:* Omani Zanzibar.

History: In 1698 the Omanis from

Arabia took control of Zanzibar. In 1862 the island became a sultanate, independent of Muscat (see **Zanzibar Sultanate**).
Omani Governors: 1698–ca. 1710 [unknown]; ca. 1710–(?) Said; (?)–1746 [unknown]; 1746–(?) Abdallah ibn Gad; (?)–ca. 1804 [unknown]; ca. 1804–ca. 1822 Yaqut; ca. 1822–ca. 1823 Muhammad ibn Nasir; ca. 1823–ca. 1832 Seyid Muhammad al-Ahabagi; ca. 1832–Nov. 1833 Hamad; Nov. 1833–1836 Tuwayni; 1836–June 1840 [unknown]; June 1840–7 Nov. 1854 Khalid; 7 Nov. 1854–10 March 1862 Seyid Madjid.

1122 Zanzibar Protectorate. 4 Nov. 1890–24 June 1963. *Location:* as **Zanzibar Republic.** *Capital:* Zanzibar. *Other names:* Zanzibar and Pemba.
History: In 1890 the British declared a protectorate over **Zanzibar Sultanate,** which also included the Island of Pemba. On July 1, 1913 it became a part of **British East Africa Protectorate,** and in 1963 self-rule was granted (see **Zanzibar [Self-Rule]**).
Sultans: 4 Nov. 1890–5 March 1893 Sayid Ali; 5 March 1893–25 Aug. 1896 Sayid Hamed; 25 Aug. 1896–27 Aug. 1896 Sayid Khalid; 27 Aug. 1896–18 July 1902 Sayid Hamud; 20 July 1902–9 Dec. 1911 Sayid Ali; 9 Dec. 1911–9 Oct. 1960 Sayid Khalifa ibn Harub (knighted 1914); 17 Oct. 1960–24 June 1963 Sayid ibn Abdallah. *First Ministers (Wazirs):* 4 Nov. 1890–11 Oct. 1901 Sir Lloyd Matthews; 11 Oct. 1901–3 Nov. 1901 vacant; 3 Nov. 1901–1906 A.S. Rogers; 1906–1908 Arthur Raikes; 1908–1914 Francis Barton. *Consuls-General:* 4 Nov. 1890–5 March 1893 Sir Charles Euan-Smith; 6 March 1891–12 Dec. 1892 Sir Gerald Portal; 12 Dec. 1892–Feb. 1894 Rennell Rodd; Feb. 1894–1900 Sir Arthur Hardinge; 1900–20 June 1904 Sir Charles Elliot; 20 June 1904–1908 Basil Cave; 1908–1909 [unknown] (acting); 1909–1 July 1913 Edward Clarke. *Residents:* 1 July 1913–1922 Francis Pearce; 1922–Dec. 1923 John Sinclair; Jan. 1924–Dec. 1929 Claud Hollis (knighted 1927); Dec. 1929–Oct. 1937 Richard Rankine (knighted 1932); Oct. 1937–1940 John Hall; 1940–1941 [unknown] (acting); 1941–1946 Sir Guy Pilling; 1946–1951 Sir Vincent Glenday; 1951–1952 [unknown] (acting); 1952–2 Nov. 1954 John Rankine; 2 Nov. 1954–1959 Henry Potter (knighted 1956); 1959–1960 [unknown] (acting); 1960–24 June 1963 Sir George Mooring.

1123 Zanzibar Republic. 12 Jan. 1964–26 Apr. 1964. *Location:* Zanzibar, off the coast of Tanzania. *Capital:* Zanzibar ("zanzibar" means "the isle of cloves"). *Other names:* Zanzibar People's Republic, People's Republic of Zanzibar.
History: In 1964 the **Zanzibar Independent Sultanate** was overthrown and the country became a republic, and later that year it joined with **Tanganyika Republic** to form **Tanganyika and Zanzibar United Republic.**
Presidents: 12 Jan. 1964–26 Apr. 1964 Abeid Amani Karume. *Prime Ministers:* 14 Jan. 1964–26 Apr. 1964 Abdullah Kassim Hanga. *Note:* in times of no Prime Minister, the President held that office.

1124 Zanzibar (Self-Rule). 24 June 1963–10 Dec. 1963. *Location:* as **Zanzibar Republic.** *Capital:* Zanzibar. *Other names:* Zanzibar.
History: In 1963 **Zanzibar Protectorate** won self-rule. Later that year it gained full independence as **Zanzibar Independent Sultanate.**
Residents: 24 June 1963–10 Dec. 1963 Sir George Mooring. *Sultans:* 24 June 1963–30 June 1963 Sayid Abdullah ibn Khalifah; 30 June 1963–10 Dec. 1963 Sayid Jamshid ibn Abdullah. *Prime Ministers:* 24 June 1963–10 Dec. 1963 Muhammad Shamte.

1125 Zanzibar Sultanate. 10 March 1862–4 Nov. 1890. *Location:* as **Zanzibar Independent Sultanate** (but with more territory inland). *Capital:* Zanzibar. *Other names:* The Isle of Cloves.

History: In 1862 **Zanzibar (Omani)** became independent, as a sultanate, separated from the previous Muscat and Omani state in Arabia which had controlled the area since the 17th century. The Sultan Barghash saw all of his interior land go to Germany and Britain (see **German East Africa Protectorate [i]** and **British East Africa Colony**). In 1890 the British proclaimed a protectorate over Zanzibar itself (see **Zanzibar Protectorate**), while the remaining portions of what had once been Zanzibar (parts of Kenya, Somalia and Tanzania) were gobbled up by the Imperial process.

Sultans: 10 March 1862–7 Oct. 1870 Seyid Madjid; 7 Oct. 1870–26 March 1888 Seyid Barghash; 27 March 1888–17 Feb. 1890 Seyid Khalifa I; 17 Feb. 1890–4 Nov. 1890 Seyid Ali. *Viziers:* 1890–4 Nov. 1890 Sir Lloyd Matthews.

Note: the Vizier (or Wazir) was, in fact, the Prime Minister. *Note:* the following were the British Consuls and Consuls-General associated with Zanzibar from 1840:

Consuls: 1840–1857 Atkins Hamerton; 1857–1860 Christopher Rigby; 1861–10 March 1862 Lewis Pelly; 10 March 1862–1865 Robert Playfair; 1865–1870 Henry Churchill; 1870–1873 John Kirk. *Consuls-General:* 1873–1886 John Kirk (knighted 1881); 1887–1888 Claude MacDonald (acting); 1888–4 Nov. 1890 Sir Charles Euan-Smith.

1126 Zaria. ca. 1578–1835. *Location:* as **Zazzau**. *Capital:* Zaria (founded 1536 and named for Chief Bakwa's daughter, Zaria). *Other names:* Zazzau.

History: About 1578 the town of Zaria was appointed capital of **Zazzau** and the name of the country changed to Zaria. Zaria became a conquering country, then a subjugated nation, and so on, as with most native kingdoms at the time, until 1804 when the **Fulani**

Empire took it over. The Hausa rulers went into exile in Zuba and founded **Abuja.** In 1808 a Fulani became ruler of Zaria, and in 1835 it became an emirate (see **Zaria Emirate**).

Sarkis (or Sarkins, or Chiefs): 1578–1584 Ali; 1584–1597 Bako Majirua; 1597–1608 Bako Su Aliyu; 1608–1608 Bako Musa; 1608–1611 Bako Mahama Gabi (or Gadi); 1611–1611 Bako Hamza (for one day); 1611–1618 Bako Abdu Ashkuku (or Abdaku); 1618–1621 Bako Brima (or Burema); 1621–1646 Bako Ali; 1646–1647 Bako Makam Rubu; 1647–1660 Bako Brima; 1660–1670 Bako Shukunu; 1670–1678 Bako Aliyu; 1678–1682 Bako Brima Hasko; 1682–1710 Bako Mahama Rubo; 1710–1718 Bako; 1718–1727 Bako Aliyu; 1727–1736 Bako Dan Musa; 1736–1738 Bako Ishihako (or Ishaq); 1738–1750 Bako Makam Danguma; 1750–1757 Bako Ruhawa; 1757–1758 Bako Makam Gaba; 1758–1760 Bako Mair ari Ashaka Okao; 1760–1762 Kao; 1762–1764 Bako Bawa; 1764–1770 Yonusa; 1770–1788 Baba (or Yakuba); 1788–1793 Aliyu; 1793–1795 Chikkoku; 1795–1796 Mai haman Maigano; 1796–1802 Ishihako Jatao (or Ishaq Jatao); 1802–1804 Makkam (or Muhamman Makau); 1804–1821 Mallam Musa; 1821–1834 Yan Musa; 1834–1835 Abdul Karim. *Sarkins in exile:* 1804–1825 Muhamman Makau; 1825–1828 Abu Ja.

1127 Zaria Emirate. 1835–March 1902. *Location:* as **Zazzau.** *Capital:* Zaria. *Other names:* Zazzau.

History: In 1835 **Zaria** officially became a Fulani emirate (see **Fulani Empire**). In 1902 it was taken by the British, but the emirate continued, even though **Northern Nigeria Protectorate** was the ruling authority.

Emirs: 1835–1846 Abdul Karim; 1846–1846 Hamada; 1846–1853 Mahoma Sani; 1853–1854 Sidi Abdulkadiri; 1854–1857 Abdul Salami; 1857–1871 Abdullahi; 1871–1874 Abubakr (Bawa); 1874–1879 Abdullahi; 1879–

1888 Sambo; 1888–1897 Yero; 1897–1902 Kwasso; 1902–1903 Nufu Aliyu; 1903–1903 Wambai Zozo; 1903–1920 Aliyu; 1920–1924 Dallatu; 1924–1937 Ibrahim; 1937–1959 Ja'afaru; 1959–Muhammadu Aminu.

Zayyanid Kingdom see **Abd-al-Wadid Kingdom**

1128 Zazzau. ca. 1010–ca. 1578. *Location:* the southernmost of the Hausa States, in northern Nigeria. *Capital:* Turunku; Wuciciri; Rikoci; Kawar. *Other names:* Zegzeg, Zakzak, Zozo.

History: Around the beginning of the 11th century the Hausa state of Zazzau was founded by King Gunguma, grandson of Bayajida (see **Kano**). The name "zazzau" means "sword." In 1536 the kingdom was moved and the town of Zaria built. At the end of the 16th century the name of the kingdom changed to **Zaria.**

Sarkis (Chiefs): ca. 1010 Gunguma; (?)–(?) Matani (or Matazo); (?)–(?) Tumso (or Tumsah); (?)–(?) Tamusa; (?)–(?) Sulimano; (?)–(?) Nasabo (or Maswaza); (?)–(?) Danzaki (or Dinzaki); (?)–(?) Saiwago (or Nayoga); (?)–(?) Kwasari (or Kauchi); (?)–(?) Nwaiku (or Nawainchi); (?)–(?) Besekal (or Machikai); (?)–(?) Kuna (or Kewo); (?)–(?) Bashikarr; (?)–(?) Maji Dadi (or Majidada); (?)–(?) Kirari (or Dihirahi); (?)–(?) Jenhako (or Jinjiku); (?)–1505 Sukana; 1505–1530 Rabon Bawa (or Monan Abu); 1530–1532 Gudumua Muska (or Gidan Dan Masukanan); 1532–1535 Tukuariki (or Nohir); 1535–1536 Uwan (or Kawanissa). *Queens:* 1536–1539 Bakwa Turunku. *Sarkis (Chiefs):* 1539–1566 Ibrihimu; 1566–1576 Karama; 1576–1578 Kafow.

Zegzeg see **Zazzau**

1129 Zeng Empire. 980–1515. *Location:* Somalia, Kenya, Tanzania, Mozambique. *Capital:* Kilwa (on the coast of what is today Tanzania). *Other names:* Zing, Zang, Kilwa.

History: In 975 Prince Ali ibn Hasan, a Shirazi nobleman from Arabia, arrived on the East coast of Africa, founded **Mombasa** that year and Kilwa in 976, and after much conquest made Kilwa the capital of his new Zeng Empire. In 1513 Kilwa, the capital, became part of the Portuguese **Sofala and Mozambique Captaincy.** The Zeng Empire brought Swahili as the language of the area. By the time the Portuguese arrived in 1507 the limits of the Empire had shrunk to between Sofala and Tanga (in today's Tanzania).

Sultans: 980–1022 Ali ibn Hasan; 1022–1027 Ali ibn Baskhat; 1027–1032 Daud ibn Ali; 1032–1035 Khalid ibn Bekr; 1035–1064 Hasan ibn Suleiman; 1064–1090 Ali ibn Daud I; 1090–1100 Ali ibn Daud II; 1100–1115 Hasan ibn Daud; 1115–1117 Suleiman the Tyrant; 1117–1158 Daud ibn Suleiman; 1158–1177 Suleiman al-Hasan the Great; 1177–1180 Daud ibn Suleiman; 1180–1181 Talut ibn Suleiman; 1181–1200 Hasan ibn Suleiman; 1200–1206 Khalid; 1206–1217 Ali ibn Suleiman the Lucky; 1217–1259 Abu Suleiman; 1259–1274 Ali ibn Daud; 1274–1293 Hasan ibn Talut; 1293–1308 Suleiman ibn Hasan; 1308–1334 Hasan abu'l Mawahib. *Regents:* 1334–1336 Daud ibn Suleiman. *Sultans:* 1336–1357 Daud ibn Suleiman; 1357–1358 Suleiman ibn Daud; 1358–1364 Hussein ibn Suleiman; 1364–1366 Talut ibn Hussein; 1366–1368 Suleiman ibn Hussein; 1368–1392 Suleiman ibn Suleiman; 1392–1416 Hussein ibn Suleiman; 1416–1425 Muhammad al-Adil; 1425–1447 Suleiman ibn Muhammad; 1447–1460 Ismail ibn Hussein. *Regents:* 1460–1461 Muhammad Yarik. *Sultans:* 1461–1462 Ahmad ibn Suleiman; 1462–1472 Hasan ibn Ismail; 1472–1482 Sa'id ibn Hasan. *Regents:* 1482–1483 Suleiman ibn Muhammad. *Sultans:* 1483–1484 Abdallah ibn Hasan; 1484–1486 Ali ibn Hasan; 1486–1487 Sabhat ibn Muhammad; 1487–1488 Hasan ibn Suleiman. *Regents:*

1488-1491 Hasan ibn Suleiman. *Sultans:* 1488-1491 Hasan ibn Suleiman (usurper); 1491-1496 Ibrahim ibn Muhammad. *Regents:* 1496-1496 Muhammad Kiwab. *Sultans:* 1496-1500 al-Fudail. *Regents:* 1500-1504 Ibrahim ibn Suleiman; 1504-1505 Muhammad Ankony; 1505-1506 Hajji Hasan; 1506-1507 Muhammad Mikat. *Sultans:* 1507-1507 Muhammad Mikat; 1507-1508 Ibrahim ibn Suleiman. *Regents:* 1508-1510 Sa'id ibn Suleiman. *Sultans:* 1510-1515 Muhammad ibn Hussein.

1130 Zimbabwe. See these **names:**
Zimbabwe (1980-)
Zimbabwe-Rhodesia British Administration (1979-1980)
Zimbabwe-Rhodesia (1979-1979)
Rhodesia Republic (1970-1979)
Rhodesia Independent State (1965-1970)
Rhodesia (1964-1965)
Southern Rhodesia Colony (1923-1964)
Southern Rhodesia (1900-1923)
South Zambesia (1894-1895)
Mashonaland Protectorate (1889-1894)
Matabeleland (1837-1894)
Mwene-Mutapa (ca. 1330-ca. 1888)
Rozwi (ca. 1430-1838)

1131 Zimbabwe. 18 Apr. 1980- . *Location:* as **Southern Rhodesia.** *Capital:* Harare (until 1981 called Salisbury). *Other names:* The Republic of Zimbabwe.
History: In 1980 **Zimbabwe-Rhodesia British Administration** became independent as The Republic of Zimbabwe.
Presidents: 18 Apr. 1980-31 Dec. 1987 Canaan Banana. *Executive Presidents:* 31 Dec. 1987- Robert Mugabe. *Prime Ministers:* 18 Apr. 1980-31 Dec. 1987 Robert Mugabe. *Note:* in times of no Prime Minister, the Executive President held that office.

1132 Zimbabwe-Rhodesia. 21 Apr. 1979-11 Dec. 1979. *Location:* as **South-**ern **Rhodesia.** *Capital:* Salisbury. *Other names:* Rhodesia, Southern Rhodesia, Zimbabwe.
History: In 1979, Rhodesia, a white-dominated country (see **Rhodesia Republic**), became Zimbabwe-Rhodesia (a temporary name used deliberately to adjust the world to the new name), a black-ruled republic almost at the point of independence (legal independence) from Britain. Later in 1979, in order to make this independence fully legal, the Gumede/Muzorewa government handed over control of the government to Britain on a temporary basis, so that Britain could oversee the legal transfer of power (see **Zimbabwe-Rhodesia British Administration**).
Presidents: 21 Apr. 1979-23 May 1979 Jade Pithey (acting); 23 May 1979-11 Dec. 1979 Josiah Gumede. *Prime Ministers:* 21 Apr. 1979-23 May 1979 Ian Smith; 29 May 1979-11 Dec. 1979 Abel Muzorewa.

1133 Zimbabwe-Rhodesia British Administration. 11 Dec. 1979-18 Apr. 1980. *Location:* as **Zimbabwe.** *Capital:* Salisbury. *Other names:* Zimbabwe-Rhodesia, Zimbabwe, Southern Rhodesia, Rhodesia.
History: In December 1979 the **Zimbabwe-Rhodesia** government of Josiah Gumede and Abel Muzorewa terminated the Unilateral Declaration of Independence pronounced by Ian Smith in 1965, and handed back authority of the country to Britain. The two statesmen wanted a clean, lawfully independent country, and by this move canceled the illegality of Smith's daring move of fourteen years before. A day later the Governor-General, Lord Soames, arrived to assume responsibility for the impending transfer of the country to an independent black regime (see **Zimbabwe**).
Governors-General: 12 Dec. 1979-18 Apr. 1980 Lord Soames. *Presidents:* 4 March 1980-18 Apr. 1980 Canaan Banana. *Prime Ministers:* 4 March 1980-18 Apr. 1980 Robert Mugabe.

Zinder see also **Damagaram**

1134 Zinder Autonomous Military Territory. 23 July 1900–22 June 1910. *Location:* Niger. *Capital:* Niamey (1903–10); Sorbo Haoussa (1900–03). *Other names:* Térritoire Militaire Autonome de Zinder.

History: In 1900 the French expanded the **Upper Senegal and Niger Territory** and created the Autonomous Military Territory of Zinder out of states like **Damagaram** and others in the area. In 1910 this area became a separate colonial unit, **Niger Military Territory.**

` *Commandants:* 23 July 1900–23 Sept. 1900 no fixed central rule; 23 Sept. 1900–1901 Lt.-Col. Péroz; 1901–Oct. 1904 Henri Gouraud; Oct. 1904–(?) Col. Noël; (?)–(?) Joseph Aymerich; (?)–(?) Col. Lamolle; (?)–22 June 1910 Col. Cristofari.

Zing see **Zeng**

1135 Zirid Kingdom. 973–July 1159. *Location:* northern Algeria, Tunisia and Libya. *Capital:* Sabra al-Mansuriyah (the last capital); Raqqada (985–[?]); al-Qayrawan (973–85).

History: Founded by Sanhaja chieftain Ziri ibn Manad al-Talkali from his base at Ashir, 80 miles southeast of Algiers. In 972 the Zirids moved their power base from Ashir to al-Qayrawan, and in 973 declared a kingdom under their leader Abu al-Futuh Buluggin (also known as Yusuf), who was the son of the Zirids' founder. The kingdom declined in the 12th century, and in 1159 became part of the **Almohad Empire** (see also **Almohad Tunis**).

Kings: 973–984 Abu al-Futuh Buluggin (or Yusuf); 984–995 al-Mansur; 995–1016 Badis; 1016–1062 al-Mu'izz; 1062–1108 Tamim; 1108–1116 Yahya; 1116–1121 Ali; 1121–1167 al-Hasan.

1136 Zirid Tripoli. 977–1148. *Location:* Tripoli, Libya. *Capital:* Tripoli. *Other names:* Tripoli (Zirid).

History: In 977 the Zirids (see **Zirid Kingdom**) took Tripoli from the Fatimids (see **Fatimid North Africa** and **Fatimid Egypt**). In 1148 they lost it to the Normans from Sicily under Roger II (see **Norman Tripolitania**).

Governors: 977–1000 Tamsulat; 1000–1001 Abu'l Hassan Yanis; 1001–1007 Yahya; 1007–1009 Fulful; 1009–1014 Warru; 1014–1022 Abu Abdallah Muhammad; 1022–1028 Khalifa; 1028–1037 Sa'id; 1037–1038 Abu'l Hassan Ali; 1038–(?) Khazrun; (?)–1053 Muhammad; 1053–(?) Abu Muhammad Abdallah; (?)–1068 al-Muntasir; 1068–1078 [unknown]; 1078–(?) Muqallab; ca. 1095 Shah Malik; (?)–1146 [unknown]; 1146–1148 Sheikh Abu Yahya.

Zitenga see **Mossi States**

1137 Zoutpansberg. 1849–Jan. 1858. *Location:* northern Transvaal, South Africa. *Capital:* Schoemansdal (founded 1849 and named for Stefanus Schoeman). *Other names:* Republic of Zoutpansberg, Soutpansberg.

History: In 1849 Hendrik Potgieter left **Ohrigstad** to found yet another republic, this time at Zoutpansberg, around the town of Schoemansdal. In 1858 it became part of the South African Republic (see **South African Republic [i]**).

Head Commandants: 1849–1851 Hendrik Potgieter. *Commandants-General:* 1851–Dec. 1852 Hendrik Potgieter; Dec. 1852–Nov. 1854 Pieter Potgieter; Nov. 1854–Jan. 1858 Stefanus Schoeman.

Zozo see **Zazzau**

Zuid-Afrikaansche Republiek see **South Africa(n) Republic**

1138 Zululand. 1817–1 Sept. 1879. *Location:* Natal, and points north, in South Africa.
Capital: Eshowe.
History: The founding of Zululand may be attributed to Chaka (or Shaka) in 1817, when he broke away from the

Mtetwa Empire that year. After that date the country changed its boundaries with the speed of the Zulu impis. In 1838 Dingaan signed away all of Natal to Piet Retief, the Trekboer (see **Natalia**) and moved north into what became the final basic stage of Zululand. The Zulu were a Bantu clan of the Transkei area, who moved north under Chaka in the early 1800s. In 1879, Sir Garnet Wolseley, following the Zulu War, split Zululand into 13 chiefdoms in order to prevent a central power (see **Zululand Province**). (See also **British Zululand** and **KwaZulu**).

Paramount Chiefs: (?)–ca. 1700 Mandalela (or Malandela); ca. 1700–ca. 1710 Zulu; ca. 1710–ca. 1727 Phunga (or Punga); ca. 1727–ca. 1745 Mageba; ca. 1745–ca. 1763 Ndaba; ca. 1763–ca. 1781 Jama; ca. 1781–1816 Senzangakhona; 1816–22 Sept. 1828 Chaka (or Shaka); 22 Sept. 1828–1828 Umthlangana; 1828–31 Jan. 1840 Dingaan (or Dingana); 10 Feb. 1840–1872 Mpande (or Panda); 1872–8 Feb. 1884 Cetewayo (or Cetshwayo); 8 Feb. 1884–Aug. 1888 Dinuzulu; Aug. 1888–1889 vacant; 1889–1933 Solomon Dinuzulu; 1933–1968 Cyprian Bhekuzulu. *Regents:* 1968–3 Dec. 1971 Gatsha Buthelezi; 3 Dec. 1971– Zwelithini Goodwill Ka Bhekuzulu.

1139 Zululand Province. 1 Sept. 1879–21 June 1887. *Location:* Zululand, northern Natal, South Africa. *Capital:* Eshowe. *Other names:* Zulu Native Reserve.

History: In 1879 the Zulus lost the Zulu War, and **Zululand** was made into a British province. Although the king continued to rule his people, his country was split into thirteen chiefdoms by Sir Garnet Wolseley, in order to prevent a strong central power, and a British resident was at the Paramount Chief's court to advise. In 1884 Dinuzulu signed away half of his land to the Boers' **New Republic** in return for their help, but most of his reign was spent in exile. In 1887 Britain annexed the country as **British Zululand.**

Kings: 1 Sept. 1879–8 Feb. 1884 Cetewayo; 8 Feb. 1884–21 June 1887 Dinuzulu. *Residents:* 8 Sept. 1879–Jan. 1880 William Wheelwright; Jan. 1880–March 1883 Sir Melmoth Osborn. *Resident-Commissioners:* 22 Dec. 1882–March 1883 John W. Shepstone; March 1883–21 June 1887 Sir Melmoth Osborn.

Bibliography

Addison, John. *Ancient Africa*. John Day: 1970.
Africa Digest. London: African Publications, pub. at regular intervals, 1949–.
Africa News. North Carolina: Africa News Science, pub. at regular intervals, 1973–.
Africa Report. Pub. at regular intervals, 1957–.
Africa Research Bulletin. United Kingdom: Africa Research, pub. at regular intervals, 1964–.
The Africa Review. United Kingdom: World of Information, pub. yearly, 1976–.
Africa South of the Sahara. London: Europa, pub. yearly, 1970–.
Africa Today. Africa Today Assocs, pub. at regular intervals, 1954–.
Africa Year Book and Who's Who. Africa Journal, pub. yearly, 1976–.
African Affairs. London: Royal African Society, pub. at regular intervals, 1901–.
African Encyclopedia. Oxford: Oxford Univ. Press, 1974.
The African Experience. Ed. John N. Paden and Edward W. Soja. 4 vols. Northwestern Univ. Press, 1970.
The African Historical Dictionary Series. Ed. Jon Woronoff. 42 vols. to date. Metuchen, N.J.: Scarecrow, 1974–.
African Recorder. Indian Publications, pub. at regular intervals, 1960–1983.
African Studies. Johannesburg: Witwatersrand Univ. Press, pub. at regular intervals, 1942–.
The Annual Register. London: Longman, pub. yearly, 1758–.
Area Handbook/Country Studies Series. 102 vols. to date. Washington DC: Government Printing Office, 1956–.
Balandier, Georges, and Jacques Maquet. *Dictionary of Black African Civilization*. New York: Amiel, 1974.
Best, Alan C., and Harm J. de Blij. *African Survey*. New York: Wiley, 1977.
Bidwell, Robin. *Bidwell's Guide to Government Ministers*. London: Cass, 1973.
Brownlie, Ian. *African Boundaries*. London: Hurst, 1979.
Budge, Wallis. *A History of Egypt*. London: Kegal, Paul, 1902.
Burns, Sir Alan. *History of Nigeria*. London: Allen and Unwin, 1929.
Butler, Audrey. *Everyman's Dictionary of Dates*. London: Dent, 1964.
The Cambridge Encyclopedia of Africa. Cambridge: Cambridge Univ. Press, 1981.
The Cambridge History of Africa. 8 vols. Cambridge: Cambridge Univ. Press, 1984.
Claridge, W. Walton. *A History of the Gold Coast and Ashanti*. 2 vols. London: Cass, 1964.
Clements' Encyclopedia of World Governments. Political Research: 1974.
Colonialism in Africa 1870–1960. 5 vols. Cambridge: Cambridge Univ. Press, 1969.
The Columbia Lippincott Gazetteer of the World. New York: Columbia Univ. Press, 1962.

Crowder, Michael, and Obaro Ikime, eds. *West African Chiefs.* New York: Africana, 1970.
Davidson, Basil. *The Growth of African Civilisation: West Africa, 1000–1800.* London: Longman, 1965.
Dickie, John, and Alan Rake. *Who's Who in Africa.* African Development, 1973.
Dictionary of African Biography. 20 vols. Encyclopedia Africana, 1977.
Diggs, Ellen Irene. *Black Chronology.* Boston: Hall, 1983.
Egan, E.W., et al., eds. *Kings, Rulers and Statesmen.* New York: Sterling, 1976.
The Encyclopedia of Africa. London: MacDonald Educational, 1976.
Encyclopedia of the Third World. New York: Facts on File, pub. yearly, 1972–.
Europa Year Book. London: Europa, pub. yearly, 1926–.
Facts on File. New York: Facts on File. Pub. monthly, 1966–.
Fage, J.D. *An Atlas of African History.* New York: Africana, 1978.
Freeman-Grenville, G.S.P. *Chronology of World History.* London: Collings, 1975.
Gailey, Harry A., Jr. *The History of Africa in Maps.* Chicago: Denoyer-Geppert, 1967.
_____. *A History of the Gambia.* New York: Praeger, 1965.
Gazetteers of the Northern Provinces of Nigeria. London: Cass, 1972.
Gerteiny, Alfred G. *Mauritania.* New York: Praeger, 1967.
Green, Lawrence M. *Islands Time Forgot.* London: Putnam, 1962.
Gurney, Gene. *Kingdoms of Asia, the Middle East and Africa.* New York: Crown, 1986.
Hallett, Robin. *Africa Since 1875.* Ann Arbor: Univ. of Michigan Press, 1974.
_____. *Africa to 1875.* Ann Arbor: Univ. of Michigan Press, 1970.
Harms, John. *Romance and Truth in the Canaries.* Acorn: 1965.
Harper Encyclopedia of the Modern World. New York: Harper & Row, 1970.
Harrabin, J.F. *An Atlas of Africa.* New York: Praeger, 1960.
Henderson, K.D.D. *Sudan Republic.* New York: Praeger, 1965.
Henige, David P. *Colonial Governors.* Madison: Univ. of Wisconsin Press, 1970.
Historical Atlas of Africa. Cambridge: Cambridge Univ. Press, 1985.
Ingham, Kenneth. *A History of East Africa.* New York: Praeger, 1962.
The International Year Book & Statesmen's Who's Who. West Sussex: Thomas Skinner Directories, pub. yearly, 1953–.
Journal of African Administration. British Government, 1949–1961.
Journal of African History. Cambridge: Cambridge Univ. Press, pub. at regular intervals, 1960–.
Journal of Modern African Studies. Cambridge: Cambridge Univ. Press, pub. at regular intervals, 1963–.
Julien, Charles-Andre. *History of North Africa.* New York: Praeger, 1970.
Keller, Helen Rex. *Dictionary of Dates.* New York: Hafner, 1971.
Kirk-Greene, Anthony H.M. *Biographical Dictionary of the British Colonial Governor.* Brighton, England: Harvester Press, 1980.
Langer, William L. *An Encyclopedia of World History.* Boston: Houghton Mifflin, 1972.
Laroui, Abdallah. *The History of the Maghrib.* Princeton, N.J.: Princeton Univ. Press, 1977.
Legum, Colin. *Africa: A Handbook to the Continent.* New York: Praeger, 1966.
_____, ed. *Africa Contemporary Record.* New York: Africana, pub. at regular intervals, 1968–.
Le Vine, Victor T. *The Cameroons: From Mandate to Independence.* Berkeley: Univ. of California Press, 1964.
Longville, Alan R. *Modern World Rulers.* Metuchen, N.J.: Scarecrow, 1979.

McEvedy, Colin. *Atlas of African History.* New York: Facts of File, 1980.
The Middle East and North Africa. London: Europa, pub. yearly, 1953–.
Oxford History of South Africa. Oxford: Oxford Univ. Press, 1969.
Pachai, B. *Malawi: The History of the Nation.* London: Longman, 1973.
Political Handbook of the World. Lakemont GA: CSA, pub. yearly, 1975–.
Reusch, Richard. *History of East Africa.* New York: Ungar, 1961.
Rosenthal, Eric. *Encyclopedia of Southern Africa.* London: Warne, 1961.
Rulers and Governments of the World. Vol. 1 by Martha Ross. Vols. 2 & 3 by Bertold Spuler. London: Bowker, 1977–78.
Schwarz, Walter. *Nigeria.* New York: Praeger, 1968.
South Africa. Official Yearbook of the Republic. South Africa: Chris Van Rensburg, pub. yearly, 1974–.
Standard Encyclopedia of Southern Africa. 12 vols. Parow, South Africa: Nasou, 1970.
The Statesman's Year Book. New York: St. Martin's, pub. yearly, 1864–.
Stratton, Arthur. *The Great Red Island.* Scribner's, 1964.
Tarikh. Essex, England: Longman, pub. at regular intervals, 1964–1980.
Theal, George M. *History of South Africa.* 10 vols. in toto. London: Allen and Unwin.
Tindall, P.E.N. *A History of Central Africa.* New York: Praeger, 1968.
Truhart, Peter. *Regents of Nations.* 4 vols. Germany: Saur, 1984.
Ufahamu. African Activist Assoc., pub. at regular intervals, 1970–.
UNESCO General History of Africa. 7 vols. 1981.
Vatikiotis, P.J. *The Modern History of Egypt.* New York: Praeger, 1969.
Vincent, Benjamin. *Haydn's Dictionary of Dates.* New York: Putnam, 1898.
Whitaker's Almanack. London: Whitaker, pub. yearly, 1868–.
Who's Who in the Arab World. London: Bowker, pub. yearly, 1966.
The World Almanac. New York: pub. yearly, 1885–.

Index of Rulers

Numbers in this index refer to individual entries rather than to pages. Names are not inverted (e.g. Niels **A**arestrup rather than Aarestrup, Niels); a **boldface** letter begins the name under which an entry is alphabetized, and everything following the boldface letter has been considered as one word in alphabetizing. Cross-references use the same device to indicate where the reader will find a given entry (e.g. "Abd al-Hamid al-Bakkush *see* Abd al-Hamid al-**B**akkush" indicates that this name is to be found under B).

Identical names have not been combined into single entries unless the author has determined with some certainty that they refer to the same person. Thus "Paul Adam 422, 1057, 1063" signifies that the Paul Adam appearing in the entries for Gabon Colony, Ubangi-Shari-Chad Colony, and Ubangi-Shari Territory is the same in each case, while such cannot *necessarily* be assumed in the case of "Abd ar-Rahman (Ottoman Egypt [i], 1651–1652)" and "Abd ar-Rahman (Ottoman Egypt [i], 1676–1680)."

A

A'alaf Sagad *see* **Y**ohannes I
Niels **A**arestrup 273
Abarshi 1119
Abayajidda 280
Abaza 272
Abba 10
Abbad al-Balkhi 1
Abbas 363
al-**A**bbas 1012
Ferhat **A**bbas 35
Abbas I 791
Abbas II Hilmi 162, 340
al-**A**bbas ibn Musa 1
Abbiye 926
Ibrahim **A**bboud 981
Abdaku *see* **B**ako Abdu Ashkuku
Abd al-Aziz 1092
Abd al-Aziz ibn Marwan 777
Abd al-Hamid al-Bakkush *see* Abd al-Hamid al-**B**akkush
Abdal Jaffar I 1012
Abdal Jaffar II 1012
Abd al-Kadir I 415

Abd al-Kadir II 415
Abd al-Karim 1092
Abd al-Karim ar-Ragrag 43
Abd al-Kedir (Baguirmi, 1846–1848) 75
Abd al-Kedir (Baguirmi, 1918–1935) 75
Abd al-Krim 1092
Ahdallah (Aghlabid Empire) 22
Abd Allah (Alawid Morocco) 28
Abdallah (Baguirmi) 75
Abdallah (Banu Khurasan Tunis) 85
Abdallah (Bornu Empire [i]) *see* **D**ala (Bornu Empire [i])
Abdallah (Harar) 502
Abdallah (Merinid Empire) 684
Abdallah (Ottoman Egypt [i]) 790
Ahmad Abdallah 245, 250
Abdallah I (Aghlabid Empire) 22
Abdallah I (Anjouan) 56
Abdallah I (Kanem) *see* **B**ikorom

Abdallah I (Timbuktu) 1012
Abdallah II (Aghlabid Empire) 22
Abdallah II (Anjouan) 56
Abdallah II (Sa'did Morocco) 863
Abdallah II (Timbuktu) 1012
Abdallah III (Anjouan) 56
Abdallah III (Timbuktu) 1012
Abdallah IV 1012
Abdallah V 1012
Abdallah al-Adil 41
Abdallah al-Ghalib 863
Abdallahi 19
Abdallah ibn Abd al-Malik 777
Abdallah ibn Abderrahman 1
Abdallah ibn Ahmad 697
Abdallah ibn Ali al-Kasri 137
Abdallah ibn al-Mussayab 1
Abdallah ibn Amr 777
Abdallah ibn Gad 1121
Abdallah ibn Hamish 690

307